Lecture Notes in Computer Sci

Commenced Publication in 1973
Founding and Former Series Editors:
Gerhard Goos, Juris Hartmanis, and Jan van Leeuwen

Aditya Bagchi   Indrakshi Ray (Eds.)

Information Systems Security

9th International Conference, ICISS 2013
Kolkata, India, December 16-20, 2013
Proceedings

 Springer

Volume Editors

Aditya Bagchi
Indian Statistical Institute
Electronics & Communication Sciences Unit
203, B. T. Road
Kolkata 700108, India
E-mail: aditya@isical.ac.in

Indrakshi Ray
Colorado State University
Computer Science Department
1873 Campus Delivery
Fort Collins, CO 80523, USA
E-mail: iray@cs.colostate.edu

ISSN 0302-9743   e-ISSN 1611-3349
ISBN 978-3-642-45203-1   e-ISBN 978-3-642-45204-8
DOI 10.1007/978-3-642-45204-8
Springer Heidelberg New York Dordrecht London

Library of Congress Control Number: 2013954264

CR Subject Classification (1998): E.3, C.2.0, D.4.6, K.6.5, K.4.4, H.2.4

LNCS Sublibrary: SL 4 – Security and Cryptology

© Springer-Verlag Berlin Heidelberg 2013

Typesetting: Camera-ready by author, data conversion by Scientific Publishing Services, Chennai, India

Printed on acid-free paper

Springer is part of Springer Science+Business Media (www.springer.com)

Foreword from the General Chairs

It was a great pleasure for us to be associated with the 9th International Conference on Information Systems Security (ICISS) during December 16–20, 2013, held at the Indian Statistical Institute Kolkata, as General Chairs. After the excellent organization of the eighth edition of the conference last year at IIT Guwahati, we believe this event also took place without glitch. During the last 8 years, ICISS has secured its place as one of the most important venues for the researchers in information systems security primarily because of the dedication and quality-consciousness of its Program Committee. The Program Committee has all along maintained a strict review policy and the average acceptance ratio has been around 25%. In each edition of the conference, excellent tutorials are also presented, which are very popular among students and researchers.

This year, the Program Committee led by Aditya Bagchi and Indrakshi Ray, and assisted by the other reviewers, did an excellent job by completing the review process within the deadline. This was done in spite of prolonged debate and discussion regarding the acceptance of papers and shepherding by the volunteers. We record our appreciation to the Program Chairs, members of the Program Committee, and other reviewers for their excellent service to this research community and for drawing up an excellent Technical Program. We are indebted to Christopher W. Clifton, Florian Kerschbaum, and Sharad Mehrotra for accepting our invitation to deliver keynote talks. Tutorial Chair R. Tamal Goswami worked hard in organizing the tutorial at Birla Institute of Technology, Mesra, Kolkata campus.

The Organizing Committee led by Pinakpani Pal and Finance Chair Subhasis Dasgupta worked tirelessly to ensure that other aspects of the event were also commensurate with the technical quality. The efforts made by Publicity Chairs Raman Adaikkalavan and Anirban Sengupta, in promoting the conference to the international community of researchers, are commendable. We take this opportunity to thank our sponsors for their contributions.

December 2013

Bimal K. Roy
Chandan Mazumdar

Preface

This volume contains the papers selected for presentation at the 9th International Conference on Information Systems Security (ICISS 2013) held during December 16–20, 2013, at the Indian Statistical Institute, Kolkata, India. In 2005, ICISS started primarily as an initiative to promote information security-related research in India. However, from the very beginning, ICISS managed to draw the attention of the research community across the globe and has become a true international event. Selecting from 82 submissions of 15 countries around the world, 20 full papers and six short papers were accepted for presentation. All the papers were rigorously reviewed by at least three members of the Program Committee. We are extremely grateful to all the members of the Program Committee and the other external reviewers for offering their time and professional expertise. We are also grateful to Prof. Christopher Clifton, Dr. Florian Kerschbaum, and Prof. Sharad Mehrotra for delivering the keynote lectures. We were fortunate to have these three leading experts as invited speakers. Special thanks are due to Prof. Bimal K. Roy and Prof. Chandan Mazumdar for serving as general chairs. We are indebted to Prof. Sushil Jajodia, the brain behind this conference and the Steering Committee chair for his continuous guidance and help. We hope this collection of papers will be both stimulating and rewarding for the research community.

December 2013

Aditya Bagchi
Indrakshi Ray

Conference Organization

Steering Committee Chair

Sushil Jajodia   George Mason University, USA

General Chairs

Bimal Kr. Roy   Indian Statistical Institute, India
Chandan Mazumdar   Jadavpur University, India

Program Chairs

Aditya Bagchi   ISI, Kolkata
Indrakshi Ray   Colorado State University, USA

Organizing Chair

Pinakpani Pal   Indian Statistical Institute, India

Tutorial Chair

R.T. Goswami   Birla Institute of Technology (Mesra), India

Publicity Chairs

Raman Adaikkalavan   Indiana University South Bend, USA
Anirban Sengupta   Jadavpur University, India

Finance Chair

Subhasis Dasgupta   Indian Statistical Institute, India

Program Committee

Vijay Atluri   Rutgers University, USA
Aditya Bagchi   Indian Statistical Institute, India
Bruhadeshwar Bezawada   International Institute of Information
                                    Technology, Hyderabad, India
Prithvi Bisht   University of Illinois at Chicago, USA

Lorenzo Cavallaro	Royal Holloway, University of London, UK
Sanjit Chatterjee	Indian Institute of Science, India
Ashok Kumar Das	International Institute of Information Technology, Hyderabad, India
Subrat Dash	The LNM Institute of Information Technology, India
Anupam Datta	Carnegie Mellon University, USA
Rinku Dewri	University of Denver, USA
William Enck	North Carolina State University, USA
Vinod Ganapathy	Rutgers University, USA
Sushil Jajodia	George Mason University, USA
Somesh Jha	University of Wisconsin, USA
Aditya Kanade	Indian Institute of Science, India
Ram Krishnan	University of Texas at San Antonio, USA
Yingjiu Li	Singapore Management University
Javier Lopez	University of Malaga, Spain
Fabio Massacci	University of Trento, Italy
Chandan Mazumdar	Jadavpur University, India
Anitha Nadarajan	PSG College of Technology, Tamil Nadu, India
Sukumar Nandi	Indian Institute of Technology, Guwahati, India
Phu H. Phung	University of Illinois, Chicago, USA
Atul Prakash	University of Michigan, USA
Indrajit Ray	Colorado State University, USA
Indrakshi Ray	Colorado State University, USA
Bimal Roy	Indian Statistical Institute, India
Anirban Sengupta	Jadavpur University, India
Indranil Sengupta	Indian Institute of Technology, Kharagpur, India
Kapil Singh	IBM T.J. Watson Research Center, USA
Scott Stoller	Stony Brook University, USA
Shamik Sural	Indian Institute of Technology, Kharagpur, India
Mahesh Tripunitara	The University of Waterloo, Canada
Vinod Yegneswaran	SRI International, USA
Stefano Zanero	Politecnico di Milano, Italy

Additional Reviewers

Albanese, Massimiliano	Cai, Shaoying
Alcaraz, Cristina	Chakraborty, Rajat Subhra
Annadata, Prasad	Chen, Yao
Aumasson, Jean-Philippe	Clark, Jeremy
Bag, Samiran	Das, Abhijit
Barenghi, Alessandro	Davidson, Drew
Barua, Rana	De Capitani Di Vimercati, Sabrina

De Carli, Lorenzo
Dutta, Ratna
Eltarjaman, Wisam
Foresti, Sara
Frossi, Alessandro
Gionta, Jason
Gupta, Kishan Chand
Harris, William
Hayawi, Kadhim
Konidala, Divyan
Le, Meixing
Luchaup, Daniel
Maggi, Federico
Moataz, Tarik
Moreno, Carlos
Mukhopadhyay, Debdeep
Mulamba, Dieudo

Muthulakshmi, Angamuthu
Nandi, Mridul
Natarajan, Venkat
Odelu, Vanga
Pandey, Sumit Kumar
Papini, Davide
Saha, Sanjoy Kumar
Schiavoni, Stefano
Sharifi, Alireza
Shi, Jie
Shin, Heechang
Strizhov, Mikhail
Sun, Kun
Uzun, Emre
Wang, Lingyu
Wang, Zhan

Table of Contents

Challenges and Opportunities for Security with Differential Privacy*

Chris Clifton and Balamurugan Anandan

Department of Computer Science and CERIAS
Purdue University West Lafayette, Indiana, USA
{clifton,banandan}@cs.purdue.edu

Abstract. Differential Privacy has recently emerged as a measure for protecting privacy in distorted data. While this seems to solve many problems, in practice it still leaves a number of security challenges, and even raises new ones. We give an example of a secure two-party dot product protocol and use this as an example to demonstrate a number of challenges arising from the interaction of information security and differential privacy. We show that independently meeting the requirements of secure multiparty computation and differential privacy does not result in a solution meeting the real goals of privacy and security. Through this, we outline challenges and opportunities for further research.

Keywords: Differential Privacy, Secure Multiparty Computation, Privacy.

1 Introduction

Data distortion has long been used as a means of protecting privacy. (e.g., for census data; see [14].) Unfortunately, standards for how to distort data, or how much noise to add, have largely been domain and application specific. There does not yet exist a general theory of data distortion that is widely accepted in practice.

Differential privacy shows promise of addressing this issue. The idea behind differential privacy is to add sufficient noise so that the impact of any single individual on the outcome is small relative to the noise. Conceptually, if the contribution (or non-contribution) of any individual is lost in the noise, nothing is being revealed about that individual that is not inherent in the general knowledge. Differential privacy developed over a series of papers, culminating in [4]. These papers introduced not only a basic definition, but also a general method that satisfies differential privacy for any outcome. The possibility does exist of getting better results for specific outcomes; some examples can be found in [5].

In spite of the volume of work that has been produced, much remains to be done. One example is graph-structured data, such as social networks. The impact of a single individual on many types of graph analysis can be huge. For example, assume we want to learn distribution of path lengths (such as the "six degrees" hypothesis; that any two individuals in a social network are linked by a path

---

* The rights of this work are transferred to the extent transferable according to title 17 U.S.C. 105.

A. Bagchi and I. Ray (Eds.): ICISS 2013, LNCS 8303, pp. 1–13, 2013.

of length six or fewer.) Since a network could exist where a single individual forms the only short path between many nodes, differential privacy requires a large amount of noise to protect such a hypothetical individual. In practice, such social networks may not exist - but how do we model this with differential privacy? Further examples and related problems can be found in [15].

One problem differential privacy does *not* solve is improper disclosure of the original data. The basic premise is to take the original data, compute a query result, then add sufficient noise to the result to protect individual privacy. The raw data still resides at the server, where it is vulnerable to malicious intrusion, insider threat, or any of the other types of disclosures that result in the majority of today's privacy breaches.

While such breaches seem to be a pure security issue, there are cases where the interplay of differential privacy and information security raises new challenges and research opportunities. This paper goes into some detail on one example, combining differential privacy and secure multiparty computation. Specifically, we introduce a protocol for a differentially private distributed dot product. This problem needs differential privacy. The idea is that each party has a vector, with each value representing a value for a particular individual. The goal is to generate an aggregate value: the sum of the products of each individual's value (e.g., independent probabilities that when combined may reveal propensity for a particular disease.) The aggregate is general knowledge, but the individual values and their multiple are private.

This is an interesting problem, because a straightforward secure multiparty computation approach (blindly computing the result, with neither party learning anything but the final result) actually has a major privacy flaw. One party can use all zeros except for a one as the value for the targeted individual. The final result is then the other party's value for that targeted individual, resulting in a privacy violation. A differentially private result would solve this, as the result would have sufficient noise to mask that single individual's value.

As we shall see in Section 4, this is actually a rather challenging problem. We sketch out a solution, but also show issues that result in flaws in either privacy or integrity. While we do not present a complete solution, we sketch several ideas and point out issues that raise more general openings for security researchers.

First, we give some background on secure multiparty computation. We then give an introduction to differential privacy. Section 4 develops a protocol for secure dot product that outlines challenges with putting these two concepts together. We conclude with some general discussion of challenges for security research in support of differential privacy.

2   Secure Multiparty Computation

Secure Multiparty Computation enables jointly computing a function over the data of two or more parties while keeping their inputs private. More precisely, it deals with problem how to compute the functionality securely. The problem originated with Yao's secure comparison problem [16], resulting in both general techniques for any (polynomial time) function and specialized methods optimized to particular problems.

There are many scenarios in which two parties may want to compute a function of their input without sharing their respective inputs. Secure scalar product has been used as a building block in several privacy preserving data mining algorithms [2]. Here we deal with the problem of securely computing the dot product of two vectors while satisfying differential privacy. The protocol combines differential privacy and cryptography to securely compute the scalar product of two vectors.

In the semi-honest setting, the parties are curious but do not deviate from the protocol to gain more information. A formal definition of private two-party computation in the semi-honest model is given below.

Definition 1. *(privacy with respect to semi-honest behavior):[7]*

Let $f : \{0,1\}^* \times \{0,1\}^* \longmapsto \{0,1\}^* \times \{0,1\}^*$ be a functionality, and $f_1(x,y)$ (resp., $f_2(x,y)$) denote the first (resp., second) element of $f(x,y)$. Let Π be two-party protocol for computing f. The view *of the first (resp., second) party during an execution of Π on (x,y), denoted $\text{VIEW}_1^{\Pi}(x,y)$ (resp., $\text{VIEW}_2^{\Pi}(x,y)$), is $(x,r,m_1,\ldots,m_t)$ (resp., $(y,r,m_1,\ldots,m_t)$), where r represents the outcome of the first (resp., second) party's internal coin tosses, and m_i represents the ith message it has received. The* OUTPUT *of the first (resp., second) party during an execution of Π on (x,y), denoted $\text{OUTPUT}_1^{\Pi}(x,y)$ (resp., $\text{OUTPUT}_2^{\Pi}(x,y)$) is implicit in the party's own view of the execution, and $\text{OUTPUT}^{\Pi}(x,y) = \left(\text{OUTPUT}_1^{\Pi}(x,y), \text{OUTPUT}_2^{\Pi}(x,y)\right)$.*

(general case) We say that Π privately computes f if there exist probabilistic polynomial-time algorithms, denoted S_1 and S_2, such that

$$\{(S_1(x, f_1(x,y)), f(x,y))\}_{x,y} \overset{C}{\equiv} \left\{\left(\text{VIEW}_1^{\Pi}(x,y), \text{OUTPUT}^{\Pi}(x,y)\right)\right\}_{x,y}$$

$$\{(S_2(y, f_2(x,y)), f(x,y))\}_{x,y} \overset{C}{\equiv} \left\{\left(\text{VIEW}_2^{\Pi}(x,y), \text{OUTPUT}^{\Pi}(x,y)\right)\right\}_{x,y}$$

where $\overset{C}{\equiv}$ denotes computational indistinguishability by (non-uniform) families of polynomial-size circuits.

While it is very useful in some scenarios, it may not be suitable for parties with malicious intent. We will introduce some examples of malicious behavior and how this affects secure multiparty computation as we go along; numerous texts (such as [7]) are available for a full tutorial.

Numerous protocols have been proposed for privacy preserving distributed data mining using cryptographic techniques. A majority of the work in privacy preserving data mining has been done in the semi-honest setting. As we shall see, for our problem it makes no sense to consider the semi-honest setting, we really need to be secure against a malicious adversary. I.e., an adversary is allowed to behave arbitrarily. Security of a protocol in the malicious model is defined using the ideal/real model paradigm. Informally, a protocol is secure, if any attack on a real protocol can be carried out in the ideal model. Security is implied because no attacks can be carried out in the ideal model. More formally it can be defined as follows.

Definition 2. *Secure two-party computation: Let f be a two party function and π be the protocol run by the two parties. Protocol π is said to securely compute f (in the malicious model) if for any non-uniform probabilistic polynomial-time adversary A in the real model, there exists a nonuniform probabilistic expected polynomial-time adversary B for the ideal model, such that*

$$\left\{ IDEAL_{f,A}(x,y) \stackrel{C}{\equiv} REAL_{\pi,B}(x,y) \right\}$$

Namely, the two distributions are computationally indistinguishable.

A few secure protocols in malicious adversary model have also been proposed. Secure Set operations like union and intersection in the presence of malicious adversaries have been proposed in [10]. They represent multisets as polynomials and used a secure implementation of oblivious polynomial evaluation for building the protocol. [9] proposes a list of protocols for set operations, scalar product in the malicious model based on paillier encryption and validating each step using zero knowledge proofs.

We how describe some cryptographic tools used in the paper.

2.1   Additive Homomorphic Encryption

Let $E_{pk}(.)$ denote the encryption function with public key pk and $D_{sk}(.)$ denote the decryption function with the secret key sk. Then, an additive homomorphic encryption system satisfies the following properties. 1) Given the encryption of m_1 and m_2, $E_{pk}(m_1)$ and $E_{pk}(m_2)$, then there exists an efficient algorithm to compute the public key encryption of $m_1 + m_2$, denoted $E_{pk}(m_1 + m_2) := E_{pk}(m_1) \oplus E_{pk}(m_2)$. 2) Given a constant c and the encryption of m_1, $E_{pk}(m_1)$, there exists an efficient algorithm to compute the public key encryption of km_1, denoted $E_{pk}(km_1) := k \otimes E_{pk}(m_1)$. In this paper, we use an additive homomorphic encryption system Paillier [13].

2.2   Zero Knowledge Proofs

Since we are dealing with the malicious model, we utilize zero knowledge proofs to make sure that the actions taken by the parties are correct. Below, we summarize the ZKFs used in our protocol.

Proving That You Know a Plain Text: A party P_i can compute the zero knowledge proof $POK(e_a)$ if he knows an element a in the domain of valid plaintexts such that $D_{sk}(e_a) = a$

Proving That Multiplication Is Correct: Assume that party P_i is given an encryption $E_{pk}(a)$ and chooses constant c and calculates $E_{pk}(a.c)$. Later on, P_i can give zero knowledge proof $POMC(e_a, e_c, e_{a.c})$ such that $D_{sk}(e_{a.c}) = D_{sk}(e_c).D_{sk}(e_a)$.

3   Differential Privacy

The key idea behind differential privacy is that the contribution of a single individual to the publicly release result is small relative to the noise. This is done by calibrating the noise based on the potential difference in results between *any* two neighboring databases (databases that differ by one individual.)

We will review differential privacy and then discuss the techniques used to achieve differential privacy. Let D, D' denote databases that differ on a single entity. Then, differential privacy is defined as follows.

Definition 3. *ϵ-Differential Privacy [4]: A randomized mechanism $\mathcal{M}$ is ϵ-differentially private if for all D, and for any $S \subseteq Range(\mathcal{M})$, the following holds*

$$P(\mathcal{M}(D) \in S) \leq e^{\epsilon} P(\mathcal{M}(D') \in S)$$

As with secure multiparty computation, differential privacy has a seminal result giving a method for any query. The technique proposed by [6] to achieve ϵ-differential privacy is by adding a suitable noise generated from the Laplace distribution to the output.

Lemma 1. *Laplace Mechanism: For a function $f : \mathcal{D} \to \mathbb{R}^k$, let the global sensitivity of f be*

$$\Delta f = \max_{D,D'} \|f(D) - f(D')\|_1$$

for any D. Then, a randomized mechanism $\mathcal{M}$ on D'' that returns $f(D'') + Lap(0, \frac{\Delta f}{\epsilon})$ is a ϵ-DP.

The difference between the results from the true world D and its neighbor D' is the difference the privatization noise will need to obfuscate in order for the privatized results to not give evidence about whether D or D' is the true world. The upper bound of this difference over $D_I \in \mathcal{D}$ is the *sensitivity* of query F. For example, if we assume a binary dot product (the count of individuals for whom both parties have value 1), the sensitivity is 1. Removing/Adding an individual (modifying a value from 1 to 0 or vice versa) will change the outcome by at most one, *regardless of the initial vectors*. In general, the sensitivity of dot product is the multiple of the maximum possible values in the domain.

Definition 3 is the strongest definition of differential privacy and is also called as information theoretic privacy. Since it is too strong, several relaxed versions of differential privacy, which holds privacy against computational adversaries were proposed in [12]. Here, we provide the definition of *SIM-CPD* privacy as it is referred later in section 4.

Definition 4. *SIM-CPD Privacy: An ensemble $\{f_k\}_{k \in \mathbb{N}}$ of randomized functions $f_k : \mathcal{D} \to \mathbb{R}_k$ provides ϵ_k-SIM-CDP if there exists an ensemble $\{F_k\}_{k \in \mathbb{N}}$ of ϵ_k-differentially-private mechanisms $F_k : \mathcal{D} \to \mathbb{R}_k$ and a negligible function negl(.) such that for every non-uniform p.p.t. TM A, every polynomial p(.), every sufficiently large $k \in \mathbb{N}$, all data sets $D \in \mathcal{D}$ of size at most $p(k)$, and every advice string z_k of size at most $p(k)$, it holds that*

$$|Pr[A_k(f_k(D)) = 1] - Pr[A_k(F_k(D)) = 1] \leq negl(k)$$

Let $\{f_k\}_{k\in\mathbb{N}}, \{g_k\}_{k\in\mathbb{N}}$ denote the ensembles of randomized interactive functions of f_k, g_k respectively and $\{\langle f_k(.), g_k(.)\rangle\}_{k\in\mathbb{N}}$ denote the ensemble of interactive protocols of $\{f_k\}_{k\in\mathbb{N}}, \{g_k\}_{k\in\mathbb{N}}$. In an execution $\langle f_k(x), g_k^*(.)\rangle$ with input x for the honest party f_k, the view of the adversary g_k^* is defined by $\text{VIEW}_{k,g_k^*}(x)$. Then, the definitions for two party differentially private computation is as follows.

Definition 5. *[12] An ensemble $\{\langle f_k(.), g_k(.)\rangle\}_{k\in\mathbb{N}}$ of interactive protocols ensures for $\{f_k\}_{k\in\mathbb{N}}$,*

- *ϵ_k-DP, if for every ensemble $\{g_k^*\}_{k\in\mathbb{N}}$ of randomized interactive functions, it holds that the ensemble $\{\text{VIEW}_{k,g_k^*}(x)\}_{k\in\mathbb{N}}$ provides ϵ_k-DP with respect to $x \in \mathcal{D}$*
- *ϵ_k-SIM-DP, if for every ensemble $\{g_k^*\}_{k\in\mathbb{N}}$ of efficiently computable randomized interactive functions, there exists an ensemble $\{F_k\}_{k\in\mathbb{N}}$ of ϵ_k-DP mechanisms $F_k(.)$ such that for every $x \in \mathcal{D}$, the probability ensembles $\{\text{VIEW}_{k,g_k^*}(x)\}_{k\in\mathbb{N}}$ and $F_k(x)_{k\in\mathbb{N}}$ are computationally indistinguishable.*

The above notions are symmetrically defined for the other ensemble $\{g_k\}_{k\in\mathbb{N}}$

The protocols we propose in the paper only need to be secure against computationally bounded adversaries because of cryptographic limitations. Any computationally unbounded adversary will be able to break the cryptographic scheme and thereby resulting in breach of privacy, so we must assume a computationally bounded adversary.

4   Secure Dot Product

The basic problem is as follows. Each party P_i has a binary input vector x_i and wish to compute the dot product of their inputs without revealing any information about them. Two parties each having an input vector run the protocol such that at the end of the protocol, both get a differential private dot product as the output while preserving the privacy of their inputs. The differentially private output of party P_i is $<x_i, x_{1-i}> + r'$ where r' is the noise randomly sampled from $Lap(0, \lambda)$ where $\lambda = \frac{1}{\epsilon}$. The perturbation technique of adding laplacian noise with zero mean and scale parameter of λ is used here to satisfy differential privacy. It is easy to see that the global sensitivity of dot product is 1.

The protocol assumes that the domain of the dataset is already known to both the parties and they have agreed on the vector space of their inputs before engaging in the dot product protocol. If their input comes from a publicly available domain then they could use it as the vector space. For example, if their inputs are documents they can use the corresponding language vocabulary as their vector space. If not, they can engage in a secure set union protocol (e.g., [10]) to determine the vector space. Before going into the details of dot product protocol, we present the notations used in the protocol.

A simple semi-honest approach would be for party P_0 to homomorphically encrypt x_0 and send it to P_1, along with an encryption of a noise value randomly selected from the laplacian distribution appropriate to the given sensitivity.

P_i	Party i
pk	Public Key
sk_i	Private key share of P_i
x_i	P_i's input vector
x_{ij}	j^{th} element of x_i
$\tilde{x}_{ij}$	Encryption of x_{ij}
$\oplus$	Homomorphic Addition
$\otimes$	Multiplication of constant with encrypted value

P_1 can then multiply each $\tilde{x}_{0j} \otimes x_{1j}$ (e.g., through repeated addition, although there are systems such as Pallier that support more efficient multiplication by a constant.) P_1 can then compute the sum, homomorphically add the noise value, and send to P_0 to decrypt.

Unfortunately, this is not quite secure even in the semi-honest model. Since, P_0 knows the noise, it can remove it to get the exact answer. A better approach is for each party to generate noise (requiring that P_1 know the encryption key), so P_1 can calculate $dotproduct \oplus noise_0 \oplus noise_1$. Then each party can subtract the noise it generated, giving each a (different) differentially private result. This is given formally in Algorithm 1.

Algorithm 1. Two Party Secure Dot Product in HbC model

Input: Party i's input vector is x_i.

Output: $f_i = <x_0, x_1> + r_{1-i}$

1: P_0 generate a pair of keys (pk, sk) using $\mathcal{KG}$ and sends the encrypted input vector $\tilde{x}_0$ and public key pk to party P_1
2: P_1 computes the dot product $\tilde{s} = E_{pk}(\sum_j^n x_{0j}.x_{1j})$ by multiplying its input vector x_1 with $\tilde{x}_0$ and summing up the values using homomorphic addition.
3: P_1 can homomorphically add suitable noise $r_1 \sim Lap(\frac{\Delta f}{\epsilon})$ to $\tilde{s}$ to obtain $\tilde{f}_0 = \tilde{s} \oplus \tilde{r}_1$ and send the differentially private value to P_0
4: P_0 decrypts the value $f_0 = D_{pk}(\tilde{f}_0)$ and sends $f_1 = f_0 + r_0$ to P_1 where r_0 is sampled from $Lap(\frac{\Delta f}{\epsilon})$ by P_0.
5: P_1 subtracts r_1 from f_1 to obtain its output.

A brief argument for the correctness and security of this protocol goes as follows. We show that the protocol ensures ϵ_k-DP for P_1 and ϵ_k-SIM-DP for P_0. For the first case, for every $\{f_k^*\}_{k \in \mathbb{N}}$, the only value dependent upon x_1 in the view of adversary during the execution of the protocol is $f_0 = <x_0, x_1> + r_1$, which is ϵ_k-differentially private based on Lemma 1. Hence, for all x_1, $\{\text{VIEW}_{k,f_k^*}(x_1)\}_{k \in \mathbb{N}}$ is ϵ_k-DP proving that the protocol ensures ensures ϵ_k-DP for P_1. For the second case, let us consider the cheating party P_1 is represented by the function ensemble $\{g_k^*\}_{k \in \mathbb{N}}$. In order to show that protocol ensures ϵ_k-SIM-DP for P_0, we need to build a simulator F_k that is ϵ_k-DP and show that $\forall x_0$, $\{F_k(x_0)\}_{k \in \mathbb{N}}$ and $\{\text{VIEW}_{k,g_k^*}(x_0)\}_{k \in \mathbb{N}}$ are computationally indistinguishable. The construction of

F_k is as follows. F_k randomly selects a input vector $x'_0 \in \{0,1\}^n$ and sends $\tilde{x}'_0$ to g^*_k. It then receives f_0 from g^*_k. F_k completes the simulation by sending $f_1 = <x_0, x_1> + r'_0$ to g^*_k, where $r'_0 \sim Lap(\frac{1}{\epsilon})$. F_k is ϵ_k-DP because for any x_0, it outputs f_1 which is ϵ_k-DP from Lemma 1. The view of the adversary that depend upon x_0 are $\tilde{x}_0$ and f_1. The indistinguishability argument for $\tilde{x}_0$ directly follows from semantic security of the Paillier encryption scheme. f_1 is identically distributed in both the views of adversary and F_k because $f_1 \sim Lap(<x_0, x_1>, \frac{1}{\epsilon})$ proving ϵ_k-SIM-DP for P_0.

Algorithm 1 is secure as long as the parties follow the protocol. But it does not guarantee that a malicious user will be caught if he deviates from the protocol. As we shall show, this can be solved using standard approaches to secure multiparty computation in the malicious model.

We now give extensions to the above protocol to address these issues. To ensure that the protocol is followed (like, proofs of consistency of cipher texts) we use zero knowledge proofs as given in [3].

Algorithm 2. Secure Dot Product in the malicious setting

Input: Two Parties holds their share sk_0 and sk_1 of the private key and a common public key pk. Party i's input vector is x_i.

Output: $f_i = <x_0, x_1> + r_{1-i}$

1: **for** P_0 **do**
2:     $\forall j \; \tilde{x}_{0j} = E_{pk}(x_{0j})$ and create $POK(\tilde{x}_{0j})$
3:     Send encryptions $\tilde{x}_{0j}, \tilde{r}_0$ and $POK(\tilde{x}_{0j})$ to P_1
4: **end for**
5: **for** P_1 **do**
6:     $\forall j$ check whether $POK(\tilde{x}_{0j})$ is correct, Else ABORT
7:     $\forall j$ create $\tilde{x}_{1j} = E_{pk}(x_{1j})$ and $\tilde{z}_{1j} = x_{1j} \otimes \tilde{x}_{0j}$
8:     $\tilde{s} = \tilde{z}_{11} \oplus \tilde{z}_{12} \ldots \tilde{z}_{1n} \oplus \tilde{r}_0 \oplus \tilde{r}_1 = E_{pk} \sum_j^n (x_{0j}.x_{1j} + \tilde{r}_0 + \tilde{r}_1)$
9:     Send $\tilde{s}, \tilde{r}_1, \forall j \; POMC(\tilde{x}_{0j}, \tilde{x}_{1j}, \tilde{z}_{1j})$ and $POK(\tilde{x}_{1j})$ to P_0
10: **end for**
11: **for** P_0 **do**
12:     Check $\forall j$ if $POK(\tilde{x}_{1j})$ are correct, Else ABORT
13:     Check $\forall j$ if $POMC(\tilde{x}_{0j}, \tilde{x}_{1j}, \tilde{z}_{1j})$ are correct, Else ABORT
14:     Calculate $\tilde{z}_{11} \oplus \tilde{z}_{12} \ldots \tilde{z}_{1n} \oplus \tilde{r}_0 \oplus \tilde{r}_1$ and verify if it matches with $\tilde{s}$
15: **end for**
16: Jointly decrypt $\tilde{s}$.
17: P_i gets the ϵ-differentially private similarity by subtracting r_i from s

---

There is a more insidious problem: A party who desires exclusive access to the result can do so without being detected. Instead of drawing noise from a Laplacian distribution, a party can always add an extremely large value. Since it can subtract this value, it obtains the correct differentially private result. But since it is possible (although highly unlikely) that a value drawn from a Laplacian distribution is extremely large, the second party will not be able to distinguish between maliciously being forced into a bad result and simple "bad luck".

While this does not result in a privacy violation (each party is still getting a result that is sufficiently noisy to hide the impact of any individual), it does make practical use of the protocol untenable.

Using existing methods from the Secure Multiparty Computation literature to convert from a semi-honest to malicious protocol does not solve the problem, as the issue is really with the noise generated, essentially part of the party's input. Such input modification is beyond the scope of malicious protocols; the ability to choose one's input (e.g., a single 1 and the rest 0s to probe for one individual's value) is what gives us the need for differential privacy in the first place. Without differential privacy, even a protocol secure in the malicious model fails to protect privacy, with a simple application of differential privacy it fails to guarantee correctness of results.

It turns out that this is a challenging issue. Methods to "check" the noise added by each party must allow for the possibility that the noise really is large; this results in at best probabilistic guarantees of correctness. Such guarantees do not really fit with existing definitions for secure multiparty computation.

5   Empirical Evaluation

One concern that arises with differential privacy is the usefulness of the results. Are they too noisy for practical utility? To do this, we look at a practical use of the protocol: document comparison using the cosine similarity metric (a differentially private solution to the problem addressed in [8].) We first review cosine similarity, and discuss how this uses and affects the differentially private secure dot product.

5.1   Cosine Similarity

There are number of situations where two parties might want to calculate the similarity of their documents without revealing the input documents. Cosine similarity is a widely used metric to measure the similarity of two documents. Cosine similarity can be viewed as the dot product of the normalized input vectors vectors.

$$\frac{\sum_j x_{0j}.x_{1j}}{\|x_0\|_2 \|x_1\|_2} = \sum_j \frac{x_{0j}}{\|x_0\|_2} . \frac{x_{1j}}{\|x_1\|_2} = <x_0'.x_1'>$$

If we assume that every term in the document has equal weight, i.e., 1 or 0 depending upon the presence or absence of a term, then the global sensitivity of the cosine similarity function is upper bounded by $\frac{1}{\sqrt{nm}}$, where n and m are the total number of terms present in the P_0 and P_1 document respectively. The notion of differential privacy allows us to assume that each party knows the size of the other party's document.

Similarity measures usually weight the terms in order to efficiently compute the metric. If tf-idf weighting mechanism is used to measure the importance of words. Let β be the highest weight of a term in the domain, then the global sensitivity of squared cosine similarity for Party P_0 is always $\leq \frac{2\beta^2}{||x_0||_2^2}$, where $||x_0||_2$ is the norm of the party P_0 input vector. Let x_1' contain one term less than x_1, the sensitivity is given as

$$\Delta s = \max_{x_1, x_1'} \left(\frac{<x_0.x_1>^2}{||x_0||_2^2 ||x_1||_2^2} - \frac{<x_0.x_1'>^2}{||x_0||_2^2 ||x_1'||_2^2} \right)$$

$$\leq \frac{<x_0.x_1>^2}{||x_0||_2^2 ||x_1||_2^2} - \frac{<x_0.x_1'>^2}{||x_0||_2^2 ||x_1||_2^2} = \frac{(\sum_j x_{0j}.x_{1j})^2 - (\sum_j x_{0j}.x_{1j}')^2}{||x_0||_2^2 ||x_1||_2^2}$$

$$= \frac{(\sum_j x_{0j}.x_{1j} - \sum_j x_{0j}.x_{1j}')(\sum_j x_{0j}.x_{1j} + \sum_j x_{0j}.x_{1j}')}{||x_0||_2^2 ||x_1||_2^2}$$

$$\leq \frac{(x_{0s}.x_{1s})(2 \sum_j x_{0j}.x_{1j})}{||x_0||_2^2 ||x_1||_2^2} \leq \frac{2\beta^2}{||x_0||_2^2}$$

In step 2 and 5, we are using the fact that $|x_1| > |x_1'|$. Since, $x_{0s}.x_{1s} \leq \beta^2$ and $\sum_j x_{0j}.x_{1j} \leq ||x_1||_2^2$, we can upper bound $\Delta s \leq 2\beta^2/||x_0||_2^2$. Similarly, we can estimate the global sensitivity for party P_1 as $2\beta^2/||x_1||_2^2$. Note that the noise distribution of P_i only depends on his input vector x_i and β (the highest term weight in the domain).

5.2   Impact of Differential Privacy

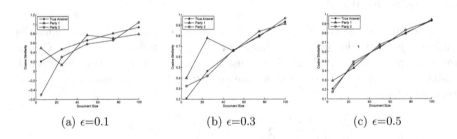

(a) ϵ=0.1   (b) ϵ=0.3   (c) ϵ=0.5

We now evaluate the utility of the protocol by computing differentially private values for different levels of security. An ϵ value of 0 in differential privacy denotes perfect privacy as the probability of seeing the output in D and D' are equal but on the downside the utility will be very less. In our experiments we have used ϵ values of 0.1, 0.3 and 0.5. We implemented the two party secure differentially private cosine similarity measure without term weighting using the secure dot product protocol and ran the tests for different values of ϵ. The global sensitivity of cosine similarity is $\frac{1}{\sqrt{nm}}$, so the random noise r' is generated from Laplace distribution with mean 0 and scale $\frac{1}{\epsilon\sqrt{nm}}$, where n, m are the number of terms in P_0 and P_1 respectively.

In order to show the deviation of the differentially private similarity score from the true score (cosine similarity without privacy), we plotted the scores of each party obtained on running the protocol along with the true scores. For each ϵ value, we fixed the input (i.e., document) of one party and varied the size of the document of other party. We can see that if the document sizes are small, then the differentially private similarity scores are far away from the true but as the size increases, the differentially private similarity score are better approximations of the true score. Hence a party without malicious intent on running the protocol will be able to obtain similarity score closer to the true value.

6   Related Work

There has been some work looking at distributed differential privacy. In [1], a secure protocol is proposed to determine the differentially private similarity of profile of users in the semi-honest setting. They measure the similarity of users using squared cosine similarity. To the best of our knowledge, all the previous papers on secure differentially private protocols are proven to be secure in the semi-honest setting. As we have seen, this is often not practically sufficient.

An interesting aside with respect to differentially private dot product. In [11] it is shown that in a two party information theoretic differential privacy setting, no party will be able to estimate the dot product of the their input vectors within an accuracy of $o(\frac{\sqrt{n}}{\log n})$.

7   Conclusion

Privacy and Security are really two different concepts, but in the computing world information privacy cannot be achieved without adequate information security. Many approaches to privacy, such as differential privacy, assume security of the underlying data. However, key security concepts such as separation of duty can be at odds with the approaches developed to produce privacy-preserving analyses of data.

Noise-based privacy approaches such as differential privacy pose a special challenge: How to ensure integrity of results when the results are falsified by design? This is the stumbling block of the protocol presented in Section 4. Expanding the theory of secure multiparty computation to deal with such noisy results and the possibility that a malicious party can succeed would enable many advances in this area.

A second opportunity arises in cryptography. Storing and computing on data in encrypted form protects against unwanted disclosure. The goal of disclosing query results only with noise added raises an interesting possibility: Can we use cryptographic methods that are inherently noisy? (E.g., probabilistic methods that may fail to properly decrypt.) If such noise/failure occurred with predictable probability, perhaps this could be used to generate encrypted datasets that inherently satisfied differential privacy when used.

Finally, for systems security researchers: What about a concept of a differentially private reference monitor? Given the "privacy budget" model of differential privacy, this raises some interesting challenges in tracking users and uses of data. However, such a model could relax other security requirements, as access to data coming through the reference monitor would not face the same constraints imposed on access to raw data.

These are only a few ideas. As evolving privacy research generates new ideas and approaches, the resulting opportunity for new information security approaches that support and enable balancing needs to use high quality data with requirements to protect individual privacy.

References

1. Alaggan, M., Gambs, S., Kermarrec, A.-M.: Private similarity computation in distributed systems: from cryptography to differential privacy. In: Fernàndez Anta, A., Lipari, G., Roy, M. (eds.) OPODIS 2011. LNCS, vol. 7109, pp. 357–377. Springer, Heidelberg (2011)
2. Clifton, C., Kantarcıoğlu, M., Lin, X., Vaidya, J., Zhu, M.: Tools for privacy preserving distributed data mining. SIGKDD Explorations 4(2), 28–34 (2003)
3. Cramer, R., Damgård, I., Nielsen, J.B.: Multiparty computation from threshold homomorphic encryption. In: Pfitzmann, B. (ed.) EUROCRYPT 2001. LNCS, vol. 2045, pp. 280–299. Springer, Heidelberg (2001)
4. Dwork, C.: Differential privacy. In: Bugliesi, M., Preneel, B., Sassone, V., Wegener, I. (eds.) ICALP 2006. LNCS, vol. 4052, pp. 1–12. Springer, Heidelberg (2006)
5. Dwork, C.: Differential privacy: A survey of results. In: Agrawal, M., Du, D.-Z., Duan, Z., Li, A. (eds.) TAMC 2008. LNCS, vol. 4978, pp. 1–19. Springer, Heidelberg (2008)
6. Dwork, C., McSherry, F., Nissim, K., Smith, A.: Calibrating noise to sensitivity in private data analysis. In: Halevi, S., Rabin, T. (eds.) TCC 2006. LNCS, vol. 3876, pp. 265–284. Springer, Heidelberg (2006)
7. Goldreich, O.: Encryption Schemes. The Foundations of Cryptography, vol. 2. Cambridge University Press (2004)
8. Jiang, W., Murugesan, M., Clifton, C., Si, L., Vaidya, J.: Efficient privacy-preserving similar document detection. VLDB Journal 19(4), 457–475 (2010)
9. Kantarcioglu, M., Kardes, O.: Privacy-preserving data mining in the malicious model. Int. J. Inf. Comput. Secur. 2(4), 353–375 (2008)
10. Kissner, L., Song, D.: Privacy-preserving set operations. In: Shoup, V. (ed.) CRYPTO 2005. LNCS, vol. 3621, pp. 241–257. Springer, Heidelberg (2005)
11. McGregor, A., Mironov, I., Pitassi, T., Reingold, O., Talwar, K., Vadhan, S.: The limits of two-party differential privacy. In: Proceedings of the 2010 IEEE 51st Annual Symposium on Foundations of Computer Science, FOCS 2010, pp. 81–90. IEEE Computer Society, Washington, DC (2010)
12. Mironov, I., Pandey, O., Reingold, O., Vadhan, S.: Computational differential privacy. In: Halevi, S. (ed.) CRYPTO 2009. LNCS, vol. 5677, pp. 126–142. Springer, Heidelberg (2009)

13. Paillier, P.: Public-key cryptosystems based on composite degree residuosity classes. In: Stern, J. (ed.) EUROCRYPT 1999. LNCS, vol. 1592, pp. 223–238. Springer, Heidelberg (1999)
14. Subcommittee on Disclosure Limitation Methodology, Federal Committee on Statistical Methodology. Report on statistical disclosure limitation methodology. Statistical Policy Working Paper 22 (NTIS PB94-16530), Statistical Policy Office, Office of Information and Regulatory Affairs, Office of Management and Budget, Washington, DC (May 1994)
15. Task, C., Clifton, C.: A guide to differential privacy theory in social network analysis. In: The 2012 IEEE/ACM International Conference on Advances in Social Networks Analysis and Mining (ASONAM 2012), Istanbul, Turkey, August 26-29 (2012)
16. Yao, A.C.: How to generate and exchange secrets. In: Proceedings of the 27th IEEE Symposium on Foundations of Computer Science, pp. 162–167. IEEE (1986)

An Encrypted In-Memory Column-Store:
The Onion Selection Problem

Florian Kerschbaum, Martin Härterich, Mathias Kohler,
Isabelle Hang, Andreas Schaad, Axel Schröpfer, and Walter Tighzert

SAP
Karlsruhe, Germany
`firstname.lastname@sap.com`

Abstract. Processing encrypted queries in the cloud has been extended
by CryptDB's approach of adjustable onion encryption. This adjustment
of the encryption entails a translation of an SQL query to an equivalent
query on encrypted data. We investigate in more detail this translation
and in particular the problem of selecting the right onion layer. Our algorithm extends CryptDB's approach by three new functions: configurable
onions, local execution and searchable encryption. We have evaluated
our new algorithm in a prototypical implementation in an in-memory
column store database system.

1 Introduction

Security is a major obstacle for widespread cloud adoption. Criminal hackers or
foreign government organizations may try to gain access to the data stored in the
cloud. Encryption of this data may provide a solution, but it may also prevent
the use of and computation with it in the cloud. A current research challenge is
therefore to enable the processing of the data in the cloud while it is encrypted.

One of the many cloud offerings is database-as-a-service [10]. A service
provider offers database store and query capabilities, e.g., through an SQL interface, and charges for storage and computation. Clearly, there is less benefit
if query processing would be done at the client and only storage in the cloud.
Therefore, when using encryption queries need to be processed over encrypted
data – ciphertexts.

This was first introduced in [9]. Relational database operators have been
adapted to allow for processing over encrypted data. Binning was introduced
as a method to handle range queries. In binning values are put in larger bins
and all bins of a range are queried using equality matching. Values which are in
the selected bins, but are not in the range are filtered using post processing on
the client.

This approach was improved by order-preserving encryption [1]. Order-
preserving encryption preserves the order of the plaintexts in the ciphertexts. It
allows implementing range queries using the same relational operators as used
in plaintext databases. Databases encrypted using order-preserving encryption

A. Bagchi and I. Ray (Eds.): ICISS 2013, LNCS 8303, pp. 14–26, 2013.

can already perform most queries (except aggregation) without modification of the database operators.

Order-preserving encryption was first put on a formal basis in [4]. Boldyreva et al. developed the concept of a random order-preserving function that mapped a smaller domain to a larger domain while preserving the order of the inputs. They proved that their encryption scheme was a uniform random choice among all random order-preserving functions. Therefore no order-preserving encryption scheme could be better than theirs.

Still, what this security guarantee entails for the user remained (and somewhat remains) unclear. Later Boldyreva et al. analyzed their own scheme [5] and concluded that roughly the upper half of the plaintext bits leaks to a passive observer. They introduced the notion of ideal security for order-preserving encryption, i.e., that nothing should be leaked except the order.

The best ideal security order-preserving encryption is replacing the plaintexts by their order. This encryption is a mapping of a larger domain of plaintexts to a smaller domain of ciphertexts. The challenge is to be able to accommodate future plaintexts not foreseen when choosing the encryption. This challenge has not yet been fully solved, but Popa et al. propose an interactive protocol to compute the ciphertexts [21].

Even with ideal security the security of order-preserving encryption remains questionable. Popa et al. developed adjustable onion encryption as a means to reveal the order-preserving ciphertexts only when necessary for a specific query. The idea is to wrap onion layers of more secure encryption schemes around the order-preserving ciphertext. These layers are only removed when a range query requiring order preservation is processed. Using this approach most queries can be handled without resorting to order-preserving encryption.

In this paper we investigate the problem of identifying the right layer of encryption for processing a query, i.e., the onion selection problem, in more detail. We define our requirements of *policy configuration, alternative resolution* and *conflict resolution*. Based on these requirements we derive and present a new onion selection algorithm.

The remainder of the paper is structured as follows: In the next section we describe the different onions and their layers in default mode. We then define the onion selection problem and present our algorithm in Section 3. Finally, in Section 4 we give an outlook on the remaining challenges in processing queries over encrypted data.

2   Adjustable Onion Encryption

Adjustable onion encryption was introduced by Popa et al. in [22]. In this section we present the layers of the onion as described in their approach. We later outline a number of alternatives and extension that complicate our problem of onion selection.

Differently from [22] which used a row-based, disk-store database management system (DBMS) we use a column-based in-memory DBMS [7]. The impact of the encryption schemes on the dictionary compression used in column-stores differs widely. We refer the interested reader to [15] for details. Still, also for onion handling column stores offer advantages. Namely, it is easy to add and remove columns on the fly during operation. This creates the opportunity to remove onions when no longer useful – a further option for future investigation.

2.1 The Onion Layers

We denote $E_C^T(x)$ the ciphertext (encryption) of plaintext x in type T (e.g. order-preserving) with key C (usually for a column). The corresponding decryption is $D_C^T(c)$, i.e., $D_C^T(E_C^T(x)) = x$ as in Dolev-Yao notation. We sometimes omit the key, if it is a single key. Note that all keys initially reside at the client. The database has no access to any key, unless revealed during the adjustment of encryption, i.e. "when peeling the onion".

In the "standard" onion there are three encryption types: order-preserving (OPE), deterministic (DET) and randomized (RND). The term onion stems from the layering of encryption, i.e., the output (ciphertext) of one encryption type is fed as in input to another. The onion of [22] looks like the following:

$$E^{RND}(E_C^{DET}(E^{OPE}(x)))$$

We describe the layers of this onion from the innermost – the plaintext – to the outermost – randomized encryption. The choice of this layering is not arbitrary. Each outer layer adds more security, i.e., the better the onion is preserved the better the security starting with industrial strength. Each inner layer adds functionality, i.e., inner layers allow more database operators to function as on plaintext. It is important to note that inner layers preserve the functionality of all outer layers, i.e., they never remove any functionality.

Plaintext. We treat the plaintext x as its own layer. This has two reasons: First, not each encryption type has the plaintext as the innermost layer – see searchable encryption (Section 2.2). Second, addressing it as its own layer enables us to make it configurable. As we describe in our requirements (Section 3.2) a user may want to prevent access to the plaintext or not encrypt certain columns at all.

Clearly, the plaintext allows processing all queries, but provides no security.

Order-Preserving Encryption. Order-preserving encryption (type: OPE) preserves the order of the encryption:

$$x \leq y \Longleftrightarrow E^{OPE}(x) \leq E^{OPE}(y)$$

We use the scheme of Boldyreva et al. [4], since the ideally secure scheme of Popa et al. [21] is incompatible with adjustable encryption. We omit the key, since we use the same key for each column of the same data type. This is necessary in order to allow joins using deterministic encryption of the upper layer.

Since the order is preserved, order-preserving encryption enables processing range queries on ciphertext in the same way as on plaintexts. Furthermore, since our order-preserving scheme is also deterministic, it also still can process equality matching and joins. As already mentioned the security of order-preserving encryption is still debated.

Deterministic Encryption. Deterministic encryption always produces the same ciphertext for a plaintext:

$$x = y \Longleftrightarrow E_C^{DET}(x) = E_C^{DET}(y)$$

Deterministic encryption used to be the standard mode before randomized encryption was introduced. Bellare et al. have proven that only deterministic encryption can allow sublinear search [2]. Therefore equality matches and joins thereon can be performed more efficiently, i.e., using an unmodified database operator. Deterministic encryption still allows statistical attacks, such as [11]. Yet, since the order is permuted, it is more secure than order-preserving encryption.

Initially we use a different key C for each column. Clearly, this prevents joins based on equality matches, since the columns are encrypted differently. Blaze et al. introduced proxy re-encryption [3] – a technique to transform a ciphertext from key A to key B without decrypting it or needing to know any of the two keys A or B. We use this proxy re-encryption in order to adjust the encryption keys just before performing a join operation. For details how to choose which column to re-encrypt we refer the reader to [16].

We use the proxy re-encryptable encryption scheme of Pohlig and Hellman for deterministic encryption [20]. A similar scheme on elliptic curves has been used in [22].

Randomized Encryption. Randomized encryption has been formalized by Goldwasser and Micali [8]. It has become the standard mode of encryption. A randomization parameter ensure that each ciphertext – even from the same plaintext – is indistinguishable. We use the AES standard in CBC mode for this encryption. We can use a single key, since each plaintext is indistinguishable.

Randomized encryption is the most secure, but allows no operation except retrieval to the client.

2.2 Alternative Encryptions

The layering of the onion does not need to be same in all cases and next to this "standard" onion other encryption schemes are necessary or useful. We introduce them in the following subsections.

Homomorphic Encryption. Homomorphic encryption allows arithmetic operations, most notably addition, using the ciphertexts. In order to support aggregation without the plaintext, it is therefore necessary to incorporate homomorphic encryption. We use the encryption scheme by Paillier [18] which allows only addition:

$$D^{HOM}(E^{HOM}(x) \cdot E^{HOM}(y)) = x + y$$

The following operation for multiplication by a plaintext can be easily derived

$$D^{HOM}(E^{HOM}(x)^y) = x \cdot y$$

Paillier's encryption scheme is indistinguishable under chosen plaintext attack – as is randomized encryption. Therefore only a single key is necessary. Furthermore Paillier's encryption scheme is public key, but we keep the public key secret and treat it like a secret key encryption scheme.

There are some difference between the above encryption schemes and homomorphic encryption scheme. First homomorphic encryption requires aggregation (sum operator) to be processed differently than on plaintexts. Additions is replaced by multiplication, actually modular multiplication. This requires implementation of one's own operator. In [22] the authors use user-defined functions, we implemented our own database operator.

A second difference is that the result of the database operator – the sum – is still encrypted. Therefore it is not possible to use this result in many subsequent operations such as range queries. Queries using a chain of such operations need to be partially executed at the client on plaintext.

Searchable Encryption. Searchable encryption allows the private or secret key holder to issue a search token for a query plaintext. This search token can be used to match ciphertexts for plaintext equality or range inclusion to the query. Unless a token has been issued searchable encryption is as secure as randomized encryption, but for search token the accessed ciphertexts are leaked. Let $T^{SRC}(x)$ denote the search token and M^{SRC} the matching operation.

$$x = / \neq y \iff M^{SRC}(T^{SRC}(x), E^{SRC}(y)) = \top/\bot$$

The research on searchable encryption has been sparked by Song et al. [24]. We use a scheme very comparable to theirs and implemented it using user-defined functions. Search time can be significantly improved by building an index, but this requires a modification of the database. Hence, we prefer the linear search.

Security for searchable encryption has been formalized by Curtmola et al. in [6] and they also present an index-based scheme. In their security definition access pattern leakage is explicitly excluded. This has been extended to dynamic searchable encryption which also allows updates [12]. Here, update patterns are also explicitly excluded which raises questions about the advantages for the user compared to deterministic encryption. Note that the scheme of [24] is more securely updateable, since it does not use an index. The technique of Shi et al. can be adapted to also enable range queries [23].

Searchable encryption must not be decryptable. In our scheme [24] – and several others – the plaintext is used to construct key and a random number is encrypted. Therefore searchable encryption may not be used for retrieval.

Efficiency of searchable encryption is significantly lower than deterministic encryption. It can therefore be advisable to not include it as an option for database operations. Before considering searchable encryption we call a function to make this decision.

Client Decryption. Next to functionality as in homomorphic encryption and security as in searchable encryption also efficiency can be a reason to add an onion. A bottleneck during encrypted query processing is decrypting the result on the client. It can therefore be more efficient to use a specific onion with efficient decryption. We use AES in CBC mode as in randomized encryption, but directly on the plaintext.

When specifying the configuration of this onion, care must be taken not to use the plaintext for database operations unless intended. We accomplish this by introducing our own layer RET for retrieval.

2.3   Common Onion Configurations

As the previous sections describe there are different alternatives for encryption. We enable the user to configure its onions for a specific column. As it is too difficult to foresee all possible onion configuration and capture all semantic restrictions of the encryption schemes, we cater for a number of common onion configurations. We successfully tested our algorithm on these onions. Other configurations are possible and often work correctly, but are not set of the defined scope.

We foresee three options: for processing queries in the cloud, for strong encryption and processing queries on the client and for no security. The option for processing queries in the cloud is our default. It is similar to [22], but extended and adapted as above. This option consists of four encryptions:

$$O_1 : [RET]$$
$$O_2 : [RND[DET[OPE]]]$$
$$O_3 : [HOM]$$
$$O_4 : [SRC]$$

We can extend this option by omitting the OPE layer and preventing from decryption to order-preserving encryption (while allowing deterministic encryption). As such, this extended option is "middle ground" between processing all queries in the cloud and our next option of processing all queries at the client.

The option for strong encryption requires all processing (except aggregation) to be processed at the client. Aggregation is done using homomorphic encryption which is as secure as randomized encryption. Hence, it can be included without sacrificing any security.

$$O_1 : [RET]$$
$$O_2 : [HOM]$$

The third option is to not use encryption at all. This can be used for non-critical data and increases the efficiency of processing. Note that it is not possible to combine this data with the encrypted data in the cloud, since the query processing option does not include an accessible plaintext.

$$O_1 : [PLN]$$

3   Onion Selection

In this section we describe the algorithm to select the onion layer – and corresponding database operator – for performing the query.

3.1   Problem Definition

The client issues its query to its database driver. The database driver intercepts and analyzes the query. It constructs an initial query plan based on relation algebra of the query. This plan consists of a tree of database operators O. The set of database operators includes projection (column selection), selection (where conditions for equality and ranges), joins (equality and ranges), grouping, sorting, aggregation (sum), union and a few others.

Each database operator's input and output are tables and each operator performs an operation on one or two columns. The semantic of this operation, e.g., an equality match, is encoded in the operator's type. Operators are connected into a tree with the root returning the result set of the query and the leaves being raw database tables (or views).

For each column there is a configurable set of onions – as described in Section 2.3. The original query executes on a virtual table that has been converted in the ciphertexts of this onion. Therefore the query needs to be rewritten in order to return the same result as the original query on the original table.

Definition 1. *The* onion selection problem *is to select the onion layer for performing an equivalent operation on the encrypted data as part of the original query on plaintext data.*

3.2   Requirements

As mentioned in the introduction, we intend to meet three requirements: *policy configuration, alternative resolution* and *conflict resolution.*

Policy Configuration. This requirement refers to the user ability to control the onion selection. A common policy could be, e.g., a security policy to never reveal a plaintext in the cloud or to never even reveal a non-randomized encryption. We implement these policies indirectly via configuration of the onions. For each column the user can specify the onion. If an onion layer, e.g., plaintext, is not available, then it is a not an option for the onion selection algorithm.

Of course, the onion configuration also has implications on efficiency and maybe even functionality. An onion configuration therefore must be carefully chosen and tested.

Alternative Resolution. This requirement refers to the availability of multiple onion layers option for a corresponding plaintext database operation. A typical example is equality matching in a where clause. This can be either fulfilled using deterministic encryption or searchable encryption. Deterministic encryption is more efficient and searchable encryption is more secure.

Our onion selection algorithm needs to make a choice. Its choice is to always select the most secure variant and if there are still multiple, then to select the most efficient remaining one. This order is motivated by the purpose of encryption: to ensure security. Furthermore, the user can influence the level of security by the onion policy configuration.

Conflict Resolution. This requirement refers to the situation where database operators are incompatible due to the encryption mode. A typical example is performing a range query on aggregated data, e.g. `SELECT x FROM t GROUP BY x HAVING SUM(y) > 10`. The aggregation can only be computed using homomorphic encryption which cannot be used for range queries on the client. Another example are joins between columns that use different onion configurations. An onion for processing data in the cloud cannot be matched to plaintext, since there is no plaintext.

Our onion selection algorithm needs to detect these situation. Furthermore, it follows a simple strategy to resolve these conflicts. As many database operators as possible are executed on the server. Once there is a conflict the intermediate result table will be transferred to the client and processing continues there on the plaintexts. As such, all queries are executable at the expense of transferring (and decrypting) additional data.

3.3 Algorithm

In order to make a selection of the most secure onion layer we impose an order on the encryption layers. We call the innermost layer the smallest or minimum layer and the outermost layer the largest or maximum layer. Let PLN be the plaintext layer.

$$T : RND, HOM, SRC, RET > DET > OPE > PLN$$

Our algorithm proceeds in five steps.

1. We build a graph of columns used in the query.
2. For each node of the graph we select the maximum layer that can fulfill the query.
3. For each connected component we select the minimum layer necessary.
4. If there are multiple parallel onions remaining, we choose the most efficient for the database operation.
5. We scan the operator tree from the leaves to the root. On the first conflict we execute the upper part on the client.

Step 1: Column Graph. We create a node for each raw table column used in the query, i.e., columns selected, columns in where or having conditions, groupings or sorted, or columns used in aggregation functions. Note that we do not create virtual columns for aggregations.

For each node we retrieve the onion configuration and attach it to the node as a structure. This may be multiple onions as in our configuration for processing encrypted queries in the cloud. We use the onion configuration as it is currently stored in the database, i.e., previous query may have already removed layers of onions.

We create an edge for each join operator between the columns used in the condition or conditions. The resulting graph is undirected, but only in rare cases connected.

An example is the query *SELECT t1.x, SUM (t2.y) FROM t1, t2 WHERE t1.i > 10 AND t1.i = t2.i GROUP BY t1.x*. This query uses the columns $t1.x$, $t2.y$, $t1.i$ and $t2.i$. In the resulting graph there is an edge between $t1.i$ and $t2.i$.

Step 2: Column Layer Selection. We iterate through all operators in the tree. For each operator we retrieve the onion and its associated onion structure. Each operator has a type (and semantics) that imply one or more necessary onion layer. For the encryption type *SRC* we call a specific function that determines whether it can be considered for this operator. If not, then it is not considered a match for the operator. If none of these onion layers is currently accessible (because it is wrapped in another layer), we successively remove layers from the onions – starting with the topmost only – until a layer appears that fulfills the semantic requirements.

Already at this step we may encounter a conflict when no onion layer for the operation is available. We then mark the structure empty as an indication that there is a conflict.

Note that we assume that layer removal increases the query processing functionality of the ciphertext. This needs to be considered when configuring the onions. It is easy to violate this assumption and then the algorithm may fail.

Consider the example query from above: *SELECT t1.x, SUM (t2.y) FROM t1, t2 WHERE t1.i > 10 AND t1.i = t2.i GROUP BY t1.x*. For simplicity assume that all onions use the same configuration for processing queries in the cloud. Furthermore, assume that no queries have been processed so far and state in the database is the initial state.

The first operator is a projection for $t1.x$. This can be fulfilled by RET, RND, DET, OPE, HOM or PLN. There are multiple layers in the current onion structure and no modification is necessary.

The second operator is an aggregation on $t2.y$. This can be fulfilled by HOM or PLN. Again, such a layer is in the current onion structure and no modification is necessary. In an alternative configuration one could drop the homomorphic encryption. Then, there would be a conflict and the structure would end up empty.

The third operator is a range query on $t1.i$. This can be fulfilled by OPE or SRC. Assume that searchable encryption is not an option due to our function call. Then there is no such layer in the current onion structure. We therefore remove the uppermost layers RND and DET.

The fourth operator is a join on equality matching. This can be fulfilled by DET, OPE or PLN. For $t1.i$ such an OPE layer is in the current onion structure due to the third operator and no further modification is necessary. For $t2.i$ no such layer is in the current onion structure. We therefore remove the uppermost layer RND.

The fifth operator is a grouping on $t1.x$. This can also be fulfilled by DET, OPE, or PLN. There are multiple layers in the current onion structure and no modification is necessary. Since the first operator made no modification there is no such layer in the current onion structure. We therefore remove the uppermost layer RND.

Step 3: Connected Component Selection. We now iterate through each connected component of the column graph. For each node in a connected component we retrieve the onion structures. For each onion we select the minimum layer in any of the structures. The resulting minimum onion structure is stored in all nodes of the connected component.

Note that the minimum for a common layer of deterministic encryption (DET) includes the use of a common key. This common also needs to be computed and proxy re-encryption to be performed. See [16] for details.

We may encounter a conflict here if the columns in a connected component use different configurations. In this case we abort and leave all onion structure as they are. We handle this conflict in step 5 of the algorithm.

We continue the example from above: *SELECT t1.x, SUM (t2.y) FROM t1, t2 WHERE t1.i > 10 AND t1.i = t2.i GROUP BY t1.x*. For the nodes $t1.x$ and $t2.y$ we are already done, since they are single nodes. The onion structure for $t1.i$ includes OPE whereas for $t2.i$ it includes DET. We set all to OPE, i.e., the minimum and perform the join on order-preserving encryption.

Step 4: Alternative Selection. We again iterate through all operators in the tree. For each operator we select the most efficient onion layer of the available choices in the current onion structure. We mark the operator with the selected onion layer.

We iterate through all operators in the tree a second time and mark all onions that are used. If a layer of an onion is supposed to be removed, but not used, we restore the onion in its structure to its current state, i.e., the layer removal will not be executed.

In the example from above there is only one operator which can use multiple layers: projection of $t1.x$. This operator can use DET or RET. The most efficient is RET and hence used.

In some databases, e.g. [7], there is a semantic dependency between grouping and projection (or sorting). Only the same column can be used in both, i.e., in our example $t1.x$ must be the same column in grouping operator and projection. Nevertheless, the RET and the DET layers are in different onions and hence columns. In our implementation we capture this dependency using a specialized operator. Then, we use the minimum operator on the RET layer in order to return a unique result.

Step 5: Local Execution Split. In the last step we scan the operator tree from the leaves to the root. If we encounter a conflict, the children of this operator are cut and it and the parents are marked to be executed on the client. Conflicts are

- There is no onion layer to fulfill the operation. Examples that can occur in a "correct" configuration are, e.g., an onion for processing on the client with an operator to be executed.
- The operation is on an *aggregate function*, but not the same aggregate function. An example is SELECT x FROM t GROUP BY x HAVING SUM(y) > 10 with our onion configuration for processing in the cloud.
- A join operation on different onion configurations.

In our running example there are no conflicts and the entire query is executed on the server. If a query is to be executed on the client, the subtrees rooted at its children are synthesized into SQL queries. These queries are then executed and their result stored in local, temporary tables on the client. The temporary tables are decrypted and the upper part of the query is synthesized. This query is then executed locally on the temporary tables.

4   Summary and Outlook

Compared to *CryptDB* [22] we introduce three main extensions. First, we allow the user to configure the onion in almost arbitrary ways directing the onion selection. Second, we introduce a local execution split in order to allow queries that cannot be otherwise fulfilled. Third, we enable the use of searchable encryption.

Already these three simple extensions make the algorithm significantly more complex. They introduce additional problems, such the availability of multiple or none encryption layers for executing the query. Furthermore, theoretically they can handle all SQL queries by executing them on the client. They also may increase security by using searchable encryption instead of deterministic or order-preserving encryption.

Still, there are many possibilities for misconfigurations by the user. An option to reduce these is a tool that checks the most important semantic constraints of an onion configuration. This tool can check for the most common problems and warn in case it does not recognize a configuration.

The use of searchable encryption is subject to further evaluation. Once our results are available we intend to publish a full report. Particularly, the implementation of the function whether to use searchable encryption is critical.

Another future problem is to enable collaboration in an encrypted database. Consider a number of organizations joining forces in intrusion detection. Each organization may want to share selected events with certain other organizations. Still all data is to be stored centrally in the cloud. Other such examples are benchmarking [13,17] and supply chain management [19].

Note that our onion selection algorithm already performs a lightweight optimization: first security, then efficiency. Clearly, it is interesting to investigate more alternatives to make such choices. An interesting example from secure computation on a generic programming language is [14]. SQL query optimization is a well studied field which can offer a number of insights.

References

1. Agrawal, R., Kiernan, J., Srikant, R., Xu, Y.: Order preserving encryption for numeric data. In: Proceedings of the ACM International Conference on Management of Data (SIGMOD) (2004)
2. Bellare, M., Boldyreva, A., O'Neill, A.: Deterministic and efficiently searchable encryption. In: Menezes, A. (ed.) CRYPTO 2007. LNCS, vol. 4622, pp. 535–552. Springer, Heidelberg (2007)
3. Blaze, M., Bleumer, G., Strauss, M.J.: Divertible protocols and atomic proxy cryptography. In: Nyberg, K. (ed.) EUROCRYPT 1998. LNCS, vol. 1403, pp. 127–144. Springer, Heidelberg (1998)
4. Boldyreva, A., Chenette, N., Lee, Y., O'Neill, A.: Order-preserving symmetric encryption. In: Joux, A. (ed.) EUROCRYPT 2009. LNCS, vol. 5479, pp. 224–241. Springer, Heidelberg (2009)
5. Boldyreva, A., Chenette, N., O'Neill, A.: Order-preserving encryption revisited: improved security analysis and alternative solutions. In: Rogaway, P. (ed.) CRYPTO 2011. LNCS, vol. 6841, pp. 578–595. Springer, Heidelberg (2011)
6. Curtmola, R., Garay, J., Kamara, S., Ostrovsky, R.: Searchable symmetric encryption: improved definitions and efficient constructions. In: Proceedings of the 13th ACM Conference on Computer and Communications Security (CCS) (2006)
7. Färber, F., May, N., Lehner, W., Groe, P., Müller, I., Rauhe, H., Dees, J.: The SAP HANA database – an architecture overview. IEEE Data Engineering Bulletin 35(1) (2012)
8. Goldwasser, S., Micali, S.: Probabilistic encryption. Journal of Computer and Systems Sciences 28(2) (1984)
9. Hacigümüs, H., Iyer, B., Li, C., Mehrotra, S.: Executing SQL over encrypted data in the database-service-provider model. In: Proceedings of the ACM International Conference on Management of Data (SIGMOD) (2002)

10. Hacigümüs, H., Iyer, B., Mehrotra, S.: Providing database as a service. In: Proceedings of the 18th IEEE International Conference on Data Engineering (ICDE) (2002)

11. Islam, M., Kuzu, M., Kantarcioglu, M.: Access pattern disclosure on searchable encryption: ramification, attack and mitigation. In: Proceedings of the 19th Network and Distributed System Security Symposium (NDSS) (2012)

12. Kamara, S., Papamanthou, C., Roeder, T.: Dynamic searchable symmetric encryption. In: Proceedings of the 19th ACM Conference on Computer and Communications Security (CCS) (2012)

13. Kerschbaum, F.: Building a privacy-preserving benchmarking enterprise system. Enterprise Information Systems 2(4) (2008)

14. Kerschbaum, F.: Automatically optimizing secure computation. In: Proceedings of the 18th ACM Conference on Computer and Communications Security (CCS) (2011)

15. Kerschbaum, F., Grofig, P., Hang, I., Härterich, M., Kohler, M., Schaad, A., Schröpfer, A., Tighzert, W.: Demo: Adjustably encrypted in-memory column-store. In: Proceedings of the 20th ACM Conference on Computer and Communications Security (CCS) (2013)

16. Kerschbaum, F., Härterich, M., Grofig, P., Kohler, M., Schaad, A., Schröpfer, A., Tighzert, W.: Optimal re-encryption strategy for joins in encrypted databases. In: Wang, L., Shafiq, B. (eds.) DBSec 2013. LNCS, vol. 7964, pp. 195–210. Springer, Heidelberg (2013)

17. Kerschbaum, F., Terzidis, O.: Filtering for private collaborative benchmarking. In: Müller, G. (ed.) ETRICS 2006. LNCS, vol. 3995, pp. 409–422. Springer, Heidelberg (2006)

18. Paillier, P.: Public-key cryptosystems based on composite degree residuosity classes. In: Stern, J. (ed.) EUROCRYPT 1999. LNCS, vol. 1592, pp. 223–238. Springer, Heidelberg (1999)

19. Pibernik, R., Zhang, Y., Kerschbaum, F., Schröpfer, A.: Secure collaborative supply chain planning and inverse optimization-the jels model. European Journal of Operational Research 208(1) (2011)

20. Pohlig, S., Hellman, M.: An improved algorithm for computing logarithms over GF(p) and its cryptographic significance. IEEE Transactions on Information Theory 24 (1978)

21. Popa, R., Li, F., Zeldovich, N.: An ideal-security protocol for order-preserving encoding. In: Proceedings of the 34th IEEE Symposium on Security and Privacy (SP) (2013)

22. Popa, R., Redfield, C., Zeldovich, N., Balakrishnan, H.: CryptDB: Protecting confidentiality with encrypted query processing. In: Proceedings of the 23rd ACM Symposium on Operating Systems Principles (SOSP) (2011)

23. Shi, E., Bethencourt, J., Chan, H., Song, D., Perrig, A.: Multi-dimensional range query over encrypted data. In: Proceedings of the 28th IEEE Symposium on Security and Privacy (SP) (2007)

24. Song, D., Wagner, D., Perrig, A.: Practical techniques for searches on encrypted data. In: Proceedings of the 21st IEEE Symposium on Security and Privacy, SP (2000)

Risk Aware Approach to Data Confidentiality in Cloud Computing

Kerim Yasin Oktay[1], Vaibhav Khadilkar[2], Murat Kantarcioglu[2], and Sharad Mehrotra[1]

[1] University Of California, Irvine, Department of Computer Science
[2] University of Texas at Dallas, Dept. of Computer Science
koktay@uci.edu, {vvk07200,muratk}@utdallas.edu,
sharad@ics.uci.edu

Abstract. This paper explores the issue of "loss of control" that results when users outsource data and computation to the clouds. While loss of control has multiple manifestations, we focus on the data privacy and confidentiality implications when cloud providers are untrusted. Instead of following the well studied (but still unsolved) path of encrypting data when outsourcing and computing on the encrypted domain, the paper advocates a risk-based approach over a hybrid cloud architecture as a possible solution. Hybrid clouds are a composition of two or more distinct cloud infrastructures (private, community, or public) that remain unique entities, but are bound together by standardized or proprietary technology that enables data and application portability. Hybrid clouds offer an opportunity to selectively outsource data and computation based on the level of sensitivity involved. The paper postulates a risk-aware approach to partitioning computation over hybrid clouds that provides an abstraction to address secure cloud data processing in a variety of system and application contexts.

Keywords: Data Confidentiality, Hybrid Clouds, Cloud Computing, Data Outsourcing.

1   Introduction

Fueled by advances in virtualization and high-speed network technologies, cloud computing has emerged as a dominant computing paradigm for the future. Cloud computing can roughly be summarized as "X as a service" where X could be a virtualized infrastructure (*e.g.*, computing and/or storage), a platform (*e.g.*, OS, programming language execution environment, databases, web servers), software applications (*e.g.*, Google apps), a service, or a test environment, *etc.* A distinguishing aspect of cloud computing is the utility computing model (aka pay-as-you-go model) where users get billed for the computers, storage, or any resources based on their usage with no up-front costs of purchasing the hardware/software or of managing the IT infrastructure. The cloud provides an illusion of limitless resources which one can tap into in times of need, limited only by the amount one wishes to spend on renting the resources.

Despite numerous benefits, organizations, especially those that deal with potentially sensitive data (*e.g.*, business secrets, sensitive client information such as credit card and

A. Bagchi and I. Ray (Eds.): ICISS 2013, LNCS 8303, pp. 27–42, 2013.

social security numbers, medical records), are slow to fully embrace the cloud model. One of the main impediments is the sense of "loss of control" over one's data wherein end-users (clients) cannot restrict access to potentially sensitive data by other entities, whether they be other tenants to the common cloud resources or privileged insiders who have access to the cloud infrastructure. Loss of control, in itself, would, perhaps, not be as much of an issue if clients/users could fully trust the service provider. In a world where service providers could be located anywhere, under varying legal jurisdictions; where privacy and confidentiality of one's data is subject to policies and laws that are at best (or under some circumstances) ambiguous; where policy compliance is virtually impossible to check; where government/agencies can subpoena cloud vendors for an individual's records; and the threat of "insider attacks" is very real - trust is a difficult property to achieve. Loss of control over resources (by migrating to the cloud) coupled with lack of trust (in the service provider) poses numerous concerns about data integrity (will a service provider serve my data correctly? Can my data get corrupted?), availability (will I have access to my data and service at any time?), security, privacy and confidentiality (will sensitive data remain confidential? Will my data be vulnerable to misuse? By other tenants? By the service provider?) to name a few.

In this paper, we focus on the privacy and confidentiality aspects of data processing in public cloud environments. An obvious approach to achieving confidentiality and privacy is to appropriately encrypt data prior to storing it on the cloud. This way, data remains secure against all types of attacks, whether they be due to using shared systems & resources also accessible to others, insider attacks, or data mining attacks leading to information leakage. While encrypting data mitigates many of the confidentiality concerns, it poses a new challenge - how does one continue to process encrypted data in the cloud? Over the past few decades, numerous cryptographic approaches as well as information hiding techniques have been developed to support basic computations over encrypted data [15, 16, 14]. For instance, a variety of semantically secure searchable encryption techniques that can support various forms of keyword search as well as range search techniques have been proposed. Likewise, work in the area of **database as a service (DAS)** [17] has explored support for SQL style queries with selections/projections/joins *etc*. When processing could not continue on the encrypted domain, the data is transferred to the secure client, which could then decrypt the data and continue the computation. The goal in such processing is to minimize the client side work, while simultaneously minimizing data exposure. In [12], we outlined how an SQL query can be split to be executed partly on the server and partly on the client to compute the final answer. Many such approaches offer sliding scale confidentiality wherein higher confidentiality can be achieved, albeit extra overheads. Significant progress has been made in designing solutions that offer viable approaches when the computation to be performed on encrypted data is suitably constrained.

Challenges and Opportunities Beyond DAS: While the techniques for query processing/search in mixed security environments developed in the literature to support the DAS model provide a solid foundation for addressing the confidentiality challenge in cloud computing, the cloud setting offers additional opportunities as well as additional challenges that have not been fully explored in the DAS literature:

– Unlike DAS, where resources were assumed to be very limited on the client-side, in the cloud setting organizations may actually possess significant resources that meet the majority of their storage and query processing needs. For instance, in the cloud setting data may only be partially outsourced, *e.g.*, only the non-sensitive part of the data may be kept on the cloud. Also, it is only at peak query loads that the computation needs to be offloaded to the cloud. This has implications from a security perspective since much of the processing involving sensitive data could be done on secure machines, *e.g.*, if a query primarily touches sensitive data, it could be executed on the private side.

– In DAS, since the goal was to fully outsource data and computations, the focus of the solutions was on devising mechanisms to operate on the encrypted representation (even though such techniques may incur significant overhead). In contrast, in hybrid cloud environments, since local machines may have significant computational capabilities, solutions that incur limited amount of data exposure of sensitive data (possibly at a significant performance gain) become attractive.

– While DAS work has primarily dealt with database query workloads (and text search [15]), in a cloud setting, we may be interested in more general computation mechanisms (*i.e.* not only database workloads). For instance, MapReduce (MR) frameworks are used widely for large-scale data analysis in the cloud. We may, thus, be interested in secure execution of MR jobs in the context of hybrid clouds.

– Another challenge is that of autonomy of cloud service providers. It is unlikely that autonomous providers will likely implement new security protocols and algorithms (specially given significant overheads associated with adding security and the restrictive nature of cryptographic security for a large number of practical purposes). For instance, it is difficult to imagine Google making changes to underlying storage models, data access protocols and interfaces used by its application services (such as Google Drive, Picasa, *etc.*) such that users can store/search/process data in encrypted form. This calls for a new, robust and more flexible approach to implement privacy and confidentiality of data in cloud-based applications.

Risk-Aware Data Processing in the Cloud: Given that general solutions that offer complete security in a cloud setting are unlikely to emerge in the near future, we promote an alternate/complementary *risk-based approach* to practical security for such settings which we are studying as part of the Radicle Project (http://radicle.ics.uci.edu) at UCI. Unlike traditional security approaches that attempt to eliminate the possibility of attacks, a risk-based approach, instead of preventing loss of sensitive data, attempts to limit/control the exposure of sensitive data on public clouds by controlling what data and computation is offloaded to the public cloud and how such data is represented. Different ways to steer data through the public and private clouds exhibit different levels of risks and expose a tradeoff between exposure risks and performance. Given such a tradeoff, the goal of risk aware computing changes from purely attempting to minimize costs (and hence maximize performance) to that of achieving a balance between performance and sensitive data disclosure risk. Let us illustrate the concept of risk-based solutions using a couple of example cloud-based scenarios.

As a first motivation, consider a hybrid cloud setting wherein an organization seamlessly integrates its in-house computing resources with public cloud services to construct a secure and economical data processing solution. A growing number of organizations have turned to such a hybrid cloud model [1, 2], since it offers flexibility on the tasks that can be offloaded to public clouds, thereby offering the advantages of increased throughput, reduced operational costs while maintaining security. Consider a data management workload (*i.e.*, a set of database queries) that the organization would like to execute periodically with some timing guarantees. The workload may be too large for a given private infrastructure and the option might be to shift some queries to the public side. There are multiple choices for data processing – either shift some queries (and the corresponding data needed for their processing) to the public side, or alternatively, one could use DAS style query operator implementations, whereby the public and private sides split the task of query execution cooperatively. In either case, the data and computation needs to be distributed and different workload distributions offer different levels of exposure risks and benefits (*e.g.*, task completion time). A risk-based approach would attempt to find a solution that optimizes the performance subject to constraints on exposure risks. Or alternatively, it may attempt to minimize the risk while ensuring certain performance guarantees. We will illustrate such tradeoffs for a static workload consisting of Hive queries based on our previous work in [4].

As another scenario, consider a system that empowers users with control over data they may store in existing (autonomous) cloud-based services such as Box, Google Drive, Google Calendar, *etc*. There are many ways to realize such a system – for instance, in our implementation, which we refer to as CloudProtect [5], the system is implemented as an intermediary privacy middleware that sits between clients and service providers that intercepts the clients' http requests, transforms requests to suitably encrypt/decrypt the data based on the user's confidentiality policies before forwarding the request to the service provider. Encrypting data, may interfere with the user's experience with the service – while requests such as create, retrieve, update, delete, share and even search can be performed over encrypted data, functions such as language translation (Google), picture printing (Shutterfly or Picasa) require data to be decrypted first. In such a case, CloudProtect executes an exception protocol that retrieves the data from the server, decrypts it, and stores the data in cleartext prior to forwarding the service request. While CloudProtect offers continued seamless availability of web services, if every user's request (or many of them) results in an exception, the user's experience will be seriously compromised due to significant overheads of exception handling. An ideal approach will adaptively choose a representation of data on the cloud side that strikes a balance between the risk of data exposure with the usability of the service (*i.e.*, reducing the number of exceptions raised in CloudProtect). Such an approach would ensure, for instance, that data at rest is always encrypted while data frequently used by requests that cannot be executed over an encrypted representation is left in cleartext form at the service provider.

Roadmap. The examples above illustrate two scenarios where a risk-based approach could be adopted to strike a balance between system specific metrics (*e.g.*, performance, usability, timeliness *etc.*) and confidentiality. Our work in the Radicle Project (http://radicle.ics.uci.edu) has explored such an approach in a few example cloud computing settings – namely, splitting database query workloads in hybrid clouds, developing a secure MapReduce (MR) execution environment (entitled SEMROD) that controls data exposure in multi-phase MR jobs, and the CloudProtect middleware that empowers users to control data that is exposed to Web applications. While each of these examples is distinct, the underlying principle and approach of realizing data confidentiality by controlling risk of exposure is common to each. In the remainder of this paper, we highlight our prior work in the context of database workload partitioning in hybrid clouds. We begin by briefly discussing the hybrid cloud model focusing on the security implications of different architectures. We then formally describe the problem of workload partitioning and illustrate a solution in the context of database queries and MR jobs. We conclude the paper with a brief discussion of challenges and opportunities in supporting a risk-based model.

2   Hybrid Cloud

A hybrid cloud is a composition of two or more distinct cloud infrastructures (private, community, or public) that remain unique entities, but are bound together by standardized or proprietary technology that enables data and application portability [6]. The emergence of the hybrid cloud paradigm has allowed end-users to seamlessly integrate their in-house computing resources with public cloud services and construct potent, secure and economical data processing solutions. A growing number of organizations have turned to such a **hybrid cloud model** [1, 2], since they offer flexibility on the tasks that can be offloaded to public cloud infrastructures (*e.g.*, Amazon EC2, Microsoft Azure) thereby offering the advantages of increased throughput, and reduced operational costs. Such a hybrid cloud creates a mixed security environment for data processing – while organizations can control (to a degree) security on their own infrastructure, the public infrastructure is susceptible to a myriad of security concerns, including information leakage through "excessive privilege abuse" (aka insider attack, which has been identified by numerous practitioners as being one of the most important database security threats). In our discussion, we will differentiate between three distinct hybrid cloud settings that target different usage scenarios and pose different tradeoffs from the perspective of risk-based security:

- An *Outsourcing* scenario, where an organization relies on a public cloud to fulfill their IT requirements, and uses their limited private cloud to perform supplementary tasks such as filtering incorrect results or decrypting encrypted results. This is similar to the DAS model studied in the literature.
- A *Cloudbursting* setting, where an organization uses their private cloud to develop, test and deploy applications, and depends on a public cloud to mitigate sudden spikes of activity in an application that arise due to unforeseen circumstances.
- A *Fully Hybrid* scenario, where companies consider the entire hybrid cloud as one big cluster of machines and are willing to keep the load imbalance across the hybrid cloud as little as possible in order to obtain the best performance. While achieving this, they prefer to handle sensitive computations within the private cloud, whereas the public side executes the workload's non-sensitive portion.

2.1   Risk-Aware Data Processing in Hybrid Clouds

A risk-based approach to data processing in hybrid clouds controls what data and computation is offloaded to the public cloud and how such data is represented, in order to control the risk of data exposure. While techniques and solutions to achieve risk-aware processing depend upon the specific instantiation of the problem and the type of hybrid cloud set up, fundamental to each approach is the underlying challenge of workload and data partitioning. A workload and data partitioning problem can be viewed as a multi-criteria optimization problem that achieves a balance between system metrics such as performance and exposure risks. Fundamental to the problem is mechanisms/metrics for assessing risks based on the representation of the data and computation performed on public machines as well as mechanisms and metrics to measure the performance that is achieved by the system given a particular load distribution and the costs incurred. Such metrics for measuring performance, costs and risks must be expressed in term of parameters that can be modified by the risk-based approach, *e.g.*, workload distribution, data partitioning, cost constraints to acquiring cloud services (and/or private machines). The risk-aware strategy can then be postulated as either optimizing for performance and costs while ensuring the exposure risks are appropriately constrained, or conversely, constraining the additional overhead of the strategy, while minimizing the risk of data loss. Solutions to such a multi-criteria optimization will allow us to determine how data should be stored and computation partitioned such that the proposed system maintains the highest level of performance while limiting/minimizing loss of sensitive data.

Two main issues in designing such a risk-based approach are: (a) Identifying metrics for the above three criteria (performance, risks, costs) in terms of parameters that can be modified by the risk-based approach, *e.g.*, workload distribution, data partitioning, cost constraints for acquiring cloud services (and/or private machines) a user may have, *etc.* (b) Designing a principled approach to determine the optimal instantiation of the parameters that meet the performance, cost and risk constraints of the user.

Both the issues of designing metrics for measuring risks, performance, and costs as well as modeling and solving the workload distribution problem in terms of the metrics pose significant challenges which we discuss in the following two subsections.

2.2   Criteria for Workload Distribution

Before we explore a risk-based framework for data processing in hybrid clouds, we first identify the key criteria of importance in designing hybrid cloud solutions. These design criteria will form the basis of postulating the risk-based strategy as will become clear later.

Performance: Consider a workload W. Let the execution of W be distributed between the private and public sides and the corresponding computations be denoted by W_{priv} and W_{pub} respectively. Note that, the execution of W_{priv} and W_{pub} together achieves W. Further, let the dataset R needed for the workload W be partitioned as R_{pub} and R_{priv}, which represents partitioning of data amongst public and private machines (note that, R_{pub} and R_{priv} may not strictly correspond to a partitioning and may overlap). The partitioning of data is such that R_{priv} (R_{pub}) includes all the data needed by the workload W_{priv} (W_{pub}). The performance of a data processing architecture over hybrid clouds is directly proportional to the overall running time of W with given W_{pub} and W_{priv}. We use the notation $RunTime(W, W_{pub})$ to express the performance factor. Estimating the expected total running time depends upon a variety of factors such as characteristics of the workload W, control flow between W_{priv} and W_{pub} (e.g., do they need to run sequentially or can they be executed in parallel), the processing speeds of machines/infrastructure, the network throughput in case data needs to be shuffled between public and private machines, the underlying representation of data, etc. In general, the execution time of tasks in W over a hybrid cloud, given that tasks in W_{pub} are executed on a public cloud can be estimated as:

$$RunTime(W, W_{pub}) = \max \begin{cases} \sum\limits_{t \in W_{pub}} runT_{pub}(t) \\ \sum\limits_{t \in W - W_{pub}} runT_{priv}(t) \end{cases}$$

where, $runT_x(t)$ denotes the estimated running time of task $t \in T$ at site x, where x is either a public ($x = pub$) or private ($x = priv$) cloud. The running time of a task on public/private machines, in itself, depends upon the machine characteristics and the task. Models for estimating these have been widely developed for database workloads in the literature and more recently for HIVE queries in the context of cluster computing [18]. We have further developed similar cost-estimation models for SPARQL queries over RDF stores. While these models determine costs of single queries, cost of a query workload can be estimated as a sum of costs of the individual queries[1].

Data Disclosure Risk: $Risk(R_{pub})$ estimates the risk of disclosing sensitive data to a public cloud service provider based on the data outsourced to public clouds or exposed during processing. Disclosure risks depend upon a variety of factors: they are directly proportional to the number of sensitive data items that R_{pub} includes. Larger the sensitive data items in R_{pub}, higher is the $Risk(R_{pub})$; the risk depends on the representation format (e.g., encryption level) used to store R_{pub} – using a less secure encryption technique incurs higher risk; the risk could depend upon the duration of time for which sensitive data is exposed in R_{pub}; the risk depends upon the vulnerability of the public cloud against outside attacks – the more vulnerable the system, the higher the exposure risk will be. While modeling such risks is an interesting direction of exploration, for now, we will limit ourselves to estimating risk simply as the number of sensitive data items exposed to the public side in R_{pub} as follows:

$$Risk(R_{pub}) = \sum_{R_i \in R_{pub}} sens(R_i),$$

where $sens(R_i)$ is the number of sensitive values contained in a data item $R_i \in R_{pub}$, which is stored on a public cloud.

Resource Allocation Cost: Resource allocation cost, $Pricing(R_{pub}, W_{pub})$, is associated with storing and processing data on public infrastructures. This criterion measures the

---

[1] Recent work has explored techniques such as shared scans in the context of executing queries over MapReduce frameworks [9], which can reduce costs of query workloads. Incorporating such optimizations will further complicate our partitioning framework.

financial cost (in terms of $) engendered by the incorporation of some type of public cloud services into hybrid cloud models. The cost can be classified into the following two broad categories:

- *On-premise Costs*: This category measures the cost incurred in acquiring and maintaining a private cloud.
- *Cloud Costs*: This category can be further sub-divided as follows: (a) *Elastic costs:* A user is charged only for the services they use (pay-as-you-use). (b) *Subscription costs*: A user is charged a decided fee on a regular basis (fixed).

The financial cost of an end-user's hybrid cloud model implementation is dependent on several factors such as the data model/query language used, storage representation, *etc.* In general, the larger the R_{pub} and W_{pub} are, the higher the cost will be. If we ignore the on-premise monetary costs and only consider the cost of storage and computation on the public cloud, we could estimate the monetary costs as follows:

$$Pricing(R_{pub}, W_{pub}) = store(R_{pub}) + \sum_{t \in W_{pub}} freq(t) \times proc(t),$$

where $store(R_{pub})$ represents the monetary cost of storing a subset $R_{pub} \subseteq R$ on a public cloud, $freq(t)$ denotes the access frequency of task $t \in W$, and $proc(t)$ denotes the monetary cost associated with processing t on a public cloud. Such monetary costs for storing and executing tasks on the public cloud depend upon the pricing models of current cloud vendors. In our experiments, we will use Amazon's pricing model to compute such monetary costs.

The above three factors – performance, risks, and costs – provide the main criteria along which different solutions of risk-based processing in hybrid clouds can be compared. It is not surprising that the spectrum of possible solutions represents tradeoffs between these factors. For instance, solutions that indiscriminately distribute work to public machines in an unconstrained way may optimize performance but they will be suboptimal from the perspective of risks. Likewise, a solution that minimizes risk by performing any operation that may leak sensitive data on private machines may either suffer significantly from the performance perspective, or require a heavy investment in the private infrastructure to meet an application's deadline, thus not leveraging the advantages of the cloud model.

2.3 Workload Partitioning Problem (WPP)

Given the three factors - performance, risks, resource allocation costs, discussed in the previous section, we can now formalize the workload partitioning problem as a multi-criteria optimization problem that chooses system parameters such as workload and data partitioning so as to simultaneously optimize the three metrics. We model the problem as a constrained optimization problem, wherein one of the metrics is optimized while ensuring that the solution is feasible with respect to the constraints specified by the user on the other metrics. In general, in WPP, a user may specify three constraints: *TIME_CONST*, *DISC_CONST* and *PRA_CONST*, where *TIME_CONST* corresponds to the deadline within which W needs to be completed, *PRA_CONST* acts as an upper bound on the maximum allowable monetary cost that can be expended on storing and processing data on a public cloud, and *DISC_CONST* denotes the maximum permissible data disclosure risk that can be taken while storing sensitive data on a public cloud. WPP can thus be envisioned as a problem that distributes a workload W (and implicitly a dataset R) over a hybrid cloud deployment model such that one of the three factors is minimized subject to constraints on the remaining two. The exact formulation of WPP varies based on whether one aims to use hybrid clouds in a cloudbursting, outsourcing or fully hybrid setting. We focus our discussion to the fully hybrid model.

WPP Definition: In the fully hybrid setting, the primary goal is to maximize performance. Additionally, an end-user may want to put an upper limit on the disclosure risk and the monetary cost while distributing computations across the cluster. Given these criteria, a WPP definition can be given as follows: Given a dataset R and a workload W, WPP can be modeled as an optimization problem whose goal is to find subsets $W_{pub} \subseteq W$ and $R_{pub} \subseteq R$ such that the overall execution time of W is minimized.

$$
\begin{aligned}
\text{minimize} \quad & RunTime(W, W_{pub}) \\
\text{subject to} \quad & (1)\ Risk(R_{pub}) \leq DISC\_CONST \\
& (2)\ Pricing(R_{pub}, W_{pub}) \leq PRA\_CONST
\end{aligned}
$$

WPP in the outsourcing and cloudbursting models can be similarly defined. In the outsourcing model, which mostly relies on public cloud resources, the goal might be to leave as much sensitive computation as possible on the private side while meeting the resource constraints on the running time and monetary costs. In contrast, in the cloudbursting model, a user may wish to minimize the outsourcing costs while ensuring that the workload finishes within a specified time and with constraints on the overall data exposure risk.

3   WPP Solution for Fully Hybrid Setting

In this section, we briefly sketch a solution to the WPP problem discussed in the previous section under a simplifying assumption that data is stored unencrypted both, on the private and public machines. Thus, exposure risks can be directly computed as the number of sensitive data items outsourced to public machines. The WPP solution thus attempts to find a subset of the given dataset R_{pub} and workload W_{pub} that can be shipped to the public cloud so as to minimize the total processing time of the workload across the hybrid cloud, while maintaining constraints on monetary costs and risks. Under our assumptions, WPP can be simplified to a more simpler version in which the problem only attempts to find W_{pub}, since R_{pub} can be considered as being equivalent to ($\bigcup\limits_{t \in W_{pub}} baseData(t)$), where $baseData(t)$ denotes the minimum set of data items required to execute task t accurately. In other words, any other solution R' that minimizes the overall performance should be a superset of $\bigcup\limits_{t \in W_{pub}} baseData(t)$ and, yet, the solution $\bigcup\limits_{t \in W_{pub}} baseData(t)$ is the one with the least sensitive data exposure risk and monetary cost. As a result, WPP can be considered to be a problem that aims to find the subset of the query workload that minimizes the workload execution time without violating the given constraints. We can solve this variant of WPP using dynamic programming; the solution produces a set of queries W_{pub} as a solution to $WPP(W, PRA\_CONST, DISC\_CONST)^2$. To develop the dynamic programming approach, we consider a general version of WPP, denoted $WPP(W^i, j, k)$, where W^j represents a prefix sequence of queries in the workload W and j and k represent the associated monetary cost and disclosure risk constraints. The original WPP problem is a subproblem of $WPP(W^i, j, k)$, and can be represented as $WPP(W^n, j, k)$, where $j = PRA\_CONST$ and $k = DISC\_CONST$. We can express the solution to WPP on W^n in terms of WPP on W^{n-1}. To see this, consider the following example where the workload W consists of 3 tasks (i.e., $W = \{t_1, t_2, t_3\}$) and $WPP(W^3, j, k)$ needs to be solved.

W	$proc(t)$	$store(baseData(t))$	$sens(baseData(t))$
t_1	$10	$15	20
t_2	$20	$10	10
t_3	$15	$10	20

W	$proc(t)$	$store(baseData(t))$	$sens(baseData(t))$
t_1	$10	$15	20
t_2	$20	$10	10
t_3	$15	$10	20

To solve WPP on t_1, t_2, t_3, let us consider deciding on whether t_3 should be assigned to the public side. First, if we ship t_3 to the public side, then the overall monetary cost and the overall disclosure risk will be at least $25 and 20 sensitive cells respectively (assume that $\forall 1 \leq i \leq 3\ freq(i) = 1$). If $j < 25$ or $k < 20$, then any solution considering t_3 as a public side query will not be a feasible one, and in turn $WPP(W^3, j, k) = WPP(W^2, j, k)$. Note that, since executing any query on the private side does not cause a violation of any constraints, this case essentially does not require a feasibility check. So let us assume that assigning t_3 to the public side does not cause a violation of constraints. To express WPP on W^i in terms of WPP on W^{i-1}, we have to consider two cases:

Case 1: If t_3 runs on the public side, then there will be more than one WPP subproblem that needs to be investigated. This is due to the fact that the possible execution of t_3 on the public side will bring at least $15 and at most $25 into the overall monetary cost value. In terms of disclosure risk, the numbers will be between 0 and 20 sensitive cells. The reason is that a portion of (or the entire) $baseData(t_3)$ could already be partially included in the solution, W_s, to some $WPP(W^2, j', k')$, and in turn storing $baseData(t_3)$ in addition to $\bigcup_{t \in W_s} baseData(t)$ may not bring as much monetary cost and disclosure risk as is represented in the table above. Consequently, $WPP(W^2, j', k')$ where $j - 25 \leq j' \leq j - 15$ and $k - 20 \leq k' \leq k$ should be investigated in order to solve $WPP(W^3, j, k)$ optimally. However, every candidate set of queries formed by taking the union of t_3 with the solution of $WPP(W^2, j', k')$ should be tested to ensure that it

---

[2] We assume that the query workload, W, and the constraints, PRA_CONST and $DISC\_CONST$ are all given beforehand.

does not violate any constraint and it is the best solution in terms of performance from amongst all solutions obtained in *Case 1*. If it does produce the best solution, it will be one of the solution candidates with the other one coming from *Case 2*.

Case 2: In case query t_3 runs on the private side, then $WPP(W^3, i, j) = WPP(W^2, i, j)$.

After computing the best solution candidate for both cases, a dynamic programming approach compares the overall expected running times of both solutions and picks the minimum one as the solution to $WPP(W^3, j, k)$.

Experimental Results

For all our experiments, we used the TPC-H benchmark with a scale factor 100. We used a query workload of 40 queries containing modified versions of TPC-H queries Q1, Q3, Q6 and Q11. In particular, we did not perform grouping and aggregate operations in any query because of the high complexity of estimating overall I/O sizes for these types of operators. Further, we assumed that each query was equally likely in the workload. The predicates in each of the queries are randomly modified to vary the range (as mandated by TPC-H) of the data that is accessed.

We first computed the running time of the query workload when all computations are performed on the private cloud (Private). The experiments subsequently use this case as a baseline to determine the performance of the dynamic programming approach that was proposed earlier to solve the WPP problem.

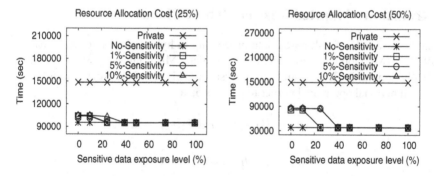

Fig. 1. Performance of the Dynamic Programming approach towards solving the WPP problem

Experiments for Dynamic Programming Approach: The goal of these experiments is to measure the performance of the dynamic programming approach that was proposed earlier for solving WPP. To perform these experiments, we varied all parameters under consideration in the following way: (1) Resource allocation cost: The resource allocation cost was varied between 25-50% of the maximum cost value that can be incurred as a result of executing the workload on the public cloud. Given the above cost metric definition, the maximum cost is incurred when dataset R is completely stored on the public cloud and the entire query workload is executed on public machines. (2) We defined four different overall sensitivity levels as, No-Sensitivity (the entire dataset is non-sensitive), 1%-Sensitivity, 5%-Sensitivity and 10%-Sensitivity (1%, 5% and 10%

of the tuples of the *lineitem* table are made sensitive). (3) We defined seven different sensitive data exposure levels as 0% (none of the sensitive data is exposed), 10%, 25%, 40%, 50%, 75% and 100% (all of the defined sensitive data may be exposed).

We then computed the overall performance of the query workload for different combinations of these three parameters, the results of which are presented in Figure 1. One of the first observations that can be made from Figure 1 is that when a user is willing to take additional risks by storing more sensitive data on the public side, they can gain a considerable speed-up in overall execution time (even greater than 50%). On the other hand, Figure 1 also shows that the monetary expenditure on public side resources is substantially low even when a user takes additional risks by storing increasing amounts of sensitive data on the public cloud (the graph for 50% resource allocation cost shows that even when more money is allowed to be spent on public side resources the overall performance is relatively the same, suggesting that a budget of only about 50% of the *PRA_CONST* is sufficient to boost the performance savings by upto 50%).

Figure 1 also shows that when a user invests more capital towards resource allocation, a considerable gain in overall workload performance (even greater than 50%) can be achieved. This is expected since when more resources are allocated on the public side, we are better able to exploit the parallelism that is afforded by a hybrid cloud. Thus, the intuition that a hybrid cloud improves performance due to greater use of inherent parallelism is justified. Finally, from Figure 1, we also notice that we can achieve a considerable improvement in query performance ($\approx 50\%$) for a relatively low risk ($\approx 40\%$) and resource allocation cost ($\approx 50\%$).

4   Risk-Aware MapReduce over Hybrid Clouds

As another example of risk-based data processing in hybrid clouds, let us consider a MapReduce (MR) job that may access sensitive data. MR frameworks such as Hadoop are widely popular for large scale data analysis [10, 11]. The MR programming model uses two functional operators in order to process data:

$$map : (k_1, v_1) \rightarrow list(k_2, v_2)$$

$$reduce : (k_2, list(v_2)) \rightarrow list(v_3)$$

MapReduce systems use a Distributed File System (DFS) as their underlying storage mechanism (HDFS for Hadoop). A *master* node manages the entire file system by keeping track of how blocks of files are distributed over all *slave* nodes. On the other hand, a process running on every slave node manages the storage infrastructure for that node. This architecture then uses the MR paradigm to process data stored in the DFS in a parallelized fashion over a cluster of nodes. The MR framework typically consists of a single master and several slaves. The master is responsible for scheduling an MR job among the slaves while a slave node is responsible for executing the given sub-task. By labeling one of the nodes as master and the remaining ones as slave nodes, the MR paradigm can be made to work on hybrid clouds.

Map operations are usually distributed across a cluster by automatically partitioning the input to possibly equivalent sized blocks (in default 64MB), which can then be processed in parallel by separate machines. Once a map operation completes on a slave, the intermediate key-value pairs are stored as partitions (hash partitioning) in local disks on that slave. The intermediate partitions are then shuffled to different reducers based on their partition-id's.

In a MR setting, sensitive data leakage can occur in multiple ways. It could occur either while storing data in the DFS or during MR processing. For instance, when an input block that contains sensitive data is assigned to a map task running on the public cloud, those sensitive data items will be directly exposed to the public side. Alternatively, if a reducer whose input partition contains sensitive information is assigned to public nodes then that sensitive information would be leaked. Mechanisms to prevent disclosure by using techniques that operate on encrypted data while interesting are not generally applicable.

Recent efforts have explored secure MapReduce techniques on hybrid clouds. *Sedic*, proposed in [13], prevents leakage by doing two things:

- A sensitivity aware data distribution mechanism that guarantees that no sensitive data is exposed to public machines, which in turn guarantees that map tasks that touch sensitive data are always only limited to private clouds, and
- constraining reducers to run exclusively on the private side.

To overcome the performance degradation during the reduce phase, Sedic attempts to use *combiners* to shift some of the work done during the reduce phase to the public side without causing any exposure. Nonetheless, combiners cannot be applied for many important data analysis tasks such as joining two tables. Therefore, Sedic has performance limitations for reduce-heavy tasks, which cannot be efficiently executed by using combiners.

One could potentially use a risk-based approach to resolve this performance issue. Consider that the user is tolerant to some risks. In this case, some reducers (especially ones with a low level of sensitive data exposure can be assigned to public machines). This will increase data exposure risks but will allow better performance and load balancing across the hybrid cloud sides. Such a technique reflects a tradeoff between risk and performance (*i.e.*, load balancing of MR jobs). On one extreme, there is Sedic, which can be regarded as 0% risk; and on the other extreme, there is original MR, which may result in unconstrained leakage of sensitive data to public clouds for performance purposes, namely full-exposure (100% risk). However, we can limit the partitions that are assigned to public machines to achieve a performance *vs.* risk tradeoff, similar to the one presented earlier in the context of workload partitioning.

While the risk-aware MR workload partitioning is relatively straightforward to formalize, there are many complexities. For instance, in the original MR setting, the assignment of partitions to reduce tasks is done when the job is initialized (deployed) and the reducer to machine assignment is done based on a policy such as FIFO. Controlling disclosure in such a setup requires us to track what data is sensitive in each map output partition so that we can then assign them to the right machines based on a given risk threshold (*i.e.*, risk aware partition assignment). Such a tracking should not be too costly so as to nullify the performance advantages obtained by using the public side for some reduce tasks. Another complexity is that if the partitioning criteria used for assigning work to reducers is completely randomized (as is generally the case for load balancing purposes), then the sensitive data may also be randomly distributed across the partitions. In such a case, the number of partitions that can be offloaded to the public side will be limited to those dictated by the risk tolerance. Designing appropriate partitioning strategies and scheduling of reduce tasks is a substantial challenge.

5   Conclusion

In this paper, we explored the challenge of "loss of control" that results from outsourcing data and computations to clouds. While loss of control has multiple manifestations, the paper focuses on the potential loss of data privacy and confidentiality when cloud providers are untrusted. Instead of using a well studied (but still unsolved) approach of encrypting data when outsourcing and computing on the encrypted domain, the paper advocates a risk-based approach over a hybrid cloud architecture as a possible solution. Hybrid clouds offer an opportunity to selectively outsource data and computations based on the level of sensitivity involved. This raises the fundamental challenge of workload and data partitioning across private and public machines. The paper formalizes such a challenge as a multi-criteria optimization problem and instantiates it for two example settings: partitioning database workloads and distributing MapReduce tasks across public and private machines.

While these approaches make a strong case for a risk-based approach for data confidentiality in the cloud setting, much work lies ahead before a risk-based approach can become an effective tool for securing data in the cloud. First, we need to develop appropriate metrics to model risks in a cloud setting. One can use simple metrics such as the number of sensitive data items exposed, and/or duration of the exposure, as a way of measuring risks (as is done in this paper). However, risks depend upon a variety of factors – *e.g.*, the vulnerability of the cloud infrastructure and steps the cloud provider has taken to secure the infrastructure, the adversaries and the nature of attacks, the degree of harm an adversary can cause to the data owner due to exposure, and the representation of data on public clouds, to name a few. A risk-based approach requires proper models and metrics to quantify risks. Risk-based approaches expose tradeoffs between security and system specific properties (*e.g.*, performance, usability, *etc.*) requiring users to make a choice. A natural question is how should the risks be communicated to the user and what kind of tools can be built to empower users to make an informed choice? Possible approaches based on HCI principles, social science research on risk communications as well as machine learning methods to learn a user's tolerances to risk could be employed. Finally, another related challenge in developing a risk-based approach is in postulating the choice of data representation on the public cloud as a multi-criteria optimization. Such a formulation requires a reasonable estimate of how the system will be used in the future (*e.g.*, what requests will a user make to cloud services in the CloudProtect context, or what analysis tasks will the user execute in the hybrid cloud setting, *etc.*). This requires mechanisms for future workload predictions. Work on autonomic computing for workload prediction (usually done in the context of performance optimization, *e.g.*, to determine what indices to create in a relational database) could possibly be exploited for such a task.

Overall, we believe that until efficient computation techniques over encrypted data representations are available (unlikely in the near future), a risk-based approach sketched above provides a viable complementary mechanism to achieve practical security and data confidentiality in a cloud computing setting. Such an approach can, of course, benefit from the ongoing work on cryptographic techniques that extend the nature/types of computations one can perform over encrypted data.

Acknowledgements. The work at UC Irvine was funded in part by NSF grants CNS 1063596, CNS 1059436, and CNS 118127. The work at UT Dallas was funded by the Air Force Office of Scientific Research MURI Grant FA9550-08-1-0265 and FA9550-12-1-0082.

References

[1] Lev-Ram, M.: Why Zynga loves the hybrid cloud (2012),
    http://tech.fortune.cnn.com/2012/04/09/zynga-2/?iid=HP_LN
[2] Mearian, L.: EMC's Tucci sees hybrid cloud becoming de facto standard (2011),
    http://www.computerworld.com/s/article/9216573/
    EMC_s_Tucci_sees_hybrid_cloud_becoming_de_facto_standard
[3] Zhang, K., Zhou, X.Y., Chen, Y., Wang, X., Ruan, Y.: Sedic: privacy-aware data intensive computing on hybrid clouds. In: ACM Conference on Computer and Communications Security, pp. 515–526 (2011)
[4] Oktay, K.Y., Khadilkar, V., Hore, B., Kantarcioglu, M., Mehrotra, S., Thuraisingham, B.: Risk-Aware Workload Distribution in Hybrid Clouds. In: IEEE CLOUD, pp. 229–236 (2012)
[5] Diallo, M., Hore, B., Chang, E.C., Mehrotra, S., Venkatasubramanian, N.: CloudProtect: Managing Data Privacy in Cloud Applications. In: IEEE CLOUD (2012)
[6] Hybrid Cloud. The NIST Definition of Cloud Computing. National Institute of Science and Technology, Special Publication, 800-145 (2011)
[7] Fouad, M.R., Lebanon, G., Bertino, E.: ARUBA: A Risk-Utility-Based Algorithm for Data Disclosure. In: Jonker, W., Petković, M. (eds.) SDM 2008. LNCS, vol. 5159, pp. 32–49. Springer, Heidelberg (2008)
[8] Trabelsi, S., Salzgeber, V., Bezzi, M., Montagnon, G.: Data disclosure risk evaluation. In: CRiSIS, pp. 35–72 (2009)
[9] Nykiel, T., Potamias, M., Mishra, C., Kollios, G., Koudas, N.: MRShare: sharing across multiple queries in MapReduce. Proc. VLDB Endow. 3, 1–2 (2010)
[10] Dean, J., Ghemawat, S.: MapReduce: simplified data processing on large clusters. Commun. ACM 51(1), 107–113 (2008)
[11] Apache Hadoop, http://hadoop.apache.org/
[12] Hacigümüş, H., Iyer, B.R., Li, C., Mehrotra, S.: Executing SQL over encrypted data in the database-service-provider model. In: SIGMOD, pp. 216–227 (2002)
[13] Zhang, K., Zhou, X., Chen, Y., Wang, X., Ruan, Y.: Sedic: privacy-aware data intensive computing on hybrid clouds. In: CCS 2011. ACM (2011)
[14] Hore, B., Mehrotra, S., Hacigm, H.: Managing and querying encrypted data. In: Gertz, M., Jajodia, S. (eds.) Handbook of Database Security, pp. 163–190. Springer, US (2008)

[15] Bagherzandi, A., Hore, B., Mehrotra, S.: Search over Encrypted Data. In: Encyclopedia of Cryptography and Security. Springer (2011)

[16] Hacigumus, H., Hore, B., Mehrotra, S.: Privacy of Outsourced Dat. In: Encyclopedia of Cryptography and Security. Springer (2011)

[17] Hacigumus, H., Iyer, B., Mehrotra, S.: Providing Database as a Service. In: IEEE International Conference in Data Engineering (2002)

[18] Wu, S., Li, F., Mehrotra, S., Ooi, B.C.: Query Optimization for massively parallel data processing. In: SoCC 2011 (2011)

Jamming Resistant Schemes for Wireless Communication: A Combinatorial Approach

Samiran Bag, Sushmita Ruj, and Bimal Roy

Indian Statistical Institute
{samiran_r,sush,bimal}@isical.ac.in

Abstract. Jamming resistant communication mechanism is essential for reliable wireless communication. In this paper, we propose two channel hopping protocols using combinatorial designs for alleviating jamming attacks. One of these protocols is for unicast communication model and the other is aimed for multicast communication model. To the best of our knowledge, this is the first paper which uses combinatorial designs as a tool to solve the anti-jamming communication problem. Our protocols guarantee that the sender and receiver rendezvous within a finite amount of time to exchange information. In our protocol, each sender and receiver has a secret hopping sequence, instead of pairwise secret codes. Our unicast-communication protocol ensures that no two pairs of nodes collide over a single channel at the same time. Besides, the channels used by node-pairs for communication keep changing after every session making it infeasible for the adversary to anticipate the common channel to be used by a particular pair of nodes. We show these protocols using combinatorial designs performs better than existing anti-jamming protocol.

1 Introduction

Wireless communication is prone to jamming attacks, in which a malicious adversary can wilfully disrupt the communication between two communicating devices by transmitting a high powered noisy signal through the same channel used by the two nodes. This noisy signal if powerful enough can render the message passed between the sender and the receiver uninterpretable. Therefore, jamming resistance is crucial for applications where reliable wireless communications is necessary.

Conventional anti jamming techniques like Frequency Hopping Spread Spectrum, Chirp Spread Spectrum and Direct Sequence Spread Spectrum (DSSS) [8] make use of the spectral diversity of the wireless medium and are well studied. These techniques rely on secret pre-shared code (key) between a pair of sender and receiver which spread the signal making it difficult for an adversary to predict channel which is being used. This kind of hopping using a predetermined sequence is known as Coordinated Frequency Hopping.

Attempts have been made to break the dependency of pre-shared key with jamming resistant communication [1,11,14]. Strasser *et al.* proposed Uncoordinated Frequency Hopping (UFH) Spread Spectrum technique [13,9]. In [9],

A. Bagchi and I. Ray (Eds.): ICISS 2013, LNCS 8303, pp. 43–62, 2013.

a jamming resistant broadcast scheme is proposed. This scheme is called UDSSS(uncoordinated direct sequence spread spectrum). UDSSS is an anti-jamming modulation technique based on the concept of DSSS. Unlike DSSS it does not rely on a pre-shared spreading sequences. In [13] the communicating devices hop over a number of available channels. The sender usually hops at a higher speed than the receiver. Whenever the receiver and the sender meets on the same channel there is a message exchange. Messages may not fit into the senders short transmission slot. Hence, messages need to be split into smaller packets by the sender.

Combinatorial designs are mathematical objects which have been used in diverse areas like constructing message authentication codes [7], key predistribution schemes in wireless sensor networks [3], secret sharing schemes [12]. We introduce a new application of combinatorial designs to construct anti-jamming protocols for wireless communication. In our scheme any pair of nodes are bound to meet on the same channel on a particular session. To the best of our knowledge, this is the first paper which discusses how designs can be used to counter jamming attacks for wireless communication.

1.1   Our Contribution

In this paper we propose two schemes that make use of combinatorial designs which enable users/nodes in a group/network to communicate with other users/nodes in presence of an active but computationally bounded jammer. We are the first to apply combinatorial design to counter jamming attacks in wireless communication. The first scheme deals with unicast communication between users. This scheme enables a set of users to communicate in presence of a jammer. The design of our protocol guarantees that the two nodes will rendezvous in $O(c)$ time, where c is the number of channels available. Other jamming–resistant communication schemes that use channel hopping as a counter measure for jamming attacks are the UFH scheme in [13] and the quorum based scheme in [4]. Our hopping protocol performs better than [4] and is more efficient than [13] with respect to the number of time slots required to accomplish the communication of a message. The second scheme is for multicast communication. This scheme assumes that there is a set of senders and a set of receivers. The senders send messages to the receivers but not vice-versa. Moreover, all the senders send the same message over different frequencies. We discuss a technique that allows the receiver to listen to the transmission from the senders while the jammer is actively present in the scenario. We have used combinatorial designs in both the schemes.

2   Related Work

Anti-jamming communication has recently drawn a lot of attention. Xu *et al.* [16] discussed channel hopping and applied node mobility to evade jammer. They focused on determining the active presence of a jammer, rather than ways to communicate in presence of them. This protocol is costly in terms of usage of energy to relocate nodes from one place to another, in order to evade an attacker. Wood *et al.* [15] presented a protocol for defeating energy-efficient jamming in networks based on IEEE 802.15.4 compatible hardware. Their protocol uses four defense mechanisms e.g. frame masking, channel hopping, packet fragmentation and redundant encoding.

Strasser *et al.* [14] proposed jamming resistant key establishment technique using uncoordinated frequency hopping. They proposed a scheme by which two devices that do not share a secret spread code (key) in presence of jammer. Their scheme is applicable to nodes having multiple transceivers, which can send and listen simultaneously on many channels. Whenever a sender and the receiver rendezvous on a common channel by chance, there is a successful message transmission from the sender to the receiver provided the channel is not jammed. This message contains a secret key or a part of it. To increase the chance of rendezvous, the sender hops faster than the receiver. Strasser *et al.* proposed a jamming resistant broadcast communication protocol in [9]. In this scheme, a publicly known set of spreading sequences is used. The sender randomly chooses a spreading sequence from this set of spreading sequences and then spreads its message with the spreading sequence. The receivers record the signal on the channel and despread the message by applying sequences from the set using a trial-and-error method. This scheme is called uncoordinated direct sequence spread spectrum scheme.

Lee *et al.* [4] proposed a quorum based channel hopping for anti-jamming communication. They used cyclic difference set to generate a quorum system. Senders hop according to this generated sequence, whereas the receiver hops much slower than the senders according to another sequence. They also proposed a jamming resistant key establishment technique in [5]. This paper proposes a novel Frequency Quorum Rendezvous (FQR) scheme for fast and resilient pre-key establishment in anti-jamming spread spectrum techniques. Their scheme guarantees a rendezvous time of each pair of node and the rendezvous time is between $O(c^2)$, where c is the number of available channels. This is quite high where there are a large number of available channels. Anti-jamming protocols using quorum based techniques have been increasingly used in cognitive radio networks [2].

So far combinatorial design has never been used for channel hopping. Also no one has been able to propose any channel hopping scheme where the sender and the receiver is bound to meet within a time bound of the order of the size of the network except the scheme in [4] which does only in best case and in the worst case the time-bound is of the order of the square of the size of the network.

3 Preliminaries

3.1 Combinatorial Design

Definition 1. *A design (def. 1.1 of [12]) is a two tuple $(X, \mathcal{A})$ where X is a set of elements and $\mathcal{A}$ is a set of subsets (also called blocks) of X. Thus,*

$$\mathcal{A} = \{x : x \subseteq X\}.$$

Definition 2. *A* Transversal Design *(def. 6.42 of [12]) $TD(k, n, \lambda)$, where $k \geq 2$, $n \geq 1$; is a triple $(X, \mathcal{G}, \mathcal{B})$ satisfying,*

1. $|X| = kn$,
2. $\mathcal{G} = \{G_1, G_2, \ldots, G_k\}$, *such that,* $|G_i| = n, 1 \leq i \leq k$, $G_i \bigcap G_j = \emptyset$, $\bigcup_{i=1}^{k} G_i = X$,
3. $\mathcal{B} = \{B : B \subset X, |B| = k\}$,
4. $\forall B \in \mathcal{B}, 1 \leq i \leq k, |B \cap G_i| = 1$,
5. $\forall i, j \in \{1, 2, \ldots, n\}, i \neq j, \forall x \in G_i, \forall y \in G_j, |\{B : B \in \mathcal{B}, x, y \in B\}| = \lambda$.

Definition 3. *A* Latin Square (LS) *(def. 6.1 of [12]) of order n is an $n \times n$ array L such that each element in the array belongs to a set X of cardinality n and each row of the L is a permutation of elements in X and each column of X is a permutation of elements in X.*

Definition 4. *(def. 6.19 of [12]) Let L_1 and L_2 are Latin Squares of order n defined on the set X_1 and X_2 respectively. Then, L_1 and L_2 are* Orthogonal Latin Squares *provided that for every $x_1 \in X_1$ and for every $x_2 \in X_2$, there is a unique cell (i, j); $i, j \in \{1, 2, 3, \ldots, n\}$ such that $L_1(i, j) = x_1$ and $L_2(i, j) = x_2$.*

Example 1. Two orthogonal Latin Squares of order 5 defined on $X_1 = X_2 = \{1, 2, 3, 4, 5\}$ are given below:

$$L_1 = \begin{array}{|c|c|c|c|c|} \hline 1 & 2 & 3 & 4 & 5 \\ \hline 2 & 3 & 4 & 5 & 1 \\ \hline 3 & 4 & 5 & 1 & 2 \\ \hline 4 & 5 & 1 & 2 & 3 \\ \hline 5 & 1 & 2 & 3 & 4 \\ \hline \end{array}, L_2 = \begin{array}{|c|c|c|c|c|} \hline 5 & 4 & 3 & 2 & 1 \\ \hline 1 & 5 & 4 & 3 & 2 \\ \hline 2 & 1 & 5 & 4 & 3 \\ \hline 3 & 2 & 1 & 5 & 4 \\ \hline 4 & 3 & 2 & 1 & 5 \\ \hline \end{array}$$

If we superpose L_1 and L_2 we get,

$$L_3 = \begin{array}{|c|c|c|c|c|} \hline (1,5) & (2,4) & (3,3) & (4,2) & (5,1) \\ \hline (2,1) & (3,5) & (4,4) & (5,3) & (1,2) \\ \hline (3,2) & (4,1) & (5,5) & (1,4) & (2,3) \\ \hline (4,3) & (5,2) & (1,1) & (2,5) & (3,4) \\ \hline (5,4) & (1,3) & (2,2) & (3,1) & (4,5) \\ \hline \end{array}$$

Note that in L_3 all 25 entries of $X \times X$ have unique position. For example the entry $(2, 1)$ is in second row and first column. Therefore according to the definition L_1 and L_2 are orthogonal Latin Squares defined on identical set of elements.

Lemma 1. *If L_1 and L_2 are two orthogonal $n \times n$ Latin Squares defined on the set $\{0, 1, 2, \ldots, n - 1\}$ and $x, y \in \{0, 1, 2, \ldots, n - 1\}$ then $L_1 + x \mod n$ and $L_2 + y \mod n$ are orthogonal LS, where $L + x \mod n$ is the LS obtained by adding an integer x to each element of the Latin Square L modulo n.*

Proof. For the proof one may refer to [12].

Theorem 1. *If $n > 1$ is odd, then there exist two orthogonal Latin Squares of order n.*

Proof. Ref. Theorem 6.23 of [12].

3.2   Construction of Orthogonal Latin Squares

For this construction, one may refer to theorem 6.23 of [12].

4   Network Description

4.1   System Model for Scheme-I in Section 5

We consider a network with a maximum of N nodes which are within communication range. The main goal is to allow the nodes to communicate with each other using the set of available frequencies C. Each node is equipped with a transceiver which is capable of sending and receiving communication signal over a range of frequencies. We assume that the transceiver does not leak information about its active reception channels. Hence, the channels on which the transceiver is actively listening on cannot be detected by monitoring its radio signal emissions. The nodes also have a clock and are loosely time synchronized in the order of seconds using GPS. The nodes are capable of computation and storage. The nodes can hop over C (where, $|C| = c$) communication frequencies. Each node has a secret key/public key pair (SK, PK) which is used for public-key encryption/decryption purpose and (K, K^{-1}) key for verification and signature. There is a base station which is also a certification authority which issues certificates to bind the public key to the respective nodes. Throughout this paper we assume that the base station cannot be compromised by any adversary. Apart from this, each node holds a secret key $\mathcal{K}$. This key is used for randomising the channel hopping sequences of the nodes. The usage of this key $\mathcal{K}$ will be discussed in later sections. The timeline is divided into time slots. A time slot is a small quantum of time during which a certain node remains on the same channel i.e it sends/receives signals on the same channel. In other words, a time slot is the minimum amount of time needed to transmit a message packet. A session consists of some number(say, ω) of consecutive time slots. A time slot t belongs to session s, where $s = (t \mod \omega)$ and $0 \leq t < \infty$.

There is a base station that controls the network. All the nodes are connected to the outside world through the base station.

4.2   System Model for Scheme-II in Section 6

We consider a different type of network model for the jamming resistant communication scheme discussed in section 6. Here we assume that there is a set S of senders and a set $\mathcal{R}$ of receivers. The senders only send messages whereas the receivers only collect these messages but not the other way round. For example, the senders can be a base station sending some broadcast messages simultaneously over multiple frequencies and thus posing as a set of senders. The receivers may be a set of nodes belonging to a wireless network. This is the basic modelling difference between the two schemes. In this scheme communication is unidirectional as opposed to the previous model where we considered bidirectional message sending. Everything else is same as discussed in section 4.1.

4.3   Attacker Model

We consider an omnipresent adversary who wants to disrupt the communication as much as possible. It is capable of eavesdropping on the network, alter messages and jam the channels by blocking the propagation of radio signals. The attacker is computationally bounded, but is present all the time. At a particular instant it can jam at most J channels where $J < c$. It jams a channel by emitting high power signal on that channel. We consider that the attacker's clock is time synchronized with the system. In every time slot t_i, the attacker jams a set of channels $S_{t_i}^J$, where $S_{t_i}^J \subset \mathcal{C}, |S_{t_i}^J| = J$. Thus, at the start of a time-slot the jammer starts jamming J randomly chosen channels. It continues to jam those channels until the beginning of the next time-slot. Thereafter, it chooses a new set of channels for jamming. In our jamming resistant communication scheme the sending sequence as well as the receiving sequence of any node changes in each session. This ensures that the jammer cannot totally disconnect the communication between two nodes by jamming a particular frequency channel. If a particular node is sending message to another node through a frequency channel x in session s, then the probability that in next session they will not be using the frequency channel i for message transfer is $\frac{c-1}{c}$. Therefore, a jammer who keeps on jamming the same set of channels at every time slot will not be able to disrupt communication between a pair of nodes every time.

4.4   Protection against Eavesdropping and Message Modification

Each message fragment (ref. section 4.5) M is encrypted with public key of the receiver. The ciphertext is $C = E_{PK}(M)$. The ciphertext is signed with the secret key. The signature is given by $\sigma = sign(C, K^{-1})$. The message (C, σ) are then sent on the channel chosen according to the Algorithm 1 given in the next section. Due to encryption, an adversary is unable to get any information by eavesdropping. The receiver checks the signature of the message to verify that it indeed was sent by a valid sender and not modified by an adversary. We will not discuss encryption and decryption techniques here, but assume that secrecy and authentication can be achieved using known protocols (as in [13]). Throughout the rest of the paper we will address only jamming attacks, in which the adversary blocks the radio signals and makes communication difficult.

4.5   Message Passing Mechanism

Since the random jammer jams randomly chosen J channels in each time-slot, there will be some messages that the adversary will be able to jam. Since there are $c = N$ channels out of which the jammer is able to jam J channels per time-slot, the probability that a particular channel will be jammed by the adversary is equal to J/c. This probability is reduced for large c. However there is a non-zero probability that the jammer will disrupt the communication between a particular pair of nodes.

To alleviate this, each message is fragmented into a number of parts and sent to the intended recipient whenever the sender and the receiver rendezvous on the same channel. The receiver collects those fragments and reassembles them to get the original message. Since the attacker has a positive probability to jam a packet, it may so happen that some of the fragments are lost because of the jammer. So, we need to send redundant packets to ensure that the receiver is successfully able to reassemble the original message from the packets it receives. Erasure code is a technique to fragment messages and has been studied in [19], [10]. Through erasure codes it is possible to fragment a message into many parts so that the receiver can reassemble the message if it is able to receive at least l of the fragments, where l is an integer whose value depends upon the coding technique used. With this technique, it has to be ensured that the authenticity and integrity of each fragment is preserved. This can be done using one way accumulators based on bilinear maps [17], [18]. An accumulator is a two-to-one collision resistant hash function $h(u; x)$, mapping from $U \times X \to U$, with the property

$$h(h(u; x_2); x_1) = h(h(u; x_1); x_2) \forall x_1, x_2 \in X$$

This property of one-way accumulators ensures that they can be used for verifying whether a particular message belongs to a chain of message or not. With one way accumulators, it is possible to verify chain of messages without bothering about the serial number of a particular message in a chain. Accumulators are used to generate witness for a fragment that can verify the fragment. To construct a witness w for a message fragment $x \in X$, where X is the set of messages originating from a particular source, the sender can pick a random $u \in U$ and can generate $w = h(\ldots h(u, x_1), x_2), \ldots), x_m)$ where $\{x_1, x_2, \ldots, x_m\} = X \setminus x$. So, the sender calculates the witness through accumulating all message fragment but the fragment for which it is generated. This witness is appended to the message fragment it corresponds to. Let the receiver receives two packets from the sender containing the message , witness pair (w_s, x_s) and (w_t, x_t). It is easy to see that

$$h(w_s, x_s) = h(h(\ldots h(u, x_{\alpha_1}), \ldots), x_{\alpha_k}), x_s) = h(u, X)$$

where $\{x_{\alpha_i}\} = X \setminus x_s$. Similarly, $h(w_t, x_t) = h(u, X)$. Hence, $h(w_s, x_s) = h(w_t, x_t)$. Hence in order to check the authenticity of the message the receiver needs to check the hash of the witness and the message fragment only. An adversary can not insert a fake packet as it can not compute a pair (u', x') such that $h(u', x') = h(u, X)$ since the hash function is collision resistant.

So, each node willing to send a message to another node, fragments the message into a number of parts through erasure coding technique and computes witnesses for each of them using one-way accumulators. Then, the sender sends the (witness, message) pair to the receiver whenever they rendezvous (which happens exactly once in each session). The receiver tries to verify each message fragment with the witness. If it is able to verify then it accepts the packet. Otherwise it rejects the packet. This way if sufficient message fragments are received, the receiver will be able to regenerate the original message.

In each session the attacker will be jamming the channel between node i and node j with a probability $\frac{J}{c}$. Hence in each session a packet will get destroyed with this probability. Let, X_i denote the number of message fragments required to be transmitted in order to communicate an l-fragmented message under erasure coding technique. The expected number of sessions required for the successful transmission of a message is given by

$$\sum_{x=l}^{x=\infty} Pr[X_i = x]x = \sum_{x=l}^{\infty} x\binom{x-1}{l-1}(1-\frac{J}{c})^l(\frac{J}{c})^{x-l} = \frac{l}{1-\frac{J}{c}}. \text{ Since, } \frac{J}{c} > 0, l < \frac{l}{1-\frac{J}{c}}.$$

This shows that the throughput of the communication scheme is reduced by a factor of $1 - \frac{J}{c}$.

5   Combinatorial Anti-jamming Protocol for Unicast Communication: Scheme-I

5.1   Definitions and Assumptions

Here we discuss some basic assumptions relating to the network model which is in addition to the system model discussed in section 4.1. Firstly, the number of available channels (c) must be more than or equal to the maximum number of nodes or users (N) in the network. In this paper we assume $c = N$. Secondly, the size of the network must be odd. If the network size is an even number then we shall have to make it odd by adding a virtual node to the network. This virtual node will cause no intricacy to the communication model.

Definition 5. *A time slot is the period during which a certain node transmits a message-fragment over a certain frequency channel. Alternately it can be defined as the period during which a certain node listens to a certain frequency channel. A session consists of N many time slots.*

Definition 6. *Sending Sequence for a node n_i is a set $\mathcal{P}$ whose elements are 3-tuples (α, β, j) such that $\alpha, \beta \in \{0, 1, \ldots, N-1\}, j \in \{\{0, 1, \ldots, N-1\}\setminus\{i\}\}$ and for all 3-tuple $(\alpha, \beta, j) \in \mathcal{P}$, node n_i sends data to node n_j at time-slot β through frequency channel α. Also sender node n_i and receiver node n_j rendezvous at time slot β on frequency channel α.*

A Receiving Sequence for a node n_i is a set $\mathcal{Q} = \{(\delta, \gamma, j) : \delta, \gamma \in \{0, 1, \ldots, N-1\}, j \in \{\{0, 1, \ldots, N-1\}\setminus i\}\}$, such that $\forall(\delta, \gamma, j) \in \mathcal{Q}$ node n_i receives data from node n_j at time-slot γ through frequency channel δ and for $i = j$, node n_i receives data from base station at time γ through frequency channel δ. Also receiver node n_i and sender node n_j rendezvous at time slot γ on frequency channel δ.

In our jamming resistant communication scheme, we map combinatorial design to frequency hopping sequence. Each element of the design is a two tuple (x, t), where x corresponds to the channel id. and t corresponds to the time slot.

Mathematically, the mapping between designs and channel allocation occurs in the following way:

Let, $(X, \mathcal{A})$ be a design where X is a set of varieties. The elements in X are two tuples. Let, $\mathcal{A} = \{B_1, B_2, \ldots, B_g\} \cup \{B'_1, B'_2, \ldots, B'_g\}$ be a set of blocks such that:

1. $\forall i, j \in \{1, 2, \ldots, g\}, B_i \cap B_j \neq \phi \Rightarrow i = j$,
2. $\forall i, j \in \{1, 2, \ldots, g\}, B'_i \cap B'_j \neq \phi \Rightarrow i = j$,
3. $\forall i, j \in \{1, 2, \ldots, g\}, |B_i \cap B'_j| \geq 1$.

We assign two blocks B_i, B'_i of $\mathcal{A}$ to node n_i of the network. These two blocks correspond to the sending and receiving sequences of the node n_i respectively. Let n_j be another node whose sending and receiving sequences correspond to block B_j and B'_j. The sending sequence of node n_i and the receiving sequence of node n_j are B_i and B'_j. $\forall (x, t) \in B_i \cap B'_j$, (x, t) corresponds to the rendezvous point of node n_i and node n_j. It means at time slot t node n_i will be sending some message to node n_j on frequency channel identified by x. Similarly, node n_i will be receiving message from node n_j in time slot t' on frequency channel y only if $(y, t') \in B_j \cap B'_i$.

Condition 1) ensures that no two senders transmit over the same channel at the same time. Similarly, condition 2) ensures that no two receivers listen to the same channel at the same time. This restriction prevents collision between two senders (or two receivers) sending (receiving) messages over the same channel at the same time. Condition 3) ensures that the design should ensure that there is atleast one element in common to two blocks of the design (used for sending and receiving). This is to guarantee that a sender and a receiver rendezvous within a finite amount of time. In the rest of the paper the terms node and user will bear the same meaning.

5.2   Channel Hopping

We now describe a channel hopping technique using Latin Squares in details. If N is odd then we can construct two orthogonal Latin Squares of order N using the method described in Theorem 6.23 of [12]. Let these two Latin Squares be L_1 and L_2. Let L_3 be the Latin Square obtained through superposition of L_1 and L_2. Load node $n_i, 1 \leq i \leq N$ with the ith row and the ith column of array L_3. A key $\mathcal{K}$ is loaded in all the nodes. This key will be used as a seed to pseudo random generators to generate pseudo random numbers modulo N. There are $c = N$ frequency channels with identifiers $0, 1, 2, \ldots, N - 1$. The entire time-line is divided into sessions. A session consists of N consecutive time slots. The time slots in every session is identified as $0, 1, \ldots, N - 1$.

Algorithm 1 is used by each node of the network for hopping through different channels. The Algorithm generates the sending and receiving sequences of any user in a session. In the Algorithm, X' and Y' are two sets that contain the sending and receiving sequences of any node. The Algorithm also uses two pseudo random-integer generators. The output generated by these two pseudo random-integer generators are used to randomize the sending and receiving sequences of a user in each session as shown in Algorithm 1. Algorithm 1 updates the content of the row X and column Y in each session using the random integers generated by the pseudo-random generators. This is to ensure that the sending and the receiving sequences become unpredictable by the jammer who does not know the key $\mathcal{K}$.

Algorithm 1. Latin Square based Channel Hopping Algorithm for unicast communication

---

Input: Key $\mathcal{K}$.

L_1 and L_2 are two orthogonal LS. L_3 is the array obtained by superposing L_1 and L_2.

r^{th} row of Superposed LS L_3 is $X = \{(\alpha_1, \beta_1), (\alpha_2, \beta_2), \ldots, (\alpha_N, \beta_N)\}$ and r^{th} column is $Y = \{(\delta_1, \gamma_1), (\delta_2, \gamma_2), \ldots, (\delta_N, \gamma_N)\}$.

Lifetime T of key $\mathcal{K}$. T is the number of sessions after which the key $\mathcal{K}$ needs to be refreshed.

Output: Channel Hopping Sequence of the rth node n_r.

  for $(i = 0; i < T; i++)$ **do**

    $X' = Y' = \phi$

    $x = Pseudorand_1(\mathcal{K}, i) \mod N$

    $y = Pseudorand_2(\mathcal{K}, i) \mod N$

    for $(j = 1; j \leq |X|; j++)$ **do**

      $\alpha'_j = \alpha_j + x \mod N, \beta'_j = \beta_j + y \mod N$

      $\delta'_j = \delta_j + x \mod N, \gamma'_j = \gamma_j + y \mod N$

      if $j \neq r$ **then**

        $X' = X' \cup (\alpha'_j, \beta'_j, j)$

      end if

      $Y' = Y' \cup (\delta'_j, \gamma'_j, j)$

    end for

    X' is the sending sequence of node r for session i.

    Y' is the receiving sequence of node r for session i.

  end for

We prove in section 7 that Algorithm 1 computes the sending and receiving sequences in such a manner that there is no collision between multiple nodes over the same frequency channel. In other words, no two nodes try to send messages over the same channel and no two nodes read the same channel at the same time. In addition to this, lemma 4 shows that any sender and any receiver must rendezvous over a certain channel on all the sessions. Hence, the average rendezvous time is bounded by $O(c)$.

The secret key $\mathcal{K}$ is used to randomise the sending and receiving sequences of a node in a session. It is applied to ensure that the adversary who does not know the key cannot compute the sending and receiving sequence of any node for any session. So, a jammer who chooses J channels out of $c = N$ available channels has a jamming probability equal to J/N as proved in Theorem 4. It is assumed that after a certain time the key might get exposed to the adversary who can take advantage of some weakness of the base station. It can be noted from Algorithm 1 that the receiving sequence of each node n_r of the network contains a triplet (α'_j, β'_j, j) and hence according to definition 6, β'_j is time slot when node n_j expects to receive some data from the base station over frequency channel α'_j in a particular session. This data is nothing but information about the new key. The key is sent at regular interval to all the nodes after encrypting it with the public key of the individual nodes. The lifetime of any key $\mathcal{K}$ is T sessions. Hence new key must be communicated to all the nodes before T many sessions have elapsed. This key refreshing is done to ensure that the secret key does not get compromised by the attacker. Once T sessions have elapsed, Algorithm 1 starts using the fresh key.

The proof of correctness is presented in Section 7.1.

Example 2. Let the number of nodes in a sensor network be 4. We take L_1 and L_2 given in Section 3 as the Latin Square to construct hopping sequence for our scheme. The superposition of L_1 and L_2 yields L_3. Now distribute i^{th} row and i^{th} column of L_3 to one node. Node n_1 will get the first row of L_3 i.e., $(1,5),(2,4),(3,3),(4,2),(5,1)$ and the first column of L_3 i.e., $(1,5),(2,1),(3,2),(4,3),(5,4)$ and so on.

Let us consider that the pseudo random integer generated by $Pseudorand_1()$ function at session $i = 1$ be 1 modulo 5. Similarly, let us consider that the pseudo random integer generated by $Pseudorand_2()$ function at session $i = 1$ be 4 modulo 5. According to the algorithm the sending sequence of node 1 is $\{(3,3,2),(4,2,3),(0,1,4),(1,0,5)\}$. Also, the receiving sequence of node 1 will be $\{(3,0,2),(4,1,3),(0,2,4),(1,3,5)\}$.

Hence, at session 1, node 1 should send a message packet to node 2 through frequency channel 3 at time slot 3 if it has some message packet to be delivered to node 2. If node 1 does not have anything to send to node 2 then it will remain idle at time slot 3. Similarly, node 1 can send message packets to node 3 through channel 4 at time slot 2, can send long channel 0 at time slot 1 to node 4. Lastly node 1 can send message packet to node 5 at time slot 0 on frequency channel 1. Therefore, node 1 will be transmitting to different nodes on different channels at different time slots.

Node 1 will listen to channel 3 at time slot 2 for incoming packets from node 2. Similarly, node 1 will listen to channel 4 at time slot 1 for message packet sent by node 3, will listen to channel 0 at time slot 2 for message packet sent by node 4 and listen to channel 1 at time slot 3 for message packet sent by node 5.

6   Anti-jamming Protocol during Multicast Communication: Scheme-II

In this section, we propose a channel hopping scheme for multicast communication using combinatorial design. In other words, this scheme is designed for such scenarios where one sender sends a message that is received by a group of receivers. We shall be using transversal design for developing this channel hopping scheme. Before we move into the details of the scheme we first state the assumptions of the scheme below.

6.1   The Scheme

Let us consider a network consisting of N nodes where $p < N \leq p^2$ and p is a prime number that equals the number of available channels. If N is less than p^2 we can regard $p^2 - N$ many nodes as virtual nodes having no physical existence. These virtual nodes will have their own receiving sequences. Let the identifier of the nodes be $(0,0), (0,1), \ldots, (p-1, p-1)$.

Recall the definition of Transversal Design stated in section 3.1. Let p be a prime number. We can compute a transversal design as in [6].

- $X = \{(x, y) : 0 \leq x < p, 0 \leq y < p\}$.
- $\forall i \in \{0, 1, 2, \ldots, p-1\}, G_i = \{(i, y) : 0 \leq y < p\}$.
- $\mathcal{A} = \{A_{ij} : 0 \leq i < p \& 0 \leq j < p\}$.
- $A_{ij} = \{(x, xi + j \mod p) : 0 \leq x < p\}$.

Now we develop a multicast channel hopping scheme for wireless communication using transversal design. The map from a transversal design to a multicast scheme is the following: each block of the design is used to generate the receiving sequence in Algorithm 2. The two tuple elements of each block will correspond to the (time slot, channel id.) pair. This mapping is discussed in detail below. This channel hopping scheme enables a set $\mathcal{S}$ of p nodes to multicast any message to a set $\mathcal{R}$ of $p^2 - p$ nodes. During one time slot one node of set $\mathcal{S}$ multicasts a message to p nodes of set $\mathcal{R}$. Let the nodes be identified by $(0,0), (0,1), (0,2), \ldots (p-1, p-1)$. This set of nodes are partitioned into two disjoint sets $viz.$ $\mathcal{R}$ and $\mathcal{S}$. $\mathcal{R} = \{(i, j) : 1 \leq i \leq p-1, 0 \leq j \leq p-1\}$ and $\mathcal{S} = \{(0, j) : 0 \leq j \leq p-1\}$. Thus, $|\mathcal{R} \cup \mathcal{S}| = p^2$.

Definition 7. A receiving sequence for a receiver node (i, j) is a set $U_{ij} = \{(\alpha, \beta, s) : 0 \leq \alpha \leq p-1, 0 \leq \beta \leq p-1, s \geq 0\}$ such that node (i, j) listens to channel β at time slot α at any session s.

Remark : The definition 7 of receiving sequence of any node is not to be confused with the definition 6 of receiving sequence

Now, we discuss the channel hopping algorithm for this scheme. We show how to find the receiving sequence of any node belonging to the receiver's group. As stated above, there are $p^2 - p$ receivers. These receivers only listen to channels for messages. The number of channels is p. Time is divided into consecutive sessions like the scheme-I in section 5. There are p timeslots in each session denoted by $0, 1, 2, \ldots, p-1$.

Algorithm 2. Transversal design based Channel Hopping Algorithm for Multicast Communication

---

Input: The set R of receivers.
Output: The frequency hopping scheme for a node r with id (i, j) in R.
   for $(s = 0; s < T; s + +)$ **do**
      $\kappa = Pseudorand(\mathcal{K}, s)$
      $U_{ij} = \phi$
      for $(x = 0; x < p; x + +)$ **do**
         $\alpha = x, \beta = xi + j + \kappa \mod p$
         $U_{ij} = U_{ij} \cup (\alpha, \beta, s)$
      end for
      U_{ij} is the receiving sequence of node r for session s.
   end for

Algorithm 2 uses Transversal design for generating the receiving sequences of the receivers for any session. T is the lifetime of the key which is fed to the pseudo-random-integer generator. The Algorithm outputs the receiving sequences of all receivers for all sessions 1 upto session T after which the key $\mathcal{K}$ needs to be refreshed. The set U_{ij} stores the receiving sequences of a node with id (i, j) for all the p timeslots in a particular session. Each block of the Transversal design is used to generate the receiving sequence of one receiver node. The output of the pseudo-random-integer generator is used to randomize the receiving sequences of a user. The integer generated by the pseudo-random-integer generator is added to β which makes it impossible for the adversary to anticipate the id of the channel to which the receiver (i, j) listens at time slot α at any session s. Here, the sender nodes have no sending sequences unlike the first scheme. This is because we have assumed that the p many senders keep sending the same messages over all the p many available channels at any time slot. A receiver node reads the messages from one of the p senders that sends identical message at any particular time slot.

Example 3. We now give an example of the channel hopping scheme discussed above. We choose a prime $p = 5$. The sender nodes are given by $(i, j) : \forall i, j \in \{0, 1, \ldots, p-1\}$. Let the $Pseudorand()$ function in Algorithm 2 returns the value 3 for some session s. Hence, the receiving sequence for the node $(2, 3)$ at session s will be given by $U_{23} = \{(0, 1, s), (1, 3, s), (2, 0, s), (3, 2, s), (4, 4, s)\}$. It can be seen that there is no pair of 3-tuples (α_1, β_1, s) and (α_2, β_2, s) such that $\beta_1 = \beta_2$. Lemma 5 gives a proof of this property of the receiving sequences. This property ensures that each sender listens to distinct channels at different time slots and thus attempt to evade a jammer.

The proof of correctness of this algorithm is given in Section 7.1.

7   Analysis of Our Schemes

We will first prove that the Algorithms 1 and 2 are correct. We then show that Scheme in Section 5.2 guarantees protection from the jammer.

7.1   Theoretical Analysis

Here we give a proof of correctness of the Algorithm 1 discussed in Section 5. We state the following theorem

Theorem 2. *Algorithm 1 is correct, which means that it satisfies the following properties:*

1. *No two nodes transmit messages through the same channel at the same time.*
2. *No two nodes listen to the same channel at the same time.*
3. *Two nodes rendezvous once in a particular session.*

We prove these properties of the channel hopping scheme below.

Lemma 2. *Algorithm 1 satisfies the condition that no two nodes transmit messages through the same channel at the same time.*

Proof. Let X'_m and X'_n be the sending sequence of node m and n respectively for some session s. Also, let the two orthogonal LS used in Algorithm 1 be L_1 and L_2 and let L_3 be the superposition of them. Let us assume that there exists a pair of nodes which transmit through the same channel at the same time. This implies that there exist tuples $(\alpha_1, \beta_1, i) \in X'_m$ and $(\alpha_2, \beta_2, j) \in X'_n$ where $(\alpha_1, \beta_1) = (\alpha_2, \beta_2)$. This further implies that for some $x, y \in \{0, 1, \ldots, N - 1\}$, there exists $L_1(m, i) \mod N$ and $L_2(m, i) \mod N$, such that $\alpha_1 = x + L_1(m, i) \mod N, \beta_1 = y + L_2(m, i) \mod N$, and there exists $L_1(n, j) \mod N$ and $L_2(n, j) \mod N$, such that $\alpha_2 = x + L_1(n, j) \mod N, \beta_2 = y + L_2(n, j) \mod N$. Here x, y are the output of $Pseudorand_1()$ and $Pseudorand_2()$ respectively.

Now since $(\alpha_1, \beta_1) = (\alpha_2, \beta_2)$, $x + L_1(m, i) \mod N = x + L_1(n, j) \mod N$. This implies that $L_1(m, i) = L_1(n, j) \mod N$ and $L_2(m, i) = L_2(n, j) \mod N$. This contradicts the fact that L_1 and L_2 are orthogonal. Hence, the first property is proved.

In similar way, we can prove that:

Lemma 3. *Algorithm 1 satisfies the condition that no two nodes listen to the same channel at the same time.*

Lemma 4. *Algorithm 1 guarantees that two nodes rendezvous once in a particular session.*

Proof. By the construction of LS for a row $i = \{(\alpha_1, \beta_1), (\alpha_2, \beta_2), \ldots, (\alpha_N, \beta_N)\}$ and column $j = \{(\gamma_1, \delta_1), (\gamma_2, \delta_2), \ldots, (\gamma_N, \delta_N)\}$ intersect at when $\alpha_j = \gamma_i$ and $\beta_j = \delta_i$. At the s-th session, $x = Pseudorandom_1(\mathcal{K}, s)$ and $y = Pseudorandom_2(\mathcal{K}, s)$. So, node i sends signal to j on channel $\alpha_j + x$ at time $\beta_j + y$. Node j receives signal from node i in session s on channel $\gamma_i + x$ at time $\delta_i + y$. Since $\alpha_j = \gamma_i$ and $\beta_j = \delta_i$, nodes i and j rendezvous on channel $\alpha_j + x$ at time $\beta_j + y$ which is the same as $\gamma_i + x$ at time $\delta_i + y$, where the additions are done modulo N.

From Lemmas 2, 3 and 4, it follows that Theorem 2 is correct.

We next prove the correctness of Algorithm 2. For this, we need to prove that all node belonging to the Receivers' group listens to distinct channels on different time slots. Since there are p time slots and p frequency channel, one receiver node listens to each of the p channels exactly once at a particular session. Lemma 5 proves this fact and hence proves the correctness of algorithm 2.

Lemma 5. *In the output of algorithm 2 for every receiver node (i,j), $\forall \gamma \in \{0,1,\ldots,p-1\}$, $\exists (\alpha, \beta, s) \in U_{ij}$ such that $\gamma = \beta$.*

Proof. for all receiver node (i,j) $|U_{ij}| = p$. It will be sufficient to prove that for any two $(\alpha_1, \beta_1, s), (\alpha_2, \beta_2, s) \in U_{ij}$, $\beta_1 = \beta_2 \Rightarrow \alpha_1 = \alpha_2$. $\beta_1 = \alpha_1 i + j + t \mod p$ and $\beta_2 = \alpha_2 i + j + t \mod p$. If $\beta_1 = \beta_2$ then $\alpha_1 i = \alpha_2 i$. Since $i \neq 0$, $\alpha_1 = \alpha_2$.

Theorem 3. *The scheme in section 6.1 ensures that any two node (i,j) and (i',j') such that $i \neq i'$ must listen to the same channel at a unique time slot in every session.*

Proof. Let s be some session for which t is the output of $Pseudorand(\mathcal{K}, s)$. At time slot x the node (i,j) will be listening to channel $xi + j + t \mod p$ while the node (i',j') will be listening to channel $(xi' + j' + t)$. Then, these two nodes will be listening to the same channel iff $xi + j + t = xi' + j' + t \mod p$ or $x = (j' - j)(i - i')^{-1} \mod p$. If $i \neq i'$ then $(i - i')^{-1}$ exists an is unique. Hence, such a time slot will exists.

We will next analyze the probability with which an attacker can jam a channel.

Theorem 4. *The scheme in Section 5 guarantees secure message exchange between a sender and a receiver with probability J/N in presence of an active jammer who jams J out of N channels.*

Proof. We first observe that all messages are encrypted and signed, which prevents an attacker to eavesdrop or change the message content, without being detected. From Lemma 4, we see that the two nodes rendezvous in finite amount of time, bounded by c. From the design, we note that the i-th sender rendezvous with the j-th receiver at time y on channel x. A jammer can jam any J channels at one time. If a sender and receiver are supposed to rendezvous on any of these channels, then they will not be able to communicate. The probability of such a situation is J/c. Since a new sending and receiving sequence is chosen at the next iteration, the jammer can jam it with a probability $J/c = J/N$.

7.2 Experimental Analysis

We now study the performance of our scheme with respect to other schemes in literature. So far it is clear that our scheme provides a better bound in rendezvous time than the scheme in [4]. Again, in our scheme-I the adversary cannot anticipate the channel that is being used by a pair of nodes for communication. Moreover, since the nodes send/listen to randomly selected channels in [14,13], it is uncertain when the two communicating nodes will rendezvous. On the contrary, our scheme ensures a rendezvous within an average time bound of $O(c)$ (c is the number of channels). Hence, any pair of communicating nodes will surely meet on some channel within a fixed time. Figure 1 shows a graphical comparison of the uncoordinated frequency hopping scheme and our scheme in section 5. We simulated the performance of the two schemes with respect to comparable values of system parameters and have plotted the experimental data. We used C program to simulate the performances of both the schemes. We compiled the source code using GNU C compiler GCC 4.5.4. The horizontal axis corresponds to the probability that a certain channel is being jammed by the adversary. The vertical axis corresponds to the probability of successful transmission of a message packet. Figure 1 shows that the proposed scheme can achieve lower probability of message loss than the well known scheme in [13].

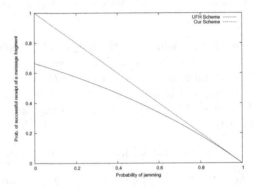

Fig. 1. Graphical comparison of the probability of successful packet transmission of of our scheme and the uncoordinated frequency hopping scheme in [13] with different parameters

Next, we do a comparative study of the time required for each node to rendezvous with other nodes for our scheme and [4]. It can be noticed that our scheme ensures an $O(c)$ time for the rendezvous of any pair of nodes. On the other hand, the scheme in [4] offers a maximum time to rendezvous of order $O(c^2)$ ($c = N$ = no. of nodes). Figure 2 shows graphical comparison of the two schemes. This graph represents the experimental data obtained through simulation of the performance of these two schemes. We used C program to simulate the performances of both the schemes. We compiled the source code using GNU C compiler GCC 4.5.4. The continuous line corresponds to our proposed scheme in section 5 and the discrete points correspond to the scheme by Lee et al. in [4]. It should be noted that the quorum based scheme in [4] requires a difference set for constructing the hopping sequences. Since, difference sets are available only at discrete points, the performance can only be evaluated at some discrete points. It can be seen that our scheme offers a lower time to rendezvous as compared to the other scheme. It can also be noticed that at some points the average

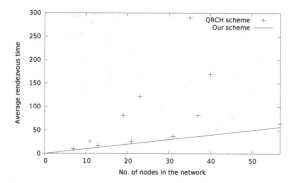

Fig. 2. Graphical comparison of the average time taken for the rendezvous of a pair of nodes by the two schemes. QRCH denotes the quorum based channel hopping scheme in [4] and the other is our proposed scheme. The graph shows that in our scheme the time to rendezvous is less than that of [4].

rendezvous time for the scheme in [4] appears very close to that of our scheme whereas at other points they appear far away from that of our scheme. This is due to the fact that the scheme in [4] yields a maximum time to rendezvous of order $O(c^2)$ but the same for our scheme is always of order $O(c)$. So, our scheme is much better than [4] as it always ensures a time to rendezvous linear in the size of the network.

Again, the performance of the channel hopping scheme in section 6.1 is compared with that of the UFH scheme [13] in figure 3. Here, we consider fragmentation of a message as discussed in section 4.5. Here the X-axis shows the total number of fragments of the original message that must be correctly transmitted to the receiver so that the receiver can successfully reconstruct the original message from the fragments. The Y-axis corresponds to the jammer's strength in terms of number of channels it can jam simultaneously. The vertical axis gives the total number of transmissions required for the message fragments. This graph is drawn by plotting the experimental data obtained through simulating the performance of the two schemes. We used C program to simulate the performance of these schemes. The upper surface in the three dimensional figure 3 corresponds to the number of message transmissions required for the UFH scheme for different size of message packets and different strength of the jammer. Similarly, the lower surface represents the number of transmissions required for our scheme. Hence, figure 3 shows that the scheme in section 6.1 requires lesser number retransmissions than the UFH scheme in [13].

Figure 3 shows how the jamming strength affects the performance of the scheme in section 6.1 for different number of message fragments. Similarly, figure 4 depicts the associativity of the jamming strength, number of nodes and the jamming probability in the scheme described in section 5. The X-axis and the Y-axis corresponds to number of nodes and the number of channels the attacker can jam respectively. The vertical axis gives the probability that a message will be jammed by the attacker.

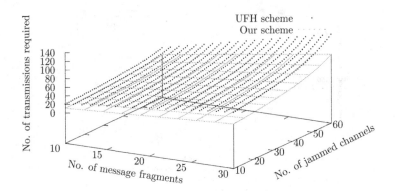

Fig. 3. Graphical comparison of the performances of the channel hopping scheme discussed in section 6.1 with the UFH scheme. The graph shows the number of transmissions required for message fragments for different jamming strength of the attacker. X-axis corresponds to the total number of fragments of the original message. Y-axis corresponds to the number of jammed channels. The vertical axis shows the number of transmissions required for communicating the fragmented message. Here we assume that the sender/receiver can send/receive messages on 8 channels simultaneously.

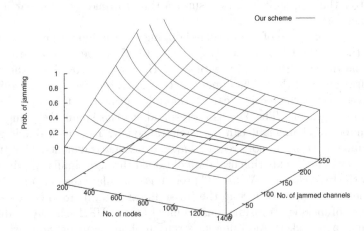

Fig. 4. Graphical presentation of dependence of parameters on our proposed scheme

8   Conclusion and Future Work

In this paper we proposed two channel hopping schemes for wireless communication using combinatorial designs. This work opens a new area of research in the field of frequency channel hopping. In the first scheme of section 5 two secret keys are used to randomize the hopping of nodes through different channels. If an attacker gets to know the keys then it will be able to disrupt the communication of some of the nodes depending upon its jamming capability. The question is whether we can design a combinatorial hopping scheme that does not require a pre-shared key? Is it possible to have distinct keys stored in different nodes and still make these nodes hop over frequency channels independently without any collision? If such a channel hopping scheme can be found then if an adversary gets to know one key or some keys by compromising some nodes then other keys will remain unaffected and hence nodes who use those keys for channel hopping can continue to do so. We leave it as an open problem to find such a channel hopping scheme. In our first channel hopping scheme, every pair of nodes may not be communicating in a particular session. Hence, at any particular time slot there could be some channels not used by any user/node. This idle channels can be given to some secondary users. In other words, we can develop a channel hopping scheme for the primary users of the radio networks and can let the secondary users use the channel only when a channel is idle. This opens a new field of research on the application of our channel hopping schemes in cognitive radio networks.

The second scheme proposed in this paper deals with multicast communication. In this scheme a set of nodes send messages to a distinct set of nodes in presence of a jammer. We have used transversal design for developing the hopping scheme. There are many other designs that could be used in this scenario. For example, if the nodes have multiple transceivers for listening and sending messages over multiple channels then symmetric balanced incomplete block design can be used for broadcast communication. Here the blocks can be replaced by channels. The sender and the receivers can randomly choose blocks and send/listen to all the channels in the block. This will ensure that there will always be a common channel between the sender and a receiver. We leave the application of other designs including symmetric BIBD as a scope for future research.

Acknowledgement. This work is partially supported by DRDO sponsored project Centre of Excellence in Cryptology (CoEC), under MOC ERIP/ER/1009002/M/01/1319/788/D(R & D) of ER & IPR, DRDO.

References

1. Baird, L.C., Bahn, W.L., Collins, M.D., Carlisle, M.C., Butler, S.C.: Keyless jam resistance. In: IEEE Information Assurance and Security Workshop, pp. 143–150 (2009)
2. Bian, K., Park, J.-M., Chen, R.: A quorum-based framework for establishing control channels in dynamic spectrum access networks. In: ACM MOBICOM, pp. 25–36 (2009)
3. Çamtepe, S.A., Yener, B.: Combinatorial design of key distribution mechanisms for wireless sensor networks. In: Samarati, P., Ryan, P.Y.A., Gollmann, D., Molva, R. (eds.) ESORICS 2004. LNCS, vol. 3193, pp. 293–308. Springer, Heidelberg (2004)
4. Lee, E.-K., Oh, S.-Y., Gerla, M.: Randomized channel hopping scheme for anti-jamming communication. IEEE Wireless Days, 1–5 (2010)

5. Lee, E.-K., Oh, S.-Y., Gerla, M.: Frequency quorum rendezvous for fast and resilient key establishment under jamming attack. SIGMOBILE Mob. Comput. Commun. Rev, 1–3 (2010)
6. Lee, J., Stinson, D.R.: A combinatorial approach to key predistribution for distributed sensor networks. In: IEEE WCNC (2005)
7. Pei, D.: Authentication Codes and Combinatorial Designs. Chapman & HallCRC (2006)
8. Poisel, R.A.: Modern Communications Jamming Principles and Techniques. Artech House Publishers (2006)
9. Pöpper, C., Strasser, M., Capkun, S.: Jamming-resistant broadcast communication without shared keys. In: USENIX Security Symposium, pp. 231–248 (2009)
10. Pöpper, C., Strasser, M., Capkun, S.: Anti-jamming broadcast communication using uncoordinated spread spectrum techniques. IEEE Journal on Selected Areas in Communications 28(5), 703–715 (2010)
11. Slater, D., Tague, P., Poovendran, R., Matt, B.J.: A coding-theoretic approach for efficient message verification over insecure channels. In: ACM WISEC, pp. 151–160 (2009)
12. Stinson, D.R.: Combinatorial Designs: Construction and Analysis. Springer, New York (2004)
13. Strasser, M., Pöpper, C., Capkun, S.: Efficient uncoordinated fhss anti-jamming communication. In: ACM MobiHoc, pp. 207–218 (2009)
14. Strasser, M., Pöpper, C., Capkun, S., Cagalj, M.: Jamming-resistant key establishment using uncoordinated frequency hopping. In: IEEE Symposium on Security and Privacy, pp. 64–78 (2008)
15. Wood, A.D., Stankovic, J.A., Zhou, G.: Deejam: Defeating energy-efficient jamming in ieee 802.15.4-based wireless networks. In: IEEE SECON, pp. 60–69 (2007)
16. Xu, W., Trappe, W., Zhang, Y., Wood, T.: The feasibility of launching and detecting jamming attacks in wireless networks. In: ACM MobiHoc, pp. 46–57 (2005)
17. Nguyen, L.: Accumulators from bilinear pairings and applications. In: Menezes, A. (ed.) CT-RSA 2005. LNCS, vol. 3376, pp. 275–292. Springer, Heidelberg (2005)
18. Barić, N., Pfitzmann, B.: Collision-free accumulators and fail-stop signature schemes without trees. In: Fumy, W. (ed.) EUROCRYPT 1997. LNCS, vol. 1233, pp. 480–494. Springer, Heidelberg (1997)
19. Luby, M.: LT Codes. In: Proc. 43rd Annual IEEE Symposium on Foundations of Computer Science (FOCS) (2002)

Improved Biometric-Based Three-factor Remote User Authentication Scheme with Key Agreement Using Smart Card

Ankita Chaturvedi, Dheerendra Mishra, and Sourav Mukhopadhyay

Department of Mathematics,
Indian Institute of Technology Kharagpur, Kharagpur-721302, India
ankitac17@gmail.com, {dheerendra,sourav}@maths.iitkgp.ernet.in

Abstract. Remote user authentication is a very important mechanism in the network system to verify the correctness of remote user and server over the insecure channel. In remote user authentication, server and user mutually authenticate each other and draw a session key. In 2012, An presented a biometric based remote user authentication scheme and claimed that his scheme is secure. In this article, we analyze An's scheme and show that his scheme is vulnerable to known session specific temporary information attack, forward secrecy attack. Moreover, we also identify that An's scheme fails to ensure efficient login phase and user anonymity. Recently, Li et al. also presented a biometric based three-factor remote user authentication scheme with key agreement. They claimed that their scheme provides three-factor remote user authentication. However, we analyze and find that scheme does not achieve three-factor remote user authentication and also fails to satisfy key security attributes. Further, the article presents an improved anonymous authentication scheme which eliminates all the drawbacks of An's and Li et al.'s scheme. Moreover, proposed scheme presents efficient login and password change mechanism where incorrect password input can be quickly detected and user can freely change his password.

Keywords: Network security, Smart card, Mutual authentication, Anonymity, Biometric, Password.

1 Introduction

The rapid development in network and communication technology has presented the platform for electronic commerce, e-medicine, e-education, e-learning and so forth. Most of the services adopt smart card based remote user authentication to facilitate secure services over the insecure public network. In general, smart card based authentication faces various attacks, a few are stolen smart card attack, password guessing attack and insider attack [1, 2]. These attacks are based on the following assumptions that is discussed by Xu et al. [3]: (A) An attacker can completely control the communication channel between user and server in login and verification phase, that is, it is capable of intercepting, modifying and

A. Bagchi and I. Ray (Eds.): ICISS 2013, LNCS 8303, pp. 63–77, 2013.

deleting the message. (B) An attacker may steel user's smart card and extract the stored values from it using one of the several techniques, a few are in [4, 5].

Instead of above mentioned assumptions, an efficient and secure anonymous user authentication scheme should meet the following requirements: (a) low computation and communication overhead with less storage requirement; (b) user anonymity during login and verification; (c) efficient login phase to detect incorrect login quickly; (d) resistance to different kinds of attacks; (e) user-friendly and efficient password change phase; (f) efficient mutually authenticate and session key agreement.

To provide smart card security, many password based authentication scheme have been proposed [1, 2, 6, 7, 8], which are widely employed because of their efficiency. The password based authentication schemes provide two-factor remote user authentication while biometric based user authentication schemes provide three-factor authentication [9]. Moreover, biometric uniqueness property increases its application in authentication protocols. Therefore, biometric-based remote user authentication schemes with password have attractive significant research attention. Recently, many biometric based authentication schemes have been proposed, a few are [2, 6, 7, 9, 10, 11, 12, 13, 14, 15, 16, 17]. These schemes have advantages of biometric keys (fingerprint, face, iris, hand geometry and palm-print, etc.), which are having following advantages: (i) biometric keys cannot be lost or forgotten; (ii) biometric keys can not be copied or shared easily; (iii) biometric keys are extremely difficult to forge or distribute; (iv) biometric keys maintain uniqueness property (v) biometric keys are hard to guess. These advantages suggest that biometric-based remote user authentications are more secure and reliable rather than traditional password-based remote user authentication.

In 2010, Li and Hwang presented a biometric based remote user authentication scheme [14], which uses user biometric identification to verify the correctness of valid user. In 2011, Li et al. [10] and Das [6] demonstrated the weaknesses of Li and Hwang's scheme and proposed a new efficient and secure protocols, independently. In 2012, An [12] demonstrated the weaknesses of Das's scheme and pointed out that Das's scheme does not resist password guessing, user impersonation, server masquerading and insider attack, and fails to achieve mutual authentication. In 2012, An [18] also demonstrated the security weaknesses of Lee et al.'s scheme and showed that Lee et al.'s scheme is vulnerable to offline password guessing attack, forgery attack and insider attack. An also presented an improved biometric based remote user authentication and key agreement scheme and claimed that his scheme is relatively more secure than related authentication schemes. Recently, Li et al. [9] showed that Das's scheme is vulnerable to forgery and stolen smart card attack. Additionally, they have presented an improved scheme.

2   Review of Li et al.'s Scheme

In this section, we will present a brief review of Li et al.'s scheme [9]. Li et al presented the improvement of Das's scheme [6]. In their scheme, registration center R selects three parameters p, q and g such that q divides $p - 1$ and g is a primitive element of $GF(q)$. Then, it chooses its master key X and provides the parameters p, q, g and X to the server.

2.1 Registration Phase

Step 1. U selects his identity ID_U and password PW_U. He also imprints biometric information B_U to the fuzzy extractor and achieves $Gen(B_U) = (R_U, P_U)$. Then, he computes $D_U = h(PW_U||R_U)$ and $h(R_U||N)$ and submits ID_U, P_U, $h(R_U||N)$ and D_U to S via secure channel.

Step 2. R computes $H = h(ID_U||X)$ and $e = h(ID_U||X) \oplus h(R_U||N)$. Then, R issues a smart card to U including the security parameters $\{e, P_U, D_U, h(\cdot), p, q, g\}$.

Step 3. On receiving the smart card, U stores N into the smart card.

2.2 Login Phase

Step 1. U inputs ID_U and PW_U, and imprints B_U at fuzzy extractor and calculates $R_U = Rep(B_U, P_U)$, then the smart card verifies $D_U =? h(PW_U||R_U)$. If condition holds, goto next step.

Step 2. Smart card achieves $M_1 = e \oplus h(R_U||N) = h(ID_U||X)$. Smart card generates a random number y, then computes $M_2 = g^y \mod p \oplus M_1$ and $M_3 = h(M_1||M_2)'$. Then, U sends the login message $< ID_U, M_2, M_3 >$ to S.

2.3 Authentication and Session Key Agreement Phase

Step 1. S verifies the ID_U format. If ID_U is valid, S computes $M_4 = h(ID_U||X)$ and then verifies $M_3 =? h(h(ID_U||X)||M_2)$. If verification holds, goto next step.

Step 2. S generates a random number z and computes $M_5 = M_2 \oplus M_4$, $Z = g^z \mod p$, $M_6 = M_5 \oplus Z$ and $M_7 = h(ID_U||ID_S||Z)$, then sends the message $< M_6, M_7 >$ to U, where ID_S is the server identity.

Step 3. Smart card achieves $M_8 = Y \oplus M_6$ and verifies $M_7 =? h(ID_U||ID_S||M_8)$. If verification holds, it computes $M_9 = h(ID_U||ID_S||h(M_8^y \mod p))$ and sends M_9 to S.

Step 4. S verifies $M_9 =? h(ID_U||ID_S||h(M_5^z \mod p))$. If verification holds, S accepts C's login.

Step 5. User and server computes the session key $sk_{SU} = h(M_1||ID_S||(g^z)^y \mod p)$ and $sk_{US} = h(M_4||ID_S||(g^y)^z \mod p)$, respectively.

2.4 Password Change Phase

- Step 1. U inputs ID_U and PW_U, and imprint B_U at fuzzy extractor and calculate $R_U = Rep(B_U, P_U)$, then the smart card verifies $D_U =? h(PW_U||R_U)$. If condition holds, goto next step.
- Step 2. U inputs a new password PW_U^{new}, then smart card computes $D_U^{new} = h(PW_U^{new}||R_U)$ and replaces D_U with D_U^{new}.

3   Cryptanalysis of Li et al.'s Scheme

In this section, we show that Li et al.'s Scheme [9] does not satisfy the key security attribute.

3.1   Three Factor Authentication

Li et al. claimed that their proposed scheme achieves three factor remote user authentication. In three factor authentication, at least three security parameters are needed to generate valid login message. In other words, user's smart card, password and biometric information are needed to generate a valid login message. However, in Li et al.'s scheme, an attacker(E) with stolen smart card and user biometric information (B_U), can generate valid login message as follows:

- E can extract the information $\{e, P_U, D_U, h(\cdot), p, q, g, N\}$ from the stolen smart card [4, 5, 19].
- E inputs B_U at fuzzy extractor and calculate $R_U = Rep(B_U, P_U)$, as P_U achieved from stolen smart card.
- E computes $h(R_U||N)$ and then $M_1' = e \oplus h(R_U||N) = h(ID_U||X)$. E also selects a random number y_E and computes $M_2' = g^{y_E} \bmod p \oplus M_1$ and $M_3' = h(M_1||M_2)$.
- E sends the login message $< ID_U, M_2', M_3' >$ to S.
- Upon receiving the message $< ID_U, M_2', M_3' >$, S verifies the ID_U format. This holds, as ID_U is extracted from user's smart card. S computes $M_4 = h(ID_U||X)$ and then verifies $M_3 =? h(h(ID_U||X)||M_2')$. The verification holds, as $M_1' = h(ID_U||X)$.

This above discussion concludes that without knowing the user's password, an attacker can generate valid login message. This proves that Li et al.'s scheme does not achieve three factor remote user authentication.

3.2   Known Session Specific Temporary Information Attack

The compromise of a short-term secret (session secret values) information should not compromise the generated session key [20, 21, 22, 23]. However, in Li et al.'s scheme, if short term session values (temporary secret) y or z are compromised, then an attacker can achieve the session key sk_{US} and sk_{SU}.
Case 1: If session secret (temporary information) y is compromised, then

- E can intercept and record the transmitted messages $< ID_U, M_2, M_3 >$ and $< M_6, M_7 >$, which transmits via public channel.
- E computes $g^y \bmod p$ and then achieve $h(ID_U||X) = M_2 \oplus g^y \bmod p$ and $g^z \bmod p = M_6 \oplus g^y \bmod p$.
- E computes $sk_{US} = h(h(ID_U||X)||ID_S||(g^z)^y \bmod p)$. E can also achieve sk_{SU}, as $sk_{SU} = sk_{US}$.

Case 2: If session secret z is compromised, then

- E computes $g^z \bmod p$ and then achieve $g^y \bmod p = M_6 \oplus g^z \bmod p$ and $h(ID_U \| X) = M_2 \oplus g^y \bmod p$.
- E computes $sk_{SU} = h(h(ID_U \| X) \| ID_S \| (g^y)^z \bmod p)$. E can also achieve sk_{US}, as $sk_{SU} = sk_{US}$.

3.3 Replay Attack

Replay attack is most common attack in which attacker used the past messages to forge the server [24, 25, 26].

An attacker can track, intercept, modify and record the message that transmits via public channel. Let the attacker has achieved a previously transmitted message $< ID_U, M_2', M_3' >$, where $M_2' = h(ID_U \| X) \oplus Y'$ and $M_3' = h(M_1 \| M_2')$. Then, he replays the message $< ID_U, M_2', M_3' >$ by sending it to server. On receiving the message $< ID_U, M_2', M_3' >$, S verifies the ID_U format. The validation holds, as the message is originally generated by user. Then, S computes $M_4 = h(ID_U \| X)$ and achieves $M_5' = M_2' \oplus M_4$, $Z = g^z \bmod p$, $M_6 = M_5' \oplus Z$ and $M_7 = h(ID_U \| ID_S \| Z)$, then sends the message $< M_6, M_7 >$ to U. The server accepts the old messages, this shows that Li et al.'s scheme does not resist replay attack.

3.4 User Anonymity

The leakage of the user's specific information, enables the adversary to track the user's current location and login history [27, 28]. Although user's anonymity ensures user's privacy by preventing an attacker from acquiring user's sensitive personal information. Moreover, anonymity makes remote user authentication mechanism more robust, as attacker could not track 'which users are interacting' [29, 30, 31].

The straightforward way to preserve anonymity is to conceal entities real identity during communication. However, in Li et al.'s scheme, user real identity is associated with the login message which reveals user's information to attacker. This shows that Li et al.'s scheme does not ensure user anonymity.

3.5 Inefficient Login Phase

In Li et al.'s scheme, smart card does not verify the correctness of identity in login phase. If a user inputs incorrect identity due to mistake, the smart card executes the login phase as follows:

- U inputs incorrect identity ID_U^* and PW_U, and imprints B_U at fuzzy extractor, then calculates $R_U = Rep(B_U, P_U)$. The smart card verifies $D_U = ? h(PW_U \| R_U)$, which holds as user inputs correct identity and password.
- Smart card achieves $M_1 = e \oplus h(R_U \| N) = h(ID_U \| X)$. Smart card generates a random number y, then computes $M_2 = g^y \bmod p \oplus M_1$ and $M_3 = h(M_1 \| M_2)$. Finally, it sends the login message $< ID_U^*, M_2, M_3 >$ to S.

Instead of incorrect login input, the smart card successfully executes the login session. This causes extra communication and computation overhead.

4   Review of An's Scheme

In 2012, An [18] proposed an improvement of Lee el al.'s [10] biometric based user authentication scheme. This comprises of three phases similar to the Lee et al.'s scheme, which are as follows: registration, login, authentication. The brief description of An's scheme is as follows:

4.1   Registration Phase

Before starting the registration, the trusted registration center R generates a large prime p and selects a primitive element g of $GF(p)$.Then, a user registers with registration center as follows:

Step 1. U generates a random number N and submits ID_U, $W = h(PW_U \oplus N)$ and $f = h(B_U)$ to S.

Step 2. S computes $J = h(PW_U \oplus N)||f$ and $e = h(ID_U||X) \oplus J$, where X is server's secret key. S issues a smart card, which includes the values $\{ID_U, f, e, h(\cdot), p, g\}$ and provides the smart card to the user.

Step 3. On receiving the smart card, U stores N into the smart card.

4.2   Login Phase

Step 1. U inputs his B_U, smart card verifies $f =? h(B_U)$. If condition holds, smart card passes biometric information.

Step 2. U inputs ID_U and PW_U, then smart card computes $J = h(PW \oplus N)||f$ and achieves $M_1 = h(ID_U||X) = e \oplus J$. Smart card generates a random number r_U, then computes $M_2 = M_1 \oplus r_U$ and $M_3 = g^{r_U} \bmod p$. U sends the login message $< ID_U, M_2, M_3 >$ to S.

4.3   Authentication Phase

Step 1. S verifies the ID_U format. If ID_U is valid, S computes $M_4 = h(ID_U||X)$ and $r'_U = M_2 \oplus M_4$, then verifies $M_3 =? g^{r'_U} \bmod p$. If verification holds, S generates r_S and computes $M_5 = M_4 \oplus r_S$ and $M_6 = g^{r_S} \bmod p$, then sends the message $< M_5, M_6 >$ to U. S also computes session key $sk_{US} = (g^{r_U})^{r_S} \bmod p$.

Step 3. Smart card computes $r'_S = M_1 \oplus M_5$ and verifies $M_6 =? g^{r'_S} \bmod p$. If verification holds, it computes the session key $sk_{SU} = (g^{r_S})^{r_U} \bmod p$.

5   Cryptanalysis of An's Scheme

In this section, we show that An's Scheme [18] does not satisfy the key security attribute.

5.1   Known Session Specific Temporary Information Attack

The compromise of a short-term secret (session secret values) information should not compromise the generated session key [20, 21, 22, 23]. However, in An's scheme, if short term session values g^{r_U} mod p or g^{rs} mod p are compromised, then an attacker can achieve the session key sk_{US} or sk_{SU} as follows:

– Attacker can intercept the message and record the transmitted messages $< M_2, M_3 >$ and $< M_5, M_6 >$, which transmits via public channel.
– Attacker can compute $sk_{SU} = (g^{rs})^{r_U}$ mod p or $sk_{US} = (g^{r_U})^{rs}$ mod p using public values and lacked values.

5.2   Forward Secrecy

The compromise of static private key of a user does not result the compromise of established session key [21, 22, 23]. Although if static private key $h(ID_U||X)$ of a user U is compromised, then An's scheme does not resist forward secrecy and an attacker can achieve the session key with the help of static private key as follows:

– Attacker can intercept the message and record the transmitted messages $< M_2, M_3 >$ and $< M_5, M_6 >$, which transmits via public channel.
– Attacker can achieve r_U and r_S as:
  $r_U = M_2 \oplus h(ID_U||X) = M_1 \oplus r_U \oplus h(ID_U||X)$,
  $r_S = M_5 \oplus h(ID_U||X) = M_4 \oplus r_S \oplus h(ID_U||X)$, as $M_1 = M_4 = h(ID_U||X)$.
– Attacker can compute $sk = g^{r_S r_U}$ mod p, using r_U and r_S.

5.3   Replay Attack

An attacker can track, intercept, modify and record the message that transmits via public channel. Let the attacker achieved a previously transmitted message $< ID_U, M_2', M_3' >$, where $M_2' = h(ID_U||X) \oplus r_U'$ and $M_3' = g^{r_U'}$ mod p. Then, he can replay the message and sends the message $< ID_U, M_2', M_3' >$ to server.

– On receiving the message $< ID_U, M_2, M_3 >$, S verifies the ID_U format. The validation holds, as the message is originally generated by user. Then, S computes $M_4 = h(ID_U||X)$ and $r_U' = M_2 \oplus M_4$, then verifies $M_3 = ?$ $g^{r_U'}$ mod p. The verification holds, as $r_U' = r_U$.
– S generates r_S and computes $M_5 = M_4 \oplus r_S$ and $M_6 = g^{rs}$ mod p, then sends the message $< M_5, M_6 >$ to U. S also computes session key $sk = (g^{r_U})^{rs}$ mod p.

5.4   Man-in-the Middle Attack

Without loss of generality, let the attacker has achieved previously transmitted message $< ID_U, M_2', M_3' >$ and $< M_5', M_6' >$, where $M_2' = h(ID_U||X) \oplus r_U'$, $M_3' = g^{r_U'}$ mod p, $M_5' = h(ID_U||X) \oplus r_S'$ and $M_6' = g^{r_S'}$ mod p. Then, he can perform the man-in-the middle attack as follows:

- When U sends the login message $< ID_U, M_2, M_3 >$ to S. E does not intercept U's message.
- On receiving the message $< ID_U, M_2, M_3 >$, S verifies the ID_U format. The validation holds, as the message is originally generated by user. Then, S computes $M_4 = h(ID_U||X)$ and achieves $r_U = M_2 \oplus M_4$, then verifies $M_3 =? g^{r_U} \bmod p$.
- S generates r_S and computes $M_5 = M_4 \oplus r_S$ and $M_6 = g^{rs} \bmod p$. Then, it computes the session key $sk_{US} = (g^{r_U})^{rs} \bmod p$.
- When S sends the message $< M_5, M_6 >$ to U. E intercepts S's message and replaces it with a old message $< M_5', M_6' >$.
- Upon receiving the message $< M_5', M_6' >$, the smart card computes $r_S' = M_1 \oplus M_5'$ and get r_S'. It verifies $M_6' =? g^{r_S'} \bmod p$. The verification holds, since $M_6' = g^{r_S'} \bmod p$. Then, smart card computes the session key $sk_{SU} = (g^{r_S'})^{r_U} \bmod p$.

Both user and server agreed upon a session key, which are not equal, that is, $sk_{SU} \neq sk_{US}$, since $r_S \neq r_S'$ and $r_U \neq r_U'$. Therefore, user and server can not communicate with each other using the session key.

5.5   User Anonymity

In An's scheme, user real identity is associated with the login message, which reveals user's information to the attacker. This shows that An's scheme does not ensure user anonymity.

5.6   Inefficient Login Phase

In An's scheme, smart card does not verify the correctness of password in login phase.

Case 1

If a user inputs wrong password due to mistake. The smart card executes the login phase, which works as follows:

- When U inputs incorrect password PW_U^* instead of PW_U, the smart card does not verify the correctness of input and computes $J^* = h(PW_U^* \oplus N)||f$ and achieves M_1^* as:

$$M_1^* = e \oplus J^* = h(ID_U||X) \oplus J \oplus J^* = h(ID_U||X) \oplus (h(PW_U \oplus N)||f) \oplus (h(PW_U^* \oplus N)||f).$$

- The smart card generates a random number r_U, then computes $M_2 = M_1^* \oplus r_U$ and $M_3 = g^{r_U} \bmod p$. Finally, U sends the login message $< ID_U, M_2, M_3 >$ to S.

- S verifies the ID_U format. If ID_U is valid, S computes $M_4 = h(ID_U\|X)$ and then r'_U as follows:

$$r'_U = M_2 \oplus M_4$$
$$= M_1^* \oplus r_U \oplus M_4$$
$$= h(ID_U\|X) \oplus (h(PW_U \oplus N)\|f) \oplus (h(PW_U^* \oplus N)\|f) \oplus r_U \oplus h(ID_U\|X)$$
$$= (h(PW_U \oplus N)\|f) \oplus (h(PW_U^* \oplus N)\|f) \oplus r_U$$

Then verifies $M_3 =? \; g^{r'_U} \bmod p$. The verification does not hold, as $r'_U \neq r_U$.
- S terminates the session, as authentication does not hold.

Case 2:
If an attacker E intercepts U's login message, as an attacker can intercept the message. Then, the following steps executes:

- E intercepts the login message and replaces it with $< ID_U, M'_2, M_3 >$, where $M'_2 = M_2 \oplus r_E$ for random value r_E, i.e., $M'_2 = M_1 \oplus r_U \oplus r_E$.
- On receiving the message $< ID_U, M'_2, M_3 >$, S verifies the ID_U format. The validation holds, as the message includes user's original identity. Then, S computes $M_4 = h(ID_U\|X)$ and achieves $r'_U = M'_2 \oplus M_4$, then verifies $M_3 =? \; g^{r'_U} \bmod p$. The verification does not hold, since $r'_U = r_U \oplus r_E$ instead of r_U.
- S terminates the session, as authentication does not hold.

In **case 1**, in spite of wrong password the smart card executes the login session. However, server terminates the session. Moreover, in case of message impersonation attack (**case 2**), the server also terminates the session in same step. Therefore, if the session terminates, it will be difficult for user to identify that exactly why the session is terminated.

6   Proposed Scheme

In this section, we present an improved scheme to overcome the weaknesses of An's schemes. The proposed scheme adopts three factor authentication. It has similar phases like Li and Hwang's scheme. In proposed scheme, a user first registers himself and achieves the smart card. Then, with the help of smart card he can login to the system and establish the session. The four phases of the proposed scheme are as follows: (i) Registration; (ii) Login; (iii) Verification; Password change.

Initially, the system chooses the large prime number p of bit size 1024, prime divisor q of $(p-1)$ of bit size 160. And, let g be a primitive element of order q in the finite field $GF(q)$, $h(\cdot)$ is a one way hash function, for example SHA-1. Then, server chooses its private key X and computes public key $Y = g^X \bmod p$.

6.1   Registration Phase

When a user wishes to register with the server to get the smart card, which works as follows:

Step R1. U selects his identity ID_U and chooses a password PW_U of his choice, then computes $W = h(PW_U || N)$, where N is a random number. Then, U imprints his personal biometric B_U at the fuzzy extractor, then the fuzzy extractor calculates $Gen(B_U) = (R_U, P_U)$, where R_U is an extracted string and P_U is a helper string. Finally, he submits ID_U and W with registration request to S via secure channel.

Step R2. Upon receiving the U's registration request, S verifies the legitimacy of ID_U. If this is invalid, it terminates the session. Otherwise, it computes $H = h(ID_U || X)$ and then $e = H \oplus W$. S embeds the values $\{e, h(\cdot), p, g, Y\}$ into the smart card and then returns the smart card to U.

Step R4. Upon receiving the smart card, U computes $L = N \oplus R_U$ and $V = h(ID_U || PW_U || N)$. Then, he stores P_U, L and V into the smart card.

6.2   Login Phase

When user wishes to login to the server, he inserts his smart card into card reader and inputs the identity ID'_U, password PW'_U and imprints his biometric B'_U at fuzzy extractor, then fuzzy extractor outputs $R'_U = Rep(B'_U; P_U)$. Note that $R_C = R'_C$, if B'_C is reasonably close to B_C. Upon getting the inputs, the smart card executes the login session as follows:

Step L1. Compute $N' = L \oplus R'_U$ and verify $V = ? h(ID'_U || PW'_U || N')$. If verification does not hold, it terminates the session. Note that the verification holds, if user enters correct identity ($ID'_U = ID_U$) and password ($PW'_U = PW_U$), and imprints biometric B'_U is reasonably close to B_U. Otherwise, goto **Step L2.**

Step L2. Compute $H = e \oplus h(PW_U || N)$, select a random number r_U and then compute $A_1 = g^{r_U} \bmod p$, $A_2 = Y^{r_U} \bmod p = (g^X)^{r_U} \bmod p$, $NID = ID_U \oplus A_2$ and $C_U = h(ID_U || H || A_1 || A_2 || T_1)$, then send the login message $< NID, A_1, C_U, T_1 >$ to S, where T_1 is the U's current timestamp.

6.3   Verification Phase

User and server perform the following steps to mutually authenticate each other:

Step R1. On receiving the message $< NID, A_1, C_U, T_1 >$ at time T_2, S verifies $T_2 - T_1 \leqslant \Delta t$, where Δt is the valid time delay in message transmission. If verification does not hold, S terminates the session. Otherwise, it computes $A_3 = (g^{r_U})^X \bmod p$ and achieves $ID_U = NID \oplus A'_2$. Then, it computes $H = h(ID_U || X)$ and verifies $C_U = ? h(ID_U || H || A_1 || A_3 || T_1)$. If verification does not hold, terminate the session. Otherwise, U is authenticated by S, then *Step R2* executes.

Step R2. S chooses a random number r_S and computes $A_4 = g^{rs} \bmod p$, $A_5 = (g^{r_U})^{rs} \bmod p$ and the session key $sk_{US} = h(ID_U||A_3||A_5||H||T_1||T_3)$, where T_3 is the current timestamp of S. Finally, it sends the message $< C_S, A_4, T_3 >$ to U, where $C_S = h(ID_U||sk_{US}||H||T_3)$.

Step R3. Upon receiving S's message $< C_S, A_4, T_3 >$ at time T_4, smart card verifies $T_4 - T_3 \leqslant \Delta t$. If time delay in message transmission is invalid, terminates the session. Otherwise, smart card achieves $A_6 = (g^{rs})^{r_U} \bmod p$ and then the session key $sk_{SU} = h(ID_U||A_2||A_6||H||T_1||T_3)$. Finally, it verifies $C_S =? h(ID_U||sk_{SU}||H||T_3)$. If verification does not hold, terminate the session. Otherwise, S is authenticated by U, then U accepts sk_{SU} as the session key.

The agreed session key $sk_{US} = sk_{SU}$, as $A_2 = A_3$ and $A_5 = A_6$.

6.4 Password Change Phase

A user with old password and smart card can change the password as follows:

Step P1. U inserts his smart card into the card reader and inputs ID'_U, old password PW'_U, a new password PW_{new} and imprints his biometric B'_U at fuzzy extractor, then fuzzy extractor outputs $R'_U = Rep(B'_U; P_U)$.

Step P2. Smart card achieves $N = L \oplus R'_U$ and verifies $V =? h(ID'_U||PW'_U||N)$. If verification does not hold, terminates the session. Otherwise, smart card computes $e_{new} = e \oplus h(PW_U||N) \oplus h(PW_{new}||N)$ and $V_{new} = h(ID_U||PW_{new}||N)$. Then, it replaces e with e_{new} and V with V_{new}.

7 Security Analysis

The detailed security analysis of the proposed scheme to verify 'how the scheme satisfying the security requirements' is as follows:

Proposition 1. The proposed scheme preserves user anonymity.

Proof. In the proposed scheme, login message includes user dynamic identity $NID = ID_U \oplus A_2$, where $A_2 = g^{XR_U} \bmod p$. The computation $g^{XR_U} \bmod p$ for given $g^{r_U} \bmod p$ and $g^X \bmod p$ is equivalent to Diffie-Hellman problem, which is intractable. Therefore, ID_U can not be achieved from NID. Moreover, NID is different for each session , as user selects r_U randomly for each session. This makes A_2 different and so NID for each session. The different NID for different session, reduces the possibility of linkability. The unlinkability and dynamic identity concept, ensures user anonymity in the proposed scheme.

Proposition 2. The proposed scheme withstands offline password guessing attack.

Proof. In proposed scheme, to verify the correctness of guessed password, an adversary can use following conditions $V = h(ID_U||PW_U||N)$ and $e = H \oplus h(PW_U||N)$, where $N = L \oplus R_U$. Each condition involves N, to achieve N, user biometric information is needed as $N = L \oplus R_U$. However, biometric information is user secret and unique information. Therefore, an attacker can not perform password guessing attack.

Proposition 4. The proposed scheme resists stolen smart card attack.

Proof. An attacker can extract the stored parameters $\{e, h(\cdot), p, g, Y, L, V\}$ of smart card. However, to generate a valid login message $< NID, A_1, C_U, T_1 >$, user's identity ID_U and user's long term key $H = h(ID_U \| X)$ are needed. The identity is neither stored in smart card nor attached with any message. The login message includes, user's dynamic identity $NID = ID_U \oplus A_2$, where computation $A_2 = g^{X R_U} \bmod p$ for given $g^{r_U} \bmod p$ and $g^X \bmod p$ is equivalent to Diffie-Hellman problem. Therefore, identity can not be achieved from login message. Additionally, the stored value $V = h(ID_U \| PW_U \| N)$ includes ID_U, but in this expression ID_U is hashed with password. Therefore, ID_U can not even be guessed.

On the other hand, the secret values $H = h(ID_U \| X)$ XORed with $h(PW_U \| N)$, i.e., $e = H \oplus h(PW_U \| N)$. Therefore, to achieve H, password PW_U and N are needed, where N is protected with biometric and password is secret. Therefore, an attacker can not achieve user long term secret H.

Proposition 5. The proposed scheme achieves known key secrecy.

Proof. In proposed scheme, the agreed session key $sk_{US} = h(ID_U \| A_3 \| A_5 \| H \| T_1 \| T_3)$ does not reveal any information about other session keys because:

1. Each key is hashed with one way hash function, therefore, no information can be drawn from the session key.
2. Each session key involves random numbers and the timestamps, which guarantees unique key for each session.
3. To construct a session key, user's secret key is needed, which is protected by password.

Proposition 6. The proposed scheme is efficient to resist stolen verifier attack.

Proof. In proposed scheme, the server does not maintain any verification table, therefore, stolen verifier attack will not work in proposed scheme.

Proposition 7. The proposed scheme achieves perfect forward secrecy.

Proof. If user's long term key H is compromised, then an attacker can not construct key $sk_{SU} = h(ID_U \| A_2 \| A_6 \| H \| T_1 \| T_3)$, as to construct the session key the values $A_2 = g^{X R_U} \bmod p$ and $A_6 = (g^{rs})^{r_U} \bmod p$ are needed. To compute $(g^{rs})^{r_U} \bmod p$ for given $g^{rs} \bmod p$ and $g^{r_U} \bmod p$, which is equivalent to computational Deffie-Helman problem. And, the computation $g^{X R_U} \bmod p$ for given $g^{r_U} \bmod p$ and $g^X \bmod p$ is also equivalent to Diffie-Hellman problem. Therefore, with the knowledge of user long term key, an attacker can not construct established session key.

Proposition 8. The proposed scheme resists Known session-specific temporary information attack.

Proof. If temporary secret r_U and r_S are compromised, then an attacker can construct $A_2 = g^{X R_U} \bmod p$ and $A_6 = (g^{rs})^{r_U} \bmod p$. However, to compute the session key $sk_{SU} = h(ID_U \| A_2 \| A_6 \| H \| T_1 \| T_3)$, the user long term secret key $H = h(ID_U \| X)$ is needed, which is protected with password.

Proposition 9. The proposed scheme forbids replay attack.

Proof. Time stamps are considered to be the counter measures to resist the replay attack [25, 26]. An attacker can not replay the message in the proposed scheme, as each transmitted message includes the time stamp. And, if the receiver finds the time delay in message transmission, he immediately terminates the session. Moreover, an attacker can not construct a new message, since a valid message includes message authentication codes M_U or M_S, where to construct them, user's secret key H is needed. Since the user's secret key is secured, the replay attack will not work.

Proposition 10. The proposed scheme ensures key freshness property.

Proof. Each session key involves random numbers and timestamp, where timestamps are unique for each session. Uniqueness property for different sessions guaranties the unique key for each session. The unique key construction for each session ensures the key freshness property.

Proposition 11. The proposed scheme achieves mutual authentication.

Proof. In mutual authentication mechanism, user must prove its identity to the server and server must prove its identity to user. In proposed scheme, user and server both authenticate each other. To achieve it, user and server exchange message authentication codes, which include entities identities and secret keys. To forge user or server, secret value H is needed, which is protected with the password. In authentication phase, server verifies user authenticity by $C_U =? h(ID_U \| H \| A_1 \| A_3 \| T_1)$ and user verifies by $C_S =? h(ID_U \| sk_{SU} \| H \| T_3)$, where C_S and C_U both involve secret key H.

Proposition 12. The proposed scheme presents efficient login and password change phase.

Proof. Upon getting the inputs, identity ID_U, biometric B_U and password PW_U, the smart card achieves $N = L \oplus R_U$ and then verifies $V =? h(ID_U \| PW_U \| N)$. If verification does not hold, terminate the session. Since the condition $V =? h(ID_U \| PW_U \| N)$ involves user's identity, password, and a random value which can only be achieved when imprints biometric B'_U is reasonably close to B_U. Therefore, if user enters any of the values incorrect, the session terminates. This shows that login and password change phases are efficient to track incorrect login.

8   Conclusion

The presented article analyzes Li et al.'s and An's biometric based remote user authentication schemes and demonstrates the weaknesses of both the schemes.

This investigation shows that both the scheme are inefficient to present three-factor remote user authentication. Moreover, both the schemes do not provide efficient login phase and fail to preserve user anonymity. Further, the article presents an improved anonymous remote user authentication scheme. It overcomes all the weaknesses of Li et al.'s and An's schemes. Moreover, proposed scheme presents efficient login and password change mechanism where incorrect input is quickly detected and user can freely change his password.

References

1. Li, X., Niu, J., Khurram Khan, M., Liao, J.: An enhanced smart card based remote user password authentication scheme. Journal of Network and Computer Applications (2013)
2. Jaspher, G., Katherine, W., Kirubakaran, E., Prakash, P.: Smart card based remote user authentication scheme–survey. In: 2012 Third International Conference on Computing Communication & Networking Technologies (ICCCNT), pp. 1–5. IEEE (2012)
3. Xu, J., Zhu, W.T., Feng, D.G.: An improved smart card based password authentication scheme with provable security. Computer Standards & Interfaces 31(4), 723–728 (2009)
4. Messerges, T.S., Dabbish, E.A., Sloan, R.H.: Examining smart-card security under the threat of power analysis attacks. IEEE Transactions on Computers 51(5), 541–552 (2002)
5. Kocher, P., Jaffe, J., Jun, B.: Differential power analysis. In: Wiener, M. (ed.) CRYPTO 1999. LNCS, vol. 1666, pp. 388–397. Springer, Heidelberg (1999)
6. Das, A.: Analysis and improvement on an efficient biometric-based remote user authentication scheme using smart cards. Information Security, IET 5(3), 145–151 (2011)
7. Wang, D., Ma, C.G.: Cryptanalysis and security enhancement of a remote user authentication scheme using smart cards. The Journal of China Universities of Posts and Telecommunications 19(5), 104–114 (2012)
8. Wen, F., Li, X.: An improved dynamic id-based remote user authentication with key agreement scheme. Computers & Electrical Engineering 38(2), 381–387 (2012)
9. Li, X., Niu, J., Wang, Z., Chen, C.: Applying biometrics to design three-factor remote user authentication scheme with key agreement. Security and Communication Networks (2013)
10. Lee, C.C., Chang, R.X., Chen, L.A.: Improvement of li-hwang's biometrics-based remote user authentication scheme using smart cards. WSEAS Transactions on Communications 10(7), 193–200 (2011)
11. Truong, T.T., Tran, M.T., Duong, A.D.: Robust biometrics-based remote user authentication scheme using smart cards. In: 2012 15th International Conference on Network-Based Information Systems (NBiS), pp. 384–391. IEEE (2012)
12. An, Y.: Security analysis and enhancements of an effective biometric-based remote user authentication scheme using smart cards. In: BioMed Research International 2012 (2012)
13. Li, X., Niu, J.W., Ma, J., Wang, W.D., Liu, C.L.: Cryptanalysis and improvement of a biometrics-based remote user authentication scheme using smart cards. Journal of Network and Computer Applications 34(1), 73–79 (2011)

14. Li, C.T., Hwang, M.S.: An efficient biometrics-based remote user authentication scheme using smart cards. Journal of Network and Computer Applications 33(1), 1–5 (2010)
15. Chang, Y.F., Yu, S.H., Shiao, D.R.: A uniqueness-and-anonymity-preserving remote user authentication scheme for connected health care. Journal of Medical Systems 37(2), 1–9 (2013)
16. Lee, T.F., Chang, I.P., Lin, T.H., Wang, C.C.: A secure and efficient password-based user authentication scheme using smart cards for the integrated epr information system. Journal of Medical Systems 37(3), 1–7 (2013)
17. Go, W., Lee, K., Kwak, J.: Construction of a secure two-factor user authentication system using fingerprint information and password. Journal of Intelligent Manufacturing, 1–14 (2012)
18. An, Y.: Improved biometrics-based remote user authentication scheme with session key agreement. In: Kim, T.-H., Cho, H.-S., Gervasi, O., Yau, S.S. (eds.) GDC/IESH/CGAG 2012. 351, vol. CCIS, pp. 307–315. Springer, Heidelberg (2012)
19. Eisenbarth, T., Kasper, T., Moradi, A., Paar, C., Salmasizadeh, M., Shalmani, M.T.M.: On the power of power analysis in the real world: A complete break of the keeloq code hopping scheme. In: Wagner, D. (ed.) CRYPTO 2008. LNCS, vol. 5157, pp. 203–220. Springer, Heidelberg (2008)
20. Cheng, Z., Nistazakis, M., Comley, R., Vasiu, L.: On the indistinguishability-based security model of key agreement protocols-simple cases. In: Proc. of ACNS, Citeseer, vol. 4 (2004)
21. Blake-Wilson, S., Johnson, D., Menezes, A.: Key agreement protocols and their security analysis. Springer (1997)
22. Blake-Wilson, S., Menezes, A.: Authenticated diffe-hellman key agreement protocols. In: Tavares, S., Meijer, H. (eds.) SAC 1998. LNCS, vol. 1556, pp. 339–361. Springer, Heidelberg (1999)
23. Menezes, A.J., Van Oorschot, P.C., Vanstone, S.A.: Handbook of applied cryptography. CRC Press (2010)
24. Aura, T.: Strategies against replay attacks. In: Proceedings of the 10th Computer Security Foundations Workshop 1997, pp. 59–68. IEEE (1997)
25. Zhen, J., Srinivas, S.: Preventing replay attacks for secure routing in ad hoc networks. In: Pierre, S., Barbeau, M., An, H.-C. (eds.) ADHOC-NOW 2003. LNCS, vol. 2865, pp. 140–150. Springer, Heidelberg (2003)
26. Malladi, S., Alves-Foss, J., Heckendorn, R.B.: On preventing replay attacks on security protocols. Technical report, DTIC Document (2002)
27. Juang, W.S., Lei, C.L., Chang, C.Y.: Anonymous channel and authentication in wireless communications. Computer Communications 22(15), 1502–1511 (1999)
28. Chang, C.C., Lee, C.Y., Chiu, Y.C.: Enhanced authentication scheme with anonymity for roaming service in global mobility networks. Computer Communications 32(4), 611–618 (2009)
29. Xu, J., Zhu, W.T., Feng, D.G.: An efficient mutual authentication and key agreement protocol preserving user anonymity in mobile networks. Computer Communications 34(3), 319–325 (2011)
30. Wang, R.C., Juang, W.S., Lei, C.L.: Robust authentication and key agreement scheme preserving the privacy of secret key. Computer Communications 34(3), 274–280 (2011)
31. Khan, M.K., Kim, S.K., Alghathbar, K.: Cryptanalysis and security enhancement of a more efficient & secure dynamic id-based remote user authentication scheme. Computer Communications 34(3), 305–309 (2011)

Signcryption from Randomness Recoverable PKE Revisited

Angsuman Das[1] and Avishek Adhikari[2]

[1] Department of Mathematics,
St. Xavier's College, Kolkata, India
angsumandas054@gmail.com
[2] Department of Pure Mathematics,
University of Calcutta, Kolkata, India
avishek.adh@gmail.com

Abstract. A new generic construction of a signcryption scheme from randomness recoverable public key encryption (PKE-RR) is proposed. This paper modifies the 'Li & Wong' construction [Information Sciences 180 (2010)] to achieve better security from weaker building blocks and thereby making it open to a larger class of encryption and signature schemes. The proposed construction achieves multi-user insider security for confidentiality in random oracle model and authenticity in standard model. It is done by incorporating one extra hashing in both signcryption and unsigncryption phases than the original construction.

Keywords: Randomness Recoverable PKE, Signcryption, Sign-then-encrypt paradigm.

1 Introduction

Signcryption is a public-key primitive which addresses both the problem of privacy and authenticity within the same protocol such that it is better in terms of ciphertext expansion, computational cost and efficiency when compared to naive combination of public-key encryption and digital signature. From the day of its introduction by Zheng [15], it has been an area of active research and as a result, a lot of techniques and security models like [1], [2], [10] etc. have evolved till date. Targeting the same goal, Li & Wong [9] proposed a generic construction of a signcryption scheme from randomness recoverable public key encryption (PKE-RR).

Informally speaking, a Randomness Recoverable Public Key Encryption (PKE-RR) is a special type of probabilistic encryption scheme where not only the plaintext but also the randomness used in the encryption algorithm can be extracted from the ciphertext with the help of the private key.[1] The idea of using PKE-RR in constructing signcryption was first noticed in [9], where the authors used

---

[1] It is to be noted here that there exist probabilistic PKE's like [6],[12] where the ephemeral key is lost i.e., there is no obvious way to recover it even with the help of private key.

A. Bagchi and I. Ray (Eds.): ICISS 2013, LNCS 8303, pp. 78–90, 2013.

an Ω-IND-CCA2 secure PKE-RR and an UF-CMA secure uniformly-distributed signature scheme as components. But, not only there exist a few known practical constructions of Ω-uniform IND-CCA2 secure PKE-RR but also the notion of Ω-uniform IND-CCA2 security[2] is somewhat artificial. In our construction, we use a weaker encryption primitive i.e., an IND-CCA2 PKE-RR (not necessarily Ω-uniform IND-CCA2 secure as used in [9]) and an UF-CMA secure signature scheme (not necessarily uniformly-distributed as used in [9]), making it open to a larger class of encryption and signature schemes. It is also shown that this transformation is better than [9], in the sense that it offers an enhanced level of security both in terms of confidentiality and unforgeability with weaker building blocks.

1.1 Organisation of the Paper

The paper is organised as follows: In Section 2, some definitions and preliminaries are discussed. The construction by Li & Wong is briefly recalled in Section 3, whereas the proposed construction is given in Section 4.2 and its security analysis is done in Section 4.3. The comparison with existing Li & Wong conversion [9] is discussed in Section 5 and finally we conclude with some open problems in Section 6.

2 Definitions and Preliminaries

We begin by formally defining the notions of *Randomness Recoverable Public-Key Encryption* (PKE-RR) and Signcryption scheme SC and then briefly recalling the security notions in the context of signcryption schemes.

2.1 Randomness-Extractable Public-Key Encryption (PKE-RR)

A Randomness Recoverable Public Key Encryption (Π) (PKE-RR) [9] is a tuple of probabilistic polynomial-time algorithms (Gen, Enc, Dec) such that:

1. The key generation algorithm, Gen, takes as input a security parameter 1^n and outputs a public-key/ private-key pair (pk, sk).
2. The encryption algorithm Enc takes as input a message m from the underlying plaintext space and a random key r from the randomness space to output a ciphertext $c := \mathsf{Enc}_{pk}(m, r)$.
3. The decryption algorithm Dec takes as input a ciphertext c to output $\mathsf{Dec}_{sk}(c) = (m, r)$.

It is required that for every n, every (pk, sk) and every message m in the corresponding plaintext space, it holds that

$$\mathsf{Dec}(\mathsf{Enc}(m, r)) = (m, r).$$

---

[2] For the definition of Ω-uniform IND-CCA2 security, see [9].

Remark 1. If we supress the decryption algorithm Dec to return only the plaintext m in the PKE-RR, we get a usual public-key scheme.

Remark 2. Paillier encryption scheme [13] and its variants like [5], OAEP [3] and its variants like OAEP+, certain lattice-based (like [8]) and code-based (variants of [11]) cryptosystems are some of the existing examples of PKE-RR.

Remark 3. Recently, in [4], an idea similar to that of PKE-RR was used while defining a new notion of security called Enhanced Chosen Ciphertext security. Our definition of PKE-RR matches with their definition of uniquely randomness recovering encryption.

Security Notions for Public-Key Encryption Scheme. Though there are various notions of security for public-key encryption schemes, but here only the relevant (CPA and CCA2) ones are discussed.

Chosen Plaintext Attack: Chosen plaintext attack to a cryptosystem is defined as a game played between a challenger C and an adversary A in a public-key encryption scheme PKE as follows:

1. Given the security parameter, C generates a pair (pk, sk).
2. A is given the public-key pk. A outputs a pair of messages (m_0, m_1) from the plaintext space associated with pk.
3. C chooses $b \in_R \{0, 1\}$ and sends the ciphertext $c^* = \mathsf{Enc}_{pk}(m_b)$ to A;
4. A outputs a bit b'.

The advantage $\mathbf{Adv}_{A,PKE}^{cpa}(n)$ is defined to be $|Pr[b' = b] - 1/2|$. The scheme PKE is said to be secure against chosen plaintext attack if for all probabilistic polynomial-time adversaries A, the advantage $\mathbf{Adv}_{A,PKE}^{cpa}(\cdot)$ is negligible.

Chosen Ciphertext Attack: Adaptive chosen ciphertext attack [14] to a cryptosystem is defined as a game played between a challenger C and an adversary A in a public-key encryption scheme PKE as follows:

1. Given the security parameter, C generates a pair (pk, sk).
2. A is given the public-key pk as well as oracle access to the decryption algorithm, $\mathsf{Dec}_{sk}(\cdot)$. A outputs a pair of messages (m_0, m_1) from the plaintext space associated with pk.
3. C chooses $b \in_R \{0, 1\}$ and sends the ciphertext $c^* = \mathsf{Enc}_{pk}(m_b)$ to A;
4. A continues to have oracle access to $\mathsf{Dec}_{sk}(\cdot)$ as in step 2, but with the restriction that it can not query c^*;
5. A outputs b'.

The advantage $\mathbf{Adv}_{A,PKE}^{cca2}(n)$ is defined to be $|Pr[b' = b] - 1/2|$. The scheme PKE is said to be secure against adaptive chosen ciphertext attack if for all probabilistic polynomial-time adversaries A, the advantage $\mathbf{Adv}_{A,PKE}^{cca2}(\cdot)$ is negligible.

Remark 4. In case of a PKE-RR, the decryption oracle in the CCA2 game returns both the message and the randomness used in the encryption process.

2.2 Signature Scheme (SS)

A Signature Scheme (SS) is a tuple of probabilistic polynomial-time algorithms (Gen, Sign, Verify) such that:

1. The key generation algorithm, Gen, takes as input the security parameter 1^n and outputs a signing-key/ verification-key pair (pk_A, sk_A).
2. The signing algorithm Sign takes as input signer's secret key sk_A and a message m from the underlying plaintext space to output a signature

$$\sigma := \text{Sign}(sk_A, m).$$

3. The verification algorithm Verify takes as input signer's verification key pk_A and a message-signature pair (m, σ) to output $\text{Verify}(pk_A, m, \sigma) = 0$ or 1.

It is required that for every n, every (pk_A, sk_A) and every message m in the corresponding plaintext space, it holds that

$$\text{Verify}(pk_A, m, \text{Sign}(sk_A, m)) = 1.$$

Security Notions for Signature Scheme (SS). A Signature Scheme (SS) is said to existentially unforgeability against chosen message attack (UF-CMA) if any probabilistic polynomial-time adversary $\mathcal{A}$ has negligible chance of winning against a challenger $\mathcal{C}$ in the following game:

1. Given the security parameter, $\mathcal{C}$ generates a signer key-pair (pk_A, sk_A) using Gen.
2. $\mathcal{A}$ is given pk_A as well as oracle access to the signer's signing algorithm, $\text{Sign}(sk_A, \cdot)$.
3. $\mathcal{A}$ outputs a message-signature pair (m^*, σ^*).

$\mathcal{A}$ wins the game if σ^* is a valid signature on m^* and if m^* was never submitted to the signing oracle $\text{Sign}(sk_A, \cdot)$.

2.3 Signcryption Scheme (SC)

A Signcryption Scheme (SC) is a tuple of probabilistic polynomial-time algorithms (Setup, KeyGen$_A$, KeyGen$_B$, Signcrypt, Unsigncrypt) such that:

1. The setup algorithm Setup, takes as input a security parameter 1^n and returns common parameters par required by the signcryption scheme.
2. The key generation algorithm for the sender A, KeyGen$_A$, takes as input the common parameters par and outputs a public-key/ private-key pair (pk_A, sk_A).
3. The key generation algorithm for the receiver B, KeyGen$_B$, takes as input the common parameters par and outputs a public-key/ private-key pair (pk_B, sk_B).

4. The signcryption algorithm Signcrypt takes as input common parameters par, sender's secret key sk_A, receiver's public key pk_B, a message m from the underlying plaintext space to output a signcryptext

$$c := \mathsf{Signcrypt}(par, sk_A, pk_B, m).$$

5. The unsigncryption algorithm Unsigncrypt takes as input common parameters par, receiver's secret key sk_B, sender's public key pk_A, a signcryptext c to output a message $m := \mathsf{Unsigncrypt}(par, sk_B, pk_A, c)$ or an error symbol $\perp$.

It is required that there exists a negligible function negl such that for every n, every (pk_A, sk_A), (pk_B, sk_B) and every message m in the corresponding plaintext space, it holds that

$$\Pr[\mathsf{Unsigncrypt}(sk_B, pk_A, (\mathsf{Signcrypt}(sk_A, pk_B, m)) \neq m] \leq \mathsf{negl}(n).$$

Security Notions for Signcryption Scheme (SC). We recall the insider security notions for signcryption schemes in multi-user setting. By multi-user setting, we mean the strongest notion of dynamic multi-user model (d-MU)[10] (and not the fixed multi-user model), where the adversary can freely choose all user keys, except the challenge receiver key in the confidentiality game and choose all user keys, except the challenge sender key in the unforgeability game.

Confidentiality: A Signcryption Scheme (SC) is said to achieve multi-user insider confidentiality in d-MU-IND-SC-iCCA2 sense if any probabilistic polynomial-time adversary $\mathcal{A}$ has negligible advantage against a challenger $\mathcal{C}$ in the following game:

1. Given the security parameter, $\mathcal{C}$ generates common parameters par and a receiver key-pair (pk_B, sk_B) using KeyGen_B.
2. $\mathcal{A}$ is given par, pk_B as well as oracle access to B's (flexible) unsigncryption algorithm, $\mathsf{Unsigncrypt}(\cdot, sk_B, \cdot)$. Each unsigncryption query consists of a pair $(pk_{A'}, c)$ where $pk_{A'}$ is a sender's public-key. Unsigncryption oracle answers it with $\mathsf{Unsigncrypt}(pk_{A'}, sk_B, c)$.
3. $\mathcal{A}$ outputs a sender key pair (pk_A, sk_A) and a pair of messages (m_0, m_1) from the associated plaintext space.
4. $\mathcal{C}$ chooses $b \in_R \{0, 1\}$ and sends the challenge signcryptext $c^* = \mathsf{Signcrypt}(sk_A, pk_B, m_b)$ to $\mathcal{A}$;
5. $\mathcal{A}$ continues to have oracle access to $\mathsf{Unsigncrypt}(\cdot, sk_B, \cdot)$ but with the restriction that it can not query (pk_A, c^*); Note that $\mathcal{A}$ can query $(pk_{A'}, c^*)$ with $pk_{A'} \neq pk_A$ and (pk_A, c) with $c \neq c^*$.
6. $\mathcal{A}$ outputs a bit b'.

The advantage $\mathbf{Adv}_{\mathcal{A}, SC}^{cca2}(n)$ is defined to be $|Pr[b' = b] - 1/2|$.

Unforgeability: A Signcryption Scheme (SC) is said to achieve multi-user insider existential signcryptext unforgeability against chosen message attack in

d-MU-UF-SC-iCMA sense if any probabilistic polynomial-time adversary $\mathcal{A}$ has negligible chance of winning against a challenger $\mathcal{C}$ in the following game:

1. Given the security parameter, $\mathcal{C}$ generates common parameters par and a sender key-pair (pk_A, sk_A) using KeyGen$_A$.
2. $\mathcal{A}$ is given par, pk_A as well as oracle access to A's (flexible) signcryption algorithm, Signcrypt$(sk_A, \cdot, \cdot)$. Each signcryption query consists of a pair $(pk_{B'}, m)$ where $pk_{B'}$ is a receiver's public-key. Signcryption oracle answers it with Signcrypt$(sk_A, pk_{B'}, m)$.
3. $\mathcal{A}$ outputs a receiver key pair (pk_B, sk_B) and a signcryptext c^*.

$\mathcal{A}$ wins the game if c^* is a valid signcryptext from A to B and if its underlying plaintext m^* of c^* was never submitted to the signcryption oracle Signcrypt$(sk_A, pk_B, \cdot)$.

3 Li and Wong Construction

Li & Wong in [9] gave the first construction of signcryption scheme using a randomness recoverable public key encryption (PKE-RR) scheme. Their construction $\mathcal{SC}'$=(Setup', KeyGen$_A$', KeyGen$_B$', Signcrypt', Unsigncrypt') from a PKE-RR scheme Π'=(Gen, Enc, Dec) and a signature scheme $\mathcal{S}'$=(Gen', Sign, Verify) was as follows:

1. Setup:
    (a) Setup$(1^n) \rightarrow par$. (par denotes the common parameters required by the signcryption scheme.)
    (b) Publish par globally.
2. KeyGen$_A$:
    (a) Gen'$(par) \rightarrow (pk_A, sk_A)$
    (b) A publishes pk_A and keeps sk_A as his signing key.
3. KeyGen$_B$:
    (a) Gen$(par) \rightarrow (pk_B, sk_B)$
    (b) B publishes pk_B and keeps sk_B as his decryption key.
4. Signcrypt: For a given message m to be sent by A to B,
    (a) $\sigma =$ Sign$_{sk_A}(m)$.
    (b) Signcrypt$(m) := c =$ Enc(m, σ).
5. Unsigncrypt: For a given signcryptext c,
    (a) $(m', \sigma') :=$ Dec(c).
    (b) If Verify$(m', \sigma') = 1$, then return m', else output $\bot$.

In [9], authors proved the following theorem:

Theorem 1. *The signcryption scheme $\mathcal{SC}'$ is*

1. *two user outsider SC-IND-CCA secure if Π' is Ω-uniform CCA2 secure and $\mathcal{S}'$ is uniformly-distributed.*
2. *two user outsider SC-UF-CCA secure if $\mathcal{S}'$ is UF-CMA secure.*

We now discuss the proposed construction which uses an weaker encryption primitive i.e., an IND-CCA2 PKE-RR and an UF-CMA secure signature scheme to achieve the same goal. It also turns out that this transformation is better than [9], in the sense that it achieves better security both in terms of confidentiality and unforgeability starting from weaker cryptographic primitives as building blocks.

4   Idea Behind the Construction

The basic idea behind the proposed construction is Fujisaki-Okamoto transformation [7] on PKE-RR. To be more specific, we discuss the utility of applying Fujisaki-Okamoto transformation [7] on an IND-CPA secure PKE-RR to achieve chosen ciphertext security with better efficiency and then translate the same to construct a secure signcryption scheme from an IND-CCA2 secure PKE-RR.

4.1   Fujisaki-Okamoto Transform on PKE-RR

In this section, as the first step, we propose a generic conversion of an IND-CPA secure PKE-RR into an IND-CCA2 secure PKE-RR. The computational overhead due to the conversion is only one hashing in both the encryption and decryption stages.

Let $\Pi = (\mathsf{Gen}, \mathsf{Enc}, \mathsf{Dec})$ be an IND-CPA secure PKE-RR. We construct an IND-CCA2 secure PKE-RR $\overline{\Pi} = (\overline{\mathsf{Gen}}, \overline{\mathsf{Enc}}, \overline{\mathsf{Dec}})$ using Π as follows:

1. Key Generation ($\overline{\mathsf{Gen}}$):
   (a) $\mathsf{Gen}(1^n) \to (pk, sk)$.
   (b) Choose a hash funstion $H : \{0,1\}^k \to \{0,1\}^l$.
2. Encryption ($\overline{\mathsf{Enc}}$): For a message $m \in \{0,1\}^{k-t}$ and public key pk,
   (a) Choose $r \in_R \{0,1\}^t$ and set $M = m\|r$.
   (b) $c = \overline{\mathsf{Enc}}_{pk}(m) = \mathsf{Enc}_{pk}(M, H(m\|r))$.
3. Decryption ($\overline{\mathsf{Dec}}$): For a ciphertext c and secret key sk,
   (a) $(M, \bar{r}) := \mathsf{Dec}_{sk}(c)$ and parse $M = m\|r$.
   (b) If $\bar{r} = H(M)$, return (m, r), else return $\perp$.

Remark 5. Though this is exactly the transformation used in [7], but, in the decryption phase, re-encryption is not required to check the validity in comparison to that in [7]. It is sufficient here to check the hashed value only.

We do not give a proof of IND-CCA2 security of this Fujisaki-Okamoto variant, as it is just an application of the F-O transform in [7]. In the next section, for our main construction, we will be using this technique to improve the Li & Wong [9] construction.

4.2 The Proposed Generic Construction

In this section, we construct a signcryption scheme $\mathcal{SC}=$(Setup, KeyGen$_A$, KeyGen$_B$, Signcrypt, Unsigncrypt) from an IND-CCA2 secure PKE-RR scheme $\Pi=$(Gen, Enc, Dec), an UF-CMA secure signature scheme $\mathcal{S}=$(Gen', Sign, Verify) and a hash function $H : \{0,1\}^{k+k'} \rightarrow \{0,1\}^l$, where k denotes the bit-length of plaintext in Π, k' denotes the bit-length of IDs and l denote the bit-length of signatures in $\mathcal{S}$, as follows:

1. Setup:
   (a) Setup$(1^n) \rightarrow par$. (par denotes the common parameters required by the signcryption scheme.)
   (b) Choose a hash function $H : \{0,1\}^{k+k'} \rightarrow \{0,1\}^l$.
   (c) Publish par, H globally.
2. KeyGen$_A$:
   (a) Gen'$(par) \rightarrow (pk_A, sk_A)$
   (b) A publishes pk_A and keeps sk_A as his signing key.
3. KeyGen$_B$:
   (a) Gen$(par) \rightarrow (pk_B, sk_B)$
   (b) B publishes pk_B and keeps sk_B as his decryption key.
4. Signcrypt: For a given message $m \in \{0,1\}^{k-t}$ to be send by A to B,
   (a) $\sigma = \text{Sign}_{sk_A}(m||ID_B)$.
   (b) Choose $r \in_R \{0,1\}^t$.
   (c) $c := \text{Enc}_{pk_B}(m||r, \sigma \oplus H(m||r||ID_A))$.
   (d) Signcrypt$(par, sk_A, pk_B, m) := (c||ID_A||ID_B)$
5. Unsigncrypt: For a given signcryptext $(c||ID_A||ID_B)$,
   (a) $(m'||r', \tau) := \text{Dec}(c)$.
   (b) Compute $\sigma' = \tau \oplus H(m'||r'||ID_A)$.
   (c) If Verify$(m'||ID_B, \sigma') = 1$, then return m', else output $\perp$.

4.3 Security Analysis of Signcryption Scheme $\mathcal{SC}$

We analyze the security of the proposed construction $\mathcal{SC}$ in the following way:

1. dynamic multi-user insider confidentiality in d-MU-IND-SC-iCCA2 sense in random oracle model;
2. dynamic multi-user insider existential signcryptext unforgeability in d-MU-UF-SC-iCMA sense in standard model;

Theorem 2. $\mathcal{SC}$ is d-MU-IND-SC-iCCA2 secure in the sense of multi-user insider confidentiality in random oracle model if Π is IND-CCA2 secure.

Proof. Let $\mathcal{A}_{\mathcal{SC}}$ be a d-MU-IND-SC-iCCA2 adversary against $\mathcal{SC}$. We construct an IND-CCA2 adversary $\mathcal{A}_\Pi$ against Π which uses $\mathcal{A}_{\mathcal{SC}}$ as a sub-routine. As an input, $\mathcal{A}_\Pi$ is fed with pk_B of Π and given the decryption oracle $\mathcal{O}$Dec of Π. $\mathcal{A}_\Pi$ simulates $\mathcal{A}_{\mathcal{SC}}$ with pk_B. Moreover, the oracle access to H-values and unsigncryption algorithm $\mathcal{SC}$ needed by the adversary $\mathcal{A}_{\mathcal{SC}}$ will be provided by $\mathcal{A}_\Pi$.

Simulation of H-Oracle: When $\mathcal{A}_{\mathcal{SC}}$ submits an H-query $(m_i\|r_i\|ID_{A_i})$, $\mathcal{A}_\Pi$ chooses a random $\alpha_i \in \{0,1\}^l$ and returns α_i to $\mathcal{A}_{\mathcal{SC}}$. Also, for each returned value, $\mathcal{A}_\Pi$ maintains a list called H-list containing $(m_i\|r_i\|ID_{A_i}, \alpha_i)$

Simulation of Unsigncryption Oracle ($\mathcal{O}$Unsigncrypt): In unsigncryption queries, when a query $(c'\|ID_{A'}\|ID_B, pk_{A'})$ is asked, $\mathcal{A}_\Pi$ queries $\mathcal{O}$Dec with c' to get (M', β') and parses M' as $m'\|r'$. $\mathcal{A}_\Pi$ then checks H-list whether $m'\|r'\|ID_{A'}$ has been previously queried or not. If it has not been queried, $\mathcal{O}$Unsigncrypt outputs $\perp$ i.e., "invalid". Whereas if $(m'\|r'\|ID_{A'}, \alpha')$ appears in the H-list, $\mathcal{A}_\Pi$ finds $\sigma' = \beta' \oplus \alpha'$ and checks whether $(m'\|ID_B, \sigma')$ is a valid message-signature pair or not, using $pk_{A'}$. If it is a valid pair, $\mathcal{O}$Unsigncrypt outputs m', else outputs $\perp$.

One thing should be noted here that $\mathcal{A}_\Pi$ should be consistent in declaring a signcryptext to be "invalid": *Suppose, $\mathcal{A}_\Pi$ has declared a signcryptext c' to be "invalid" as the corresponding $m'\|r'\|ID_{A'}$ has not been H-queried till then. Let us look into $\mathcal{A}_\Pi$'s view towards c': $\mathcal{A}_\Pi$ queries $\mathcal{O}$Dec with c' to get $(m'\|r', \beta')$, where β' is of the form $\sigma' \oplus \hat{\alpha}$, σ' being a signature on $m'\|ID_B$ and $\hat{\alpha}$ is a random string chosen by $\mathcal{A}_{\mathcal{SC}}$. Though $\mathcal{A}_{\mathcal{SC}}$ knows both σ' and $\hat{\alpha}$, none of them are known to $\mathcal{A}_\Pi$. (As, in most of the cases, $\mathcal{S}$ is a probabilistic signature scheme, m' can have many valid signatures.) Now suppose $\mathcal{A}_{\mathcal{SC}}$ submits an H-query for that same $m'\|r'\|ID_{A'}$ in a later stage to receive α' as response and submits $\hat{c} = \mathsf{Enc}(pk_B, m'\|r', \sigma'' \oplus \alpha')$ as an unsigncryption query. Observe that $\hat{c}$ is a valid-signcryptext for m' according to $\mathcal{B}$ where σ'' is another signature on $m'\|ID_B$, other than σ'. So, the simulated unsigncryption oracle will return m'. This will lead to an inconsistency, in part of $\mathcal{A}_\Pi$ if $\alpha' = \hat{\alpha}$ and it will occur only when $\mathcal{A}_\Pi$'s response α' matches with the random string $\hat{\alpha}$ chosen by $\mathcal{A}$ while generating c'. (As $\mathcal{A}_\Pi$ does not know $\hat{\alpha}$, he can not choose α' to be different from $\hat{\alpha}$ while responding to the H-query.) So, the probability of one such inconsistency of* unsigncryption oracle of $\mathcal{A}_\Pi$ is $1/2^l$.

This provides an almost perfect simulation since the probability of producing a valid signcryptext without previously making the corresponding H-query is $1/2^l$, which is negligible. If q_U is the total number of unsigncryption queries, then $\mathcal{A}_\Pi$ will be consistent in responding to the unsigncryption queries with probability $\geq (1 - 1/2^l)^{q_U}$.

Once the first query phase is over, $\mathcal{A}_{\mathcal{SC}}$ returns two plaintexts $m_0, m_1 \in \{0,1\}^{k-t}$ and an attacked sender key-pair (pk_A, sk_A) to $\mathcal{A}_\Pi$. $\mathcal{A}_\Pi$ randomly chooses $r_0, r_1 \in_R \{0,1\}^t$ and submits $m_0\|r_0, m_1\|\|r_1$ to the IND-CCA2 challenger $\mathcal{C}$ of Π. $\mathcal{C}$ randomly chooses a bit $b \in \{0,1\}$, $r \in_R \{0,1\}^l$. $\mathcal{C}$ returns $\mathcal{A}_\Pi$ the challenge ciphertext $c^* = \mathsf{Enc}(pk_B, m_b\|r_b, r)$ and $\mathcal{A}_\Pi$ passes c^* to $\mathcal{A}_{\mathcal{SC}}$ as the challenge signcryptext.

In the second query phase, $\mathcal{A}_{\mathcal{SC}}$ is allowed to make any H-query and any unsigncryption query other than the challenge signcryptext c^*. If $\mathcal{A}_{\mathcal{SC}}$ makes an H-query with $m_b\|r_b\|ID_A$ with $b \in \{0,1\}$, $\mathcal{A}_\Pi$ returns b to $\mathcal{C}$ and stops the game. If $m_b\|r_b\|ID_A$ is not queried, then $\mathcal{A}_\Pi$ outputs b' (the output of $\mathcal{A}_{\mathcal{SC}}$) after the second query phase is over.

The theorem now follows immediately from the following lemma.

Lemma 1. *If ϵ be the probability that given a valid signcryptext, $\mathcal{A}_{SC}$ can correctly guess the bit b, then $\mathcal{A}_{\Pi}$ can win the IND-CCA2 game with a probability greater or equal to*

$$\epsilon - \left(\frac{q_H}{2^t} + \frac{q_U}{2^l} \right)$$

Proof. Let $\mathsf{Succ}\mathcal{A}_{SC}$ denote the probability of $\mathcal{A}_{SC}$ returning the correct bit b and $\mathsf{Succ}\mathcal{A}_{\Pi}$ be that of $\mathcal{A}_{\Pi}$. Let $\mathsf{E_0}$ be the event that $\mathcal{A}_{SC}$ queries H-oracle with $m_b||r_b||ID_A$, where b is the encrypted bit and $\mathsf{E_1}$ be the event that $\mathcal{A}_{SC}$ queries H-oracle with $m_{\bar{b}}||r_{\bar{b}}||ID_A$, where $\bar{b}$ is the complement of b. Then

$$Pr[\mathsf{Succ}\mathcal{A}_{SC}] = Pr[\mathsf{Succ}\mathcal{A}_{SC}|\mathsf{E_0}] \cdot Pr[\mathsf{E_0}]$$

$$+ Pr[\mathsf{Succ}\mathcal{A}_{SC}|(\sim \mathsf{E_0}) \wedge \mathsf{E_1}] \cdot Pr[(\sim \mathsf{E_0}) \wedge \mathsf{E_1}]$$

$$+ Pr[\mathsf{Succ}\mathcal{A}_{SC}|(\sim \mathsf{E_0}) \wedge (\sim \mathsf{E_1})] \cdot Pr[(\sim \mathsf{E_0}) \wedge (\sim \mathsf{E_1})].$$

and

$$Pr[\mathsf{Succ}\mathcal{A}_{\Pi}] = Pr[\mathsf{Succ}\mathcal{A}_{\Pi}|\mathsf{E_0}] \cdot Pr[\mathsf{E_0}]$$

$$+ Pr[\mathsf{Succ}\mathcal{A}_{\Pi}|(\sim \mathsf{E_0}) \wedge \mathsf{E_1}] \cdot Pr[(\sim \mathsf{E_0}) \wedge \mathsf{E_1}]$$

$$+ Pr[\mathsf{Succ}\mathcal{A}_{\Pi}|(\sim \mathsf{E_0}) \wedge (\sim \mathsf{E_1})] \cdot Pr[(\sim \mathsf{E_0}) \wedge (\sim \mathsf{E_1})].$$

Now, as per the simulation, we have $Pr[\mathsf{Succ}\mathcal{A}_{\Pi}|\mathsf{E_0}] = 1$, $Pr[\mathsf{Succ}\mathcal{A}_{\Pi}|(\sim \mathsf{E_0}) \wedge \mathsf{E_1}] = 0$ and $Pr[\mathsf{Succ}\mathcal{A}_{SC}|(\sim \mathsf{E_0}) \wedge (\sim \mathsf{E_1})] = Pr[\mathsf{Succ}\mathcal{A}_{\Pi}|(\sim \mathsf{E_0}) \wedge (\sim \mathsf{E_1})]$. So,

$$Pr[\mathsf{Succ}\mathcal{A}_{\Pi}] - Pr[\mathsf{Succ}\mathcal{A}_{SC}] = (1 - Pr[\mathsf{Succ}\mathcal{A}_{SC}|\mathsf{E_0}]) \cdot Pr[\mathsf{E_0}]$$

$$- Pr[\mathsf{Succ}\mathcal{A}_{SC}|(\sim \mathsf{E_0}) \wedge \mathsf{E_1}] \cdot Pr[(\sim \mathsf{E_0}) \wedge \mathsf{E_1}]$$

$$\geq -Pr[(\sim \mathsf{E_0}) \wedge \mathsf{E_1}] = -\frac{q_H}{2^t}.$$

Thus, $Pr[\mathsf{Succ}\mathcal{A}_{\Pi}] \geq Pr[\mathsf{Succ}_{SC}] - \frac{q_H}{2^t}$

Thus, $\mathcal{A}_{\Pi}$ can win the IND-CCA2 game with probability

$$\epsilon \left(1 - \frac{1}{2^l} \right)^{q_U} - \frac{q_H}{2^t} \geq \epsilon - \left(\frac{q_H}{2^t} + \frac{q_U}{2^l} \right)$$

$\square$

Theorem 3. *SC is d-MU-UF-SC-iCMA secure in the sense of multi-user insider existential signcryptext unforgeability in standard model if S is UF-CMA secure.*

Proof. To prove this, we will construct a UF-CMA forger ζ against S using a d-MU-UF-SC-iCMA forger $\mathcal{F}$ against SC. As an input, ζ is fed with pk_A of S and given the signing oracle $\mathcal{O}Sign(sk_A, \cdot)$ of S. ζ simulates $\mathcal{F}$ with pk_A. In addition to this, ζ publishes a hash function $H : \{0,1\}^{k+k'} \rightarrow \{0,1\}^l$.

Simulation of Signcryption Oracle ($\mathcal{O}Signcrypt(sk_A, \cdot, \cdot)$)**:** When $\mathcal{F}$ submits a signcryption query $(pk_{B'}, m)$, ζ queries $\mathcal{O}Sign(sk_A, \cdot)$ with $m||ID_{B'}$ to receive a signature σ on $m||ID_{B'}$. Then, ζ chooses $r \in_R \{0,1\}^t$ and outputs $c = \text{Enc}(pk_{B'}, m||r, \sigma \oplus H(m||r||ID_A))$ to $\mathcal{F}$.

After the query phase is over, $\mathcal{F}$ outputs a receiver key pair (pk_B, sk_B) and a signcryptext (c^*, ID_A, ID_B) to ζ. ζ decrypts c^* with $\text{Dec}(sk_B, c^*)$ to get $(m^*||r^*, \beta^*)$ and compute $\sigma^* = \beta^* \oplus H(m^*||r^*||ID_A)$. ζ outputs σ^*.

Now, the theorem follows from the following lemma.

Lemma 2. *The following are true:*

1. *If c^* is a valid signcryptext from A to B, then σ^* is a valid signature of A on $m^*||ID_B$.*
2. *If m^*, the underlying message of c^*, have not been submitted to the signcryption oracle $\mathcal{O}\text{Signcrypt}(sk_A, pk_B, \cdot)$, then $m^*||ID_B$ have not been queried to the signing oracle $\mathcal{O}\text{Sign}(sk_A, \cdot)$.*

Proof. 1. If c^* is a valid signcryptext from A to B, then $\text{Ver}(sk_A, \sigma^*, m^*||ID_B) = 1$. Hence, the result.

2. If m^*, the underlying message of c^*, have not been submitted to the signcryption oracle $\mathcal{O}\text{Signcrypt}(sk_A, pk_B, \cdot)$, then, as per the simulation, $m^*||ID_B$ have not been queried to the signing oracle $\mathcal{O}\text{Sign}(sk_A, \cdot)$. $\qquad\square$

Theorem 4. *$\mathcal{SC}$ is d-MU-IND-SC-iCCA2 secure in the sense of multi-user insider confidentiality in random oracle model and d-MU-UF-SC-iCMA secure in the sense of multi-user insider existential signcryptext unforgeability in standard model if Π is IND-CCA2 secure and $\mathcal{S}$ is UF-CMA secure.*

Proof. The proof follows from Theorems 2 & 3. $\qquad\square$

5   Comparison with Li and Wong Construction [9]

It is to be noted that the proposed conversion relies on weaker buliding blocks both in terms of the encryption and signature primitives than [9], as the authors in [9] used an Ω-uniform IND-CCA2 secure PKE-RR and an UF-CMA secure uniformly-distributed signature scheme as components. But, not only there exist a few known constructions of Ω-uniform IND-CCA2 secure PKE-RR but also the notion of Ω-uniform IND-CCA2 security is somewhat artificial. In our construction, we use an weaker encryption primitive i.e., an IND-CCA2 secure PKE-RR and a UF-CMA secure signature scheme (not necessarily uniformly-distributed), making it open to a larger class of encryption and signature schemes by incorporating just one hashing (described above) in each of signcryption/ unsigncryption phases. Moreover the proposed construction is secure in dynamic multi-user insider setting whereas [9] is only secure in two-user outsider model.

One can point out that the security in the Li-Wong construction was in standard model, whereas in the proposed one, confidentiality relies on random oracle model[3]. But, we argue that relying on a more general primitive (like IND-CCA2

---

[3] It is to be noted that we still managed to achieve unforgeability in standard model.

security) in random oracle model is better than to depend on a 'less-common' primitive (like Ω-uniform IND-CCA2 security) in standard model, keeping in mind the generic nature of the conversion and the enhanced level of security that we achieved.

6   Conclusion and Open Issues

In this paper, we have presented a provably secure generic construction of signcryption scheme $\mathcal{SC}$ from an IND-CCA2 randomness recoverable public-key encryption scheme (PKE-RR) Π and a UF-CMA secure signature scheme $\mathcal{S}$. The construction is shown to be d-MU-IND-SC-iCCA2 secure in random oracle model and d-MU-UF-SC-iCMA secure in standard model, both in dynamic multi-user insider setting. The proposed scheme $\mathcal{SC}$ is more acceptable than its obvious counterpart [9] due to its reliance on weaker building blocks. As a by-product, we also showed that Fujisaki-Okamoto transform on PKE-RR can yield better efficiency than using it on a normal PKE.

Clearly, the proposed construction can not achieve efficiency like [10], but the main objective of this paper is to demonstrate the fact that the novel idea of using PKE-RR in constructing signcryption schemes, introduced in [9], can be modified to achieve enhanced security and to make it open to a larger class of cryptographic primitives. As future research, it can be a novel issue to design a generic conversion that uses a one-way PKE-RR rather than an IND-CCA2 one.

Acknowledgements. The authors would like to thank Summit Kumar Pandey of C.R.Rao Institute, Hyderabad, India and Partha Sarathi Roy and Sabyasachi Dutta of Department of Pure Mathematics, University of Calcutta, India for several fruitful comments and discussions in the initial phase of the work.

References

1. An, J.H., Dodis, Y., Rabin, T.: On the security of joint signature and encryption. In: Knudsen, L.R. (ed.) EUROCRYPT 2002. LNCS, vol. 2332, pp. 83–107. Springer, Heidelberg (2002)
2. Baek, J., Steinfeld, R., Zheng, Y.: Formal proofs for the security of signcryption. Journal of Cryptology 20(2), 203–235 (2007)
3. Bellare, M., Rogaway, P.: Optimal Asymmetric Encryption. In: De Santis, A. (ed.) EUROCRYPT 1994. LNCS, vol. 950, pp. 92–111. Springer, Heidelberg (1995)
4. Dachman-Soled, D., Fuchsbauer, G., Mohassel, P., O'Neill, A.: Enhanced Chosen-Ciphertext Security and Applications. Eprint archive (2012), http://eprint.iacr.org/2012/543
5. Das, A., Adhikari, A.: An Efficient IND-CCA2 secure Paillier-based cryptosystem. Information Processing Letters 112, 885–888 (2012)
6. Elgamal, T.: A Public Key Cryptosystem And A Signature Scheme Based On Discrete Logarithms. IEEE Trans. on Information Theory, IT-31(4), 469–472 (1985)
7. Fujisaki, E., Okamoto, T.: How to Enhance the Security of Public-Key Encryption at Minimum Cost. In: Imai, H., Zheng, Y. (eds.) PKC 1999. LNCS, vol. 1560, pp. 53–68. Springer, Heidelberg (1999)

8. Hoffstein, J., Pipher, J., Silverman, J.H.: NTRU: A ring-based public key cryptosystem. In: Buhler, J.P. (ed.) ANTS 1998. LNCS, vol. 1423, pp. 267–288. Springer, Heidelberg (1998)

9. Li, C.K., Wong, D.S.: Signcryption from randomness recoverable public key encryption. Information Sciences 180, 549–559 (2010)

10. Matsuda, T., Matsuura, K., Schuldt, J.C.N.: Efficient Constructions of Signcryption Schemes and Signcryption Composability. In: Roy, B., Sendrier, N. (eds.) INDOCRYPT 2009. LNCS, vol. 5922, pp. 321–342. Springer, Heidelberg (2009)

11. McEliece, R.: A public key cryptosystem based on algebraic coding theory. DSN Progress Report 42-44, 114–116 (1978)

12. Nieto, J.M.G., Boyd, C., Dawson, E.: A Public Key Cryptosystem Based On A Subgroup Membership Problem. Designs, Codes and Cryptography 36, 301–316 (2005)

13. Paillier, P.: Public-Key Cryptosystems Based on Composite Degree Residuosity Classes. In: Stern, J. (ed.) EUROCRYPT 1999. LNCS, vol. 1592, pp. 223–238. Springer, Heidelberg (1999)

14. Rackoff, C., Simon, D.: Noninteractive zero-knowledge proof of knowledge and chosen ciphertext attack. In: 22nd Annual ACM Symposium on Theory of Computing, pp. 427–437 (1990)

15. Zheng, Y.: Digital signcryption or how to achieve cost (signature & encryption) << cost(signature) + cost(encryption). In: Kaliski Jr., B.S. (ed.) CRYPTO 1997. LNCS, vol. 1294, pp. 165–179. Springer, Heidelberg (1997)

Auctions with Rational Adversary

Sourya Joyee De and Asim K. Pal

Management Information Systems Group,
Indian Institute of Management Calcutta, India

Abstract. Security of various types of online auctions has received a
considerable attention from researchers. However, very few works have
analyzed the problem of security in online sealed-bid auctions from the
point of view of rational participants. The paper deals with an online
auction scenario where two types of participants co-exist: 1) a party
corrupted by a rational adversary that have positive utilities from information gained and that has no valuation for the items on auction
enabling them to bid arbitrarily and 2) rational parties that are privacy
conscious, positively value information gain and have a valuation for
items on auction. The secure auction protocol proposed here addresses
1) privacy concerns of the rational players from themselves as well as the
rational adversary; 2) prevention of 'throwing away' of contracts by rational adversaries and 3) prevention of sellers from obtaining their copy
of the contract while winners do not receive theirs.

1 Introduction

Security of various types of online auctions (such as combinatorial, Vickery-Clarke-
Groves, first price etc) has received considerable attention from researchers during
the past two decades [1–3, 8, 11–13]. Important security concerns in online auctions include bid privacy, bidder anonymity, correct evaluation and declaration
of winner etc. Both the auctioneer and the bidders can be considered dishonest –
while bidders may try to know the bid values of other bidders, the auctioneer may
not only try to know the bid values (for e.g. the knowledge of the second highest bid value helps to set reservation price in second price auction) but also ma-
nipulate results. Incorrect outcome may result from introduction of false bids or
modification of submitted bids, undue extension or shortening of bidding period
and introduction of new bids based on information about submitted bids, bidder-
auctioneer collusion, collusion among bidders etc. For bidders, bid values may be
sensitive information and loss of bid-privacy may reveal important information
such as financial status etc. against their wishes. Cryptographic techniques have
been predominantly used to overcome these difficulties. However, very few works
have analyzed the problem of security in online sealed-bid auctions from the point
of view of rational participants. Traditionally, cryptographic protocols for secure
computation in auctions have achieved privacy and security not as an equilibrium
strategy to the game which every party will find in their best interest to follow
but as "...a second-phase technical level outside of the scope of game and parties'
strategies.." [10].

A. Bagchi and I. Ray (Eds.): ICISS 2013, LNCS 8303, pp. 91–105, 2013.
© Springer-Verlag Berlin Heidelberg 2013

In [10], the authors discuss about privacy-enhanced auctions with rational cryptography and propose a protocol that is in computational Nash Equilibrium for even privacy-conscious players to follow. Here, bidders wish to know information about other bidders' valuations or types while not revealing any information about its own type. More formally, rational players have a hybrid utility i.e. a monetary utility from winning an item in the auction as well as an information utility from learning about others' bids while not giving up any information about ones own bid. Bidders participate in a secure multi-party computation simulating the mediator of a mediated auction mechanism Mec and at the end each winner receives a contract which is a document digitally signed by all participants associating the winner with the correct item-value pair. The seller is assumed to have made a commitment to sell his items to bidders who can show him a valid contract. Fair distribution of contracts has been achieved in non-simultaneous, point-to-point channel using concepts from rational secret reconstruction mechanisms [4, 5, 7, 9] where a winner receives its contract in a randomly chosen epoch. Each player obtains a list of shares of the contracts after the computation of Mec and in each epoch, players communicate their shares one by one so that at the end of the epoch a player can reconstruct a value which is either the contract or some other default value. When there are multiple winners, a privacy-conscious winner who has been able to reconstruct its contract at the end of a particular epoch shall find it beneficial to stop communicating its shares henceforth because contracts of other winners may reveal some information about its valuation. So other winners are unable to reconstruct their contract. This problem is solved by revealing the information in the contract in a round prior to the one in which the actual contract is to be received. If any player aborts in this round then nobody gets the contracts due to be revealed in the next round. Since each player has a monetary utility of obtaining this contract they continue communicating shares even in the next round. A winner can reject the contract he won, modelled by the mediated setting with reject. However, the authors consider that when winners opt for 'reject' they gain zero monetary utility instead of the contract. Winners do not 'throw away' their contracts without buying the item simply because they assign a positive utility for the contract.

Given this background, we are interested in what happens when at least one player is only interested in the information revealing round rather than the contract reconstruction round that comes after it, other players being rational in the sense described earlier? Such a player is only interested in knowing the information revealed in the contracts but not in the item won i.e. it positively valuates the information it learns while it has no valuation of the items being sold in the auction. We call a player behaving in this way a rational adversary. We assume the availability of non-simultaneous channel for communication and deal with only first price and second price auctions. If a rational adversary were to participate in the privacy-enhanced auction mechanism just described, no winner will be able to reconstruct his contract because the adversary will have no incentive to continue after the information-revealing round and hence will abort immediately. The following practical examples suitably describe this situation.

Example 1. Bob is selling an old painting using Vickery auction through an online auction website. Coincidentally, Alice also possesses a painting of the same painter but has no idea how much price such a painting could fetch her if she sold it. However, she is certain that no one will be willing to pay more than a million dollars for that painting. So, she bids a million dollars for Bob's painting and waits to hear the winning price. As a rule, the winning price is only announced to the winner and the seller. Alice wins the auction and comes to know that the best bid next to hers was only a thousand dollars. She does not buy the painting of course. Bob can only mark her with a negative reputation as a buyer.

Example 2. Bob is selling a painting using a first price sealed bid auction in an online site. Alice wants to know whether a similar painting will fetch her a thousand dollars or not. The auction site enables buyers to blacklist any seller who does not deliver a sold item. So instead of directly putting up the painting for auction, she bids a thousand dollars at Bob's auction; if she wins then she knows that the painting may not actually fetch her as much money as she requires. This information can enable her to decide whether to put up the painting for auction. Throwing away of the contract leads to a loss for other bidders who would have bought the item if they won and the seller who has to conduct yet another auction for the same item to sell it, still being unsure whether someone like Alice will not participate again. Additionally, bidders may also wish to know information on the types of other bidders. Bidders who are privacy conscious have disincentives to participate in an auction protocol which leaks information about their types. On the other hand, sellers are revenue conscious and thus will not have any incentive to hold an auction of their items if adversaries place arbitrary bids in the auction to win and then never actually buy the item.

Our Contributions. We discuss a problem scenario consisting of two types of participants that co-exist: 1) a party corrupted by a rational adversary that have positive utilities from information gained and that has no valuation for the items on auction enabling them to bid arbitrarily (leading to "gain information, win and throw away contract" behavior) and 2) rational parties that are privacy conscious, positively value information gain and have a valuation for items on auction. Neither privacy conscious rational participants nor revenue-conscious sellers will find it beneficial to participate in online auctions that are not secure against a rational adversary. Our secure auction protocol addresses 1) privacy concerns of the rational players from themselves (because of conflicting interest in information gain and privacy-consciousness) as well as the rational adversary; 2) prevention of 'throwing away' of contracts by rational adversaries and 3) prevention of sellers from obtaining their copy of the contract while winners do not receive theirs. It uses the concept of rational secret reconstruction. Each winner is to receive a contract which is a legal document stating the item-value pair it has won. The seller possesses a counter-part of this contract having the same information. If either of them fails to honor the commitment associated with the contract then the other can seek suitable compensation in the court of law. Each winner partially reconstructs its contract by participating in a fair reconstruction mechanism with other players while the contract is fully recovered only after the winner communicates with the seller. We show that it is in computational strict Nash Equilibrium for rational adversaries, rational players and a seller to follow this protocol while rational adversaries only bid values that are upper-bounded by their information utility of the contract.

Online auctions inevitably result in the transfer of physical goods from the buyer to the seller (unless the item on auction is an electronic file). To enforce the physical transfer of goods and payment for the same, the contract must be enforced. Many popular vendors such as eBay do this by means of reputation scores, user agreements etc. The reputation score of a buyer has to be computed over a period of time, based on many instances of the buyer's participation. So, new buyers do not have reputation scores. Moreover, sometimes reputed buyers may also behave like a rational adversary. It is not necessary that a buyer always exhibits the same kind of behavior, whether honest or adversarial. He may honestly buy the items he has won most of the times, thus obtaining a good reputation score, but once in a while, he may wish to deviate. Reputation score can limit the number of instances of rational adversarial behavior but cannot totally eradicate the problem. The legal contract in our system is no better or no worse than that being used by eBay, as both are expected to operate under the same domestic or international laws. The major difference between eBay and our system is that eBay acts as a trusted third party (TTP) that computes the result of the auction, while, in our case, the bidders and sellers can themselves compute the output without relying on any TTP. In the absence of a trusted mediator, if fairness is not ensured then even if the contract is enforced or there is a user agreement, the winner (seller) can abort early so that the seller (winner) may not even know who has won. The situation is further complicated by the fact that the communication takes place over an unreliable channel, the Internet, so that a bidder may have to abort early, not intentionally but due to failure of communication. Under this situation our protocol ensures fairness even after allowing early abort in the presence of rational adversary, rational players and the seller.

Organization of the Paper. This paper is organized as follows. In section 2, we describe the preliminaries such as utilities of rational adversary, rational players and the seller and finally define what we mean by a secure auction protocol. In section 3, we propose our secure auction mechanism while in section 4 we finally conclude.

2   Sealed-Bid Auctions and Its Participants

In this section we describe sealed-bid auctions followed by equilibrium notions and nature of participants in an online auction and their utilities. We finally use these concepts to define secure online auctions in our settings.

Table 1. Symbols Used

Symbol	Meaning
$Mec()$	The auction/allocation mechanism
k	Security parameter
$\mu', \mu'', negl$	Negligible functions
r	Index of a run of the unmediated auction mechanism
$P_i\ (P_{-i})$	ith player or bidder or participant (any player other than P_i)
A	Rational adversary
T_i	Type space of bidder P_i
t_i	Type of bidder P_i
t	Vector of types of bidders
b_i	Bid value of bidder P_i
o_i	Output of the auction mechanism for P_i
(Γ, σ)	A mechanism consisting of the game Γ and the strategy $\sigma = (\sigma_i, \sigma_{-i})$ suggested by the protocol designer
$\sigma_i, (\sigma_{-i})$	Suggested strategy for $P_i\ (P_{-i})$
σ_i'	Any strategy other than the suggested strategy followed by P_i
$u_i(\sigma)$	Utility of P_i when everybody (including itself) follows σ
$u_i(\sigma_i', \sigma_{-i})$	Utility of P_i when it follows σ_i' while everybody else follows σ_{-i}
$Info_i^r\ (Info_{-i}^r, Info_A^r)$	Information set consisting of pieces of information collected by $P_i\ (P_{-i}, A)$ about other participants in run r of an unmediated auction mechanism
$u_A^I(Info_A^r, Info_{-i}^r)$	Information utility of A when its information set is $Info_A^r$ and that of others are $Info_{-i}^r$
$u_i^I(Info_i^r, Info_{-i}^r)$	Information utility of P_i when its information set is $Info_i^r$ and that of others are $Info_{-i}^r$
o_r	Vector of outputs received by all participants at the end of run r
$o_i^r\ (o_A^r, o_{r,s})$	Output received by $P_i\ (A,$ seller) at the end of run r
$u_i^{auc}(o_r, t)\qquad (u_A^{auc}(o_r, t),$ $u_S^{auc}(o_{r,s}, t))$	Auction utility of $P_i\ (A,$ seller)
$u_i(r, t)$	Overall utility of P_i for run r

2.1 Sealed-Bid Auctions

Classical sealed bid auctions can be looked upon as Bayesian games of incomplete information. The n players $P_1, \ldots, P_n$ participating in this game are called bidders. At the beginning of the game, each bidder P_i receives private information regarding its type $t_i \in T_i$ where T_i is the type space of that bidder. The vector of bidders types $t = (t_1, \ldots, t_n)$ is drawn from $T = T_1 \ldots T_n$ according to a probability density $\phi(.)$. Each bidder P_i then strategically chooses and submits his bid b_i according to its type t_i (a bidder's type is its valuation of the item on auction). The allocation mechanism Mec, depending on the received bids $b = (b_1, \ldots, b_n)$ allocates items to bidders as well as computes a price of each item won. We have $o = (o_1, \ldots, o_n) = Mec(b)$ where o_i represents whether P_i is the winner or not and if he is the winner then the price of the item he has won. For a single item auction, if it wins P_i has the positive utility of $(t_i - p)$ where t_i is P_i's true valuation of the item and p is the price of the item; otherwise its utility is 0. In the particular case of Vickery auction, if P_i is the winner then, $p = Max(b_1, \ldots, b_{i-1}, b_{i+1}, \ldots, b_n)$.

A secure rational unmediated auction mechanism consists of the game Γ and a suggested strategy σ. The game can be looked upon as a tree of all possible paths formed by combination of all possible strategies that participants may follow. Each such path can be called a run. The root node of the tree is the initial state of the game, whereas later nodes depict states as the game progresses (for example, as participants exchange messages) [7]. For different runs, participants will have different information gains and obtain different outcomes (i.e. all winners receive contract or only one receives etc). The suggested strategy or protocol will lead to a run that each player will find it in its best interest to follow. Such a strategy is said to be in equilibrium, such as Nash Equilibrium.

2.2 Equilibrium Notions

A suggested strategy σ of a mechanism (Γ, σ) is said to be in Nash equilibrium when there is no incentive for a player P_i to deviate from the suggested strategy, given that everyone else is following this strategy. In the setting of cryptography, in many cases, players are assumed to be computationally bounded which calls for a suitable modification in the notion of Nash equilibrium used. Here we reiterate the definition of computational strict Nash Equilibrium [4] which we use for our protocol.

Definition 1. *(Computational strict Nash Equilibrium [4]) The suggested strategy σ in the mechanism (Γ, σ) is a computational strict Nash Equilibrium if for every P_i and for any probabilistic polynomial time strategy σ_i', $u_i(\sigma_i', \sigma_{-i}) < u_i(\sigma) + \mu''(k)$ for some negligible μ''.*

2.3 Nature of Participants and Utilities

The first consideration of rational adversaries appears in the context of the Byzantine Agreement problem in [6] where a rational adversary is said to be characterized by some utility function describing its preference over the outcomes of the protocol in question. In their case, at most t players are controlled by this rational adversary who wishes to achieve a particular outcome (different from the intended one) for the Byzantine agreement protocol while the rest are honest. In our case, the utility of the rational adversary is defined over the information it gains during the protocol execution as well as the outcome of the protocol itself i.e. over a run of the unmediated auction mechanism. We assume that a corrupted player is controlled by the rational adversary. Uncorrupted players are rational with preferences as mentioned earlier. We do not model envy i.e. neither the rational players nor the rational adversary prevents others from gaining monetary utility due to the item on sale. All players are computationally bounded. The seller finds it beneficial to participate in protocols where contracts are honored by winners. This is depicted by the auction utility of the seller. However, the seller may try to be unfair and try to obtain the contract alone. This is because the contract is assumed to have a monetary value for the seller. We define two types of utilities: the information utility and the auction utility. However we distinguish between the information and auction utilities of the rational adversary from those of the rational players. For sellers only auction utility is defined. The overall utility of a player is the combined value of the auction utility and the information utility.

Information Utilities. Suppose $Info_i^r$ is the information set consisting of pieces of information I_{ij}^r collected by a participant P_i about another participant P_j ($j \neq i$) in a run r of an unmediated auction mechanism.

Information Utility of Rational Adversary. Suppose the rational adversary A controls the bidder P_i while the remaining bidders are rational players, denoted by P_{-i}. Then, I_A denotes the set of information pieces gathered by the adversary A and I_{-i} denotes the sets of information pieces gathered by the rational player P_{-i} in a particular run of the unmediated auction mechanism. Then the information utility for the adversary is expressed by the function u_A^I such that:

1. $u_A^I(Info_A^r, Info_{-i}^r) > 0$ whenever $Info_A^r \neq \phi$ and $u_A^I(Info_A^r, Info_{-i}^r) \leq 0$ otherwise,
2. $u_A^I(Info_A^r, Info_{-i}^r) \geq u_A^I(Info_A^{r'}, Info_{-i}^r)$ whenever $Info_A^{r'} \subseteq Info_A^r$.

In other words, the rational adversary has a positive information utility whenever it gains a piece of information about any other participant. Moreover, it is not privacy conscious; it is only interested in gaining whatever information it can. The utility maximizing rational adversary thus prefers a run for which it gathers the most information, irrespective of the information gathered by others.

Information Utility of Rational Party. Suppose P_j is a rational party. The information utility for any rational party P_j is expressed by the function u_j^I such that it captures any arbitrary privacy concern with the constraint that [10]:

1. $u_j^I(Info_j^{r'}, Info_{-j}^r) \leq u_j^I(Info_j^r, Info_{-j}^r) + \epsilon$ whenever $Info_j^r \subset Info_j^{r'}$ and $Info_{-j}^r = Info_{-j}^r$ where ϵ is negligible.
2. u_j^I is poly-time computable.

Therefore, a rational party prefers a run of the unmediated auction mechanism which has the least privacy concern and the most information gain. We assume privacy concerns that are sufficiently small with respect to the expected utility of participating in the game. Note that the seller does not have any information utility.

Auction Utilities. Suppose o^r denotes the vector of outputs received by all participants at the end of run r and t denotes the vector of types of the different participants. The seller obtains a corresponding vector $o^{r,s}$ at the end of the run r. The auction utility of a rational player P_i is expressed by the function u_i^{auc} such that: $u_i^{auc}(o^r, t) > 0$ if o_i^r is the contract; else $u_i^{auc}(o^r, t) = 0$. On the other hand, the rational adversary has the following utilities: $u_A^{auc}(o^r, t) = 0$ if it does not win the auction i.e. o_A^r is not the contract or if he does not have to buy the item he won whereas $u_A^{auc}(o^r, t) < 0$ if o_A^r is the contract and it must buy the item he won. In fact, $u_A^{auc} = -p$ where p is the winning price for the item. The auction utility of a seller is expressed as follows: $u_S^{auc}(o^{r,s}, t) > 0$ when at least one of the participants in the auction is a rational player with positive auction utility when it wins. The overall utility of a participant P_i (which is either a rational adversary A or a rational party) for run r in the unmediated auction mechanism is given by:

$$u_i(r, t) = u_i^I(Info_i^r, Info_{-i}^r) + u_i^{auc}(o^r, t)$$

We can write the overall utility for a rational party simply as $u_R = u_R^I + u_R^{auc}$ and that of a rational adversary as $u_A = u_A^I + u_A^{auc}$. The seller's utility is simply represented as u_S which is the same as his auction utility. Suppose the suggested strategy i.e. the secure protocol for the unmediated auction mechanism for each party P_i is $\sigma_{i,s}$. Then, the utility of a participant to follow this protocol is $u_i(\sigma_{i,s}, \sigma_{-i,s}) = u_i^I(Info_i^{\sigma_{i,s},\sigma_{-i,s}}, Info_{-i}^{\sigma_{i,s},\sigma_{-i,s}}) + u_i^{auc}(o^{\sigma_{i,s},\sigma_{-i,s}}, t)$.

2.4   Secure Online Auction

The security of an auction protocol in the presence of rational adversary, rational parties and the seller with information and auction utilities as described in the last section must address 1) privacy concerns of the rational players from themselves (because of conflicting interest in information gain and privacy-consciousness) as well as the rational adversary; 2) prevention of 'throwing away' of contracts by rational adversaries and 3) prevention of sellers from obtaining their copy of the contract while winners do not receive theirs. The secure protocol must be such that it is in the best interest of all participants to follow the protocol i.e. the suggested strategy should be an equilibrium strategy. We define a computationally secure auction protocol in the following way:

Definition 2. *(Computationally Secure Auction Protocol.) An auction protocol π^{auc} which is a suggested strategy $\sigma_s = (\sigma_{i,s}, \sigma_{-i,s})$ in an unmediated auction* game Γ^{auc} is said to be computationally secure against a rational adversary with overall utility $u_A = u_A^I + u_A^{auc}$, a rational party with overall utility $u_R = u_R^I + u_R^{auc}$ and a seller with utility u_S if the following conditions are satisfied:

1. σ_s is a computational strict Nash equilibrium for the rational players for every deviating strategy σ_{dev} i.e. $u_R(\sigma_{dev}) < u_R(\sigma_s) + negl(k)$.
2. The rational adversary bids a value $b_A < u_A^I$. In addition, σ_s is a computational strict Nash equilibrium for the rational adversary for every deviating strategy σ_{dev} i.e. $u_A(\sigma_{dev}) < u_A(\sigma_s) + negl(k)$.
3. It is beneficial for the seller to participate in the protocol i.e. $u_S(\sigma_s) > 0$ and σ_s is a computational strict Nash equilibrium for the seller for every deviating strategy σ_{dev} i.e. $u_S(\sigma_{dev}) < u_S(\sigma_s) + negl(k)$. Here k is a security parameter and $negl(k)$ is a negligible function in k and the above conditions hold for infinitely many values of k.

3   Secure Auction Protocol

For a second price auction bidding infinity becomes the dominant strategy whenever the contract is not enforced. Even in the ideal/mediated setting that does not allow reject (and ends in distributing the contract to the bidders), presence of the rational adversary in addition to the rational players has the same effect as the mediated setting with reject where only rational players participate. This implies that simply associating monetary utility of players with the contract does not solve our problem. Instead, we must enforce the contract. For a player who has no monetary utility for the item on auction, enforcement of the contract acts as a deterrent to bid arbitrarily. If players are allowed to reject or if they come to know that they have obtained the required information in the contract in the revealing epoch itself then for the rational adversary who assigns no monetary value to the contract itself but only to the information in the contract this epoch then is the point where one can deviate or to reject the contract after having a look at it. To avoid this problem, rejection should not be allowed.

We define the contract obtained as the outcome of the auction to be a legal document containing the information about the winner, the price the winning bidder has to pay and the item it has won if different items are being auctioned by the same seller. It has a seller's copy and a winner's copy. So, the seller can claim an amount of money equal to the winning price of an item by showing his copy of the contract to an appropriate authority, say a bank. On the other hand the winner of a contract gets information about the item he won and the price he has to pay for it from the contract and can also legally claim the item by showing the contract to the appropriate person i.e. the seller. Since the contract has legal validity, the winner can also seek compensation if the seller does not honor his commitment to sell the item won. Thus, when the seller obtains his copy of the contract it can be assumed to be as good as obtaining the payment for the item the particular winner has won. Similarly when the winner has obtained the contract it is as good as obtaining the item he has won. Each winner reconstructs his share of the contract from sub-shares obtained from each of the bidders using the principles of rational secret reconstruction. This share is meaningless until it is used to reconstruct the contract along with the seller's share. Therefore, at the end, each winner has a contract and the seller also has a contract corresponding to each winner. The main idea is that the contract and the information in the contract are obtained simultaneously. If a party aborts the protocol at any stage before the last, it has to forgo both the contract and the information. Therefore we allow abort. This takes into account technical failures, such as, problems in network connectivity while the transaction occurs. But it ensures that no party (neither the seller nor the rational players nor the rational adversary) interested in the result of the auction intentionally aborts at any stage. Our protocol is thus the real world implementation of an ideal world that allows abort but not reject. Each players share is signed with information theoretic MAC so that a player cannot send a false share undetected. So, in each round, a player can either send the designated share or keep silent.

Choice of β. Following the general method of rational secret reconstruction [4, 5, 7, 9] the contract can be reconstructed only at a randomly chosen epoch so that it is possible to correctly guess the contract revelation round with a probability of β. Since there are three types of players (rational adversary, rational participant and seller), the choice of β must be made depending on the utility of obtaining the contract alone for each. When the rational adversary wins and obtains the contract alone, it need not buy the item it won and hence its overall utility is $u_A = u_A^I = p_A$ where p_A is its valuation of the information in the contract. When the rational participant wins and obtains the contract alone, its overall utility is $u_R = u_R^I + u_R^{auc} = p_R + v_w$. Note that the rational player does not pay the winning price p_w for the item. When the seller obtains the contract alone, its overall utility for each winner is $u_S = u_S^{auc} = p_w + v_S$ where v_S is the sellers personal valuation of the item he is selling (it is most likely that $v_S \leq p_w$). Therefore, β must be chosen such that $\beta.Max(\alpha_A p_A, \alpha_R(p_R + v_w), p_w + v_S) < Min(\alpha_A(p_A - p_w), \alpha_R(p_R + v_w - p_w), p_w)$ where the RHS denotes the minimum of the utilities when not deviating and α_A and α_R denote the probabilities that the rational adversary wins and the rational player wins respectively. We assume here that the protocol designer has an idea about the winning price of the item on auction.

3.1   Our Protocol

The Mediated Setting without Abort and without Reject. Let $C_{med}^{non-adv}$ be the communication device that also acts as the mediator.

Input: Obtain as input the bid b_i from each bidder P_i and the identity sel_{id} from the seller S.

Compute result: Compute $(o_1, \ldots, o_n) = Mec(b)$.

Send contract: Each bidder P_i is given its contract o_i and the seller S is given a copy of the contract for each P_i. The recommended strategy $\pi_{med}^{non-adv}$ for each bidder P_i is to input a bid $b_i \leftarrow B_i(t_i)$ and for the seller is to input the correct sel_{id}.

We next consider mediation with abort to account for undesired protocol abortion by rational parties/adversaries.

The Mediated Setting with Abort and without Reject. Here we want to have a protocol that is secure against following deviations. First, privacy conscious rational parties may abort at appropriate points in the protocol so as to prevent other parties from receiving their contract and hence any information about types of the aborting parties. Secondly, the rational adversary is only interested in the information about the winner. So, it may prevent the seller from receiving his contract and other parties from receiving their outputs. Such deviations are not allowed in our protocol. Lastly, a seller may want to receive his copy of the contract alone and hence abort early. Therefore, the mediated setting only allows aborts that do not allow any of the parties or the adversary to receive any output, i.e., the ideal world allows either everybody to receive the output or nobody to receive the output. This takes into account unintentional aborts over Internet like communication medium.

Input

The input of each bidder P_j is his bid b_j and that of the seller his identity sel_{id}. The trusted mediator does the following:

Computation Phase

Computes the winning bidder using an auction mechanism Mec as $(o_1, \ldots, o_n) = Mec(b)$.

Pre-processing Phase

1. Choose an i_I^* according to a geometric distribution with parameter β.
2. For each output o_j corresponding to each party P_j do the following for $i \in 1, \ldots, m$:
   - For $i < i_I^*$, set $o_{ij}^p \leftarrow D_p$ and $o_{ij}^s \leftarrow D_s$.

   - For $i \geq i_I^*$, set $o_{ij}^p = o_i$ and $o_{ij}^s = o_i$.

Abort phase

- During any of the above phases, the trusted mediator can receive an $abort_j$ instruction from any party P_j. In that case the trusted mediator must inform all the bidders and the seller that the protocol has been aborted and then quit.

Communication Phase

- In rounds $1 \leq i \leq m$, corresponding to party P_j, send o_{ij}^p to party P_j.
- In rounds $1 \leq i \leq m$, corresponding to party P_j, send o_{ij}^s to the seller.

Each rational party P_j does the following:

- Outputs o_{ij}^p as received from the trusted mediator.
- If an abort message is received from the trusted mediator then output a special symbol denoting failed transaction and quit.

The seller does the following:

- Outputs o_{ij}^s corresponding to each party P_j as received from the trusted mediator.
- If an abort message is received from the trusted mediator, then output a special symbol denoting failed transaction and quit.

The Unmediated Setting
Functionality ShareGen
Input
Each bidder P_j inputs his bid b_j and the seller his identity sel_{id}.
Computation Phase
Computes the winning bidder using an auction mechanism Mec as $(o_1, \ldots, o_n) = Mec(b)$.
Pre-processing Phase I

1. Choose an i_I^* according to a geometric distribution with parameter β.
2. For each output o_j corresponding to each party P_j do the following for $i \in 1, \ldots, m$:
   - For $i < i_I^*$, set $o_{ij}^p \leftarrow D_p$ and $o_{ij}^s \leftarrow D_s$.
   - For $i \geq i_I^*$, set $o_{ij}^p = o_i$ and $o_{ij}^s = o_i$.
3. Set A_{ij}^p and B_{ij}^p to be the random shares of o_{ij}^p and A_{ij}^s and B_{ij}^s to be the random shares of o_{ij}^s.

Pre-processing Phase II

1. Choose an i_{II}^* according to a geometric distribution with parameter β.
2. For each share A_{ij}^p corresponding to each party P_j do the following for $i \in 1, \ldots, m$:
   - For $i < i_{II}^*$, set $a_{ij}^b \leftarrow f(x_b')$ for $b \in 1, \ldots, n$ where following Shamir's secret sharing f is an $(n-1)$ degree polynomial with A_{ij}^{fake} as the free coefficient.
   - For $i \geq i_{II}^*$, set $a_{ij}^b \leftarrow f(x_b)$ for $b \in 1, \ldots, n$ where following Shamir's secret sharing f is an $(n-1)$ degree polynomial with A_{ij}^p as the free coefficient.

Output
Send shares to bidder:

- Send the shares a_{ij}^k to player P_k corresponding to the output of player P_j.
- Send the shares a_{ik}^k and B_{ik}^s to player P_k corresponding to its own output.

Send shares to seller:

- Send shares A_{ij}^s and B_{ij}^p to seller corresponding to the output of player P_j.

Protocol π_I^{auc}
Stage 1
Players use their inputs to execute a secure protocol for *ShareGen* and obtains outputs as specified by functionality *ShareGen*.
Stage 2
Using the outputs of the previous stage each player P_k does the following:

1. In round $r = i$, epoch j sends the shares a_{rj}^k to each player P_j.
2. In round $r = i$, epoch k remains silent and receives the shares a_{rk}^j from each player P_j.
3. Reconstructs all A_{rj}^p.
4. In each round $r' = i$, epoch 1, each player P_k sends his share B_{rk}^s to the seller. Similarly, in each round $r' = i$, epoch 2, each player P_k receives the share A_{rk}^s from the seller.
5. Reconstructs o_{ik}^p.

The seller does the following:

1. In each round $r' = i$, epoch 1, the seller receives the share B_{rk}^s from P_k. Similarly, in each round $r' = i$, epoch 2, the seller distributes the share A_{rk}^s to each player P_k.
2. Reconstructs o_{ik}^s for each player P_k.

Outputs
For each player P_k

- If some other party aborts before any o_{ik}^p can be reconstructed, then output a special symbol denoting failed transaction and quit.
- If the seller or some other player aborts after at least one o_{ik}^p is recontsructed, then output the last reconstructed o_{ij}^p.

For the seller

- If a bidder aborts before any o_{ik}^s can be reconstructed, then output a special symbol denoting failed transaction and quit.
- If the bidder P_k aborts after at least one o_{ik}^s can be reconstructed, then output the last reconstructed o_{ik}^s.

3.2   Analysis

Theorem 1. *Protocol π_I^{auc} is computationally secure.*

Proof. We shall prove that our auction protocol π_I^{auc} is computationally secure (according to Definition 3) in three steps. First, we show for rational adversaries, $b_A < u_A^I$. Next we show that for sellers it is always beneficial to participate in the protocol. Lastly, we show that for each participant (rational adversary/ rational player/ seller) it is in computational strict Nash Equilibrium to follow the protocol.

In our protocol π_I^{auc}, each winner and the seller obtains a contract at the end of the protocol. No information related to the contract is released in any intermediate step. Also, the contracts are enforced causing each winner to pay for the item it has won. For a first price auction where a winner has to pay an amount equal to its bid value for the item it won, the rational adversary can only bid an amount less than its valuation of the information gained from the contract in order to gain a positive utility, if it wins, by participating in the protocol. So, for a first price auction, $b_A < u_A^I$. For a second price auction, the rational adversary's overall utility gain from the auction i.e. u_A will depend on the second highest bid value. However, this is not known to the rational adversary. For it to be beneficial for the rational adversary to participate in the auction, $(u_A^I - p) > 0$. But, since p is unknown beforehand, the rational adversary's overall utility from participating in the auction (u_A) is less than 0 whenever $u_A^I \leq p$. So participation in the auction does not guarantee a positive utility. On the other hand if the rational adversary bids $b_A \leq u_A^I$ then 1) if it does not win then $u_A = 0$ and 2) if it wins then $u_A > 0$ since $p < u_A^I$. So the rational adversary finds it beneficial to bid a value less than u_A^I. Since contracts are enforced, a winner always pays for the items it wins. Therefore the seller always has a utility $u_S(\sigma_s) > 0$ so that it is beneficial to participate in the protocol. In each round, each participant can either send the designated message or keep silent. Since messages are signed by information theoretic MACs, a participant cannot send a false message undetected. Now suppose a participant quits at the qth round. For a rational adversary or a rational player to benefit from quitting in this round: 1) it must have won the auction and 2) this is the round where the contract is reconstructed. With probability β, this is the round where the participant wins and the contract is revealed whereas with probability $(1 - \beta)$ it is not so. Then expected utility of a rational adversary on quitting in round q is βu_A^I. But, by our choice, $\beta p_A < \alpha_A(p_A - p_w)$ where p_A is the rational adversary's valuation of the information in the contract, p_w is the winning price of the item and α_A is the probability that the rational adversary wins the auction. Therefore, it is in computational strict Nash Equilibrium for a rational adversary to follow the protocol. Similarly we can show that for rational parties and the seller, it is in computational strict Nash Equilibrium to follow the protocol.

4   Conclusion

We introduce a new problem scenario for online auctions where rational adversaries 'throw away' the contracts they win because they only value the information in the contract but do not want to buy the item they won. Other participants in such an auction scenario are referred to as rational players who buy the item if they win but are selfish and privacy-conscious. The seller can also misbehave by trying to obtain the legal contract alone and then exercising it. We propose a new auction protocol that is computationally secure in this scenario.

Acknowledgement. We would like to thank the anonymous reviewers for their useful comments and suggestions that helped us improve our work.

References

1. Bogetoft, P., Damgård, I.B., Jakobsen, T., Nielsen, K., Pagter, J.I., Toft, T.: A practical implementation of secure auctions based on multiparty integer computation. In: Di Crescenzo, G., Rubin, A. (eds.) FC 2006. LNCS, vol. 4107, pp. 142–147. Springer, Heidelberg (2006)
2. Bradford, P.G., Park, S., Rothkopf, M.H., Park, H.: Protocol completion incen-tive problems in cryptographic Vickrey auctions. Electronic Commerce Research 8(1-2), 57–77 (2008)
3. Franklin, M.K., Reiter, M.K.: The design and implementation of a secure auction service. IEEE Transactions on Software Engineering 22(5), 302–312 (1996)
4. Fuchsbauer, G., Katz, J., Naccache, D.: Efficient rational secret sharing in standard communication networks. In: Micciancio, D. (ed.) TCC 2010. LNCS, vol. 5978, pp. 419–436. Springer, Heidelberg (2010)
5. Gordon, S.D., Katz, J.: Rational Secret Sharing, Revisited. In: De Prisco, R., Yung, M. (eds.) SCN 2006. LNCS, vol. 4116, pp. 229–241. Springer, Heidelberg (2006)
6. Groce, A., Katz, J., Thiruvengadam, A., Zikas, V.: Byzantine agreement with a rational adversary. In: Czumaj, A., Mehlhorn, K., Pitts, A., Wattenhofer, R. (eds.) ICALP 2012, Part II. LNCS, vol. 7392, pp. 561–572. Springer, Heidelberg (2012)
7. Halpern, J., Teague, V.: Rational secret sharing and multiparty computation: extended abstract. In: Proceedings of the Thirty-Sixth Annual ACM Symposium on Theory of Computing, STOC 2004, pp. 623–632. ACM, New York (2004)
8. Juels, A., Szydlo, M.: A two-server, sealed-bid auction protocol. In: Blaze, M. (ed.) FC 2002. LNCS, vol. 2357, pp. 72–86. Springer, Heidelberg (2003)
9. Kol, G., Naor, M.: Games for exchanging information. In: Proceedings of the 40th Annual ACM Symposium on Theory of Computing, STOC 2008, pp. 423–432. ACM, New York (2008)
10. Miltersen, P.B., Nielsen, J.B., Triandopoulos, N.: Privacy-enhancing auctions using rational cryptography. In: Halevi, S. (ed.) CRYPTO 2009. LNCS, vol. 5677, pp. 541–558. Springer, Heidelberg (2009)
11. Naor, M., Pinkas, B., Sumner, R.: Privacy preserving auctions and mechanism design. In: Proceedings of the 1st ACM Conference on Electronic Commerce, pp. 129–139. ACM (November 1999)
12. Parkes, D.C., Rabin, M.O., Thorpe, C.: Cryptographic combinatorial clock-proxy auctions. In: Dingledine, R., Golle, P. (eds.) FC 2009. LNCS, vol. 5628, pp. 305–324. Springer, Heidelberg (2009)
13. Suzuki, K., Yokoo, M.: Secure generalized Vickrey auction using homomorphic encryption. In: Wright, R.N. (ed.) FC 2003. LNCS, vol. 2742, pp. 239–249. Springer, Heidelberg (2003)

A Framework for Formal Reasoning about Privacy Properties Based on Trust Relationships in Complex Electronic Services

Koen Decroix[1], Jorn Lapon[1], Bart De Decker[2], and Vincent Naessens[1]

[1] KU Leuven, Technology Campus Ghent, Department of Computer Science
Gebroeders Desmetstraat 1, 9000 Ghent, Belgium
firstname.lastname@kahosl.be
[2] KU Leuven, iMinds-DistriNet,
Celestijnenlaan 200A, 3001 Heverlee, Belgium
firstname.lastname@cs.kuleuven.be

Abstract. This paper presents a formal approach for the analysis of privacy properties of complex electronic services. A flexible framework for logic reasoning allows for formally modeling these services in a typed first-order logic and for inferring privacy properties that can be interpreted by all the stakeholders including consumers. The inference strategy consists of compiling user profiles according to the expectations of the consumer about the data practices of the service providers involved. The data in these profiles originates from information that has been disclosed by the consumer during the service interactions or that may have been exchanged between organizations thereafter. The framework can infer relevant privacy properties from these profiles. To validate our work, the approach is applied to the modeling of a web shop.

Keywords: privacy, trust, electronic services, formal model.

1 Introduction

During the last decades, web services have evolved from simple services offered by a single service provider towards complex web mashups in which multiple stakeholders are involved. For instance, when a user books a trip, an online travel agency may interact with an airline company, a hotel chain, and a payment provider to fulfill the booking request. Similarly, an online music store can rely on a social network service provider to ease registration. In fact, advanced web services are often decomposed in a set of tasks (or sub-services) that are handled by different service providers with strict liabilities and accountabilities. Each provider has acquired experience in specific tasks which may increase the quality of the overall service. Many composite web services present a high level of interaction in which consumer information is exchanged between companies that handle part of the service request. In many cases, information exchange is necessary to accomplish a task. For instance, an online travel agency must pass certain consumer data (like her name and address) to the hotel chain involved

A. Bagchi and I. Ray (Eds.): ICISS 2013, LNCS 8303, pp. 106–120, 2013.

in the booking. Sometimes, information exchange purposes are less clear. Additional consumer data may be collected and thereafter exchanged between service providers to offer a higher degree of personalization or to discriminate users. For instance, an online music store can collect the user's age and country of residence to personalize recommendations which is beneficial for both the consumer and the service provider. However, the latter can also collect additional information from social networking sites to compile advanced profiles that can later be used to impose higher prices to prosperous users. Due to highly complex collaborations between companies in web services, the user has no transparent view on the information that is released to each entity.

Although legislation can oblige organizations to apply data practices that are compliant with their publicly available service policies, conflicts may arise when different organizations, each with their own service policies, collaborate [3]. Privacy policies are often described informally and verifying that a particular policy is correctly applied is often hard. The lack of transparency affects both service providers participating in the composite web service, as well as consumers. Privacy infringements caused by one service provider can decrease the reputation of other organizations participating in the composite web service. Similarly, due to a lack of transparency, users fall back on trust perceptions [12,16,9] when selecting a particular web service.

Contribution. This paper presents a formal approach for the analysis of privacy properties of complex electronic services. A flexible framework for logic reasoning allows for formally modeling these services in a typed first-order logic. These models are expressed using concepts introduced in previous work [6], such as the user and organizations involved in these services, the identifiers to which a user can be linked with, the user's credentials, and the trust relations. Furthermore, the framework's strategy for inferring privacy properties that can be interpreted by all the stakeholders including consumers is elaborated. This strategy consists of compiling user profiles according to the expectations of the consumer about the data practices of the service providers involved. The data in these profiles originates from information that has been disclosed by the consumer during the service interactions or that may have been exchanged between organizations thereafter. The framework can infer relevant privacy properties from these profiles. To validate our work, the approach is applied to the modeling of a web shop.

The rest of this paper is structured as follows. Section 2 gives an overview of related work. The web shop use case is presented in Section 3. It is used throughout in the remainder of this paper. Section 4 describes the framework for logic reasoning and explains the functionality of each component. The input model, that formally specifies the electronic services, is presented in Section 5. Section 6 elaborates on the inference strategy, and demonstrates how privacy properties are derived. The framework is evaluated in section 7. Section 8 summarizes the major contributions and suggests future work.

2 Related Work

Multiple approaches have been presented to inspect privacy related properties. For instance, during the last decade, a lot of research focused on measuring the level and degree of anonymity of users. L. Sweeney [13] introduced the concept of k-anonymity. A set of disclosed data exhibits k-anonymity if this set maps to at least k entities. A. Serjantov and G. Danezis [11] present an information theoretical approach to quantify anonymity. They measure the likelihood to identify an individual as the sender of a message. A user is considered anonymous if no threshold has been exceeded. Our approach focuses on the automatic generation of user profiles that an organization may compile about its customers. These user profiles can serve as input to the approaches above to measure the anonymity level of a particular profile.

Formal protocol models, such as the ones based on π-calculus, can deliver communication level data that is released by communicating entities. For instance, IP addresses, session identifiers and possibly cookies are exchanged in many communication protocols. Recent work applies this strategy for the analysis of an e-voting and e-auction system [5,8]. Another formal approach is proposed by Veeningen et al. [14]. They use a deductive reasoning framework for the analysis of identity management protocols. Whereas those approaches can yield all the data released at the level of communication, ours can inspect the impact of releasing such identifiers on the privacy in user profiles (i.e., when combining them with data disclosed at application level).

The research community also identifies and recognizes the complexity of reasoning about privacy policies and correctly implementing them, especially in systems in which many stakeholders are involved (such as composite web services). Breaux et al. [3] illustrate this with a real-world Facebook-app that forwards data to a third-party advertiser. The latter provides personalized in-app advertisements. They show the complex privacy conflicts that arise due to the privacy policies of each individual organization. They have mapped the privacy policies in human language to formal specifications in description logic. The latter allows to automatically detect conflicts between privacy policies claimed by individual organizations, and to verify if services are consistent with them. Moreover, legislation (e.g., the US privacy act) or directives may constrain data practises applied by organizations. Possibly, conflicts may arise between corporate level service polices and the ones imposed by legislation. To detect conflicts, the authors of [2,7] formally define legislative rules. Le Métayer [10] proposes a formal framework to reason about the impact of design choices on the privacy in advanced decentralized services. Our approach is situated in the same field. In contrast to their work, ours presents higher flexibility in the sense that multiple trust perceptions and identifiability models can be applied to inspect the impact on the profiles collected by different stakeholders.

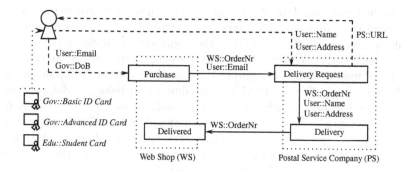

Fig. 1. Overview of the composite web service

3 A Web Shop and Delivery Service

This section presents a composite web service that is used as an example to clarify the concepts throughout the rest of this paper. The major components are depicted in Figure 1. It consists of two service providers, namely a web shop (WS) and a postal service company (PS). A consumer can purchase products at an online website managed by WS. As the shop wants to exclude minors, a consumer needs to prove to be older than 18. The web shop supports two credential technologies to fulfill that prerequisite. Either the consumer uses a basic electronic identity card or a more privacy-friendly one. We assume that the former consists of an X.509 certificate which embeds the customer's *name*, *address*, *date of birth* (DoB), and *social security number* (SSN), and the latter can be an anonymous credential which contains the same attributes. Anonymous credentials allow to selectively disclose attributes. More specifically, a user can prove to be older than 18 without revealing his date of birth. Students can purchase goods at a reduced prize if they show their electronic student card. It consists of an X.509 certificate with the student's *name, address,* and *institute* as attributes. Consumers also need to disclose their email address when they want to buy a product. When a purchase transaction is completed, WS sends transaction details together with personalized recommendations to the consumer's email address. Also, WS shares the order number (OrderNr) and email address (Email) with PS, and the user is redirected to PS. The consumer additionally needs to fill in his *name* and *address* in the registration form provided by PS. PS collects the data and sends a unique hyperlink to the user's mailbox which can be used to track the delivery status. After delivery, PS informs WS that the delivery corresponding to *OrderNr* was successful. Note that, for simplicity, we make abstraction of the data exchanged at communication level.

4 Approach

When invoking a service, information is disclosed to the organization providing the service. This information can contain attributes that are disclosed by the user to the service (e.g., his date of birth and his email address), or data generated by the service or the user during service consumption (e.g., an order number). The information can both be stored by the organization providing the service or be forwarded to other services. These services can, in turn, also store or forward the collected information. The organizations involved can use this information to compile user profiles (i.e., a collection of attributes that belong to the same user). The user profiles that organizations may possibly collect, form the basis from which conclusions about the privacy of the user are drawn. The analysis process requires users to express their trust in the service providers first. For instance, a highly mistrusted service provider is suspected to store – and possibly distribute – more attributes than specified in its service policy.

Figure 2 gives an overview of the major components in the framework of the modeling approach. The *System Independent Modeling component* (i.e., $\mathcal{E} \cup R$) consists of a set of formal sentences that denote generic propositions on systems and can be reused in whatever system (or application) is modeled. For instance, sentences that describe the properties of X.509 certificates. The *Input Model* consists of a *User Model* ($\mathcal{M}_U$), a *System Model* ($\mathcal{M}_S$), and an *Identifiability Model* ($\mathcal{M}_{ID}$). $\mathcal{M}_U$ defines the user's initial state and trust perceptions. Therefore, this component needs to be replaced if a new type of user is modeled. Similarly, $\mathcal{M}_S$ is application specific and needs to be replaced if a new application is modeled. $\mathcal{M}_{ID}$ defines sets of attributes that are each sufficient to distinguish a single user. Some sets are identifiable, others are pseudonymous. For instance, the user's name and date of birth can be an identifiable set, while an email address can be a pseudonymous singleton. A modeler can then decide how strict the notion of identifiability and pseudonymity should be. Finally, the *Logic Component* represents a knowledge-based tool that automatically infers *privacy conclusions* ($\mathcal{M}_O$) based on the System Independent Model and the Input Model. The rest of this section discusses the major components in more detail.

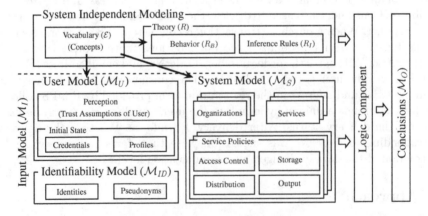

Fig. 2. Framework for logic reasoning about privacy properties in complex electronic services

Vocabulary. The Vocabulary $\mathcal{E}$ consists of three parts, namely $\mathcal{E}_I$, $\mathcal{E}_R$ and $\mathcal{E}_O$. The *input vocabulary* $\mathcal{E}_I$ includes the symbols required for the specification of new systems (or services), $\mathcal{E}_R$ defines theory dependent symbols for reasoning (i.e., they are meant for internal use only), and the *output vocabulary* $\mathcal{E}_O$ includes the symbols necessary to express conclusions. Consequently, new symbols will be defined when new types of conclusions need to be supported.

Theory. The Theory R comprises a set of first-order logic sentences and inductive definitions that are expressed over the vocabulary $\mathcal{E}$. It is divided into a fixed *behavior* theory R_B and an interchangeable *inference* theory R_I. R_B defines the concepts that are fixed for the same kind of inferences. For instance, the non-functional properties of authentication technologies are expressed here. More specifically, formal rules express that multiple transactions with the same X.509 certificate can be linked and that all attributes within an X.509 certificate are released to the service provider, whereas anonymous credentials support unlinkability and selective disclosure of attributes. R_I contains the theory that is required to draw conclusions from a given input model. Depending on the type of conclusions, another (pluggable) inference theory component is used. Section 6 focuses on an instance of R_I that is used to draw conclusions from user profiles kept at different organizations.

System Model. The System Model $\mathcal{M}_S$ defines (a) the set of organizations involved in the composite web service, (b) the set of services they offer, and (c) a set of service policies assigned to those services. Four types of policies are assigned to each service: the access control policy defines the attributes that must be disclosed (or proven) before a service can be consumed; the storage policy defines the set of attributes that will be stored by the service provider (i.e., typically a subset of the attributes released by the user); the distribution policy defines the set of attributes forwarded to other service providers (i.e., also a subset of attributes released by the user); and the output policy defines data generated during service consumption. For instance, a new account that is created or the list of purchased goods.

User Model. The User Model $\mathcal{M}_U$ defines the set of credentials of a single user (only one user of the services is considered in this appraoch). A credential, such as an electronic identity card, is a collection of attributes, certified by an issuer and managed by the user. Credentials and profiles can be used to fulfill access control policies. $\mathcal{M}_U$ also defines the trust perception of the user. More specifically, the framework allows for specifying whether a user trusts that the expressed storage and distribution practices are observed by an organization. Different users may have different trust assumptions. For instance, privacy addicts may have a lower trust in specified data practices than other individuals. The framework allows to model multiple types of individuals.

Logic Component. The Logic Component consists of a logic tool that automates the reasoning on formal models. IDP [15] has been selected for the realization of this logic reasoning system. IDP reasons on models specified in the IDP language which is a formal language based on typed first-order logic. This language has successfully been used for the formal specification of services. IDP reasons about an input model $\mathcal{M}_I$ using a theory R. The results are presented in the output model $\mathcal{M}_O$.

5   Specification of the Input Model

This section shows what elements and relations a modeler needs to express when modeling a particular system. The elements and relations are instantiations of the symbols in the input vocabulary $\mathcal{E}_I \subset \mathcal{E}$, and together form the Input Model $\mathcal{M}_I = \mathcal{M}_S \cup \mathcal{M}_U \cup \mathcal{M}_{ID}$. The presented input specification is based on the web shop scenario described in section 3.

Organizations and Attributes. The organizations that are involved in the system being modeled are part of the *Organization* domain. They participate in services provided to the user or they can issue credentials required by services. The data that is exchanged when invoking services are modeled by attributes that are part of the *Attribute* domain. These represent data types instead of the actual data values. This abstraction is possible due to the single-user approach.

$\mathcal{M}_S$ :: Organization $= \{Government, University, WS, PS\}$
$\mathcal{M}_S$ :: Attribute $= \{Name, Address, DoB, SSN, Institute, OrderNr, URL, Email\}$

Identities and Pseudonyms. The *Identifier* domain groups the elements that allow for linking profiles. Each identifier belongs either to the *Identity* or to the *Pseudonym* domain. The former allows to link a profile to the user, while the latter does not. These are relations that assign a set of attributes to each identity and pseudonym. In our system, one identity $Identity_1 \in \mathfrak{I}$ and four pseudonyms (i.e., singletons) $Nym_i \in \mathfrak{N}$ are defined. The modeler specifies that the user's *Name* and *Address* belong to $Identity_1$ (i.e., collecting both attributes will make someone identifiable), and that the user's *SSN*, *OrderNr*, the unique *URL* provided by the delivery service provider, and *Email* address are unique pseudonyms. Note that another modeler could specify the user's *SSN* as an identity instead of a pseudonym, or specify that the user's *Name* is sufficient to identify the user.

$\mathcal{M}_{ID}$ :: Identifier $= \{Identity_1, Nym_1, Nym_2, Nym_3, Nym_4\}$
$\mathcal{M}_{ID}$ :: Identity $= \{Identity_1\}$
$\mathcal{M}_{ID}$ :: Pseudonym $= \{Nym_1, Nym_2, Nym_3, Nym_4\}$
$\mathcal{M}_{ID}$ :: IdentifierAttr(Identifier, Attribute) $= \{$
        $(Identity_1, Name), (Identity_1, Address),$
        $(Nym_1, SSN), (Nym_2, OrderNr), (Nym_3, URL), (Nym_4, Email)\}$

User Trust Perception. These relations (part of $\mathcal{M}_U$) allow to specify trust perceptions of the user with respect to the organizations in the model. The relations below specify that the user only believes that the postal service company abides his storage policy, and that the web shop observes his distribution policy.

$\mathcal{M}_U$ :: StorageTrust(Organization) = $\{PS\}$
$\mathcal{M}_U$ :: DistributionTrust(Organization) = $\{WS\}$

Credential Specification. All credentials owned by the user are listed in the *Credential* domain. In the web shop scenario, the user may have three credentials, namely, a basic identity card, a privacy-friendly identity card, and optionally a student card. For each credential, multiple properties need to be defined, namely the set of attributes included in the credential, the underlying credential technology that is used, and the credential issuer. In the example, three credential elements are specified in *Credentials*. For instance, the user's name and address are embedded in the *BasicIDCard*, which is an X.509 certificate issued by the *Government*.

$\mathcal{M}_U$ :: Credential = $\{BasicIDCard, PrivIDCard, StudentCard\}$
$\mathcal{M}_U$ :: CredAttr(Credential, Attribute) = {
    $(BasicIDCard, Name), (BasicIDCard, Address), \ldots,$
    $(PrivIDCard, Name), \ldots\}$
$\mathcal{M}_U$ :: CredTech(Credential, ClaimbasedTech) = {
    $(BasicIDCard, X509), (PrivIDCard, Idemix), \ldots\}$
$\mathcal{M}_U$ :: CredIssuer(Credential, Organization) = {
    $(BasicIDCard, Government), (PrivIDCard, Government), \ldots\}$

Services and Service Policies. Each service is uniquely identified by a *ServiceIdentifier* and consists of the *ServiceType* and the organization providing the service. The relations below focus on the specification of a service identified by *BasicPurchaseServ*. In addition, for each service the applicable policies are specified. The access control policy (e.g., PurchaseAccessPol) specifies the attributes that need to be disclosed and their source in order to grant access (e.g., reveal *DoB* from the *BasicIDCard*). The storage policy specifies the attributes that are stored and the distribution policy defines which attributes are sent to another service. As shown below, *BasicPurchaseServ* forwards *OrderNr* to the postal company when invoking *DeliveryRequestServ*. Optionally, an output policy specifies the data returned to the user when the service was invoked.

$\mathcal{M}_S$ :: ServiceType = $\{Purchase, Delivery, DeliveryRequest, Delivered\}$
$\mathcal{M}_S$ :: ServiceIdentifier = $\{BasicPurchaseServ, PrivPurchaseServ,$
    $DeliveryRequestServ, \ldots\}$
$\mathcal{M}_S$ :: Service(ServiceIdentifier, ServiceType, Organization) = {
    $(BasicPurchaseServ, Purchase, WS),$
    $(PrivPurchaseServ, Purchase, WS),$
    $(DeliveryRequestServ, DeliveryRequest, PS), \ldots\}$
$\mathcal{M}_S$ :: ServicePolicies(ServiceIdentifier, AccessPolicy, StoragePolicy,
    DistributionPolicy, OutputPolicy) = {
        $(BasicPurchaseServ, PurchaseAccessPol, PurchaseStorePol,$
        $PurchaseDistrPol, PurchaseOutPol), \ldots\}$
$\mathcal{M}_S$ :: RevealAttr(AccessPolicy, AttrSrc, Attribute) = {
    $(PurchaseAccessPol, BasicIDCard, DoB), \ldots\}$

$\mathcal{M}_S$ :: StoreAttr(StoragePolicy, Attribute) = {$PurchaseStorePol$, $OrderNr$), ...}
$\mathcal{M}_S$ :: DistrAttrTo(DistributionPolicy, ServiceIdentifier, Attribute) = {
   ($PurchaseDistrPol$, $DeliveryRequestServ$, $OrderNr$), ...}
$\mathcal{M}_S$ :: OutputAttr(OutputPolicy, Attribute) = {($PurchaseOutPol$, URL)}

6 Inferring Privacy Based on Trust

This section presents the general idea behind the inference rules R_I that the automated reasoning system applies to the input model $\mathcal{M}_I$. The inference strategy starts from a *service invocation graph*, which is a representation of the possible invocations of services which may either be directly or indirectly invoked by a user. It is used to compile user profiles that belongs to organizations, based on the user's trust in the involved organizations. These user profiles show for each organization the personal information that can be linked to the same user and possibly make him identifiable. In the rest of this section, this inference strategy is further discussed and demonstrated using the web shop scenario.

Service Invocation Graph. This is an acyclic directed graph $G = \langle \Delta, \mathcal{F} \rangle$, where each node $\delta_o \in \Delta_o$ represents a service provided by organization $o \in O$, with $\Delta_o \subseteq \Delta$ the set of services provided by o. Each edge $f \in \mathcal{F} \subseteq \Delta \times \Delta$ defines the invocation of a service by another service. These edges are derived from the data distribution specifications of the service policies. Nodes without incoming edges, denoted by $\delta_o^* \in \Delta^* \subseteq \Delta$, are only invokable by users. We assume that services can neither directly nor indirectly invoke themselves. As a result, this graph is acyclic and a *strict order relation* $<_G$ on Δ can be defined that expresses the relative invocation order between services. For instance, $\delta_o^i <_G \delta_{o'}^j$, expresses that $\delta_{o'}^j$ is invoked by δ_o^i (directly or indirectly), with $\delta_o^i, \delta_{o'}^j \in \Delta$. Note that a service policy is assigned to each service.

The service invocation graph for the web shop scenario is illustrated in Figure 3. As an example, when a user makes a purchase at the web shop, the web shop sends a delivery request to the postal service. There are four alternative invocations that depend on the selected purchase option. One of them is presented by an edge in the service invocation graph from the *WS:BasicPurchase* service (δ_{WS}^{a*}) to the *PS:DeliveryRequest* service (δ_{PS}^1). The other incoming edges of δ_{PS}^1 represent the other alternatives.

Figure 3 also shows the sub-graph $G_{\delta_{\text{WS}}^{a*}}$ of G. This sub-graph includes all services that are invoked when invoking δ_{WS}^{a*}. Semantically, it corresponds to the services in the web shop scenario that are invoked when a product is purchased with a basic ID card. More formally, $G_{\delta_o^*} = \langle \Delta_{\delta_o^*}, \mathcal{F}_{\delta_o^*} \rangle$ is the sub-graph for a user invocable service δ_o^* that is defined by $\Delta_{\delta_o^*} = \{\delta_{o'} \in \Delta \mid \delta_o^* <_G \delta_{o'}\} \cup \{\delta_o^*\}$ and $\mathcal{F}_{\delta_o^*} = \{(\delta_{o'}^i, \delta_{o''}^j) \in \mathcal{F} \mid \delta_{o'}^i \in \Delta_{\delta_o^*} \wedge \delta_{o''}^j \in \Delta_{\delta_o^*}\}$, with $o', o'' \in O$. We assume that the sub-graph contains no alternative service invocations (i.e., nodes have at most one incoming edge). Therefore, it forms a tree with root node δ_o^*. Starting from these sub-graphs $G_{\delta_o^*}$, user profiles are compiled.

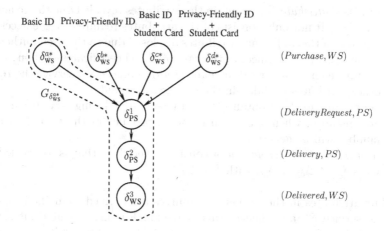

Fig. 3. Service invocation graph G of the web shop scenario

User Profiles. In this approach, we analyze the user's privacy even when organizations are not trustworthy. Therefore, the user profiles that are built, are not only based on what is specified in the service policies, but also on the user's trust perception. In other words, profiles satisfy the user's expectations. The user's trust is specified in relation to the data storage and data distribution policies of organizations:

- *Storage trust* ($o \in T_S$), specifies that for each service $\delta_o \in \Delta_o$, the user believes that only the attributes Ω_{δ_o} specified in the storage policy of δ_o, are actually stored. Without storage trust, all data possibly collected by these services, is expected to be stored.
- *Distribution trust* ($o \in T_D$), specifies that for each service $\delta_o \in \Delta_o$, the user believes that only the attributes Θ_{δ_o} specified in the distribution policy of δ_o, are forwarded to the specified service. Otherwise, all data possibly collected by these services, is expected to be forwarded.

The compilation of user profiles, that organizations build by executing a *user invokable service* δ_o^*, consists of two steps. In the first step, the sub-profile $P(\delta_{o'}|\delta_o^*)$ is compiled for each service $\delta_{o'} \in \Delta_{\delta_o^*}$. It defines the attributes that are kept persistently by o' when executing $\delta_{o'}$. Next, the sub-profiles of different services that are kept by an organization, are combined to compile its user profiles.

STEP1: compiling sub-profiles for δ_o^*. A sub-profile $P(\delta_{o'}|\delta_o^*)$ is compiled for each of the nodes $\delta_{o'}$ of the sub-graph $G_{\delta_o^*}$ and consists of the attributes that are collected by $\delta_{o'}$ with respect to the user's expectations. In case of storage trust, generating the sub-profile $P(\delta_{o'}|\delta_o^*)$, given by Eq. (1a), is trivial. The stored attributes are specified explicitly in the storage policy of that service. On the other hand, Eq. (1b) specifies the compilation of a sub-profile when there is no storage trust. This involves different sources of attributes, namely:

- *disclosed attributes* $\Upsilon_{\delta_{o'}}$ contain the attributes revealed due to the access policy of $\delta_{o'}$. It not only consists of the attributes required by the access policy, but also of the additional attributes disclosed due to the used authentication technology. For instance, in the case of X.509 certificates, although the user is only required to reveal his *date of birth* to access a service, he reveals all other attributes included in the certificate as well.
- *generated data* $\Gamma_{\delta_{o'}}$ contains the data generated during service consumption. For instance, when a user purchases a product in the web shop an order number will be generated.
- *forwarded attributes* $\Phi(\delta_{o'}|\delta_o^*)$ consist of the data that is forwarded by services $\delta_{o''} \in \Delta_{\delta_o^*}$ to $\delta_{o'}$, with $\delta_{o''} <_G \delta_{o'}$.

The attributes in the former two sources are derived from the access policy of the service $\delta_{o'}$ and, hence, this is trivial. Finding the attributes that are forwarded to $\delta_{o'}$ is more complex and depends on the distribution trust with respect to the services that are forwarding data to this service.

$$P(\delta_{o'}|\delta_o^*) = \begin{cases} \Omega_{\delta_{o'}}, & o' \in T_S \quad (1a) \\ \Upsilon_{\delta_{o'}} \cup \Gamma_{\delta_{o'}} \cup \Phi(\delta_{o'}|\delta_o^*), & o' \notin T_S \quad (1b) \end{cases}$$

$$\Phi(\delta_{o'}^i|\delta_o^*) = \begin{cases} \Theta_{\delta_{o''}^j}, & o'' \in T_D \quad (2a) \\ \Upsilon_{\delta_{o''}^j} \cup \Gamma_{\delta_{o''}^j} \cup \Phi(\delta_{o''}^j|\delta_o^*), & o'' \notin T_D \quad (2b) \end{cases}$$

with $\Phi(\delta_{o'}|\delta_o^*) = \emptyset$ for $\delta_{o'} = \delta_o^*$, and $\delta_{o''}^j = pred(\delta_{o'}^i)$

Equations (2a) and (2b) express the data that is forwarded to service $\delta_{o'}^i$ by the service $\delta_{o''}^j$ that directly invokes it (i.e., $\delta_{o'}^i = pred(\delta_{o'}^j)$). The attributes forwarded by $\delta_{o''}^j$, in case of distribution trust, are given by Eq. (2a) and are specified in its distribution policy. Equation (2b) shows the attributes that are forwarded by $\delta_{o''}^j$ in case when there is no distribution trust. It forwards all the attributes that it generates itself ($\Gamma_{\delta_{o''}^j}$) and that are disclosed to it due to its own access policy ($\Upsilon_{\delta_{o''}^j}$) or that have been forwarded by its predecessor ($\Phi(\delta_{o'}^j|\delta_o^*)$). When applied to the web shop scenario presented in Figure 1, the data received by the *WS::Delivered* service depends on how much trust the customer has in the parties involved. The service will only receive the order number *OrderNr* from the *PS:Delivery* service, when the user has distribution trust in the postal service company PS ($PS \in T_D$). Whereas when $PS \notin T_D$, *WS:Delivered* may not only receive *OrderNr* from *PS:Delivery*, but also the *Name* and *Address* of the user and the *URL* to track the delivery status of the purchase.

STEP 2: Compiling user profiles. Organizations compile their user profiles using their sub-profiles they generated in the previous step. This requires the presence of one or more shared identifiers $id \in \mathfrak{I} \cup \mathfrak{N}$. Initially, all sub-profiles that include an identifier, are considered as user profiles. User profiles sharing a same identifier are merged into a single user profile that contains all the attributes from these user profiles. Since identifiers may be defined as a set of attributes (see Section 5), and these attributes may be spread over different user profiles, merging these profiles may have as side-effect that a new identifier appears in the resulting profile. Therefore, this step is repeated until no new identifiers are formed in the merged user profiles. As a result, a number of user profiles $P_{o'}^{id}(G|\delta_o^*)$ are compiled with attributes that can be linked by organization o' to a unique identifier id after the user invoked service δ_o^*. Hence, the organization may keep multiple user profiles of the same user that cannot be linked to each other (i.e., they have no shared identifiers). Note that the same user profile may contain multiple identifiers.

Impact of Multiple Service Invocations on Profiles. Until now, we have focused on the profiles that can be compiled when a user invokes a single service δ_o^*. However, in practice, a user typically invokes multiple services over time. Hence, user profiles often grow gradually. For instance, in the web shop scenario, the user purchases a product with a *BasicIDCard* and *StudentCard* (i.e., service invocation δ_{ws}^{b*}). Later on, he receives an *PrivIDCard* from the government and quits high school. If he then purchases an item, service invocation δ_{ws}^{b*} is applied. Similarly, consider a web shop that offers three services to users, namely *Register*, *Browse*, and *Purchase*. When browsing the site, a persistent cookie is installed that is requested each time to personalize offers. Before a user can *Purchase* a product, he must *Register*. At that phase, additional attributes are possibly disclosed. In that case, it does not make sense to only evaluate the impact of the service invocation *Purchase* on the profiles kept by organizations. On the contrary, the impact of multiple types of service invocations on the profiles is relevant. Our framework easily compiles profiles that result from multiple invocations. $P_{o'}^{id}(G|[\delta_{o_a}^{a*}, \delta_{o_b}^{b*}, ..., \delta_{o_x}^{x*}])$ defines the expected profile kept by o' with attributes linked to id after a sequence of services $[\delta_{o_a}^{a*}, \delta_{o_b}^{b*}, ..., \delta_{o_x}^{x*}]$ are invoked by the user. $P_{o'}^{id}(G|[\delta_{o_a}^{a*}, \delta_{o_b}^{b*}, ..., \delta_{o_x}^{x*}])$ is constructed by merging all the profiles $P_{o'}^{id}(G|\delta_{o_i}^{i*})$ with $\delta_{o_i}^{i*} \in [\delta_{o_a}^{a*}, \delta_{o_b}^{b*}, ..., \delta_{o_x}^{x*}]$.

7   Evaluation

To validate the framework, both the Theory R – including the behavior R_B and inference rules R_I – and the input model $\mathcal{M}_I$ for the web shop scenario were realized[1] in IDP.This is used to compare the alternative services of *WS::Purchase* (i.e., δ_{ws}^a, δ_{ws}^{b*}, δ_{ws}^{c*}, and δ_{ws}^{d*}) under different trust perceptions of the user. When considering the case in which both the web shop and postal service company, comply with their service policies (i.e., this corresponds with a user perception where services are fully trusted), the resulting user profiles are independent of the used credentials. WS stores only the *OrderNr* and *Email*. PS instead, stores the user's *Name* and *Address*, the *OrderNr* and the tracking *URL*. Both organizations have user profiles that are pseudonymous. The postal service can also identify the user by his *Name* and *Address* from its user profile. When no storage trust

---

[1] See http://code.google.com/p/inspect-privacy-and-trust/, 2013

Table 1. User's additional attributes in the web shop's user profile related to the case where both organizations are trusted

	$T_S = \{PS\}, T_D = \{WS, PS\}$	$T_S = \{PS\}, T_D = \{WS\}$
$P^{id}_{ws}(G|\delta^{a*}_{ws})$	Name, Address, DoB, SSN	Name, Address, URL, DoB, SSN
$P^{id}_{ws}(G|\delta^{b*}_{ws})$	—	Name, Address, URL
$P^{id}_{ws}(G|\delta^{c*}_{ws})$	Name, Address, DoB, SSN, Institute	Name, Address, URL, DoB, SSN, Institute
$P^{id}_{ws}(G|\delta^{d*}_{ws})$	Name, Address, Institute	Name, Address, URL, Institute

is present in both WS and PS, extra attributes are part of the user profiles and it depends on the distribution trust of the user. Table 1 presents the extra attributes collected in the web shop's user profile for the alternative services of *WS::Purchase* under different trust perceptions. In the second column, the user has distribution trust in both organizations, while in the third column he only trusts WS. The table clearly shows that, except for service δ^{b*}_{ws} that uses the privacy-friendly ID card (when $T_D = \{WS, PS\}$), the user is always identifiable by the web shop. These two examples illustrate some of the conclusions generated by the framework. For instance, to remain unidentifiable towards WS, the user needs to trust the storage and distribution policies of both WS and PS.

In addition, user profiles are bounded by a minimum and maximum. For the user profile $P^{id}_{o'}(G|\delta^*_o)$ we get that $P^{id}_{o'}(G|\delta^*_o)^{\mathfrak{T}_{max}} \subseteq P^{id}_{o'}(G|\delta^*_o) \subseteq P^{id}_{o'}(G|\delta^*_o)^{\mathfrak{T}_{min}}$. The minimum user profile corresponds to a full user trust perception $\mathfrak{T}_{max} = \{T^{max}_S, T^{max}_D\}$, where $\forall o' \in O : o' \in T^{max}_S \wedge o' \in T^{max}_D$. The maximum user profile instead, corresponds to a user that has no trust $\mathfrak{T}_{min} = \{T^{min}_S, T^{min}_D\}$, with $T^{min}_S = \emptyset$ and $T^{min}_D = \emptyset$. It is trivial to show this order between user profiles using equations, (1a), (1b), (2a), and (2b). This requires the definition of the order relation between two trust perceptions $\mathfrak{T}_u = \{T^u_S, T^u_D\}$ and $\mathfrak{T}_v = \{T^v_S, T^v_D\}$, namely $\mathfrak{T}_u \geq \mathfrak{T}_v$, with $\mathfrak{T}_u \geq \mathfrak{T}_v \Leftrightarrow T^v_S \subseteq T^u_S \wedge T^v_D \subseteq T^u_D$.

Flexibility. Different *types of users* are easily modeled based on the user's initial state (e.g., the credentials the user owns) and his trust perception. Modelers can use this to estimate the acceptance of a system for different types of real-world users, since their perceptions influence their attitude towards the attributes they disclose [16,9]. Furthermore, our framework supports a less strict definition of *identifiability* and *pseudonymity* represented in the identifiability model $\mathcal{M}_{ID}$, which may be closer to their real-world counterparts.

Basic Framework. The approach presented here, is a basic framework for the analysis of the privacy of users across different organizations. This framework already allows to analyze many real-world scenarios and offers interesting conclusions. Nevertheless, the framework can easily be extended to include many more features, and coarse grained concepts proposed here can be further refined. Extra inference rules R_I can be added to the theory R to extract more conclusions. For instance, inference rules can be defined to show the gradual growth of the user's profiles over time for each additional invocation of a service. Other inference rules may be used to verify the correctness (consistency) of the input model or show the resulting user profiles when organizations collude. Extensions to the vocabulary $\mathcal{E}$ may be necessary when defining new conclusions and adding new inference rules to the framework. However, both inference rules and vocabularies can be part of a library that is available to modelers. Currently, the user's trust perception is rather coarse grained based on storage and distribution trust. Although it may express many real-world settings, the framework can easily be extended with more fine-grained trust perceptions.

Usability. Current service policies often vaguely describe their data practices. It is, therefore, not trivial to use them as an input to automatically generate the system model. Recent research [4,1] presents proposals that enforce organizations to act according to the service policies that accurately describe their data practices. These formal representations can be used to automatically derive the system model in our framework. To make the system modeling more comprehensive for non-experts, an input and output component can be added to the framework. For instance, the input component can automatically generate a user model $\mathcal{M}_U$ and identifiability model $\mathcal{M}_{ID}$ from a graphical representation made by the modeler. Similarly, a graphical representation of the conclusions can be created to ease the interpretation of the generated output.

8 Conclusion

A formal approach to analyze privacy properties of complex electronic services is presented. We describe a framework and its components to model these services in a typed first-order logic. An inference strategy is proposed to compile user profiles from service policies of involved service providers. These profiles, from which privacy properties are derived, are according to the user's expectations about the provider's actual data practices. To show the framework's flexibility, it is realized and applied to a modeled web shop. The inference strategy that is used, focuses on the privacy of a single service invoked by a user. However, we argue that it is relevant to consider multiple service invocations and we show how the inference can be extended for this. Future work will elaborate on this.

Acknowledgements. This work was made possible through funding from the MobCom project, granted by the Flemish *agency for Innovation by Science and Technology (IWT)*.

References

1. Ardagna, C.A., De Capitani di Vimercati, S., Neven, G., Paraboschi, S., Preiss, F.-S., Samarati, P., Verdicchio, M.: Enabling privacy-preserving credential-based access control with xacml and saml. In: Proceedings of the 2010 10th IEEE International Conference on Computer and Information Technology, CIT 2010, pp. 1090–1095. IEEE Computer Society, Washington, DC (2010)
2. Barth, A., Datta, A., Mitchell, J.C., Nissenbaum, H.: Privacy and contextual integrity: Framework and applications. In: Proceedings of the 2006 IEEE Symposium on Security and Privacy, SP 2006, pp. 184–198. IEEE Computer Society, Washington, DC (2006)

3. Breaux, T.D., Rao, A.: Formal analysis of privacy requirements specifications for multi-tier applications. In: RE 2013: Proceedings of the 21st IEEE International Requirements Engineering Conference, RE 2013. IEEE Society Press, Washington, DC (2013)
4. Camenisch, J., Mödersheim, S., Neven, G., Preiss, F.-S., Sommer, D.: A card requirements language enabling privacy-preserving access control. In: Proceedings of the 15th ACM Symposium on Access Control Models and Technologies, SACMAT 2010, pp. 119–128. ACM, New York (2010)
5. Cortier, V., Wiedling, C.: A formal analysis of the norwegian e-voting protocol. In: Degano, P., Guttman, J.D. (eds.) Principles of Security and Trust. LNCS, vol. 7215, pp. 109–128. Springer, Heidelberg (2012)
6. Decroix, K., Lapon, J., De Decker, B., Naessens, V.: A formal approach for inspecting privacy and trust in advanced electronic services. In: Jürjens, J., Livshits, B., Scandariato, R. (eds.) ESSoS 2013. LNCS, vol. 7781, pp. 155–170. Springer, Heidelberg (2013)
7. DeYoung, H., Garg, D., Jia, L., Kaynar, D., Datta, A.: Experiences in the logical specification of the hipaa and glba privacy laws. In: Proceedings of the 9th Annual ACM Workshop on Privacy in the Electronic Society, WPES 2010, pp. 73–82. ACM, New York (2010)
8. Dreier, J., Lafourcade, P., Lakhnech, Y.: Formal verification of e-auction protocols. In: Basin, D., Mitchell, J.C. (eds.) POST 2013 (ETAPS 2013). LNCS, vol. 7796, pp. 247–266. Springer, Heidelberg (2013)
9. Dwyer, C., Hiltz, S.R., Passerini, K.: Trust and privacy concern within social networking sites: A comparison of facebook and myspace. In: Proceedings of the Thirteenth Americas Conference on Information Systems, AMCIS 2007, Paper 339 (2007)
10. Métayer, D.L.: Privacy by design: a formal framework for the analysis of architectural choices. In: Proceedings of the Third ACM Conference on Data and Application Security and Privacy, CODASPY 2013, pp. 95–104. ACM, New York (2013)
11. Serjantov, A., Danezis, G.: Towards an information theoretic metric for anonymity. In: Dingledine, R., Syverson, P.F. (eds.) PET 2002. LNCS, vol. 2482, pp. 41–53. Springer, Heidelberg (2003)
12. Shin, D.-H.: The effects of trust, security and privacy in social networking: A security-based approach to understand the pattern of adoption. Interact. Comput. 22(5), 428–438 (2010)
13. Sweeney, L.: k-anonymity: a model for protecting privacy. Int. J. Uncertain. Fuzziness Knowl. -Based Syst. 10(5), 557–570 (2002)
14. Veeningen, M., de Weger, B., Zannone, N.: Formal privacy analysis of communication protocols for identity management. In: Jajodia, S., Mazumdar, C. (eds.) ICISS 2011. LNCS, vol. 7093, pp. 235–249. Springer, Heidelberg (2011)
15. Wittocx, J., Mariën, M., Denecker, M.: The IDP system: a model expansion system for an extension of classical logic. In: LaSh, pp. 153–165 (2008)
16. Young, A.L., Quan-Haase, A.: Information revelation and internet privacy concerns on social network sites: a case study of facebook. In: Proceedings of the Fourth International Conference on Communities and Technologies, CT 2009, pp. 265–274. ACM, New York (2009)

Correctness Verification in Outsourced Databases: More *Reliable* Fake Tuples Approach

Ganugula Umadevi and Ashutosh Saxena

Infosys Labs, Infosys Limited, Hyderabad, India
{Uma_Ganugula,Ashutosh_Saxena01}@Infosys.Com

Abstract. Enterprises outsource data to storage service providers in order to avail resources at lower costs and for ensuring economy of scale. Prime concerns of organizations are privacy of data and quality of service provided, which include correctness of query results and integrity of data. In earlier works, integrity of data is verified by preserving hash of tuple data as *header* attribute and completeness is assured by inserting and retrieving fake tuples. In this work, we propose a secret sharing based approach for deterministic generation of fake tuples used for verifying completeness and integrity of data, where we eliminate the dependency on header attribute. Our integrity check mechanisms work faster than existing approaches in this direction as depicted in our experimental results. Furthermore, we show that our approach is information theoretically secure, where an adversary without knowledge of underlying security parameters can never be able to break the scheme.

Keywords: Database Outsourcing, Query Integrity, Fake Tuples.

1 Introduction

The necessity for economical solutions for organizations drive them towards options like Storage as a Service (SaaS) [1]. SaaS provides the opportunity to preserve the organization's data in external servers at a reasonable cost for storage. However, the benefits of this facility do not stop the organizations from being skeptical about the security and privacy issues of their outsourced data. To provide security to the data, organizations usually opt for encrypting critical data before it is uploaded to the third party servers. They employ indices to search upon the encrypted data. Another aspect of concern for organizations is the integrity of query results, which means the results are accurate and data is not altered at the server's end. This process of checking for data integrity is referred to as correctness verification of the outsourced databases.

In correctness verification of outsourced databases, three aspects are considered: a) Completeness b) Freshness c) Integrity. Completeness ensures that the query results are correct and complete. Freshness ensures that the query results are up to date. Integrity ensures that the data is not tampered in transit or at rest. In the literature, there are multiple approaches for addressing the problem of verifying correctness of query results in outsourced databases. In [2–4],

A. Bagchi and I. Ray (Eds.): ICISS 2013, LNCS 8303, pp. 121–132, 2013.

hash of encrypted data is computed and stored, for checking integrity. Since, any change in the encrypted data is reflected in the hash, changes in original data are detected. In [5], the database is restructured as a Merkle-Hash tree for verification. In [6], hash of the tuple is computed and stored as an extra attribute in each tuple. For verifying correctness, the solution proceeds by insertion of check points in the database. These check points, which are referred to as *fake tuples or artificial tuples*, are created and inserted into the database along with the original data. When query results are retrieved, the number of fake tuples returned are compared against the number of tuples originally inserted; change in the count value of fake tuples indicate adversarial changes to original data [6]. In [7], random and deterministic ways to generate fake tuples are proposed. There are techniques which use secret sharing [8] for generating fake tuples. Hash based techniques are mainly used for integrity check. The fake tuple techniques are used for completeness verification of query results.

The drawbacks of the solutions discussed in literature are (a) approaches discussed in [5, 13] are computationally heavy or (b) fail to ensure integrity for complete query results. In [6], an extra attribute holding hash is used to identify tuple/data integrity. An adversary who has knowledge of this scheme can delete the entire attribute and disturb the integrity check process completely. Approaches for completeness discussed in [7], focus on the verification of the retrieved fake tuples for completeness check and discusses majorly on building trust on the storage server. Approaches discussed in [5] require fake tuples be stored at the organization's desk, which is space-consuming and is conflicting with the idea of using SaaS.

In the data outsourcing scenario, we propose an approach to ensure integrity for the entire query result set. Unlike existing approaches, data for integrity check is not stored as an explicit attribute but is stored as a tuple along with the original data; so that it can not be easily tampered. We ensure information theoretic strength for the approach, when the security parameters are not disclosed to an adversary. The computation and communication overhead of our approach are comparable to existing works [6]. For completeness, we use the fake tuple based approach which can be used to build trust [7]. Unlike the work of [8], we use data available in the database along with the concept of secret sharing to generate fake tuples which can be used for integrity and completeness check; and the proposed approach is storage-efficient.

Paper Organization. In section 2, we explain the notations and well-known techniques that we have used in the work. Section 3 explains the approach for correctness verification, where we discuss how integrity and completeness are checked for outsourced databases. In section 4, we analyze the functionality of the approach, in formal terms for strength and security aspects, cost and computation effort and also in terms of features and limitations with respect to handling database updates. We conclude and discuss future work in section 5.

2   Notations and Preliminaries

We refer to the SaaS providers as servers S and organizations storing data at S as the client C. Let Q be test query, which is associated with the fake tuples. We denote the result set of query Q as R_Q. $T_1, T_2, \ldots, T_n$ are the tuples returned by Q, where n is a symbolic indication of the number of tuples returned by Q. $A_1, A_2, \ldots, A_\omega$ are the attributes, where A_p is the primary key attribute of the table. Without loss of generality, we assume that values of attributes $A_1, A_2, \ldots, A_\omega \in \mathbb{R}$, where $\mathbb{R}$ is the set of real numbers and the domain for $A_1, A_2, \ldots, A_\omega$. Table 1 gives the list of notations used in rest of the paper.

Table 1. Notations

Notation	Description
PRG	Pseudo random number generator
V_{F_T}	Verifier Fake Tuple
S_{F_T}	Supporting Fake Tuples
L	Set of storage locations of the supporting fake tuples
k	Count of tuples used for V_{F_T} generation
δ	Count of supporting fake tuples inserted into the database

Shamir Secret Sharing: Shamir Secret Sharing(SSS)[11] is a cryptographic technique where a secret value is distributed among a group of players. Each player gets a share which is computed by evaluating a polynomial at the unique player *id*. In SSS, a polynomial $f(.)$ is considered such that, for the threshold of k players (k players can reconstruct the secret), a $k-1$ degree polynomial is constructed such that $f(0) = s$, where s is the secret to be shared amongst the players. When k players come together, the polynomial is reconstructed and secret value is retrieved from the polynomial. SSS is information theoretically secure. The strength of SSS comes from theorem 1. The proof of the theorem discussed in [9, 10] plays a critical role for ensuring unique reconstruction property of Shamir secret sharing scheme [11]. We use the secret sharing technique in our fake tuple generation process discussed in the later sections.

Theorem 1. (Lagrange interpolation theorem). Let $\mathbb{R}$ be a field and $a_0, \ldots, a_n$, $y_0, \ldots, y_n \in \mathbb{R}$ so that all values a_i are distinct. Then there exists only one polynomial f over $\mathbb{R}$ so that $deg(f) \leq n$ and $f(a_i) = y_i$, $(i = 0; \ldots; n)$.

3   Query Integrity Verification: The Approach

The idea is to insert fake tuples along with original data in the database, such that integrity and completeness of result set for a given query (R_Q) is verified. In this section, we discuss the approach for generating the fake tuples for numeric data in a deterministic way. For non-numeric data types like varchar, char, string,

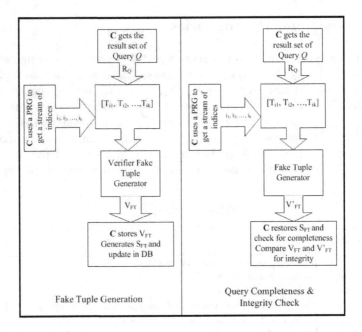

Fig. 1. Query Integrity and Completeness Verification

blob, they can be converted to numeric by doing a character-wise ascii conversion for char datatypes and by doing base conversion for blob datatypes, based on design requirements.

Figure 1 shows the outline of the approach. When the client C submits the query Q to the server S, then the server returns the result set R_Q. We create a set $PA = \{A_{p1}, A_{p2}, \ldots, A_{p\tau}\}$, where the elements A_{pi} are the primary key values of of ith tuple of R_Q, and τ indicates the number of tuples in R_Q. We pick a non-empty subset of the result set R_Q using a pseudo random generator PRG to get some indices in PA. We observe that, dependency on PA and A_p can be reduced by associating a dummy id to the chosen tuples and by storing the hash of the tuple for its unique identification from R_Q. In detail, the PRG generates a stream of indices, from which we select first k values $(i_1, i_2, \ldots, i_k)$ which lie in the set PA. From the result set R_Q, the tuples corresponding to these indices are retrieved. These tuples are input to the Fake Tuple Generator, which produces the verifier fake tuple V_{F_T}. V_{F_T} is used to generate the supporting fake tuples S_{F_T}. This V_{F_T} is split into supporting fake tuples S_{F_T} according to a deterministic function. These supporting fake tuples are inserted into the database at locations L. The query Q, the PRG with its seed, the value k, the fake tuple V_{F_T}, location set L and functions associated with S_{F_T} are stored at C.

In the verification phase, V'_{F_T} is generated and checked against the stored values for query completeness and integrity as explained in tables 2,3 and 4. While computing V_{F_T} and S_{F_T}, the queries of generic nature are chosen, such that they can be applied anytime for insert into a given table. An example query is, SELECT * FROM *Table* where $A_i \geq V_1$ *and* $A_i \leq V_2$, where V_1 and V_2 are values in the range of A_i. When an integrity check needs to be performed, a random query can be given to the database along with the clause on A_i. Since the results returned by random query has the data used for V_{F_T} and S_{F_T}, the returned results can be verified. Based on this kind of range queries, for every instance of database insert update, fake tuples can be created and included into the original data before inserting into the original database. C being the owner of the data, decides the queries applicable for integrity check.

Table 2. Verifier Fake Tuple Generation

Method for generating Verifier Fake tuple
1. For each of $T_{i1}, T_{i2}, \ldots, T_{ik}$, C collects the A_x, A_p value pairs to form points $P_{i1}, P_{i2}, \ldots, P_{ik}$; where point $P_{ij} = $ (attribute A_p value of R_{ij}, attribute A_x value of R_{ij}).
2. $\mathcal{F}_1$ can be explained as: Using a curve fitting algorithm, C interpolates these points to get a $k-1$ degree polynomial.
3. A_x of V_{F_T} is assigned the value of the constant term of the resulting polynomial.

3.1 Fake Tuple Generator

Verifier Fake Tuple Generation. Given the result set of the query Q, R_Q and the chosen indices from the stream of indices generated from the PRG, we explain the deterministic approach used by the client C to generate the fake tuple. Let $T_{i1}, T_{i2}, \ldots, T_{ik}$ be the tuples chosen for creating the fake tuple. As defined earlier, $A_1, A_2, \ldots, A_\omega$ are the attributes of the table, where A_p is the primary key attribute. To generate attribute A_x for V_{F_T}, the function $\mathcal{F}_1 : (\mathbb{R}, \mathbb{R})^k \to \mathbb{R}$, where $x \in \{1, \ldots, \omega\} \backslash \{p\}$ is an indicator of the location in the list of attributes, the method used by C is given in table 2.

Supporting Fake Tuple Generation. Once the verifier fake tuple is constructed, C uses this V_{F_T} to construct the supporting fake tuples. In table 3, we discuss the supporting fake tuple generation using secret sharing schemes, whereas in table 4, we use *PRG* for generating S_{F_T}. Here $V_{F_T}^{A_x}$ is the A_x attribute of V_{F_T}.

3.2 Integrity Check of Database

In the scenario where the database has not undergone any updates, the process for verifying the result set for query Q is explained as follows:

Table 3. Secret Sharing Based S_{F_T} Generation

Method for generating Supporting Fake tuples
1. C chooses a random value δ based on his choice of number of supporting fake tuples.
2. C computes $S_{F_T}^{A_x} = f_{A_x}(i)$, where $f_{A_x}(0) = V_{F_T}^{A_x}$. $S_{F_T}^{A_x}$ are shares generated by SSS using $f_{A_x}(.)$, which is a polynomial of degree $\delta - 1$ defined over $\mathbb{Z}_p$, where p is the prime closer to $max(A_x)$.
3. These $S_{F_{Ti}}$ form the supporting fake tuples, which are inserted into the database.
Reconstructing V_{F_T}: For the chosen query Q, C gets R_Q from the database and using the *secret reconstructing* algorithm, V_{F_T} is reconstructed from δ S_{F_T}s.

1. C submits the query Q and obtains the result set R_Q. C gathers all the A_p values of tuples in the resulting set.
2. Using the PRG definition along with the seed, it generates and gathers k indices falling in the A_p set in a deterministic way. Using the Fake Tuple Generator, it generates the fake tuple V'_{F_T}.
3. Once the original verifier fake tuple V_{F_T} is extracted, it is compared against V'_{F_T}. For each of the attributes, other than A_p, if $V'_{F_T} = V_{F_T}$, it indicates that the integrity of query results is preserved.

3.3 Completeness Check of Database

Completeness of the query results is checked using the supporting fake tuples. In the scenario where the database has not undergone any updates, we explain the completeness verification process for result set of Q.

1. C fires the query Q and obtains the result set R_Q.
2. Using the location information L, C gathers all supporting tuples, $S_{F_{Ti}}$, and reconstructs V'_{F_T} using the techniques discussed in table 3 and table 4.
3. C verifies V'_{F_T} against V_{F_T}, which is stored at his end. For each of the attributes if V_{F_T} and V'_{F_T} has same values, it indicates that the query results are complete.

In both the cases, where some of the tuples are modified or removed at the database end, it can be observed at step 3 of the verification process, where $V'^{A_x}_{F_T}$ generated is different from the stored $V^{A_x}_{F_T}$.

4 Analysis

4.1 Functioning of Proposed Approach

We use the following lemmas to prove that the proposed approach is functionally correct as per the requirements.

Table 4. PRG Based S_{F_T} Generation

Method for generating Supporting Fake tuples
1. C chooses a random value δ based on his choice of number of supporting fake tuples.
2. C represents $V_{F_T}^{A_x} = \oplus_{i=1}^{\delta} S_{F_T i}^{A_x}$, where $S_{F_T i}$ are random value chosen from $\mathbb{R}$, for each attribute A_x in V_{F_T}.
3. These $S_{F_T i}$ form the supporting fake tuples, which are inserted into the database.
Reconstructing V_{F_T}: For the chosen query Q, C gets R_Q from the database and using the Step 2, V_{F_T} is reconstructed from δ S_{F_T}.s.

Lemma 1. *Changes in R_Q will result in changes in V_{F_T}.*

Proof. Assume to the contrary, that even if the tuples in R_Q change, the values in V_{F_T} remain same. This means different points can end up at the same polynomial which contradicts Theorem 1. This proves that changes in R_Q results in changes in V_{F_T}.However, since we consider constant term of the resulting polynomial, there is a negligible probability that the constants remain the same for different unique polynomials. The probability is $\frac{1}{(q-1)(q)^{k-2}}$, for a k-degree polynomial and q is the field size which is $|\mathbb{R}|$ in our case. □

Lemma 2. *When $V_{F_T} = V'_{F_T}$ then the database records preserve integrity.*

Proof. Without chance in notations, V_{F_T} is the verifier fake tuple originally stored at C's end and V'_{F_T} is the fake tuple generated at a later point of time, to verify integrity of database records. In this setup, if $V_{F_T} \neq V'_{F_T}$, it indicates that at least one of the tuples have been tampered with. This indicates that the data is not same as the original data and hence, database records lost their integrity. □

Lemma 3. *When V_{F_T} can be reconstructed from S_{F_T}, R_Q is complete.*

Proof. When secret sharing approach is used, theorem 1 ensures that for a given set of δ S_{F_T}s, V_{F_T} is unique. Hence, with the same success probability of integrity check as discussed in section 4.2, R_Q is complete. □

4.2   Success Probability

In this part of work, we discuss the success probabilities of the integrity check mechanism as well as successful escape probability of the adversary.

Success of Integrity Check: There are two levels at which integrity check success can be discussed: a) query result integrity b) database integrity. In a given instance, when k out of n of R_Q are used for generating V_{F_T}, query results preserve integrity with probability $\frac{k}{n}$. For sure verification, all the n tuples in R_Q need to be used to generate V_{F_T}. In the case, where entire database integrity has to be verified, instead of a single query, multiple queries have to be considered for V_{F_T} generation. Let r be number of tuples covered by all the possible queries in V_{F_T} generation process from y tuples present in the database, then database record integrity is preserved with probability of $\frac{r}{y}$.

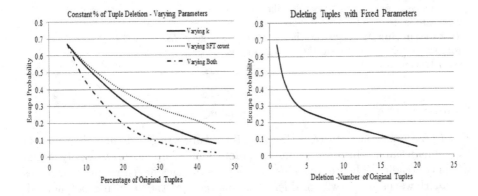

Fig. 2. Escape Probability of Adversary

Escape Probability of Adversary: An adversary can modify(update or delete) some tuples from the database and still get unnoticed. The escape probability of the adversary is the success with which he can delete a tuple from the database which does not belong to the k tuples associated with V_{F_T} generation, and also which do not belong to S_{F_T}s. For a given instance, if Q returns n tuples, which has δ S_{F_T}s and k out of n are used to construct V_{F_T}, then the escape probability of adversary for deleting *one* tuple and being unnoticed is $\frac{n-k}{n+\delta}$. This value decreases exponentially when multiple fake tuples are deleted, depending on both k and δ. Figure. 2 shows how the escape probability reduced to negligible value when $|S_{F_T}|$ varies as a percentage of n. In figure 2(a), the number of fake tuples deleted is fixed and the security parameters are varied; and the decrease in escape probability is observed. It can be observed the when both the security parameters k and δ are set to a small percentage of count of original tuples, the escape probability of adversary becomes negligible. Similarly in figure 2(b), the security parameters are fixed and increasing the number of fake tuple deletions, escape probability is observed.

4.3 Cost Analysis

Here, we analyze the communication and computation cost incurred at C using the proposed approach.

Communication Cost: The cost of communication is the cost incurred in sending a tuple to a outsourced database. If Φ is the cost incurred for sending a tuple to a outsourced database and if C decides to have δ fake tuples for a query Q, then the cost incurred in $\delta.\Phi$.

Computation Cost: At C's end, the following computation costs are involved. Some computations like *generation* are performed once in the query integrity process whereas other computations like *verification* are performed everytime integrity check is done.

Verifier Fake tuple Generation: For a given query, the computing for V_{F_T} is equivalent to getting the constant term for the polynomial coming from a set of points. Getting the constant term involves evaluating a simple expression, which involves mere substitution of x and y values.

$$constant = \sum_{i=1}^{k} \frac{(-1)^k . \prod_{j}^{k; j \neq i} x_j}{\prod_{j}^{k; j \neq i} (x_i - x_j)} * y_i$$

Supporting Fake tuple Generation: For a given query Q, the number of fake tuples inserted depends on the client's demand for robustness. For a given query, computing δ fake tuples as discussed in table 3 and table 4 involves two types of computations. Using the first technique involves triggering $\delta - 1$ PRGs with their respective seeds to produce $\delta - 1$ random values, identifying the remaining S_{F_T} value involves simple *xor* of generated random values with corresponding value in V_{F_T}. This is also a constant time operation. Using the second technique of using *secret sharing* polynomial, generating supporting fake tuples involves evaluating various polynomials at different values. Evaluating a polynomial is also a constant time operation.

Verifier Fake Tuple Verification: For any given query Q, cost of retrieving R_Q is a communication cost. After retrieving R_Q, the fake tuple generation involves constant time operation as explained in fake tuple generation process.

Supporting Fake Tuple Verification: After retrieving R_Q which has the supporting fake tuples, using the same operations discussed in supporting fake tuple generation process, verification is done. This verification involves performing ex-or or constructing V_{F_T}, which are constant time operations.

4.4   Security Analysis

In this section, we prove the security of our system in an *ideal* setting. The data outsourcing scheme is considered broken if an adversary can reconstruct the polynomial used either in the generation of the verifier fake tuple or in the generation of supporting fake tuples.

Lemma 4. *The scheme is information-theoretically secure, that is, an adversary with unlimited computing power also, can not break the scheme.*

Proof. It is well known that the secret sharing schemes such as Shamir's are informationally theoretically secure, in that, less than the requisite number of shares of the secret provide no information about the secret or equivalently the polynomial used in the generation of the shares. As the number of shares required for reconstructing the polynomial used either in the verifier fake tuple/supporting fake tuples is unknown to the adversary (both k and δ are secret), even an adversary with unlimited computational power cannot break the scheme. Even if we assume that k and δ are known to the adversary, he cannot distinguish whether the value of an attribute in a tuple is a share or any arbitrary value in the domain of that attribute. Therefore, our scheme is information-theoretically secure. □

In the case of outsourced databases, the possible adversary is a curious server who would like to differentiate between the fake tuples and normal data. Since the server could not differentiate the tuples without the knowledge of δ and k, the S_{F_T} tuples are indistinguishable from the normal data and hence, the server can not treat the fake tuples seperately. For a new query, when the fake tuples are inserted along with the normal data, following this theorem, the server can not differentiate between a normal data insert and insert with fake tuples.

4.5   Empirical Evaluation

We used a PC with AMD Athlon IIX2 processor and 4GB RAM to act as C and S. The approach is simulated using Java language and Microsoft SQL Server DBMS is used to store the outsourced tuples. A table with medical records is used as test table with five attributes namely Record-ID, BP-Observed, Sugar-Observed, Weight and Height. C fires the queries to S, which hosts the table having 1 million tuples. Fake tuple sets of different sizes are constructed with respect to different *range* queries and inserted into the database. We implemented our approach and Hash Attribute approach discussed in [6] and observed the difference in processing time at C's end for completeness check which is seen in Figure 3(b). Our approach has comparable results for processing time at client. We also analyzed the efforts for generating supporting fake tuples at the client using the two deterministic approaches discussed in table 3 and table 4, results on computation effort at C are shown in Figure 3(a).

4.6   Features and Limitations

Here, we discuss the limitations and features of our approach.

Handling Database Updates: Updates to a database include insert, delete and drop. The client has to ensure that the appropriate update is reflected at the server. We discuss how each update affects the query integrity process and how to ensure integrity despite running updates on database.

Insert Update. In insert operation, new tuples are inserted into the database. This process may not effect the existing integrity related tuples. However, the process discussed in section 2 , should be applied again for these tuples as well, if there is a noticeable amount of data inserted into the database. If the insert changes will be reflected in the result set R_Q of a query Q which is covered by C, then supporting fake tuples can be inserted according to technique (a) or (b) discussed in generating supporting fake tuples. Since this leads to a change from δ to δ_1, C updates the new δ_1 along with Q.

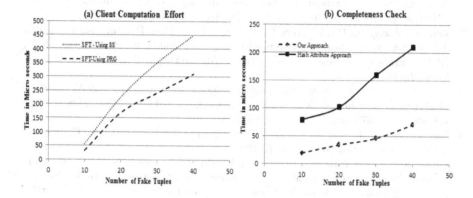

Fig. 3. Computation Effort at Client

Delete Update. Delete is a complex operation to incorporate in the existing setup, because delete could lead to deletion of S_{F_T} tuple associated with V_{F_T} at C. Since locations associated with S_{F_T} are known to C, it can verify the delete query before executing and exclude deletion of fake tuples.

5 Conclusion and Future Work

Earlier works in completeness verification in outsourced databases ensured query integrity by adding an extra attribute to the table. However, deleting this attribute hinders integrity check. In this work, we eliminated the dependency on adding new attribute. Integrity check and also, completeness check are ensured by using fake tuples. We proposed two deterministic ways to generate fake tuples. These generated fake tuples are used for completeness check. Our integrity check mechanism works faster than existing approaches, as depicted in our empirical evaluation. And also discussed the aspects of cost and computation complexity of the approach along with its features and limitations as well. We showed that our approach is information theoretically secure, where an adversary without knowledge of the underlying security parameters can never be able to break the scheme. Future work involves utilization of the proposed approach for public auditing in cloud.

References

1. Hacigumus, H., Iyer, B.: Providing Database as a Service. In: International Conference of Data Engineering (2002)
2. Narasimha, M., Tsudik, G.: Authentication of Outsourced Databases Using Signature Aggregation and Chaining. In: Li Lee, M., Tan, K.-L., Wuwongse, V. (eds.) DASFAA 2006. LNCS, vol. 3882, pp. 420–436. Springer, Heidelberg (2006)
3. Noferesti, M., Hadavi, M.A., Jalili, R.: A Signature-Based Approach of Correctness Assurance in Data Outsourcing Scenarios. In: Jajodia, S., Mazumdar, C. (eds.) ICISS 2011. LNCS, vol. 7093, pp. 374–378. Springer, Heidelberg (2011)
4. Zhu, Y., Wang, H., Hu, Z., Ahn, G.-J., Hu, H., Yau, S.S.: Dynamic audit services for integrity verification of outsourced storages in clouds. In: Proceedings of the ACM Symposium on Applied Computing (SAC 2011), pp. 1550–1557. ACM, New York (2011)
5. Goodrich, M.T., Tamassia, R., Triandopoulos, N.: Super-Efficient Verification of Dynamic Outsourced Databases. In: Malkin, T. (ed.) CT-RSA 2008. LNCS, vol. 4964, pp. 407–424. Springer, Heidelberg (2008)
6. Xie, M., Wang, H., Yin, J.: Integrity Auditing of Outsourced Data. In: Conference on Very Large Databases, VLDB (2007)
7. Ghasemi, S., Noferesti, M., Hadavi, M.A., Dorri Nogoorani, S., Jalili, R.: Correctness Verification in Database Outsourcing: A Trust-Based Fake Tuples Approach. In: Venkatakrishnan, V., Goswami, D. (eds.) ICISS 2012. LNCS, vol. 7671, pp. 343–351. Springer, Heidelberg (2012)
8. Hadavi, M.A., Jalili, R.: Secure Data Outsourcing Based on Threshold Secret Sharing; Towards a More Practical Solution. In: Proceeding of VLDB PhD Workshop, pp. 54–59 (2010)
9. Waring, E.: Problems concerning interpolations. Philosophical Transactions of Royal Society 69, 59–67 (1779)
10. Lagrange, J.L.: Leons Imentaires sur les mathamatiques donnes a lcole normale. In: Serret, J. (ed.) OEuvres de Lagrange, Paris, France, vol. 7, pp. 183–287 (1877)
11. Shamir, A.: How to share a secret. Communications of the ACM 22, 612–613 (1979)
12. Shacham, H., Waters, B.: Compact Proofs of Retrievability. In: Pieprzyk, J. (ed.) ASIACRYPT 2008. LNCS, vol. 5350, pp. 90–107. Springer, Heidelberg (2008)
13. Wang, C., Wang, Q., Ren, K., Lou, W.: Privacy-Preserving Public Auditing for Data Storage Security in Cloud Computing. In: Proceedings of INFOCOM, pp. 1–9 (2010)

Policy Mining: A Bottom-Up Approach toward a Model Based Firewall Management

Safaà Hachana[1,3], Frédéric Cuppens[2],
Nora Cuppens-Boulahia[1,2], Vijay Atluri[4], and Stephane Morucci[1]

[1] Swid Web Performance Service, France
{safa,stephane.morucci}@swid.fr
[2] Institut Telecom-Mines/Telecom Bretagne, Dépt. LUSSI, France
{frederic.cuppens,nora.cuppens}@telecom-bretagne.eu
[3] École Nationale Supérieure de Mécanique et d'Aérotechnique, Dépt. LIAS, France
[4] CIMIC, Rutgers University, USA
atluri@rutgers.edu

Abstract. Todays enterprises rely entirely on their information systems, usually connected to the internet. Network access control, mainly ensured by firewalls, has become a paramount necessity. Still, the management of manually configured firewall rules is complex, error prone, and costly for large networks. The use of high abstract models such as role based access control RBAC has proved to be very efficient in the definition and management of access control policies. The recent interest in role mining which is the bottom-up approach for automatic RBAC configuration from the already deployed authorizations is likely to further promote the development of this model. Recently, an extension of RBAC adapted to the specificities of network access control, which we refer to as NS-RBAC model, has been proposed. However, no effort has been made to extend the bottom-up approach to configure this model. In this paper, we propose an extension of role mining techniques to facilitate the adoption of a model based framework in the management of network access control. We present policy mining, a bottom-up approach that extracts instances of the NS-RBAC model from the deployed rules on a firewall. We provide a generic algorithm that could adapt most of the existing role mining solutions to the NS-RBAC model. We illustrate the feasibility of our solution by experimentations on real and synthetic data.

Keywords: IT Security, Access Control, Network Security, Firewall, RBAC, Role Mining.

1 Introduction

Nowadays, most of the enterprises are completely dependent on their information systems, either for their internal functioning, or for their commercial web interface. A reliable access control policy is essential to ensure the good and continuous working of these systems. The access control policy is mainly deployed on firewalls. The configuration and the management of these firewalls are hard tasks. Filtering rules are enforced in a vendor specific low level language, the

A. Bagchi and I. Ray (Eds.): ICISS 2013, LNCS 8303, pp. 133–147, 2013.
© Springer-Verlag Berlin Heidelberg 2013

number of rules is usually high, and the rules are order sensitive. Performed manually, operations such as migration, updates, and delegation to a new administrator are real challenges. The firewall management problem becomes more and more urgent with the increasing complexity of modern security policies. One of the most important proposed approaches is to configure and manage firewalls from a high level language down to device specific low level language [1–3]. This methodology is likely to overcome the problems encountered when using low level languages by providing the administrator with the benefit of hindsight, decreasing the probability of human error and allowing a reliable configuration of a system of firewalls.The greatest stumbling block to the wholesale adoption of high level models is that no solution has been proposed to handle the already deployed rules on firewalls. This implies to throw away the already deployed rules, and start from scratch the specification of the whole access control policy. To bypass this problem, we advocate for a bottom-up approach that parses the configured rules in the firewalls and leverages data mining techniques to automatically reach an instance of the high level model corresponding to the deployed policy. Recently, the emergence of *Role Mining* [4] has become a new catalyst of the expansion of *Role Based Access Control (RBAC)* [5] in organizations. Role mining is the discipline of automating the extraction of RBAC roles from the already deployed set of direct authorizations in a system, using data mining tools. However, applying the role mining solutions proposed in literature directly to firewall rules can not provide interesting outcome. Indeed, though *RBAC* model has imposed itself as the standard high abstraction level access control policy model, and has proved to be very efficient in a wide area of access control applications such as physical security package, environmental security, operating system security, and staff security [6], it still does not fully capture the specificities of network access control policies. From the perspective of the RBAC model, the access control security rules are considered to follow the pattern: [*a user u is allowed access to permission p*], with *p* an operation over an object. The users are the central entities, and RBAC introduces the concept of *role* to structure them. However, when we focus on the structure of a network access control rule, it is of the form [*allow source_host sh to send service of type s to destination_host dh*]. In this pattern, the three involved entities are semantically at the same level of importance from the network access control perspective. Cuppens et al. have showed that a model that captures this ternary relation allows to define a network security policy efficiently [3]. The *Network Security RBAC (NS-RBAC)* model contains and generalizes the concept of *role* from RBAC by adding the concepts of *activity* to structure the services, and *view* to structure the destination_hosts, the same as *role* structures the source_hosts into higher level of abstraction entities. Role mining techniques do not fit the NS-RBAC model since they structure only one of the three entities. Applying role mining to structure each of the three entities separately is not feasible since it would output unconnected abstract entities that can not be related with security rules to express the original access control policy.

In this paper, we propose policy mining: a bottom-up approach to extract instances of the NS-RBAC model from a set of firewall rules. Policy mining is an extension of role mining that calculates roles, activities and views to meet network security requirements. We intend to reuse existing role mining techniques to leverage the achievements realized in this filed. Due to the fact that the three concrete entities in a rule are structured in consistency, policy mining generates also a set of *abstract rules* that constitute the high level policy. Policy mining handles the problem of factorization of a three-dimensional matrix where the traditional role mining is usually assimilated to a problem of factorization of a two-dimensional matrix.

Paper Organization. Section 2 presents NS-RBAC model and shows how it models a network security policy. Then, it introduces the policy mining problem. Section 3 proposes an algorithm that solves the policy mining problem. Section 4 provides experimental results. Section 5 surveys the approaches that address firewall management problems in literature. Section 6 concludes the paper and discusses some perspectives.

2   Formalization of the Proposed Approach

2.1   NS-RBAC Model to Specify Network Security Policies

In the last couple of decades, the *Role Based Access Control model (RBAC)* has become the dominant model for access control in both commercial and research communities. Definition 1 presents the basic model $RBAC_0$ [5].

Definition 1. *RBAC*
An RBAC configuration denoted $RC = (ROLES, UR, RP)$ is characterized by:

- *U, ROLES, OPS, and OBJ, the sets of users, roles, operations, and objects*
- *$UR \subseteq U \times ROLES$, a many-to-many mapping user-to-role assignment relation*
- *$PRMS \subseteq \{(op, obj) | op \in OPS \wedge obj \in OBJ\}$, a set of permissions, where a permission is an operation over an object*
- *$RP \subseteq ROLES \times PRMS$, a many-to-many mapping of role-to-permission assignment relation*
- *$assigned\_users(R) = \{u \in U | (u, R) \in UR\}$, the mapping of role R onto a set of users*
- *$assigned\_permissions(R) = \{p \in PRMS | (R, p) \in RP\}$, the mapping of role R onto a set of permissions.*

RBAC introduces the concept of *role* in order to make the access control system more compact, structured and stable, compared to the direct user-permission assignments. From this perspective, the security rules are considered to follow the pattern: [*a user u is allowed access to permission p*], with p an operation over an object. The users are the central entities in RBAC. They are expected to be the active entities who require authorizations in the system. Users are dynamic entities, so it is safer and more efficient to structure them into higher level of abstraction entities. Roles are defined by security experts according to the organization functioning, and this task is called *role engineering*. Permissions are granted to the roles. Users are assigned to roles and can gain permissions through these roles. However, the structure of a network access control rule is of the form [*allow source_host sh to send service of type s to destination_host dh*] where *sh is an IP address or a panel of addresses* that send packets of service *s defined by protocol, source_port, and destination_port, to dh which is also an IP address or a panel of addresses*. If we assimilate the *source_host* to user, the *service* to operation and the *destination_host* to object according to the terminology of Definition 1, then we note that in this pattern, the three entities are semantically at the same level of importance from the network access control perspective. They are equally dynamic and should be handled by the system as so. Thus it is not appropriate to structure only the users and not the operations and the objects. In this optic, the NS-RBAC model extends the basic RBAC model to structure the three concrete entities into higher level of abstraction entities equally [1, 3, 7, 8].

Definition 2. *NS-RBAC*

An NS-RBAC configuration denoted NS-RC = (ROLES, UR, ACTIVITIES, OPA, VIEWS, OBV, RAV) is characterized by:

- *U, ROLES, OPS, ACTIVITIES, OBJ, and VIEWS which are the sets of users, roles, operations, activities, objects and views*
- $UR \subseteq U \times ROLES$, *a many-to-many mapping user-to-role assignment relation*
- $assigned\_users(R) = \{u \in U | (u, R) \in UR\}$, *the mapping of role R onto a set of users*
- $OPA \subseteq OPS \times ACTIVITIES$, *a many-to-many mapping operation-to-activity assignment relation*
- $assigned\_operations(A) = \{op \in OPS | (op, A) \in AD\}$, *the mapping of activity A onto a set of operations*
- $OBV \subseteq OBJ \times VIEWS$, *a many-to-many mapping object-to-view assignment relation*
- $assigned\_objects(V) = \{obj \in OBJ | (obj, V) \in OBV\}$, *the mapping of view V onto a set of objects*
- $RAV \subseteq ROLES \times ACTIVITIES \times VIEWS$, *a many-to-many-to-many mapping of role-to-activity-to-view assignment relation.*

Definition 2 adds two new abstract entities: *activity* which structures the operations, and *view* which structures the objects, the same as *role* structures the users. More importantly, the fact that the three concrete entities are structured induces the definition of *abstract rules* represented by the relation *RAV*. An abstract rule is of the form [*role r is granted to perform activity a over view v*]. The concrete access control rule involving a given user u, operation op and object ob exists if u is assigned to a role R, op is assigned to an activity A, and ob is assigned to a view V, and the triplet (R, A, V) belongs to the relation *RAV*. This feature allows to significantly aggregate the firewall rules.

2.2   Policy Mining

The role mining approach extracts a configuration of roles from the already deployed direct user-to-permission assignments using data mining techniques.

The users granted with similar permissions are gathered into similar roles. Symmetrically, permissions with common users are assigned together, so that they belong to the same roles. Several role mining techniques are proposed in the literature, with different assumptions and optimization criteria leading to different solutions. For instance, the first formal definition for the *role mining problem* is given in [9] where Vaidya et al. suggest the optimization criteria to be the minimization of the number of generated roles. Solutions with different objectives have been proposed, which are necessary to deal with the changing requirements and contexts of application. The solution should be tied to the nature of the input data and the constraints related to the application field. Hachana et al. [4] have surveyed the role mining research field and identified the main directions and perspectives. However, traditional role mining techniques can not be directly applied to firewall rules. Indeed, the targeted high level model is not RBAC but NS-RBAC. We still need a more adapted bottom-up approach to the network security application. In this paper, we handle the problem of *policy mining*. We aim at extracting not only roles from the deployed rules, but activities and views as well. Moreover, we aim at mining the abstract rules that define the relations between these abstract entities. The problem is formalized as an extension of the *inference role mining problem* [10]:

Definition 3. *Policy Mining Problem*
  Let U be a set of users, OPS a set of operations, OBJ a set of objects, and UOO a user-operation-object assignment relation. Infer the unknown NS-RBAC configuration NS-RC = (RAV, ROLES, UR, ACTIVITIES, OPA, VIEWS, OBV), under the following assumptions:

1. *An underlying NS-RBAC configuration exists*
2. *Exceptions (may) exist.*

By exceptions we mean that direct user-operation-object assignment may still be allowed in the NS-RBAC configuration. This may be necessary in some cases: a compromise with the solution performance, a flexibility required by an organization, or a tip to discard noise and errors in the initial set of rules.

3   Policy Mining Algorithm

Starting from the configured rules in a firewall, Algorithm 1 solves the *policy mining problem* by calculating an equivalent NS-RBAC configuration. We assume that the input rules are not order sensitive and are accept only. This is a realistic assumption since there exist in literature tools that transform a set of overlapping prioritized firewall rules into a set of flat rules. For instance, in [11] Tongaonkar proposes an algorithm that transforms the set of rules into an equivalent directed acyclic graph (DAG) where the nodes are the packet header fields (dest_host, src_host, dest_port, etc.), the leaf nodes are the firewall actions (accept/deny), and the edges going from a node are labeled with the different values assigned to its packet header field in the set of rules. The algorithm optimizes the DAG by a pruning and node merging process. Then it returns a set of flat and accept only firewall rules. The number of flat rules is generally higher than the number of original order sensitive rules, but this does not matter since our policy mining algorithm aggregates the rules afterward. We also assume in this paper that we handle rules from only one firewall. We deal with rules deployed on several network security policy components in a forthcoming paper.

To unify the representation of the inputs and outputs of the algorithm and to perform calculations, the involved data is represented with Boolean matrices. Algorithm 1 takes as input a set of firewall rules represented by a 3-dimentional Boolean matrix of user-operation-object assignment UOO. In a preprocessing stage, the firewall rules are parsed, and the different instances of source_hosts, services and destination_hosts are saved respectively in the sets of U, OPS, and OBJ. Given m users, n operations and k objects, the UOO relation is built as an $m \times n \times k$ 3-dimentional matrix of zeroes. For each original rule where user i is allowed to perform operation j on object l, the cell $\{ijl\}$ in UOO is set to 1. The output of Algorithm 1 is an NS-RBAC configuration consisting of a set of abstract rules represented by the 3-dimensional Boolean relation RAV modeled as an $M \times N \times K$ 3-dimensional Boolean matrix of M roles, N activities and K views, where a 1 in cell $\{ijl\}$ indicates that role i is allowed to perform activity j on view k. The NS-RBAC configuration includes also three relations of assignment of user-to-Role UR, operation-to-Activity OPA, and object-to-View OBV. UR is modeled as an $n \times N$ boolean matrix where 1 in cell $\{ijl\}$ indicates the assignment of role j to user i. Similarly, OPA and OBV are represented as respectively an $m \times M$ and a $k \times K$ Boolean matrices.

3.1   Extending Existing Matrix Factorization Techniques

This paper does not aim to propose another role mining algorithm, but rather to show how to adapt existing role mining techniques to the policy mining problem. Role mining is mainly about leveraging already existing data mining techniques to define roles. It has explored and borrowed solutions from different fields such as matrix compression, formal concept analysis, probabilistic models, NPC problem reduction, graph theory, etc [4].

Thus, Algorithm 1 takes as input, in addition to the relation UOO, a *matrix factorization method*. We refer by *factorization method* to any algorithm that takes as input a Boolean matrix C and gives as output two Boolean matrices A and B such that $A \otimes B \approx C$. The Boolean matrix multiplication is defined as:

Definition 4. *Boolean matrix multiplication*
A Boolean matrix multiplication between Boolean matrices $A \in \{0,1\}^{n \times k}$ and $B \in \{0,1\}^{k \times m}$ is denoted $A \otimes B = C$ where $C \in \{0,1\}^{n \times m}$ and $c_{ij} = \bigvee_{l=1}^{k} \wedge a_{il} b_{lj}$.

This notation allows us to reuse most of the role mining techniques proposed in literature. In an RBAC configuration, matrix C would represent the relation UPA, and matrices A and B would match UR and RP relations such that $UPA = UR \otimes RP$. The Boolean multiplication can be interpreted as: a user i is granted permission j in UPA if and only if, at least, one of the roles to which he is assigned in *UR* is assigned to this permission in *RP*. Role mining tries to extract *UR* and *RP* from *UPA* using a given factorization method. Usually, there exist several possibilities of factorization for the same initial matrix. The choice depends on the optimization objectives of the factorization method. We intentionally leave open the possibility of different factorization techniques to benefit from their different optimization objectives and be able to easily adapt Algorithm 1 according to the requirements.

To reuse existing factorization methods for policy mining purpose, we have to address two main issues. The first issue is that these methods generally handle 2-dimensional Boolean matrices whereas the input relation of authorizations *UOO* is a 3-dimentional Boolean matrix. To solve this problem, we define a polynomial mapping that transforms a 3-dimensional Boolean matrix into a 2-dimensional Boolean matrix, and vice versa, as required by Algorithm 1. Figure 1 provides an illustration of this transformation. Given an $m \times n \times k$ matrix, we merge the second and third dimensions with regard to the first dimension by presenting in the second dimension all the possible combinations of elements from dimensions 2 and 3. For example if we have a users×operations×objects 3D matrix, we transform it into a user to permission relation, provided that a permission is a combination of an operation and an object. This transformation is obviously reversible with a simple Euclidian division to get back to the 3-dimensional matrix from the 2-dimentional matrix. We also note that the size of data is still the same: $m \times n \times k$. The second issue is the normalization of the inputs and outputs of the different factorization methods that we use, in such a way to integrate them automatically in the policy mining Algorithm 1. We intend to use any data mining or role mining algorithm that could be leveraged to solve $M = A \otimes B$. In practice, they do not always give directly matrices A and B as output. For example, some role mining algorithms provide only a list of candidate roles from where we have to choose the pertinent roles according to some prioritization criteria. That is to say, we may need specific processing for each factorization method before integrating it in Algorithm 1. Moreover, some methods give only an approximation of the factorization of $M \approx A \otimes B$. The approximation error $(M - A \otimes B)$ may be assimilated to the exceptions in Definition 3. We consider both cases of approximate and exact factorizations in our framework.

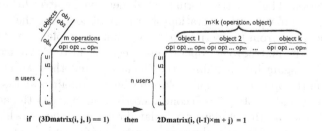

Fig. 1. Transforming a Boolean Matrix from 3-dimensions to 2-dimensions

3.2   The Algorithm

Algorithm 1. PolicyMining(UOO, FactorizationMethod, parameters of FactorizationMethod)

Input: *UOO* : the firewall rules expressed as a 3-dimentional Boolean relation between users, operations and objects
Input: FactorizationMethod
Input: Further parameters may be required by the used factorization method
Output: An NS-RBAC configuration: user-role *UR*, operation-activity *OPA*, object-view *OBV* and a Role-Activity-View *RAV* Boolean relations

1: 2D transformation: from user-operation-object to user-permission *UPA*
2: mine Roles : FactorizationMethod(*UPA*) to get : $UPA \approx UR \otimes RP$
3: 3D transformation: from role-permission matrix to role-operation-object
4: Permutation : role-operation-object to operation-object-role
5: 2D transformation: operation-object-role to operation-domain *OPD*
6: mine Activities: FactorizationMethod(*OPD*) to get : $OPD \approx OPA \otimes AD$
7: 3D transformation: activity-domain into activity-object-role
8: Permutation : activity-object-role to object-role-activity
9: 2D transformation : object-role-activity to object-capacity *OBC*
10: mind Views : FactorizationMethod(*OBC*) to get : $OBC \approx OBV \otimes VC$
11: 3D transformation: view-capacity into view-activity-role
12: Permutation : view-activity-role into role-activity-view
13: **return** *RAV*, *UR*, *OPA*, and *OBV*

The driven idea of Algorithm 1 is to use the *factorization method* to extract the three abstract entities: roles, activities, and views, sequentially, but while taking into account the abstract entities calculated in the previous steps at each new step in order to preserve consistency. By consistency we mean that the three abstract entities should be related by abstract rules such that the users assigned to a given role be allowed to perform activities assigned to a given activity using objects belonging to a same View. Initially, the deployed firewall rules are presented as a 3-dimensional Boolean matrix *UOO*. We transform it to a 2-dimentional Boolean matrix *UPA*, the same as in usual role mining applications. Then we apply the factorization method to extract the roles as sets of permissions in *RP*, and calculate also the user-to-role assignment relation *UR* of the NS-RBAC configuration. Then, we transform the 2-dimensional matrix *RP* to obtain a new 3-dimensional matrix role-operation-object, by dissociating the operation and object dimensions from the permissions. We make a simple permutation of the dimensions of the matrix to get operation-object-role instead. We transform the latter relation again into a 2-dimentional matrix, and then we apply the factorization over the operation-domain relation where a domain is an association between an object and a role. This second factorization extracts the activities while taking into account the previously calculated roles since the users have been substituted by the roles. We keep the operation-to-activity assignment relation *OPA* in the NS-RBAC configuration, and we repeat the same process to extract the Views while substituting the users by the roles and the operations by the activities. We obtain the relation between the roles, activities and views which constitutes the abstract rules *RAV*.

Theorem 1 *Correctness.* *If the used factorization method provides exact decomposition (without approximation errors), then the authorizations granted to the concrete entities by the NS-RBAC configuration calculated by Algorithm 1 are exactly the same as the authorizations granted by the input rules UOO.*

Proof. All the steps of Algorithm 1 are reversible. The 2D transformation is reversible by the 3D transformation and vice versa. The permutation of matrix dimensions is reversible by the opposite permutation. And the factorization is reversible by the Boolean multiplication. So starting from the NS-RBAC configuration, we can calculate *UOO* by following the opposite way. This means that [*a user u is allowed to do an operation op over an object ob*] in the input relation *UOO* *if and only if* there exists a role R to which u is assigned in *UR*, and there exists an activity A to which op is assigned in *OPA*, and there exists a view V to which ob is assigned in *OBV*, and the relation between R, A and V equals to 1 in *RAV*.

Complexity of the Algorithm: The time complexity of Algorithm 1 is at least polynomial on the size of the input matrix *UOO* ($n \times m \times k$) and depends on the complexity of the used factorization algorithm. We run the factorization algorithm three consecutive times, with a decreasing input data size. There exist several role mining algorithms in literature with polynomial complexity on the number of users n and the number of permissions $m \times k$ such as FastMiner [12] with a $O(n^2 \times (m \times k))$ complexity. The operations of changing the dimension of matrices and of permutation of matrices dimensions are polynomial.

4 Experimental Results

4.1 Synthetic Data

We have implemented a proof of concept framework for Algorithm 1. Our experiments follow this scenario: we generate a random NS-RBAC configuration, we calculate the deriving *UOO* from it, then we perform policy mining on the *UOO* relation to extract an NS-RBAC configuration in a reverse engineering process. We have first implemented a random NS-RBAC configuration generator. This tool takes as input the number of users, operations, objects, roles, activities and views, in addition to the density of the concrete-to-abstract entities assignments and the density of the abstract rules, and generates randomly the matrices *UR*, *OPA*, *OBV* and *RAV* of an NS-RBAC configuration. The probability to have 1 in a cell is equal to density. We have generated four data sets with increasing sizes and with the density parameters set to 0.1. Then, we have adapted two different factorization methods for our experiments: SVD as an example for approximate factorization method, and FCA for exact factorization. The Singular

Value Decomposition SVD [13] decomposes a matrix into its eigenvectors which represent its directing patterns. We assimilate them to the abstract entities. We keep only the eigenvectors corresponding to the largest eigenvalues to recompose the initial matrix while discarding the weak patterns which may be assimilated to errors or exceptions. We set a threshold to decide of the amount of discarded data automatically. Since this factorization is not Boolean, we set the obtained values to one if they are higher than a given binarization threshold, and to zero otherwise. The Formal Concept Analysis FCA [14] is a discipline that has a solid theoretical foundation in mathematics and has been widely used in role mining. A formal context represents binary relations between objects and attributes. A formal concept is defined by a set of objects and a set of attributes which represents mutually all the objects that share the given attributes, and all the attributes shared by the given objects. It may be assimilated to an abstract entity in the NS-RBAC model. There exists several efficient algorithms that calculate all the formal concepts corresponding to a given formal context. We have used the implementation described in [15]. There exist in the role mining literature sophisticated criteria to select the relevant concepts [16]. We assign to each concrete entity the minimal set of formal concepts to cover all its attributes. We have implemented the plateform of test in MATLAB_R2011a. The results of the experiments are summarized in Figure 2. Figure 2(a) shows that the number of abstract rules is much lower than the number of concrete rules, especially with SVD factorization method with all the four synthetic data sets. Policy mining obviously aggregates the firewall rules. Since we perform three successive factorizations in Algorithm 1, we were interested in the evolution of the approximation error. We have plotted the distance between the matrix of the initial concrete rules and the matrix of the obtained concrete rules after each of the factorizations that calculate the roles, then the activities and finally the views (lines 2,6 and 10 in Algorithm 1). We use the Frobenius norm ($||X||_f = \sqrt{\sum x_{ij}^2}$) to evaluate the difference between the matrices. The results are presented in Figure 2(b). When using the SVD method, we note that the error increases with the data size. However, the cumulative error is not increasing. In the contrary, it tends to decrease. For example, the divergence from the initial set of rules after the factorization of the activities tends to be lower than the divergence after the factorization of the roles. When using the FCA factorization method, there is no approximation error as expected. Besides, we have chosen to calculate the roles first, then the activities and finally the views in Algorithm 1. This choice is totally arbitrary, and can be changed by a simple permutation of the dimensions of the input matrix UOO. We were interested in the effect of changing the order of mining on the obtained abstract entities. Figures 2(c) and 2(d) show the distance between the roles, activities and views obtained when mining roles then activities then views and when mining activities then roles then views for the same input set of rules. The obtained entities are not the same neither with the approximate nor with the exact factorization method. There are usually several possible factorizations for the same set of data. What makes the difference is the

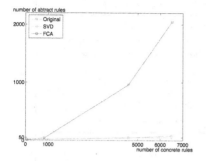

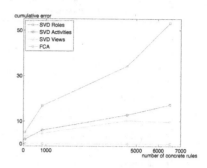

(a) Compacity of the mined abstract rules vs the original concrete rules

(b) Cumulative error with approximate factorization method

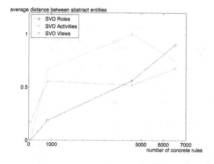

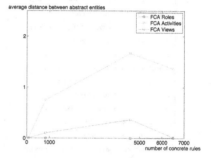

(c) Changing abstract entities mining order effect on the mined abstract entities with SVD

(d) Changing abstract entities mining order effect on the mined abstract entities with SVD

Fig. 2. Experimental Results with the Policy Mining Algorithm

optimization objectives. We could orientate the resulting abstract entities if we use factorization methods with more precise objectives in real applications.

4.2 Real Data

We show the results of applying the bottom-up approach on an actual set of firewall rules borrowed from [17] in Figure 3. The left column represents the set of original firewall rules implemented in a firewall that protects an informatics department. The right column represents the NS-RBAC instance resulting from policy mining. First we have parsed all the instances of source_hosts to build the set of users, for example $192.168.1.126/25$ is a user. We found four different source_hosts that constitute the set of users. We note that, since some rules are defined from *any* source_host then *any* is also considered a user. We have done the same operation with services and dest_hosts. We have found twenty different operations and ten objects. We have built the UOO matrix of size $4 \times 20 \times 10$ as a 3D-matrix of zeroes, then we have set to one cells corresponding to the different rules. We have performed policy mining on that matrix using SVD then

Original Set of FW iptables Rules	Policy Mining Results
	Abstract Rules:
	1- FROM *Corporate_Zone* TO *SSH_Server* FOR *Secured_Traffic*
	2- FROM *Any* TO *Web_Server* FOR *Secured_Web_Service*
Concrete Rules:	3- FROM *Any* TO *Corporate_Zone* FOR *Protocol_Control*
1- -p tcp -d 192.168.1.250 --dport domain	4- FROM *Exterior* TO *Printer* FOR *Printing*
2- -p tcp -d 192.168.1.251 --dport smtp	5- FROM *DMZ* TO *SUN_NFS_Server* FOR *UNIX_Services*
3- -p tcp -d 192.168.1.251 --dport smtps	6- FROM *Any* TO *DNS_Server* FOR *DNS*
4- -p tcp -d 192.168.1.251 --dport imaps	7- FROM *Any* TO *Messaging_Server* FOR *E-mailing*
5- -p tcp -d 192.168.1.251 --dport pop3s	
6- -p tcp -d 192.168.1.252 --dport www	*Source_Host to Role assignment:*
7- -p tcp -d 192.168.1.126/25 --dport auth	1- *Corporate_Zone*= *{192.168.1.126/25}*
8- -s 192.168.1.126/25 -p tcp -d 192.168.1.13 --dport ssh	2- *Exterior* = *{192.168.1.236}*
9- -s 192.168.1.126/25 -p tcp -d 192.168.1.14 --dport ssh	3 -*DMZ* = *{192.168.1.254/28}*
10- -s 192.168.1.126/25 -p tcp -d 192.168.1.15 --dport ssh	4- *Any* = *{any}*
11- -s 192.168.1.126/25 -p tcp -d 192.168.1.20 --dport ssh	*Service to Activity assignment:*
12- -p tcp -d 192.168.1.252 --dport https	1- *Secured_Traffic* = *{-p tcp -dport ssh}*
13- -s 192.168.1.254/28 -d 192.168.1.11 -p tcp --dport sunrpc	2- *Secured_Web_Service* = *{{-p tcp -dport auth}, {-p tcp -dport https}}*
14- -s 192.168.1.236 -p tcp -d 192.168.1.35 --dport ipp	3 -*Ptrotocol_Control* = *{{tcp FOR auth}, {-p icmp -icmp-type: destination unreachable},{ -p icmp -icmp-type parameter-problem}, { -p icmp -icmp-type source-quench}}*
15- -s 192.168.1.254/28 -d 192.168.1.11 -p udp --dport nfs	
16- -s 192.168.1.254/28 -d 192.168.1.11 -p udp --dport 4000:4002	4- *Printing* = *{{-p tcp -dport ipp}, {-p udp -dport ipp}}*
17- -p udp -d 192.168.1.251 --dport smtp -j accept	5- *UNIX_Services* = *{-p tcp -dport sunrpc}, { -p udp -dport sunrpc}, {-p udp -dport nfs}, {-p udp -dport 4000:4002}}*
18- -p udp -d 192.168.1.250 --dport domain -j accept	
19- -s 192.168.1.254/28 -p udp -d 192.168.1.11 --dport sunrpc	6- *DNS* = *{{-p tcp -dport domain},{-p udp -dport domain}}*
20- -s 192.168.1.236 -p udp -d 192.168.1.35 --dport ipp	7- *E-mailing* = *{{-p tcp -dport smtp}, {-p tcp -dport smtps}, {-p tcp -dport imaps}, {-p tcp -dport pop3s}, {-p udp -dport smtp}}*
21- -d 192.168.1.126/25 -p icmp --icmp-type destination-unreachable	*Destination_Host to View assignment:*
22- -d 192.168.1.126/25 -p icmp --icmp-type parameter-problem	1- *SSH_Server* = *{[192.168.1.13 - 15] and 192.168.1.20}*
23- -d 192.168.1.126/25 -p icmp --icmp-type source-quench	2- *Web_Server* = *{192.168.1.252}*
24- IPTABLES -A FORWARD -j REJECT	3 - *Corporate_Zone* = *{192.168.1.126/25}*
	4- *Printer* = *{192.168.1.35}*
	5- *Sun_NFS_Server* = *{192.168.1.11}*
	6- *DNS_Server* = *{192.168.1.250}*
	7- *Messaging_Srever* = *{192.168.1.251}*

Fig. 3. Results of Policy Mining on a Real Set of Data

FCA. Both methods have outputted the same NS-RBAC configuration, without approximation error, mainly because it is relatively a small data set. In the resulting configuration we have four roles, seven activities and seven views, and seven abstract rules. We have observed the set of concrete entities assigned to each abstract entities and named it accordingly. This could help to detect anomalies. For example if a source_host has nothing to do with a set of source_hosts assigned to the same role, this should draw the attention of the security administrator. The obtained set of abstract rules is obviously more compact and offers better readability. The obtained structures of concrete entities can usually be easily associated to significant entities in the network.

5   Related Work

While the constructors focus mainly on enhancing the firewall performance related to speed, transparency, and capacity of filtering, enhancing the management of firewalls is still an academic concern. Different approaches in literature address firewall management problems, including penetration testing, offline simulation based query tools, and misconfiguration detection. All these approaches aim at analyzing the behavior of already configured firewalls but they are usually difficult to conduct. They are intrusive and/or they require an active interaction with the user whose queries and envisaged scenarios may be not exhaustive and nor precise. A more comparable approach to our work is the approach that tries to refactor the rules deployed on a firewall by rewriting them in a more readable and optimized way. In particular, refactoring may involve aggregating the rules. For example in [18], Marmorstein et al. has proposed a solution to aggregate firewall rules by classifying each of the source_hosts and destination_hosts into homogeneous groups. In [17], Tongaonkar et al. have extended this work by classifying the services as well. Abedin et al. [19] have proposed to apply data mining techniques combined with specific heuristics to perform a similar work of aggregating but in a different usage context. They do not process on the firewall rules, but on the logs of the firewalls. They try to extract the effective firewall rules through aggregating the logs and compare them to the original rules. These solutions of aggregation of firewall rules do not target a well defined model of higher level policy, and thus they may produce too much unstructured output to be useful. What we propose is a bottom-up approach to reach a standard model based level of abstraction. This model guarantees portability, interoperability, integration of the network security policy in the global organization policy, and facilitates the information transmission to new security administrators. It allows to correct and update the configuration of the policy at high level, then deploy it on the firewalls in a cyclic manner. Moreover, we leverage different existent tools from other areas of research that have a sound theoretical background. Regarding role mining approaches, Ene et al. [20] have applied a standard role mining solution on two firewall sets. To get a 2-dimensional input data matrix, they have merged two dimensions of the firewall rules which are source_hosts and destination_hosts into one dimension considering them to be the permissions in the RBAC model, while they have clustered the services into roles. This initiative did not have much impact because it is not adapted to network security. Compared to policy mining, it corresponds to only one step in our algorithm. Besides, we have surveyed factorization tools for multi-dimensional tensors. Kemp et al. [21] have defined a learning systems of concepts with an infinite relational model (IRM) that could be used to cluster multiple dimensions at the same time. However, this approach considers that a concrete entity belongs to only one cluster which is not a good assumption when it comes to firewall policies. We have not been able to make comparison with our solution because the available implementation of IRM does not allow for concrete entities to be involved in multiple rules neither.

6   Conclusions and Perspectives

Adopting a standard high abstraction model is likely to make firewall management much simpler and safer. We have proposed a bottom-up approach for the NS-RBAC model configuration. We have showed the limits of existing role mining techniques to satisfy network security requirements. We have proposed a formalization of the policy mining problem, and an algorithm to solve it. This solution allows to extend and leverage existing mining tools to the network security application. Bottom-up and top-down approaches should be used together in a cyclic manner: the bottom-up approach is used to reach a general high level programming language from the already configured firewall rules, then the policy is updated or corrected at the abstract level before being deployed in the concrete level again with the top-down approach. This work has several interesting perspectives. Policy mining could be used for the analysis of other access control devices such as *Intrusion Detection Systems (IDS)*, and for examining firewall logs. It could be extended to the management of a system of firewalls by merging the results of policy mining on each firewall. Some further semantics in the NS-RBAC model such as *context* could be used to manage stateful firewalls. Finally, the ternary relation in access control rules that is emphasized by the NS-RBAC model could be useful in other applications than firewall management, and policy mining could be useful for these applications as well.

References

1. Macfarlane, R., Buchanan, W.J., Ekonomou, E., Uthmani, O., Fan, L., Lo, O.: Review of security policy implementations. Computers & Security (COMPSEC) 2(31), 253–270 (2011)
2. Titov, A., Zaborovsky, V.: Firewall configuration based on specifications of access policy and network environment (2010)
3. Cuppens, F., Cuppens-Boulahia, N., Sans, T., Miège, A.: A formal approach to specify and deploy a network security policy. In: Dimitrakos, T., Martinelli, F. (eds.) Formal Aspects in Security and Trust, pp. 203–218. Springer, Heidelberg (2004)
4. Hachana, S., Cuppens-Boulahia, N., Cuppens, F.: Role mining to assist authorization governance: How far have we gone? International Journal of Secure Software Engineering (IJSSE) 3(4) (2012)
5. Ferraiolo, D.F., Sandhu, R., Gavrila, S., Kuhn, D.R., Chandramouli, R.: Proposed NIST standard for role-based access control. standard, NIST (2001)
6. Fuchs, L., Pernul, G., Sandhu, R.S.: Roles in information security - a survey and classification of the research area. Computers & Security 30(8), 748–769 (2011)
7. Macfarlane, R., Buchanan, W.J., Ekonomou, E., Uthmani, O., Fan, L., Lo, O.: Formal security policy implementations in network firewalls. Computers & Security (COMPSEC) 31(2), 253–270 (2012)
8. Mallouli, W., Orset, J.M., Cavalli, A., Cuppens, N., Cuppens, F.: A formal approach for testing security rules (2007)
9. Vaidya, J., Atluri, V., Guo, Q.: The role mining problem: finding a minimal descriptive set of roles. In: Proceedings of the 12th ACM Symposium on Access Control Models and Technologies, SACMAT 2007, pp. 175–184. ACM (June 2007)

10. Frank, M., Buhmann, J.M., Basin, D.: On the definition of role mining. In: Proceeding of the 15th ACM Symposium on Access Control Models and Technologies, SACMAT 2010, pp. 35–44. ACM (June 2010)

11. Tongaonkar, A.S.: Fast pattern-matching techniques for packet filtering. The graduate school in partial fulfillment of the requirements for the degree of master of science in computer science, Stony Brook University (May 2004)

12. Vaidya, J., Atluri, V., Warner, J.: Roleminer: mining roles using subset enumeration. In: Proceedings of the 13th ACM Conference on Computer and Communications Security, CCS 2006, pp. 144–153. ACM (November 2006)

13. Klema, V.C., Laub, A.J.: The singular value decomposition: Its computation and some applications. IEEE Transactions on Automatic Control 25(2), 164–176 (1980)

14. Ganter, B., Wille, R.: Formal Concept Analysis - Mathematical Foundations. Springer (1999)

15. Krajca, P., Outrata, J., Vychodil, V.: Parallel recursive algorithm for FCA. In: Proceedings of the Sixth International Conference on Concept Lattices and Their Applications, vol. 433, pp. 71–82 (2008)

16. Molloy, I., Chen, H., Li, T., Wang, Q., Li, N., Bertino, E., Calo, S., Lobo, J.: Mining roles with multiple objectives. ACM Transactions on Information and System Security (TISSEC) 13, 36:1–36:35 (2010)

17. Tongaonkar, A., Inamdar, N., Sekar, R.: Inferring higher level policies from firewall rules. In: Proceedings of the 21st Large Installation System Administration Conference, LISA 2007 (November 2007)

18. Marmorstein, R.M., Kearns, P.: Firewall analysis with policy-based host classification. In: Proceedings of the 20th conference on Large Installation System Administration, LISA 2006, pp. 41–51. USENIX Association, Berkeley (2006)

19. Abedin, M., Nessa, S., Khan, L., Al-Shaer, E., Awad, M.: Analysis of firewall policy rules using traffic mining techniques. Int. J. Internet Protocol Technology 5(1-2) (2010)

20. Ene, A., Horne, W., Milosavljevic, N., Rao, P., Schreiber, R., Tarjan, R.E.: Fast exact and heuristic methods for role minimization problems. In: Proceedings of the 13th ACM Symposium on Access Control Models and Technologies, SACMAT 2008, pp. 1–10. ACM (June 2008)

21. Kemp, C., Tenenbaum, J.B., Griffiths, T.L., Yamada, T., Ueda, N.: Learning systems of concepts with an infinite relational model. In: Proceedings of the 21st National Conference on Artificial Intelligence, vol. 1, pp. 381–388 (2006)

Secure States *versus* Secure Executions
From Access Control to Flow Control

Mathieu Jaume[1], Radoniaina Andriatsimandefitra[2],
Valérie Viet Triem Tong[2], and Ludovic Mé[2]

[1] University Pierre & Marie Curie, LIP6, MOVE, Paris, France
[2] SUPELEC, SSIR Group (EA 4039), Rennes, France

Abstract. Several points of view exist about security policies among which two main approaches can be distinguished: policies can be defined by some properties over states of a system or by some properties over executions of a system. While enforcing a policy specified by some properties over states is rather easy, designing enforcement mechanisms to ensure security properties over executions is more complex. However, enforcing a property over states is sometimes sufficient to ensure a property over executions. In this paper, we investigate these two approaches in order to provide a formal framework that permits to make the bridge between the definition of secure states and security properties over sequences of secure states corresponding to executions. Along the lines of this paper, we illustrate our definitions by considering access control policies defined as properties over states and flow properties over executions of a system.

Keywords: Security policies, access control, information flows.

1 Introduction

One way to define a security policy consists in specifying a (decidable) property over some entities that can be observed from states of a system. By following such an approach, enforcement mechanisms over transition systems can be easily defined: it suffices to observe the current state and to perform a transition if and only if it leads to a state satisfying the security property. As a typical example, access control policies are often defined by specifying some properties over accesses that can be done simultaneously in the system, and can be enforced by simply observing the set of current accesses during the lifetime of the system. Another way to define a security property consists in specifying a property over executions of a system. Of course, the definition of enforcement mechanisms for such policies is more complex than for policies expressed by properties over states, and is strongly dependent on the formalism used to define the property over executions. A large litterature already exists on this topic (see [8,9] for a – non-exhaustive – survey). As a typical example, flow policies often specify granted flows that can be generated by executions of a system. In this paper, we investigate these two approaches by following a semantical point of view and we illustrate our definitions by considering access control and flow control.

A. Bagchi and I. Ray (Eds.): ICISS 2013, LNCS 8303, pp. 148–162, 2013.

We first recall previous works [6] on interpretations and comparison of security policies as properties over states. This leads to a formal framework in which we can characterize access control policies whose secure states are states generating granted flows (according to a flow-based interpretation of access control policies). However, even if each state of an execution is secure (according to a policy over states), it may happen that the whole execution does not satisfy a policy over executions. For instance, composing several granted information flows may lead to a forbidden flow. Hence, we extend here our framework to deal with such issues. To achieve this goal, we introduce abstract semantical definitions in order to characterize policies over states that ensure security properties over executions. This leads to a generalization of previous results on access control policies. Often, when a property over executions cannot be enforced by preserving a property over states, this means that the information needed to ensure the property over executions is not observable on states. In this case, a solution consists in enriching the structure of states in order to make available such information. Hence, we also describe in our framework this mechanism and we illustrate our definitions by considering a tags system over objects of a system that permits to enrich discretionary access control policies over states in order to ensure properties over flows generated by sequences of secure states. Such an approach provides a new semantical reading of a mechanism of detection of illegal information flows previously introduced in [7], which corresponds to a dual point of view of this tags system.

2   Secure States

Security Properties over States. In [5], a security policy is defined as the specification of properties over entities of a system. More formally, a policy is a tuple $\mathbb{P} = (\mathbb{T}, \mathcal{C}, \Vdash)$ where $\mathbb{T}$ is the set of "things" that the policy aims to control, called the targets (these "things" can be the actions simultaneously done in the system, or some information about the entities of the system), $\mathcal{C}$ is the set of configurations corresponding to the information needed to characterize secure elements of $\mathbb{T}$ according to the policy, and $\Vdash \subseteq \mathcal{C} \times \mathbb{T}$ is the relation specifying secure targets according to configurations: $c \Vdash t$ means that the target t is secure according to the configuration c. Enforcing such a policy according to a configuration $c \in \mathcal{C}$ over a transition system $\mathbb{S} = (Q, Q_0, L, \delta)$ (where Q is a set of states, $Q_0 \subseteq Q$ is a set of initial states, L is a set of labels and $\delta \subseteq Q \times L \times Q$ is a transition relation) can be done by considering an interpretation of states by targets $I : Q \to \mathbb{T}$ (which can be viewed as the interface between the policy and the system, or as an output function on states) from which we define the secure system $\mathbb{S}_{|\mathbb{P}}[I, c] = (Q, Q_0', L, \delta_c)$ where:

$$Q_0' = \{q_0 \in Q_0 \mid c \Vdash I(q_0)\} \text{ and } \delta_c = \{(q_1, l, q_2) \in \delta \mid c \Vdash I(q_1) \Rightarrow c \Vdash I(q_2)\}$$

As formally implemented and proved in [2], by construction, each reachable state of this system is secure according to the configuration c.

Table 1. Access Control Policies

Policy	Configuration	$c \Vdash t \Leftrightarrow$
$\mathbb{P}_{\text{hru}}$	$m \in \mathcal{C}_{\text{hru}}$	$t \subseteq m$
$\mathbb{P}_{\text{mls}}^{\uparrow}$	$(\mathcal{L}, \preceq, f_O)$ $\in \mathcal{C}_{\text{mls}}$	$\forall s \in \mathcal{S} \ \forall o_1, o_2 \in \mathcal{O}$ $((s, o_1, \text{read}) \in t \wedge (s, o_2, \text{write}) \in t) \Rightarrow f_O(o_1) \preceq f_O(o_2)$
$\mathbb{P}_{\text{mls}}^{\downarrow}$	$(\mathcal{L}, \preceq, f_O)$ $\in \mathcal{C}_{\text{mls}}$	$\forall s \in \mathcal{S} \ \forall o_1, o_2 \in \mathcal{O}$ $((s, o_1, \text{read}) \in t \wedge (s, o_2, \text{write}) \in t) \Rightarrow f_O(o_2) \preceq f_O(o_1)$
$\mathbb{P}_{\text{mls}}^{C}$	$(\mathcal{L}, \preceq, f_O, f_S)$ $\in \mathcal{C}_{\text{mls}}^{S}$	$\forall s \in \mathcal{S} \ \forall o_1, o_2 \in \mathcal{O}$ $((s, o_1, \text{read}) \in t \wedge (s, o_2, \text{write}) \in t) \Rightarrow f_O(o_1) \preceq f_O(o_2)$ $\wedge \ \forall (s, o, \text{read}) \in t \ f_O(o) \preceq f_S(s)$
$\mathbb{P}_{\text{mls}}^{I}$	$(\mathcal{L}, \preceq, f_O, f_S)$ $\in \mathcal{C}_{\text{mls}}^{S}$	$\forall s \in \mathcal{S} \ \forall o_1, o_2 \in \mathcal{O}$ $((s, o_1, \text{read}) \in t \wedge (s, o_2, \text{write}) \in t) \Rightarrow f_O(o_2) \preceq f_O(o_1)$ $\wedge \ \forall (s, o, \text{write}) \in t \ f_O(o) \preceq f_S(s)$

Access Control Policies. Access control policies aim at controlling sets of accesses that can be simultaneously done by active entities, the subjects in $\mathcal{S}$, over some passive entities, the objects in $\mathcal{O}$, according to some access modes belonging to a set $\mathcal{A}$ (in this paper, we consider the set $\mathcal{A} = \{\text{read}, \text{write}\}$). An access can be represented by a triple (s, o, a) expressing that the subject s has an access over the object o according to the access mode a. In this context, we define the set $\mathbb{T}_A = \wp(\mathcal{S} \times \mathcal{O} \times \mathcal{A})$ of security targets of access control policies as the powerset of the cartesian product $\mathcal{S} \times \mathcal{O} \times \mathcal{A}$: targets are sets of accesses. In this paper, we focus on two main approaches for access control: the HRU policy [4] which is a discretionary policy based on a set of granted accesses (which can be extended to consider RBAC [11] policies based on permissions respectively associated with subjects and roles), and MLS policies [12], like the mandatory part of the well-known Bell & LaPadula [1] or Biba [10] policies, which are based on a partially ordered set $(\mathcal{L}, \preceq)$ of security levels (or sensitivities). Formal definitions of these policies are summarized in table 1. A configuration for HRU is just a set $m \in \mathcal{C}_{\text{hru}}$ of authorized accesses (thus both targets and configurations are sets of accesses and we have $\mathcal{C}_{\text{hru}} = \mathbb{T}_A$), and the HRU policy specifies secure sets of accesses as sets only containing authorized accesses. MLS policies are defined by associating security levels in $\mathcal{L}$ with objects and/or subjects and specify what are authorized accesses in terms of security levels. We consider here four classical examples showing how to define confinement, confidentiality and integrity policies as MLS policies. As we will formally see later, the main purpose of these access control policies is to constrain information flows. We define two confinement policies, $\mathbb{P}_{\text{mls}}^{\uparrow}$ ("no write down") and $\mathbb{P}_{\text{mls}}^{\downarrow}$ ("no write up"), which are both based on the set $\mathcal{C}_{\text{mls}}$ of configurations containing tuples $(\mathcal{L}, \preceq, f_O)$ where $f_O : \mathcal{O} \to \mathcal{L}$ defines the security level of objects. By considering configurations in the set $\mathcal{C}_{\text{mls}}^{S}$ containing tuples $(\mathcal{L}, \preceq, f_O, f_S)$, where $f_S : \mathcal{S} \to \mathcal{L}$, specifying security levels to both objects and subjects, it becomes possible to define the confidentiality policy $\mathbb{P}_{\text{mls}}^{C}$ and the integrity policy $\mathbb{P}_{\text{mls}}^{I}$.

Flow Policies. Flow policies aim at controlling information flows between entities during the lifetime of a system. Of course, generally, flows generated by executions of a system cannot be deduced by observing final states of these executions and are often defined by considering each transition and/or state occurring in executions. Hence, flows are usually defined by a semantics interpretation of executions. However, we explicitly specify here control flow by considering sets of flows occurring in a system as targets of a flow policy, without any consideration about the origin of such flows (execution of a program, sequences of accesses done in a system, etc). Hence, such policies can be seen as abstract policies since we do not take here into account how such flows are generated. These flows can be flows between objects (confinement flow policy), flows from objects to subjects (confidentiality flow policy), and flows from subjects to objects (integrity flow policy). Hence, targets of such policies are tuple $(\stackrel{oo}{\rightsquigarrow}, \stackrel{os}{\rightsquigarrow}, \stackrel{so}{\rightsquigarrow})$ where:

$$\stackrel{oo}{\rightsquigarrow} \subseteq \stackrel{oo}{\hookrightarrow} = \mathcal{O} \times \mathcal{O} \qquad \stackrel{os}{\rightsquigarrow} \subseteq \stackrel{os}{\hookrightarrow} = \mathcal{O} \times \mathcal{S} \qquad \stackrel{so}{\rightsquigarrow} \subseteq \stackrel{so}{\hookrightarrow} = \mathcal{S} \times \mathcal{O}$$

specifying three sets of flows done in the system: $o_1 \stackrel{oo}{\rightsquigarrow} o_2$ means that the information contained into o_1 flows into o_2, $o \stackrel{os}{\rightsquigarrow} s$ means that the subject s has (in a direct or indirect way) a read access over the information initially contained into o, and $s \stackrel{so}{\rightsquigarrow} o$ means that the subject s has (in a direct or indirect way) a write access to o. Of course, these sets are "coherent" and belongs to the set:

$$\mathbb{T}_F = \left\{ \begin{array}{l} (\stackrel{oo}{\rightsquigarrow}, \stackrel{os}{\rightsquigarrow}, \stackrel{so}{\rightsquigarrow}) \mid \stackrel{oo}{\rightsquigarrow} = \left(\stackrel{oo}{\rightsquigarrow}\right)^* \wedge \stackrel{oo}{\rightsquigarrow} = \left(\stackrel{so}{\rightsquigarrow} \circ \stackrel{os}{\rightsquigarrow}\right) \cup \{ o \stackrel{oo}{\rightsquigarrow} o \mid o \in \mathcal{O} \} \\ \wedge \forall s \in \mathcal{S} \; \forall o_1, o_2 \in \mathcal{O} \; (o_1 \stackrel{oo}{\rightsquigarrow} o_2 \wedge o_2 \stackrel{os}{\rightsquigarrow} s) \Rightarrow o_1 \stackrel{os}{\rightsquigarrow} s \\ \wedge \forall s \in \mathcal{S} \; \forall o_1, o_2 \in \mathcal{O} \; (s \stackrel{so}{\rightsquigarrow} o_1 \wedge o_1 \stackrel{oo}{\rightsquigarrow} o_2) \Rightarrow s \stackrel{so}{\rightsquigarrow} o_2 \end{array} \right\}$$

Indeed, the relation characterizing flows between objects is clearly transitive and flows between objects are only generated by read and write accesses done by subjects over objects, and thus are obtained by composition[1] of flows between subjects and objects. Furthermore, if there is an information flow from o_1 to o_2 and if a subject s has a read access to o_2 (resp. has a write access to o_1), then s has also a read access to the information contained into o_1 (resp. has a write access to o_2). Flows policies are based on configurations specifying sets of authorized flows, from which we define several flow policies, summarized in table 2. We write $\stackrel{oo}{\rightsquigarrow}$, $\stackrel{os}{\rightsquigarrow}$ and $\stackrel{so}{\rightsquigarrow}$ the subsets of $\stackrel{oo}{\hookrightarrow}, \stackrel{os}{\hookrightarrow}$ and $\stackrel{so}{\hookrightarrow}$ specifying authorized sets of flows of a configuration. Note that when considering configurations of the form $(\stackrel{oo}{\rightsquigarrow}, \stackrel{os}{\rightsquigarrow})$, a flow between objects granted by $\stackrel{oo}{\rightsquigarrow}$ may lead a subject s, which is not allowed (by $\stackrel{os}{\rightsquigarrow}$) to know the information contained into an object o, to access to this information if another subject allowed to read o generates a flow from o to an object o' such that s is allowed to know o' according to $\stackrel{os}{\rightsquigarrow}$. Hence, it may be relevant to constrain configurations by considering the set $\mathcal{C}_{oos}^C$. Similarly, when considering configurations of the form $(\stackrel{oo}{\rightsquigarrow}, \stackrel{so}{\rightsquigarrow})$, a flow between objects granted

---

[1] Given two relations $R_1 \subseteq A \times B$ and $R_2 \subseteq B \times C$, $R_2 \circ R_1 \subseteq A \times C$ is the relation defined by $\forall a, c \in A \times C \; (a, c) \in R_2 \circ R_1 \Leftrightarrow \exists b \in B \; (a, b) \in R_1 \wedge (b, c) \in R_2$.

Table 2. Abstract flow policies

Policy	Configurations	$c \Vdash (\overset{oo}{\rightsquigarrow}, \overset{os}{\rightsquigarrow}, \overset{so}{\rightsquigarrow}) \Leftrightarrow$
$\mathbb{P}_{oo}^T$	$\mathcal{C}_{oo} = \{\overset{oo}{\rightsquigarrow} \subseteq \overset{oo}{\rightsquigarrow}\}$	$\overset{oo}{\rightsquigarrow} \subseteq (\overset{oo}{\rightsquigarrow})^*$
$\mathbb{P}_{oos}^C$	$\mathcal{C}_{oos}^C = \left\{ \begin{array}{l} (\overset{oo}{\rightsquigarrow}, \overset{os}{\rightsquigarrow}) \mid \forall o_1, o_2 \in \mathcal{O}\ \forall s \in \mathcal{S} \\ (o_1(\overset{oo}{\rightsquigarrow})^* o_2 \wedge o_2 \overset{os}{\rightsquigarrow} s) \Rightarrow o_1 \overset{os}{\rightsquigarrow} s \end{array} \right\}$	$\overset{oo}{\rightsquigarrow} \subseteq (\overset{oo}{\rightsquigarrow})^* \wedge \overset{os}{\rightsquigarrow} \subseteq \overset{os}{\rightsquigarrow}$
$\mathbb{P}_{soo}^I$	$\mathcal{C}_{soo}^I = \left\{ \begin{array}{l} (\overset{oo}{\rightsquigarrow}, \overset{so}{\rightsquigarrow}) \mid \forall o_1, o_2 \in \mathcal{O}\ \forall s \in \mathcal{S} \\ (s \overset{so}{\rightsquigarrow} o_1 \wedge o_1(\overset{oo}{\rightsquigarrow})^* o_2) \Rightarrow s \overset{so}{\rightsquigarrow} o_2 \end{array} \right\}$	$\overset{oo}{\rightsquigarrow} \subseteq (\overset{oo}{\rightsquigarrow})^* \wedge \overset{so}{\rightsquigarrow} \subseteq \overset{so}{\rightsquigarrow}$
$\mathbb{P}_{ci}$	$\mathcal{C}_{ci} = \left\{ \begin{array}{l} (\overset{os}{\rightsquigarrow}, \overset{so}{\rightsquigarrow}) \mid \forall o_1, o_2 \in \mathcal{O}\ \forall s \in \mathcal{S} \\ ((o_1, o_2) \in (\overset{so}{\rightsquigarrow} \circ \overset{os}{\rightsquigarrow}) \wedge o_2 \overset{os}{\rightsquigarrow} s) \Rightarrow o_1 \overset{os}{\rightsquigarrow} s \end{array} \right\}$ $\cap$ $\left\{ \begin{array}{l} (\overset{os}{\rightsquigarrow}, \overset{so}{\rightsquigarrow}) \mid \forall o_1, o_2 \in \mathcal{O}\ \forall s \in \mathcal{S} \\ ((o_1, o_2) \in (\overset{so}{\rightsquigarrow} \circ \overset{os}{\rightsquigarrow}) \wedge s \overset{so}{\rightsquigarrow} o_1) \Rightarrow s \overset{so}{\rightsquigarrow} o_2 \end{array} \right\}$	$\overset{os}{\rightsquigarrow} \subseteq \overset{os}{\rightsquigarrow} \wedge \overset{so}{\rightsquigarrow} \subseteq \overset{so}{\rightsquigarrow}$

by $\overset{oo}{\rightsquigarrow}$ may lead a subject s, which is not allowed (by $\overset{so}{\rightsquigarrow}$) to write information into an object o, to perform this action by writing into an object o' such that there is a granted flow from o' to o. We define $\mathcal{C}_{soo}^I$ in order to avoid such situation. For similar reasons, the set $\mathcal{C}_{ci}$ is defined in order to take into account flows between objects generated by composition of flows between objects and subjects.

Embeddings of Policies. Embeddings are defined to compare the expressive power of policies over the same domain (i.e. over the same targets). For example, this can be useful when considering two access control policies based on different notions of configurations (for instance, when trying to know if authorizations induced by a hierarchy of roles for a RBAC policy can be obtained with a partial order of security levels for a MLS policy). Intuitively, we say that $\mathbb{P}_1 = (\mathbb{T}, \mathcal{C}_1, \Vdash_1)$ can be embedded into $\mathbb{P}_2 = (\mathbb{T}, \mathcal{C}_2, \Vdash_2)$, which is written $\mathbb{P}_1 \trianglelefteq \mathbb{P}_2$, iff the control done by $\mathbb{P}_1$ can be done by $\mathbb{P}_2$. Hence, $\mathbb{P}_1 \trianglelefteq \mathbb{P}_2$ iff each configuration $c_1 \in \mathcal{C}_1$ can be interpreted by a configuration $c_2 \in \mathcal{C}_2$ which authorizes exactly the same targets. An interpretation $\mathfrak{I} : \mathcal{C}_1 \to \mathcal{C}_2$ of configurations of $\mathbb{P}_1$ by configurations of $\mathbb{P}_2$ is an embedding operator of $\mathbb{P}_1$ into $\mathbb{P}_2$ iff:

$$\forall c_1 \in \mathcal{C}_1\ \forall t \in \mathbb{T} \quad c_1 \Vdash_1 t \Leftrightarrow \mathfrak{I}(c_1) \Vdash_2 t$$

In fact, $\mathbb{P}_1 \trianglelefteq \mathbb{P}_2$ means that $\mathbb{P}_2$ has at least the same expressive power than $\mathbb{P}_1$. The relation $\trianglelefteq$ defines a preorder relation and we write $\mathbb{P}_1 \equiv \mathbb{P}_2$ when $\mathbb{P}_1 \trianglelefteq \mathbb{P}_2$ and $\mathbb{P}_2 \trianglelefteq \mathbb{P}_1$. For example, for the flow policies $\mathbb{P}_{oo}^T$ and $\mathbb{P}_{oos}^C$ introduced in table 2, we have $\mathbb{P}_{oo}^T \trianglelefteq \mathbb{P}_{oos}^C$, since, clearly, the interpretation $\mathfrak{I} : \mathcal{C}_{oo} \to \mathcal{C}_{oos}^C$ such that:

$$\forall \overset{oo}{\rightsquigarrow} \in \mathcal{C}_{oo} \quad \mathfrak{I}(\overset{oo}{\rightsquigarrow}) = \left((\overset{oo}{\rightsquigarrow})^*, \overset{os}{\hookrightarrow} \right) \in \mathcal{C}_{oos}^C$$

defines an embedding operator of $\mathbb{P}_{oo}^T$ into $\mathbb{P}_{oos}^C$. Of course, since $\mathbb{P}_{oo}^T$ does not constrain flows from objects to subjects, the converse does not hold ($\mathbb{P}_{oos}^C \ntrianglelefteq \mathbb{P}_{oo}^T$): for configurations $c = (\overset{oo}{\rightsquigarrow}, \overset{os}{\rightsquigarrow}) \in \mathcal{C}_{oos}^C$ such that $\overset{os}{\rightsquigarrow} \neq \overset{os}{\hookrightarrow}$, there does not exist a configuration in $\mathcal{C}_{oo}$ allowing exactly the same targets than c. In [6], the relation $\trianglelefteq$ has been used to compare several access control policies (not surprisingly, HRU and RBAC policies have the same expressive power in terms of authorizations, which does not mean that they are equivalent from an administrative point of view, and HRU and MLS cannot be compared according to $\trianglelefteq$).

Interpretation of Policies. In practice, it can also be useful to compare policies over different domains. As a typical example, some access control policies are designed for ensuring flow properties: such policies do not deal with information flow but only with objects containing information to be traced. Characterizing flow properties induced by an access control policy first requires to interpret the access control policy by a flow policy and then to compare this flow policy with other known flow policies by using embeddings. This can be done by considering a generic notion of interpretation of policies allowing to understand security properties expressed over some entities induced by a policy whose domain is based on different entities. Given a policy $\mathbb{P} = (\mathbb{T}, \mathcal{C}, \Vdash)$ and a $\mathbb{D}$-interpretation $\mathcal{I} : \mathbb{T} \to \mathbb{D}$ of targets over a domain $\mathbb{D}$, we define the interpreted policy $[\![\mathbb{P}]\!]_{\mathcal{I}} = ([\![\mathbb{T}]\!]_{\mathcal{I}}, [\![\mathcal{C}]\!]_{\mathcal{I}}, [\![\Vdash]\!]_{\mathcal{I}})$ where:

- $\forall T \subseteq \mathbb{T} \; [\![T]\!]_{\mathcal{I}} = \{\mathcal{I}(t) \mid t \in T\}$
- $\forall C \subseteq \mathcal{C} \; [\![C]\!]_{\mathcal{I}} = \{[\![c]\!]_{\mathcal{I}} \mid c \in C\}$ where $\forall c \in \mathcal{C} \; [\![c]\!]_{\mathcal{I}} = \{\mathcal{I}(t) \mid c \Vdash t\}$
- $\forall c' \in [\![\mathcal{C}]\!]_{\mathcal{I}} \; \forall t' \in [\![\mathbb{T}]\!]_{\mathcal{I}} \quad c' [\![\Vdash]\!]_{\mathcal{I}} t' \Leftrightarrow t' \in c'$

The interpretation $\mathcal{I}$ provides a way to obtain an extensional representation of $\mathbb{P}$: targets belong to $\mathbb{D}$ and configurations are some subsets of $\mathbb{D}$ (a configuration c is represented by the set of the interpretations of targets that c authorizes).

Flow-Based Interpretation of Sets of Accesses. Accesses done in a system generate information flows between objects, and between subjects and objects and we can define the $\mathbb{T}_F$-interpretation $\mathcal{I}_F : \mathbb{T}_A \to \mathbb{T}_F$. An elementary flow of the information contained into an object o_1 to an object o_2 can occur iff there exists a subject s reading o_1 and writing into o_2 and given a set $t_A \in \mathbb{T}_A$ of accesses, the set of elementary flows generated by t_A is defined by:

$$\mapsto_{t_A} = \left\{ o_1 \overset{oo}{\hookrightarrow} o_2 \mid \exists s \in \mathcal{S} \; (s, o_1, \text{read}) \in t_A \wedge (s, o_2, \text{write}) \in t_A \right\}$$

We can now introduce a $\overset{oo}{\hookrightarrow}$-interpretation $\mathcal{I}_{oo}$ of $\mathbb{T}_A$ allowing to characterize flows between objects generated by a set t_A of accesses: the information contained into o_1 can flow into o_2 iff there exists in t_A a chain of read and write accesses starting from a read access over o_1 and ending at a write access over o_2. This can be simply defined by considering the reflexive and transitive closure of $\mapsto_{t_A}$:

$$\mathcal{I}_{oo}(t_A) = \mapsto_{t_A}^{*}$$

For example, the set of flows generated by the following set t_A of accesses:

$$\left\{ \begin{array}{l} (s_1, o_1, \text{read}), \; (s_3, o_2, \text{read}), \; (s_1, o_3, \text{read}), \; (s_2, o_1, \text{read}), \; (s_2, o_2, \text{read}), \\ (s_2, o_2, \text{write}), \; (s_1, o_1, \text{write}), \; (s_3, o_2, \text{write}), \; (s_3, o_4, \text{write}) \end{array} \right\} \quad (1)$$

is defined by : $\stackrel{oo}{\hookrightarrow}_{t_A} = \left\{ \begin{array}{l} o_1 \stackrel{oo}{\hookrightarrow} o_1,\, o_2 \stackrel{oo}{\hookrightarrow} o_2,\, o_3 \stackrel{oo}{\hookrightarrow} o_3,\, o_4 \stackrel{oo}{\hookrightarrow} o_4,\, o_3 \stackrel{oo}{\hookrightarrow} o_1, \\ o_1 \stackrel{oo}{\hookrightarrow} o_2,\, o_2 \stackrel{oo}{\hookrightarrow} o_4,\, o_1 \stackrel{oo}{\hookrightarrow} o_4,\, o_3 \stackrel{oo}{\hookrightarrow} o_2,\, o_3 \stackrel{oo}{\hookrightarrow} o_4 \end{array} \right\}$

Note that we assume here the "worst" case: we suppose here that if there is a potential for information flow then the flow actually occurs (the definition of $\stackrel{oo}{\hookrightarrow}_{t_A}$ over-estimates the information flow generated by t_A since temporal aspect of accesses is not considered, but it can be refined by observing sequences of elementary flows). We can now introduce the $\stackrel{os}{\hookrightarrow}$-interpretation $\mathcal{I}_{os}$ and the $\stackrel{so}{\hookrightarrow}$-interpretation $\mathcal{I}_{so}$ of $\mathbb{T}_A$ allowing to characterize flows occurring between subjects and objects generated by a set of accesses t_A:

$$\mathcal{I}_{os}(t_A) = \left\{ o_1 \stackrel{os}{\hookrightarrow} s \mid o_1 \stackrel{oo}{\hookrightarrow} o_2 \in \mathcal{I}_{oo}(t_A) \wedge (s, o_2, \mathrm{read}) \in t_A \right\}$$
$$\mathcal{I}_{so}(t_A) = \left\{ s \stackrel{so}{\hookrightarrow} o_2 \mid (s, o_1, \mathrm{write}) \in t_A \wedge o_1 \stackrel{oo}{\hookrightarrow} o_2 \in \mathcal{I}_{oo}(t_A) \right\}$$

We can finally introduce the flow-based $\mathbb{T}_F$-interpretation $\mathcal{I}_F$ of $\mathbb{T}_A$ as follows:

$$\forall t_A \in \mathbb{T}_A \; \mathcal{I}_F(t_A) = (\mathcal{I}_{oo}(t_A), \mathcal{I}_{os}(t_A), \mathcal{I}_{so}(t_A)) \in \mathbb{T}_F$$

Access Control Policies *versus* **Flow Policies.** Flow-based interpretation of access control policies can now be compared with flow policies.

Proposition 1 ([6]). *There is a path from* $\mathbb{P}_1$ *to* $\mathbb{P}_2$ *in figure 1 iff* $\mathbb{P}_1 \trianglelefteq \mathbb{P}_2$.

Hence, the flow-based interpretations of MLS policies are equivalent to flow policies (furthermore, note that the "no-write-down" and "no-write-up" policies are equivalent up to an inversion of the partial order over security levels, and thus can both be viewed as a confinement policy), while the flow-based interpretation of $\mathbb{P}_{hru}$ cannot be embedded into a flow policy.

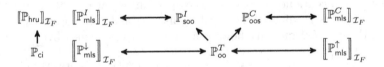

Fig. 1. Flow-based interpretation of access control policies

Equivalent Policies. Combining embeddings and interpretations provides a powerful way to analyse and to compare security policies from a semantical point of view. For example, it becomes formally possible to know if the control done by a policy $\mathbb{P}_1$ can be done by a policy $\mathbb{P}_2$ according to an interpretation of its targets. More precisely, as stated by the following proposition, proving that interpreting a policy $\mathbb{P}_1$ according to an interpretation (of targets) $\mathcal{I}$ leads to a policy equivalent (by embeddings) to a policy $\mathbb{P}_2$, can be done by mapping each configuration $c_1 \in \mathcal{C}_1$ by an "equivalent" configuration $c_2 \in \mathcal{C}_2$.

Proposition 2 ([6])**.** *Let* $\mathbb{P}_1 = (\mathbb{T}_1, \mathcal{C}_1, \Vdash_1)$ *and* $\mathbb{P}_2 = (\mathbb{T}_2, \mathcal{C}_2, \Vdash_2)$ *be two policies, and* $\mathcal{I} : \mathbb{T}_1 \to \mathbb{T}_2$ *be a* $\mathbb{T}_2$-*interpretation of* $\mathbb{T}_1$. $[\![\mathbb{P}_1]\!]_{\mathcal{I}} \equiv \mathbb{P}_2$ *iff there exists an interpretation* $\mathfrak{I} : \mathcal{C}_1 \to \mathcal{C}_2$ *such that* $[\![\mathbb{P}_1]\!]_{\mathcal{I}} = [\![(\mathbb{T}_2, \mathfrak{I}(\mathcal{C}_1), \Vdash_2)]\!]_{Id} = [\![\mathbb{P}_2]\!]_{Id}$ *where* $Id : \mathbb{T}_2 \to \mathbb{T}_2$ *is the identity interpretation.*

Hence, as illustrated by figure 2, semantic equivalence between policies can be defined as follows: $\mathbb{P}_1 = (\mathbb{T}_1, \mathcal{C}_1, \Vdash_1)$ is equivalent to $\mathbb{P}_2 = (\mathbb{T}_2, \mathcal{C}_2, \Vdash_2)$ according to the interpretations $\mathcal{I} : \mathbb{T}_1 \to \mathbb{T}_2$ and $\mathfrak{I} : \mathcal{C}_1 \to \mathcal{C}_2$ iff $\mathfrak{I}$ is surjective and:

$$\forall t_1 \in \mathbb{T}_1 \; \forall c_1 \in \mathcal{C}_1 \quad c_1 \Vdash_1 t_1 \Leftrightarrow \mathfrak{I}(c_1) \Vdash_2 \mathcal{I}(t_1)$$

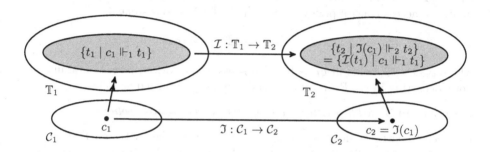

Fig. 2. Equivalent security policies

Flow Policies Induced by Access Control Policies. As stated by proposition 1, for each MLS access control policy $\mathbb{P}_A = (\mathbb{T}_A, \mathcal{C}_A, \Vdash_A)$, there exists a flow policy $\mathbb{P}_F = (\mathbb{T}_F, \mathcal{C}_F, \Vdash_F)$ such that $[\![\mathbb{P}_A]\!]_{\mathcal{I}_F} \equiv \mathbb{P}_F$. Hence, by proposition 2, there exists an interpretation $\mathfrak{I} : \mathcal{C}_A \to \mathcal{C}_F$ such that $\mathbb{P}_A$ and $\mathbb{P}_F$ are equivalent according to $\mathcal{I}_F$ and $\mathfrak{I}$. This means that $\mathfrak{I}$ is a surjective function such that:

$$\forall c_A \in \mathcal{C}_A \; [\![c_A]\!]_{\mathcal{I}_F} = \{\mathcal{I}_F(t_A) \mid c_A \Vdash_A t_A\} = \{t_F \in \mathbb{T}_F \mid \mathfrak{I}(c_A) \Vdash_F t_F\}$$

In other words, sets of flows generated by authorized sets of accesses specified by configurations in $\mathcal{C}_A$ and sets of authorized flows specified by configurations in $\mathcal{C}_F$ are the same. For example, the equivalence $\left[\!\left[\mathbb{P}^{\uparrow}_{\mathsf{mls}}\right]\!\right]_{\mathcal{I}_F} \equiv \mathbb{P}^T_{\mathsf{oo}}$ can be proved by considering the interpretation $\mathfrak{I} : \mathcal{C}_{\mathsf{mls}} \to \mathcal{C}_{\mathsf{oo}}$ defined by:

$$\mathfrak{I}((\mathcal{L}, \preceq, fo)) = \{o_1 \overset{\mathsf{oo}}{\hookrightarrow} o_2 \mid fo(o_1) \preceq fo(o_2)\}$$

Such a definition can be generalized since it leads us to consider $\mathfrak{I}$ as an embedding operator of the flow-based interpretation of $\mathbb{P}_A$ into $\mathbb{P}_F$ (interpreted by the identity $\mathbb{T}_F$-interpretation Id). Indeed, we define the "generic" flow-based interpretation scheme $\mathfrak{I}_F : \mathcal{C}_A \to \mathcal{C}_F$ of configurations of access control policies as the mapping such that $\mathfrak{I}_F(c_A)$ specifies a configuration based on the following sets of authorized flows:

$$\overset{oo}{\leadsto}_{c_A} = \{o_1 \overset{oo}{\hookrightarrow} o_2 \mid \exists t_A \in \mathbb{T}_A \; c_A \Vdash_A t_A \wedge \; o_1 \overset{oo}{\hookrightarrow} o_2 \in \mathcal{I}_{oo}(t_A)\}$$
$$\overset{os}{\leadsto}_{c_A} = \{o \overset{os}{\hookrightarrow} s \mid \exists t_A \in \mathbb{T}_A \; c_A \Vdash_A t_A \wedge \; (s, o, \text{read}) \in t_A\} \quad (2)$$
$$\overset{so}{\leadsto}_{c_A} = \{s \overset{so}{\hookrightarrow} o \mid \exists t_A \in \mathbb{T}_A \; c_A \Vdash_A t_A \wedge \; (s, o, \text{write}) \in t_A\}$$

This can be viewed as the definition of a flow policy induced by an access control policy, whose configurations are sets of authorized flows.

Consistent Access Control Policies. We are now in position to define consistent access control policies as policies whose flow-based interpretations are equivalent to their induced flow policies (according to $\mathcal{I}_F$ and $\mathcal{J}_F$). More formally, an access control policy $\mathbb{P}_A = (\mathbb{T}_A, \mathcal{C}_A, \Vdash_A)$ is consistent iff:

$$\forall t_A \in \mathbb{T}_A \; \forall c_A \in \mathcal{C}_A \quad c_A \Vdash_A t_A \Leftrightarrow \mathcal{J}_F(c_A) \Vdash_F \mathcal{I}_F(t_A)$$

where $c_F \Vdash_F t_F$ holds iff c_F is based on sets of authorized flows containing all flows occurring in t_F. Proposition 1 can now be generalized as follows.

Proposition 3. *MLS policies are consistent access control policies.*

For access control policies which are not consistent, like HRU or RBAC, there exists at least a configuration $c_A \in \mathcal{C}_A$ such that $\{t_A \in \mathbb{T}_A \mid c_A \Vdash_A t_A\}$ contains a set of accesses generating an illegal flow according to $\overset{oo}{\leadsto}_{c_A}$, $\overset{os}{\leadsto}_{c_A}$, or $\overset{so}{\leadsto}_{c_A}$ (and in this case $[\![c_A]\!]_{\mathcal{I}_F} \not\subseteq \{t_F \in \mathbb{T}_F \mid \mathcal{J}_F(c_A) \Vdash_F t_F\}$). For example, if we consider the configuration c_A of HRU specifying that authorized accesses are those in the set defined by (1):

- s_1 can read o_3 and write into o_1 on which s_2 can make a read access, even if s_2 cannot read o_3 (hence the flow $o_3 \overset{os}{\hookrightarrow} s_2$ can be generated by a secure set of accesses according to c_A while it is not authorized by $\overset{os}{\leadsto}_{c_A}$ since a target containing the access (s_2, o_3, read) is not secure according to c_A),
- s_2 can write into o_2 and then s_3 can read o_2 and write into o_4, even if s_2 cannot write into o_4 (hence the flow $s_2 \overset{so}{\hookrightarrow} o_4$ can be generated by a secure set of accesses according to c_A while it is not authorized by $\overset{so}{\leadsto}_{c_A}$ since a target containing the access (s_2, o_4, write) is not secure according to c_A).

In fact, only a subset of configurations of such policies can be viewed as a consistent (according to $\mathcal{C}_{ci}$) specification of authorized flows. Hence, the policy $\mathbb{P}_{hru}^{ci} = (\mathbb{T}_A, \mathcal{C}_{hru}^{ci}, \Vdash_{hru})$, where $\mathcal{C}_{hru}^{ci} \subset \mathcal{C}_{hru}$ contains configurations c_A which are sets of authorized accesses such that $\mathcal{I}_{os}(c_A) = \overset{os}{\leadsto}_{c_A}$ and $\mathcal{I}_{so}(c_A) = \overset{so}{\leadsto}_{c_A}$, is equivalent to the flow policy $\mathbb{P}_{ci}$. Indeed, in this case $(\overset{os}{\leadsto}_{c_A}, \overset{so}{\leadsto}_{c_A})$ belongs to $\mathcal{C}_{ci}$. This formally explains why $\mathbb{P}_{ci} \trianglelefteq [\![\mathbb{P}_{hru}]\!]_{\mathcal{I}_F}$ holds. However, since we have only $\mathcal{C}_{hru}^{ci} \subset \mathcal{C}_{hru}$ (and not $\mathcal{C}_{hru}^{ci} = \mathcal{C}_{hru}$), the converse does not hold and $[\![\mathbb{P}_{hru}]\!]_{\mathcal{I}_F} \ntrianglelefteq \mathbb{P}_{ci}$.

3   Secure States *versus* Secure Executions

Security Properties over Executions. Security policies can also be defined by specifying a subset of secure executions of a transition system $\mathbb{S} = (Q, Q_0, L, \delta)$. This often leads to define a property X characterizing secure executions of $\mathbb{S}$:

$$\mathbb{S}[X] = \{r \in Run(\mathbb{S}) \mid X(r)\}$$

where $Run(\mathbb{S}) \subseteq Q^\star$ denotes the set of all executions of $\mathbb{S}$. Such approaches can be refined by considering properties X depending on some configurations of the system and in this case we write X_c the property characterizing secure executions according to the configuration $c \in C$. When states of a transition system are not just names but can be interpreted to provide information on some entities of the system, secure executions can sometimes be characterized from the semantics $[\![\ ]\!]_\mathbb{D} : Q^\star \to \mathbb{D}$ of executions of $\mathbb{S}$ over a domain of interpretation $\mathbb{D}$:

$$\forall r \in Run(\mathbb{S}) \quad X_c(r) \Leftrightarrow c \Vdash [\![r]\!]_\mathbb{D}$$

where $\Vdash \subseteq C \times \mathbb{D}$ specifies secure executions by considering their semantics over $\mathbb{D}$. Hence, by following such an approach, the specification of $\mathbb{S}[X]$ is split into two parts: the definition of a semantics of executions over a domain $\mathbb{D}$, and the definition of a policy $\mathbb{P} = (\mathbb{D}, C, \Vdash)$ whose targets are in $\mathbb{D}$. However, the policy $\mathbb{P}$ does not aim at monitoring a transition system but only specifies secure executions of a system according to a family of properties defined from configurations.

States as Traces. In the most favorable case, observing a state q according to $I : Q \to \mathbb{D}$ provides exact information about executions leading to q:

$$\forall (q_0, \cdots, q_n) \in Run(\mathbb{S}) \quad [\![(q_0, \cdots, q_n)]\!]_\mathbb{D} = I(q_n) \tag{3}$$

In this case, enforcing the property X_c specified by a configuration c of a policy $\mathbb{P} = (\mathbb{D}, C, \Vdash)$ over the executions of $\mathbb{S}$ is easy: it suffices to build $\mathbb{S}_{|\mathbb{P}}[I, c]$. Indeed, in this case, each execution $r \in Run(\mathbb{S}_{|\mathbb{P}}[I, c])$ is such that $c \Vdash [\![r]\!]_\mathbb{D}$.

Proposition 4. *Let $I : Q \to \mathbb{D}$ and $[\![\ ]\!]_\mathbb{D} : Q^\star \to \mathbb{D}$ be interpretations satisfying (3).*

1. *Soundness.* $\forall r \in Run(\mathbb{S}_{|\mathbb{P}}[I, c]) \quad c \Vdash [\![r]\!]_\mathbb{D}$
2. *Completeness. If*

$$\forall (q_0, \cdots, q_n) \in Run(\mathbb{S}) \quad c \Vdash [\![(q_0, \cdots, q_n)]\!]_\mathbb{D} \Rightarrow \forall i \leq n \ c \Vdash [\![(q_0, \cdots, q_i)]\!]_\mathbb{D}$$

then $\forall r \in Run(\mathbb{S}) \quad c \Vdash [\![r]\!]_\mathbb{D} \Rightarrow r \in Run(\mathbb{S}_{|\mathbb{P}}[I, c])$.

Note that completeness requires a supplementary assumption since, by construction, $Run(\mathbb{S}_{|\mathbb{P}}[I, c])$ is prefix-closed.

From Secure States to Secure Executions. Of course, in practice, the assumption (3) is seldom satisfied. However, enforcing a property specified by a policy $\mathbb{P}_2 = (\mathbb{T}_2, \mathcal{C}_2, \Vdash_2)$ over executions of a system $\mathbb{S}$ by enforcing a policy $\mathbb{P}_1 = (\mathbb{T}_1, \mathcal{C}_1, \Vdash_1)$ over states during the lifetime of a system $\mathbb{S}$ is sometimes possible. It suffices that the following property holds:

$$\forall (q_0, \cdots, q_n) \in Run(\mathbb{S}) \quad \bigwedge_{i=0}^{n} c_1 \Vdash_1 I(q_i) \Rightarrow [\![c_1]\!]_{\mathcal{I}} \Vdash_2 [\![(q_0, \cdots, q_n)]\!]_{\mathbb{T}_2} \qquad (4)$$

where $I : Q \to \mathbb{T}_1$, $\mathcal{I} : \mathbb{T}_1 \to \mathbb{T}_2$ and $[\![\,]\!]_{\mathbb{T}_2} : Q^\star \to \mathbb{T}_2$.

Proposition 5. *Let $I : Q \to \mathbb{T}_1$, $\mathcal{I} : \mathbb{T}_1 \to \mathbb{T}_2$ and $[\![\,]\!]_{\mathbb{T}_2} : Q^\star \to \mathbb{T}_2$ be interpretations satisfying (4).*

1. *Soundness.* $\forall r \in Run(\mathbb{S}_{|\mathbb{P}_1}[I, c_1]) \quad [\![c_1]\!]_{\mathcal{I}} \Vdash_2 [\![r]\!]_{\mathbb{T}_2}$
2. *Completeness. If*

$$\forall (q_0, \cdots, q_n) \in Run(\mathbb{S}) \quad [\![c_1]\!]_{\mathcal{I}} \Vdash_2 [\![(q_0, \cdots, q_n)]\!]_{\mathbb{T}_2} \Rightarrow \forall i \le n \; c_1 \Vdash_1 I(q_i)$$

then $\forall r \in Run(\mathbb{S}) \quad [\![c_1]\!]_{\mathcal{I}} \Vdash_2 [\![r]\!]_{\mathbb{T}_2} \Rightarrow r \in Run(\mathbb{S}_{|\mathbb{P}_1}[I, c_1])$.

Moreover, when $[\![\mathbb{P}_1]\!]_{\mathcal{I}} \equiv \mathbb{P}_2$, by proposition 2, there exists an interpretation $\mathfrak{J} : \mathcal{C}_1 \to \mathcal{C}_2$ such that (4) is equivalent to:

$$\forall (q_0, \cdots, q_n) \in Run(\mathbb{S}) \quad \bigwedge_{i=0}^{n} c_1 \Vdash_1 I(q_i) \Rightarrow \mathfrak{J}(c_1) \Vdash_2 [\![(q_0, \cdots, q_n)]\!]_{\mathbb{T}_2} \qquad (5)$$

Runtime Flow Policies. Proposition 5 can be useful to ensure that constraining executions of a system $\mathbb{S}$ according to a consistent access control policy $\mathbb{P}_A = (\mathbb{T}_A, \mathcal{C}_A, \Vdash_A)$ leads to a system whose executions satisfy a flow property specified by the flow policy $\mathbb{P}_F$ induced by $\mathbb{P}_A$ as specified by (2). In this case, $\mathbb{P}_A$ is said to be a consistent runtime flow policy for $\mathbb{S}$ and (4) is equivalent to:

$$\forall (q_0, \cdots, q_n) \in Run(\mathbb{S}_{|\mathbb{P}_A}[I, c_A]) \quad \mathfrak{J}_F(c_A) \Vdash_F [\![(q_0, \cdots, q_n)]\!]_{\mathbb{T}_F}$$

For example, let us consider the system whose states are sets of accesses and whose transitions are obtained by adding or by removing an access to a state:

$$\mathbb{S}_A = (\mathbb{T}_A, \{\emptyset\}, \{\mathrm{add}(s, o, a), \mathrm{remove}(s, o, a) \mid (s, o, a) \in \mathcal{S} \times \mathcal{O} \times \mathcal{A}\}, \delta_A)$$

$$\text{where: } (t_1, l, t_2) \in \delta_A \Leftrightarrow \left(\begin{array}{l} (l = \mathrm{add}(s, o, a) \wedge t_2 = t_1 \cup \{(s, o, a)\}) \\ \vee \; (l = \mathrm{remove}(s, o, a) \wedge t_2 = t_1 \backslash \{(s, o, a)\}) \end{array} \right)$$

The flow-based interpretation of executions of $\mathbb{S}_A$ can be defined as follows. First, flows between objects are defined by composition:

$$\forall n > 0 \; \forall (t_1, \cdots, t_n) \in \mathbb{T}_A^\star \stackrel{\infty}{\hookrightarrow}_{(t_1, \cdots, t_n)} = \begin{cases} \mathcal{I}_{oo}(t_1) & \text{if } n = 1 \\ \mathcal{I}_{oo}(t_{k+1}) \circ \stackrel{\infty}{\hookrightarrow}_{(t_1, \cdots, t_k)} & \text{if } n = k + 1 \end{cases}$$

Then, flows from objects to subjects (resp. from subjects to objects) characterizing which subject can read which information initially contained into an object (resp. can write into which object) are defined as follows:

$$\overset{\text{os}}{\hookrightarrow}_{(t_1,\cdots,t_n)} = \bigcup_{i=1}^{n} \left\{ o_1 \overset{\text{os}}{\hookrightarrow} s \mid o_1 \overset{\text{oo}}{\hookrightarrow}_{(t_1,\cdots,t_i)} o_2 \wedge (s,o_2,\text{read}) \in t_i \right\}$$

$$\overset{\text{so}}{\hookrightarrow}_{(t_1,\cdots,t_n)} = \bigcup_{i=1}^{n} \left\{ s \overset{\text{so}}{\hookrightarrow} o_2 \mid (s,o_1,\text{write}) \in t_i \wedge o_1 \overset{\text{oo}}{\hookrightarrow}_{(t_i,t_{i+1},\cdots,t_n)} o_2 \right\}$$

Finally, semantics of non-empty executions of $\mathbb{S}$ is defined by :

$$[\![(t_1,\cdots,t_n)]\!]_{\mathbb{T}_F} = \left(\overset{\text{oo}}{\hookrightarrow}_{(t_1,\cdots,t_n)}, \overset{\text{os}}{\hookrightarrow}_{(t_1,\cdots,t_n)}, \overset{\text{so}}{\hookrightarrow}_{(t_1,\cdots,t_n)} \right)$$

We can now formally characterize flows generated by executions of the system $\mathbb{S}_{A|\mathbb{P}_A}[Id, c_A]$ (where $Id : \mathbb{T}_A \to \mathbb{T}_A$ is the identity function) and compare them to the flows authorized by the induced configuration $\mathbb{J}_F(c_A)$. Not surprisingly, for MLS policies we have the following proposition.

Proposition 6. *MLS policies are consistent runtime flow policies for $\mathbb{S}_A$.*

Hence, for MLS policies, controlling sets of accesses suffices to enforce a flow property over executions. On the contrary, enforcing an access control policy $\mathbb{P}_A$, like HRU, is clearly not sufficient to control flows according to the induced flow policy $\mathbb{P}_F$. Indeed, if we consider again the configuration $c_A \in \mathcal{C}_{\text{hru}}$ defined by (1), we would like for example that:

- s_2 can read o_1 while o_1 does not contain information coming from objects that s_2 is not authorized to read,
- s_3 can write into o_4 while objects read by s_3 do not contain information coming from subjects that are not authorized to write into o_4.

Of course, such a control cannot be done by only observing sets of accesses since it requires to know the origin of information contained into objects during the lifetime of the system. Hence, in this case, a supplementary information has to be considered together with sets of accesses.

From Secure Executions to Secure States. Enforcing a property over the executions of a system $\mathbb{S} = (Q, Q_0, L, \delta)$ by preserving a property over states during its executions is not always possible. This is the case when the property over executions is not deducible by observing states and a solution consists in enriching the structure of states with some new information belonging to a set K (the relation δ must also be enriched in order to describe how the added information is modified during transitions). This leads to the definition of a new system $\mathbb{S}^+ = (Q \times K, Q_0 \times K_0, L, \delta^+)$ such that $K_0 \subseteq K$ and:

$$\forall q_1, q_2 \in Q \; \forall k_1, k_2 \in K \; \forall l \in L \; ((q_1, k_1), l, (q_2, k_2)) \in \delta^+ \Rightarrow (q_1, l, q_2) \in \delta$$
$$\wedge \; \forall q_1, q_2 \in Q \; \forall l \in L \; (q_1, l, q_2) \in \delta \Rightarrow \exists k_1, k_2 \in K \; ((q_1, k_1), l, (q_2, k_2)) \in \delta^+$$

$$\tag{6}$$

Such a system is well-suited to enforce a property specified by $\mathbb{P}_2 = (\mathbb{T}_2, \mathcal{C}_2, \Vdash_2)$ over executions of $\mathbb{S}$ by enforcing $\mathbb{P}_1 = (\mathbb{T}_1, \mathcal{C}_1, \Vdash_1)$ over states of $\mathbb{S}^+$ iff:

$$\forall((q_0, k_0), \cdots, (q_n, k_n)) \in Run(\mathbb{S}^+) \bigwedge_{i=0}^{n} c_1 \Vdash_1 I(q_i, k_i) \Rightarrow [\![c]\!]_{\mathcal{I}} \Vdash_2 [\![(q_0, \cdots, q_n)]\!]_{\mathbb{T}_2}$$

where $I : Q \times K \to \mathbb{T}_1$, $\mathcal{I} : \mathbb{T}_1 \to \mathbb{T}_2$ and $[\![\,]\!]_{\mathbb{T}_2} : Q^\star \to \mathbb{T}_2$. Indeed, in this case, this property is similar to the assumption (4).

From Access Control to Flow Control. As we said, some access control policies $\mathbb{P}_A = (\mathbb{T}_A, \mathcal{C}_A, \Vdash_A)$, like HRU or RBAC, are neither consistent nor runtime flow policies. Hence, enforcing a flow property (specified by the configuration $\mathcal{I}_F(c_A)$) over executions of the access system $\mathbb{S}_A$ requires to enrich the structure of states in a way that for each state q, some information (or property) about flows previously done before reaching q can be observed (or characterized). Of course, such an information has to be "minimal" (it should not correspond to a complete trace of previous flows). In [3,13], intrusion detection systems have been designed in different contexts to detect illegal information flows according to (the flow-based interpretation of) an access control policy. These systems are based on tags attached to objects and a fomalization of such an approach has been presented in [7]. We present here a dual formalization of this approach by following the framework introduced in this paper (which can here be viewed as the development *a posteriori* of theoretical foundations of previous works). Tags describe what flows still can happen during the lifetime of the system and correspond to the information added to states. Tags belong to the set:

$$K = \{k : \mathcal{E} \to \wp(\wp(\mathcal{E}) \times \mathcal{E})\} \quad \text{where } \mathcal{E} = \mathcal{O} \cup \mathcal{S}$$

Each tag provides information about what is still authorized by the flow policy according to the configuration $\mathcal{I}_F(c_A)$ and to the flows that have previously occurred. The set K_0 contains one single element k_0 defined by:

$$\forall e \in \mathcal{E} \ k_0(e) = \left\{ \begin{array}{l} (E, e') \mid e \in E \\ \wedge (e' \in \mathcal{O} \Rightarrow \forall o \in \mathcal{O} \cap E \ \mathcal{I}_F(c_A) \Vdash_F o \overset{oo}{\leadsto} e') \\ \wedge (e' \in \mathcal{S} \Rightarrow \forall o \in \mathcal{O} \cap E \ \mathcal{I}_F(c_A) \Vdash_F o \overset{os}{\leadsto} e') \\ \wedge (e' \in \mathcal{O} \Rightarrow \forall s \in \mathcal{S} \cap E \ \mathcal{I}_F(c_A) \Vdash_F s \overset{so}{\leadsto} e') \end{array} \right\}$$

Now, the transition system $\mathbb{S}_A^+ = (\mathbb{T}_A \times K, \{(\emptyset, k_0)\}, L, \delta_A^+)$ can be defined from the transition relation (satisfying (6)):

$$((t_1, k_1), l, (t_2, k_2)) \in \delta_A^+ \Leftrightarrow ((t_1, l, t_2) \in \delta_A \ \wedge \forall e \in \mathcal{E} \ k_2(e) = \bigcap_{e' \in J} k_1(e'))$$

$$\text{where: } J = \left\{ e' \in \mathcal{E} \mid e \overset{oo}{\leadsto} e' \in \mathcal{I}_{oo}(t_2) \vee e \overset{os}{\leadsto} e' \in \mathcal{I}_{os}(t_2) \vee e \overset{so}{\leadsto} e' \in \mathcal{I}_{so}(t_2) \right\}$$

Enforcing the flow property $\mathcal{I}_F(c_A)$ over executions of $\mathbb{S}_A^+$ can now be done by enforcing a property over states specified by the policy $\mathbb{P}_A^+ = (\mathbb{T}_A \times K, \mathcal{C}_A, \Vdash_A^+)$ where:

$$c_A \Vdash_A^+ (t_A, k) \Leftrightarrow (c_A \Vdash_A t_A \wedge \forall e \in \mathcal{E} \ k(e) \cap W(e) \neq \emptyset)$$

where W is a constant defined from c_A by:

$$W(e) = \left\{ \begin{array}{l} (E,e) \mid (e \in \mathcal{O} \Rightarrow \forall o \in \mathcal{O} \cap E \; \mathfrak{I}_F(c_A) \Vdash_F o \overset{oo}{\hookrightarrow} e) \\ \wedge (e \in \mathcal{S} \Rightarrow \forall o \in \mathcal{O} \cap E \; \mathfrak{I}_F(c_A) \Vdash_F o \overset{os}{\hookrightarrow} e) \\ \wedge (e \in \mathcal{O} \Rightarrow \forall s \in \mathcal{S} \cap E \; \mathfrak{I}_F(c_A) \Vdash_F s \overset{so}{\hookrightarrow} e) \end{array} \right\}$$

In [7], a dual reading of this tags system leads to the definition of a mechanism that aims at detecting illegal information flows (by raising alerts). Soundness and completeness can be reformulated in our new framework as follows:

$$\forall((t_0, k_0), \cdots, (t_n, k_n)) \in Run(\mathbb{S}_{A|\mathbb{P}_A^+}[Id, c_A])$$
$$\bigwedge_{i=1}^{n} c_A \Vdash_A^+ (t_i, k_i) \Rightarrow \mathfrak{I}_F(c_A) \Vdash_F [\![(t_0, \cdots, t_n)]\!]_{T_F} \tag{7}$$

$$\forall(t_0, \cdots, t_n) \in Run(\mathbb{S}_A) \; \mathfrak{I}_F(c_A) \Vdash\!\!\!/_F [\![(t_0, \cdots, t_n)]\!]_{T_F}$$
$$\Rightarrow \exists i \leq n \; \forall((t_0, k_0), \cdots, (t_i, k_i)) \in Run(\mathbb{S}_A^+) \; c_A^+ \Vdash\!\!\!/_A^+ (t_i, k_i)$$

Note that the property (7) corresponds to the property (5), since it can be proved that $[\![\mathbb{P}_A^+]\!]_{\mathcal{I}_F'} \equiv \mathbb{P}_F$ according to $\mathfrak{I}_F$, where forall (t, k), $\mathcal{I}_F'(t, k) = \mathcal{I}_F(t)$ and:

$$\forall((t_0, k_0), \cdots, (t_n, k_n)) \in Run(\mathbb{S}_A^+) \; [\![((t_0, k_0), \cdots, (t_n, k_n))]\!]_{T_F} = [\![(t_0, \cdots, t_n)]\!]_{T_F}$$

In other words, $\mathbb{P}_A^+$ can be viewed as a consistent runtime flow policy for $\mathbb{S}_A^+$.

4 Conclusion

The goal of security policies is to achieve security properties. On the other hand, the relation between these properties and the properties on which security mechanisms are based is not always obvious. Hence, a question naturally emerges: how to bridge the gap in such a case? In this paper, to answer this question, we have introduced formal definitions based on the semantics of secure states and secure executions providing methodological tools allowing to handle such situations. Thanks to these definitions, we've focused on the consistency between the protection of information obtained from an access control and the flow of information that may occur when a system is under control of the access control policy. More generally, this paper addresses the problem of enforcing security properties over executions by preserving security properties over states occurring in executions, focusing in particular on the relationship between access control policies on one side and flow control policies on the other. Our approach extend a formal framework introduced in previous works [5,7,6]. In fact, when designing this framework, our main motivation was to be able to provide some methodological guidelines to specify security policies but also to be able to compare these policies. This framework can be used to consider many developments since it does not depend on the syntax used to described policies but only on some semantics aspects of policies. It allows to identify the various entities involved in the definition of a policy and their role. The main developments done within our framework is concerned with flow analysis of access control policies.

In fact, access control policies allow to grant or to revoke the rights for some subjects to access some objects, but cannot always control how the information is used once it has been accessed (there is no control on its propagation). Intuitively, a link is needed between "what you do" (the policy) and "what you want" (the goal for which the policy is designed). Comparing and understanding relationship between policies requires attention in emerging contexts where policies under different domains might need to be compared or merged. Our work can be viewed as a first step in this direction. However, several issues remain to be addressed. For example, we plan to work on composition of security policies (for example on the way to compose a policy P with an administrative policy that aims at controlling modification of configurations of P).

References

1. Bell, D., LaPadula, L.: Secure Computer Systems: a Mathematical Model. Technical Report MTR-2547 (Vol. II), MITRE Corp., Bedford, MA (May 1973)
2. Doligez, D., Jaume, M., Rioboo, R.: Development of secured systems by mixing programs, specifications and proofs in an object-oriented programming environment. In: Proceedings of the ACM SIGPLAN Seventh Workshop on Programming Languages and Analysis for Security (PLAS 2012), pp. 80–91. ACM (2012)
3. Geller, S., Hauser, C., Tronel, F., Viet Triem Tong, V.: Information flow control for intrusion detection derived from MAC policy. In: IEEE International Conference on Communications (ICC 2011) (2011)
4. Harrison, M., Ruzzo, W., Ullman, J.: Protection in operating systems. Communications of the ACM 19, 461–471 (1976)
5. Jaume, M.: Security rules *versus* security properties. In: Jha, S., Mathuria, A. (eds.) ICISS 2010. LNCS, vol. 6503, pp. 231–245. Springer, Heidelberg (2010)
6. Jaume, M.: Semantic comparison of security policies: From access control policies to flow properties. In: IEEE Symposium on Security and Privacy Workshops, pp. 60–67. IEEE Computer Society (2012)
7. Jaume, M., Viet Triem Tong, V., Mé, L.: Flow-based interpretation of access control: Detection of illegal information flows. In: Jajodia, S., Mazumdar, C. (eds.) ICISS 2011. LNCS, vol. 7093, pp. 72–86. Springer, Heidelberg (2011)
8. Khoury, R., Tawbi, N.: Which security policies are enforceable by runtime monitors? a survey. Computer Science Review 6(1), 27–45 (2012)
9. Ligatti, J., Reddy, S.: A theory of runtime enforcement, with results. In: Gritzalis, D., Preneel, B., Theoharidou, M. (eds.) ESORICS 2010. LNCS, vol. 6345, pp. 87–100. Springer, Heidelberg (2010)
10. Sandhu, R.S.: On five definitions of data integrity. In: Database Security, VII: Status and Prospects. In: Proceedings of the IFIP WG11.3 Working Conference on Database Security. IFIP Transactions, vol. A-47, pp. 257–267 (1993)
11. Sandhu, R.S., Coyne, E.J., Feinstein, H.L., Youman, C.E.: Role-based access control models. IEEE Computer 29(2), 38–47 (1996)
12. Sandhu, R.S.: Lattice-based access control models. IEEE Computer 26(11), 9–19 (1993)
13. Viet Triem Tong, V., Clark, A., Mé, L.: Specifying and enforcing a fined-grained information flow policy: Model and experiments. Journal of Wireless Mobile Networks, Ubiquitous Computing and Dependable Applications, JOWUA (2010)

Monitoring for Slow Suspicious Activities Using a Target Centric Approach

Harsha K. Kalutarage, Siraj A. Shaikh, Qin Zhou, and Anne E. James

Digital Security and Forensics (SaFe) Group, Faculty of Engineering and Computing
Coventry University, Coventry, CV1 5FB, UK
{kalutarh,aa8135,cex371,csx118}@coventry.ac.uk

Abstract. Slow, suspicious and increasingly sophisticated malicious activities on modern networks are incredibly hard to detect. Attacker tactics such as source collusion and source address spoofing are common. Effective attribution of attacks therefore is a real challenge. To address this we propose an approach to utilise destination information of activities together with a data fusion technique to combine the output of several information sources to a single profile score. The main contribution of the paper is proposing a radical shift to the focus of analysis. Experimental results offer a promise for target centric monitoring that does not have to rely on possible source aggregation.

1 Introduction

Slow, suspicious and increasingly sophisticated malicious activities on modern networks are incredibly hard to detect. An attacker may take days, weeks or months to complete an attack life cycle. Attacks may blend into the network noise in order to never exceed detection thresholds and to exhaust detection system state. A particular challenge is to monitor for such attempts deliberately designed to stay beneath detection thresholds. Attacker tactics such as source collusion and source address spoofing are common, and therefore make such attacker detection very hard. To address this we propose a method that does not require correlating to a common source. We shift the focus away from potential sources of attacks to potential targets of such activity. The proposed approach is designed to utilise destination information of activities together with a data fusion technique to combine the output of several information sources to a single profile score. We analyse for suspicious activities based on (or around) the destination information of the activities only.

2 Methodology

The problem of *target-centric* monitoring is broken down into two sub problems: *profiling* and *analysis*. Profiling provides for evidence fusion across spaces and accumulation across time, updating the normal node profiles dynamically based on changes in evidence. A multivariate version of simple Bayesian formula is

A. Bagchi and I. Ray (Eds.): ICISS 2013, LNCS 8303, pp. 163–168, 2013.

used as the method for evidence fusion to profile destination of activities during a smaller observation window. Those short period profiles are accumulated over the time to generate profiles for extended period of times (larger windows). It reduces the sheer volume of information such as raw logs and events [1], provided by number of different type of sources (e.g. SIDSs, anomaly detection components, file integrity checkers, AV, information from L3 switches), to a single value profile score for each node. Analysis distinguishes between anomalous and normal profiles using Grubbs' test [2]. Let H_1 and H_2 be two possible states of a node in computer network. We define H_1 as a node under attack and H_2 as a node not under attack. H_1 and H_2 are mutually exclusive and exhaustive states. P(H_1) expresses the belief, in term of probability, that the node is in state H_1 in absence of any other knowledge. Once we obtain more knowledge on our proposition H_1 through multiple information sources, in form of evidence $E=\{e_1,e_2,e_3,...,e_m\}$, our belief is expressed as a conditional probability $p(H_1/E)$. Using Bayes theorem, and assuming statistical independence between information sources:

$$p(H_1/E) = \frac{\prod\limits_{j=1}^{m} p(e_j/H_1).p(H_1)}{\sum\limits_{i=1}^{2} \prod\limits_{j=1}^{m} p(e_j/H_i).p(H_i)} \tag{1}$$

The assumption on statistical independence above is reasonable as we propose to use distinct types of information sources, which operate independently. In practice, a good Security Information Event Management (SIEM) deployment aggregates a number of solutions from many independent vendors [1]. When likelihoods $p(e_j/H_i)$ and priors $p(H_i)$ are known, the posterior $p(H_1/E)$ can be calculated. $p(H_1/E)$ terms in Equation 1 can be accumulated by time and used as a metric to distinguish targeted nodes from other nodes. We use the univariate version of Grubbs' test [2] to detect anomalies points in a given set of node profiles, subject to the assumption that *normal* node profiles in a given set follow an unknown Gaussian distribution. For each profile score x, its z score is computed as $z = \frac{|x-\bar{x}|}{s}$; where $\bar{x}$ and s are the mean and standard deviation of data set. A test instance is declared anomalous at significance level α if

$$z \geq \frac{N-1}{\sqrt{N}} \sqrt{\frac{t^2_{\alpha/N,N-2}}{N-2+t^2_{\alpha/N,N-2}}} \tag{2}$$

where N is the number of profiles points in the set, and $t_{\alpha/N,N-2}$ is the value taken by a t-distribution (one tailed test) at the significance level of $\frac{\alpha}{N}$. The α reflects the confidence associated with the threshold and indirectly controls the number of profiles declared as anomalous [3]. This is a vertical analysis to detect one's aberrant behaviour with respect to her peers.

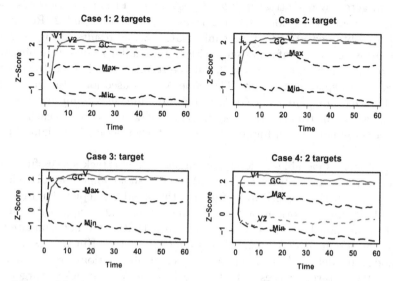

Fig. 1. Monitoring utilising the destination information of slow activities

3   Experimental Analysis

Network simulator $NS3$ is used to build a network topology consisting of a server farm and 10 subnets of varying size. Anonymous attackers, located in 3 subnets, are launching slow attacks on nodes in the server farm in a random manner. Anomalous traffic, by means of unusual port numbers, is generated along with normal traffic within and between networks using a Poisson arrival model. To simulate innocent events like user mistakes, suspicious traffic is also generated by normal nodes, but at different rates. If λ_a, λ_n are mean rates of generating suspicious events by attacker and innocent nodes respectively, we ensured maintaining $\lambda_a = \lambda_n \pm 3\sqrt{\lambda_n}$ and $\lambda_n (\le 0.1)$ sufficiently smaller for all our experiments to characterise slow suspicious activities which aim at staying beneath the threshold of detection and hiding within the background noise. The idea to use the above relationship for generating attacker activities was to keep them within the *normalilty range* of innocent activities (i.e. background noise). $\sqrt{\lambda_n}$ is the standard deviation of rates of suspicious events generated by normal nodes. Each simulation was run for a reasonable period of time to ensure that enough traffic is generated. For the purposes of simulation prior probabilities $p(H_1) = \frac{1}{2}$ and likelihoods $p(e_j/H_1) = k$ (arbitrary values ≥ 0.5 and ≤ 1) were used to distinguish different types of events. Estimation of these probabilities for real networks can be found in [3,4,5].

Figure 1 shows how the targets of slow attacks are detected. In case 1 two nodes on the server farm are targeted by three attackers, in case 2 one node on the server farm is targeted by three attackers, in case 3 one node on the server farm is targeted by a single attacker, and in case 4 two nodes on the server farm are targeted by one attacker. The Bayesian model from equation 1 is used to generate profile scores for obtaining results in Figures 1 and 2. Results in Figure 1 are obtained utilising target information while results in Figure 2 are obtained utilising source information. In Figure 2, similar results were obtained for all three attackers in cases 1 and 2, but the results for only one attacker are presented due to space constraints. The same trace is used for obtaining results in both Figures. *Min*, *Max* and *GC* are the minimum, maximum and Grubbs' critical value (i.e. the threshold) for profile scores of normal nodes in each subnet where a targeted node (V in Figure 1) and an attacker node (A in Figure 2) are located.

Our approach is capable of detecting targets under attack successfully (see Figure 1). Targets cut off (or very close to) the threshold while normal nodes in target's subnet are significantly away from the threshold. As depicted in Figure 2, attackers hide among normal nodes, and the source-centric approach fails to detect them as quickly. Case 4, where colluded activities are not simulated, is an exception here as it detects only one target out of two. But in case 1, both target nodes are detected; a minimum number of observations are required in order to detect a target successfully. In case 1, since three attackers target two victims, there is a better chance for the monitoring system to observe enough evidence against each victim than it is in case 4. Finding the relationship between detectability and minimum number of observations required is future work.

Detection potential measures how likely an activity could be detected as a suspicious slow activity. It is expressed in terms of deviations of profile scores from the threshold line. The higher the deviation the better the chances of detection. On that basis the detection potential d is defined as: $d = z - GC$. Figure 3 compares this across the two approaches in each case. A (or A_i) represents the detection potential for attackers while V (or V_i) represents the detection potential for targets. The latter has a higher detection potential in all cases. Higher variations (fluctuations) on detection potential indicate a higher chance for false alarms.

4   Related Work

[6] offers a different direction for security monitoring by proposing a class of scanning detection algorithms that focus on what is being scanned for instead of who is scanning. But such an approach is not completely independent from the source information either. It uses the source information of scan packets for victim detection. Our approach does not require any information about the source. It completely depends on destination information and allows for any suspicious event on the network to be accounted for. Most importantly, we acknowledge two types of uncertainties of events defined in [7,4] in a Bayesian framework. Hence our effort is completely different from [6], but has been inspired from that work. Using Bayesian technique and its variants for intrusions detection can be found in [5]. The relevance of information fusion for network security monitoring has been widely discussed [3,8]. Our method is based on anomaly detection.

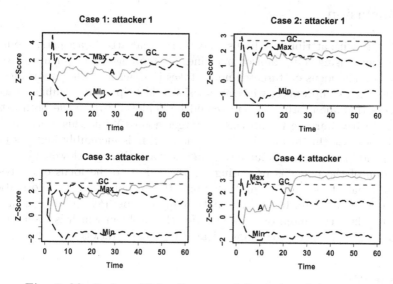

Fig. 2. Monitoring utilising the source information of slow activities

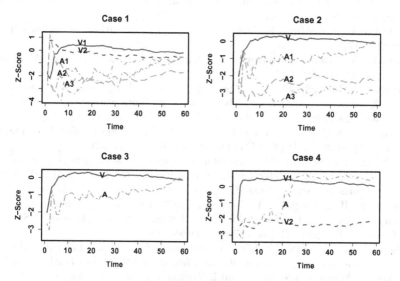

Fig. 3. A comparison of detection potential for each case

A number of other anomaly based detection approaches have been proposed, but most are general in nature [9,10,11]. Most of current incremental anomaly detection approaches focus on rapid attacks, have high rate of false alarms, are non-scalable, and are not fit for deployment in high-speed networks (refer to survey paper [12]), whereas our focus is on slow attacks.

5   Conclusion

One difficulty with attribution discussed earlier is that attacks are carried out in multiple stages using compromised machines as stepping stones (or in the form of bot-nets). The focus on targeted nodes takes into account the importance of preventing such compromise, which in itself should help to undermine attacks. One argues that monitoring systems could be deployed to achieve both attribution and early warning for attacks on target nodes. While this is feasible in theory, in practice this means the cost of monitoring is incredibly high, as networks expand in size, traffic volume rise, and slow attackers get slower. The main contribution of the paper is proposing a radical shift to the focus of analysis. We utilise a data fusion algorithm to combine the output of several information sources to a single score. It acts as a data reduction method and enables us to propose a lightweight monitoring scheme for the problem which is essential in near-real-time analysis of slow, sophisticated targeted attacks.

References

1. (CSIEM): Cisco security information event management deployment guide (August 2013), http://www.cisco.com
2. Grubbs, R.E.: Procedures for Detecting Outlying Observations in Samples. Technometrics 11(1), 1–21 (1969)
3. Chandola, V., Banerjee, A., Kumar, V.: Anomaly detection: A survey. ACM Comput. Surv. 41(3), 15:1–15:58 (2009)
4. Kalutarage, H.K., Shaikh, S.A., Zhou, Q., James, A.E.: Sensing for suspicion at scale: A bayesian approach for cyber conflict attribution and reasoning. In: 4th International Conference on Cyber Conflict (CYCON), pp. 1–19 (2012)
5. Siaterlis, C., Maglaris, B.: Towards multisensor data fusion for dos detection. In: ACM Symposium on Applied Computing, pp. 439–446 (2004)
6. Whyte, D., van Oorschot, P.C., Kranakis, E.: Exposure maps: removing reliance on attribution during scan detection. In: Proceedings of the 1st USENIX Workshop on Hot Topics in Security, HOTSEC 2006. USENIX Association (2006)
7. Kalutarage, H.K., Shaikh, S.A., Zhou, Q., James, A.E.: Tracing sources of anonymous slow suspicious activities. In: Lopez, J., Huang, X., Sandhu, R. (eds.) NSS 2013. LNCS, vol. 7873, pp. 122–134. Springer, Heidelberg (2013)
8. Vokorokos, L., Chovanec, M., Látka, O., Kleinova, A.: Security of distributed intrusion detection system based on multisensor fusion. In: 6th International Symposium on Applied Machine Intelligence and Informatics, pp. 19–24 (2008)
9. Patcha, A., Park, J.M.: An overview of anomaly detection techniques: Existing solutions and latest technological trends. In: Computer Networks. Elsevier (2007)
10. Kumar, S., Spafford, E.H.: An application of pattern matching in intrusion detection. In: Technical Report CSDTR-94-013 Purdue University, IN, USA (1994)
11. Chandola, V., Banerjee, A., Kumar, V.: Anomaly detection: A survey. ACM Computing Surveys 41 (2009)
12. Bhuyan, M.H., Bhattacharyya, D., Kalita, J.K.: Survey on incremental approaches for network anomaly detection. International Journal of Communication Networks and Information Security 3(3), 226–239 (2012)

RAPID-FeinSPN: A Rapid Prototyping Framework for Feistel and SPN-Based Block Ciphers*

Ayesha Khalid[1], Muhammad Hassan[1], Anupam Chattopadhyay[1], and Goutam Paul[2],**

[1] MPSoC Architectures Research Group,
RWTH Aachen University, Aachen 52074, Germany
{ayesha.khalid,hassanm,anupam.chattopadhyay}@ice.rwth-aachen.de
[2] R.C. Bose Centre for Cryptology and Security,
Indian Statistical Institute, Kolkata 700 108, India
goutam.paul@isical.ac.in

Abstract. In this paper we propose RAPID-FeinSPN, an extensible framework designed for rapid prototyping of Feistel Network and Substitution-Permutation Network (SPN) based symmetric ciphers. The framework tries to bridge the gap between the designer of cryptographic schemes and the VLSI implementation engineers of that cryptographic systems. Using a GUI-based interface the user has the freedom either to choose a well-known Feistel or SPN based cryptosystem for implementation or to specify the configuration of a new cipher. RAPID-FeinSPN supports multiple configurations of cryptographic settings and using the modular design principles generates a customized C code as well as a customized hardware implementation without significant performance degradation. This approach allows a quick hardware resource estimation, early functional validation of desirable cipher properties and can be used for benchmarking various design parameters of a cipher that vary in terms of security, complexity or both for a security-throughput trade-off. We have implemented some well known block ciphers using RAPID-FeinSPN and benchmarked the performance against software as well as hardware implementations.

Keywords: Block cipher, Feistel network cipher, High-level Synthesis, Rapid Prototyping, SPN cipher, VLSI Implementation.

1 Introduction and Motivation

Security is an essential part of today's information systems. Multiple cryptographic primitives including block ciphers, stream ciphers, hash functions, message authentication codes (MAC) and public key cryptography ensure privacy,

---

* The work of this author was done in part during his visit at RWTH Aachen, Germany as an Alexander von Humboldt Fellow.
** Corresponding author.

A. Bagchi and I. Ray (Eds.): ICISS 2013, LNCS 8303, pp. 169–190, 2013.

authenticity and security required in a wide range of application domains. To fulfill the demanding need of high bandwidth for multimedia applications, dedicated accelerators or customized ASICs for most of the cryptographic algorithms are extensively taken up [3,29,31,51,52,9,10]. These custom ASIC implementations try to economize a particular or multiple hardware resources i.e., area, throughput, energy efficiency or various possible design points as a compromise between these critical parameters. For software based algorithms, implementation results on a flexible processor, sometimes with algorithm specific customizations is usually presented [1,2]. In their basic proposal documentation, most of the newer cryptographic algorithms have throughput figures for C implementation on a known General Purpose Processor (GPP) or area and throughput results of a VLSI implementation on a known FPGA or CMOS technology library. These parameters are used to evaluate the usability of algorithms; e.g., NIST eliminated algorithms in SHA-3 competition based on its performance on a software/ hardware platform, in addition to the typical parameters to judge the quality of a cryptographic algorithm (security, diversity, attack resilience) [63]. A rapid prototyping framework can generate required implementations in C and HDL to significantly shorten the design cycle for these algorithms.

1.1   When Change Is Constant

The field of cryptography is dynamic; newer, faster and more secure algorithms and successful cryptanalytic attacks are frequently reported. The justifications of having a rapid prototyping framework for cryptographic algorithms are as following.

1. *Countering cryptanalysis*: Newer cryptanalytic methods and successful attempts against algorithms generally suggest countermeasures that may have a deteriorating effect on resource utilization of its implementation. For example, to increase the resistance against cryptanalysis, a proposed countermeasure against attack on Threefish-512 requires additional operations [7]. In several cases, the attack is reported against a family of ciphers [32,7].
2. *Versions of cryptographic algorithms*: Throughput requirements often require designers to switch between various versions of the same algorithm and achieve a performance-security trade-off e.g., varying the number of rounds in salsa20 [20] or switching to more a secure version of an RC4 [8].
3. *Newer cryptographic subclasses*: Rigorous constraints on resource utilization in terms of computational complexity and area have led way to light-weight cryptography. The need of benchmarking resources for newer algorithms against the existing ones is critical.

1.2   Computational Dwarfs

Despite a lot of interest of multiple active research groups undertaking the VLSI implementation of various cryptographic workloads individually, an effort to tackle the problem in a generic way is still missing. For a cryptographic rapid prototyping framework, we propose to take up the architectural design of an entire class of cryptographic algorithms based on common operations. Quite a few library-based software implementations exist for many applications. Library based processor design approach in hardware is offered by Tensilica [4] (user-customizable processor configuration designs) and ARC configurable cores [5]. For both of these approaches the ease of pre-verification accelerates design cycle but at the cost of compromising optimization for application specific architectures over generality.

The idea of combining computational workloads under a class or dwarf that captures a pattern of computation and communication was presented at [11]. Each of the 13 proposed Berkeley dwarfs capture the major functionality and data movement pattern across an entire class of important application. Hence the insight of the major characteristic computation kernels belonging to one dwarf can be reused for different applications of the same dwarf class [11]. A similar idea of combining computational workloads under a class that captures a pattern of computation and communication is presented by Intel Recognition-Mining-Synthesis (RMS) view [12].

The concept of computational kernels has been exploited in the domain of cryptography as well. In [31], a high-level synthesis framework for fast hardware implementation of elliptic curve arithmetic operations is proposed. However, most of the parametrized toolflows concentrate on the cryptanalysis [33,34]. The reported efforts of rapid prototyping frameworks for cryptographic protocols remains limited to generation of software codes [61,62]. Given the increasing importance of hardware performance and in absence of concrete analytical measures against low-level hardware attacks, it is imperative to prepare a framework, which covers both the algorithmic design as well as efficient hardware implementation. This is exactly what we propose in this work.

1.3 Our Contributions

RAPID-FeinSPN is a robust, efficient and extensible framework for cryptographic researchers to develop software and hardware implementations of SPN and Feistel network based ciphers. The framework collects configuration, via a Graphical User Interface (GUI), related to algorithm and architecture before generating the software and hardware implementation. The noteworthy features of the framework are as follows

1. It simultaneously shelters the algorithms designer from low level implementation details of the algorithms as well as aids them by providing a powerful and flexible API to rapidly incorporate improvements in the design.
2. A key challenge addressed in this work is to identify the (valid) algorithm sub-structures and map those to efficient hardware/software blocks.
3. We have successfully implemented some prominent block ciphers. The ciphers are validated against specified test vectors. Furthermore, we have compared our implementation efficiency via runtime on a GPP and via area-time performance for the software and hardware implementations.

It should also be noted that we are not targeting for the best possible optimized implementation, but an implementation, which is

- reasonably efficient,
- allows exploring algorithmic and implementation choices simultaneously,
- can be easily used by a person without strong expertise in implementation of cryptographic primitives.

Rest of the paper is organized as follows. In Section 2, several construction primitives for symmetric-key cryptography are reviewed. This is followed by a detailed study of block ciphers based on SPN and Feistel networks in Section 3. The generation of hardware from the proposed framework is presented in Section 5. The overall RAPID-FeinSPN toolflow is presented in Section 4. The paper is concluded with experiments and summary in Section 6 and Section 7 respectively.

2   Building Blocks for Symmetric Key Cryptography

Considering the building blocks for various types of symmetric key cryptography algorithms, block ciphers stand out due to their security guarantee. *Block ciphers are often used to construct other cryptographic primitives like hash functions, stream ciphers, and MACs.* To achieve that, a number of different operation modes for block ciphers are defined [13]. To quote a few recent examples, we consider two finalists for hash function competition SHA-3 [14]. BLAKE [16] and Skein [15] are both based on block cipher primitives, namely BLAKE and Threefish, respectively. For MAC algorithms, ISO defines the recipe of their construction from hash functions (e.g., HMAC) [18] or from block cipher algorithms [17]. The same holds true for stream ciphers as well. Considering eS-TREAM finalists [19], we see that Salsa20 [20] and ChaCha [22] make use of hash function in counter mode to generate keystream and SOSEMANUK [23] uses design principles of stream cipher SNOW 2.0 and block cipher SERPENT for its construction. Newer algorithms for light-weight cryptography also utilize block cipher primitives for their construction. The study and implementation of these primitives is therefore of critical importance.

We list below some major subclasses belonging to symmetric-key cryptography, based on the structure of construction. It should be highlighted that this list is neither complete nor non-exclusive for all symmetric-key cryptographic algorithms, however, captures major subclasses of block ciphers.

1. *ARX*: This subclass includes block ciphers, stream ciphers and hash functions that use Addition (A), Rotation (R) and Xor (X) operations as building blocks. A few examples include Salsa20 [20] and ChaCha [22] belonging to stream cipher category, BLAKE [16] and Skein [15] that are hash functions and BLAKE and Threefish that are block cipher primitives [7].

2. *Sponge Constructions*: Sponge constructions gained popularity when NIST selected Keccak [25] as the winner of Secure Hash Algorithm (SHA-3) competition [14]. Keccak is a hash function, however, Sponge Constructions make primitive blocks for block ciphers, stream ciphers, PRNGs and MACs as well.

3. *Feistel Networks*: Feistel network [24] is a symmetric block cipher primitive used for Data Encryption Standard (DES) [27]. Encryption transformations apply to half of the data per round and encryption and decryption operations are similar. Some popular examples of Feistel network based block ciphers include CLEFIA, CAST-128/256, TEA, Blowfish.

4. *SPN*: An SPN cipher applies several alternating rounds of substitution boxes (S-boxes), permutation boxes (P-boxes) and modular arithmetic to produce the ciphertext block. Its a block cipher primitive. The most noticeable example of this category is AES (Rijndael) [26].

Both Feistel networks and SPN ciphers belong to the class of product ciphers and make the most popular class of block cipher primitives today. The idea of product ciphers was proposed by Claude Shannon [28] suggesting a systems security by iteratively using rounds of simple operations such as substitutions and permutations. These iterated product ciphers encrypt and decrypt data in multiple rounds, where each round uses a different subkey derived from the original key. Our framework is applicable to all block ciphers belonging to the category of SPN and Feistel networks, which are more frequently used for block ciphers construction.

3   An Overview of Feistel and SPN-Based Block Ciphers

We first analyze components of a typical Feistel and SPN based block cipher, identify the common building blocks and develop a generic library for our framework.

3.1   Typical Features of Feistel and SPN Based Block Ciphers

In a Feistel cipher, the plaintext data block is partitioned into two equally sized parts. The round function is applied to one half, using a subkey, and then the output is xor-ed with the other half. The two halves are then switched. The iterative structure is required for an SPN ciphers as well, however, halving of plaintext before substitution and permutation is not required. Fig. 1 shows typical implementations of a Feistel network cipher and a SPN cipher.

Some common nomenclature terms, for both Feistel and SPN based block ciphers are enumerated below.

1. The data input to a block cipher is *plaintext*. The output is *ciphertext* and has the size same as that of the input plaintext. This size is referred as *blocksize* (S_B in bits).

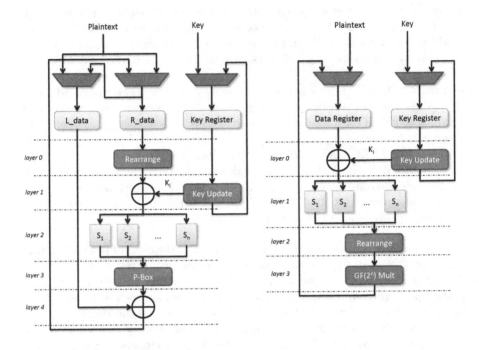

Fig. 1. Block diagram of typical Feistel network cipher (left) and SPN cipher (right)

2. Encryption/ decryption on the data operates under a a **key**. The size of key (in bits) is referred as **keysize** (S_K).

3. Block ciphers usually iterate simple operations, we call this combination of operations as a **round**. For many block ciphers, the initial round or final round or both differ in operations from rest of the rounds. To distinguish we name them as **first_round**, **middle_round** and **final_round**.

4. Rounds involve an iteration, **roundcount** (Num_{round}) number of times during encryption and decryption. Software as well as hardware implementations of block ciphers must maintain a **counter** to keep track of the number of iterations. This counter counts up and down during encryption and decryption of data, respectively.

5. Each round of a block cipher is defined by a series or **layers** of operations that take blocksize of bits at a time as shown in Fig. 1. These layers may require one or more operations. Since the round definition for the initial, middle or final round may be different the definition of layers, their number **layernumber** and order **layerorder** may be different for the three kinds of rounds.

6. One or more **operations** can define a layer. We list below some operations used in the layer of block ciphers (this list could be conveniently extended to accommodate newer operations). Each layer may use one or more of these operations.

(a) A substitution box or an **S-Box** has the same size of inputs and outputs, defined as **wordsize**. The number of S-Boxes required for a layer in case of an SPN cipher is obtained by division of blocksize and wordsize, for Feistel networks this number is half.

(b) For Feistel networks, the swapping operation of left and right halves of the data word can be defined as a Permutation box or a **P-Box**.

(c) Galois field multiplication or **GF-mul**.

(d) Bitwise operations include **rotation, shifting, addition, subtraction, xor-ing, bit-rearrangement**

7. The key is updated for every round and the new keys generated are called the **subkeys**. Just as the rounds are defined by one or more layers of operations, a **key_update** for calculation of subkeys requires multiple layers of operations.

3.2 Configuration Space of Feistel and SPN-Based Block Ciphers

The different parameter values for prominent SPN-based block ciphers are presented in Table 1. A similar configuration space is required for Feistel ciphers. In the reference papers for some ciphers, no information about a few parameters could be found and these are marked by (-).

Table 1. SPN block cipher configurations

| Algorithm | Size (in bits) | | | | Rounds | S-Box | | P-Box | Reference | Year |
	Key	Block	Input	Output		In×Out	Count			
SXAL/MBAL	64	64	64	64	8	8×8	1	Yes	[35]	1993
3 WAY	96	96	96	96	11	-	-	-	[36]	1993
BaseKing	192	192	192	192	11	-	-	-	[37]	1994
AKELARRE	128	128	128	128	4	-	-	Yes	[38]	1996
SHARK	128	64	64	64	6	-	-	Yes	[39]	1996
SQUARE	128	128	128	128	8	8×8	16	Yes	[41]	1997
AES	128,192,256	128	128	128	10,12,14	8×8	16	No	[26,40]	1998
SERPENT	128,192,256	128	128	128	32	4×4	32	Yes	[42]	1998
CRYPTON	128,192,256	128	128	128	12	8×8	16	Yes	[43]	1998
ANUBIS	128-320	128	128	128	≥ 12	8×8	16	Yes	[44]	2000
Hierocrypt-3	128,192,256	128	128	128	6.5,7.5,8.5	8×8	16	Yes	[46]	2000
KHAZAD	128	64	64	64	8	8×8	8	Yes	[45]	2000
NOEKEON	128	128	128	128	16	4×4	32	Yes	[47]	2000
ICEBERG	128	64	64	64	16	8×8	8	Yes	[48]	2000
MESH	128,192,256	64,96,128	128	128	8.5,10.5,12.5	-	-	Yes	[49]	2002
ARIA	128,192,256	128	128	128	12,14,16	8×8	16	Yes	[50]	2003
PRESENT	80,128	64	64	64	32	4×4	16	Yes	[51]	2007
PUFFIN	128	64	64	64	32	4×4	16	Yes	[52]	2008
HummingBird	64	16	16	16	4	4×4	4	Yes	[53]	2010
PrintCipher	80,160	48,96	48,96	48,96	48,96	3×3	16,32	Yes	[54]	2011
LED	64,128	64	64	64	32,48	4×4	25	Yes	[55]	2011
KLEIN	64,80,96	64	64	64	12,16,20	4×4	16	Yes	[56]	2012
PRINCE	128	64	64	64	-	4×4	16	-	[57]	2012

4   RAPID-FeinSPN Toolflow

The toolflow of RAPID-FeinSPN is graphically shown in Fig. 2. The user specifies block cipher template customizations or chooses from a list of well known-ciphers. This is controlled by a sophisticated GUI-based environment. The configurations undergo a set of rule-checks. Using templates from a function template library, RAPID-FeinSPN Generator generates a regular and reasonably optimized C-code implementation having good code readability. The hardware implementation is generated via a commercial high-level synthesis framework that is explained in Section 5.2.

4.1   Configuration Design Space

In a Feistel or SPN block cipher, the plaintext is operated upon by a key to generate ciphertext. Plaintext, ciphertext and other parameters that combine to form a cipher can be easily configured using the RAPID-FeinSPN GUI. It offers the flexibility to configure most of the cipher parameters and layers of operations. A list of known ciphers is available to instantly load the configurations. The configuration can be altered for generating a dual of the known cipher [30].

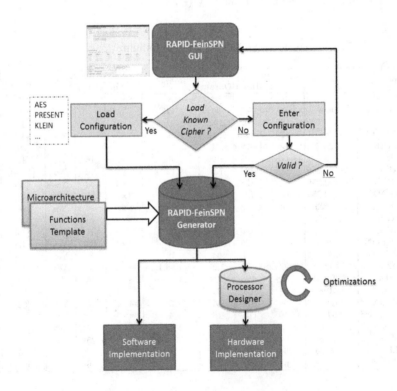

Fig. 2. RAPID-FeinSPN toolflow

For convenient construction of the cipher, the configuration space is exposed stepwise as following.

1. Basic cipher parameters are specified; keysize (S_K), blocksize (S_B), rounds(Num_{round}), wordsize (S_W).
2. Layers of operations are defined by layer number and layer order.
3. Pipelining and subpipelining is specified between rounds and inside rounds between layers respectively.
4. Definition of plaintext and key is also entered in the GUI.

The configuration undergoes a set of basic rule-checks before initiating the RAPID-FeinSPN Generator. The generator engine loads the template library and microarchitectures for efficient implementation. The parametrized template functions are put together using glue logic to generate a C code for software implementation and a LISA code for hardware implementation.

4.2 Configuration Validation

The flexibility of RAPID-FeinSPN framework is exploited by modifying the configurations of known ciphers as well as entering new configurations. The framework validates the configuration of the cipher for the basic parameters. The configuration is checked against a list of defined rules for violations in a defined order. The list can be conveniently extended to accommodate new rules. Exemplary rules are as following.

− *Blocksize* $S_B = 2m$, where $m \geq 1$.
− *Wordsize* $S_W < S_B$.
− *Keysize* $S_K \geq S_B$ and $= 2m$, where $m \geq 1$.
− *Plaintext size* $S_P = S_B$.
− Unrolling factor $l < Num_{round}$.
− S-Box input $W_{SUB} \in [0.. \ S_B/S_W]$.
− The S-Box values $\in [0..2^{S_W}]$.
− The Xor operation input bits $\in [0..S_B]$.
− Rotation and shifting operation has arguments $\in [0..S_B]$.
− The permutation or P-Box operation has arguments $\in [0..S_B]$.
− The polynomial coefficients for GF-mul are not $\varnothing$.

An example of the generated code for AES is presented in the appendix.

5 Efficient Hardware Implementation

This section describes the microarchitecture templates for the cipher hardware generated using RAPID-FeinSPN together with its hardware generation toolflow.

5.1   Microarchitecture Template

Considering the hardware implementation of a block cipher, several different configurations are of interest to the designer, depending on the area budget and performance requirements. These configurations boost cipher speed by duplicating the hardware for implementing rounds where each round has layers of operations as shown in Fig. 3. These configuration variations effect parameters like maximum frequency of circuit, latency, power, throughput and area of the design, emphasizing the need of rapid prototyping for a wise choice of design. The user may choose any of these templates, based on the target application in mind, give specifications of the design and get these parameters. Some commonly used templates are listed below.

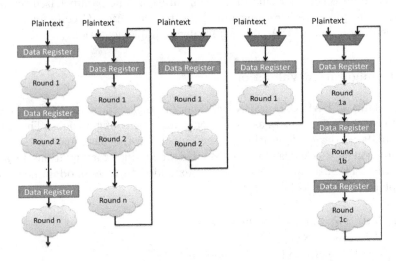

Fig. 3. Various hardware configurations depicting the option of area-throughput trade-off (left to right) a) pipelined rounds b) fully unrolled round c) round unrolled by 2 d) round without unrolling e) subpipelined round

1. **Pipelining.** The pipelined architecture is realized by inserting registers between each round. For an algorithm with n rounds, the implementation requires hardware for n rounds plus n data registers. Each round can have multiple layers with several different operations. The operations work on blocksize and keysize. Registers are not inserted inside each round i.e., between these layers of operations.
2. **Subpipelining.** Similar to the pipelining, subpipelining inserts registers in the combinational paths. However, registers are inserted both in between and inside each round. For an algorithm with n rounds and k times subpipelined round, a total number of $n \times k$ data registers will be required.
3. **Loop-unrolling.** In the last two approaches, multiple blocks of data are processed simultaneously due to pipelining. Comparatively, loop unrolled or unfolded architectures can process only one block of data at a time, but

multiple rounds may be processed in each clock cycle, depending on the unroll factor. Fig. 3(b), (c) and (d) show the various possibilities of an unroll factor l, while l could vary between 1 to n (for and n round block cipher) for a *folded architecture* or a *fully unrolled architecture* respectively. *Unrolling by a factor l, where $1 < l < n$, results in design variants with hardware area lesser than that of a fully unrolled design and higher latency, comparatively.*

Among these architectural optimization approaches, subpipelining can achieve maximum speedup and optimum speed/area ratio for block ciphers [29].

5.2   Toolflow for Hardware Implementation

For efficient hardware implementation via a suitable high-level synthesis framework, we adopted Synopsys Processor Designer [6]. In Processor Designer, it is permitted to describe a hardware implementation with or without programmability/configurability [21,7]. The description is captured using a language known as LISA[58]. The language offers rich programming primitives to capture an implementation with full programmability such as a RISC processor to an implementation with no configurability at all e.g., an ASIC. From LISA, the hardware implementation as well as the software toolsuite, e.g., C compiler, simulator, assembler, linker can be automatically generated as shown in LISA implementation flow in Fig. 5. The high-level synthesis environment allows easy control of the design parameters and fast exploration of design alternatives. The language allows full control over minute design decisions and preserves the overall structural organization neatly in the generated hardware description. This is especially important for verifying the design costs (area, timing) and accordingly modifying the design at high level.

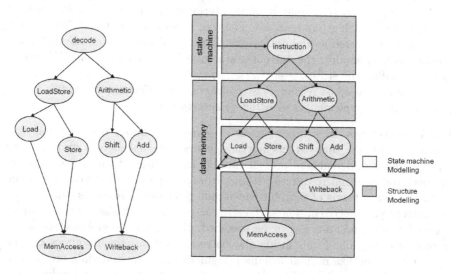

step 1 : capturing the state machine   step 2 : structuring the state machine

Fig. 4. Development of hardware implementation

Before starting with the language semantics, it is useful to understand the key ideas of the high level modeling using LISA. In LISA, the complete implementation is viewed as a Directed Acyclic Graph (DAG) of LISA operations. The operations contain state encoding, state behavior and *activation* to successor operations. On top of this description, the structural information such as, pipelining, memory partitioning, storage accesses are added. This process of state machine modeling using LISA is shown in Fig. 4. One common operation can be activated by multiple parent operations. Again, one operation can activate multiple children operations. The complete structure is an annotated Directed Acyclic Graph (DAG) $\mathcal{D} = \langle V, E \rangle$. V represents the set of LISA operations, E the graph edges as set of child-parent relations.

Behavior Description. LISA operations' *behavior section* contains the behavior description. The behavior description of a LISA operation is based on extended C programming language. On top of regular C like syntax, bitwise manipulations and user defined datatypes are supported. By the behavior description, the combinatorial logic is implemented. The clocked resources, declared in a global *resource* section, can be accessed from the behavior section as well.

   The combinational blocks of the SPN and Feistel ciphers, e.g., Key update, $GF(2^n)$ multiplication are implemented using the behavior description.

State Encoding Description. LISA operations' *coding section* is used to describe the state's encoding. The encoding of a LISA operation is described as a sequence of several *coding* elements. Each coding element is either a terminal bit sequence with "0", "1", "don't care" bits or a nonterminal. The nonterminal coding element can point to either an *instance* of LISA operation or a *group* of LISA operations. The behavior of a LISA operation is executed only if all terminal coding bit patterns match, all non-terminal instances match and at least one member of each group matches. The root LISA operation containing a coding section is referred as the *coding root*. For a FSM description, the individual operations may modify the current state encoding or an external PIN can be used for feeding the states.

   The data flow of SPN and Feistel ciphers, e.g., first_round, middle_round, final_round are implemented in encoding description.

LISA Resources. Resources consist of general hardware resources for storage and structure such as, memory, registers, internal signals and external pins. Memory and registers provide storage capabilities. Signals and pins are internal and external resources without storage capabilities. Resources can be parametrized in terms of sign, bit-width and dimension. Memories can be more extensively parametrized. There the size, accessible block size, access pattern, access latency, endian-ness can be specified. Resources are globally accessible from any operation. From inside the behavior section, the resources can be read and written like normal variables. Memories are accessed via a pre-defined set of interface functions. These interface functions comprise of blocking and non-blocking memory access possibilities. Resource section allows definition of microarchitecture by using the keywords PIPELINE and PIPELINE_REGISTER.

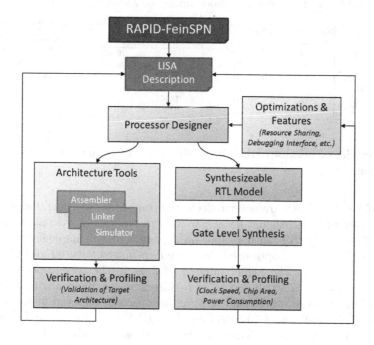

Fig. 5. Implementation flow with LISA

With the pipeline definition, all the LISA operations need to be assigned in a particular pipeline stage.

Depending on the unrolling and pipelining decisions, the microarchitecture is constructed using LISA with proper assignments of LISA operations.

6   Experimental Results

This section talks about the results obtained by the implementation of some noticeable block ciphers using RAPID-FeinSPN. Studies with selected ciphers for both software and hardware implementation efficiency has been carried out.

6.1   Software Efficiency

The experimental results of 3 mainstream ciphers are presented here. The automatically generated software implementation was compiled using gcc version 4.4.6 and run on AMD Phenom^{TM} II X6 1100T Processor running at 3.3 GHz operating frequency with 8 GB RAM and Linux operating system. The AES-128 software implementation is executed on Intel$^{®}$ Core^{TM} i7-2670QM CPU running at 2.2 GHz operating frequency. AES, PRESENT and KLEIN are chosen for performance benchmarking. AES is chosen because of its highly optimized software and hardware implementations and widespread acceptance. PRESENT and

Table 2. SPN and Feistel block cipher software efficiency results

Algorithm	Key Size (S_K) (Bits)	Block Size (S_B) (Bits)	Execution Time (Cycles/byte)		Lines of Code (lines)	
			This work	From Others	This work	From Others
AES-128 [59]	128	128	315	10.43	272	318
PRESENT-80 [60]	80	64	4595	4034	165	90 and 259
PRESENT-128	128	64	6241.12	-	166	-
KLEIN-64	64	64	1208	-	205	-
KLEIN-96	96	64	1278	-	205	-
KLEIN-128	128	64	1344.75	-	205	-

KLEIN are chosen because of their increasing importance in resource-constrained application areas.

Lines of Code. This parameter reflects the complexity of generated software implementation, which should be at par with the manually written implementations. The PRESENT authors [60] have presented two implementations of the cipher that are size optimized and speed optimized with 90 and 259 lines of code, respectively. The higher number of lines in the speed optimized implementation of [60] is attributed to its architecture-specific configurations and optimizations. On the other hand, size optimization is achieved at the cost of code readability [60]. For PRESENT-80, RAPID-FeinSPN generated 165 lines of code in comparison, a moderate number, as shown in Table 2. For AES-128, we found an online C implementation at [59], which has 318 lines of code compared to only 272 lines of code generated by RAPID-FeinSPN. It could be easily appreciated that the software implementation generated from RAPID-FeinSPN is compact.

Software Execution Time. The performance comparison in Table 2 shows the execution time for the 3 ciphers. A significant increase in number of cycles per byte in AES is due to the unoptimized code generation from RAPID-FeinSPN. A close inspection revealed that RAPID-FeinSPN, due to its compositional library-based software generation uses high amount of function calls. Optimized AES implementations instead store the complete or partial round transformations in form of look-up tables, which are missing in our automated framework. We intend to explore in future, whether such optimizations can be generally achieved for all Feistel and SPN-based ciphers thereby preserving the flexibility of a template-based generation environment. Despite this, the software execution time of PRESENT-80 is quite close to the best results reported by the authors [60], possibly due to the absence of look-up tables in the transformation, which increases overhead in a resource-constrained environment. The execution times for KLEIN and PRESENT-128 were not available.

6.2 Hardware Efficiency

We implemented PRESENT (with $S_K = 80, 128$ bits) and AES (with $S_K = 128$ bits) in Verilog HDL and synthesized it using the Faraday standard cell libraries in topographical mode. We used three technology nodes for synthesis, namely, UMC L180E High Speed FSG Generic II Process $0.18\mu m$ CMOS, UMC L90 Standard Performance Low-K (Regular VT) Process 90nm CMOS and UMC SP/RVT Low-K process 65nm CMOS.

A folded block cipher architecture (round with no unrolling) of encryption only block was implemented in which one clock cycle is required for one round. For PRESENT, data encryption uses 16 S-Box in parallel (S_B/S_W) while key scheduling uses 1 and 2 S-Boxes for key size of 80 and 128 bits, respectively. Consequently, 32 rounds are executed in 32 clock cycles. For comparison with the manually optimized implementations reported so far, the smallest area implementation of PRESENT-80 reportedly require 1000 gates only [64]. What makes it incomparable in the context is that its a serialized architecture, having a bit sliced hardware (4 bits at a time). The same work reports round-based PRESENT-80 implementations consuming 1650 and 1706 gates at 100 KHz and 10 MHz respectively which we take up for comparison. As given in Table 3 our area is only 30 and 85 gates more than the reported manual implementation [64]. This area-gap is far too small to be considered an overhead and possibly can be attributed to the difference in the vendor libraries used in the two implementations.

For AES synthesis results, a fair comparison is hard to carryout. The reason is that most of the reported implementations manifest S-Box optimizations for area reduction while our implementation uses simple LUTs. The closest implementation we could find of a folded AES-128 architecture with same number of S-boxes used as ours was available at [65] with 12K (area optimized) and 21K GE area (speed optimized) budgets when the core is synthesized at 145 MHz and 224 MHz, respectively, using 110 nm technology node. The area gap with the RAPID-FeinSPN generated results can be explained, as the comparison is

Table 3. Feistel and SPN block cipher hardware synthesis results (Typical case values)

Algorithm	Key Size S_K(Bits)	Block Size S_B(Bits)	Cycles/Block (Cycles)	S-boxes used Enc + Key sch.	Technology Node (nm)	Area (GE) @100 KHz	@10 MHz
RAPID-FeinSPN generated RTL							
PRESENT-80	80	64	32	16+1	65	1618	1617
PRESENT-80	80	64	32	16+1	90	1574	1574
PRESENT-80	80	64	32	16+1	180	1735	1735
PRESENT-128	128	64	32	16+2	65	1956	1956
PRESENT-128	128	64	32	16+2	90	1915	1915
PRESENT-128	128	64	32	16+2	180	2132	2130
AES-128	128	128	11	16+4	65	14659	14659
AES-128	128	128	11	16+4	90	14620	14620
AES-128	128	128	11	16+4	180	16389	16385
PRESENT-80	80	64	32	16+1	180	1650	1706
AES-128	128	128	11	16+4	65	14745	14745
AES-128	128	128	11	16+4	90	14315	14313
AES-128	128	128	11	16+4	180	16438	16388

loose for several reasons. Firstly, a simplistic S-box optimization is being applied at [65]. Secondly, the technology nodes used for synthesis are different. Presumably the difference is contributed by synthesis settings or different versions of synthesis tools as well. For a fair comparison we took up the RTL of a round based AES-128 encryption core available at Open Cores [66] and synthesized it at 10 MHz and 100 KHz using the same technology libraries as used by RAPID-FeinSPN. The results are promising since the area overhead of RAPID-FeinSPN is within the range of -0.5% till $+2\%$, which is far too small to be considered an overhead. Consequently, RAPID-FeinSPN can serve as a very good starting point for Verilog HDL generation before optimizations are applied to specific parts of the core as these optimizations are only complementary to the basic implementation.

7   Conclusion and Future Work

We presented RAPID-FeinSPN, a fast prototyping platform for Feistel and SPN-based block ciphers. After structural analysis of such block ciphers, a unified microarchitectural template and a set of software functions implementations are determined. The framework gives freedom to the user to select a known configuration of a cipher or specify it using a GUI. A set of rule-checks indicates errors in the configurations if any. The hardware implementation is aided by a commercial high-level synthesis framework. RAPID-FeinSPN allows a cryptographer to quickly do the software/hardware evaluation of a cipher design without extensive knowledge of hardware implementation. A reasonably efficient generated implementation may be further manually optimized for a specific platform.

RAPID-FeinSPN is the first step towards a generic extensible cryptographic workbench development environment. We are enthusiastic to add the provision of choosing duals of a known cipher [30] and the support for customized irregular operations occurring in some block ciphers. We also plan to address the efficiency-gap in some of the generated ciphers by plugging in optimizations in the generation process. The choice of applying novel hybrid microarchitectures like bit-sliced subpipelined cores for block ciphers is also on the roadmap. For feedback, RAPID-FeinSPN tool will soon be made available for download.

References

1. Tillich, S.: Instruction Set Extensions for Support of Cryptography on Embedded Systems. PhD thesis, Graz University of Technology, Austria (2008),
https://online.tugraz.at/tug_online/
voe_main2.getvolltext?pCurrPk=39243
2. Constantin, J., Burg, A., Gürkaynak, F.: Investigating the potential of custom instruction set extensions for SHA-3 candidates on a 16-bit microcontroller architecture. Cryptology ePrint Archive, Report 2012/050 (2012),
http://eprint.iacr.org/2012/050

3. Guo, X., Srivastav, M., Huang, S., Ganta, D., Henry, M.B., Nazhandali, L., Schaumont, P.: ASIC implementations of five SHA-3 finalists. In: IEEE DATE 2012, pp. 1006–1011 (2012)
4. Tensilica (now part of Cadence), http://tensilica.com
5. Synopsys DesignWare ARC Configurable Cores, http://www.synopsys.com.
6. Synopsys Processor Designer, http://www.synopsys.com/Systems/BlockDesign/processorDev/Pages/default.aspx
7. Shahzad, K., Khalid, A., Rákossy, Z.E., Paul, G., Chattopadhyay, A.: CoARX: a coprocessor for ARX-based cryptographic algorithms. In: Proceedings of the 50th Annual Design Automation Conference (DAC 2013) (2013), doi:10.1145/2463209.2488898
8. Chattopadhyay, A., Paul, G.: Exploring security-performance trade-offs during hardware accelerator design of stream cipher RC4. In: 20th International Conference on VLSI and System-on-Chip (VLSI-SoC 2012). IEEE (2012)
9. Gupta, S.S., Chattopadhyay, A., Khalid, A.: Designing integrated accelerator for stream ciphers with structural similarities. Cryptography and Communications 5(1), 19–47 (2013)
10. Sen Gupta, S., Chattopadhyay, A., Khalid, A.: HiPAcc-LTE: an integrated high performance accelerator for 3GPP LTE stream ciphers. In: Bernstein, D.J., Chatterjee, S. (eds.) INDOCRYPT 2011. LNCS, vol. 7107, pp. 196–215. Springer, Heidelberg (2011)
11. Asanovic, K., Bodik, R., Catanzaro, B.C., Gebis, J.J., Husbands, P., Keutzer, K., Patterson, D.A., Plishker, W.L., Shalf, J., Williams, S.W., Yelick, K.A.: The landscape of parallel computing research: A view from berkeley. UCB/EECS-2006-183, EECS Department, University of California, Berkeley
12. Dubey, P.: Teraflops for the masses: Killer apps of tomorrow. In: Workshop on Edge Computing Using New Commodity Architectures (UNC), vol. 23 (2006)
13. Dworkin, M.: Recommendation for block cipher modes of operation. methods and techniques. In: NIST Special Publication 800-38A (2001)
14. SHA-3 Cryptographic Hash Algorithm Competition, http://csrc.nist.gov/groups/ST/hash/sha-3/index.html
15. Ferguson, N., Lucks, S., Schneier, B., Whiting, D., Bellare, M., Kohno, T., Callas, J., Walker, J.: The Skein Hash Function Family, Version 1.3 (October 2010), http://www.skein-hash.info/sites/default/files/skein1.3.pdf
16. Aumasson, J., Henzen, L., Meier, W., Phan, R.: SHA-3 proposal BLAKE ver 1.3 (2010), https://www.131002.net/blake
17. ISO/IEC 9797-1: Authentication Codes (MACs) Part 1: Mechanisms using a block cipher. In: Information Technology-Security Techniques (1999)
18. ISO/IEC 9797-2: Authentication Codes (MACs) Part 2: Mechanisms using a dedicated hashfunction. In: Information Technology-Security Techniques (1999)
19. eSTREAM: the ECRYPT Stream Cipher Project, http://www.ecrypt.eu.org/stream
20. Bernstein, D.J.: The Salsa20 family of stream ciphers. In: Robshaw, M., Billet, O. (eds.) New Stream Cipher Designs. LNCS, vol. 4986, pp. 84–97. Springer, Heidelberg (2008)
21. Kammler, D., Zhang, D., Schwabe, P., Scharwaechter, H., Langenberg, M., Auras, D., Ascheid, G., Mathar, R.: Designing an ASIP for Cryptographic Pairings over Barreto-Naehrig Curves. In: Clavier, C., Gaj, K. (eds.) CHES 2009. LNCS, vol. 5747, pp. 254–271. Springer, Heidelberg (2009)

22. Bernstein, D.J.: ChaCha, a variant of Salsa20. In: Workshop Record of SASC, The State of the Art of Stream Ciphers (2008), http://cr.yp.to/papers.html#chacha

23. Berbain, C., et al.: SOSEMANUK, a fast software-oriented stream cipher. In: Robshaw, M., Billet, O. (eds.) New Stream Cipher Designs. LNCS, vol. 4986, pp. 98–118. Springer, Heidelberg (2008)

24. Luby, M., Rackoff, C.: How to Construct Pseudorandom Permutations and Pseudorandom Functions. SIAM Journal on Computing 17(2), 373–386 (1988)

25. Bertoni, G., Daemen, J., Peeters, M., Van Assche, G.: Keccak sponge function family main document. Submission to NIST, round 3 (2011)

26. Advanced encryption standard. Federal Information Processing Standard, FIPS-197, 12 (2001)

27. Data encryption standard. National Bureau of Standards, U.S. Department of Commerce, Washington D.C., FIPS 46 (1977)

28. Shannon, C.E.: Communication theory of secrecy systems. Bell System Technical Journal 28(4), 656–715 (1949)

29. Zhang, X., Parhi, K.: High-speed VLSI architectures for the AES algorithm. IEEE Transactions on Very Large Scale Integration (VLSI) Systems 12(9), 957–967 (2004)

30. Barkan, E., Biham, E.: In How Many Ways Can You Write Rijndael? In: Zheng, Y. (ed.) ASIACRYPT 2002. LNCS, vol. 2501, pp. 160–175. Springer, Heidelberg (2002)

31. Ernst, M., Klupsch, S., Hauck, O., Huss, S.A.: Rapid Prototyping for Hardware Accelerated Elliptic Curve Public-Key Cryptosystems. In: Proceedings of the 12th International Workshop on Rapid System Prototyping (RSP 2001) (2001)

32. Khovratovich, D., Nikolić, I.: Rotational cryptanalysis of ARX. In: Hong, S., Iwata, T. (eds.) FSE 2010. LNCS, vol. 6147, pp. 333–346. Springer, Heidelberg (2010)

33. Leurent, G.: ARX Toolkit, http://www.di.ens.fr/~leurent/arxtools.html

34. Mouha, N., Velichkov, V., De Cannière, C., Preneel, B.: S-function Toolkit, http://www.ecrypt.eu.org/tools/s-function-toolkit

35. Fujii, M., Torigai, M.: Data transfer method, communication system and storage medium. In US Patent US6038321 A (March 14, 2000)

36. Daemen, J., Govaerts, R., Vandewalle, J.: A New Approach to Block Cipher Design. In: Anderson, R. (ed.) FSE 1993. LNCS, vol. 809, pp. 18–32. Springer, Heidelberg (1994)

37. Daemen, J.: Cipher and Hash Function Design: Strategies based on linear and differential cryptanalysis (Ph.D. Dissertation), ch. 7. Katholieke Universiteit Leuven (1994)

38. Álvarez Marañón, G., Fúster Sabater, A., Guía Martínez, D., Montoya Vitini, F., Peinado Domínguez, A.: Akelarre: a New Block Cipher Algorithm. In: Proceedings of SAC 1996, Third Annual Workshop on Selected Areas in Cryptography, Queen's University, Kingston, Ontario, pp. 1–14 (1996)

39. Rijmen, V., Daemen, J., Preneel, B., Bosselaers, A., De Win, E.: The Cipher SHARK. In: Gollmann, D. (ed.) FSE 1996. LNCS, vol. 1039, pp. 99–111. Springer, Heidelberg (1996)

40. Daemen, J., Rijmen, V.: The Design of Rijndael: AES–The Advanced Encryption Standard. Springer (2002) ISBN 3-540-42580-2

41. Daemen, J., Knudsen, L.R., Rijmen, V.: The Block Cipher Square. In: Biham, E. (ed.) FSE 1997. LNCS, vol. 1267, pp. 149–165. Springer, Heidelberg (1997)

42. Biham, E., Anderson, R.J., Knudsen, L.R.: Serpent: A new block cipher proposal. In: Vaudenay, S. (ed.) FSE 1998. LNCS, vol. 1372, pp. 222–238. Springer, Heidelberg (1998)

43. Lim, C.H.: CRYPTON: A new 128-bit Block Cipher. NIST AES Proposal (1998)
44. Rijmen, V., Barreto, P.S.L.M.: The ANUBIS Block Cipher. New European Schemes for Signatures, Integrity, and Encryption (NESSIE) (2000)
45. Barreto, P.S.L.M., Rijmen, V.: The Khazad Legacy-level Block Cipher. In: First open NESSIE Workshop, p. 15 (2000)
46. Ohkuma, K., Muratani, H., Sano, F., Kawamura, S.: The Block Cipher Hierocrypt. In: Stinson, D.R., Tavares, S. (eds.) SAC 2000. LNCS, vol. 2012, pp. 72–88. Springer, Heidelberg (2001)
47. Daemen, J., Peeters, M., Van Assche, G., Rijmen, V.: Nessie Proposal: Noekeon (2000)
48. Standaert, F.-X., Piret, G., Rouvroy, G., Quisquater, J.-J., Legat, J.-D.: ICEBERG: An Involutional Cipher Efficient for Block Encryption in Reconfigurable Hardware. In: Roy, B., Meier, W. (eds.) FSE 2004. LNCS, vol. 3017, pp. 279–299. Springer, Heidelberg (2004)
49. Nakahara Jr., J., Rijmen, V., Preneel, B., Vandewalle, J.: The MESH Block Ciphers. In: Chae, K.-J., Yung, M. (eds.) WISA 2003. LNCS, vol. 2908, pp. 458–473. Springer, Heidelberg (2004)
50. Kwon, D., Kim, J., Park, S., Sung, S.H., Sohn, Y., Song, J.H., Yeom, Y., Yoon, E., Lee, S., Lee, J., Chee, S., Han, D., Hong, J.: New Block Cipher: ARIA. In: Lim, J.-I., Lee, D.-H. (eds.) ICISC 2003. LNCS, vol. 2971, pp. 432–445. Springer, Heidelberg (2004)
51. Bogdanov, A.A., Knudsen, L.R., Leander, G., Paar, C., Poschmann, A., Robshaw, M., Seurin, Y., Vikkelsoe, C.: PRESENT: An Ultra-Lightweight Block Cipher. In: Paillier, P., Verbauwhede, I. (eds.) CHES 2007. LNCS, vol. 4727, pp. 450–466. Springer, Heidelberg (2007)
52. Cheng, H., Heys, H.M., Wang, C.: PUFFIN: A Novel Compact Block Cipher Targeted to Embedded Digital Systems. In: 11th EUROMICRO Conference on Digital System Design Architectures, Methods and Tools, DSD 2008, pp. 383–390 (2008), doi:10.1109/DSD.2008.34.
53. Engels, D., Fan, X., Gong, G., Hu, H., Smith, E.M.: Hummingbird: Ultra-Lightweight Cryptography for Resource-Constrained Devices. In: Sion, R., Curtmola, R., Dietrich, S., Kiayias, A., Miret, J.M., Sako, K., Sebé, F. (eds.) RLCPS, WECSR, and WLC 2010. LNCS, vol. 6054, pp. 3–18. Springer, Heidelberg (2010)
54. Knudsen, L., Leander, G., Poschmann, A., Robshaw, M.J.B.: PRINTcipher: A Block Cipher for IC-Printing. In: Mangard, S., Standaert, F.-X. (eds.) CHES 2010. LNCS, vol. 6225, pp. 16–32. Springer, Heidelberg (2010)
55. Guo, J., Peyrin, T., Poschmann, A., Robshaw, M.: The LED Block Cipher. In: Preneel, B., Takagi, T. (eds.) CHES 2011. LNCS, vol. 6917, pp. 326–341. Springer, Heidelberg (2011)
56. Gong, Z., Nikova, S., Law, Y.W.: KLEIN: A New Family of Lightweight Block Ciphers. In: Juels, A., Paar, C. (eds.) RFIDSec 2011. LNCS, vol. 7055, pp. 1–18. Springer, Heidelberg (2012)
57. Borghoff, J., Canteaut, A., Güneysu, T., Kavun, E.B., Knezevic, M., Knudsen, L.R., Leander, G., Nikov, V., Paar, C., Rechberger, C., Rombouts, P., Thomsen, S.S., Yalçın, T.: PRINCE – A Low-Latency Block Cipher for Pervasive Computing Applications. In: Wang, X., Sako, K. (eds.) ASIACRYPT 2012. LNCS, vol. 7658, pp. 208–225. Springer, Heidelberg (2012)
58. Chattopadhyay, A., Meyr, H., Leupers, R.: LISA: A Uniform ADL for Embedded Processor Modelling, Implementation and Software Toolsuite Generation. In: Mishra, P., Dutt, N. (eds.) Processor Description Languages, pp. 95–130. Morgan Kaufmann (2008)

59. Doeffinger, R.: AES C Implementation,
    `stuff.mit.edu/afs/sipb/project/vlcplayer/old/src/ffmpeg/libavutil/`

60. Klose, D.: PRESENT C Implementation (32 bit),
    `http://www.lightweightcrypto.org/implementations.php`.

61. Akinyele, J.A., et al.: Charm: A framework for rapidly prototyping cryptosystems.
    Journal of Cryptographic Engineering, 1–18 (2013)

62. Lacy, J.B., Donald, P.: Mitchell, and William M. Schell. CryptoLib: Cryptography
    in software. In: Proc. of Fourth USENIX Security Workshop, pp. 1–18 (1993)

63. SHA-3 Finalists Announced by NIST Blog post quoting NIST's announcement in
    full, `http://crypto.junod.info/2010/12/10/`
    `sha-3-finalists-announced-by-nist/`

64. Rolfes, C., Poschmann, A., Leander, G., Paar, C.: Ultra-lightweight implementa-
    tions for smart devices security for 1000 gate equivalents. In: Grimaud, G., Stan-
    daert, F.-X. (eds.) CARDIS 2008. LNCS, vol. 5189, pp. 89–103. Springer, Heidel-
    berg (2008)

65. Satoh, A., Morioka, S., Takano, K., Munetoh, S.: Ultra-lightweight implementations
    for smart devices security for 1000 gate equivalents. In: Boyd, C. (ed.) ASIACRYPT
    2001. LNCS, vol. 2248, pp. 239–254. Springer, Heidelberg (2001)

66. Simple AES (Rijndael) IP Core, `http://opencores.org/project,aes_core`

Appendix

AES encryption block with on-the-fly subkey calculation C-code generated by
RAPID-FeinSPN.

```c
#include "define.h"
#include "functions.h"

ARRAY state[ARRAY_SIZE] = {};
ARRAY key[ARRAY_SIZE] = {};
ARRAY result[ARRAY_SIZE] = {};
ARRAY key_from_user[ARRAY_SIZE_USER_KEY] = {};
#define OUTPUT_CIPHER_FILE  "key_output.txt"

int main (void)
{
    char i, rounds_idx = 1;
    FILE * pOutputFile = NULL;
    for (rounds_idx = ROUNDS_START; rounds_idx < (ROUNDS_END); rounds_idx++) {
        key_schedule(key,key_from_user, rounds_idx);
        add_round_key (state,key);
        sbox_function (state);
        ARRAY sr_0[4], sr_1[4], sr_2[4], sr_3[4];
        for (i = 0 ; i < 4 ; i ++) {
            sr_3 [i] = state[(i*4) + 3];
            sr_2 [i] = state[(i*4) + 2];
            sr_1 [i] = state[(i*4) + 1];
            sr_0 [i] = state[(i*4) ];
        }
```

```
ShiftRows (sr_3,0);
ShiftRows (sr_2,1);
ShiftRows (sr_1,2);
ShiftRows (sr_0,3);
// writing the values from 4 Bytes chunks to 16 Bytes state.
for (i = 0; i < 4; i++) {
    state [(i*4)]     = sr_0[i];
    state [(i*4) + 1] = sr_1[i];
    state [(i*4) + 2] = sr_2[i];
    state [(i*4) + 3] = sr_3[i];
}
// Galois field mul
ARRAY st0 [4], st1 [4], st2 [4], st3 [4];
for (i = 0; i < 4; i++) {
    st0 [3-i] = state[i];
    st1 [3-i] = state[i+4];
    st2 [3-i] = state[i+8];
    st3 [3-i] = state[i+12];
}
galois_field_mul (st0);
galois_field_mul (st1);
galois_field_mul (st2);
galois_field_mul (st3);
// writing the values from 4Bytes chunks to 16 Bytes state.
for (i = 0; i < 4; i ++) {
    state [i]   = st0[3-i];
    state [i+4] = st1[3-i];
    state [i+8] = st2[3-i];
    state [i+12]= st3[3-i];
}
}
key_schedule(key, key_from_user, rounds_idx);
add_round_key (state,key);
sbox_function (state);
// Shift ROWS
ARRAY sr_0[4];
ARRAY sr_1[4];
ARRAY sr_2[4];
ARRAY sr_3[4];
// writing the values from 16Bytes state to 4 Bytes chunks.
// Input to Galois field mul is 4 Bytes.
for (i = 0; i < 4; i++) {
    sr_3 [i] = state[(i*4) + 3];
    sr_2 [i] = state[(i*4) + 2];
    sr_1 [i] = state[(i*4) + 1];
    sr_0 [i] = state[(i*4) ];
}
```

```
ShiftRows (sr_3,0);
ShiftRows (sr_2,1);
ShiftRows (sr_1,2);
ShiftRows (sr_0,3);
// writing the values from 4Bytes chunks to 16 Bytes state.
for (i = 0; i < 4; i++) {
    state [(i*4)]     = sr_0[i];
    state [(i*4) + 1] = sr_1[i];
    state [(i*4) + 2] = sr_2[i];
    state [(i*4) + 3] = sr_3[i];
}
key_schedule(key,key_from_user, rounds_idx);
add_round_key (state,key);
pOutputFile = fopen(OUTPUT_CIPHER_FILE, "w+");
if (pOutputFile == NULL) {
    perror ("Error opening file");
    exit(0);
}
for(i = ARRAY_SIZE -1; i > -1; i--)
    fprintf(pOutputFile,"%x",state[i]);
fprintf(pOutputFile," \n ");
fclose(pOutputFile);
return 0;
}
```

Simple and Efficient Time-Bound Hierarchical Key Assignment Scheme
(Short Paper)

Naveen Kumar, Anish Mathuria, and Manik Lal Das

DA-IICT, Gandhinagar, India
{naveen_kumar,anish_mathuria,maniklal_das}@daiict.ac.in

Abstract. We propose a simple and efficient hash-based time-bound hierarchical key assignment scheme that requires a single key per user per subscription. It is more efficient than existing schemes in terms of public storage.

Keywords: Time-bound access, Hierarchical access control, Key management.

1 Introduction

There exist many on-line applications where data access is restricted to a specific time interval. The total system time is divided into distinct *time slots*. A time slot is the smallest possible subscription period. Each time slot has a set of data blocks associated with it. A contiguous sequence of time slots is called a *time interval*. A user can subscribe for one or more time intervals (subscription intervals).

A monthly *subscription hierarchy* with 3 time slots (one for each January, February and March) is shown in Figure 1. For each possible subscription interval, there is a distinct node in the hierarchy. Each leaf node represents a time slot. A directed edge in the subscription hierarchy represents an access to a subscription interval with a subsequence of time slots. For example, an edge from node $Jan - Mar$ to $Jan - Feb$ implies that a user with subscription of node $Jan - Mar$ can access to node $Jan - Feb$.

To cryptographically enforce time-bound access control, each node in the subscription hierarchy is assigned a key using appropriate Hierarchical Key Assignment Scheme ($HKAS$) [1]. Resources associated with a time slot are encrypted with its associated encryption key. User is given secret information using which one can easily compute all authorized encryption keys. The secret information must be distributed securely to the user by a trusted Central Authority (CA). An edge in the hierarchy represents direction of key derivation. A user subscribed for the month of Jan and Feb is given a single secret information $K_{Jan-Feb}$ through which he can compute encryption keys K_{Jan} and K_{Feb} for the nodes Jan and Feb respectively.

When designing an efficient scheme, the objective is to minimize the amount of secret key storage, public storage and key derivation time. Tzeng [2] proposed

A. Bagchi and I. Ray (Eds.): ICISS 2013, LNCS 8303, pp. 191–198, 2013.

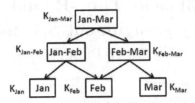

Fig. 1. An example subscription hierarchy

the first time-bound $HKAS$ based on RSA [3] cryptosystem. However, Yi and Ye [4] found a three party collusion attack on [2]. In a survey paper on time-bound $HKAS$, Zhu et al [5] suggest that hash-based constructions are more promising than expensive modular exponentiation based constructions.

Ateniese, Santis, Ferrara and Masucci [6][7] proposed two constructions, one based on bilinear pairing and another based on symmetric encryption. First requires large key storage (i.e. $O(z)$ where z is the number of time slots) to a user per subscription. Second uses worst case two-level structure to reduce key derivation cost at the expense of huge public storage ($O(z^3)$).

Atallah, Blanton and Frikken [8] proposed an improved construction that requires at most $z - 1$ hash operations as key derivation cost and $z(z-1)$ public edge values. Using $2 - Hop$ shortcut edge scheme [8], it requires key derivation cost as 4 hash operations with a cost of $O(z^2 \log z)$ additional public shortcut edge values. Shortcut edges are used to reduce key derivation cost. A $2 - Hop$ shortcut edge scheme is such that distance between any two nodes in a linear hierarchy is at most 2 edges (Hops). Using $\log z - Hop$ shortcut edge scheme [8], it requires key derivation cost as $2 \log z$ with $O(z \log z)$ additional public shortcut edge values.

Crampton [9,10] exploits the fact that it is not necessary to derive keys for non-leaf nodes in a subscription hierarchy. He proposed an improved time-bound $HKAS$ with single key per user where he divides the nodes in the subscription hierarchy into triangle, rectangle and square blocks and edges are inserted between different blocks for key derivation. He was able to reduce key derivation cost up to $\log z$ hash operations. Number of public edge values required with a subscription hierarchy is $z(z - 1)$ similar as in Atallah et al. [8]. In [9], he discussed one more construction (for single key/user), with key derivation cost of 2 hash operations but with a significant increase in public edge values ($O(z^3)$, similar to [7]). Recently Crampton [11] proposed another similar (for single key per user) construction with a reduced key derivation cost of $\log \log z$ hash operations but with a public storage cost of $z^2(1 + (1/6) \log \log z)$. The aforementioned constructions illustrate the trade-offs between key derivation cost and public storage cost.

In this work, we propose a new construction for time-bound $HKAS$ with single key storage per user per subscription. Our scheme uses indirect key derivation with dependent keys. As shown in Section 3, our scheme requires less public storage $(z(z-1) - \lceil (1/8)z(3z+2) \rceil)$ and only one key private storage at CA. It requires at most $\log z$ hash operations as key derivation cost. The security of our scheme relies on the one-way property of cryptographic hash functions.

In the next section, we describe our proposed time-bound $HKAS$. We analyze and compare performance of our proposed construction with other time-bound $HKAS$ in Section 3.

2 Proposed Scheme

We propose a time-bound $HKAS$ that uses xor and hash functions. A time-bound $HKAS$ generates system public information and, secret information for each existing subscription interval such that a user with a secret information can derive any authorize subscription node's key in the hierarchy. Time-bound $HKAS$ is said to be secure if it is sound, even if user's collude. A scheme is sound if a user will not have secret information using which he can compute any unauthorized encryption key in the system. Our scheme uses indirect key derivation with dependent keys. In indirect key derivation, a user can derive key of any immediate successor node directly and hence can compute key of any descendant node working along the path towards the target node ([12]). In case of dependent keys, key of a node is dependent on the keys of its predecessor nodes [1]. CA will generate, assign and maintain secret keys in the system.

Key Assignment. Keys are assigned using following steps.

Step 1. Let, system consists of z time slots $t_1, ..., t_z$. CA generates a subscription hierarchy structure with z leaf nodes, one for each time slot t_i, with $1 \le i \le z$. It contains a node for every possible subscription interval in a system of z time slots. Nodes are arranged in such a way that at each level l in the subscription hierarchy structure, there are $l + 1$ nodes with subscription interval of size $z - l$ each. Therefore, at level $l = 0$ (root level) there is only one $(0 + 1)$ node with subscription interval size z, i.e., node with time interval (t_1, t_z) represented as $(1, z)$. An example subscription hierarchy structure (or a subscription hierarchy) for $z = 4$ time slots is shown in Figure 2(a).

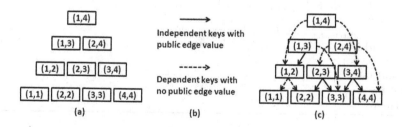

Fig. 2. (a) An example subscription hierarchy, (b) Arrow types in Fig.(c), (c) Key derivation structure corresponding to subscription hierarchy in Fig.(a)

Step 2. CA chooses a public cryptographic one-way hash function $h()$ for key generation. $h()$ is also used by the subscribers for key derivation purpose. A secret key K_s is generated and stored by the CA. CA assigns a random public label $l_{(a,b)}$ to each node (t_a, t_b) in the subscription hierarchy. In order to assign keys to the nodes in subscription hierarchy, CA will call procedure *Key_Assignment()*, defined in Algorithm 1. Step 1 in Algorithm 1, moves to each level from top to bottom in the subscription hierarchy. Step 2 initializes counter i to one, to point left most node in a level. Step 3 moves to each node from left to right in a level. If no key is assigned to the selected node, it compute and assign key to the node using $h()$ and K_s (Step $4-6$). Steps $7, 8$ computes two child nodes named *left* and *right* child nodes respectively of the selected node. In steps $9-13$, if key to *left* child node is *Null*, then compute and assign dependent key $K_{(i,left)}$ as in Step 10. Else, compute public edge value $r_{(i,j),(i,left)}$ for key derivation between nodes (Step 12). Steps $14-18$ gives similar treatment to *right* child. Step 19 will increment i by one, to move next node in same level.

Algorithm 1. *Key_Assignment*$(SH, z, K_s, h())$

DESCRIPTION: Given a subscription hierarchy SH, number of time slots z, secret key K_s associated with SH and $h()$, assign keys to nodes in SH.

1: **for** $l = 0 \rightarrow (z-2)$ **do**
2:     $i = 1$
3:     **for** $j = (z-l) \rightarrow z$ **do**
4:         **if** $(K_{(i,j)} = Null)$ **then**
5:             $K_{(i,j)} = h(K_s, l_{(i,j)})$
6:         **end if**
7:         $left = \lfloor (i+j)/2 \rfloor$
8:         $right = left + 1$
9:         **if** $K_{(i,left)} = Null$ **then**
10:            $K_{(i,left)} = h(K_{(i,j)}, l_{(i,left)})$
11:        **else**
12:            $r_{(i,j),(i,left)} = h(K_{(i,j)}, l_{(i,left)}) \oplus K_{(i,left)}$
13:        **end if**
14:        **if** $K_{(right,j)} = Null$ **then**
15:            $K_{(right,j)} = h(K_{(i,j)}, l_{(right,j)})$
16:        **else**
17:            $r_{(i,j),(right,j)} = h(K_{(i,j)}, l_{(right,j)}) \oplus K_{(right,j)}$
18:        **end if**
19:        $i = i + 1$
20:     **end for**
21: **end for**
22: **return**

Figure 2(*c*) shows output of *Key_Assignment()* (Algorithm 1) considering subscription hierarchy shown in Figure 2(a). In Figure 2(*c*), a smooth directed edge denotes a public edge value between two end nodes and dotted directed edge denotes a dependent key generation as shown in Figure 2(b). A dotted directed edge from node u to v shows that the key of node v is computed using key of node u. Table 1 shows output of *Key_Assignment()* (Algorithm 1) with respect to subscription hierarchy shown in Figure 2(c).

Table 1. Key assignment to the subscription hierarchy given in Figure 2(c)

node	Key	left child	right child	public edge values left child	right child
$(1,4)$	$h(K_s, l_{(1,4)})$	$(1,2)$	$(3,4)$	–	–
$(1,3)$	$h(K_s, l_{(1,3)})$	$(1,2)$	$(3,3)$	$r_{(1,3),(1,2)}$	–
$(2,4)$	$h(K_s, l_{(2,4)})$	$(2,3)$	$(4,4)$	–	–
$(1,2)$	$h(K_{(1,4)}, l_{(1,2)})$	$(1,1)$	$(2,2)$	–	–
$(2,3)$	$h(K_{(2,4)}, l_{(2,3)})$	$(2,2)$	$(3,3)$	$r_{(2,3),(2,2)}$	$r_{(2,3),(3,3)}$
$(3,4)$	$h(K_{(1,4)}, l_{(3,4)})$	$(3,3)$	$(4,4)$	$r_{(3,4),(3,3)}$	$r_{(3,4),(4,4)}$
$(1,1)$	$h(K_{(1,2)}, l_{(1,1)})$	–	–	–	–
$(2,2)$	$h(K_{(1,2)}, l_{(2,2)})$	–	–	–	–
$(3,3)$	$h(K_{(1,3)}, l_{(3,3)})$	–	–	–	–
$(4,4)$	$h(K_{(2,4)}, l_{(4,4)})$	–	–	–	–

Key Derivation. A user with a subscription key can derive any authorize encryption key within its subscription using procedure *Key_Derivation()*, defined in Algorithm 2. Suppose that there is a user with secret information $K_{(t_a,t_b)}$ corresponding to a subscription interval (t_a, t_b). To derive an encryption key $K_{(t,t)}$ with $t_a \leq t \leq t_b$, the user will do the following.

Step 1. Let $(t_a < t_b)$, user will find two nodes with subscription (t_a, t_{mid}) and (t_{mid+1}, t_b) where $t_{mid} = \lfloor (t_a + t_b)/2 \rfloor$.

(a). Let $t \in (t_a, t_{mid})$. To compute key $K_{(t_a,t_{mid})}$, if public edge value $r_{(t_a,t_b),(t_a,t_{mid})}$ exists then user will compute $K_{(t_a,t_{mid})} = h(K_{(t_a,t_b)}, l_{(t_a,t_{mid})}) \oplus r_{(t_a,t_b),(t_a,t_{mid})}$ where $h()$ and $l_{(t_a,t_{mid})}$ are public. Otherwise, user will compute $K_{(t_a,t_{mid})} = h(K_{(t_a,t_b)}, l_{(t_a,t_{mid})})$.

(b). Let $t \in (t_{mid+1}, t_b)$. To compute key $K_{(t_{mid+1},t_b)}$, if public edge value $r_{(t_a,t_b),(t_{mid+1},t_b)}$ exists then user will compute $K_{(t_{mid+1},t_b)} = h(K_{(t_a,t_b)}, l_{(t_{mid+1},t_b)}) \oplus r_{(t_a,t_b),(t_{mid+1},t_b)}$. Otherwise, he will compute $K_{(t_{mid+1},t_b)} = h(K_{(t_a,t_b)}, l_{(t_{mid+1},t_b)})$.

Step 2. User will repeat Step 1 using fresh computed key $K_{(t_x,t_y)}$ ((t_x, t_y) is either (t_a, t_{mid}) or (t_{mid+1}, t_b)) with $t_x \leq t \leq t_y$ until get target encryption key $K_{(t,t)}$.

Since, there is a path from each subscription node to its all descendant leaf nodes in the subscription hierarchy; one will surely get any authorize leaf node encryption key following above steps.

Algorithm 2. $Key\_Derivation(K_{(i,j)}, i, j, t, Pub)$

DESCRIPTION: Given a subscription key $K_{(i,j)}$, subscription start time slot i, subscription expiry time slot j, target time slot t with $i \leq t \leq j$ and public information, it returns target node encryption key $K_{(t,t)}$.

1: **if** $(t < i)$ or $(t > j)$ or $(j < i)$ **then**
2:     **return** $Null$
3: **end if**
4: **while** $j > i$ **do**
5:     $m = \lfloor (i+j)/2 \rfloor$
6:     **if** $(t \leq m)$ **then**
7:        **if** $r_{(i,j),(i,m)}$ **then**
8:           $K_{(i,m)} = h(K_{(i,j)}, l_{(i,m)}) \oplus r_{(i,j),(i,m)}$
9:        **else**
10:         $K_{(i,m)} = h(K_{(i,j)}, l_{(i,m)})$
11:       **end if**
12:       $j = m$
13:     **else**
14:        **if** $r_{(i,j),(m+1,j)}$ **then**
15:          $K_{(m+1,j)} = h(K_{(i,j)}, l_{(m+1,j)}) \oplus r_{(i,j),(m+1,j)}$
16:        **else**
17:          $K_{(m+1,j)} = h(K_{(i,j)}, l_{(m+1,j)})$
18:       **end if**
19:       $i = m + 1$
20:     **end if**
21: **end while**
22: **return** $K_{(i,j)}$

3 Performance Analysis

Each node in the subscription hierarchy excluding leaf nodes has at most two outgoing edges and each edge has one associated public edge value. Hence, there are at most $z(z - 1)$ public edge values. The nodes in lower half levels of the subscription hierarchy are having dependent keys and hence each such node has one incoming edge which does not have associated public edge value. The number of nodes (X) in lower half levels is computed below,

```
X = # nodes in full hierarchy - # nodes in upper half levels
  = (1/2)z(z+1) - (1/2)(z/2)((z/2)+1)
  = (1/8)z(3z+2)
```

Hence, out of $z(z - 1)$ edges, up to $(1/8)z(3z + 2)$ (nodes in lower half levels of subscription hierarchy) nodes have dependent incoming edges without public edge value. Hence, a total of $z(z - 1) - (1/8)z(3z + 2)$ public edge values are required.

In our scheme, each key in the subscription hierarchy is computed with single key (e.g. K_s). Hence, only one key is required with CA to derive all other keys. In [9,10], since keys are independently assigned to the nodes in the subscription hierarchy, there are many nodes whose parent does not exists (are root nodes). A key for each root node must be stored at CA. We can see in their hierarchy that at least upper half of the levels do not have parents (hence are root nodes. Therefore, $(1/2)(z/2)((z/2)+1) = (z/8)(z+2)$ keys must be stored at CA. In [8], since using root node key, CA can derive every key in the hierarchy, it requires only one key to store. In [7], there are two levels. Upper level will have a node corresponding to each subscription interval with more than one time slots. In other way, it includes all nodes in the considered subscription hierarchy other than leaf nodes (nodes in upper $z-1$ levels) i.e. $(z/2)(z-1)$.

Table 2 compares cost associated with a subscription hierarchy in the existing time-bound $HKAS$. Ateniese et al [7] scheme requires one decryption operation for key derivation with an expense of huge ($O(z^3)$) public storage. Atallah et al base scheme [8] requires at most z hash operations as a key derivation. When using $log\ z - Hop$ shortcut edge scheme, Atallah et al improved scheme reduces key derivation cost up to $2 log z$ with an expense of additional ($> z^2$) public edge values. Crampton [9,10] was able to reduce key derivation cost up to $log z$ without using any additional (shortcut) public edge value by using independent keys. In our scheme, we use dependent keys and are able to further reduce public storage by a factor of $(1/8)z(3z+2)$. Key derivation cost in our scheme is similar (at most $log z$ steps) to [9,11], as a user can jump half of the existing levels towards target leaf node in every step.

Table 2. Comparison of single key time-bound $HKAS$

Scheme	Type of keys	Public edge values	Secret storage at CA	Key derivation cost
Ateniese et al Scheme [7]	independent	$z(z-1)(z+4)/6$	$z(z-1)/2$	1 decryption
Atallah et al base Scheme [8]	independent	$z(z-1)$	1	z
Atallah et al Impv. Scheme [8] with $log\ z - Hop$ scheme	independent	$> z(z-1) + z^2$	1	$2.log\ z$
Crampton Scheme [9]	independent	$z(z-1)$	$> z/8(z+2)$	$log\ z$
Our proposed Scheme	dependent	$z(z-1)- \lceil (1/8)z(3z+2) \rceil$	1	$log\ z$

Note that, allowing more number of outgoing edges to a node in subscription hierarchy will reduce key derivation cost. There is a trade-off between outgoing edges to a node and key derivation cost. In our scheme, if we allow $log\ z$ outgoing edges to a node (with the same spirit as in [11]), key derivation cost will be reduced to $log\ log\ z$ as in [11]. Public storage cost in our construction will be still less with a factor of $(1/8)z(3z+2)$ since these number of nodes are still require an incoming edge with dependent key derivation i.e. without any public edge value.

4 Future Work

Future direction to this work includes: extending system hierarchy to consider dynamic operations like add or delete user subscription in the system and formal security analysis with appropriate adversary model.

References

1. Akl, S.G., Taylor, P.D.: Cryptographic solution to a problem of access control in a hierarchy. ACM Trans. on Computer Systems 1(3), 239–248 (1983)
2. Tzeng, W.G.: A time-bound cryptographic key assignment scheme for access control in the hierarchy. IEEE Trans. on Know. and Data Eng. 14, 182–188 (2002)
3. Rivest, R.L., Shamir, A., Adleman, L.M.: A method for obtaining digital signatures and public-key cryptosystems. Communications of the ACM 21(2), 120–126 (1978)
4. Yi, X., Ye, Y.: Security of Tzeng time-bound key assignment scheme for access control in hierarchy. IEEE Trans. on Know. and Data Eng. 15(4), 1054–1055 (2003)
5. Zhu, W.T., Deng, R.H., Zhou, J., Bao, F.: Time-bound hierarchical key assignment: An overview. IEICE Trans. 93-D(5), 1044–1052 (2010)
6. Ateniese, G., De Santis, A., Ferrara, A.L., Masucci, B.: Provably-secure time-bound hierarchical key assignment schemes. In: ACM Conference on Computer and Communications Security, pp. 288–297 (2006)
7. Ateniese, G., De Santis, A., Ferrara, A.L., Masucci, B.: Provably-secure time-bound hierarchical key assignment schemes. Journal of Cryptology 25(2), 243–270 (2012)
8. Atallah, M.J., Blanton, M., Frikken, K.B.: Incorporating temporal capabilities in existing key mgmt. schemes. In: Biskup, J., López, J. (eds.) ESORICS 2007. LNCS, vol. 4734, pp. 515–530. Springer, Heidelberg (2007)
9. Crampton, J.: Trade-offs in cryptographic implementations of temporal access control. In: Jøsang, A., Maseng, T., Knapskog, S.J. (eds.) NordSec 2009. LNCS, vol. 5838, pp. 72–87. Springer, Heidelberg (2009)
10. Crampton, J.: Time-storage trade-offs for cryptographically-enforced access control. In: Atluri, V., Diaz, C. (eds.) ESORICS 2011. LNCS, vol. 6879, pp. 245–261. Springer, Heidelberg (2011)
11. Crampton, J.: Practical and efficient cryptographic enforcement of interval-based access control policies. ACM Trans. on Inf. Syst. Secur. 14(1), 14 (2011)
12. Atallah, M.J., Frikken, K.B., Blanton, M.: Dynamic and efficient key management for access hierarchies. In: ACM Conference on Computer and Communications Security, pp. 190–202 (2005)

Traitor-Traceable Key Pre-distribution Based on Visual Secret Sharing

Sheethal Kumar[1], Pai B.J. Jaipal[1], Sourav Sen Gupta[2,*],
and Vigesh R. Ungrapalli[1]

[1] National Institute of Technology Karnataka, Surathkal, India
{sheethalk.49,vigshru23}@gmail.com, redevils_jaipal_710@hotmail.com
[2] Indian Statistical Institute, Kolkata, India
sg.sourav@gmail.com

Abstract. In this paper, we study the problem of traitor-traceable key pre-distribution for general access structures. We propose a new scheme for key pre-distribution using visual secret sharing, where the keys are generated based on certain combinatorial block designs. Our scheme naturally extends for general access structures, and provides a flexible many-to-one function using visual secret sharing concepts to efficiently avoid the problem of pixel expansion. In addition, our proposal accommodates a simple traitor-tracing functionality for video broadcast applications; using efficient PBIBD based combinatorial constructs and visual secret sharing based on random grids. In effect, our scheme provides a novel technique for secure video and image broadcast, using general access structures to reduce collusions, trace forgery, and identify traitors in case there is a collusion. We duly analyze and discuss the efficiency of our scheme for varying number of users in the broadcast network.

Keywords: key pre-distribution, general access structure, traitor tracing, combinatorial block design, visual secret sharing, random grids.

1 Introduction

Secure transmission of intellectual properties of commercial value to a large number of recipients has beckoned the rise of data encryption in broadcast networks. In the past two decades, several techniques related to encryption of broadcast data have found diverse applications in video distribution, streaming video applications, area-specific media devices (CD, DVD etc.), access-controlled databases, and even in SaaS frameworks of the cloud architecture.

Naive idea to achieve data security in broadcast mode of transmission is to establish a secret-key secure channel between the distributor and each authorized recipient. Establishment of a common secret key between the transmitter and the receiver may be achieved either by using a public key framework for key

* Supported by DRDO sponsored project Centre of Excellence in Cryptology (CoEC), under MOC ERIP/ER/1009002/M/01/1319/788/D(R&D) of ER&IPR, DRDO.

A. Bagchi and I. Ray (Eds.): ICISS 2013, LNCS 8303, pp. 199–213, 2013.
© Springer-Verlag Berlin Heidelberg 2013

exchange, or by a simpler and alternative method of key pre-distribution. In case of key pre-distribution, it is hard to cater to a large user-base if single unique keys are provided to each user. The most compelling requirement for such an access control structure comes from the domain of image and video broadcast, where the transmitter generally caters to a large number of users.

1.1 Preliminaries of Media Broadcast

Conventional method of video broadcasting involves encrypting the video frames and broadcasting them across the network. It is expected that only authorized users can decrypt the video stream using an authenticated set of keys given to them by the transmitter, and no other individual may have a similar access to the data. The transmitter builds a main key-pool, and pre-distributes authorized subsets of keys to each authorized user. The user may thereafter construct an authorized decoder using his/her user key-set, and access the encrypted video broadcast on the network. The pre-distribution of the user key-sets are expected to satisfy the following conditions.

- When used together, the keys of a particular authorized user key-set must map to a single value – the final decryption key.
- None of the sub-sets of the main key-pool, apart from the authorized user key-sets, should map to the final decryption key.

Many-to-one Functions. The key pre-distribution described above suggests access-control using a many-to-one function, which maps each of the authorized user key-sets to the final decryption key; but no other subset of the main key-pool to the final key. By definition, a many-to-one function is a relation $\mathcal{R} \subseteq S \times T$ where every element of the domain of $\mathcal{R}$ relates to exactly one element of its co-domain, that is,

$$(x, y_1) \in \mathcal{R} \wedge (x, y_2) \in \mathcal{R} \Rightarrow y_1 = y_2 \qquad \text{if and only if} \quad x \in \mathrm{Dom}(\mathcal{R}).$$

The key-sets meant for the authorized users lie within $\mathrm{Dom}(\mathcal{R})$, while the final decryption key is a member of the co-domain of $\mathcal{R}$. Several techniques have been proposed in the literature to construct such functions; many based on suitable combinatorial designs like BIBD and PBIBD [8, 7, 9–11, 13].

A specific technique of realizing these functions may be conceived using Visual Secret Sharing (VSS). The basic concept of Secret Sharing was independently proposed by Shamir [12] and Blakley [2] in 1979. Visual Secret Sharing (VSS) appeared in 1994 as a special sub-domain of secret sharing, where a single image is divided into secret shares and a combination of certain shares (defined by some access structure) results in the original image. The very first VSS scheme was proposed by Naor and Shamir [6], and later this was further extended to general access structure based VSS schemes by Ateniese, Blundo, Santis and Stinson [1]. In 2012, Wu and Sun [15] proposed a general access structure based VSS scheme using random grids, which efficiently overcame the critical problem of pixel expansion.

Traitor-Tracing. The many-to-one functions solve the two conditions required for a key pre-distribution scheme. However, this introduces a new problem of potential collusion amongst authorized users to produce a new authorized key-set, which had not been provided by the distributor. Suppose that the main key-pool is $\mathcal{K}$, and N key-sets $K_1, K_2, \ldots, K_N \subset \mathcal{K}$ have been distributed to authorized users. Some of these authorized users may attempt a collusion to construct a new key-set K_{N+1} which maps to the final decryption key as well. The colluding users may choose to sell this pirated key-set K_{N+1} to enable unauthorized users to decrypt the contents of the encrypted media without proper consent or authorization by the original distributor.

In such a scenario, it is required to identify the colluding authorized users, hereafter called *traitors*, who have violated their contract by jointly producing a pirate key-set out of their own authorized keys. Solution to this problem requires a traitor tracing scheme to trace at least one traitor from the coalition of users. Traitor tracing is necessary to provide a legal proof for cheating. Traitor tracing methods were first proposed by Chor, Fiat and Naor [4], and traitor tracing techniques using combinatorial approach were proposed by Stinson and Wei [13], Safavi-Naini and Wang [10], and Ruj and Roy [7]. It is worth noting that traitor-tracing schemes are a special subclass of many-to-one functions, and not all such functions allow for tracing traitors within colluding groups.

1.2   Motivation for This Paper

We consider the scenario of video or image broadcast on a network where the media is encrypted for security, and can be decrypted only by the authorized users who possess certain key-sets pre-distributed by the authentic distributor of the media. This warrants for a many-to-one function with general access structure in case of the key pre-distribution. The broadcaster/distributor gives a set of keys to authorized receivers, which maps to a particular final decryption key, and a 'black-box' decoder decrypts the media using this decryption key. We call the domain of the many-to-one function *qualified sets*, which are to be acquired by authorized users.

Dealing with the encryption and decryption of video and image media becomes conceptually easier (and quite efficient) if the keys used in the process are also of a similar format. If images are used as keys, the process of encryption or decryption of digital images and videos (frame-by-frame) may be performed easily by simple arithmetic operations like XOR and OR; especially if we consider visual secret sharing techniques. Moreover, we noticed that visual secret sharing schemes offer a natural many-to-one function, which may be extended to a general access structure to provide a more flexible form of the function.

Although general access structures based on visual secret sharing have been proposed in the literature, we could find none that addresses the problem of traitor tracing in practical scenarios of video broadcast. However, there exist efficient general access structures based on combinatorial block designs to achieve traitor tracing in practice. We attempt at combining the two apparently disjoint ideas to form a general access structure based on visual secret sharing that would as well provide an efficient mechanism for traitor tracing in practical cases of broadcast of image and videos. A concrete practical instantiation of our motivation for this paper is as follows.

Practical Instantiation of Our Motivation: Consider a video broadcaster who wants only authorized users to access the video. To achieve this, he encrypts the video frame-by-frame using the encryption key – an image similar to a single frame of the video – and broadcasts the resulting data to the network. Decryption by an authorized user will have to use the pre-distributed key-set provided by the broadcaster well in advance. We require the following properties for the scheme.

1. General access structure for the pre-distributed authorized key-sets.
2. Traitor traceable mechanism built within the key-set pre-distribution.
3. Conceptually simple implementation of encryption-decryption routine.

1.3 Contribution of This Paper

We propose a visual secret sharing based traitor traceable key pre-distribution scheme which distributes sets of shares to each user, such that, on combining the shares of each authorized user, the final decryption key is recovered in form of an image. The desired properties can be achieved using VSS scheme which distributes the personal sets of keys in form of images for easy media operation during encryption and decryption. Traitor tracing is possible in cases of collusion through the use of a traitor traceable key pre-distribution scheme, as proposed in [7], where the proposed general access structure arising from PBIBD may be implemented through visual secret sharing using random grids, as in [15].

The advantage of our scheme is that if any set formed by collusion is not from any of the authorized user key-sets, then the combination of keys of this set will not yield the secret image. In other words we have a many-to-one function whose domain is strictly the set of authorized user key-sets and range is the secret image. This reduces the chances for collusion, and even if there is any, the broadcaster can trace the traitors quite efficiently.

Practical Instantiation of Our Contribution: In line with our motivating example, as earlier, our proposal may be practically applied in case of video broadcast. Our proposal achieves the following desirable properties.

1. PBIBD based general access structure for traitor-tracing.
2. General access structure based on visual secret sharing.
3. Easy media encryption-decryption using images as shares.

Roadmap. In Section 2, we discuss general access control schemes based on visual secret sharing. Later in Section 3, we propose our scheme for VSS-based traitor tracing and key pre-distribution, describe its details, and analyze the efficiency of our proposal. Finally, Section 4 concludes the paper with a summarized discussion of our proposal, and future scope for research in this direction.

2   VSS Based Access Control

In this section, we discuss some aspects regarding VSS based many-to-one functions and access control designs. Based on Naor and Shamir's [6] VSS schemes, several related works have been published over the last two decades. The VSS schemes for general access structure proposed in [13, 15] are noteworthy.

VSS Based Many-to-One Functions. Naor and Shamir [6] proposed a (k, n)-VSS. This scheme is one possible realization of many-to-one functions using VSS, where any subset of size k, taken from the main key-pool, successfully maps to a single image; the 'secret image' of the scheme. The domain of the function is the set of all subsets of size k, and the range is a unique secret image.

Contrary to accepting all subsets of size k in the domain of the many-to-one function, certain access control applications may require to allow only certain subsets (of varying sizes) to map to the secret image. This requires a general access control structure using VSS; a brief overview is as follows.

2.1   General Access Structure Using Conventional VSS

Let $P = \{1, 2, \ldots, n\}$ be a set of participants (users) in a VSS scheme and let 2^P denote the power set (set of all subsets) of P. Let $\Gamma_{Qual} \subseteq 2^P$ be the *qualified sets* of the scheme, and $\Gamma_{Forb} \subseteq 2^P$ be the *forbidden sets*. Then the pair $(\Gamma_{Qual}, \Gamma_{Forb})$ is called the access structure of this VSS scheme [13].

In conventional VSS, a secret pixel is encoded into n shared pixels. Each shared pixel contains m black and white sub-pixels, where m is called the pixel expansion of the scheme. The construction can be described by an $n \times m$ boolean matrix $S = [s_{ij}]$, where $s_{ij} = 1$ if and only if the j-th sub-pixel in the i-th share is black. The grey level of each pixel of the final image, obtained by stacking the shares $i_1, i_2, \ldots, i_s$, is interpreted by the human eye as black or white in accordance with the contrast of the pixel. The contrast is proportional to the hamming weight $H(V)$ of the m-dimensional vector V obtained by a logical OR of the row vectors $r_{i_1}, r_{i_2}, \ldots, r_{i_s}$ from the matrix S, associated with the shares given out to the participants $i_1, i_2, \ldots, i_s$, respectively.

Let $(\Gamma_{Qual}, \Gamma_{Forb})$ be an access structure defined on a set of n participants. A $(\Gamma_{Qual}, \Gamma_{Forb})$-VSS scheme with pixel expansion m, relative difference $\alpha(m)$, and set of thresholds $\{(X, t_X)\}_{X \in \Gamma_{Qual}}$ is realized using the two collections of $n \times m$ boolean matrices C_0 and C_1 if the following two conditions are satisfied.

1. If $X = \{i_1, i_2, \ldots, i_p\} \in \Gamma_{Qual}$, then the V-vector produced by logical OR of the rows $r_{i_1}, r_{i_2}, \ldots, r_{i_p}$, meets $H(V) \leq t_X - \alpha(m) \cdot m$ for any $M \in C_0$, whereas it results in $H(V) \geq t_X$ for any $M \in C_1$.
2. If $X = \{i_1, i_2, \ldots, i_q\} \in \Gamma_{Forb}$, the two collections of $q \times m$ matrices D_0, D_1 obtained by restricting the $n \times m$ matrices C_0, C_1 to rows $r_{i_1}, r_{i_2}, \ldots, r_{i_q}$, respectively, are indistinguishable from one another.

The first condition is to ensure that any qualified set $Q \in \Gamma_{Qual}$ recovers the 'secret image' whereas the second condition is to ensure that the recovery of the secret image in this scheme is immune against any forbidden set $F \in \Gamma_{Forb}$.

2.2   General Access Structure Using VSS Based on Random Grids

An alternative method of visual secret sharing was proposed by Kafri and Keren [5] in 1987. This was a $(2,2)$-VSS based on random grids, which eliminates the problems of pixel expansion and shape distortion in practice. The scheme was extended to an (n,n)-VSS scheme in 2008 by Chen and Tsao [3], and was further extended by Wu and Sun [15] in 2012 to a VSS based on general access structure.

Construction of Shares: In the VSS scheme based on general access structure, proposed in [15], n binary shares $R_1, \ldots, R_n$ are constructed from an $M \times N$ secret image S for a pre-specified access structure $(\Gamma_{Qual}, \Gamma_{Forb})$. It defines the set of all minimal qualified sets for the VSS as

$$\Gamma_0 = \{Q \in \Gamma_{Qual} \; : \; Q' \notin \Gamma_{Qual} \; \forall \; Q' \subset Q\},$$

and for each pixel $(i,j) \in S$, a minimal qualified set $Q = i_1, \ldots, i_p \in \Gamma_0$ is selected at random $(p \le n)$. For each of the first $p-1$ shares in Q, the pixel (i,j) is randomly assigned a value 0 (for white) or 1 (for black).

Thereafter the pixel (i,j) of the p-th share is obtained by performing a logical XOR on the (i,j)-th pixel of each of the $p-1$ shares and the (i,j)-th pixel of the secret image:

$$r_{i_p}(i,j) = S(i,j) \oplus r_{i_1}(i,j) \oplus r_{i_2}(i,j) \oplus \cdots \oplus r_{i_{p-1}}(i,j) \qquad \forall \text{ pixel } (i,j) \in S.$$

For the remaining $n-p$ binary shares not in the minimal qualified set Q, the (i,j)-th pixel is randomly assigned a value 0 (for white) or 1 (for black). The process is repeated for each pixel in the secret image.

Proof of Correctness: As a result of the above construction, participants belonging to any qualified set can reconstruct the image by performing a logical XOR operation on the corresponding pixels of the shares in the qualified sets; however, stacking of the shares in any of the forbidden sets does not provide any information of the secret image. This has theoretically been proved in the original proposal [15].

Contrast of the Recovered Image: The original scheme [15] also proves a quantitative measure of the contrast of the recovered image. Let $k = |\Gamma_0|$ be the number of minimal qualified sets. $X = \{i_1, i_2, ..., i_p\} \in \Gamma_{Qual}$ be a qualified set whose elements can form d minimal qualified sets $(1 \le d \le k)$. Then the contrast of the image by stacking shares $R_{i_1}, ..., R_{i_p}$ from the qualified set X, as proved in [15, Theorem 2], is as follows:

$$\alpha = \frac{2d}{(2^p + 1)k - d} \tag{1}$$

Thus, it is evident that as the number of qualified sets increases, the contrast of the recovered image obtained from each qualified set decreases considerably. In our proposal, we try to rectify this issue and provide perfect contrast.

3   Our Proposal – VSS-Based Traitor-Tracing

Traitor tracing schemes were first proposed by Chor, Fiat and Naor [4]. The key distributor distributes a set of keys $K = \{K_1, K_2, ..., K_b\}$ to b users, where the base set or key-pool consists of v keys. Each user U is given a set of k keys which form the personal user key-set, and we denote this set by $P(U)$. If user U is authorized by the broadcaster to access the encrypted content, then $P(U) \in \Gamma_{Qual}$. It is assumed that a set $C = \{K_1, K_2, ..., K_c\}$ of c malicious users (traitors) may collude and construct a pirate decoder F, not originally (or not yet) authorized by the broadcaster, such that

$$F \subset \bigcup_{U \in C} P(U), \quad F \in \Gamma_{Qual}, \quad \text{and} \quad |F| = k.$$

The goal of the broadcaster is to assign the keys to the users in such a way that once the pirate decoder F is found and the keys are examined, at least one traitor within the colluding set C will be identified.

Traitor Tracing Schemes Based on PBIBD. The first PBIBD based traitor tracing scheme was proposed by Ruj and Roy [7]. A partially balanced incomplete block design with m associate classes [14], denoted by PBIBD(m), is a design on a v-set X, with b blocks each of size k and with each element of X being repeated r times, such that if there is an association scheme with m classes defined on X where, two elements x and y are i-th associates ($1 \leq i \leq m$), then they occur together in λ_i blocks. Such a design is denoted by $PB[k, \lambda_1, \lambda_2, ..., \lambda_m; v]$. One may refer to [14] for a comprehensive mathematical treatment of PBIBD and similar combinatorial designs.

The proposal of [7] achieves a PBIBD-based key distribution scheme for N users, with the size of each personal set $|P(U)| \sim O(N^{1/2})$, and a mechanism to trace a collusion of at most $|C| \sim O(N^{1/4})$ traitors. In this paper, we try to combine this idea with VSS-based general access structures, while keeping the bounds on personal key-set and collusion detection the same as [7].

3.1   Combination of VSS and PBIBD

In this section, we describe our proposal of mapping of PBIBD scheme to a general access structure based on VSS. The PBIBD-based scheme distributes a set of k keys based on the number of users b. In our proposal, each key in the PBIBD scheme is mapped to a particular share obtained from a secret image in the VSS scheme. Thus, the concept of many-to-one function realized by the PBIBD approach is naturally extended to the VSS scheme.

The set of shares in the VSS scheme corresponding to the qualified user key-set, when combined together, results in the original secret image. However, when the set of shares corresponding to the set of keys other than the qualified user key-set are combined together, the secret image is not recovered. Thus, the set of shares corresponding to the user key-set in the PBIBD scheme forms the access structure of the VSS scheme, where the set of shares given to authorized users form the qualified sets, and the other sets automatically become forbidden. To achieve this map from PBIBD based key distribution scheme to VSS, we need a general access structure based VSS, with a mechanism to map the set of user key-sets in the PBIBD scheme to the qualified sets for generating shares.

Choosing the Appropriate VSS Construction. In the general access structure based VSS scheme provided in [13], the construction of shares is based on the minimal forbidden sets, and not on the minimal qualified sets. The complexity of determining all the forbidden sets, given a small number of qualified sets, increases exponentially with the increase in the number of shares. Thus the complexity of the determining all the shares using the construction in [13] is impractical if only the qualified sets are specified. However, that is the situation in our case, as PBIBD based traitor-tracing generally prescribes only the qualified sets in the access structure.

In order to reduce the complexity of the construction of shares, we consider the random grid based VSS scheme, proposed in [15], as this construction considers the minimal qualified sets for designing the access structure. In practical applications, the number of users U and hence the number of personal user key-sets $P(U)$ is usually high. But it is evident from Eqn. (1) that as the number of qualified sets increases, the contrast of the image obtained by combining all the shares in a qualified set decreases exponentially, which results in poor 'visual' recovery of the secret image. To overcome this problem we introduce a new scheme based on random grids in the next section.

3.2   Design of the Proposed Scheme

As discussed earlier, we propose a key-distribution scheme based on VSS and general access structure, along the following line of construction.

Step 1 – PBIBD based general access structure for traitor-tracing.
Step 2 – General access structure based on visual secret sharing.
Step 3 – Visual secret sharing using random grid based approach.

Designing the Access Control Structure. Assuming b users in the scheme, each user is assigned k keys as his/her user key-set, where $k \sim O(b^{1/2})$. The PBIBD based construction with $PB[k, \lambda_1, \lambda_2, ..., \lambda_m; v]$ gives us the set of all personal user key-sets $Z = \{P(B_1), P(B_2), ...P(B_b)\}$ where $P(B_i)$ is the user key-set of the i-th user U_i. This set Z forms the access structure for the VSS based key pre-distribution scheme.

Let $(\Gamma_{Qual}, \Gamma_{Forb})$ be the access structure, where $\Gamma_{Qual} = Z$, and let Γ_0 be the set of all minimal qualified sets. As no subset of a set $P(B_i) \in Z$ belongs to Z, the minimal qualified set is Z itself, that is, we may write $Z = \Gamma_{Qual} = \Gamma_0$.

Designing the VSS Scheme for the Access Control Structure. Now we design a random grid based VSS scheme which provides access control as well as good contrast of the recovered image irrespective of the size of the minimal qualified set $\Gamma_0 = Z$.

In [15], for a given pixel in the secret image, a qualified set is selected at random and then the corresponding pixels of the shares are calculated. Hence, a pixel in the recovered image will have the same value as that in the secret image only when the shares of that particular random qualified set are stacked together. However, as discussed earlier, we know that this results in poor contrast.

Design for High Contrast Image Recovery: We consider all shares in the qualified sets of Z simultaneously for a particular pixel in the secret image. For a pixel $(i, j) \in S$ of the secret image, we calculate the corresponding (i, j)-th pixel of all the shares in the first qualified set $P(B_1) \in Z$; followed by that in all shares of the second qualified set $P(B_2) \in Z$, and the process is repeated for all the qualified sets $P(B_i) \in Z$.

Dummy Share: Now it may be so that for a qualified set $P(B_j) \in Z$, all the shares within have already been computed as a part of the previously considered qualified sets $P(B_1), P(B_2), \ldots, P(B_{j-1}) \in Z$. In such a scenario, we add a dummy share to $P(B_j)$ such that, when all the shares of the qualified set $P(B_j)$ along with the dummy share are stacked together, the secret image is recovered with a very high contrast. Thus with a little overhead (at most one per user) of dummy shares, we achieve near-perfect contrast in the recovered image, which is a significant improvement over [15].

Designing the Traitor-Tracing Mechanism. To achieve the traitor-tracing feature, we have to make sure that the traitor tracing technique based on PBIBD, as proposed in [7], is still applicable to our new modified sets of secret user keys.

Security Analysis: There are two possible scenarios.

Case 1. The collusion is such that a colluded set consists one of the dummy keys that we have introduced in the user key-sets. If this happens, the traitor(s) contributing the dummy key will be trivially exposed, as all dummy keys are randomly and uniquely chosen for each user.

Case 2. The other possibility is that there are no dummy keys in the pirate user key-set resulting from the collusion. This reduces the problem to traitor tracing without considering the dummy keys at all; precisely the condition where the traitor tracing techniques of [7] are applicable.

Thus, we conclude that our modified scheme satisfies the requirement for traitor tracing, in a way similar to that proposed in the PBIBD construction of [7].

Suppose the pirate user key-set formed through collusion is present in the set of qualified sets Γ_{Qual}, but has not been distributed to an authorized user yet. This is possible as some extra qualified sets are expected to be kept in reserve for the scope of expansion in user base. In such a case, the traitors can be traced as in [7], within a bound of $O(N^{1/4})$ traitors, where N is the number of users.

Advantage over [7]: If two or more users collude and form a pirate set of keys which is not present in the set of qualified sets Γ_{Qual}, then the access control structure achieved through our random grid based VSS assures that stacking the shares present in this pirate set does not reveal the secret image. In other words, if the pirate user key-set is not in Γ_{Qual}, our scheme assures that this key-set is not present in the set of minimal qualified sets $\Gamma_0 = Z$ of our design as well. This was not guaranteed in the scheme proposed by Ruj and Roy [7].

Algorithm for the Proposed Scheme. The discussion above confirms that we have created a VSS based on random grid methods to address the problem of general access structure based key pre-distribution with traitor tracing. Algorithm 1 illustrates our design.

Input: Number of users b, size of user key-set k and an $M \times N$ binary image Im.

Output: b user key-sets $Z = \{PS_1, PS_2, \ldots, PS_b\}$, v binary shares $R_1, \ldots, R_n$ corresponding to v keys of the key-pool, and d dummy shares.

Generate a PBIBD framework $PB[k, \lambda_1, \lambda_2, \ldots, \lambda_m; v]$;

Generate the user key-sets $Z = \{P(B_1), P(B_2), \ldots, P(B_b)\}$ using PB;

Construct the access structure $(\Gamma_{Qual}, \Gamma_{Forb})$, where $\Gamma_{Qual} = \Gamma_0 = Z$;

for *each minimal qualified set* $P(B_i) \in Z = \Gamma_0$ **do**

    $PS_i = P(B_i)$;

    if *last share in PS_i is already visited* **then**

        if *there exists a share $X \in PS_i$, which is not already visited* **then**

            | Swap last share with X;

        end

    else

        | Create a dummy share d of size $M \times N$;

        | Expand the key-set $PS_i = P(B_i) \cup d$;

    end

    end

    for *each share $S \in PS_i$* **do**

        for *each pixel $(i, j) \in S$* **do**

            if *S is not visited and it is not the last share in PS_i* **then**

                | $S(i, j) = \text{RandomBit}(0, 1)$;

            end

            if *S is the last share in PS_i* **then**

                | $S(i, j) = \bigoplus_{R \in PS_i, R \neq S} R(i, j) \oplus Im(i, j)$;

            end

        end

    end

end

Algorithm 1: The proposed VSS scheme based on a traitor-traceable access structure generated by PBIBD

3.3   Implementation of the Proposed Scheme

In this section we demonstrate an example implementation of our proposed key pre-distribution scheme. We consider the PBIBD construction $PB[10, 1, 0; 82]$ from [7], with total number of users $N = 41$. Each user is given a set of $k = 10$ keys. For completeness, we replicate the construction from [7], as follows.

$P(B_1) = \{1, 6, 25, 27, 33, 46, 64, 76, 77, 80\}$ $P(B_2) = \{2, 7, 26, 28, 34, 47, 65, 77, 78, 81\}$
$P(B_3) = \{3, 8, 27, 29, 35, 48, 66, 78, 79, 82\}$ $P(B_4) = \{4, 9, 28, 30, 36, 49, 67, 79, 80, 42\}$
$P(B_5) = \{5, 10, 29, 31, 37, 50, 68, 80, 81, 43\}$ $P(B_6) = \{6, 11, 30, 32, 38, 51, 69, 81, 82, 44\}$
$P(B_7) = \{7, 12, 31, 33, 39, 52, 70, 82, 42, 45\}$ $P(B_8) = \{8, 13, 32, 34, 40, 53, 71, 42, 43, 46\}$
$P(B_9) = \{9, 14, 33, 35, 41, 54, 72, 43, 44, 47\}$ $P(B_{10}) = \{10, 15, 34, 36, 1, 55, 73, 44, 45, 48\}$
$P(B_{11}) = \{11, 16, 35, 37, 2, 56, 74, 45, 46, 49\}$ $P(B_{12}) = \{12, 17, 36, 38, 3, 57, 75, 46, 47, 50\}$
$P(B_{13}) = \{13, 18, 37, 39, 4, 58, 76, 47, 48, 51\}$ $P(B_{14}) = \{14, 19, 38, 40, 5, 59, 77, 48, 49, 52\}$
$P(B_{15}) = \{15, 20, 39, 41, 6, 60, 78, 49, 50, 53\}$ $P(B_{16}) = \{16, 21, 40, 1, 7, 61, 79, 50, 51, 54\}$
$P(B_{17}) = \{17, 22, 41, 2, 8, 62, 80, 51, 52, 55\}$ $P(B_{18}) = \{18, 23, 1, 3, 9, 63, 81, 52, 53, 56\}$
$P(B_{19}) = \{19, 24, 2, 4, 10, 64, 82, 53, 54, 57\}$ $P(B_{20}) = \{20, 25, 3, 5, 11, 65, 42, 54, 55, 58\}$
$P(B_{21}) = \{21, 26, 4, 6, 12, 66, 43, 55, 56, 59\}$ $P(B_{22}) = \{22, 27, 5, 7, 13, 67, 44, 56, 57, 60\}$
$P(B_{23}) = \{23, 28, 6, 8, 14, 68, 45, 57, 58, 61\}$ $P(B_{24}) = \{24, 29, 7, 9, 15, 69, 46, 58, 59, 62\}$
$P(B_{25}) = \{25, 30, 8, 10, 16, 70, 47, 59, 60, 63\}$ $P(B_{26}) = \{26, 31, 9, 11, 17, 71, 48, 60, 61, 64\}$
$P(B_{27}) = \{27, 32, 10, 12, 18, 72, 49, 61, 62, 65\}$ $P(B_{28}) = \{28, 33, 11, 13, 19, 73, 50, 62, 63, 66\}$
$P(B_{29}) = \{29, 34, 12, 14, 20, 74, 51, 63, 64, 67\}$ $P(B_{30}) = \{30, 35, 13, 15, 21, 75, 52, 64, 65, 68\}$
$P(B_{31}) = \{31, 36, 14, 16, 22, 76, 53, 65, 66, 69\}$ $P(B_{32}) = \{32, 37, 15, 17, 23, 77, 54, 66, 67, 70\}$
$P(B_{33}) = \{33, 38, 16, 18, 24, 78, 55, 67, 68, 71\}$ $P(B_{34}) = \{34, 39, 17, 19, 25, 79, 56, 68, 69, 72\}$
$P(B_{35}) = \{35, 40, 18, 20, 26, 80, 57, 69, 70, 73\}$ $P(B_{36}) = \{36, 41, 19, 21, 27, 81, 58, 70, 71, 74\}$
$P(B_{37}) = \{37, 1, 20, 22, 28, 82, 59, 71, 72, 75\}$ $P(B_{38}) = \{38, 2, 21, 23, 29, 42, 60, 72, 73, 76\}$
$P(B_{39}) = \{39, 3, 22, 24, 30, 43, 61, 73, 74, 77\}$ $P(B_{40}) = \{40, 4, 23, 25, 31, 44, 62, 74, 75, 78\}$
$P(B_{41}) = \{41, 5, 24, 26, 32, 45, 63, 75, 76, 79\}$

User Set-Keys in the Proposed Scheme: In the above PBIBD construction, there are 82 unique keys. An additional 22 keys are appended as dummy shares (to certain sets) after applying Algorithm 1. The key-sets after applying Algorithm 1 are as follows, where the user key-sets from PS_{20} to PS_{41} have been appended with one dummy share each; numbered 83 to 104 in the presentation.

$PS_1 = \{1, 6, 25, 27, 33, 46, 64, 76, 77, 80\}$ $PS_2 = \{2, 7, 26, 28, 34, 47, 65, 77, 78, 81\}$
$PS_3 = \{3, 8, 27, 29, 35, 48, 66, 78, 79, 82\}$ $PS_4 = \{4, 9, 28, 30, 36, 49, 67, 79, 80, 42\}$
$PS_5 = \{5, 10, 29, 31, 37, 50, 68, 80, 81, 43\}$ $PS_6 = \{6, 11, 30, 32, 38, 51, 69, 81, 82, 44\}$
$PS_7 = \{7, 12, 31, 33, 39, 52, 70, 82, 42, 45\}$ $PS_8 = \{8, 46, 32, 34, 40, 53, 71, 42, 43, 13\}$
$PS_9 = \{9, 47, 33, 35, 41, 54, 72, 43, 44, 14\}$ $PS_{10} = \{10, 48, 34, 36, 1, 55, 73, 44, 45, 15\}$
$PS_{11} = \{11, 49, 35, 37, 2, 56, 74, 45, 46, 16\}$ $PS_{12} = \{12, 50, 36, 38, 3, 57, 75, 46, 47, 17\}$
$PS_{13} = \{13, 51, 37, 39, 4, 58, 76, 47, 48, 18\}$ $PS_{14} = \{14, 52, 38, 40, 5, 59, 77, 48, 49, 19\}$
$PS_{15} = \{15, 53, 39, 41, 6, 60, 78, 49, 50, 20\}$ $PS_{16} = \{16, 54, 40, 1, 7, 61, 79, 50, 51, 21\}$
$PS_{17} = \{17, 55, 41, 2, 8, 62, 80, 51, 52, 22\}$ $PS_{18} = \{18, 56, 1, 3, 9, 63, 81, 52, 53, 23\}$
$PS_{19} = \{19, 57, 2, 4, 10, 64, 82, 53, 54, 24\}$ $PS_{20} = \{20, 25, 3, 5, 11, 65, 42, 54, 55, 58, 83\}$
$PS_{21} = \{21, 26, 4, 6, 12, 66, 43, 55, 56, 59, 84\}$ $PS_{22} = \{22, 27, 5, 7, 13, 67, 44, 56, 57, 60, 85\}$
$PS_{23} = \{23, 28, 6, 8, 14, 68, 45, 57, 58, 61, 86\}$ $PS_{24} = \{24, 29, 7, 9, 15, 69, 46, 58, 59, 62, 87\}$
$PS_{25} = \{25, 30, 8, 10, 16, 70, 47, 59, 60, 63, 88\}$ $PS_{26} = \{26, 31, 9, 11, 17, 71, 48, 60, 61, 64, 89\}$
$PS_{27} = \{27, 32, 10, 12, 18, 72, 49, 61, 62, 65, 90\}$ $PS_{28} = \{28, 33, 11, 13, 19, 73, 50, 62, 63, 66, 91\}$
$PS_{29} = \{29, 34, 12, 14, 20, 74, 51, 63, 64, 67, 92\}$ $PS_{30} = \{30, 35, 13, 15, 21, 75, 52, 64, 65, 68, 93\}$
$PS_{31} = \{31, 36, 14, 16, 22, 76, 53, 65, 66, 69, 94\}$ $PS_{32} = \{32, 37, 15, 17, 23, 77, 54, 66, 67, 70, 95\}$
$PS_{33} = \{33, 38, 16, 18, 24, 78, 55, 67, 68, 71, 96\}$ $PS_{34} = \{34, 39, 17, 19, 25, 79, 56, 68, 69, 72, 97\}$
$PS_{35} = \{35, 40, 18, 20, 26, 80, 57, 69, 70, 73, 98\}$ $PS_{36} = \{36, 41, 19, 21, 27, 81, 58, 70, 71, 74, 99\}$
$PS_{37} = \{37, 1, 20, 22, 28, 82, 59, 71, 72, 75, 100\}$ $PS_{38} = \{38, 2, 21, 23, 29, 42, 60, 72, 73, 76, 101\}$
$PS_{39} = \{39, 3, 22, 24, 30, 43, 61, 73, 74, 77, 102\}$ $PS_{40} = \{40, 4, 23, 25, 31, 44, 62, 74, 75, 78, 103\}$
$PS_{41} = \{41, 5, 24, 26, 32, 45, 63, 75, 76, 79, 104\}$

Example Verification for Correctness. We stack the shares of the qualified set $P(B_1) = \{1, 6, 25, 27, 33, 46, 64, 76, 77, 80\}$, as shown in Table 3.3. It is clear that contrast of the recovered image is same as that of the original secret image.

Table 1. Original Image, Recovered Image and the shares of Set PS_1

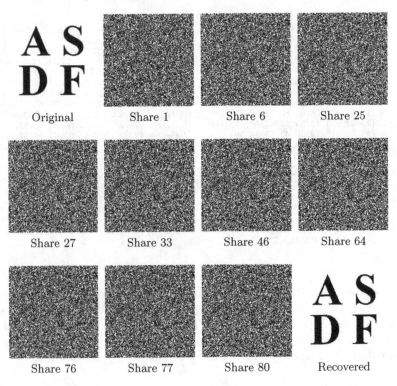

For the user key-set $P(B_{20}) = \{20, 25, 3, 5, 11, 65, 42, 54, 55, 58\}$ from the PBIBD construction of [7], notice that as all the shares have been calculated in the previous sets $P(B_1), \ldots, P(B_{19})$. Thus, Algorithm 1 introduces a dummy share 'Share 83' in $P(B_{20})$; turning the new user key-set into

$$PS_{20} = \{20, 25, 3, 5, 11, 65, 42, 54, 55, 58, 83\}.$$

Stacking of the shares in this set, along with the dummy share 83, also reveals the original image with full contrast, as expected from our scheme. The results are shown in Table 3.3.

Collusion Resistance: Let users U_1 and U_2 collude to form a pirate key-set $F = \{1, 2, 6, 7, 9, 28, 62, 69, 76, 77\}$, as in the example of [7]. Note that F is not present in the set of minimal qualified sets $\Gamma_0 = Z$ of our design. Hence, stacking the shares of F would not reveal the secret image in our access control structure.

Table 2. Shares of set PS_{20} and Recovered Image

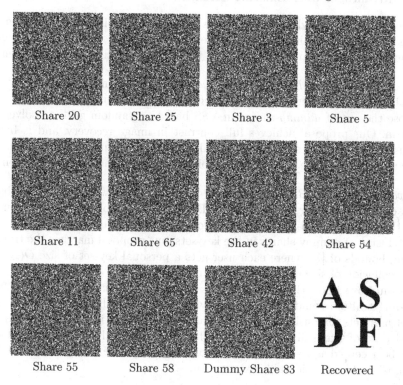

| Share 20 | Share 25 | Share 3 | Share 5 |

| Share 11 | Share 65 | Share 42 | Share 54 |

| Share 55 | Share 58 | Dummy Share 83 | Recovered |

Efficiency of the Proposed Scheme. The proposed scheme was implemented on a 2.3GHz Intel processor running GNU/Linux. Table 3 illustrates the efficiency of our proposal through experiments with different number of users.

Table 3. Experimental results to check the efficiency of the proposed scheme

Number of Users	Size of Key-pool	Number of Dummy keys	Time in seconds for	
			Share generation	Share stacking
3	4	1	1.210 sec	0.306 sec
12	40	3	10.830 sec	0.427 sec
16	17	6	1.908 sec	0.110 sec
25	30	13	12.600 sec	0.314 sec
41	82	22	33.470 sec	0.400 sec

The only extra overhead in our case, compared to the proposal of [7], originates due to the dummy shares. From Table 3 it is clear that the number of dummy shares is reasonably less than the number of users in each case. For N users, each user gets k keys, where $k \sim O(N^{1/2})$, and a collusion of up to $O(N^{1/4})$ traitors can be traced. Compared to [7], we do not lose on these bounds.

3.4   Advantages over Existing Schemes

To the best of our knowledge, there exists no scheme for using VSS-based general access structures in traitor tracing. However, there exist several VSS-based general access structures and PBIBD-based traitor tracing schemes, independently.

Comparison with VSS-Based General Access Structures: In general access structures based on VSS, the contrast of the final recovered image is quite poor. We propose the use of *dummy shares* in VSS based on random grids to solve this problem. Our proposal achieves full contrast in image recovery, and is better in this sense from the schemes proposed in [3, 13, 15]. In addition, the use of random grids eliminate the problem of pixel expansion and shape distortion.

Comparison with PBIBD-Based Traitor Tracing Schemes: We borrow the basic ideas of traitor-tracing from the PBIBD-based scheme of [7], and combine it with the aforesaid VSS-based general access structure. We show that even with the inclusion of dummy shares in the key-sets, our proposal matches the traitor-tracing bounds of [7], where each user gets a personal key-set of size $O(N^{1/2})$, and a collusion of size up to $O(N^{1/4})$ can be traced.

We improve upon the idea of [7] in one major aspect. In case of [7], the colluding traitors could generate a new key-set which did not belong to the preset user-sets, but still qualifies as a valid key. However in our proposal, if the colluded set of shares did not belong to the preset qualified user-sets, then it will never be accepted as a valid key. Thus, compared to [7], we reduce the possibility of collusions to a considerable extent.

4   Conclusion

We have constructed a key distribution scheme which is based on VSS. We have used general access structure based VSS for key distribution, where the access structure is defined by PBIBD blocks to reduce the size of the main key pool. We have used the concept of random grids in our VSS scheme which eliminates the problem of pixel expansion and shape distortion of the recovered image.

In addition, we have introduced the concept of dummy shares in the PBIBD construction to completely recover the secret image in VSS with a contrast same as that of the original. Using VSS as the many-to-one function, our key pre-distribution scheme reduces the number of possible collusions, and provides a mechanism alike [7] to trace collusions up to $O(N^{1/4})$ where N is the number of total users in the design.

Our proposed scheme is particularly suitable for applications like video and image broadcast, where the recovered VSS image can directly be applied as a key towards data encryption by simple logical operations between the similar data structures. In such cases, our proposal also guarantees low collusion and traitor tracing for the distributor based on the PBIBD access control structure; once again, particularly suitable for commercial broadcast applications.

Future Scope: One may try to design new schemes in this line to eliminate the necessity of dummy shares. A practical implementation of the proposed scheme for secure video broadcast would also be an appealing direction.

Acknowledgments. The authors would like to thank the anonymous reviewers for their valuable comments that helped improve the quality of the paper. Sheethal Kumar, Jaipal Pai B J and Vigesh R Ungrapalli would also like to thank Prof. Bimal Roy, Director, Indian Statistical Institute, for supporting them during the tenure of the project at ISI Kolkata under a Summer Internship grant from Microsoft Research India, and for sparking their motivation towards this project through an instructive talk on combinatorial designs in cryptology.

References

1. Ateniese, G., Blundo, C., Santis, A.D., Stinson, D.R.: Visual cryptography for general access structures. Inf. Comput. 129(2), 86–106 (1996)
2. Blakley, G.: Safeguarding cryptographic keys. In: Proceedings of the 1979 AFIPS National Computer Conference, pp. 313–317. AFIPS Press (1979)
3. Chen, T.-H., Tsao, K.-H.: Visual secret sharing by random grids revisited. Pattern Recognition 42(9), 2203–2217 (2009)
4. Chor, B., Fiat, A., Naor, M.: Tracing traitors. In: Desmedt, Y.G. (ed.) CRYPTO 1994. LNCS, vol. 839, pp. 257–270. Springer, Heidelberg (1994)
5. Kafri, O., Keren, E.: Encryption of pictures and shapes by random grids. Opt. Lett. 12(6), 377–379 (1987)
6. Naor, M., Shamir, A.: Visual cryptography. In: De Santis, A. (ed.) EUROCRYPT 1994. LNCS, vol. 950, pp. 1–12. Springer, Heidelberg (1995)
7. Ruj, S., Roy, B.K.: Key distribution schemes using combinatorial designs to identify all traitors. Congressus Numerantium 193, 195–214 (2008)
8. Ruj, S., Roy, B.K.: Key predistribution using combinatorial designs for grid-group deployment scheme in wireless sensor networks. TOSN 6(1) (2009)
9. Ruj, S., Roy, B.K.: Key pre-distribution using partially balanced designs in wireless sensor networks. IJHPCN 7(1), 19–28 (2011)
10. Safavi-Naini, R., Wang, Y.: A combinatorial approach to asymmetric traitor tracing. In: Du, D.-Z., Eades, P., Sharma, A.K., Lin, X., Estivill-Castro, V. (eds.) COCOON 2000. LNCS, vol. 1858, pp. 416–425. Springer, Heidelberg (2000)
11. Safavi-Naini, R., Wang, Y.: Sequential traitor tracing. In: Bellare, M. (ed.) CRYPTO 2000. LNCS, vol. 1880, pp. 316–332. Springer, Heidelberg (2000)
12. Shamir, A.: How to share a secret. Commun. ACM 22(11), 612–613 (1979)
13. Stinson, D.R., Wei, R.: Combinatorial properties and constructions of traceability schemes and frameproof codes. SIAM J. Discrete Math. 11(1), 41–53 (1998)
14. Street, A.P., Street, D.J.: Combinatorics of experimental design. Clarendon Press, Oxford University Press, Oxford, New York (1987)
15. Wu, X., Sun, W.: Visual secret sharing for general access structures by random grids. IET Information Security 6(4), 299–309 (2012)

Web Services Based Attacks against Image CAPTCHAs

David Lorenzi[1], Jaideep Vaidya[1], Shamik Sural[2], and Vijayalakshmi Atluri[1]

[1] Rutgers University, USA
{dlorenzi,jsvaidya,atluri}@cimic.rutgers.edu
[2] IIT Kharagpur, India
shamik@sit.iitkgp.ernet.in

Abstract. CAPTCHAs provide protection from automated robot attacks against online forms and services. Image recognition CAPTCHAs, which require users to perform an image recognition task, have been proposed as a more robust alternative to character recognition CAPTCHAs. However, in recent years, a number of web services that deal with content based image retrieval and analysis have been developed and released for public consumption. These web services can be used in completely unexpected ways to attack image CAPTCHAs. Specifically, in this paper, we consider three specific kinds of web services: 1) Reverse Image Search (RIS), 2) Image Similarity Search (ISS), and 3) Automatic Linguistic Annotation (ALA). We show how the functionality of these image based web services, used in conjunction with regular expressions, keyword ontologies and some statistical analysis/inference, can pose a dangerous attack that easily bypasses the hard AI problem used in challenges for typical image CAPTCHAs. We also discuss effective defensive measures that can be utilized to make CAPTCHAs more resistant to the attack vectors these web services provide.

Keywords: Web Security, CAPTCHA, Web Services.

1 Introduction

Automated spam in all of its forms (email, garbage comments, link farming etc.) has become pervasive throughout the World Wide Web. To deal with this, webmasters have utilized CAPTCHAs as a successful method for differentiating legitimate human users from spam bots, helping to curtail online form abuse. While many different types of CAPTCHAs exist, in this paper we are primarily interested in image CAPTCHAs, which are a type of CAPTCHA that use images as a primary focus for personhood verification. Image CAPTCHAs have been proposed as an alternative to the ubiquitous alphanumeric "text" based CAPTCHAs (a la ReCAPTCHA) currently in use with popular public facing large scale web services (email services, blog services, message board services etc.). The key advantage of image CAPTCHAs lies in the variety of the hard AI problems they can present to the user [18].

A. Bagchi and I. Ray (Eds.): ICISS 2013, LNCS 8303, pp. 214–229, 2013.

The real task for any attacker is attempting to either directly solve the hard AI problem put forth by the CAPTCHA, or find other ways to "work around" the problem (side channel attacks, mechanical turks, remote farming, exploitable implementation flaws etc.) However, many spambots simply look for low hanging fruit, that is, online forms that are unsecured or have easily circumvented protections. When viewed from an economic perspective (often this is the motivation for a majority of spam), this behavior on behalf of the spambot is logical, as it is not as cost effective expending effort to break into hardened targets. A vast majority would not bother developing advanced attacks against image CAPTCHAs that would presumably require sophisticated computer vision techniques to attempt to break.

However, with the rise of image based web services providing a comparable result to that of CV algorithms, much of the difficult work traditionally associated with utilizing CV algorithms has been circumvented and can now be obtained quickly and easily from these online services. In this paper, we demonstrate how these image based web services can be used to directly solve or circumvent some of the challenges faced by attackers when presented with various hard AI problems found in image CAPTCHAs. Our proposed attack method relies on the aforementioned image based web services, a few CAPTCHA design flaws/exploits, word ontologies, and the power of regular expressions coupled with probabilistic computations, culminating in an answer that provides a "best guess" response to the CAPTCHA.

Image based web services are nothing new – they have existed in some capacity since 2001, when Google released its image search capabilities. The image search query results provide the filename of the image, the link text pointing to the image, and text adjacent to the image. These results are straightforward and can be interpreted as information directly relating to describing the image itself or what the image is depicting. Google image search also recently added some advanced features, greatly enhancing the utility of its image search capabilities. In 2009, Google image search introduced image similarity search (ISS) [2,8,9], enabling finding images that are similar in composition or content to the image uploaded. Google also provides reverse image search (RIS) capabilities, as well as a textual "best guess" as to what the image is depicting. In addition to Google, other advanced image based web services have been developed, such as TinEye, a web service that provides RIS capabilities exclusively. TinEye currently has about 3 billion images in its search index. The TinEye FAQ states that, "it finds exact and altered copies of the images that you submit, including those that have been cropped, color adjusted, resized, heavily edited or slightly rotated" [7]. However, it does not return similar matches and it cannot recognize the contents of any image. We also explore the use of automated linguistic annotation (ALA), which takes a given image and provides tagging suggestions as to the content of the image. The ALIPR [11] service which provides real-time computerized image tagging based on statistical modeling, learning, and wavelet transforms [10] is used for ALA. The overall functionality in each case can be considered a subset of content based image retrieval (CBIR), although each is distinct enough in its implementation and purpose to warrant separation. While it is important to understand how each of these services perform their tasks to utilize them to their maximum potential, an in depth discussion of their operation is beyond the scope of this paper. We are more interested in what results are provided (e.g associated image metadata) for a given image input and how they can be used to attack CAPTCHAs.

2   Preliminaries

In order to design competent attacks against image CAPTCHAs we must understand the types of hard AI problems (henceforth referred to as challenge questions) used by the CAPTCHA to distinguish if the form submission presented to the server is from a legitimate human or a spam bot. Computer vision tasks are considered to be AI-complete or AI-hard, that is, CV tasks cannot be solved in the general case by a simple specific algorithm – hence their use as the primary challenge in an image CAPTCHA.

Image CAPTCHA challenge questions generally fall into the following categories/styles as defined by Chew & Tygar[3]: naming images, distinguishing images, and identifying anomalies. These categories essentially define the task(s) the user is asked to perform to "solve" the CAPTCHA and can be considered as a subset of problems in the domain of computer vision (CV). For naming images, the test subject is asked to identify a word associated with a set of images. The task in distinguishing images is to determine if two subsets of images are associated with the same word or not. For identifying anomalies, the test subject is shown a set of images where all but one image is associated with a word and asked to identify the anomalous image.

While image CAPTCHAs use at least one of these categories/styles in its challenge question, many use a combination to add layers of complexity making it more difficult for attackers using a single tool or technique to defeat. To create a direct attack, one must attempt to align the challenge(s) provided by the image CAPTCHA and the CV tasks that would best answer the question posed by the challenge. For example, in a naming images CAPTCHA, the CV tasks of image recognition (correctly ID the image(s)) and image labeling (report the string describing the images) would need to be performed by the attacker to correctly answer the challenge question in an "human cognitive" way. However, the clever attacker has no need to approach the problem directly with CV techniques, as existing image based web services can provide related metadata that can be used to answer the CAPTCHA challenge that otherwise only humans and the appropriate combination of CV algorithms would be able to answer.

2.1   IRC Exploitable Vulnerabilities and Design Flaws

It is important to note that any and all CAPTCHAs that use images that are indexed by/scraped/acquired from a web image search are potentially vulnerable to our attack. Using an image search to populate a database with images for use in CAPTCHA challenges is a recipe for disaster from a security perspective. It is easy to perform a RIS to find a specific image used in CAPTCHA that was generated using the aforementioned method, making solving the challenge much easier than the author intended. Even attempts to distort (crop, color adjust, resize, edited or slightly rotate) the image can be accounted for (to varying degrees of success) by these services. ISS makes finding related images very easy, and if the CAPTCHA presents multiple images from the same word category there exists the possibility that an ISS search will find a number (or potentially all - which can be found by a regular image search once the term is discovered) of the images used to populate a CAPTCHA database. ALA makes it possible to attempt to generate useful information in the form of tags via annotation that can lead to image identification if no other contextual data/metadata can be gathered from RIS or ISS, and offers a last ditch effort to ascertain what is depicted in the image.

One important aspect to the success of these web services is that they frequently return filenames within the hyperlink where the image is used on the web. This hyperlink is also accompanied by related text information, often describing the image or a scenario depicted by the image. Since a majority of images are used within the context of the text around them - these two pieces of information in particular can give strong clues as to the content of the image. Figure 4 shows an example of this.

Naming images (identifying the correct keyword that describes the series of images) can be best attacked through RIS to attempt to find other places online that use the image in a contextually accurate situation that relates directly to how it is being used in the challenge. ISS can also find similarly composed images that fall into a contextual situation that matches the suspected keyword. If no keywords can be found, ALA provides a chance to generate annotations/tags that describe the image and are also potential keywords. When these textual clues are used in conjunction with a related word ontology, either a direct correct answer can be given (direct keyword) or a probabilistic "best guess" can be made. There exist three scenarios for distinguishing images, based on whether the keyword is 1) provided directly, 2) provided in a list of keywords, or 3) not provided. When these textual clues are used with the keyword ontology, either a direct correct answer can be given (direct keyword) or a probabilistic "best guess" (searching the ontology for related words) can be made. Anomaly images can only be handled by process of elimination - that is - each image needs to be RIS and/or ALA queried and the results evaluated against one another. From this, we can determine the "odd image out" and answer the challenge accordingly.

2.2   Related Keyword Ontologies

Related word ontologies provide unique capabilities in that they are designed to find and relate a series of keywords from an image filename or link that could potentially be a correct response to an image challenge. They are designed to use domain knowledge of a subject matter in a meaningful way. For example, if the challenge category word answer is "drinks" and you receive a filename of "350pxtomcollins.jpg" you want to be able to relate that a Tom Collins is a type of drink and thus belongs to the "drinks" category - even though the word "drink" is never explicitly given. The same is true if the link points to a website URL *http://www.nationwidebarcrawl.com*. The association between barcrawls, bars and "drinks" can be discerned by the bot attacker using the ontology.

pdictionary is a pictoral dictionary of 627 English words designed for illustrations (i.e., these words will likely be the keywords used by CAPTCHAs). Therefore, pdictionary forms a good foundation for the core words of the related word ontologies (meaning other words are related to these 627 probable keywords), and can be used as the base ontology for such reasoning.

It is important to note that these ontologies will be organized in a hierarchical structure, as some CAPTCHAs could potentially use words that will be subcategories of a core word. For example, a naming images challenge uses the keyword "horses" - which would be a subcategory of the keyword "animal". If the images shown have associated URLs such as "thoroughbredhorseranch.com" the ontology needs to be able to know that the word "horse" can be a potential candidate keyword and not choose "animal" as the response. A weighting algorithm designed for word handling can solve this problem. The algorithm computes the number of images used in the CAPTCHA challenge along with the frequency of each word appearing in the return searches from a RIS and an ISS query. Thus, if the keyword "horse" appears in two of the four images' RIS and ISS results, the probability that "horse" is the keyword and not "animal" is strong. The threshold value for deciding on choosing a core keyword or a subcategory keyword is different for each CAPTCHA, and must be altered accordingly based on a statistical sampling of challenges. In the event that the RIS and ISS turn up no textual clues, the ALA can provide guesses in the form of annotations (tags) as to what the image is depicting. These tags can then be used by the ontology to guess at the context of the image and provide a keyword to solve the challenge. Under these circumstances, a core keyword will always be used.

3   Related Work

Much of this work in this paper is based upon careful evaluation of prior literature in the subject domain of CAPTCHA design [19,5]. Ross et. al [14] briefly mention an instance where RIS was used to find the original images when dealing with an image orientation CAPTCHA, but did not expand their testing beyond this. Datta et. al [4] mention that image CAPTCHAs can potentially be vulnerable to ISS and ALA, but make no mention of RIS. Once image based web services evolved to the point where they could perform tasks that were previously considered difficult and/or time consuming, they became a legitimate threat vector and a reason to reevaluate the security provided by image CAPTCHAs. It is important to note that most authors of image CAPTCHAs frequently point out that a traditional database attack against their CAPTCHA would technically be effective, but that the required effort to mount such an attack is usually more than all but the most determined spammers and bots will employ. In most circumstances, this remains a truism - generating a database of images from a CAPTCHA for the purposes of brute force comparison answers remains a painstaking process. However, the critical design flaw of populating an image database with indexed/tagged/publicly available images from the web [15,17,6] from which the CAPTCHA challenges are generated is now more easily exploitable using these image based web services. Attempts to evade the publicly available images problem have been proposed, by generating images in real time from cameras and asking users to identify what the scene is depicting [16]. As a consequence of this, ALA engines like ALIPR, which work in real time as well, provide the ability to annotate an image, with the annotations it generates serving as a potential solution to the challenge. The designers of ALIPR note that it has problems providing accurate annotation when an image is fuzzy or of extremely low resolution or low contrast - which is most likely the case when sourcing images from inexpensive camera-phones. Currently, the THINK CAPTCHA can most likely evade the attack - however, as time goes on ALIPR will become stronger and more accurate as it accrues more training data and its algorithms improve, while camera-phones will provide clearer pictures. Eventually the threat vector ALA poses will become legitimate, and the authors of such systems should be aware of its potential to compromise security.

Another example would be Asirra [1], a CAPTCHA that asks users to determine which images out of a set of 12 are cats or dogs. It uses the petfinder.com database of pet images to populate its challenges - which is constantly changing and expanding in size as new pet images are added daily. Since this dataset is not publicly indexed, it is very resistant to RIS (unless someone cross posted images elsewhere and they were indexed) - ALA and ISS provide options as alternate attack vectors but neither is accurate enough (alone or in conjunction) currently to pose a threat to Asirra's challenge (a nuanced binary classification) in a meaningful way. Sketcha [14] also is based on a similar principle of rotating images in the database and generating them from a 3D model. Even if the 3D model is indexed, the fact that it can be rotated and is stripped down into a basic line model make it resistant to RIS and ISS attacks. Typical attacks against image captchas have been based on image recognition [12], however this paper highlights the grave new threat posed by image web services.

4 Methodology

We now provide a generalized framework through which an attack can be created against an image based CAPTCHA. Since there exist a wide variety of implementations of image CAPTCHAs, each requiring customized attack parameters, we instead focus on the core ideas and tools that enable an attack vector against any implementation that uses indexed images in its generated challenges. The goal is to provide the basis for a viable attack model that can then be modified and/or augmented as needed to defeat the security of a particular image based CAPTCHA.

The basic attack method proceeds once the image based CAPTCHA generates a challenge using indexed images and provides it to the attacker, and consists

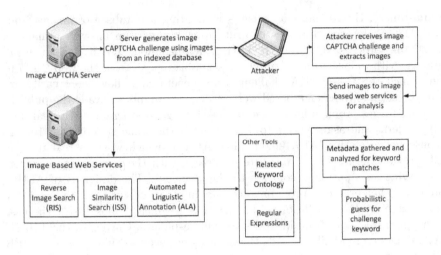

Fig. 1. General Attack Method for Image Based Web Services

of the following steps: 1) The attacker receives the challenge and extracts the images from the challenge. 2) The attacker then runs the images through each of the three online tools: RIS (Google and TinEye – since each uses different indexed databases, both are required), ISS (Google), and ALA (ALIPR). 3) The search results are prioritized – RIS results are the most important, as this tool attempts to find exact matches and thus the metadata gathered from the results is the most "accurate" of the three. Metadata gathered from the ALA analysis of the image is the next most accurate and finally metadata from ISS is the least important. 4) The metadata from the RIS and the ALA can be analyzed for any potential keyword matches, as this signifies a strong probability of the what is depicted in the image. 5) From this metadata, a probabilistic guess can be made for the response to the challenge. This requires the use of the custom generated ontologies that aid in handling keyword relationships for more accurate guesses. If the guess is correct, the images and the keyword(s) are saved in a database for reuse in the future. The basic attack flow is depicted in Figure 1.

We now demonstrate the effectiveness of the online image based tools through a sampling of images from popular image based CAPTCHAs. This enables us to see what types of metadata could be gathered in order to get around the requirements of performing an image classification task. The only assumption the attacker must make is that the CAPTCHA is using images that are indexed online. If the metadata gathered from the image search is descriptive enough, this information can be used to "solve" the classification task.

4.1 Reverse Image Search

Figure 2 shows an example of the SQ-PIX CAPTCHA challenge. The task here is to trace an outline around the instances of the keyword requested in the given

Fig. 2. Example challenge for SQ-PIX

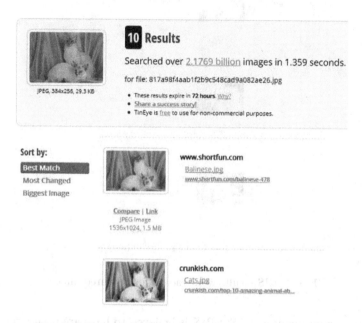

Fig. 3. RIS results w/metadata for an extracted image

images. Since SQ-PIX uses indexed images, the images are vulnerable to all of the online tools in image search, especially RIS in particular.

Figure 3 shows an example result from a Reverse Image Search (TinEye) done on an image of "cats" provided by the SQ-PIX challenge. The power of the "exact" match is that RIS tells you where else on the web the image is being used. It also provides the metadata that accompanies the use of that image (filename, URL, image properties etc.). Using the "best match" functionality, the second hit in a list of exact matches has a descriptive filename, "cats.jpg" - a match to the challenge keyword of "cats". Note that the file submitted by the attacker has a long and obfuscated filename (a straight extraction from the challenge HTML) and is a different size than the resulting matches. The first hit is actually too accurate - the proper name for the breed of cat depicted in the image - but this requires a related word ontology to be able to discern that "Balinese" is indeed a breed of cat.

Fig. 4. RIS results w/metadata for obscured image

From our experimentation, SQ-PIX is believed to have approximately 34 different keyword categories from which challenges are generated, although we have no way of knowing the exact number of keywords - this figure was derived from a statistical sampling. The accompanying word ontology can then be generated from this list of keywords with some effort on behalf of the attacker. There have been attempts by some CAPTCHA developers to obstruct and obscure their images with noise to foil attackers that attempt to use image classification and object recognition tools to discern what is depicted in the image. However, TinEye is robust against alterations to images, and can find exact matches of images that have been obstructed, obscured, or altered in a meaningful way. Figure 4 shows an example of an obscure image. The image used in this challenge was generated by the IMAGINATION CAPTCHA [4] – which is a two stage CAPTCHA. IMAGINATION uses obfuscation of its images as an added layer of security from automated image recognition/object recognition attacks. The image in the example comes from the second stage, which is a image classification/object recognition challenge - asking the user to match the image with the keyword from a list. Figures 5 and 6 show the two stage challenges.

The first stage has a compelling attack developed by Zhu et. al. [20], but none have been provided for the second stage excepting ours. Overall, if an existing image is used by the CAPTCHA (which is normally the case for scalability), reverse image lookup can find it.

4.2   Automated Linguistic Annotation

Automated Linguistic Annotation is a useful tool when the metadata gathered by RIS and ISS does not provide any easily distinguishable clues as to the content contained in the challenge images. Since it uses advanced algorithms to discern what is depicted in the image, an attacker uses it as a last resort to attempt to generate some metadata that may be relevant and lead to the ability to generate a guess against a list of keywords, or just provide a slightly more accurate random guess. We use ALIPR as the tool for ALA. ALIPR generates 15 tags based on an analysis of the image provided to it. These tags can then be saved and compared against a keyword list from the CAPTCHA. For the image in Figure 6, Figure 7 shows the automated linguistic annotation (note that *train* is indeed one of the tags generated). One additional benefit is that images submitted to ALIPR are saved to its index, so that over time it will have more images with correct tags and more accurate tags provided by humans – allowing for an increase in accuracy when used by an automated service like this attack bot.

While this seems like a very powerful approach to solving the problem, appearing to be a better solution than RIS, it is not without its shortcomings. ALA is not very accurate - most of the tags generated are too broad to be of use. Li and Wang [10], the developers of ALIPR, state that the goal of their automatic annotator is to be able to provide 98% of images with at least one correct

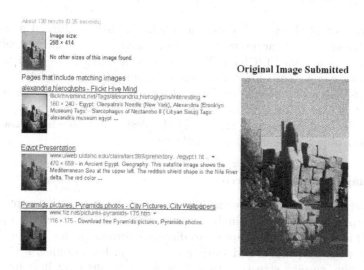

Fig. 5. RIS Results w/ obfuscated image - IMAGINATION Stage 1

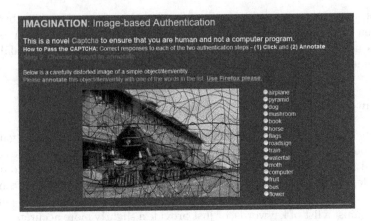

Fig. 6. Example second stage challenge for IMAGINATION

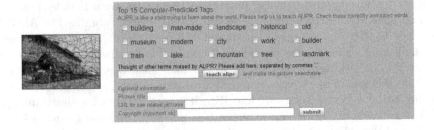

Fig. 7. ALA results generate 15 tags - exact match "train"

annotation out of the top 15 tags generated. The highest ranked annotation word for each image is accurate with a rate above 51% (in their experiments with image data from FLICKR). Knowing this fact, ALA is best used along with RIS for comparison of metadata and as a generator of metadata when RIS or ISS fails – never by itself exclusively. However, this research is very interesting and it is easy to imagine that it will improve in speed and accuracy with time, which should give pause to CAPTCHA designers who wish to use image recognition/object recognition as a challenge.

4.3   Image Similarity Search

Google currently provides the capabilities to upload images to its search engine and returns images that are similar in color and composition to the uploaded image. This is useful for attempting to discern information that can be derived based on some conjectures and statistical sampling. For example, if the image has a unique, specific structure to it (e.g. a car, a bus etc.) it is likely that similar images featuring these same properties will show up – this is the composition component of ISS. The color component plays a different role, that of

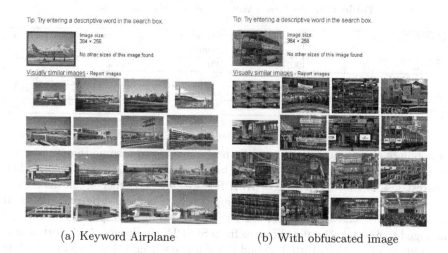

(a) Keyword Airplane   (b) With obfuscated image

Fig. 8. Google ISS Results

discerning broad generalities about the image - e.g. if a certain percentage of the image contains large amounts of certain shades of green or blue pixels – there is a probability it could be sky, water, grass etc. or if an image contains skin tone shades within a specified range for people. In addition to this, the metadata for the top results can be gathered and analyzed against information from the CAPTCHA. Figure 8(a) shows the result for a search with a standard image – note that in the top 16 results, there is one image featuring an airplane. Depending on how much information the CAPTCHA provides, a high probability guess can be wagered if used in conjunction with the related keyword ontology. Image similarity search also works to a degree with obscured images. However, since the similarity algorithm looks at the composition of the image, the distortions and obfuscations play a role in influencing what images it returns as results. Figure 8(b) shows an example of results for an obscured image. While the strong features of the grid have influenced the results, another bus image is still seen in the top 16 results. Metadata extraction would now help to breach the source CAPTCHA.

5 Experimental Results and Analysis

We now present the results of a few brief experiments to demonstrate the capabilities of the image based web services in action on real world image CAPTCHAS. However, we proceed with a few caveats. Unfortunately, many of the CAPTCHAs (ESP-PIX, SQ-PIX, IMAGINATION) and some of the tools (ALA) are not available, as their web sites time out, have broken image links or are in some other way unusable for a significant period of time. Additionally, many of the CAPTCHAs described in the literature have not yet been deployed publicly or are unavailable for evaluation. If the authors of the CAPTCHA explicitly mention their method

Table 1. Image Based Web Services - Accuracy Results

CAPTCHA	Reverse Image Search (Google)	Reverse Image Search (TinEye)	Image Similarity Search (Google)	Total
SQ-PIX	90%	60%	30%	90%
IMAGINATION Stage 1	25%	25%	12%	37.5%
IMAGINATION Stage 2	30%	30%	12%	38%
Control Images (Not Online)	0%	0%	20%	20%

to populate their image database, it is probably safe to assume that similar results to the ones we do provide would be achievable by a clever attacker. The greatest loss is that of the use of ALIPR - we have no other online ALA tool and therefore cannot report any meaningful results to its use beyond the small number of test cases performed for the methodology examples. However, we managed to extract 82 unique images from SQ-PIX challenges, 11 distorted first stage images and 13 distorted second stage images from IMAGINATION while they were still online. We also include a control group of images that are not indexed / available on the web. The control group images are immune to RIS and can only be attacked by ISS and ALA. We would like to make note that the composition of the image directly influences the results of the ISS e.g. if you take a picture of a cat that is focused primarily on the cat, ISS results will have pictures of cats in the top 16 results. However, if the shot is composed such that the cat is part of a larger scene, the results will vary greatly and most likely will not return an image of a cat in the results (cat is small percentage of overall composition of the image). The influence of the structure and composition of the image on ISS results is certainly worthy of further study but is beyond the scope of this paper.

Our two selected CAPTCHAs in particular serve the evaluation purposes sufficiently. SQ-PIX images serve as the clear/free of distortions challenge, and IMAGINATION images serve as the distorted/altered challenge. Note that the results should be taken with a grain of salt. The sample size is limited and there exists the possibility that the challenges received were "easy" in comparison to what would have been generated in a larger sample. Nevertheless, we believe the attack method is strong and our results validate the argument that any and all CAPTCHAs that use images that are indexed by/scraped/acquired from a web image search are potentially vulnerable to attack.

5.1   RIS Results

Table 1 gives the results in terms of ability to crack the challenge.

IMAGINATION. Out of 11 images for RIS on stage 1, with each image consisting of 8 smaller images that must be tested individually after segmenting them (88 imgs total), on average, tineye found 2/8 and google found 2/8 (frequently they would share the same hit or all hits – each hit can only be counted once), thus the average combined total for RIS is 25%. Out of 13 images total for RIS on stage 2, tineye found 4/13 (cat, tiger, flower, peppers) and google found 4/13 (cat, tiger, flower, train) thus the combined total, counting identical matches once (cat, tiger, flower, peppers, train) for RIS on stage 2 would be 5/13=38.4%.

SQ-PIX. Out of 82 unique images, Google was able to find 74/82=90% of the images we sampled. Tineye was able to find 49/82=60% of the images we sampled. In our test, every miss was a miss by both tineye and google but every match for tineye was also a match for google. Thus we end up with an average accuracy of 90% for the SQ-PIX CAPTCHA.

5.2 ISS Results

The ISS results are based on whether or not a meaningful result (i.e. a similar image that was accurate - e.g. a cat picture provides more cat pictures and not landscapes) could be given from the top 16 hits returned. In the case of SQ-PIX, about 24/82=30% images had meaningful results in the top 16 hits. For IMAGINATION, stage 1 had a 1/8=12% and stage 2 had a 1/8=12% meaningful result. ISS was more useful on stage 2 than on stage 1, as stage 1 needs an exact match if there is any hope of finding the geometric center of the image - in this case a similar image is useless (the challenge solution to stage 1). One shortcoming was that almost every meaningful result from ISS was with an image that also had a match from RIS for both SQ-PIX and IMAGINATION - thus the ISS is not as useful as it seems on the surface.

6 Effective Defensive Measures

There are a number of limitations in using these tools to mount an effective attack. However, some of these shortcomings affect both attackers and the designers of CAPTCHAs. We now list some of the major points for consideration:

- Non-Indexed images: RIS cannot provide any help if the images in question are not part of its index. Relying on ISS and ALA is not as strong as having identical matches and their related information to work with, and as such these images provide strong security against these attack vectors.
- Service Throttling: Free image based web services only allow limited number of free queries without paying a fee for premium service or having their IP banned or throttled for a period of time. Ironically enough, this is intentional in design to discourage abuse of the systems by bots.
- Composite images with distortions: composite images provide a challenge for RIS as they do not have an image fingerprint to find. While they are composed of other images that may be indexed, finding the original images can prove to be a difficult challenge. When distortions and obfuscations are added this makes it even more difficult. As such, these images provide strong security against RIS and ISS. However, if the composed image is too "unnatural" (i.e., images added to the base image stand out easily), they can be identified by ALA or segmented out from the image and analyzed individually. In this case, they provide weak security.

7   Conclusions and Future Work

In this paper, we have demonstrated a dangerous new attack against image CAPTCHAs using image web services. In the future, we plan to examine further the use of composite images and images with distortions as methods to foil image search engines ability to find exact matches. Further investigation into the utility of results from a similarity search will be done to see if a compelling attack can be developed using metadata that is similar or near to that of an exact match, providing enough context for the challenge to be solved irrespective of the ability to find an "exact" answer.

References

1. Asirra: a captcha that exploits interest-aligned manual image categorization. In: Proceedings of the 14th ACM Conference on Computer and Communications Security, CCS 2007, pp. 366–374 (2007)
2. Chechik, G., Sharma, V., Shalit, U., Bengio, S.: Large scale online learning of image similarity through ranking. J. Mach. Learn. Res. 11, 1109–1135 (2010)
3. Chew, M., Tygar, J.D.: Image recognition captchas. Technical Report UCB/CSD-04-1333, EECS Department, University of California, Berkeley (June 2004)
4. Datta, R., Li, J., Wang, J.Z.: Imagination: a robust image-based captcha generation system. In: Proceedings of the 13th Annual ACM International Conference on Multimedia, MULTIMEDIA 2005, pp. 331–334 (2005)
5. Fidas, C.A., Voyiatzis, A.G., Avouris, N.M.: On the necessity of user-friendly captcha. In: Proceedings of the SIGCHI Conference on Human Factors in Computing Systems, CHI 2011, pp. 2623–2626 (2011)
6. Gossweiler, R., Kamvar, M., Baluja, S.: What's up captcha?: a captcha based on image orientation. In: Proceedings of the 18th International Conference on World Wide Web, WWW 2009, pp. 841–850 (2009)
7. Idee. Tineye reverse image search (July 2013), http://www.tineye.com
8. Jing, Y., Baluja, S.: Pagerank for product image search. In: Proceedings of the 17th International Conference on World Wide Web, WWW 2008, pp. 307–316 (2008)
9. Jing, Y., Rowley, H., Wang, J., Tsai, D., Rosenberg, C., Covell, M.: Google image swirl: a large-scale content-based image visualization system. In: Proceedings of the 21st International Conference Companion on World Wide Web, WWW 2012 Companion, pp. 539–540 (2012)
10. Li, J., Wang, J.Z.: Real-time computerized annotation of pictures. IEEE Trans. Pattern Anal. Mach. Intell. 30(6), 985–1002 (2008)
11. Li, J., Wang, J.Z.: Automatic linguistic indexing of pictures in real-time (October 2012), http://www.alipr.com/
12. Lorenzi, D., Vaidya, J., Uzun, E., Sural, S., Atluri, V.: Attacking image based captchas using image recognition techniques. In: Venkatakrishnan, V., Goswami, D. (eds.) ICISS 2012. LNCS, vol. 7671, pp. 327–342. Springer, Heidelberg (2012)
13. Matthews, P., Mantel, A., Zou, C.C.: Scene tagging: image-based captcha using image composition and object relationships. In: Proceedings of the 5th ACM Symposium on Information, Computer and Communications Security, ASIACCS 2010, pp. 345–350 (2010)

14. Ross, S.A., Halderman, J.A., Finkelstein, A.: Sketcha: a captcha based on line drawings of 3d models. In: Proceedings of the 19th International Conference on World Wide Web, WWW 2010, pp. 821–830 (2010)
15. Shirali-Shahreza, S., Shirali-Shahreza, M.: Categorizing captcha. In: Proceedings of the 4th ACM Workshop on Security and Artificial Intelligence, AISec 2011, pp. 107–108 (2011)
16. Srikanth, V., Vishwanathan, C., Asati, U., Iyengar, N.C.S.N.: Think-an image based captcha mechanism (testifying human based on intelligence and knowledge). In: Proceedings of the International Conference on Advances in Computing, Communication and Control, ICAC3 2009, pp. 421–424 (2009)
17. Vikram, S., Fan, Y., Gu, G.: Semage: a new image-based two-factor captcha. In: Proceedings of the 27th Annual Computer Security Applications Conference, ACSAC 2011, pp. 237–246 (2011)
18. von Ahn, L., Blum, M., Langford, J.: Telling humans and computers apart automatically. Commun. ACM 47(2), 56–60 (2004)
19. Yan, J., El Ahmad, A.S.: Usability of captchas or usability issues in captcha design. In: Proceedings of the 4th Symposium on Usable Privacy and Security, SOUPS 2008, pp. 44–52 (2008)
20. Zhu, B.B., Yan, J., Li, Q., Yang, C., Liu, J., Xu, N., Yi, M., Cai, K.: Attacks and design of image recognition captchas. In: Proceedings of the 17th ACM Conference on Computer and Communications Security, CCS 2010, pp. 187–200 (2010)

New Long-Term *Glimpse* of RC4 Stream Cipher

Subhamoy Maitra and Sourav Sen Gupta[*]

Indian Statistical Institute, Kolkata, India
subho@isical.ac.in, sg.sourav@gmail.com

Abstract. In 1996, Jenkins pointed out a correlation between the hidden state and the output keystream of RC4, which is well known as the *Glimpse* theorem. With a permutation of size N-bytes, the probability of guessing one location by random association is $1/N$, whereas the existing correlations related to *glimpse* allow an adversary to guess a permutation location, using the knowledge of the keystream output bytes, with probability $2/N$. To date, this is the best known state-leakage based on glimpse. For the first time in RC4 literature, we show that there are certain events that leak state information with a probability of $3/N$, considerably higher than the existing results. Further, the new glimpse correlation that we observe is a *long-term* phenomenon; it remains valid at any stage of the evolution of RC4 Pseudo Random Generation Algorithm (PRGA). This new glimpse with a considerably higher probability of state-leakage may potentially have serious ramifications towards state-recovery attacks on RC4.

Keywords: stream cipher, RC4, glimpse, long-term, correlation.

1 Introduction

Over the last three decades of research in stream ciphers, several designs have been proposed and analyzed by the community. The RC4 stream cipher, 'allegedly' designed by Rivest in 1987, has sustained to be one of the most popular ciphers in this category for more than 25 years. The cipher has continued gaining its fabled popularity for its intriguing simplicity that has made it widely accepted in the community for various software and web applications.

The cipher consists of two major components, the Key Scheduling Algorithm (KSA) and the Pseudo-Random Generation Algorithm (PRGA). The internal permutation of RC4 is of N bytes, and so is the key K. The original secret key is of length typically between 5 to 32 bytes, and is repeated to form the final key K. The KSA produces the initial permutation of RC4 by scrambling an identity permutation using key K. The initial permutation S produced by the KSA acts as an input to the next procedure PRGA that generates the output keystream. The RC4 algorithm is as shown in Fig. 1.

---

[*] Supported by DRDO sponsored project Centre of Excellence in Cryptology (CoEC), under MOC ERIP/ER/1009002/M/01/1319/788/D(R&D) of ER&IPR, DRDO.

A. Bagchi and I. Ray (Eds.): ICISS 2013, LNCS 8303, pp. 230–238, 2013.

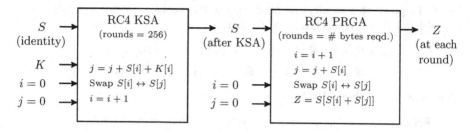

Fig. 1. Key-Scheduling Algorithm and Pseudo-Random Generation Algorithm of RC4

1.1 Notation and Assumptions

For round $r \geq 1$ of RC4 PRGA, we denote the indices by i_r, j_r, the output byte by Z_r, the index location of output Z_r as t_r, and the permutations before and after the swap by S_{r-1} and S_r respectively. Thus, round r of RC4 is defined by the operations

$$i_r = i_{r-1} + 1; \quad j_r = j_{r-1} + S_{r-1}[i_r]; \quad \text{Swap } S_{r-1}[i_r] \leftrightarrow S_{r-1}[j_r];$$
$$t_r = S_r[i_r] + S_r[j_r]; \quad Z_r = S_r[t_r].$$

The initial permutation of PRGA is denoted by S_0, and all arithmetic operations in the context of RC4 are to be considered modulo N.

During the course of this paper, we shall assume uniform randomness of certain events for the proofs. In most of these cases, the randomness assumption will be based on natural pseudo-randomness assumptions of the RC4 stream cipher, as appropriate. In some cases, we shall assume randomness based on experimental evidences, run over atleast a billion trials of RC4 with random keys. For all such assumptions, a random association probability $1/N$ will be assumed if there is no significant bias, of the order $1/N$ or similar. Some of these events may have prominent biases when treated conditionally with certain other events, but we shall only treat them in their unconditional forms, where they exhibit no significant biases. We shall state, and justify if required, the randomness assumptions as and when required in this paper.

1.2 Motivation and Contribution

In 1996, Jenkins [4] pointed out that the RC4 keystream provides a glimpse of the RC4 state as follows, which is known as Glimpse theorem or Jenkins' correlation. We present the complete proof of the theorem for clarity.

Theorem 1 (Glimpse theorem). *After the r-th round of RC4 PRGA, for $r \geq 1$, we have*

$$\Pr(S_r[j_r] = i_r - Z_r) \; = \; \Pr(S_r[i_r] = j_r - Z_r) \; \approx \; \frac{2}{N}.$$

Proof. To prove this result, one needs to use the paths $i_r = S_r[i_r] + S_r[j_r]$ and $j_r = S_r[i_r] + S_r[j_r]$ respectively. Note that

$$i_r = S_r[i_r] + S_r[j_r] \Rightarrow Z_r = S_r[i_r] = i_r - S_r[j_r], \text{ and}$$
$$j_r = S_r[i_r] + S_r[j_r] \Rightarrow Z_r = S_r[j_r] = j_r - S_r[i_r].$$

Thus, one may evaluate $\Pr(S_r[j_r] = i_r - Z_r)$ as

$$\Pr(Z_r = i_r - S_r[j_r] \mid i_r = S_r[i_r] + S_r[j_r]) \cdot \Pr(i_r = S_r[i_r] + S_r[j_r])$$
$$+ \Pr(Z_r = i_r - S_r[j_r] \mid i_r \neq S_r[i_r] + S_r[j_r]) \cdot \Pr(i_r \neq S_r[i_r] + S_r[j_r])$$
$$\approx 1 \cdot 1/N + 1/N \cdot (1 - 1/N) \approx 2/N,$$

where it is assumed that the desired event $(S_r[j_r] = i_r - Z_r)$ occurs with the probability of random association $1/N$ if $i_r \neq S_r[i_r] + S_r[j_r]$. One may prove the bias in $(S_r[i_r] = j_r - Z_r)$ similarly. □

One may note that this glimpse correlation can be observed at any point of the RC4 keystream. Later, in Asiacrypt 2005, Mantin [6] has also explored a general set of similar events in this direction that leak state information with probability more than that of random association. There exist several related works that look only at the initial keystream bytes of RC4 to obtain information regarding the state and eventually the secret keys (a few recent examples are in [13]). However, these observations never work in the long term scenario.

The question that we ask here is:

"Can one discover a correlation between the RC4 keystream and the state that offers a glimpse with a probability significantly more than 2/N in long term evolution of the cipher?"

We answer to this question affirmatively. We prove the following: given that two consecutive bytes Z_r, Z_{r+1} of RC4 are equal to the specific value $(r + 2)$ during the consecutive two rounds r and $r + 1$ (modulo N), the probability that the $(r + 1)$-th location of the state array during round r (denoted as $S_r[r + 1]$ as per our notation) will be equal to $(N - 1)$ is $3/N$, significantly higher than the probability of random association $1/N$. The result is presented in Section 2.

2   Long-Term *Glimpse* of RC4

We start with our most important observation which we made while trying to obtain the scenario where the S array comes back to the same permutation after two consecutive rounds.

2.1   The Main Observation Motivating Our Result

As one may note in Fig. 2, if in the r-th round, $j_r = i_r + 1$ and $S_r[j_r] = N - 1$, then the two places swapped in round $(r + 1)$ will be restored in round $(r + 2)$. That is, we shall have S_{r+2} identical to S_r in such a case. This motivated our first result, as in Theorem 2.

Theorem 2. *After the r-th round ($r \geq 1$) of RC4 PRGA, we have*

$$\Pr(S_r[r+1] = N - 1 \mid Z_{r+1} = Z_r) \approx \frac{2}{N}.$$

Proof. We shall first prove $\Pr(Z_{r+1} = Z_r \mid S_r[r+1] = N - 1) \approx 2/N$, and then apply Bayes' theorem to get the desired result. The condition $S_r[r+1] = N - 1$, and the path $j_r = r + 1$ results in $j_{r+1} = j_r + S_r[r+1] = r + 1 + N - 1 = r$, which eventually gives

$$
\begin{aligned}
t_{r+1} &= S_{r+1}[i_{r+1}] + S_{r+1}[j_{r+1}] \\
&= S_r[j_{r+1}] + S_r[i_{r+1}] \\
&= S_r[r] + S_r[r+1] \\
&= S_r[i_r] + S_r[j_r] = t_r.
\end{aligned}
$$

Thus, $Z_{r+1} = S_{r+1}[t_{r+1}] = S_{r+1}[t_r]$ is equal to $Z_r = S_r[t_r]$ in almost all cases, except when t_r equals either i_{r+1} or j_{r+1}, the only two locations that get swapped in transition from S_r to S_{r+1}. Thus,

$$\Pr(Z_{r+1} = Z_r \mid S_r[r+1] = N - 1 \wedge j_r = r + 1) \approx 1.$$

This scenario is as illustrated in Fig. 2.

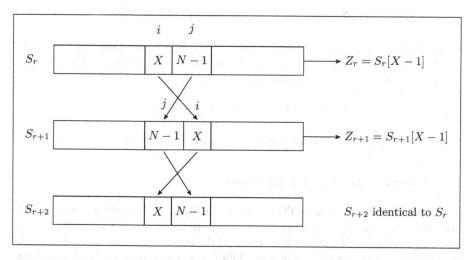

Fig. 2. The scenario for $(Z_{r+1} = Z_r \mid S_r[r+1] = N - 1 \wedge j_r = r + 1)$

We may now evaluate $\Pr(Z_{r+1} = Z_r \mid S_r[r+1] = N - 1)$ as

$$
\begin{aligned}
&\Pr(Z_{r+1} = Z_r \mid S_r[r+1] = N - 1 \wedge j_r = r + 1) \cdot \Pr(j_r = r + 1) \\
&+ \Pr(Z_{r+1} = Z_r \mid S_r[r+1] = N - 1 \wedge j_r \neq r + 1) \cdot \Pr(j_r \neq r + 1) \\
&\approx 1 \cdot 1/N + 1/N \cdot (1 - 1/N) \approx 2/N.
\end{aligned}
$$

Applying Bayes' theorem to the above result, we obtain

$$\Pr(S_r[r+1] = N - 1 \mid Z_{r+1} = Z_r) \cdot \Pr(Z_{r+1} = Z_r)$$
$$= \Pr(Z_{r+1} = Z_r \mid S_r[r+1] = N - 1) \cdot \Pr(S_r[r+1] = N - 1)$$
$$\approx 2/N \cdot 1/N.$$

Assuming pseudo-randomness of RC4 keystream bytes, we may write $\Pr(Z_{r+1} = Z_r) \approx 1/N$ (experimentally verified over a billion trials). This gives $\Pr(S_r[r+1] = N - 1 \mid Z_{r+1} = Z_r) \approx 2/N$. □

Thus the event $(Z_{r+1} = Z_r)$ leaks the information of a single permutation location with probability twice that of random association.

2.2   Corollary of the Glimpse Theorem from [4]

Before proceeding further, we would like to point out a simple corollary of the Glimpse theorem (Theorem 1) that leaks the information of a permutation location with the same probability.

Corollary 1. *After the r-th round of RC4 PRGA, for* $r \geq 1$*, we have*

$$\Pr(S_r[r+1] = N - 1 \mid Z_{r+1} = r + 2) \approx \frac{2}{N}.$$

Proof. In RC4 transition between rounds r and $r + 1$, we have $i_{r+1} = r + 1$, and $S_{r+1}[j_{r+1}] = S_r[i_{r+1}] = S_r[r+1]$, due to the swap in round r. Thus, by the Glimpse theorem (Theorem 1), we have

$$\Pr(S_r[r+1] = r + 1 - Z_{r+1}) \approx 2/N.$$

In case of $Z_{r+1} = r + 2$, we get the desired conditional result. □

2.3   The Main Result of This Paper

In the scenarios presented in Theorem 2 and Corollary 1, we find two different cases that leak the value of a specific location in the S array, namely $S_r[r + 1]$, with probability $2/N$ in each case. Moreover, the two events seem to be unrelated, or atleast not completely dependent. Thus, it is quite natural to expect that considering the events together, one may have better confidence about the value in that specific location $S_r[r + 1]$. In this direction, we present our main result of this paper in the form of Theorem 3.

Theorem 3. *After the r-th round* $(r \geq 1)$ *of RC4 PRGA, we have*

$$\Pr(S_r[r+1] = N - 1 \mid Z_{r+1} = Z_r \ \wedge \ Z_{r+1} = r + 2) \approx \frac{3}{N}.$$

Proof. Let us define the main events as follows:

$$A := (S_r[r+1] = N-1), \; B := (Z_{r+1} = Z_r), \; C := (Z_{r+1} = r+2).$$

The result requires $\Pr(A|B \wedge C)$, and it seems that a naive composition of Theorem 2 (which gives $\Pr(A|B)$) and Theorem 1 (which gives $\Pr(A|C)$) will produce the desired result. However, this is not the case. If we try to compute $\Pr(A \wedge B \wedge C)$ as $\Pr(B \wedge C|A)\Pr(A)$, then the first part is not easily computable as events B and C, conditional to event A, are not independent (verified experimentally over a billion trials). Hence we try the following route.

$$\Pr(A \wedge B \wedge C) = \Pr(C|B \wedge A) \cdot \Pr(B|A) \cdot \Pr(A).$$

Still there remains a problem with the first part, as event C occurs simultaneously with the occurrence of Z_{r+1} in event B. This is easy to observe experimentally, but not so easy to prove in theory.

To avoid the aforesaid problem in computing $\Pr(C|B \wedge A)$, we rewrite the problem definition slightly, and try to prove

$$\Pr(S_r[r+1] = N-1 \mid Z_r = r+2 \;\wedge\; Z_{r+1} = r+2) \;\approx\; 3/N.$$

We compute this as $\Pr(A \wedge B' \wedge C) = \Pr(C|B' \wedge A) \cdot \Pr(B'|A) \cdot \Pr(A)$, where $A := (S_r[r+1] = N-1)$, $C := (Z_{r+1} = r+2)$ as before, and $B' := (Z_r = r+2)$. Now we may compute $\Pr(C|B' \wedge A)$ easily, as event C occurs after completion of both the events A and B'.

Computing $\Pr(C|B' \wedge A)$: Note that event $A := (S_r[r+1] = N-1)$ implies $Z_{r+1} = S_{r+1}[S_{r+1}[r+1] + S_r[r+1]] = S_{r+1}[S_{r+1}[r+1] - 1]$. And of course, event $B' := (Z_r = r+2)$ implies $Z_r = S_r[t_r] = r+2$. We consider the following paths for the proof.

- *Case I:* $(S_{r+1}[r+1] = r+2)$. In case of this path, we shall have $Z_{r+1} = S_{r+1}[(r+2)-1] = S_{r+1}[r+1] = r+2$, with probability of occurrence 1.
- *Case II:* $(S_{r+1}[r+1] = t_r + 1)$. In case of this path, we shall have $Z_{r+1} = S_{r+1}[(t_r+1)-1] = S_{r+1}[t_r] = S_r[t_r] = r+2$, with probability of occurrence approximately 1, disregarding the two cases when t_r may be equal to either i_{r+1} or j_{r+1}.

In almost all other cases, we may assume that $C := (Z_{r+1} = r+2)$ happens with probability of random association $1/N$ (verified experimentally over a billion trials). We compute $\Pr(C|B' \wedge A)$ as

$$\begin{aligned}
&\Pr(C|B' \wedge A \wedge (S_{r+1}[r+1] = r+2)) \cdot \Pr(S_{r+1}[r+1] = r+2) \\
&+ \Pr(C|B' \wedge A \wedge (S_{r+1}[r+1] = r+2)) \cdot \Pr(S_{r+1}[r+1] = t_r + 1) \\
&+ \sum_{\substack{X \neq r+2 \\ X \neq t_r+1}} \Pr(C|B' \wedge A \wedge (S_{r+1}[r+1] = X)) \cdot \Pr(S_{r+1}[r+1] = X) \\
&\approx 1 \cdot 1/N + 1 \cdot 1/N + (1 - 2/N) \cdot 1/N \approx 3/N.
\end{aligned}$$

Computing $\Pr(A|B' \wedge C)$: As no glimpse-like connection has been found between $S_r[r+1]$ and Z_r in the literature to date, we may assume $\Pr(B'|A) \approx 1/N$ (verified experimentally over a billion trials), and we may of course take $\Pr(A) \approx 1/N$ as per natural pseudo-randomness assumptions of RC4. Thus,

$$\Pr(A \wedge B' \wedge C) = \Pr(C|B' \wedge A) \cdot \Pr(B'|A) \cdot \Pr(A) \approx 3/N \cdot 1/N \cdot 1/N.$$

We may assume $\Pr(B' \wedge C) = \Pr(B') \cdot \Pr(C) \approx 1/N \cdot 1/N$ (verified experimentally over a billion trials), and this produces the desired conditional result $\Pr(A|B \wedge C) = \Pr(A|B' \wedge C) \approx 3/N$. ☐

2.4 Experimental Results

We have performed extensive experiments to obtain accurate practical estimates of each of the results presented in this paper. Each correlation reported in this paper is of order $1/N$ with respect to a base event of probability $1/N$. Thus, $O(N^3)$ trials are sufficient to identify the biases with considerable probability of success (refer to [5,9] for detailed explanation on the complexity).

The experimental results presented in this section are based on an average of N^4 trials of RC4, in each case, with keys chosen uniformly at random. The experiments were carried out using GCC-compiled C-code on a Unix machine with 3.34 GHz processor and 8 GB of memory. Table 2.4 lists the theoretical estimates against the experimental values for each of the results presented in Section 2.

Table 1. Experimental values and theoretical estimates pertaining to our results, where $A := (S_r[r+1] = N-1)$, $B := (Z_{r+1} = Z_r)$ and $C := (Z_{r+1} = r+2)$

Biased Event	Probability (experimental value)	Probability (theoretical estimate)	Result (as in Section 2)
$(A \mid B)$	0.0077881670	$2/N = 0.0078125$	Theorem 2
$(A \mid C)$	0.0078166422	$2/N = 0.0078125$	Corollary 1
$(A \mid B \wedge C)$	0.0117323766	$3/N = 0.01171875$	Theorem 3

The values presented in Table 2.4 testify that our theoretical estimates for the higher-order glimpse correlation and associated results closely match their respective experimental values. Slight deviations, if any, are due to marginal gaps of order $1/N^2$ or less, which we have purposefully disregarded in case of the theoretical results.

2.5 Discussion of Our Results

The glimpse correlations have been quite well studied in RC4 literature, as they provide practical leaks into the state permutation of the cipher from the knowledge of the output keystream. Glimpse correlations can be exploited towards state-recovery and key-recovery attacks on RC4. One may find some important results in state-recovery attacks on RC4 in [7,3], and a few attacks along the lines of RC4 key-recovery from the permutation in [8,2,1].

Although glimpse biases provide practical cryptanalytic tools against RC4, not many have been identified over the last two decades of analysis. Jenkins [4] was the first to report a glimpse into RC4 state from the keystream with probability $2/N$, and it has since been the best one that persists in the long-term evolution of the PRGA. Later in 2001 and 2005, Mantin [5,6] generalized the glimpse correlations into 'useful states' of RC4, which included Jenkins' correlations as a special case. These biases were again of magnitude $2/N$, and persisted in the long-term evolution of PRGA. In recent times, several correlations between the state permutation and keystream have been observed, mainly by Sepehrdad et al [12,13], and later proved by Sen Gupta et al [10,11]. Although these correlations are larger in magnitude, none persist in the long-term evolution of RC4 PRGA, and only pertain to the initial bytes of the output.

Our result in this paper provides the following.

Strong long-term glimpse correlation: It provides a long-term glimpse correlation of magnitude $3/N$, the best to date. It is interesting to note that no long-term glimpse bias of magnitude more than $2/N$ has been reported in the literature over the last 15 years, since the first one [4] in 1996.

Guessing single permutation location using two output bytes: The long-term glimpse correlations reported in the literature to date generally relate a keystream output byte to a single location of the state permutation, typically at a specific round of RC4. Thus, simultaneous knowledge of two or more keystream bytes may help in guessing two or more permutation locations, but does not always provide additional benefits in guessing a single location of the permutation over any one of them. Our result combines the knowledge of two consecutive output bytes Z_r, Z_{r+1} to obtain a significant advantage in guessing a single permutation location $S_r[r+1]$. To the best of our knowledge, such a correlation has never been proposed in the literature.

3   Conclusion

In this paper we have shown that there exist long term correlations during the evolution of RC4 PRGA, even with a higher magnitude compared to the existing Jenkins' correlations [4], leaking information (providing a glimpse) about certain locations in the S array from the knowledge of the keystream output bytes.

The new glimpse association that we prove occurs with a probability of $3/N$, which is considerably higher than the probability of random association $1/N$, as well as higher in magnitude compared to the best known existing glimpse correlation probability $2/N$, as in the current literature [4].

Acknowledgments. The authors would like to thank the anonymous reviewers for their valuable comments that helped improve the quality of the paper.

References

1. Akgün, M., Kavak, P., Demirci, H.: New Results on the Key Scheduling Algorithm of RC4. In: Chowdhury, D.R., Rijmen, V., Das, A. (eds.) INDOCRYPT 2008. LNCS, vol. 5365, pp. 40–52. Springer, Heidelberg (2008)
2. Biham, E., Carmeli, Y.: Efficient Reconstruction of RC4 Keys from Internal States. In: Nyberg, K. (ed.) FSE 2008. LNCS, vol. 5086, pp. 270–288. Springer, Heidelberg (2008)
3. Golic, J.D., Morgari, G.: Iterative Probabilistic Reconstruction of RC4 Internal States. IACR Cryptology ePrint Archive, Report 2008/348 (2008), http://eprint.iacr.org/2008/348
4. Jenkins, R.J.: ISAAC and RC4 (1996), Published on the Internet at http://burtleburtle.net/bob/rand/isaac.html (last accessed on December 28, 2012)
5. Mantin, I.: Analysis of the stream cipher RC4. Master's thesis, The Weizmann Institute of Science, Israel (2001), http://www.wisdom.weizmann.ac.il/~itsik/RC4/rc4.html
6. Mantin, I.: A Practical Attack on the Fixed RC4 in the WEP Mode. In: Roy, B. (ed.) ASIACRYPT 2005. LNCS, vol. 3788, pp. 395–411. Springer, Heidelberg (2005)
7. Maximov, A., Khovratovich, D.: New State Recovery Attack on RC4. In: Wagner, D. (ed.) CRYPTO 2008. LNCS, vol. 5157, pp. 297–316. Springer, Heidelberg (2008)
8. Paul, G., Maitra, S.: Permutation After RC4 Key Scheduling Reveals the Secret Key. In: Adams, C., Miri, A., Wiener, M. (eds.) SAC 2007. LNCS, vol. 4876, pp. 360–377. Springer, Heidelberg (2007)
9. Paul, G., Maitra, S.: RC4 Stream Cipher and Its Variants, 1st edn. CRC Press, Boca Raton (November 16, 2011)
10. Gupta, S.S., Maitra, S., Paul, G., Sarkar, S.: Proof of Empirical RC4 Biases and New Key Correlations. In: Miri, A., Vaudenay, S. (eds.) SAC 2011. LNCS, vol. 7118, pp. 151–168. Springer, Heidelberg (2012)
11. Sen Gupta, S., Maitra, S., Paul, G., Sarkar, S.: (Non-)Random Sequences from (Non-) Random Permutations - Analysis of RC4 stream cipher. To appear in Journal of Cryptology. Springer (accepted November 3, 2012)
12. Sepehrdad, P., Vaudenay, S., Vuagnoux, M.: Discovery and exploitation of new biases in RC4. In: Biryukov, A., Gong, G., Stinson, D.R. (eds.) SAC 2010. LNCS, vol. 6544, pp. 74–91. Springer, Heidelberg (2011)
13. Sepehrdad, P., Vaudenay, S., Vuagnoux, M.: Statistical Attack on RC4 - Distinguishing WPA. In: Paterson, K.G. (ed.) EUROCRYPT 2011. LNCS, vol. 6632, pp. 343–363. Springer, Heidelberg (2011)

A Voucher Assisted Adaptive Acknowledgement Based Intrusion Detection Protocol for MANETs

Soumyadev Maity and R.C. Hansdah

Dept. of Computer Science and Automation
Indian Institute of Science, Bangalore, India
{soumya,hansdah}@csa.iisc.ernet.in

Abstract. In MANETs, supporting a routing protocol with an intrusion detection system (IDS) is crucial in ensuring secure communication. This paper proposes a novel Voucher assisted Adaptive ACKnowledgement (VAACK) mechanism for the detection of routing misbehaviors in MANETs. The protocol uses a novel voucher acknowledgment technique which is assisted by an efficient route scanning module. The proposed protocol is complete in the absence of node collusions and, it is also sound. Moreover, the protocol can partially fight against node collusion. The analytical and the simulation results confirm the effectiveness of the proposed protocol.

1   Introduction

In mobile ad hoc networks (MANETs), the key management protocols [1, 2] act as the first line of defense, whereas, the intrusion detection systems (IDS) act as the second line of defense. An IDS protocol is said to be *complete*, if it can detect all compromised nodes. The protocol is said to be *sound*, if it never reports a well-behaving node as compromised. The watchdog based IDS protocols [3–6] are not complete as they depend upon transmission overhearing. The two-hop acknowledgement based protocols (TWOACK [7], AACK [8]) do not depend on transmission overhearing, and they are complete in the absence of node collusions. All of the above mentioned protocols do not have a mechanism to detect false misbehavior reports, hence, they are not sound. The EAACK protocol [9] incorporates a misbehavior report authentication (MRA) module to solve the false misbehavior reporting problem. In this protocol, whenever an intermediate node F_i sends a misbehavior report about its next hop node F_{i+1} to the source node S, node S sends an MRA packet to the destination node D asking it to inform whether it received the data packets properly. The source node blacklists node F_{i+1} only when the destination does not receive the packets, otherwise, it blacklists node F_i for sending false misbehavior report. The EAACK protocol is complete in the absence of node collusions. However, in the following, we show that the EAACK protocol also is not sound.

Suppose the intermediate node F_{i+2} in the above example is compromised. Node F_{i+2} does not send any TWOACK packet to F_i for the data packets

A. Bagchi and I. Ray (Eds.): ICISS 2013, LNCS 8303, pp. 239–246, 2013.

received from F_{i+1}, but, forwards the received data packets properly towards the destination D. Hence, node F_i would send a misbehavior report to the source S. When node S enquires the destination D by sending an MRA packet, it comes to know that D has received all data packets sent by S. So, F_i gets blacklisted by the source node S. In this way, an adversary can always exhaust the resources of a compromised node (F_{i+2}) to detach a well-behaving node (F_i) from the rest of the network.

In this paper, we propose a novel routing layer IDS protocol, named Voucher assisted Adaptive ACKnowledgement (VAACK) protocol, for MANETs. The proposed protocol adopts the adaptive acknowledgement mechanism used in the AACK protocol [8], and uses a special type of acknowledgement process called the voucher acknowledgement which is implemented using one way hash chains. The voucher acknowledgement mechanism is accompanied with a novel route scanning module for the detection of misbehaving nodes in a route. The VAACK protocol is complete in the absence of node collusion, and is sound. Moreover, the protocol can partially fight against node collusion.

The rest of the paper is organized as follows. In section 2, we provide a detailed description of the proposed VAACK protocol. Section 3 analyzes the completeness and the soundness properties of the protocol. The simulation results are shown in section 4 and finally, section 5 concludes the paper.

2   The VAACK Protocol

The VAACK protocol uses an adaptive acknowledgement mechanism as in [8]. The protocol defines two modes of data transmissions, viz., *1*) the *destination acknowledgement* (DACK) mode, and *2*) the *voucher assisted destination acknowledgement* (CK) mode. A source node starts a data session in the DACK mode. The DACK mode uses only an end-to-end acknowledgement mechanism. After sending a data packet, a source node waits for a predefined duration of time (τ_{ack}) for an acknowledgement (ACK) packet to come from the destination node. If no ACK packet is received during the interval, the source node switches to the CK mode till the end of the session.

2.1   Voucher Assisted Destination Acknowledgement

In the CK mode, in addition to the end-to-end acknowledgement process, a voucher acknowledgement mechanism runs in parallel where each node in a data route acknowledges its previous hop node, for each of the data packets it receives, by sending a VOUCHER packet to it (see figure 1). Unlike a normal acknowledgement process which possesses only the *originator authentication* property, the voucher acknowledgement mechanism used in our protocol possesses the *originator non-repudiation* property also. To authenticate the VOUCHER packets, a node F_{i+1} makes use of a one-way hash chain $\langle h_0, .., h_{n-1} \rangle$. During the setup phase of the data session, node F_{i+1} sends the final value h_{n-1} of its hash chain, signed by its private key $(E_{PrK_{F_{i+1}}}[h_{n-1}])$, to node F_i. Subsequently, F_{i+1}

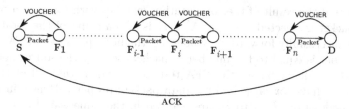

Fig. 1. The VAACK Protocol: Voucher Assisted Destination Acknowledgement Mode

incorporates the elements from its reverse hash chain $\langle h_{n-2}, .., h_0 \rangle$ sequentially and one at a time, into the VOUCHER packets sent to F_i. Here, we assume that the length of a chain n is larger enough than the total number of packets that can be sent during a data session. Node F_i can easily verify the authenticity of a VOUCHER packet by computing the *Hash* of the hashvalue contained in the current VOUCHER packet and matching the result with the hashvalue contained in the previous VOUCHER packet.

After forwarding each data packet, node F_i waits for a predefined duration of time (τ_{vouch}) for a VOUCHER packet to come from F_{i+1}. If no valid VOUCHER is received, F_i stops data transmission and sends a route error (RERR) packet to the source node. The RERR packet is handled by the underlying routing protocol as usual. In the CK mode, if the source node does not receive an ACK packet from the destination, it suspends the session and invokes the *route scanning module* of the protocol.

2.2 Route Scanning

The protocol incorporates a route scanning module which is designed for the purpose of detecting misbehaving nodes in a data route. The route scanning module uses a distributed binary search mechanism which is initiated by the source node S (see figure 1) in a route. This iterative scan process starts by selecting the node in the middle position (say node F_i) of the data route. The source node S executes a packet forwarding activity (PFA) test on node F_i. The PFA test is done on a node to determine whether the node has forwarded all the data packets sent by the source node during the session so far or not.

The test process is initialized by the source node S by sending an enquiry packet (ENQRY) to node F_i. As a response to the ENQRY packet, node F_i sends a reply packet (REPLY) to S. The REPLY packet contains three pieces of information, viz., 1) $\mathcal{N}_{vouchs}$: the total number of vouchers received by node F_i so far, 2) h_f: the hashvalue contained in the last received VOUCHER packet and 3) $E_{Pr K_{F_{i+1}}}[h_{n-1}]$: the final value of the hash chain used and signed by node F_{i+1}. The source node computes $Hash^{\mathcal{N}_{vouchs}}(h_f)$, where $Hash^x$ denotes x times successive application of the *Hash* function. Node S considers the REPLY packet as valid only if the result of the computation matches with h_{n-1}, otherwise, the REPLY packet is rejected. Now, as $\mathcal{N}_{vouchs}$ is also a count of the total number of packets successfully forwarded by node F_i, the node passes the PFA test only if, this number is equal to the number of packets sent by the source node.

When the node F_i passes the PFA test, it is evident that all of the nodes from F_1 to F_i have forwarded all the data packets properly. Hence, in the next iteration, nodes from F_{i+1} to F_n are scanned in the same way. However, if the node F_i fails the PFA test, it can be due to the reason that some of the nodes from F_1 to F_i has dropped some packets. Hence, nodes F_1 to F_i are scanned in the next iteration. When there remains only one node left for scanning, the route scanning module terminates after executing the PFA test on the node. If the node fails the PFA test, the module reports the node as a misbehaving node, otherwise, no node is reported as misbehaving. If an intermediate node is reported by the route scanning module as misbehaving, the source node blacklists it and finds an alternative route (avoiding blacklisted nodes) to send the rest of the data packets of the session. If no misbehaving node is reported by the module, the source node resumes the packet transmission of the session in CK mode again.

2.3   Timeout Values for τ_{ack} and τ_{vouch}

Let N_{hops} denote the length (hop-count) of a data traffic route, and D_{hop} denote the single hop transmission delay for a data packet. A node after transmitting a data packet in the CK mode, must wait for a duration of time which is sufficient enough for the corresponding VOUCHER packet to come from the next hop node. Hence, it is essential that τ_{vouch} satisfy the following condition.

$$\tau_{vouch} > D_{hop} \tag{1}$$

When a node does not receive a VOUCHER packet corresponding to a data packet forwarded to its next hop node, it send a RERR packet to the source. Let d_{rerr} denote the duration of time from the instant when the source node completes the transmission of a data packet to the instant when the eventual RERR packet is received from the intermediate node at the source node. Clearly, d_{rerr} is maximum (d_{rerr}^{max}) when the concerned intermediate node is the last intermediate node of the route. Hence, if τ_{ack} is shorter than d_{rerr}^{max}, an intermediate node may not get sufficient time to alert the source node and to stop the session, by sending the RERR packet, before the source initiates a route scanning. Thus, the timer τ_{ack} must satisfy the following condition.

$$\tau_{ack} > d_{rerr}^{max} \tag{2}$$

As the last intermediate node, after transmitting the packet to the destination node, waits at least τ_{vouch} duration of time before sending a RERR packet, $d_{rerr}^{max} > 2(N_{hops} - 1) \times D_{hop} + \tau_{vouch}$. Hence, the following condition holds for τ_{ack}.

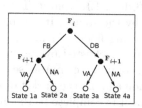

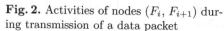

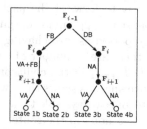

Fig. 2. Activities of nodes (F_i, F_{i+1}) during transmission of a data packet

Fig. 3. Activities of nodes (F_{i-1}, F_i, F_{i+1}), when F_i is uncompromised

$$\tau_{ack} > 2(N_{hops} - 1) \times D_{hop} + \tau_{vouch} \tag{3}$$

It can be noted here that, a timeout value for τ_{ack} satisfying the above condition, also ensures that a source node can receive an ACK packet corresponding to a data packet before the timer expires.

3   Analysis

Completeness of the VAACK Protocol. Suppose F_i and F_{i+1} are two consecutive nodes in a data route (see figure 1). Assume that all the nodes in the route other than nodes F_i and F_{i+1} are not compromised. Let us consider a two player game between F_i and F_{i+1} which starts when the first player, node F_i, receives a data packet. The extensive form of the game is represented by the game tree in figure 2. Each vertex in the tree corresponds to one of the two players. An edge going out of a vertex indicates a possible move by the corresponding player. A leaf of the tree represents the state of the protocol after both the players have executed their moves. The first player F_i has two possible moves: 1) it can forward the received data packet to F_{i+1} (move FB), 2) it can drop the packet (move DB). The moves available for the second player (F_{i+1}) are: 1) it can send a VOUCHER acknowledgement to F_i (move VA), 2) it can send no acknowledgement to F_i (move NA). Now, state 1a in figure 2 is reached when there is no unexpected activity from any nodes in the route. When node F_i does not receive the required VOUCHER for the data packet forwarded to F_{i+1}, the protocol reaches state 2a. In this case, F_i sends RERR packet to the source, as a result of which, the session is terminated. When node F_{i+1} is not compromised, state 4a is reached if F_i drops the data packet. In this case, as the destination D does not receive the data packet, it does not send an ACK packet to the source S. As a result, S initiates route scanning. Since F_i does not have the required VOUCHER, it is reported as misbehaving and blacklisted by the source. State 3a is reached when F_i drops data packet, and F_{i+1} sends a VOUCHER to F_i for a packet which it does not receive from F_i. This is an example of *node collusion*. Due to the reason mentioned in the earlier case, in this case also, source node S initiates route scanning. Now, node F_i has the required VOUCHER. However, since F_i has not forwarded the data packet to F_{i+1}, F_{i+1}

has no way to forward the packet to its next hop node F_{i+2}. As F_{i+2} is not compromised, F_{i+1} cannot obtain the required VOUCHER from it. Thus, node F_{i+1} is reported as misbehaving and blacklisted by the source. It can be noted that, if there are x number of compromised colluding nodes, $F_i, .., F_{i+x-1}$, the last node F_{i+x-1} in the collusion would always be blacklisted by the protocol. The above analysis shows that, when there are no colluding compromised nodes, the protocol is always able to detect and take action against the packet dropping activity of a node in the route. Hence, the protocol is complete in the absence of node collusion. In presence of node collusion, the protocol is able to blacklist one of the compromised nodes in the collusion.

Soundness of the VAACK Protocol. Consider three consecutive nodes in a route F_{i-1}, F_i and F_{i+1}. Assume that node F_i is not compromised. Figure 3 shows the game tree corresponding to the data transmission game for the three players F_{i-1}, F_i and F_{i+1}. When the first player F_{i-1} forwards the data packet, the second player F_i must send a VOUCHER to F_{i-1}, and must forward the packet to F_{i+1} (move VA+FB). Otherwise, F_i must not send any acknowledgement to F_{i-1} (move NA). It can be noted that, when F_{i-1} does not forward the data packet, F_i cannot forward it to F_{i+1}. However, the third player F_{i+1} is free to decide whether it would send a VOUCHER to F_i irrespective of whether it receives the data packet from F_i as shown in figure 3.

To prove the soundness property, we argue by contradiction and assume that the uncompromised node F_i gets blacklisted by the source node S. For a node to be blacklisted by a source node, the route scanning module must be initiated by the source. Moreover, the route scanning module reports a node as misbehaving only if the following two conditions are satisfied: 1) all the nodes preceding the concerned node holds the required number of VOUCHERs and 2) the concerned node does not have the required number of VOUCHERs. Now, in state 2b in figure 3, as F_i does not receive VOUCHER for the data packet forwarded to F_{i+1}, it sends RERR to the source. Receiving the RERR, the source terminates the current session. The route scanning module is invoked by the source only when the timer τ_{ack} expires for a data packet sent. But, as the protocol ensures that $\tau_{ack} > D_{rerr}^{max}$, in state 2b, route scanning module is not invoked. In state 3b and 4b, F_{i-1} does not have the required VOUCHER. This violates the condition 1 mentioned above. Thus, in state 3b and 4b, F_i is not blacklisted. Hence, F_i is blacklisted in state 1b. However, in state 1b F_i has obtained the required voucher. This contradicts with the condition 2 mentioned above. Thus, it is proved that an uncompromised node is never blacklisted by the source node.

4   Simulation Results

Using the QualNet simulator [10], we have compared the performance of the proposed VAACK protocol with the watchdog [3], TWOACK [7], AACK [8] and EAACK [9] protocols. We have used 50 nodes in a 700 m × 700 m simulation

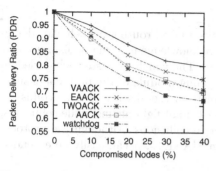

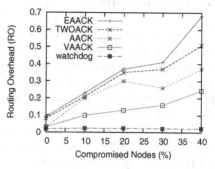

Fig. 4. Comparison of Packet Delivery Ratios

Fig. 5. Comparison of Routing Overheads

area. The random way-point mobility model has been used with an average node speed of 10 m/second. Total simulation time is 1000 seconds. Each simulation uses 10 randomly chosen source nodes. A source node executes 4 constant bit rate (CBR) sessions with four randomly chosen destinations during the simulation. The duration of each CBR session is 200 seconds and data packet size is 512 bytes. Timeout values for τ_{vouch} and τ_{ack} are set to 170 ms and 1.5 seconds respectively.

Figure 4 compares the packet delivery ratio (PDR) for all the protocols. As obvious, the acknowledgement based protocols perform better than the watchdog based protocol. Among the two hop acknowledgement protocols, the EAACK protocol can detect false misbehavior reports unlike the AACK and the TWOACK protocol. In the VAACK protocol, there is no scope for misbehavior reporting. Moreover, unlike the VAACK protocol, the EAACK protocol cannot fight against the compromised nodes which forward data packets but do not send acknowledgements. For these reasons, the EAACK and VAACK protocols outperform the AACK and the TWOACK protocols in terms of the PDR. Moreover, the VAACK protocol achieves a higher PDR value than the EAACK protocol.

Figure 5 compares the routing overhead (RO) values for different protocols. The watchdog protocol and the EAACK protocol possesses the lowest and the highest RO values respectively as compared to the other protocols. This is due to the fact that, the watchdog protocol does not use any acknowledgement packets, whereas, the EAACK protocol uses large size digital signatures to authenticate its acknowledgement packets. Due to the adaptive acknowledgement mechanism used in the AACK and VAACK protocols, the two protocols enjoy lower RO values as compared to the TWOACK protocol. The size of a VOUCHER packet used in the VAACK protocol is much smaller than the the size of a two hop acknowledgement (TWOACK) packet used in the AACK protocol. In addition, unlike a TWOACK packet which is transmitted over two hops, a VOUCHER packet is transmitted only over one hop. For these reasons, the RO value for the VAACK protocol is even lesser than that for the AACK protocol.

5 Conclusions

This paper describes the VAACK protocol - a novel routing misbehavior detection protocol for MANETs. The adaptive acknowledgement mechanism used by the protocol ensures lower routing overhead. The voucher assisted acknowledgement mechanism along with the route scanning module of the protocol ensures protocol soundness. The protocol is complete in the absence of node collusion. However, unlike the existing schemes which cannot fight against node collusions, our protocol can partially fight against node collusions. Although the protocol is designed for source routing protocols in MANETs, it can easily be extended for the next hop routing protocols.

References

1. Maity, S., Hansdah, R.C.: Certificate-Less On-Demand Public Key Management (CLPKM) for Self-organized MANETs. In: Venkatakrishnan, V., Goswami, D. (eds.) ICISS 2012. LNCS, vol. 7671, pp. 277–293. Springer, Heidelberg (2012)
2. Maity, S., Hansdah, R.C.: A Secure and Efficient Authentication Protocol (SEAP) for MANETs with Membership Revocation. In: Proc. of the 27th International Conference on Advanced Information Networking and Applications Workshops (WAINA 2013), Barcelona, Spain, pp. 363–370 (March 2013)
3. Marti, S., Giuli, T.J., Lai, K., Baker, M.: Mitigating routing misbehavior in mobile ad hoc networks. In: Proc. of the 6th Annual International Conference on Mobile Computing and Networking, vol. 6(11), pp. 255–265 (2000)
4. Patcha, A., Mishra, A.: Collaborative security architecture for black hole attack prevention in mobile ad hoc networks. In: Proc. of the IEEE Radio and Wireless Conference (RAWCON 2003), pp. 75–78 (2003)
5. Parker, J.P.A.J.J., Undercoffer, J., Pinkston, J., Joshi, A.: On intrusion detection and response for mobile ad hoc networks. In: Proc. of the IEEE International Conference on Performance, Computing, and Communications, pp. 747–752 (2004)
6. Nasser, N., Chen, Y.: Enhanced intrusion detection system for discovering malicious nodes in mobile ad-hoc networks. In: Proc. of the IEEE International Conference on Communications (ICC 2007), pp. 1154–1159 (2007)
7. Liu, K., Deng, J., Varshney, P.K., Balakrishnan, K.: An acknowledgment-based approach for the detection of routing misbehavior in MANETs. IEEE Transactions on Mobile Computing 6(5), 536–550 (2007)
8. Sheltami, T., Al-Roubaiey, A., Shakshuki, E., Mahmoud, A.: Video transmission enhancement in presence of misbehaving nodes in MANETs. Multimedia Systems 15(5), 273–282 (2009)
9. Shakshuki, E., Kang, N., Sheltami, T.: EAACK - A Secure Intrusion Detection System for MANETs. IEEE Transactions on Industrial Electronics 60(3), 1089–1098 (2013)
10. QualNet 5.0: Scalable Network Technologies, Inc., 6100 Center Drive, Suite 1250, Los Angeles, CA 90045, http://www.scalable-networks.com

Cryptanalysis of Pairing-Free Identity-Based Authenticated Key Agreement Protocols

Dheerendra Mishra and Sourav Mukhopadhyay

Department of Mathematics
Indian Institute of Technology Kharagpur
Kharagpur–721302, India
{dheerendra,sourav}@maths.iitkgp.ernet.in

Abstract. The pairing-free ID-based authenticated key agreement (ID-AKA) protocol provides secure and efficient communication over the public network, which is introduced by Zhu et al. in 2007. Afterwards, a number of identity-based authenticated key agreement protocols have been proposed to meet a variety of desirable security and performance requirements. In this paper, we analyze Fiore and Gennaro's scheme and demonstrate key off-set and forgery attack. We identify that Farash and Attari's protocol is vulnerable to the forgery attack, key compromise impersonation attack, key off-set attack and known session key specific temporary information attack. We also show that Hou and Xu's scheme also fails to resist key off-set and forgery attack.

Keywords: Identity-based key agreement, elliptic curve, pairing-free cryptography, cryptanalysis.

1 Introduction

Advancement in network technology has presented various online services for remote users. These services are highly efficient and useful. Although a user communicates to other user or server over the public network, although an attacker can get full control over the public channel, such that he can track, intercept, modify and delete the message. Therefore, an adversary is always considering being capable to perform active and passive attacks, which makes communication vulnerable over the public network. Although, the identity based key agreement (ID-KA) protocols tries to ensure authorized and secure communication, which is introduced in early '90s. It allows the users to agree upon a session, which is constructed by their key shares such that authorized participant can construct the session key [3, 9, 11, 12].

Most of the existing protocols [3, 4, 10] are pairing based, which requires computation of bilinear pairing on elliptic curve group with large element size. The comparative computation cost of the pairing is higher than the elliptic curve point multiplication. Therefore, pairing free ID-KA protocol seems to be an efficient mechanism, as it requires no computation of bilinear pairing or map to point hash function [1, 2, 7, 8, 12]. Zhu et al. [12] initiated the work of pairing-free ID-KA protocol by presenting a new pairing-free ID-KA protocol based on

A. Bagchi and I. Ray (Eds.): ICISS 2013, LNCS 8303, pp. 247–254, 2013.

elliptic curve cryptography (ECC). In 2010, Cao et al. [1] presented an efficient ID-KA protocol, which exchanges two message of less size in order to achieve the session key. In 2010, Fiore1 and Gennaro [6] also presented a new identity based key agreement protocol. Recently, Hou and Xu [7] demonstrated that Cao et al.'s protocol does not resist known session key specific temporary information attack. Additionally, they proposed improved ID-KA protocol and claimed that their protocol satisfies all known security attributes. However, in general, pairing-free ID-KA protocols [1, 2, 7, 8] only the users from same network can communicate, i.e., users with different KGCs cannot establish a secure session. Farash and Attari [5] extended Cao et al. pairing-free ID-KA protocol and presented an efficient protocol based on ECC in which two users of independent organizations or networks with separate KGCs can establish secure session.

2   Review and Analysis of Pairing-Free Identity-Based Authentication Protocols

2.1   Review and Cryptanalysis of Fiore and Gennaro's Protocol

In this section, we present a review and cryptanalysis of Fiore and Gennaro's protocol[6]. Fiore and Gennaro's protocol comprises three phases, namely, setup, key derivation and key exchange. The brief description is as follows:

Setup: The Key Generation Center (KGC) selects a group G of l-bits prime order q, a random generator g of G and hash functions $h_1 : \{0,1\}^* \to Z_q$ and $h_2 : Z_q \times Z_q \to \{0,1\}^l$. It selects a master key $x \in Z_q$ and set public key $y = g^x$. The KGC publishes system parameters $\langle G, g, y, h_1, h_2 \rangle$ and keeps the master key x secret.

Key Derivation: When user U submits its public identity ID_U to KGC. KGC verifies the proof of the identity. If verification succeeds, then it takes the following steps:

- Generate $k \in Z_q$.
- Compute $r_U = g^k$ and generate U's private key $s_U = k + h_1(ID_U, r_U)x$, then deliver (r_U, s_U) to U via secure channel.

On receiving private key, U can verify it by $g^{s_U} = r_U + y^{h_1(ID_U, r_U)}$.

Key Agreement: When a user Alice with identity ID_A and secret key (r_A, s_A) wants to establish a session key with another user Bob with identity ID_B and secret key (r_B, s_B). A selects a random number $t_A \in Z_q$ and sends $< ID_A, r_A, u_A >$ to B where $u_A = g^{t_A}$. Analogously, B chooses a random number $t_B \in Z_q$ and computes $u_B = g^{t_B}$, then sends $< ID_B, r_B, u_B >$. Once the participants exchanged the messages, they compute the session key. A and B calculate the session key as follows:

- A computes $K_{AB}^1 = (u_B r_B y^{h_1(ID_B, r_B)})^{t_A + s_A} = g^{(t_B + s_B)(t_A + s_A)}$, and $K_{AB}^2 = u_B^{t_A} = g^{t_B t_A}$, then achieves $sk_{AB} = h_2(K_{AB}^1, K_{AB}^2)$.
- B computes $K_{BA}^1 = (u_A r_A y^{h_1(ID_A, r_A)})^{t_B + s_B} = g^{(t_A + s_A)(t_B + s_B)}$ and $K_{BA}^2 = u_A^{t_B} = g^{t_A t_B}$, then achieves $sk_{BA} = h_2(K_{BA}^1, K_{BA}^2)$.

Cryptanalysis of Fiore and Gennaro's Protocol. We analyze Fiore and Gennaro's protocol [6] and find that their protocol does not present efficient key exchange protocol.

1) **Key Off-set Attack:** Fiore and Gennaro's protocol does not withstand key off-set attack. The attacker can execute the key off-set attack as follows:

- When A sends the message $< ID_A, r_A, u_A >$ to B, E intercepts A's message and selects $t_E \in Z_q$ and computes $u_E = g^{t_E}$, then replaces $< ID_A, r_A, u_A >$ with $< ID_A, r_A, u_E >$.
- When B sends the message $< ID_B, r_B, u_B >$ to A, E intercepts B's message, then replaces $< ID_B, r_B, u_B >$ with $< ID_B, r_B, u_E >$.
- A computes $K_{AB}^1 = (u_E r_B y^{h_1(ID_B, r_B)})^{t_A + s_A} = g^{(t_E + s_B)(t_A + s_A)}$ and $K_{AB}^2 = u_E^{t_A} = g^{t_E t_A}$, then achieves session key $sk_{AB} = h_2(K_{AB}^1, K_{AB}^2)$.
- B computes $K_{BA}^1 = (u_E r_A y^{h_1(ID_A, r_A)})^{t_B + s_B} = g^{(t_E + s_A)(t_B + s_B)}$ and $K_{BA}^2 = u_E^{t_B} = g^{t_E t_B}$, then achieves session key $sk_{BA} = h_2(K_{BA}^1, K_{BA}^2)$.

It is easy to see that both Alice and Bob compute the keys which are not equal, i.e., $sk_{AB} \neq sk_{BA}$, since $K_{BA}^1 \neq K_{AB}^1$ and $K_{AB}^2 \neq K_{BA}^2$. Due to key offset attack, users agree upon a key that is differing at both ends. This violates the **key integrity property** in which each participant should assure that secret session key is a function of only the individual contributions of all involved parties.

2) **Forgery Attack:** The Fiore and Gennaro's Protocol is vulnerable to a forgery attack, where an eavesdropper intercepts the communication message $< ID_A, r_A, u_A >$ of legal user A that broadcasts through public channel. Then, it can achieve user's identity ID_A and r_A that allows it to easily masquerade as a legal users to forge other user. This works as follows:

- E selects $t_E \in Z_q$ and computes $u_E = g^{t_E}$, then masquerades as a legal user A and sends $< ID_A, r_A, u_E >$ to B. When B sends the message $< ID_B, r_B, u_B >$ to A, E intercepts B's message.
- B computes $K_{BA}^1 = (u_E r_A y^{h_1(ID_A, r_A)})^{t_B + s_B} = g^{(t_E + s_A)(t_B + s_B)}$ and $K_{BA}^2 = u_E^{t_B} = g^{t_E t_B}$, then achieves $sk_{BA} = h_2(K_{BA}^1, K_{BA}^2)$. It is clear that B computes the session key without identifying the validity of message. Thus, the attacker can easily impersonate as valid user.

2.2 Review and Analysis of Farash and Attari's Protocol

In this section, we briefly review the Farash and Attari's ID-KA Protocol [5] and show some of the weaknesses of this protocol. Farash and Attari's pairing-free identity-based key agreement protocol for independent KGCs involves the following three phases: (i) Setup, (ii) Extract (iii) Key Agreement.

Setup: Private key generator takes security parameter 1^k and returns security parameters and master key $x^{(i)}$. The system keeps n number of KGCs where each i'th KGC_i defines its parameters as follows:

Step S1. Choose a k-bit prime $P^{(i)} \in G^{(i)}$. Select a master key $x^{(i)} \in Z_q^*$ and set public key $\mathsf{P}_{pub}^{(i)} = \mathsf{x}^{(i)} P^{(i)}$, where $P^{(i)}$ is a generator of elliptic curve group $G^{(i)}$.

Step S2. Choose two hash functions H_1 and H_2.

Step S3. Publish system parameters $\langle F_{q^{(i)}}, E^{(i)}/F_{q^{(i)}}, G^{(i)}, P^{(i)}, \mathsf{P}_{pub}^{(i)}, H_1^{(i)}, H_2^{(i)} \rangle$ and keep master key $\mathsf{x}^{(i)}$ secret.

Extract: User submits its public identities ID_U to KGC, then KGC generates user's private key as follows:

Step E1. Generate $r_U \in Z_{q^{(i)}}^*$.

Step E2. Compute $R_U = r_U P^{(i)}$ and $h_U = H_1^{(i)}(ID_U \| R_U)$, generate private key $s_U = r_U + \mathsf{x}^{(i)} h_U$ and deliver private key (R_U, s_U) to U via secure channel.

On receiving private key, U verifies $s_U P^{(i)} = R_U + H_1^{(i)}(ID_U \| R_U)\mathsf{P}_{pub}^{(i)}$. If verification succeeds, U sets its public key $P_U = s_U P^{(i)}$.

Key Agreement: To establish the session key, users A and B of independent networks proceed as follows:

Step K1. A selects two random numbers $a^{(1)} \in Z_{q^{(1)}}^*$ and $a^{(2)} \in Z_{q^{(2)}}^*$. He computes $T_A^{(1)} = a^{(1)} P^{(1)}$ and $T_A^{(2)} = a^{(2)} P^{(2)}$, then sends $< ID_A, T_A^{(1)}, T_A^{(2)}, R_A >$ to B.

Step K2. B chooses two random numbers $b^{(1)} \in Z_{q^{(1)}}^*$ and $b^{(2)} \in Z_{q^{(2)}}^*$. He computes $T_B^{(1)} = b^{(1)} P^{(1)}$ and $T_B^{(2)} = b^{(2)} P^{(2)}$, then sends $< ID_B, T_B^{(1)}, T_B^{(2)}, R_B >$ to A.

Step K3. Finally, A and B compute their respective session key K_{AB} and K_{BA} as follows:
$$K_{AB} = H_2\{ID_A, ID_B, T_A^{(1)}, T_A^{(2)}, T_B^{(1)}, T_B^{(2)}, a^{(1)}T_B^{(1)}, a^{(2)}T_B^{(2)}, K_A^{(1)}, K_A^{(2)}\}$$
$$K_{BA} = H_2\{ID_A, ID_B, T_A^{(1)}, T_A^{(2)}, T_B^{(1)}, T_B^{(2)}, b^{(1)}T_A^{(1)}, b^{(2)}T_A^{(2)}, K_B^{(1)}, K_B^{(2)}\}$$
where $K_A^{(1)} = s_A T_B^{(1)}$, $K_A^{(2)} = a^{(2)} P_B^{(2)}$, $K_B^{(1)} = b^{(1)} P_A^{(1)}$ and $K_B^{(2)} = s_B T_A^{(2)}$.

Cryptanalysis of Farash and Attari's Protocol. We analyze the Farash and Attari's protocol and identify that their protocol does not resist some of the known attacks. The description is as follows:

1) **Known Session Specific Temporary Information Attack:** Farash and Attari's protocol does not resist this attack. In other words, if the short-term secrets $a^{(1)}, a^{(2)}, b^{(1)}$ and $b^{(2)}$ compromised, then an adversary can construct the session key as follows:

- E can achieve $ID_A, T_A^{(1)}, T_A^{(2)}, R_A, ID_B, T_B^{(1)}, T_B^{(2)}, R_B, P_{pub}$, as all these information broadcast over public channel. From these information, E can construct the public key of A and B, namely, $P_A^{(1)}$ $P_B^{(2)}$.
- E can compute $K_A^{(2)} = a^{(2)}P_B^{(2)}, a^{(1)}T_B^{(1)}, a^{(2)}T_B^{(2)}$, and $K_B^{(1)} = b^{(1)}P_A^{(1)}$ from leaked $a^{(1)}, a^{(2)}, b^{(1)}, b^{(2)}$ and publicly known values $T_A^{(1)}, T_A^{(2)}, P_B^{(2)}$ and $P_A^{(1)}$.
- E can construct $K_{AB} = H_2\{ID_A, ID_B, T_A^{(1)}, T_A^{(2)}, T_B^{(1)}, T_B^{(2)}$ $, a^{(1)}T_B^{(1)}, a^{(2)}T_B^{(2)}, K_A^{(1)}, K_A^{(2)}\}$, as $K_A^{(1)} = K_B^{(1)}$.
- E can also achieve K_{BA} as $K_{AB} = K_{BA}$.

2) **Key Compromise Impersonation Attack:**   Assume that E achieves private key s_A of A. Then, key compromise impersonation attack activates as follows:

- When A initiates the session with B. He selects two random numbers $a^{(1)} \in Z_{q^{(1)}}^*$ and $a^{(2)} \in Z_{q^{(2)}}^*$. He computes $T_A^{(1)} = a^{(1)}P^{(1)}$ and $T_A^{(2)} = a^{(2)}P^{(2)}$, then sends $< ID_A, T_A^{(1)}, T_A^{(2)}, R_A >$ to B. E does not intercept the A's message.
- On receiving A's message, B chooses two random numbers $b^{(1)} \in Z_{q^{(1)}}^*$ and $b^{(2)} \in Z_{q^{(2)}}^*$. He computes $T_B^{(1)} = b^{(1)}P^{(1)}$ and $T_B^{(2)} = b^{(2)}P^{(2)}$, then sends $< ID_B, T_B^{(1)}, T_B^{(2)}, R_B >$ to A.
- E intercepts the B's message, then generates two random numbers $e^{(1)} \in Z_{q^{(1)}}^*$ and $e^{(2)} \in Z_{q^{(2)}}^*$, and computes $T_B'^{(1)} = e^{(1)}P^{(1)}$ and $T_B'^{(2)} = e^{(2)}P^{(2)}$, then replaces B's message by $< ID_B, T_B'^{(1)}, T_B'^{(2)}, R_B >$. Upon receiving the message, A computes session key K_{AB} as follows:
$K_{AB} = H_2\{ID_A, ID_B, T_A^{(1)}, T_A^{(2)}, T_B'^{(1)}, T_B'^{(2)}, a^{(1)}T_B'^{(1)}, a^{(2)}T_B'^{(2)}, K_A'^{(1)}, K_A'^{(2)}\}$, where $K_A'^{(1)} = s_A T_B'^{(1)}$ and $K_A^{(2)} = a^{(2)}P_B^{(2)}$.
- E can also compute K_{AB}' as follows:
  - E can compute $K_A'^{(1)} = s_A T_B'^{(1)}, K_B'^{(1)} = e^{(1)}P_A^{(1)}, e^{(1)}T_A^{(1)}$ and $e^{(2)}T_A^{(2)}$.
  - E can achieve $K_{AB}' = H_2\{ID_A, ID_B, T_A^{(1)}, T_A^{(2)}, T_B'^{(1)}, T_B'^{(2)}, a^{(1)}T_B'^{(1)}, a^{(2)} T_B'^{(2)}, K_A'^{(1)}, K_A'^{(2)}\}$, as $K_A^{(2)} = K_B'^{(1)}, a^{(1)}T_B'^{(1)} = e^{(1)}T_A^{(1)}$ and $a^{(2)}T_B'^{(2)} = e^{(2)}T_A^{(2)}$

It is clear from the discussion that in Farash and Attari's protocol, if user's private key is compromised, then an attacker can impersonate other user.

3) **Forgery Attack:**   Eavesdropper can intercept the legal user message if it transmits via public channel. And, it can achieve user identity ID_A and partial key R_A information that allow it to easily masquerade as a legal users to other user as follows:

- E masquerades as a legal user A and sends $< ID_A, T_A^{(1)}, T_A^{(2)}, R_A >$ to B where $T_A^{(1)} = a^{(1)}P^{(1)}$ and $T_A^{(2)} = a^{(2)}P^{(2)}$ for $e^{(1)} \in Z_{q^{(1)}}^*$ and $e^{(2)} \in Z_{q^{(2)}}^*$.
- On receiving the message, B sends $< ID_B, T_B^{(1)}, T_B^{(2)}, R_B >$ to A. Then, he computes $sk_{BA} = H_2(ID_A||ID_B||T_A'||T_B||K_{BA}^1||K_{BA}^2)$ where $K_{BA}^1 = s_B eP + bs_A P$, and $K_{BA}^2 = beP$. E intercepts B's message.

The user B computes the session key without identifying the validity of messages sender. This shows that an adversary can perform forgery attack.

4) **Key Offset Attack:** In Farash and Attari's protocol, an active eavesdropper can off-set the agreed session key by an exponent, which remains unknown to both participants. This occurs as follows:

- E eavesdrops the communication of user A and B.
- When A sends $< ID_A, T_A^{(1)}, T_A^{(2)}, R_A >$ to B. E intercepts A's message and replaces it by $< ID_A, T_A'^{(1)}, T_A'^{(2)}, R_A >$ where $T_A'^{(1)} = ea^{(1)}P^{(1)}$ and $T_A'^{(2)} = ea^{(2)}P^{(2)}$ for a random value e.
- When B sends his message $< ID_B, T_B^{(1)}, T_B^{(2)}, R_B >$ to A. E intercepts A's message and replaces it by $< ID_B, T_B'^{(1)}, T_B'^{(2)}, R_B >$ where $T_B'^{(1)} = eb^{(1)}P^{(1)}$ and $T_B'^{(2)} = eb^{(2)}P^{(2)}$.
- A and B compute their respective session key K_{AB} and K_{BA} as follows:
$K_{AB} = H_2\{ID_A, ID_B, T_A^{(1)}, T_A^{(2)}, T_B'^{(1)}, T_B'^{(2)}, a^{(1)}T_B'^{(1)}, a^{(2)}T_B'^{(2)}, K_A'^{(1)}, K_A^{(2)}\}$
$K_{BA} = H_2\{ID_A, ID_B, T_A'^{(1)}, T_A'^{(2)}, T_B^{(1)}, T_B^{(2)}, b^{(1)}T_A'^{(1)}, b^{(2)}T_A'^{(2)}, K_B^{(1)}, K_B'^{(2)}\}$
where $K_A^{(1)} = s_A e T_B^{(1)}$, $K_A^{(2)} = a^{(2)}P_B^{(2)}$, $K_B^{(1)} = b^{(1)}P_A^{(1)}$ and $K_B^{(2)} = e s_B T_A^{(2)}$.
- A and B both compute their keys, however, $K_{AB} \neq K_{BA}$, as $K_A^{(1)} \neq K_B^{(1)}$ and $K_A^{(2)} \neq K_B^{(2)}$.

2.3   Review and Analysis of Huo and Xu's Key Agreement Protocol

In 2011, Hou and Xu [7] demonstrated the weaknesses of Cao et al.'s protocol [1] and introduced an improved one-round ID-AKA protocol without pairing. Huo and Xu one-round ID-AKA protocol comprises of three phases: Setup, Extract and Key Agreement. The setup and extract phase is similar to the discussed above except the fact that the scheme is applicable of single KGC system. Therefore, we are only discussing key agreement phase of Hou and Xu's protocol.

Key Agreement: To establish session key, A and B proceed as follows:

- A chooses a random ephemeral key $a \in Z_q^*$ and sends $< ID_A, R_A, T_A >$ to B where $T_A = aP$.
- On receiving the A's message, B chooses a random ephemeral key $b \in Z_q^*$, then sends $< ID_B, R_B, T_B >$ to A where $T_B = bP$.
- A and B compute their respective session keys as:

$$sk_{AB} = H_2(ID_A || ID_B || T_A || T_B || K_{AB}^1 || K_{AB}^2 || K_{AB}^3)$$

$$sk_{BA} = H_2'(ID_A || ID_B || T_A || T_B || K_{BA}^1 || K_{BA}^2 || K_{BA}^3)$$

where $K_{AB}^1 = s_A T_B + a(R_B + H_1(ID_B || R_B)P_{pub})$, $K_{AB}^2 = aT_B$, $K_{AB}^3 = r_A R_B$ and $K_{BA}^1 = s_B T_A + b(R_A + H_1(ID_A || R_A)P_{pub})$, $K_{AB}^2 = bT_A$, $K_{AB}^3 = r_B R_A$.
- They agree upon a session key, as $sk_{AB} = sk_{BA}$.

Cryptanalysis of Hou and Xu's Protocol. In this section, we show that Hou and Xu's Protocol does not resist 'key off-set attack' and 'forgery attack'.

1) **Key Offset Attack.** An adversary performs the key offset attack when initiator and responder communicate as follows:

- A chooses a random ephemeral key $a \in Z_q^*$ and sends $< ID_A, R_A, T_A >$ to B where $T_A = aP$.
- E intercepts A's message and selects $e \in Z_q^*$, then replaces $< ID_A, R_A, T_A >$ by $< ID_A, R_A, T_A^* >$ where $T_A^* = eT_A^*$.
- B chooses a random ephemeral key $b \in Z_q^*$, then sends $< ID_B, R_B, T_B >$ to A where $T_B = bP$.
- E intercepts B's message, then replaces $< ID_B, R_B, T_B >$ by $< ID_B, R_B, T_B^* >$ where $T_B^* = eT_B$.
- A and B compute their respective session keys as:
  $sk_{AB} = H_2(ID_A||ID_B||T_A||T_B^*||K_{AB}^1||K_{AB}^2||K_{AB}^3)$
  $sk_{BA} = H_2'(ID_A||ID_B||T_A^*||T_B||K_{BA}^1||K_{BA}^2||K_{BA}^3)$,
  where $K_{AB}^1 = s_A T_B' + a(R_B + H_1(ID_B||R_B)P_{pub})$, $K_{AB}^2 = aT_B' = aeT_B$, $K_{AB}^3 = r_A R_B$ and $K_{BA}^1 = s_B T_A' + b(R_A + H_1(ID_A||R_A)P_{pub})$, $K_{AB}^2 = bT_A' = beT_B$, $K_{AB}^3 = r_B R_A$.
- They agree upon a key, which is different at both ends, i.e., $sk_{AB} \neq sk_{BA}$ because $K_{AB}^1 \neq K_{BA}^1$.

Due to key off-set attack, users agree upon a key that is differing from his calculated key. This violates the key integrity property where it suggests that agreed session key should be same and depends only on the inputs of participated users.

2) **Forgery Attack.** Eavesdropper intercepts the communication messages of legal user, say A over public channel. It can gain user legal identity ID_A and partial key R_A information that allow it to easily masquerade as a legal user to other user as follows:

- E masquerades as a legal user A and sends $< ID_A, R_A, T_E >$ to B where $T_E = eP$ and $e \in Z_q^*$.
- On receiving the message, B selects ephemeral key $b \in Z_q^*$ and compute $T_B = bP_A$, then sends $< ID_B, R_B, T_B >$ to A. E intercept the B's message.
- B computes $sk_{BA} = H_2'(ID_A||ID_B||T_E||T_B||K_{BA}^1||K_{BA}^2||K_{BA}^3)$, where $K_{BA}^1 = s_B T_E + b(R_A + H_1(ID_A||R_A)P_{pub})$, $K_{AB}^2 = bT_E$, $K_{AB}^3 = r_B R_A$.

The user B computes the session key without identifying the invalid user. Thus, the attacker can easily impersonate as valid user and can perform forgery attack.

3   Conclusion

In this article, we have presented the cryptanalysis of Farash and Attari's protocol and show that it is vulnerable to the forgery attack, key compromise impersonation attack, key off-set attack and known session key specific temporary information attack. We have demonstrated that Fiore and Gennaro's, Hou and Xu's protocols are also failed to resist key off-set attack and forgery attack.

References

1. Cao, X., Kou, W., Du, X.: A pairing-free identity-based authenticated key agreement protocol with minimal message exchanges. Information Sciences 180(15), 2895–2903 (2010)
2. Xue-Fei, C., Kou Wei-Dong, F.K., Jun, Z.: An identity-based authenticated key agreement protocol without bilinear pairing. Chinese Journal of Electronics & Information Technology 31(5), 1241–1244 (2009)
3. Chen, L., Cheng, Z., Smart, N.P.: Identity-based key agreement protocols from pairings. International Journal of Information Security 6(4), 213–241 (2007)
4. Chen, L., Kudla, C.: Identity based authenticated key agreement protocols from pairings. In: 2003 Proceedings of the 16th IEEE Computer Security Foundations Workshop, pp. 219–233 (2003)
5. Farash, M.S., Attari, M.A.: An id-based key agreement protocol based on ecc among users of separate networks. In: 2012 9th International ISC Conference on Information Security and Cryptology (ISCISC), pp. 32–37 (2012)
6. Fiore, D., Gennaro, R.: Identity-based key exchange protocols without pairings. Transactions on Computational Science X, 42–77 (2010)
7. Hou, M., Xu, Q.: A one-round id-based authenticated key agreement protocol with enhanced security. In: 2011 2nd International Conference on Intelligent Control and Information Processing (ICICIP), vol. 1, pp. 194–197 (2011)
8. Islam, S., Biswas, G.: An improved pairing-free identity-based authenticated key agreement protocol based on ecc. Procedia Engineering 30, 499–507 (2012)
9. Just, M., Vaudenay, S.: Authenticated multi-party key agreement. In: Kim, K.-c., Matsumoto, T. (eds.) ASIACRYPT 1996. LNCS, vol. 1163, pp. 36–49. Springer, Heidelberg (1996)
10. Smart, N.: Identity-based authenticated key agreement protocol based on weil pairing. Electronics Letters 38(13), 630–632 (2002)
11. Xu, J., Zhu, W.T., Feng, D.G.: An efficient mutual authentication and key agreement protocol preserving user anonymity in mobile networks. Computer Communications 34(3), 319–325 (2011)
12. Zhu, R.W., Yang, G., Wong, D.S.: An efficient identity-based key exchange protocol with kgs forward secrecy for low-power devices. Theoretical Computer Science 378(2), 198–207 (2007)

Information Theoretical Analysis
of Side-Channel Attack

Hiroaki Mizuno, Keisuke Iwai, Hidema Tanaka, and Takakazu Kurokawa

Department of Computer Science, National Defense Academy of Japan,
Hashirimizu 1-10-20, Yokosuka, Kanagawa, Japan
{em51045,iwai,hidema,kuro}@nda.ac.jp

Abstract. This paper presents a proposal of a new information-the-oretical evaluation method for the side-channel resistance. This method provides some benefits: (1) It provides a rationale for evaluation. (2) Moreover, it enables numerical execution of mutual evaluation among countermeasures of several kinds. In an evaluation of side-channel resistance, the feasibility of attack, such as the number of observations or experimental time for revealing secrets, is discussed. In conventional methods, these numbers are examined experimentally using actual attacks. Therefore such experimental methods present several problems: (1) the rationale of the numbers used in evaluation is poor; (2) executing mutual evaluation is difficult; and (3) some experimental constraints exist such as time, cost, and equipment specifications. Our proposed method regards side-channel attack as a communication channel model. Therefore, this method estimates its channel capacity as the upper bound of the amount of leakage information. As described herein, we apply this approach to correlation power analysis against implementations of stream cipher Enocoro-128 v2 and underscore its effectiveness.

Keywords: Side-Channel Attack, Correlation power analysis, Amount of information, Enocoro-128 v2.

1 Introduction

A side-channel attack (SCA) reveals secret information through the observation of physical phenomena that a cipher module causes in device execution. At such times, an attacker exploits physical phenomena such as power consumption and electromagnetic emanation, in addition to phenomena arising from characteristics such as running time and cache memory. Here, the attacker observes physical phenomena. The observed data include various errors and noise. Therefore, the attacker must collect numerous observed data and perform proper statistical processing for convergence of the error or noise. In contrast to the attacker, a designer of a cipher module takes countermeasures so that some characteristics do not appear.

Relating to SCA, many papers have reported various applied attacks and countermeasures. However, proper indexes for evaluation do not exist. Such indexes should have rationale, be unified and be easy to use. For the evaluation of

A. Bagchi and I. Ray (Eds.): ICISS 2013, LNCS 8303, pp. 255–269, 2013.

SCA, a numerical index is helpful for general users to understand the security of implementations or effectiveness of countermeasures. As an example of such indexes, some studies have used the number of observed data ($\#_{obs}$) necessary for successful attacks. Similarly, $\#$ of plain texts, the required time for observation and others were also used. Some studies present evaluations such as "The advantage of implementation $\mathcal{Z}$ is confirmed from comparison of index $\mathcal{X}$ calculated using $\mathcal{Y}$ observed data in actual attacks" [1–3]. For example, the CRYPTREC project [4] portrays a policy. In the policy, the results of actual power analysis (PA) using 100,000 power consumption waveforms are needed. Such implementation is evaluated as "secure" if $\#_{obs}$ for successful attacks is greater than 100,000. They cannot compare the effectiveness of each implementation if there are some "secure" implementations. They conclude that their effectiveness is equivalent.

These conventional evaluations are intuitive and heuristic metrics. Moreover, such evaluation presents some problems. First, the necessary $\#_{obs}$ for a successful attack is confirmed experimentally only by results of actual attacks. Second, such results of actual attacks are known to depend on the internal state, secret key, other inputs, and implementation characteristics. Therefore, evaluation using such index or metrics is difficult to use as common (see Sect.6.3.). Finally, effects can arise from experimental constraints such as the execution time or specifications of experimental equipment. For example, mutual evaluation among several kinds of countermeasures might require high costs. That is true because the relative predominance cannot be judged until an attack against either of the implementations succeeds.

We propose an information-theoretical index and evaluation method. In our method, the amount of information related to secret information received from observed data is defined as the amount of leakage information. Moreover, this proposed method incorporates SCA as a communication channel model. Thereby, the upper bound of the amount of leakage information can be estimated as the channel capacity. In contrast to conventional and experimental methods, our proposed method estimates the amount of leakage information using the Shannon–Hartley theorem.

In a related work, Standaert et al. proposed an information-theoretical framework unifying various theory and practice related to SCA [5]. The achievements of their framework are similar to those of our proposed method in several ways: (1) information-theoretical evaluation with rationale and (2) the fair and adaptive evaluation of some adversary, their attack methods, and implementations. Their framework uses Shannon conditional entropy and mutual information as information-theoretic metrics for evaluation. Various studies have used similar metrics [6, 7]. The amount of information that our method uses is derived as the channel capacity in analog continuous communication channel. Therefore, we discuss not only the Signal-to-Noise Ratio but also the definition of bandwidth in SCA observations. Tanaka also proposes an evaluation method for Tempest attack from a similar viewpoint [8]. Additionally, the definitions of "signal" and "noise" in our method differ from those used in previous works.

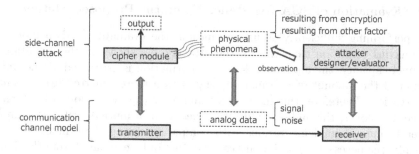

Fig. 1. Communication Channel Model and SCA

As described in this paper, we perform Correlation Power Analysis [9] against stream cipher Enocoro-128 v2 [10], for the evaluation of examples. Enocoro is adopted as an international standard for lightweight cryptography by ISO/IEC. It is expected to be useful in compact devices. The establishment of the standard for lightweight cryptography has progressed recently. Therefore, evaluation related to such cryptography is expected to become increasingly important. We use Enocoro for the evaluation examples described herein.

2 Overview of Our Proposed Method

2.1 Communication Channel Model and Side-Channel Attack

Figure 1 presents an overview of the proposed method. In this model, the transmitter sets inputs into a cipher module and produces some physical phenomena. Then the receiver observes it. In a communication channel model, the receiver must distinguish signal from noise. On the other hand, an attacker takes notice of a certain related process to infer secret information in the cipher module. The attacker must distinguish between physical phenomena resulting from such process and those resulting from other factors. Therefore, we regard the transmitter, receiver, "signal" and "noise", respectively, as the cipher module, attacker, the physical phenomena caused by a certain process of which the attacker takes notice in the cipher module and physical phenomena caused by other factors. Hereinafter, we describe these physical phenomena as "signal" and "noise" in SCA. We assume additive white Gaussian noise.

In the communication channel model, the channel capacity denotes communication efficiency, which is defined when the transmitter and receiver exist. This is calculable using "signal" and "noise" based on the Shannon–Hartley theorem. We define the channel capacity calculated from the "signal" and "noise" in SCA as the amount of leakage information related to a secret that the receiver can infer. We can use the amount of leakage information for the evaluation of SCA resistance as a numerical index.

2.2   Evaluation of SCA Resistance Using the Proposed Method

For performing sufficiently secure evaluation, the evaluator needs a more advantageous condition than that of the attacker. As shown in the definition of channel capacity, the amount of leakage information is estimated as the upper bound of the amount of information related to a secret inferred from a single observation. Therefore, this index is adequate for the evaluation of SCA resistance. Moreover, this index enables the execution of mutual evaluation among several kinds of implementations with comparison using these indexes. Additionally, the necessary $\#_{obs}$ for successful SCA can be estimated from this index (See Sect. 6.4.).

3   Preliminaries

3.1   Side-Channel Attack

In the first step, the attacker chooses the attack target in the cipher module, such as the register, memory, and selector. The attack target must affect physical phenomena according to internal processing. Moreover, the states or values of the attack target must be predictable from known information, with the assumption of secrets such as key, internal state, and a specific condition. Next, the attacker selects a statistical processing method and an assumption model. This model must indicate some kind of relation between the attack target and physical phenomena. Models of two kinds are used as the premise for power consumption, the Hamming distance model and the Hamming wait model. This paper presents an example evaluation of Correlation Power Analysis (CPA) [9] and employs a Hamming distance model. In this evaluation, we specifically examine a register as an attack target and denote it as the "attack register".

Hamming Distance Model. In this model, we specifically examine the power consumption which results from a standard CMOS device, such as bit-flip in the attack register at a certain process. A linear relation exists between # of action of bit-flip and power consumption. Therefore, the amount of power consumption can be estimated from the value of the Hamming distance (HD) of the attack register.

Correlation Power Analysis. There may appear a correlation between a specific internal state and observed data. In CPA, the attacker exploits such characteristics to infer secret information. The outline of the CPA is the following. We assume that the secret information is fixed.

Step 1. Inside the cipher circuit, find an attack register that is operable or knowable in a specific timing. The registers are expected to enable the determination of secret information. The value of the register is expected to be predictable after specific internal processing. We devote attention to the value of HD of attack register with the processing.

Table 1. Variables used in calculation of the correlation coefficient

n	Total number of observations
t	Time ($t_1 \leqq t \leqq t_2$)
i	i-th observation($1 \leqq i \leqq n$)
j	j-th candidate for the secret key
	Letting J be the total number of assumption, then j is in the range ($1 \leqq j \leqq J$)
$h_{i,j}$	Hamming distance of attack register ($0 \leqq h_{i,j} \leqq \log_2 J$)
$W_{i,t}$	Power consumption at time t in i-th observed data

Step 2. For appropriate statistical processing, the attacker collects observed data so that the transition of the attack register becomes uniform over all observed data. Therefore, the attack register is operated so that the value is distributed uniformly. In actual observation, it is difficult to recognize the transition of the attack register accurately, so it is observed in a certain time difference ($t_1 \sim t_2$).

Step 3. Make an assumption about secrets, and calculate HD of the attack register with the specific process. This HD is regarded as an index of the predictive power consumption. Calculate the correlate coefficient value between HD and the observed data.

Step 4. Perform Step 2 and 3 for all candidates of secrets, and compare all correlation coefficient values. Finally, the secret can be determined as the value of candidate for which the correlation is the strongest.

At calculation of the correlate coefficient, the Pearson product–moment correlation coefficient is used,

$$\rho_{t,j} = \frac{\sum_{i=1}^{n}(h_{i,j} - \overline{h_j})(W_{i,t} - \overline{W_t})}{\sqrt{\sum_{i=1}^{n}(h_{i,j} - \overline{h_j})^2}\sqrt{\sum_{i=1}^{n}(W_{i,t} - \overline{W_t})^2}}, \tag{1}$$

where $-1 \leq \rho_{t,j} \leq 1$. Details of variables in Eq. (1) are presented in Table 1. $\overline{h_j}$ and $\overline{W_t}$ respectively denote the mean values of $h_{i,j}$ and $W_{i,t}$,

$$\overline{W_t} = \frac{1}{n}\sum_{i=1}^{n} W_{i,t} \qquad \overline{h_j} = \frac{1}{n}\sum_{i=1}^{n} h_{i,j}. \tag{2}$$

The value of $\rho_{t,j}$ takes a peak if the prediction related to the secret key is true.

3.2 Channel Capacity

In a continuous channel and additive white Gaussian noise model, the channel capacity is calculated using the Shannon–Hartley theorem [11] as follows.

$$C = B \log_2 \left(1 + \frac{S}{N}\right) \text{ [bit/s]} \tag{3}$$

Therein, C, B, S, and N respectively denote the channel capacity [bps], bandwidth [Hz], power of signal, and noise. In this theorem, the transmission is performed at the Nyquist rate $2B$ [Hz]. The observed data are discrete values on evaluation points according to the sampling rate of experimental equipment. Therefore, Eq. (3) is rewritten as the channel capacity per sample, as follows.

$$C = \frac{1}{2} \log_2 \left(1 + \frac{S}{N}\right) \text{ [bit/sample]} \tag{4}$$

4   Proposed Evaluation Method with the Amount of Leakage Information

We discuss the evaluation of CPA resistance employing a Hamming Distance model from an evaluator's perspective. As shown in Sect. 2.2, the evaluator performs methods with more beneficial conditions than those of the attacker. An evaluator can set any value as a secret key and treat it as known information.

4.1   Estimation of the Amount of Leakage Information

The values of HD of attack register and power consumption show a linear relation. When applying this model to a communication channel model (Fig. 1), the information related to HD is regarded as a signal at a transmitter. The transmitter attempts to send information that "The value of HD of attack register is p-bit". The observed power consumption is regarded as received information containing noise at the receiver. A receiver attempts to identify "What is the value of HD of attack register?". From Eq. (4), the amount of leakage information per observation can be rewritten as follows.

$$C = \log_2 \sqrt{\frac{N + S}{N}} \text{ [bit/sample]} \tag{5}$$

The description above indicates a communication channel that can distinguish $\sqrt{(N + S)/N}$ kinds of signal by a single observation. Generally, N and S are defined as the average power. In our evaluation, we follow the definition of the Shannon–Hartley theorem and treat N and S as the variance of observed voltage values.

All observed data are regarded as some signal containing noise. Therefore, we define $N+S$ as the variance of voltage value of all observed data. We treat the factor which disturbs our ability to distinguish it as noise: we define N as the variance of voltage value for each value of HD. Consequently, Eq. (4) can be rewritten as follows.

$$I_L = \frac{1}{2} \log_2 \frac{\frac{1}{n} \sum_{i=1}^{n} (V_i - \overline{V})^2}{\frac{1}{n} \sum_{p=0}^{q} (\sum_{k=1}^{m^p} (V_k^p - \overline{V^p})^2)} \text{ [bit/sample]} \tag{6}$$

Table 2. Variables in Equation (6)

n	Total number of observations
i	i-th observation($1 \leqq i \leqq n$)
V_i	Voltage value at the i-th observation
$\overline{V}$	Mean value of V_i
q	Bit-width of the attack register
p	Value of HD of the attack register ($0 \leqq p \leqq q$)
m^p	Total observations for HD=p ($\sum_{p=0}^{q} m^p = n$)
k	k-th observation for HD=p ($1 \leqq k \leqq m^p$)
V_k^p	Voltage value at the k-th observation for HD=p
$\overline{V^p}$	Mean value of V_k^p

Details of variables in Eq. (6) are presented in Table 2. In the evaluation, if I_L is estimated as small value, then the evaluator can see such implementation as strong against the attack. Actual observations are performed in a certain time difference ($t_1 \leq t \leq t_2$), so that I_L is estimated for each sampling point. The proposed method adopts the point that derives the largest I_L. This way holds the definition of channel capacity.

From the viewpoint of a designer, a maximum value of I_L is needed. Therefore, we assume that all variables also including a secret key are operable and knowable to obtain the largest value of I_L. We perform the following evaluation scheme from the standpoint of a designer.

Step 1. Fix the value of a secret such as a key.
Step 2. Operate the attack register uniformly at random. Then observe power consumption from a voltage value.
Step 3. Calculate $\overline{V}$ from the result of Step 2.
Step 4. Calculate $\overline{V^p}$ from the result of Step 2 for each p.
Step 5. Calculate the amount of leakage information I_L from Eq. (6).

Step 2 requires numerous observed data. We mention the required $\#_{obs}$ in Sect.6.

4.2   Relation between the Proposed Method and SCA Resistance

For successful SCA, the attacker must distinguish signals from all observed data. When we discuss SCA resistance, we consider factors that enable attackers to distinguish a "signal" clearly from all observed data. For example, Fig. 2 shows our assumption related to the strength of SCA resistance presuming the use of a Hamming distance model. Therein, N^p is N in the case of HD=p and $N^p = \frac{1}{m^p} \sum_{k=1}^{m^p} (V_k^p - \overline{V^p})^2$. In Fig. 2, the left panel shows the power consumption distribution of an implementation, which makes it easy to distinguish each "signal" from all observed data. The right one shows that it is difficult to distinguish them. We can ascertain two facts that influence SCA resistance. First, the slope of power consumption distribution relates to the strength of SCA resistance of the implementation. It is decided only by $S+N$. Therefore, the value of $S+N$ affects the SCA resistance: the smaller $S+N$ improves SCA resistance.

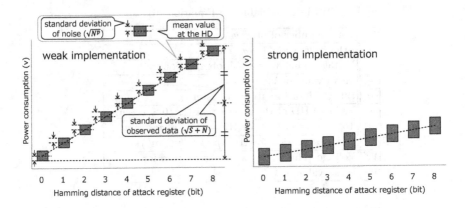

Fig. 2. Assumption related to the Hamming distance model (Presuming 8-bit attack register)

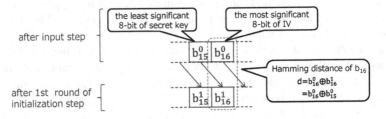

Fig. 3. Attack target of CPA against Enocoro-128 v2

Second, the more widely the "noise" is distributed (range of noise), the more difficult it is to distinguish. That is, greater N improves the SCA resistance. Considering the two facts above, decreasing the "signal" and increasing the "noise" are effective as SCA resistance. Some papers note only that increasing "noise" is effective to improve SCA resistance [5]. For our approach, we assume that not only the strength of "noise" but also that of a "signal" is important. In Sect. 5.3, we again discuss our assumption using a concrete observation.

5   Example Experimentation and Evaluation

5.1   Correlation Power Analysis against Enocoro-128 v2

This section explains a CPA against Enocoro [10] based on an attack method shown in [2]. This attack treats IV, which is a kind of input, as known information for the attacker. The attacker controls the value of IV in each boot of the cipher module. The attack target is shown in Fig. 3. This attack selects a buffer b_{16} as the attack register. During the setup phase of Enocoro, the least significant 8-bit of secret key is set to b_{15}. The most significant 8-bit of IV is set to b_{16}. Subsequently, the value of b_{16} transits to the value of b_{15} at the first round of

Table 3. Environment of Measurement

Oscilloscope	Tektronix TDS 2024B
Sampling rate	2Giga samples per second
measuring probe	Coaxial cable (50Ω)
Clock of cipher module	2 MHz

Table 4. Example implementation of Enocoro-128 v2

Implementation	Specification
S_4-table	Implementation with a simple circuit using a small substitution table
S_8-table	Implementation with a circuit using a big substitution table. S_8-table might entail more weakness against PA than S_4-table.
S_4-table-RSL	Implementation with a circuit using small substitution table which is taken countermeasure against PA (We apply Random Switching Logic[14] method, a kind of gate level countermeasure.) It is expected that S_4-table-RSL has more resistance than S_4-table.

the initialization phase. In this attack, the attacker makes the assumption of $\widetilde{b_{15}^0}$, the least significant 8-bit of the secret key. Then, the attacker calculates the predictive Hamming distance $\widetilde{d}$ of b_{16} at the first transition from $\widetilde{b_{15}^0}$ and b_{16}^0.

$$\widetilde{d} = \widetilde{b_{16}^1} \oplus b_{16}^0 = \widetilde{b_{15}^0} \oplus b_{16}^0 \text{ [bit]} \tag{7}$$

Moreover, the attacker calculates the correlation coefficient between $\widetilde{d}$ and observed data.

5.2 Experimental Environment

We implemented Enocoro into SASEBO-GII [12], side-channel attack standard evaluation board, and performed CPA. The environment used for measurements is presented in Table 3. For collecting the pairs of IV and the power consumption waveform, we used SEASON [13], which is software used for SCA. We measured the power consumption with 30 sampling points ($1 \leq t \leq 30$). As an attack target, three implementations of Enocoro were prepared as shown in Table 4. In this paper, 0x55 is used as the secret key as an example. Use of the secret key and its effects on evaluation results are mentioned in Sect. 6.1. Then we choose inputs uniformly random, except the secret key.

5.3 Estimation Using the Proposed Method

Using Eq.(6), we can calculate the amount of leakage information I_L from the observed data. In this evaluation, $N + S$ is the variance of all observed data and N is the variance of observed data for each value of HD. The evaluator knows the secret information. Table 5 shows the estimation result of I_L and variances used for its calculation as an example (secret key: 0x55). We show detailed analyses in Sect. 6.1 for the use of $\#_{obs}$ for calculating each I_L.

Table 5. Calculation result for I_L (secretkey: 0x55)

Implementation	I_L [bit/sample]	$N+S$ [v^2]	N [v^2]	$(N+S)-N$ [v^2]	Using $\#_{obs}$ [sample]
S_4-table	0.00225	9.926	9.895	0.031	25,000
S_8-table	0.00566	11.31	11.23	0.08	20,000
S_4-table-RSL	0.000335	11.41	11.40	0.01	55,000

As shown in Table 5, we can estimate I_L of each implementation as clearly comparable indexes. We can compare their CPA resistances numerically. Hereinafter, I_{S4}, I_{S8} and I_{S4R} respectively denote I_L of S_4-table, S_8-table and S_4-table-RSL. I_{S8} is about 2 times of I_{S4}. S_8-table uses big substitution and is weak against SCA. Therefore, I_{S8} is the largest. In contrast, I_{S4R} is about 1/7th of I_{S4}. S_4-table-RSL shows implementation with countermeasures against SCA. It works effectively; therefore, I_{S4R} is the smallest. Consequently, it can be concluded that S_4-table-RSL has the strongest SCA resistance and that the S_8-table has the least SCA resistance among them.

When attention is devoted to the variances $N+S$, N and $(N+S)-N$ in Table 5, then we can analyze the effects of "signal" and "noise". $(N+S)-N$ can be considered as a factor caused by "signal". The variances of S_8-table and S_4-table-RSL are large in comparison with that of S_4-table because of their respective circuit sizes. The values of $N+S$ and N of S_8-table are about 1.14 times as large as those of S_4-table, whereas the value of $(N+S)-N$ is about 2.6 times. Therefore, it is concluded the "signal" is a main factor that increases I_{S8}. The values of $N+S$ and N of S_4-table-RSL are about 1.15 times as high as those of S_4-table, although the value of $(N+S)-N$ is about one third. Therefore, it is concluded that the "signal" factor of S_4-table-RSL is suppressed and that I_{S4R} is the smallest. We obtained similar results even if the other value excluding 0x55 is used as the secret key. Therefore, we can confirm the effect of a "signal" as described in Sect. 4.2 and can conclude that our assumption is valid.

6   Discussion

6.1   Convergence and Accuracy of the Amount of Leakage Information

There are two matters of concern related to the validation of evaluation, which are the convergence of I_L and the effects of input such as the secret key.

The convergence of I_L affects the accuracy of its estimation. Hereinafter, we present discussion of the estimation scheme of the $\#_{obs}$ required to converge I_L, that is the column "Using $\#_{obs}$" in Table 5. The implementation method affects the convergence of I_L. We discuss the range of error of I_L using s observed data. We specifically examine the rate of change of I_L resulting from increase of $\#_{obs}$ for use. Let r be the rate of change of I_L as follows.

$$r = \frac{I_L(s) - I_L(s - \delta_s)}{I_L(s)} \times 100 \ [\%]. \qquad (8)$$

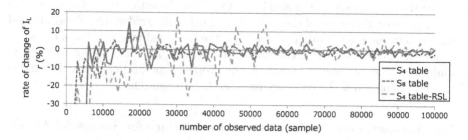

Fig. 4. Rate of change of I_L resulting from increase by 1,000 observed data (secret key: 0x55)

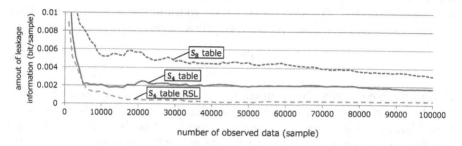

Fig. 5. Convergence of the leakage information (secret key: 0x55)

Therein, $I_L(x)$ means I_L estimated with x observed data. In addition, δ_s represents the rate of increase of observed data. Any integer value can be set as $(1 \leqq \delta_s)$. The value of r is estimated every δ_s observed data. Therefore, small δ_s provides a frequent check of r and requires a huge computational cost. The value of r indicates that the error range of I_L with s observed data is less than r. If the evaluator defines permissible error of I_L as $\pm e$ [%], then the evaluator must increase the $\#_{obs}$ until the value of r is suppressed within error range $\pm e$ [%]. At this time, the evaluator can conclude the value of I_L.

In the example evaluation shown in Sect. 5, we define e and δ_s as 10% and 1,000 samples respectively. Fig. 4 shows the relation of r and s. The r of I_{S4}, I_{S8}, and I_{S4R} are suppressed within $\pm 10\%$ when s are 25,000, 20,000, and 55,000 samples or more, respectively. With each value of s, we can judge their convergence and stop the observation. Fig. 5 shows the relation between I_L and $\#_{obs}$. From this figure, we can confirm that each I_L converges with s certainly. Our method is reliable.

In the scheme presented above, it is our future work to derive a method of determining the appropriate permissible error e. In Sect. 5, we choose e as 10% because we expected that such error will not affect mutual evaluation seriously. The validity of a 10% permissible error can be judged from the result of mutual evaluation. However, evaluation among implementations for which the effectiveness is quite high will require high accuracy and less permissible error. In such a case, we need more $\#_{obs}$ for convergence.

For stable evaluation, it is also important that the estimation of each I_L does not depend on the value of the secret key or other internal states. We confirmed that also in the case of other secret keys, the proposed method shows the same results as those above with the same convergence. The other inputs are set as uniformly random values. Therefore, the proposed method can provide reliable mutual evaluation if the convergence of each I_L is guaranteed.

6.2   Estimation of the Number of Observations for Successful Attack

The I_L value is estimated as the amount of leakage information concerning attack target (secret information) from a single observation. Therefore, we can estimate the necessary $\#_{obs}$ to reveal all bits of the attack register, which is the required $\#_{obs}$ for a successful attack. Let q be the bit-width of the attack register. Then the required $\#_{obs}$ for successful attack is estimated as

$$M = \left\lfloor \frac{q}{I} \right\rfloor \text{ [sample].} \tag{9}$$

Hereinafter, we describe the required $\#_{obs}$ for successful CPA against S_4-table, S_8-table and S_4-table-RSL respectively as M_{S4}, M_{S8} and M_{S4R}. In this evaluation, M_{S4}, M_{S8} and M_{S4R} are estimated respectively as about 4,000, 2,000 and 24,000 samples from Eq. (9). These estimations are the necessary $\#_{obs}$ for ideal successful CPA.

6.3   Comparison of the Proposed Method with Conventional Method

In conventional evaluation, actual attacks are performed and the SCA resistance is checked experimentally. Fig. 6~8 shows the actual results of CPA with three secret keys against implementations shown in Sect. 5.2, i.e, relations between $\#_{obs}$ used for attack and number of true bit in the assumed secret key. In this CPA, we prepared 100,000 observed data.

Based on these results, using conventional estimation method, M_{S8} is estimated as around 10,000 for any secret key. M_{S4R} is estimated as 45,000–80,000, which depends on the secret key. M_{S4} is estimated as 20,000–30,000 in the case of secret keys of 0x55 and 0xf0. However, the true key cannot be determined in the case of a secret key 0x00 within 100,000 observed data; M_{S4} for secret key 0x00 cannot be determined. Therefore, the necessary $\#_{obs}$ for determining all of the 8-bit attack register depends on the value of a secret key or other internal state. Conventional evaluation methods need more attack results to confirm the evaluation. Alternatively, the results might be improved by changing experimental environment. Consequently, with the conventional method, it can be mentioned experimentally that S_4-table-RSL has the strongest SCA resistance and S_8-table has the least among the three implementations. However, S_4-table might have more resistance than S_4-table-RSL for some secret key. Therefore these conclusions are unreliable.

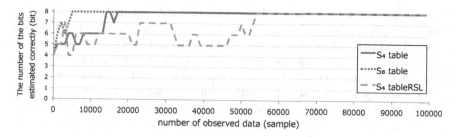

Fig. 6. Result of CPA (secret key: 0x55)

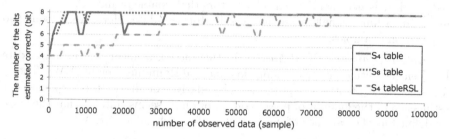

Fig. 7. Result of CPA (secret key: 0xf0)

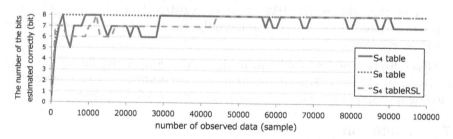

Fig. 8. Result of CPA (secret key: 0x00)

In comparison with the conventional method, the proposed method is advantageous in terms of rationale and low-cost experimentation. Moreover, the proposed method facilitates mutual evaluation among several implementations or countermeasures. Then, the required $\#_{obs}$ for reliable numerical evaluation can be estimated. Additionally, the proposed method can verify the respective effects of "signal" and "noise".

6.4   Definitions of Signal and Noise

For adequate evaluation using the proposed method, "signal" and "noise" should be defined. In this paper, noise is defined as the variance of power consumption for each value of HD of attack register. Therefore, the amount of leakage information is estimated as a positive value. In actual observations, the range of noise depends on the value of HD. In an ideal situation, the entire range of noise is the same value. Therefore, if we can determine the value of noise as HD=0, we can determine noise for any value of HD. Letting basic noise be the observed value at HD=0 and letting the basic noise model be the evaluation method using basic noise, then if we can apply a basic noise model, we will expect to produce a more definite evaluation. However, if we use basic noise model for actual evaluation, then it might generate a negative evaluation value against the definition of information theory. Therefore, we calculate noise as the variance of each value of HD for these reasons. The analysis of evaluation method using the basic noise model is a subject of our future work.

For application to other SCA or assumption model, signal and noise should be redefined. It is necessary to consider factors that enable or disturb the attacker in distinguishing signals from the overall observed data. Here, we present two application examples.

Example 1 (Hamming Wait Model). In this model, a linear relationship exists between the actual power consumption and the Hamming weight (HW). Therefore the value of attack register is particularly examined. It is exploited for estimation of the amount of power consumption. It seems suitable that the noise be defined as the variance of power voltage for each value of HW.

Example 2 (Differential Power Analysis (DPA)). On DPA, the behavior of a one-bit attack register is specifically examined. There are two kinds of signal caused by the value of HD/HW of attack register (1 or 0). Therefore if the variance of basic noise converges sufficiently, the use of the basic noise alone might be efficient.

Generalization of the definitions of signal and noise is our future work. By achievement of these adequate definitions, mutual evaluation among several implementations, countermeasures, attacks and others can be realized.

7   Conclusion

We propose a new evaluation method of SCA that enables execution of a theoretical mutual evaluation. We regard SCA as channel communication model and define the amount of leakage information related to secret information by application of the Shannon–Hartley theorem. Moreover, for the application of proposed method to CPA, we define the "signal" and "noise" and show the estimation method of leakage information. Then we confirmed the effectiveness of the proposed method by example evaluation. When the evaluation method is performed to an implementation that is completely secure against CPA, then the value of I_L will converge to 0. Therefore, it can be said that the value of I_L of implementation with ideal countermeasures equals 0.

Our future works include the generalization of the definition of "signal" and "noise" and the clarification of the relation between the accuracy of I_L and evaluation targets. These problems are expected to be solved by the application of our method to various evaluation targets. By applying the proposed method to various attacks, ciphers and countermeasures, the generalization and unification of mutual evaluation will become possible.

Acknowledgements. This work was supported by JSPS KAKENHI Grant Number 24560791 (Grant-in-Aid for Scientific Research C).

References

1. Research Center for Information Security: Power Analysis Attacks on SASEBO. Technical report, National Institute of Advanced Industrial Science and Technology (2010),
   http://www.morita-tech.co.jp/SASEBO/pdf/SASEBO_PA_Report_English.pdf
2. Mikami, S., Watanabe, D.: Correlation power analysis against stream cipher enocoro-128 v2. Technical Report of IEICE. ISEC 111, 1–6 (2011)
3. Mikami, S., Yoshida, H., Watanabe, D., Sakiyama, K.: A correlation power analysis countermeasure for stream cipher enocoro-128 v2 using threshold implementation. In: Proceedings of the 2012 Symposium on Cryptography and Information Security, SCIS 2012, pp. 2C2-1 (2012)
4. Cryptography Research and Evaluation Committees: CRYPTREC Report 2011, Report of the Cryptographic Module Committee (2011),
   http://www.cryptrec.go.jp/report/c11_mod_web_v1.pdf
5. Standaert, F.-X., Malkin, T.G., Yung, M.: A unified framework for the analysis of side-channel key recovery attacks. In: Joux, A. (ed.) EUROCRYPT 2009. LNCS, vol. 5479, pp. 443–461. Springer, Heidelberg (2009)
6. Köpf, B., Basin, D.: An information-theoretic model for adaptive side-channel attacks. In: Proceedings of the 14th ACM Conference on Computer and Communications Security, CCS 2007, pp. 286–296. ACM, New York (2007)
7. Gierlichs, B., Batina, L., Tuyls, P., Preneel, B.: Mutual information analysis. In: Oswald, E., Rohatgi, P. (eds.) CHES 2008. LNCS, vol. 5154, pp. 426–442. Springer, Heidelberg (2008)
8. Tanaka, H.: Evaluation of information leakage via electromagnetic emanation and effectiveness of tempest. IEICE Transactions on Information and Systems 91, 1439–1446 (2008)
9. Brier, E., Clavier, C., Olivier, F.: Correlation power analysis with a leakage model. In: Joye, M., Quisquater, J.-J. (eds.) CHES 2004. LNCS, vol. 3156, pp. 16–29. Springer, Heidelberg (2004)
10. Hitachi, Ltd.: Stream cipher Enocoro (2010),
    http://www.hitachi.com/rd/yrl/crypto/enocoro/index.html
11. Shannon, C.E.: A mathematical theory of communication. SIGMOBILE Mob. Comput. Commun. Rev. 5, 3–55 (2001)
12. Research Center for Information Security: Side-channel Attack Standard Evaluation Board SASEBO-GII (2009),
    http://www.morita-tech.co.jp/SASEBO/ja/board/sasebo-g2.html
13. Iwai, K., Kurokawa, T.: An implementation of a software platform for evaluation of side channel attacks. The IEICE Transactions on Information and Systems (Japanese edition) 95, 1242–1254 (2012)
14. Suzuki, D., Saeki, M., Ichikawa, T.: Random switching logic: A new countermeasure against dpa and second-order dpa at the logic level. IEICE Transactions 90-A, 160–168 (2007)

Efficient Multi-bit Image Steganography
in Spatial Domain

Imon Mukherjee[1] and Goutam Paul[2]

[1] Dept. of Computer Science & Engineering,
St. Thomas' College of Engineering & Technology, Kolkata 700 023, India
mukherjee.imon@gmail.com
[2] R. C. Bose Centre for Cryptology and Security,
Indian Statistical Institute, Kolkata 700 108, India
goutam.paul@isical.ac.in

Abstract. An LSB-based image steganography algorithm hides information in the least significant bits of the pixel intensities of a cover image. But such a method has a very low embedding capacity compared to a multi-bit embedding scheme. The latter is very challenging in the sense that the possibility of a large change in the pixel value of the cover image becomes very high and only a few algorithms based on multi-bit embedding exist in the literature. In this paper, we improve the multi-bit embedding technique of Park et al. (2005), and achieve higher capacity of embedding (at most 5 bits per pixel) and higher embedding efficiency (at most 5.33) into an image with lower distortion. We compare our performance with existing techniques and support our claim with theoretical and experimental results.

Keywords: Data Hiding, Multi-bit Steganography, Spatial Domain, Steganalysis, Information Security.

1 Introduction

Steganography [1, 2] involves communicating secret data in an appropriate cover media, e.g., image, audio, video and text. It comes under the assumption that if the communication is visible, the point of attack is evident, and thus the goal here is always to conceal the very existence of the embedded data. In most of the steganographic algorithms [1, 6], the least significant bit (LSB) based data hiding have been carried out where the embedding capacity is very low. Only a few of the existing steganographic algorithms are capable of multi-bit embedding in the cover media. Gutub [7] has proposed the pixel indicator based steganographic technique using the two least significant bits of one channel to indicate the existence of data in the other two channels of RGB in an image. The size of the secret data is used here as the selection criteria for the first indicator channel in order to enhance the security by randomly choosing pixel indicator. This algorithm has no need to depend on a separate key to take out the key management overhead. Bailey et al. [8] have proposed an image based

A. Bagchi and I. Ray (Eds.): ICISS 2013, LNCS 8303, pp. 270–284, 2013.

multi-bit steganography technique which increases the capacity of hiding information. Their approach can embed information in at most 4 bits of each pixel. Stego Color Cycle (SCC) technique [9] provides the secured high capacity least significant bit (LSB) image steganography by cycling the hidden data among the Red, Green, and Blue channels. Fridrich et al. [16] have described the grid coloring steganographic technique based on Hamming code, keeping their limits of embedding modification ±1. In another work, Fridrich et al. [17] have estimated the embedding efficiency by measuring the average distance to code rather than considering the covering radius and also they have improved this embedding efficiency using q-ary codes with q matched to the steganographic embedding operation.

In [3–5], high capacity embedding techniques are developed where embedding in each pixel is influenced by its neighbours. Wu et al. [3] have proposed a new scheme to hide more data with outstanding quality of stego image pixel value-differencing (PVD) method. Park et al. [4] have proposed a multi-bit image steganographic technique based on pixel characteristics. Recently, Mandal et al. [5] have proposed a multi-bit steganographic technique that provides more security in data hiding and also better stego image quality than Wu-Tsai's PVD method.

Our proposed algorithm is based on visual characteristics of eight neighbours of the target pixel such that it achieves better capacity and visual quality than [3–5]. We discuss our method in Section 2. A detailed theoretical analysis of our technique with respect to some existing state of the art techniques is explained in Section 3. We also discuss resistance against statistical tests in Section 4 and present detailed experimental results in Section 5. Our method enjoys easy implementation with low computational complexity.

2   Proposed Method

The proposed method refers to a neighbourhood-based multi-bit steganographic technique in spatial domain by altering the pixel value as minimum as possible. Without any loss of generality we discuss the detailed steps for embedding message bits into one pixel $\pi_{x,y}$ of an image. The process has to be repeated for each pixel in row-major order until the entire message is embedded. We consider the 8 neighbours (except at the boundaries) of a pixel $\pi_{x,y}$ as shown below.

$\pi_{x-1,y-1}$	$\pi_{x-1,y}$	$\pi_{x-1,y+1}$
$\pi_{x,y-1}$	$\pi_{x,y}$	$\pi_{x,y+1}$
$\pi_{x+1,y-1}$	$\pi_{x+1,y}$	$\pi_{x+1,y+1}$

Let $\gamma_{x,y}$ denote the intensity of the pixel $\pi_{x,y}$. We first calculate the maximum γ_{max} and the minimum γ_{min} of the (at most eight) neighbouring pixel intensities and their difference $\gamma_{diff} = \gamma_{max} - \gamma_{min}$. Next, the *embedding capacity* of the pixel, i.e., the number of bits to be embedded in the pixel is determined as

$$n = \begin{cases} min(5, \lfloor \log_2 \gamma_{diff} \rfloor - 1), & \text{if } \gamma_{diff} \in [4, 255], \\ 1 & \text{, otherwise.} \end{cases} \quad (1)$$

Based on the value of n, a temporary value $\psi_{x,y}$ is estimated (as shown in step 2 of Algorithm 1). If we replace the pixel intensity value, $\gamma_{x,y}$ with $\psi_{x,y}$, then distortion may be perceptible in the stego image, which violates the basic criteria of image steganography. We target to adjust the distortion without compromising with embedding capacity. If $-2^{n-1} \leq \psi_{x,y} \leq 2^{n-1}$ then we compute a value of q, known as the quality factor, which helps to reduce the distortion by transforming $\psi_{x,y}$ into $\psi'_{x,y}$ which, in turn, is used to determine the new pixel value. On the other hand, if $\psi_{x,y}$ does not belong to the above range, then first we do a normal embedding (by overriding the n least significant bits of the pixel by the n message bits) to obtain a potential stego pixel value $\gamma'_{x,y}$. Next, we complement the $(n+1)$-th bit of $\gamma'_{x,y}$ to obtain $\gamma''_{x,y}$. Then we calculate the difference between $\gamma_{x,y}$ and $\gamma'_{x,y}$ and also the difference between $\gamma_{x,y}$ and $\gamma''_{x,y}$. The value amongst $\gamma'_{x,y}$ and $\gamma''_{x,y}$ that gives the smaller difference is considered as the best choice for replacing the cover pixel to form the stego pixel. We present step-by-step descriptions of our embedding and extraction methods in Algorithm 1 and Algorithm 2 respectively.

Input: Cover pixel intensity $\gamma_{x,y}$ and message bits to be hidden.
Output: Stego pixel intensity $\gamma^*_{x,y}$.

1 Calculate the *embedding capacity* n of the pixel by Equation (1);
2 Calculate a temporary value $\psi_{x,y}$ as follows: $\psi_{x,y} = M - \gamma_{x,y} \bmod 2^{n-1}$, where M is the decimal representation of the selected n bits of the hidden message;
3 **if** $-2^{n-1} \leq \psi_{x,y} \leq 2^{n-1}$ **then**

> $\psi'_{x,y} = \psi_{x,y} + q.2^{n-1}$, where q, the quality factor, is determined as follows: $q =$
>
> $$\begin{cases} 1 & \text{if } -(2^{n-1}+1) \leq \psi_{x,y} < \left\lfloor -\frac{2^{n-1}-1}{2} \right\rfloor, \\ 0 & \text{if } \left\lfloor -\frac{2^{n-1}-1}{2} \right\rfloor \leq \psi_{x,y} < \left\lceil \frac{2^{n-1}-1}{2} \right\rceil, \\ -1 & \text{if } \left\lceil \frac{2^{n-1}-1}{2} \right\rceil \leq \psi_{x,y} < 2^{n-1}. \end{cases}$$
>
> Set $\gamma^*_{x,y} = \gamma_{x,y} + \psi'_{x,y}$;

  end
4 **else**

> Calculate $\varepsilon'_{x,y} = |\gamma_{x,y} - \gamma'_{x,y}|$, $\varepsilon''_{x,y} = |\gamma_{x,y} - \gamma''_{x,y}|$, where
> $\gamma'_{x,y}$ = pixel value after normal embedding, and
> $\gamma''_{x,y}$ = pixel value after complementing the $n+1$-th bit.
> Set
>
> $$\gamma^*_{x,y} = \begin{cases} \gamma''_{x,y} \text{, if } \varepsilon''_{x,y} \leq \varepsilon'_{x,y} \\ \gamma'_{x,y} \text{, otherwise.} \end{cases}$$

  end
5 Replace the value $\gamma_{x,y}$ with $\gamma^*_{x,y}$;

Algorithm 1. Algorithm for embedding multiple bits in a cover pixel

---

Input: Stego pixel intensity $\gamma_{x,y}$.
Output: Message bits hidden in the pixel.

1 Calculate the *embedding capacity* n of the pixel by Equation (1);
2 The hidden message is given by $\gamma_{x,y} \bmod 2^n$;

Algorithm 2. Algorithm for extracting message bits from a stego pixel

2.1 Some Examples

To illustrate the algorithm, we will discuss two examples. For both the examples, consider the same eight neighbouring pixels as follows.

76	110	120
37	$\gamma_{x,y}$	120
100	100	120

We have $\gamma_{max} = 120$, $\gamma_{min} = 37$, $\gamma_{diff} = 120 - 37 = 83$.
Now, $n = \lfloor \log_2 \gamma_{diff} \rfloor - 1 = \lfloor \log_2 83 \rfloor = 5$.

Example 1. Suppose $\gamma_{x,y} = 100$ and the message bits are

$$\left(\ldots \underbrace{1\ 0\ 0\ 1\ 1}0\ 1\ 0\ \ldots \right)_2$$

$$\Downarrow$$

$$(19)_{10}$$

According to the algorithm, $\psi'_{x,y} = \psi_{x,y} = 19 - (100 \bmod 2^{5-1}) = 15$, and the new pixel value would be $\gamma^*_{x,y} = \gamma_{x,y} + \psi'_{x,y} = 100 + 15 = 115$.
To extract the message bits, one computes $115 \bmod 2^5 = 19$.

Example 2. Suppose $\gamma_{x,y} = 96$ and the message bits are

$$\left(\ldots \underbrace{1\ 1\ 1\ 1\ 1}0\ \ldots \right)_2$$

$$\Downarrow$$

$$(31)_{10}$$

Since $\psi_{x,y} = 31 - (96 \bmod 2^{5-1}) = 31 > 2^{5-1}$, we consider the following.

$$\gamma_{x,y} = (96)_{10} = (01100000)_2$$
$$\psi_{x,y} = (31)_{10} = (00011111)_2$$

$$\gamma'_{x,y} = (01111111)_2 = (127)_{10}$$

Complementing the underlined bit, we get $\gamma''_{x,y} = (01011111)_2 = (95)_{10}$. Thus, $\varepsilon'_{x,y} = |96 - 127| = 31$ and $\varepsilon''_{x,y} = |96 - 95| = 1$. Since $\varepsilon''_{x,y} < \varepsilon'_{x,y}$, we have the new pixel value as $\gamma^*_{x,y} = 95$. To extract the message bits, one computes $95 \bmod 2^5 = 31$.

The second example shows that the intensity value has been changed from 96 to 95. Like an LSB based image steganographic embedding technique, the intensity value gets changed (increased/decreased) by ±1. In this case we are able to embed 5 bits in one component of a pixel of the image only by changing the intensity value by one. Since a 24-bit color image contains three components (Red, Green and Blue), so one pixel may contain 15 bits of information (if $n = 5$ for all three components) with minor change of pixel value. This demonstrates that our algorithm tries to embed multi-bit information per pixel without sacrificing the image quality.

3   Theoretical Analysis with Respect to Existing Methods

Here we analyze our algorithms with respect to the other existing methods, e.g., the methods of [4, 17].

3.1   Method [4] and Our Proposed Method

The existing algorithm [4] for multi-bit image steganography has considered four neighbours in order to calculate the number of bits to be embedded into the cover image, whereas we have considered 8 neighbours to calculate the same. As we have considered 2^{n-1} in adjustment rather than considering 2^n, the changed intensity value of the pixel of the cover image will be reduced. It indicates that our proposed algorithm distort the image quality very less compared to the existing algorithm [4]. Figure 1 shows the cover image and the stego image which are alike with respect to visualization.

Theorem 1. *If Δ_{old} and Δ_{new} are the changes in pixel intensities due to algorithm [4] and our method respectively, then their relationship with $\psi_{x,y}$ is given as in Table 1.*

Proof. Let $b_{i..j}$ denote the decimal number corresponding to the bit-string from the ith to the jth least significant bit positions and let n be the length of the message M to be embedded in a pixel, as calculated in Equation (1). Then, any k-bit pixel intensity $\gamma_{x,y}$ can be expressed as

$$\gamma_{x,y} = b_{k-1...(n+1)} \cdot 2^{n+1} + b_n \cdot 2^n + b_{(n-1)...0}.$$

Hence, after Step 2 of Algorithm 1, $\psi_{x,y} = M - b_{(n-1)...0}$ for the old method [4] and $\psi_{x,y} = M - b_{(n-2)...0}$ for our new method. Depending on the range of $\psi_{x,y}$, in Step 3 and 4, the pixel value is changed by a certain amount, say Δ. We consider five different ranges of $\psi_{x,y}$, and for each of these ranges, we have estimated the comparative values of Δ from the old method and that from our proposed method in Table 1. Note that Case 1 and 5 fall under Step 4. For these two cases, Δ of our method can be determined by

$$\Delta_{new} = min\{M - b_{(n-1)..0}, M - b_{(n-1)...0} \pm 2^n\}.$$

$\square$

Table 1. Comparative study of the values of Δ calculated in method [4] and our proposed method

	$\psi_{x,y}$	Δ_{old} of method [4]	Δ_{new} of our method
Case 1	$(-2^n+1,-2^{n-1})$	$(1,2^{n-1})$	$(-2^{n-1}+1,0)$
Case 2	$(-2^{n-1}+1,-2^{n-2})$	$(-2^{n-1}+1,-2^{n-2})$	$(1,2^{n-2})$
Case 3	$(-2^{n-2}+1,2^{n-2}+1)$	$(-2^{n-2}+1,2^{n-2}+1)$	$(-2^{n-2}+1,2^{n-2}+1)$
Case 4	$(2^{n-2},2^{n-1}-1)$	$(2^{n-2},2^{n-1}-1)$	$(-2^{n-2},-1)$
Case 5	$(2^{n-1},2^n-1)$	$(-2^{n-1},-1)$	$(0,2^{n-1}-1)$

For example, an 8-bit pixel intensity is given as

$$\gamma_{x,y} = b_7\ b_6\ b_5\ b_4\ b_3\ b_2\ b_1\ b_0.$$

Assuming $n = 5$, we can write

$$\gamma_{x,y} = b_{7..6} \cdot 2^6 + b_5 \cdot 2^5 + b_{4..0} = b_{7..5} \cdot 2^5 + b_4 \cdot 2^4 + b_{3..0}.$$

Hence, after Step 2, $\psi_{x,y} = M - b_{4..0}$ for the old method [4] and $\psi_{x,y} = M - b_{3..0}$ for our new method. For the 5 different ranges of $\psi_{x,y}$, the comparative values of Δ from the old method and that from our proposed method are estimated as in Table 2.

Table 2. Example of Δ values for $n=5$, in method [4] and our proposed method

	$\psi_{x,y}$	Δ of method [4]	Δ of our method
Case 1	(-31,-16)	(1,16)	(-15,0)
Case 2	(-15,-8)	(-15,-8)	(1,8)
Case 3	(-7,7)	(-7,7)	(-7,7)
Case 4	(8,15)	(8,15)	(-8,-1)
Case 5	(16,31)	(-16,-1)	(0,15)

3.2   Method [17] and Our Proposed Method

According to Fridrich et al. [17], all stego-detecting tools rely on bit flipping. For least significant bit (LSB) flipping, the only possibility is $2i \leftrightarrow 2i+1$ where $i \in [0, 127]$. The probability of changing the intensity to $2i - 1$ from $2i$ after least significant bit (LSB) flipping is strictly zero. In our method, we did not use any bit flipping technique, rather we have considered simple arithmetic operations like addition, subtraction etc. Hence our algorithm can withstand all such detecting tools. The following definition of *embedding efficiency* appears in [17].

Definition 1. *The embedding efficiency is defined as the expected number of message bits embedded per embedding change.*

For a random bit-stream embedding with uniform distribution of 0's and 1's, embedding 1 bit per pixel causes a change in the pixel intensity with probability $\frac{1}{2}$. Hence the embedding efficiency for LSB stenagography is $\frac{1}{1/2} = 2$. Considering the random ternary symbols with uniform distribution, the pixel intensity value may remain unchanged or be modified by ± 1. Hence the probability of change in intensity is $\frac{2}{3}$. Thus, the embedding efficiency can be estimated by $\left(\frac{\log_2 3}{2/3}\right) \approx 2.3774$ which is higher than normal LSB embedding. The authors of [17] have shown that they have achieved maximum embedding efficiency of 4.4 theoretically for ternary ± 1 embedding. We derive the embedding efficiency of our method in the following result.

Theorem 2. *If n is the number of bits to be embedded per pixel of the cover image, then the maximum embedding efficiency of Algorithm 1 can be estimated as $\frac{n \cdot 2^{n-1}}{2^{n-1}-1}$.*

Proof. According to Table 1, the possible values of distortions for embedding n bits is given by $\{1, 2, \ldots, 2^{n-1} - 1\}$. Note that from 2^{n-1} possible $(n-1)$-bit patterns, the all-zero bit pattern is excluded from this set. Assuming uniform distribution, the probability of change in pixel intensity is given by $\frac{2^{n-1}-1}{2^{n-1}}$. Dividing n by this probability, we get the embedding efficiency.   □

For example, say $n = 5$. Hence theoretically, the maximum embedding efficiency can be determined by $\frac{5 \cdot 2^{5-1}}{2^{5-1}-1} \approx 5.33$, which is higher than the value 4.4 obtained by Fridrich et al. [17].

Since in our method, the embedding efficiency changes from pixel to pixel, we introduce the following definition of *average embedding efficiency*.

Definition 2. *The sum of embedding efficiency for each pixel divided by the total number of pixels in an image is defined as the average embedding efficiency over that image.*

Average embedding efficiency for an image with m pixels can be formulated as, $\alpha_{avg} = \frac{1}{m} \sum_{i=1}^{m} \frac{n_i}{p_i}$, where n_i denotes the number of message bits embedded in the i-th pixel and p_i represents the probability of change for the ith pixel.

Corollary 1. *The average embedding capacity per pixel cannot exceed the product of the average embedding efficiency per pixel and the sum of the probability of distortion of each pixel.*

Proof. Let m be the total number of pixels in an image and let n_i be the number of message bits embedded in the i-th pixel. As shown in Theorem 2, the probability of distortion of the i-th pixel is given by $p_i = \frac{2^{n_i-1}-1}{2^{n_i}-1}$ and the embedding efficiency for the i-th pixel is given by $\alpha_i = \frac{n_i}{p_i}$. Hence the average embedding efficiency is given by $\alpha_{avg} = \frac{1}{m} \sum_{i=1}^{m} \alpha_i$ and the average embedding capacity is given by $\beta = \frac{1}{m} \sum_{i=1}^{m} n_i$. We know that,

$$\frac{n_1}{p_1} + \frac{n_2}{p_2} + \frac{n_3}{p_3} + \cdots + \frac{n_m}{p_m} \geq \frac{n_1 + n_2 + n_3 + \cdots + n_m}{p_1 + p_2 + p_3 + \cdots + p_m}$$

$$\Rightarrow \sum_{i=1}^{m} \alpha_i \geq \frac{m \cdot \beta}{\sum_{i=1}^{m} p_i}$$

$$\Rightarrow \beta \leq \frac{1}{m} \sum_{i=1}^{m} \alpha_i \cdot \sum_{i=1}^{m} p_i = \alpha_{avg} \cdot \sum_{i=1}^{m} p_i.$$

□

4   Resistance against Statistical Attacks

Most of the steganalysis techniques [11, 13, 14] can detect the stego information from the least significant bits of the image pixel. Hence our multi-bit steganographic technique can easily withstand these steganalytic attacks. Another very good steganalysis tool is "Stegdetect" [12]. But it works in the frequency domain, e.g., for JPEG images. On the other hand, our method is prescribed for uncompressed images in spatial domain. Below we argue why our method survives some other standard statistical tests for steganalysis.

4.1   Chi-Square Test

The Chi-square test enables us to explain whether the two attributes (or two random variables) are associated or not. We perform the test using the pixel intensities of the cover and the stego images as the two attributes. This evaluation of the proposed algorithm gives a measure whether it can survive statistical steganalysis or not. If the calculated value of χ^2 is less than the standard table value at a certain level of confidence for a given degree of freedom, we conclude that the null hypothesis stands which means that the two attributes are independent, i.e., the proposed algorithm is effective in protecting the steganalysis attack. On the other hand, if the calculated value of χ^2 is greater than the standard table value at a certain level of confidence for a given degree of freedom then the null hypothesis does not hold good, i.e., the proposed algorithm is not effective in order to protect the steganalysis attack. This test operates on a mapping of observations into categories. The degree of similarity is determined using this test. The χ^2 statistic is given as:

$$\chi^2_{K-1} = \sum_{i=1}^{n} \frac{(n_i - n_i^*)^2}{n_i^*}$$

with K-1 degrees of freedom where, n_i^* is the expected frequency in category i after embedding an message and n_i is the measured frequency of occurrence in our random sample. Here the calculated value of χ^2 for 13 degree of freedom at 0.95 level of confidence (shown in Table 3) is much higher than the standard table

Table 3. Test Result of χ^2 Test

	stegoBlue
Chi-Square	8.545*
df	13
Asymp. Sig.	0.806

*: The minimum expected cell frequency is 1.6.

value 5.892. Hence the result of experiment does not support the hypothesis. Thus we can conclude that the proposed algorithm is effective in preventing the steganalysis attack.

4.2 Dual Statistics Method

Fridrich et al. [15] describe one statistical test that partitions an image with a total number of pixels N into N/n disjoint groups of n adjacent pixels. For a group of pixels $G = (\pi_1, \pi_2, \ldots, \pi_n)$, the authors consider a discrimination function $g(\pi_1, \pi_2, \ldots, \pi_n) = \sum_{i=1}^{n-1} |\pi_{i+1} - \pi_i|$.

They define two LSB flipping functions $F_1 = 0 \leftrightarrow 1, 2 \leftrightarrow 3, \ldots, 254 \leftrightarrow 255$ and $F_{-1} = -1 \leftrightarrow 0, 1 \leftrightarrow 2, \ldots, 255 \leftrightarrow 256$, along with an identity flipping function $F_0(\pi) = \pi$. The assignment of flipping to a group of n pixels can be captured by a mask $M = (M(1), M(2), \ldots, M(n))$, where $M(i) \in \{-1, 0, +1\}$ denotes which flipping function is applied to which pixel.

The flipped group of a group $G = (\pi_1, \pi_2, \ldots, \pi_n)$ is given by $F(G) = (F_{M(1)}(\pi_1), F_{M(2)}(\pi_2), \ldots, F_{M(n)}(\pi_n))$. They classify the pixel groups as Regular, Singular, or Unchanged, according as $g(F(G)) > g(G)$, $g(F(G)) < g(G)$, or $g(F(G)) = g(G)$, respectively. The counts of such classified group helps to determine the length of the hidden message.

The authors mention that their method does not work well for images that are noisy, or of low-quality, or over-compressed, or of small size. Moreover, Dumitrescu et al. [13] point out that the above scheme is based on the following two assumptions:

Assumption 1: Suppose X is the set of all pixel pairs (u, v) such that $(v = even \wedge u < v) \vee (v = odd \wedge u > v)$. Suppose Y is the set of all pixel pairs (u, v) such that $(v = even \wedge u > v) \vee (v = odd \wedge u < v)$. The assumption is that statistically we have $|X| = |Y|$.

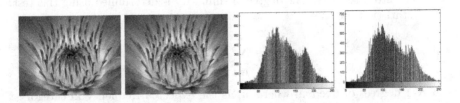

Fig. 1. Sample cover image (leftmost), stego image (right of leftmost), histogram of cover image (left of rightmost) and histogram of its stego version (rightmost)

Assumption 2: The message bits of LSB steganography are randomly scattered in the image space, independent of image features.

Our method does not make any of the above assumptions. Dumitrescu et al. [13] mention that Assumption 1 is valid only for natural images. Our method does not assume any particular type of cover image. It works on cartoons as well. Moreover, the core of our steganographic algorithm is not only limited to LSB based embedding - at most five bits per 8-bit pixel can be embedded in our algorithm. Its depends on the intensity values of its neighbouring pixels and hence it directly violates Assumption 2. So theoretically, our method is not breakable by the dual statistics method.

5 Performance Evaluation through Experimental Results

In this section, we provide experimental evidence towards efficiency of our algorithm and compare our results with state-of-the-art techniques. We have performed the experiments on 250 24-bit color images and 100 8-bit greyscale images of three types, e.g., nature, busy nature and cartoon images (downloaded from [18]), taking different text files containing the story of Sherlock Holmes (downloaded from [19]).

5.1 Embedding Metric and Visual Distortion Analysis

Recall that the Average Embedding Capacity (AEC) is defined as the number of embedded bits per pixel, i.e.,

$$AEC = \frac{Number\ of\ Embedded\ Bits}{Total\ Number\ of\ Pixels}.$$

The imperceptibility of hidden information in a stego image is measured by the image quality in terms of Mean Square Error (MSE) that represents the cumulative squared error between the two images. The mean square error measure is very popular because it can correlate reasonably with subjective visual tests and it is mathematically tractable. The lower the mean square error, the higher is the degree of imperceptibility. Consider a discrete image $A(m, n)$, for $m = 1, 2, 3, \ldots, M$ and $n = 1, 2, 3, \ldots, N$, which is treated as a reference image. Consider a second image $B(m, n)$, of the same spatial dimension as $A(m, n)$, that is to be compared to the reference image. Then mean square error (MSE) is given by

$$MSE = \frac{1}{MN} \sum_{M,N} (A(m, n) - B(m, n))^2$$

and the peak signal-to-noise ratio (PSNR) is given by

$$PSNR = 10 \log_{10} \left(\frac{T^2}{MSE} \right),$$

where T is the maximum intensity value of all pixels.

Table 4 and Table 5 provide the comparative numerical values of the dimension of the images, number of embedded bits (ϑ) per pixel in each component, average embedding capacity (AEC) and mean square error (MSE) analysis for the method in [4] and our proposed method. As we have obtained less MSE value, hence it is obvious to get higher PSNR value. Table 7 shows that the peak signal-to-noise ratio (PSNR) provides a satisfactory result. The average AEC (for 24-bit color images) that we have obtained lies between 7 to 13 bits/pixel which seems to be a satisfactory result. Wu et al. [3] and Mandal et al. [5] show that the average embedding capacity is almost 1.6 bits per pixel and 1.48 bits per pixel respectively in each component of the image. Figure 2 gives the comparative study of our method with existing method [4]. It shows that in each

Table 4. Performance analysis of the algorithm of [4]

Image Name	Dimension	No. of Pixels	Red Component	Green Component	Blue Component
BLOCK.BMP	8×3	24	ϑ=67 AEC_r=2.7917 MSE_r=0.436250	ϑ=67 AEC_g=2.7917 MSE_g=0.604583	ϑ=53 AEC_b=2.2083 MSE_b=0.6975
F1.BMP	210×280	58800	ϑ=144784 AEC_r=2.4623 MSE_r=0.129828	ϑ=151696 AEC_g=2.5799 MSE_g=0.159991	ϑ=152333 AEC_b=2.5907 MSE_b=0.159877
F15.BMP	210×280	58800	ϑ=176710 AEC_r=3.0053 MSE_r=0.192291	ϑ= 171453 AEC_g=2.9159 MSE_g=0.157917	ϑ=204201 AEC_b=3.4728 MSE_b=0.423873
F32.BMP	210×280	58800	ϑ=210766 AEC_r=3.5845 MSE_r=0.327371	ϑ= 201071 AEC_g=3.4196 MSE_g=0.228170	ϑ=233919 AEC_b=3.9782 MSE_b=0.536027
F34.BMP	210×280	58800	ϑ=180096 AEC_r=3.0629 MSE_r=0.237768	ϑ=155073 AEC_g=2.6373 MSE_g=0.221902	ϑ=159462 AEC_b=2.7119 MSE_b=0.213574
F68.BMP	210×280	58800	ϑ=157205 AEC_r=2.6736 MSE_r=0.318571	ϑ=157446 AEC_g=2.6773 MSE_g=0.232771	ϑ=173058 AEC_b=2.9432 MSE_b=0.365554

Table 5. Performance analysis of our proposed Algorithm

Image Name	Dimension	No. of Pixels	Red Component	Green Component	Blue Component
BLOCK.BMP	8×3	24	ϑ=120 AEC_r=5 MSE_r=0.644167	ϑ=96 AEC_g=4 MSE_g=0.539583	ϑ=96 AEC_b=4 MSE_b=0.32250
F1.BMP	210×280	58800	ϑ=172217 AEC_r=2.9289 MSE_r=0.104754	ϑ=179820 AEC_g=3.0582 MSE_g=0.123336	ϑ=179902 AEC_b=3.0694 MSE_b=0.123102
F15.BMP	210×280	58800	ϑ= 203250 AEC_r=3.4566 MSE_r=0.161443	ϑ=199119 AEC_g=3.3864 MSE_g=0.137972	ϑ=227505 AEC_b=3.8691 MSE_b=0.262393
F32.BMP	210×280	58800	ϑ=243810 AEC_r=4.1464 MSE_r=0.231387	ϑ=231324 AEC_g=3.9341 MSE_g=0.187569	ϑ=261211 AEC_b=4.4424 MSE_b=0.322234
F34.BMP	210×280	58800	ϑ=212645 AEC_r=3.6164 MSE_r=0.176045	ϑ=186011 AEC_g=3.1635 MSE_g=0.096013	ϑ=190477 AEC_b=3.2394 MSE_b=0.123315
F68.BMP	210×280	58800	ϑ= 178156 AEC_r=3.0299 MSE_r=0.181113	ϑ=178398 AEC_g=3.0340 MSE_g=0.146939	ϑ=196807 AEC_b=3.3479 MSE_b=0.187123

pixel component, the embedding capacity in our method is higher with respect to same PSNR value than [4]. The average embedding efficiency of our proposed algorithm is experimentally found as 4.3707 which is much higher than 3.9725 obtained using method [4].

5.2   Histogram Analysis

Figure 1 shows a sample cover image and the corresponding stego image. The main purpose to analyze the histogram is to detect significant changes in frequency of appearance of each color component in an image by comparing the cover image with the steganographic image. Figure 1 shows the histogram of an image of a flower in two stages: before stego insertion, after stego insertion. Visibly as well as statistically the histogram of the cover image and that of the stego image are almost similar.

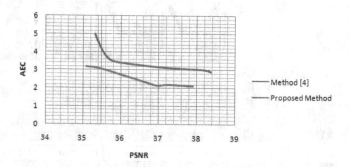

Fig. 2. Graphical representation of *Embedding Capacity* vs *PSNR* of our proposed method and method [4]

5.3   Bitplane Analysis

Grey level image can be decomposed into bitplane images [10]. Each pixel in the image is represented by 8 bits. Therefore the image is decomposed into eight 1-bit planes, ranging from 7th bitplane for MSB to 0th bitplane for LSB. The 7th bitplane contains all the bits in the pixels comprising the image and 0th bitplane contains all the LSB's as shown in Figure 3. Decomposition of original and stego image in to 8 bitplanes is shown in Table 6. Separating a digital image into its bitplanes is useful for analyzing the relative importance played by each bit of the image. It determines the adequacy of numbers of bits used to quantize each pixel. The bitplane of the Lena image and its stego version (provided in Table 6) shows no difference in normal sense.

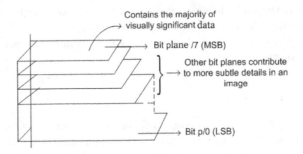

Fig. 3. Bitplane of an image

Table 6. Bitplane analysis of Lena.bmp and sLena.bmp

cover	stego	cover	stego	cover	stego
All bitplanes	All bitplanes	bitplane 7	bitplane 7	bitplane 6	bitplane 6
bitplane 5	bitplane 5	bitplane 4	bitplane 4	bitplane 3	bitplane 3
bitplane 2	bitplane 2	bitplane 1	bitplane 1	bitplane 0	bitplane 0

5.4 StirMark Analysis

In order to establish strength and robustness, the steganographic algorithm should resist some standard attacks like Self Similarities Test, Small Random Distortions Test, Geometric Distortions Test, Median Cut Test etc. There is a special tool called StirMark 4.0 [20] that implements these tests. We have applied StirMark on our cover and stego images and found that the test values for the two types of images are not significantly different. Table 7 summarizes the results of different attacks.

Table 7. StirMark Analysis of Flower.bmp (cover image) and sFlower.bmp (stego image)

	FACTOR	COVER COLOR IMAGE	STEGO COLOR IMAGE
Dimension of Image	N.A.	280 x 210	280 x 210
TestSelf Similarities	1	30.1594 dB	30.1581 dB
TestSelf Similarities	2	45.7146 dB	45.7138 dB
TestSelf Similarities	3	27.7947 dB	27.7947 dB
PSNR	10	38.3476dB	38.3477 dB
TestAddNoise	20	9.60953 dB	9.64482 dB
TestAddNoise	60	7.87685 dB	7.88188 dB
TestAddNoise	100	7.5588 dB	7.58339 dB
TestSmallRandom Distortions	0.95	17.2706 dB	16.3975 dB
TestSmallRandom Distortions	1.00	17.0821 dB	16.2232 dB
TestSmallRandom Distortions	1.05	16.8358 dB	15.9981 dB
TestLatestSmall RandomDistortions	0.95	17.1030 dB	17.0479 dB
TestLatestSmall RandomDistortions	1.00	16.7566 dB	16.7814 dB
TestLatestSmall RandomDistortions	1.05	16.5792 dB	16.5647 dB
TestConvFilter	1.00	11.0467 dB	11.0467 dB
TestConvFilter	2.00	-7.54787 dB	-7.5479 dB
TestMedianCut	3.00	29.1881 dB	29.1873 dB
TestMedianCut	5.00	26.6277 dB	26.6276 dB

6 Conclusion

Mandal et al. [5] have proposed a multi-bit steganographic algorithm that compromises with the capacity to keep the visual and computational quality high as compared with the method proposed by [3]. But both the algorithms suffers with respect to embedding capacity when compared with the multi-bit image steganography scheme [4] that embeds message in a number of least significant bits of a pixel intensity value. The number of embedding bits depend on the pixel characteristics. In this paper, we propose a modification of the scheme of [4] so that the maximum number of bits used for embedding is limited to 5. Our maximum embedding efficiency is 5.33, which is higher than that of [17]. Moreover, we give theoretical justifications as well as empirical support that our method gives a lower average distortion per pixel than the previous methods.

As part of our future work, we plan to analyze resiliency of our method against different adversary models. We also plan to analyze the scope for further improvement of embedding capacity and embedding efficiency, without compromising image quality and security.

References

1. Paul, G., Davidson, I., Mukherjee, I., Ravi, S.S.: Keyless Steganography in Spatial Domain using Energetic Pixels. In: Venkatakrishnan, V., Goswami, D. (eds.) ICISS 2012. LNCS, vol. 7671, pp. 134–148. Springer, Heidelberg (2012)
2. Zhang, X., Wang, S., Zhou, Z.: Multibit Assignment Steganography in Palette Images. IEEE Signal Processing Letters 15 (2008)
3. Wu, H.C., Wu, N.I., Tsai, C.S., Hwang, M.S.: Image steganographic scheme based on pixel value differencing and LSB replacement method. In: IEEE Proceedings on Vision, Image and Signal Processing, vol. 152(5), pp. 611–615 (2005)

4. Park, Y., Kang, H., Shin, S., Kwon, K.: An Image Steganography Using Pixel Characteristics. In: Hao, Y., Liu, J., Wang, Y.-P., Cheung, Y.-m., Yin, H., Jiao, L., Ma, J., Jiao, Y.-C. (eds.) CIS 2005. LNCS (LNAI), vol. 3802, pp. 581–588. Springer, Heidelberg (2005)
5. Mandal, J.K., Das, D.: Colour Image Steganography Based on Pixel Value Differencing in Spatial Domain. International Journal of Information Sciences and Techniques (IJIST) 2(4) (July 2012)
6. Kahn, D.: The History of Steganography. In: Anderson, R. (ed.) IH 1996. LNCS, vol. 1174, pp. 1–17. Springer, Heidelberg (1996)
7. Gutub, A.A.: Pixel Indicator Technique for RGB Image Steganography. Journal of Emerging Technologies in Web Intelligence 2(1), 56–64 (2010)
8. Bailey, K., Curran, K.: An evaluation of image based steganography methods. Journal of Multimedia Tools and Applications 30(1), 55–88 (2006)
9. Neeta, D., Snehal, K., Jacobs, D.: Implementation of LSB Steganography and Its Evaluation for Various Bits. In: 1st International Conference on Digital Information Management, pp. 173–178 (December 2006)
10. Kejgir, S., Kokare, M.: Optimization of Bit Plane Combination for Efficient Digital Image Watermarking. International Journal of Computer Science and Information Security (IJCSIS) 4 (August 2009)
11. Provos, N.: Defending against Statistical Steganalysis. In: Tenth USENIX Security Symposium, pp. 325–335 (2001)
12. Provos, N., Honeyman, P.: Detecting Steganographic Content on the Internet. In: ISOC NDSS 2002, San Diego, CA (February 2002)
13. Dumitrescu, S., Wu, X., Memon, N.: On Steganalysis of Random LSB Embedding in Continuous-tone Images. In: IEEE ICIP 2002, New York, USA, vol. III, pp. 641–644 (September 2002)
14. Westfeld, A., Pfitzmann, A.: Attacks on Steganographic Systems. In: Pfitzmann, A. (ed.) IH 1999. LNCS, vol. 1768, pp. 61–76. Springer, Heidelberg (2000)
15. Fridrich, J., Goljan, M., Dui, R.: Reliable Detection of LSB Steganography in Color and Grayscale Images. In: Proceedings of the ACM Workshop on Multimedia and Security, Ottawa, CA, pp. 27–30 (October 5, 2001)
16. Fridrich, J., Lisoněk, P.: Grid Colorings in Steganography. IEEE Trans. on Information Theory 53(4), 1547–1549 (2007)
17. Fridrich, J., Lisoněk, P., Soukal, D.: On Steganographic Embedding Efficiency. In: Camenisch, J.L., Collberg, C.S., Johnson, N.F., Sallee, P. (eds.) IH 2006. LNCS, vol. 4437, pp. 282–296. Springer, Heidelberg (2007)
18. http://www.webshots.com
19. http://221bakerstreet.org
20. http://www.petitcolas.net/fabien/watermarking/stirmark

Evolutionary Multibit Grouping Steganographic Algorithm*

Nabanita Mukherjee[1], Ayon Bhattacharya[2], and Siddhartha Sekhar Bose[3]

[1] Dept. of Information Technology,
Pailan College of Management & Technology, West Bengal, India
nabanitaganguly0@gmail.com
[2] Dept. of Computer Science & Engineering,
Neotia Institute of Technology, Management and Science, West Bengal, India
ayonbhattacharya90@yahoo.com
[3] Dept. of Information Technology,
Neotia Institute of Technology, Management and Science, West Bengal, India
siddhartha.sekhar@gmail.com

Abstract. The increasing rise of vulnerability of data-in-transit in the 21st century has proven time and again that significant emphasis must be given to improving and developing sound techniques to combat data interception in transit. Audio steganography is one of the most promising methods providing security to messages in transit. Our proposed method of audio steganography focuses on encrypting the file and then encapsulating the encrypted file inside the cover audio. Our method uses advanced deviation of the common least-significant-bit (LSB) encoding technique to achieve higher embedding capacity, increased data rate and dynamic implementation.

Keywords: Information Security, Multi-bit, Audio Steganography, Steganalysis.

1 Introduction and Motivation

Derived from the Greek words *steganos* (covered or secret) and *graphy* (writing or drawing) and meaning, literally, covered writing, steganography [2–4] is the practice of hiding private or sensitive information within something that appears to be nothing out of the usual. Steganography is different from cryptography as in steganography the information is hidden such that it appears that no information is hidden at all. This gives an extra advantage as information may be hidden in innocuous objects like every day sound or picture files that are shared over the internet. Steganography in digital communication is a growing field with excellent future scope.

---

* This work was done in part while the third author was visiting European Organization for Nuclear Research (CERN), Geneva 23, Switzerland as an Associate Member of this organization.

A. Bagchi and I. Ray (Eds.): ICISS 2013, LNCS 8303, pp. 285–296, 2013.

Apart from upkeep of the overall carrier signal quality, steganography in most cases has the additional need of robustness against external manipulations intended to remove the embedded information from the carrier signal. This makes steganography appropriate for cases where data is hidden inside a carrier medium such as audio file. One of the primary methods of implementing least significant bit (LSB) based steganography is through bit level encryption key [6]. The encryption allows the improvement of robustness while retaining the conservative and well tested approach to LSB based steganography. In general, LSB embedding suffers from poor bit rate and carrying capacity. The steganographic algorithm [5] clearly suggests improved methods for utilizing LSB embedded steganography. Here a 4-bit compensation technique is implemented to lower distortion levels in single bit audio steganography. The novel approach in [12] has put forward two innovative ways to implement audio based information hiding. The first concept is to randomize bit number of host message used for embedding secret message while the second way is to randomize sample number containing next secret message bit. In depth explanation is given of the concept of frequency masking and spread spectrum sound steganography and their comparisons to basic LSB embedding. Nugraha et al. [13] are of the opinion, based on test results, that the implementation of direct-sequence spread spectrum steganography on audio cover object is possible and practical to use. However it is more expensive than LSB methods. A novel method of synchronized audio-to-audio steganography has been put forward [2]. Here secret speech data is recorded and embedded into audio data when it is playing. This is done synchronously as trusted receiver extracted secret speech from stego with shared secret key. However, even knowledge of an existing hidden message should not be sufficient for the removal of the message without knowledge of additional parameters such as secret keys or in the case of our proposed algorithm the dynamic embedding pattern. A comprehensive description and succinct summary of the current popularly used techniques and benchmarks in audio steganography is provided [11].

The quality of a particular steganographic algorithm can be characterized by a number of defining properties. Three of them, which are most important for audio steganographic algorithms, are defined:

Transparency is a benchmark for evaluating the audible distortion due to signal modifications like message embedding or attacking. The fidelity of the steganography algorithm is usually defined as a perceptual similarity between the cover and stego audio sequences. However, the quality of the stego audio is usually degraded, either intentionally by an adversary or unintentionally in the transmission process, before a person perceives it. In that case, it is more adequate to define the fidelity of a steganography algorithm as perceptual similarity between the stego audio and the original host audio at the point at which they are presented to a consumer. In this work Mean Opinion Score (MOS) can be considered as a qualitative measure of the transparency benchmark in audio steganography.

Payload of a particular cover audio to embed information is algorithm specific. It may be defined as the maximum amount of data that can be hidden in a cover audio. Generically,

$$Payload(\%) = \frac{Number\ of\ embedded\ bits}{Total\ number\ of\ bits} \times 100$$

Robustness in broad terms, gives the ability to maintain data integrity for a particular data hiding algorithm against intentional and unintentional attacks. Robustness is therefore the ability of the proposed algorithm to resist detection and if detected the ability to resist giving up plain text. As suggested by Watkins et al. [7] robustness is an important benchmark for data hiding algorithms.

The motivation behind the paper is to separate the encryption and embedding process while at the same time increasing capacity without increasing distortion of audio to unacceptable levels. The method [15] proposes encryption using key sharing. Our algorithm uses a level of encryption achieved using decision values from the payload text itself. This alleviates the necessity of devising a method to share the secret key which itself is prone to attacks and interception. Moreover, the text file based encryption makes the assumption that the receiver has successfully extracted the encrypted text from the stego audio. Any wrong extraction changes the ability of the decryption algorithm to successfully generate meaningful clear text. This in our view contributes greatly to enhanced security.

The proposed algorithm attempts to improve both on the capacity and dynamicity of the embedding logic. Dynamicity is the ability of the algorithm to have a different embedding pattern each time it is run. If the stego audio is subjected to attacks it will be difficult to determine the position of the embedded bits as it changes for every input. Not being able to correctly identify and extract even a few bits for every sequence results in complete change in the ASCII value. This error gets further compounded when the attacker tries to decrypt making meaningful clear text generation difficult at best. The algorithm improves capacity by implementing the data hiding on multiple bits and thus greatly increasing the payload with minimum and inaudible distortion of the vessel media. In general, the payload is thrice that of generic LSB based embedding. Moreover, attempts have been made to make the embedding logic dependent on the cover audio itself, thus making the embedding algorithm dynamic on each run. The advantage of making the embedding process dynamic is that there are no fixed patterns and thus the audio file cannot be decrypted unless in-depth knowledge of the algorithm is present. This improves the overall security of the algorithm.

2 Proposed Method

The cover audio file is read by the system and converted into its digital stream. The stream is then converted to binary sample. Each sample (s) is 16 bits in length.

The text message is read by the system and converted into its binary form R, where n is the total number of characters in the text file. Each character in the message is converted to its corresponding 7 bit data instance. In this algorithm R represents the binary representation of ASCII values of each character of the text file. Thus for each text character, say T_k, R_k will be corresponding collection of binary bits. B is the pool of binary bits which 7 in turn make up each collection of R, i.e. $B_1, B_2,...B_7$ would make up R_1 and so on.

A pair of bits P_j is found out from the text file binary stream containing the nth and $(n-1)^{th}$ bits of every successive odd row. If the values are $(0,0)$ or $(1,1)$ then XOR operation is done on every element of the two rows and the values are replaced in the second of the two rows. However, if the values are $(0,1)$ or $(1,0)$ then XNOR operation is done between corresponding elements of the rows and replaced in the second of the two rows.

Likewise the pair of bits P_j is found out from the text file binary stream containing the nth and $(n-1)^{th}$ bits of every successive even row. If the value are $(0,1)$ or $(1,0)$ then XNOR operation is done on every element of the two rows and the values are replaced in the second of the two rows. Again if the values are $(0,0)$ or $(1,1)$ then XOR operation is done on the corresponding elements of the rows and replaced in the second of the two rows. These steps allow encryption of the text file from plain text and thus improve the degree of robustness. Once the file has been fully encrypted the embedding is done using the proposed Multi-bit Steganographic Algorithm. At first each sample of the binary representation of the audio file (of lossless .wav audio file format) in which the text file is to be embedded is grouped into groups of two from the 6th to the 1st bits. Thus 6th and 5th bits, 4th and 3rd bits and 2nd and 1st bits form a set of tuples. The proposed algorithm compares the most significant bit (MSB) and the next bit of MSB, i.e. $MSB + 1$ (i.e. b_{16} and b_{15} respectively as shown in Figure 1) bits of each 16 bit sample of the audio file, if it is $(0, 1)$ or $(1, 0)$ then the E_{dir} value is set $Left\text{-}to\text{-}Right$ (LR). The E_{dir} refers to the direction of embedding and is the primary point of dynamicity of the Evolutionary Multibit Grouping Steganographic Algorithm (EMGSA). Again if, MSB and $MSB + 1$ bits are $(0,0)$ or $(1,1)$ the E_{dir} value is set $Right\text{-}to\text{-}Left$ (RL).

The embedding is done based on the value of the E_{dir}. If E_{dir} is $Left\text{-}to\text{-}Right$ (LR) then the next bit (say, B_k) is XOR-ed with an even bit (S_{2j}) of the audio sample and the result replaces the prior odd bit position (i.e. S_{2j-1}) of the sample. However, if the E_{dir} value is $Right\text{-}to\text{-}Left$ then a particular bit, (say, B_k) is XOR-ed with an odd bit (S_{2j-1}) of the audio sample and the result replaces the next even bit position (i.e. S_{2j}) of the sample. The tuple position then moves left again till number of tuples run out.

$$\overrightarrow{LR}$$

$$\overline{b_{16}\ b_{15}\ ...\ b_6\ b_5\ b_4\ b_3\ b_2\ b_1}$$

$$\overleftarrow{RL}$$

Fig. 1. LR and RL movement of E_{dir}

Input: An audio component with s samples, a text message $T_1, \ldots, T_n$ of known length n.
Output: The stego audio component containing the embedded message.

1 Find MSB odd-successive pair set
$P_j \leftarrow \{MSB_{2j-1}, MSB_{2j+1}\}, \forall \, T_1 \leqslant j \leqslant T_n$ and $mod(j, 2) = 1$ from the text T_n containing n characters;
2 **if** $P_j \in \{00, 11\}$ **then**
3 $\quad \mid \quad R_{2j+1} \leftarrow R_{2j+1} \bigoplus R_{2j-1};$
   end
4 **else**
5 $\quad \mid \quad R_{2j+1} \leftarrow \overline{R_{2j+1} \bigoplus R_{2j-1}};$
   end
6 Find MSB even-successive pair set
$P_{j+1} \leftarrow \{MSB_{2j}, MSB_{2j+2}\}, \forall \, T_1 \leqslant j \leqslant T_n$ and $mod(j, 2) = 1$ from the Text T_n containing n characters;
7 **if** $P_{j+1} \in \{01, 10\}$ **then**
8 $\quad \mid \quad R_{2j+2} \leftarrow R_{2j} \bigoplus R_{2j+2};$
   end
9 **else**
10 $\quad \mid \quad R_{2j+2} \leftarrow \overline{R_{2j} \bigoplus R_{2j+2}};$ where R_k represents the binary
$\quad \mid \quad$ representation of kth character of the text message.
   end
11 $k \leftarrow 0;$
12 **for** i *from 1 to s* **do**
13 $\quad \mid \quad$ **if** $MSB_0 \neq MSB_1$ **then**
14 $\quad \mid \quad \mid \quad E_{dir} \leftarrow$ "LR";
   $\quad \mid \quad \mid \quad$ **for** j *from 3 to 1* **do**
15 $\quad \mid \quad \mid \quad \mid \quad S_{2j-1} \leftarrow S_{2j} \bigoplus B_k;$ The entire pool of binary bits for the
   $\quad \mid \quad \mid \quad \mid \quad$ entire text file is $B_1 \ldots B_m$ where m is equal to $k * 7$.
16 $\quad \mid \quad \mid \quad \mid \quad k \leftarrow k + 1;$
   $\quad \mid \quad \mid \quad$ **end**
   $\quad \mid \quad$ **end**
   $\quad \mid \quad$ **else**
   $\quad \mid \quad \mid \quad$ **for** j *from 1 to 3* **do**
17 $\quad \mid \quad \mid \quad \mid \quad E_{dir} \leftarrow$ "RL";
18 $\quad \mid \quad \mid \quad \mid \quad S_{2j} \leftarrow S_{2j-1} \bigoplus B_k;$
19 $\quad \mid \quad \mid \quad \mid \quad k \leftarrow k + 1;$
   $\quad \mid \quad \mid \quad$ **end**
   $\quad \mid \quad$ **end**
   end
20 Output the transformed audio component;

Algorithm 1. Multi-bit Audio Steganographic Algorithm for Embedding the Message

Input: The stego audio file.
Output: The hidden text message.

1 $k \leftarrow 0$;
2 **for** i *from 1 to s* **do**
3   **if** $MSB_0 \neq MSB_1$ **then**
4        $E_{dir} \leftarrow$ "LR";
       for j *from 3 to 1* **do**
5           $T_k \leftarrow S_{2j} \bigoplus S_{2j-1}$;
6           $k \leftarrow k + 1$;
       end
    end
    else
       for j *from 1 to 3* **do**
7           $E_{dir} \leftarrow$ "RL";
8           $T_k \leftarrow S_{2j-1} \bigoplus S_j$;
9           $k \leftarrow k + 1$;
       end
    end
    end
10 Find MSB odd-successive pair set
$P_j \leftarrow \{MSB_{2j-1}, MSB_{2j+1}\}, \forall\ T_1 \leqslant j \leqslant T_n$ and $mod(j,2) = 1$ from the text T_n containing n characters;
11 **if** $P_j \in \{00, 11\}$ **then**
12     $R_{2j+1} \leftarrow R_{2j+1} \bigoplus R_{2j-1}$;
    end
13 **else**
14     $R_{2j+1} \leftarrow \overline{R_{2j+1} \bigoplus R_{2j-1}}$;
    end
15 Find MSB even-successive pair set
$P_{j+1} \leftarrow \{MSB_{2j}, MSB_{2j+2}\}, \forall\ T_1 \leqslant j \leqslant T_n$ and $mod(j,2) = 1$ from the Text T_n containing n characters;
16 **if** $P_{j+1} \in \{01, 10\}$ **then**
17     $R_{2j+2} \leftarrow R_{2j} \bigoplus R_{2j+2}$;
    end
18 **else**
19     $R_{2j+2} \leftarrow \overline{R_{2j} \bigoplus R_{2j+2}}$;
    end
20 Each R is converted to corresponding ASCII value and nally to text character.

Algorithm 2. Multi-bit Audio Steganographic Algorithm for Extracting the Hidden Message

For extracting the embedded text file the same process is applies in reverse. As explained in Algorithm 2, the stego audio with s number of samples is fed as input. Once again depending on the MSB and MSB+1 bits the E_{dir} value is determined. Depending on the E_{dir} value the algorithm determines which direction was used for embedding the values and thus proceeds to extract using that direction. E_{dir} may be either *Left-to-Right* (LR) when the MSB and MSB+1 values are unequal or *Right-to-Left*(RL) when they are equal.

3   Theoretical Analysis and Comparison with Existing Algorithms

Definition 1. *Payload can be defined as the ratio of average number of bits to be embedded per sample and the total number of bits present in each sample of the PCM audio file.*

A theoretical bound on the capacity for the embedding schemes is expressed in Theorem 1 and in Theorem 2.

Theorem 1. *Let S be the total number of samples in each audio channel and S' be the number of bits per sample after normalization. The total number of message bits that can be embedded at most in each of the channel is independent of S'.*

Proof. In Algorithm 1, each S' bit normalized sample can store exactly three message bits. In other word, three message bits are incorporated in each sample. Hence, if S be the total number of samples present in each audio channel, then the total number of bits embedded in each normalized audio channel is $3S$ which is independent of S'.   □

Theorem 2. *The maximum number of message bits that can be embedded in each of the channel after normalization using Algorithm 1 is directly proportional to the number of samples present in each audio channel.*

Proof. If S be the total number of samples in each audio channel and S' be the number of bits per sample after normalization, then each S' bit normalized sample can store exactly three message bits using Algorithm 1. Hence total number of bits (say, N) in each channel can be expressed as $N = CS$, where C is the bit-embedding constant. Here, the value of this bit-embedding constant is 3. In other word we can say, $N \alpha S$, i.e. N is directly proportional to S.   □

In LSB based algorithm [9] embedding is done in 1 out of 16 bits giving maximum payload as 6.25%. In method [15] the bit-embedding constant is 2, where as in our method, we have consider this constant as 3. Theoretically the average payload using Algorithm 1 can be estimated as $\frac{3}{16}$% i.e. 18.75% which is in method [15].

4 Experimental Results

The proposed Algorithm has been widely tested over primarily four varieties of audio lossless uncompressed .wav files viz. Animal Sounds, Pop music, Melody, Punk music. The experimental outcomes in order to prove our algorithm efficient are as follows:

4.1 Payload Analysis

Embedding is done on 3 bits out of 16 total number of bits of each sample, therefore theoretically giving an average payload of 18.75% of each sample bit. Comprehensive testing also shows the exactly same result as theoretical estimation. Therefore for a 100 KB audio file, we can hide approximately 18.75 KB of text message. The above test data are generated at 18.75% payload. In LSB based algorithm [9] embedding is done in 1 out of 16 bits giving capacity if 6.25%. The embedding capacity value of our method is three times compared to the 6.25% payload achieved by the various LSB embedding algorithms.

4.2 Signal-to-Noise Ratio

Definition 2. *If $S(n)$ and $S'(n)$ denote the cover signal and stego signal respectively then Signal-to-Noise Ratio (SNR) can be defined as a quantitative estimator of embedding perceptibility measured from quantization error of each sampling point of cover and stego media as follows:*

$$SNR = 10 \log_{10} \frac{\Sigma_n S^2(n)}{(\Sigma_n S(n) - S'(n))^2}$$

Here the difference between $S(n)$ and $S'(n)$ basically determines the noise.

4.3 Mean Opinion Score

Definition 3. *Mean Opinion Score can be defined by the average of a large set sample score given by the common people based on the distinguishable ability of cover and stego audio based on Table 1.*

Mean Opinion Score (MOS) has been evaluated by listening to test sound files involving numerous people. A large number of sound sequences were used. Audio files were 44.1 kHz sampled stereo audio files, represented by 16 bits per sample. Each person listened to the original and the embedded sound sequences in pairs. The study was based on the opinion of the focus groups who were asked to report on the differences between the two sound signals. The data gathered was then statistically compiled using a 5-point impairment scale:

Table 1. Score chart for calculating MOS

> 5: imperceptible
> 4: perceptible but not annoying
> 3: slightly annoying
> 2: annoying
> 1: very annoying.

4.4 Bit Error Rate

Apart from Signal-to-Noise Ratio (SNR) and Mean Opinion Score (MOS), *Bit Error Rate* (BER) has also been calculated.

Definition 4. *Bit Error Rate can be defined as the ratio of the number of changed bits (dirty bits) as reflected after implementation of steganographic algorithm to the total number of bits in the cover audio.*

$$BER = \frac{Number\ of\ Dirty\ bits}{Total\ number\ of\ bits}$$

Bit 1 is considered as the least significant bit (LSB) while Bit 16 is considered the most significant bit (MSB). The values obtained from testing on Animal Sounds, Pop music, Melody and Punk music cover audio files are represented separately for comparison.

The summarized results have been shown in Table 2.

Table 2. Summary of Test data (SNR, MOS and BER) on huge number of audio files of four types viz. Animal sounds, Pop, Melody and Punk music

Sound Type	SNR (dB)	MOS	BER
Animal Sound	61.92	4.2	0.09740
Pop	64.00	4.5	0.09371
Melody	63.70	4.25	0.09370
Punk	63.25	4.5	0.09375

4.5 Analysis through Waveform and Other Graphical Representations

Besides the audibility distortion testing (viz. mean opinion testing), the waveform analysis is equally important in order to test the distortion graphically. Figure 2 shows a portion of the cover audio and the same portion of its stego version which is hardly detectable.

Our method has been innovated to be extremely adaptive to end user requirements. If the user requirement encompasses higher SNR values, the payload percentage may be decreased. However if the SNR requirement is tolerant then a high payload percentage may be achieved by the same adaptive algorithm. In Figure 3

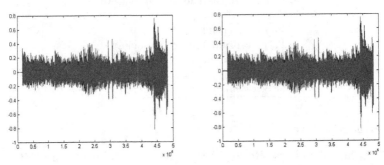

Fig. 2. Waveform of sample cover audio (at left) and that of stego version (at right)

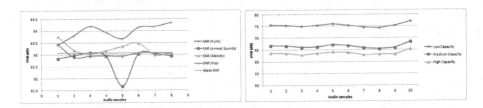

Fig. 3. SNR of sample audio files of four types viz. Animal sounds, Pop music, Melody and Punk music (at left) and variation of SNR of different audio files with respect to varying payloads viz. large, medium and small (at right)

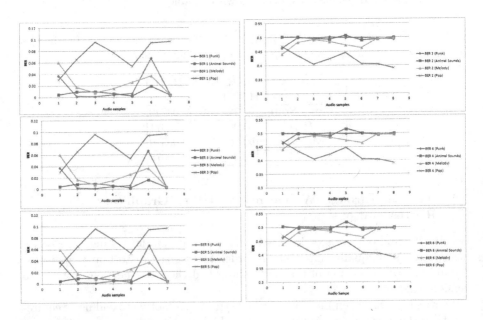

Fig. 4. BER values (from BER1 to BER6) on 4 types of sounds viz. Animal sounds, Pop, Melody and Punk music

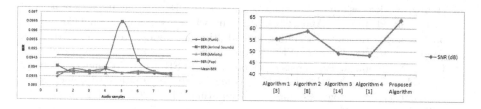

Fig. 5. Mean BER of sample audio files of four types viz. Animal sounds, Pop music, Melody and Punk music (at left) and performance analysis of existing algorithms [1, 3, 8, 14] and proposed algorithm (at right)

we can see the variation in SNR values corresponding to three different range of payloads viz. large text which is of size 40 KB, medium text which is of size 20 KB and small text which is of size 2 KB. These three different variations of payloads are tested with audio samples of size 400 KB exclusively to portray the payload graph. However, testing on several other audio samples have been conducted with the same approximations of size of payloads as described above.

Figure 2 shows a comparative waveform study of the cover audio and stego audio. There is minimal change evident from in depth analytical study of the waveforms. The left part of Figure 3 gives a graphical overview of the SNR values for different types of sound file and the right side of the figure denotes the SNR values obtained through comprehensive testing on different size of text. From Figure 4, a comparative graphical representation of the BER results (BER 1 to BER 6) in which embedding is using proposed algorithm can be obtained. Figure 5 presents a comparison between the end result of steganographic algorithms by [8], [3], [14] and [1] having the SNR of 55.37 dB, 59 dB, 49.15 dB and 48.18 dB respectively and our proposed algorithm has a mean SNR of 63.62 dB, thus improving over the previous methods.

5   Conclusion

In this paper a novel approach for multi-bit steganography of a payload text file into a cover audio has been proposed. The stress of our Multi-bit Audio Steganographic Algorithm has been on improving the capacity as compared to standard single bit LSB encoding method and improving the robustness from intended attacks by improving the dynamicity of the embedding technique. The robustness is further increased by encrypting the text file based on the text itself. Subjective testing reflects, there is a remarkable increase in the carrying capacity of the stego audio. Further more rigorous comprehensive listening tests prove a high degree of transparency between the cover and stego audio files.

References

1. Sun, W., Shen, R., Yu, F., Lu, Z.: Data Hiding in Audio Based on Audio-to-Image Wavelet Transform and Vector Quantization. In: Eighth International Conference on Intelligent Information Hiding and Multimedia Signal Processing (IIHMSP), Piraeus, China, July 18-20, pp. 313–316. IEEE Xplore (2012)

2. Huang, X., Kawashima, R., Segawa, N., Abe, Y.: Design and Implementation of Synchronized Audio to Audio Steganography scheme. In: International Conference on Intelligent Information Hiding and Multimedia Signal Processing (IIHMSP), August 15-17, pp. 331–334. IEEE Xplore (2008)

3. Cvejic, N., Seppnen, T.: Increasing Robustness of LSB Audio Steganography using a novel embedding method. In: Proceedings of the International Conference on Information Technology: Coding and Computing (ITCC 2004), vol. 2, p. 533–537. IEEE Xplore (2004)

4. Paul, G., Davidson, I., Mukherjee, I., Ravi, S.S.: Keyless Steganography in Spatial Domain Using *Energetic* Pixels. In: Venkatakrishnan, V., Goswami, D. (eds.) ICISS 2012. LNCS, vol. 7671, pp. 134–148. Springer, Heidelberg (2012)

5. Bandyopadhyay, S., Datta, B.: Higher LSB Layer Based Audio Steganography Technique. International Journal of Electronics & E-Communication Technology 2(4) (October 2011)

6. Sridevi, R., Damodaram, A., Narasimham, S.V.L.: Efficient Method of Audio Steganography By Modified LSB Algorithm and Strong Encryption Key with Enhanced Security. Journal of Theoretical and Applied Information Technology (2005-2009)

7. Watkins, J.: "Steganography - Messages Hidden in Bits", Multimedia Systems Coursework, Dept. of Electronics and Computer Science, University of Southampton, UK (December 15, 2001)

8. Divya, S., Reddy, M.: Hiding text in audio using multiple LSB steganography and provide security using cryptography. International Journal of Scientific & Technology Research 1(6) (July 2012)

9. Jayaram, P., Ranganatha, H., Anupama, H.: Information Hiding Using Audio Steganography A Survey. The International Journal of Multimedia and Its Applications (IJMA) 3(3) (August 2011)

10. Atoum, M.S.: A Steganography Method Based on Hiding Secrete Data in MPEG/Audio Layer. International Journal of Computer Science and Network Security (IJCSNS) 11(5) (May 2011)

11. Djebbar, F., Ayad, B., Hamam, H., Meraim, K.: A view on latest audio steganography techniques. In: International Conference on Innovations in Information Technology, April 25-27, pp. 409–414 (2011)

12. Asad, M., Gilani, J., Khalid, A.: An Enhanced Least Significant Bit Modification Technique for Audio Steganography. In: International Conference on Computer Networks and Information Technology (ICCNIT), July 11-13, pp. 143–147 (2011)

13. Nugraha, R.M.: Implementation of Direct Sequence Spread Spectrum Steganography on Audio Data. In: 2011 International Conference on Electrical Engineering and Informatics, Bandung, Indonesia, July 17-19. pp. 1–6. IEEE Xplore (2011)

14. Zhu, J., Wang, R., Yan, D.: The Sign bits of Huffman Codeword-based Steganography for AAC Audio. In: International Conference on Multimedia Technology (ICMT), Ningbo, China, October 29-31, pp. 1–4. IEEE Xplore (2010)

15. Huang, X., Abe, Y., Echizen, I.: Capacity Adaptive Synchronized Acoustic steganography Scheme. International Journal of Information Hiding and Multimedia Signal Processing 1(2) (April 2010)

Let the Right One in:
Discovering and Mitigating Permission Gaps

Beng Heng Ng and Atul Prakash

University of Michigan, Ann Arbor MI 48105, USA
{bengheng,aprakash}@eecs.umich.edu

Abstract. Permissions that are granted but unused, or *permission gaps*, are needless risks to systems and should be removed expeditiously. More insidiously, granted permissions may not always be revoked when they are no longer required. In practice, identifying permission gaps can be hard since another reference point besides granted permissions is usually unavailable. Therefore, we argue that permission gaps often must be estimated. We propose DeGap, a framework that uses standard system logs as a reference point and a common logic for estimating the gaps in various services. DeGap identified potentially overly relaxed SSH server configurations, incorrect permissions on sensitive files, and dormant user groups. Just discovering permission gaps may be insufficient; administrators need to know how they can be fixed. DeGap can also identify changes to service configurations towards reducing permission gaps.

Keywords: permission gaps, permissions, system security.

1 Introduction

Permissions for system objects (e.g., files and network sockets) serve as a first line of defense against misuse by unauthorized users. Ideally, only permissions needed by legitimate users to access objects are granted. Unfortunately, this can be hard to achieve in reality. Granted permissions that are not needed, or *permission gaps*[1], often arise due to administrator oversights or new software, which is less scrutinized. The gaps can remain undetected and be exploited [1–3].

One method for identifying potential permission gaps is static analysis. In several works on Android apps [4–6], using static code analysis, the authors compared permissions requested by an Android app *from* the user with permissions that could be used by the app. Unfortunately, even legitimately granted permissions can be exploited by, say, code injection. Thus permissions, which are granted but not actually used, should be removed. Besides, using static analysis to identify gaps is not broadly applicable. In [6], a firewall with too liberal permissions is used to motivate the need for closing permission gaps. But, static analysis of services listening on the ports and comparing them with firewall permissions is unlikely to identify the gaps because, usually, only the firewall is

---

[1] Other terms, such as *over-provisioning* and *over-assignment* of permissions, have been used to describe permission gaps.

A. Bagchi and I. Ray (Eds.): ICISS 2013, LNCS 8303, pp. 297–313, 2013.
© Springer-Verlag Berlin Heidelberg 2013

responsible for blocking the remote requests. There is only one reference point, i.e., the firewall policy, to compare with for identifying potential gaps.

Furthermore, any permission gap analysis is likely to be computing an *estimate* of a gap. Security requirements change over time and may not even be precisely known. For example, an administrator may miss out revoking the access right of a user who has left the job. Even in the static analysis example, there could be a rare app that wants to acquire extra permissions from users, anticipating a future capability in the app.

The above leads to the question: what is the best that we can do in an automated manner, given that permission gaps exist in systems but static analysis is infeasible and any analysis must necessarily be an estimate? We propose a framework, DeGap, that analyzes potential permission gaps using a common logic for different services. DeGap can determine a lower bound on the set of permissions for an object that is consistent with its usage during a selected period. These permissions are then compared with the assigned permissions to expose potential permission gaps. DeGap then proposes a set of suggested configurations for achieving that lower bound. While we demonstrate the feasibility of our framework in the setting of system objects, it should be readily applicable to other scenarios, such as improving privacy settings in social networks. Overall, we make the following core contributions:

- We describe DeGap's core components while highlighting the design nuances for components that need customization for different services. We elaborate the common logic used for analyzing permission gaps.
- We implemented and applied DeGap for three scenarios: SSHD, file permissions, and user groups in /etc/group. For SSHD, DeGap found that (i) unused access for two users were not revoked, and (ii) password-based authentication was unnecessarily allowed for a server that had been the target of password brute-force attacks. For auditd, DeGap found a private key for one service that was set to be world-readable, as well as two additional files on the servers that could be exploited to execute a privilege escalation attack. Finally, DeGap identified unused user groups during monitoring.
- DeGap was able to automatically suggest changes that can be made to configurations for reducing permission gaps for all three scenarios.

Section 2 provides the related work. Section 3 discusses the limitations. Section 4 presents definitions and the basic techniques. Section 5 describes the system architecture. Section 6 presents evaluation results. Section 7 presents conclusions and possible future work.

2   Related Work

The concept of permission gaps (aka "over-provisioning of permissions" [7])has been discussed previously in works on securing Android applications by Felt et al. [4], Au et al. [5], and Bartel et al. [6]. The key distinction between DeGap and these works is that in these works, the application is considered to be the subject, G is the set of authorizations requested *from* the user during application installation, and R is an upper bound on the set of permissions usable by the application, based on static code analysis (which tends to be exhaustive). DeGap examines a different scenario where R is incomputable by static analysis. DeGap could still be useful in the context of Android applications. An application could make use of more restricted permissions than it actually does. In that case, DeGap may identify opportunities for tightening permissions within the code.

Leveraging actual permission usage, such as those recorded in logs, to generate access control policies is not new [8, 9]. While these works attempt to model roles and their granted permissions from logs, DeGap focuses on identifying and removing unused accesses.

DeGap is not an access control mechanism; it complements existing access control mechanisms by providing a means to verify the correctness of access control policies. Access control mechanisms, such as SELinux [10] and AppArmor [11], adopt a different philosophy from DeGap; SELinux and AppArmor begin by restricting accesses to objects and relaxing the limits when needed, while DeGap aims to identify accesses that are no longer required and then restricting these accesses.

Other efforts to improve a system's permissions resulted in integrated tools that perform functions beyond permission checking, such as vulnerability analysis. These tools, which include COPS [12], Tiger Analytical Research Assistant [13], and Bastille Linux [14], return a list of files and directories with world-readable or writable permissions. This is also achievable using the `find` command on Linux-based systems [15]. We argue that the challenge is not in finding such a list, since it is likely to be huge. Instead, the fundamental problem that we are solving with DeGap is in determining if permissions are indeed unused.

3 Limitations

DeGap uses logs, which record past object accesses over the analysis period. Clearly information about prior accesses provides no guarantee regarding future access patterns. But in the absence of the ability to accurately predict future uses and despite the possibility of false positives, DeGap provides a means for identifying potential permission gaps so long as access patterns remain unchanged.

An adversary may have accessed an object prior to or during log analysis. DeGap is not able to distinguish legitimate accesses from illegitimate ones. Illegitimate accesses can be filtered out if they are known prior to analysis, for example using reports from an intrusion detection system (IDS). DeGap provides a database and a query engine that allows the exclusion of known illegitimate accesses. For unknown illegitimate accesses, an attacker's activity will be treated as normal; in that case, DeGap is still useful in tightening the system to prevent other attacks that did not occur during the monitored period.

Since accesses are logged after they have occurred, DeGap is by design incapable of preventing illegitimate accesses as they happen. Without reinventing the wheel, we leave this responsibility to existing tools such as IDS. The same approach is taken by other security alerting systems [16], such as Tripwire, a system that detects changes to file system objects [17].

4   Tightening Permission Gaps

We now define the notion of permission gap and its usage in DeGap. Using the same terminologies as Lampson [18], *subjects* access *objects* using a set of *rights*. We represent a *permission* as a tuple (s, o, r) that denotes subject s as having the right r to access object o. In turn, system objects are collectively guarded by a set of *granted permissions* $G = \{g_1, g_2, \ldots, g_n\}$, where each g_i is a permission tuple (s_i, o_i, r_i). A subset $TrueGap$ of granted permissions G are not required for all legitimate accesses to succeed. This subset constitutes the *true permission gap* for the system. These extraneous permissions potentially increase the attack surface of the system, and the goal is to help users discover these gaps and recommend ways of fixing them.

The challenge is that computing $TrueGap$ is generally not possible for an automated tool in the sense that the precise set of legitimate accesses that should be allowed normally cannot be automatically inferred if the only reference point available is the set of granted permissions. A second reference point is needed to compute an estimate of the gap.

We attempt to compute an estimate of the $TrueGap$ by using past accesses, usually recorded in system logs, as a second reference point that can be compared with G. Let R be the set of permissions that were appropriately authorized, as per log files. We define the notion of *permission gap*, P, to be $G \setminus R$. '$\setminus$' denotes set subtraction. There is no permission gap if and only if $P = \emptyset$.

In a static system (where G and $TrueGap$ do not change), the permission gap P from the above definition is an upper bound on $TrueGap$. How tight this bound is will generally depend on both the quality of the log files and the period of time that they cover. The approach we take is that since $TrueGap$ must be estimated, a reasonable choice, as good as any available for most services, is to estimate the gaps based on past usage. At least, that way, users have some well-defined reference point when deciding whether to tighten permissions. Using this definition also permits users to ask the question, *"Given a permission that is proposed to be revoked, were there past actions that would have been denied had the permission never been granted in the first place?"*

Answering the preceding question is critical before revoking permissions as it may be indicative of denial-of-service problems caused by the revocations. Using a firewall analogy, if blacklisting a sub-domain of IP addresses is proposed as solution to prevent attacks from a subset of nodes in that domain, it is important to consider whether there have been legitimate accesses from that sub-domain in recent past. If so, then blacklisting the entire sub-domain may be unacceptable.

Our approach of using best-effort estimation of gaps is consistent with the approach in other areas of applied security. IDS and virus detection systems do not always guarantee correctness, but they are still useful to administrators as an aid in securing systems.

Without loss of generality, our approach could be extended to support more detailed models of permissions, e.g., where subjects, objects, and rights have attributes and granted permission is viewed as a combination of approved attributes of subjects, objects, and rights. The key requirement is that there be a way to compute $G \setminus R$, given G and R.

4.1   Gap Analysis and Traceability

Our goal is not only to determine whether a permission gap exists, but exactly the setting in a configuration file or the permission on an object that contributes to the gap, i.e., the question of mapping $G \setminus R$ back to specific configuration settings; ideally, the administrator should be told the specific setting that contributes to the gap without guessing. This is particularly important because gaps are likely to be reported at a lower abstraction level by the tool than what an administrator is accustomed to.

The challenge in identifying the settings in a configuration file that are candidates for tightening is that a reverse mapping from P to a configuration setting may not always be available or straightforward to provide. For example, if logs indicate that remote root login to SSHD is not required, identifying the specific place to make the change (e.g., `PermitRootLogin` field or the `AllowUsers` field) will require a fair amount of domain knowledge. One potentially has to write two parsers, one to go from a configuration file to G and another from gaps to specific settings in a configuration file.

DeGap supports two approaches to the problem for discovering changes in configuration settings that lead to reducing the permission gap. In the first approach, the existence of a reverse map from gaps to configuration settings is assumed to be available for a service and can be provided to DeGap.

In the second approach, the existence of a reverse map from gaps to configuration settings is assumed to be unavailable. We only require the availability of a one-way transform from configuration settings to G. This requires less work in applying DeGap to a new service since a reverse map from gaps to configuration settings does not have to be defined. However, the first approach can sometimes be more efficient. We will primarily discuss the second approach since we have found it to work sufficiently well in practice that the extra work of creating a reverse map is probably not worthwhile.

In the second approach, to identify changes in settings that could reduce the gap, the basic idea is to generate potential deltas to a configuration file that tighten permissions and map the modified configuration files to a set of granted permissions G'. We then determine if G' helps close the permission gap with respect to a set of required permissions R.

A permission gap P, where P is $G \setminus R$, can be tightened by restricting G to G' where $G' \subset G$. This involves eliminating permissions. To eliminate the gap P completely, one must choose $G' = G \setminus P$. Realistically, this is not always possible due to limits on the granularity of the granted permissions that can be influenced by the configuration settings. For example, for Unix file permissions, changing the **other** mode bits will impact all non-owner and non-group users.

Removing permissions by changing configuration settings leads to three possible outcomes: under-tightening, over-tightening, or both. Over-tightening affects usability; some rights in R would have been denied. Under-tightening exposes the system to accesses that are not in R. For a static system (where G has not changed over the logging period), we claim the following propositions:

Proposition 1. (Over-Tightening Rule) G' *is over-tightened with respect to required permissions R if and only if $R \setminus G' \neq \emptyset$.*

Proposition 2. (Under-Tightening Rule) G' *is under-tightened with respect to required permissions R if and only if $G' \setminus R \neq \emptyset$.*

It is possible for a configuration change to result in G' that is both over-tightened and under-tightened with respect to R. This could theoretically occur if the configuration change results in revocation of multiple permissions that are insufficient to close the gap, but some of the revoked permissions are in the set R. For Unix files, removing group permissions could result in such a situation.

The over-tightening rule is a simplification of the reality. Since G is really a snapshot of granted permissions, it is possible that $R \setminus G$ is not empty – permissions could have been tightened during or after the logging period, because of a change in security requirements and removal of some objects, but before a snapshot of G was taken. If so, $(R \setminus G') \subset (R \setminus G)$ should hold. If true, then the configuration change contributes to reducing the permission gap between G and R; otherwise not. We accommodated this scenario by *normalizing R* (replacing it with $R \setminus G$) thereby removing requests in the log that pertain to objects that no longer exist or permissions that administrators have revoked. Once R is normalized, the over-tightening and under-tightening rules continue to apply.

To test if a configuration setting contributes to the permission gap, we can simply simulate a change to the setting to obtain G', and compute $R \setminus G'$. If $R \setminus G' = \emptyset$, the setting contributes to the permission gap. On the other hand, if new tuples show up in $R \setminus G'$, that means that changing the setting caused some actions in R to be denied. The setting does not contribute to the permission gap. Additionally, we check that $G' \setminus R = \emptyset$. Otherwise, some of the previously granted subjects will be denied access with the changed setting.

In general, if there are n possible atomic deltas to an existing configuration setting, it will require $O(n)$ checks to identify all the deltas that can lead to tightening the gap without over-tightening. The above idea also applies to finding potentially stale members in a group. As an example, for `SSHD`, the `AllowUsers` field specifies a list of authorized users. To detect users in the list that could be contributing to a permission gap, one simply needs to simulate removing each user one by one and, for each G', determine if $R \setminus G' = \emptyset$; if yes, the user's authorization was not used for login and may be removed from `AllowUsers`.

5   System Architecture

Figure 1 shows the architecture of DeGap. Shaded boxes in the figure are specific to each service being analyzed. Bulk of the gap analysis system and the database is automatically generated from schemata that describe the attributes of subjects, objects, rights, and format of the service configuration files.

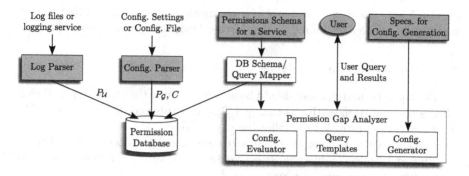

Fig. 1. Conceptual model for DeGap. Arrows indicate dataflow. Shaded components are specific to the service being analyzed.

A Log Parser extracts permissions used from either log files or directly from a service logging facility and system activities and puts it in a database. For services, writing logs to a file is usually more efficient than writing to the database on the fly [19]. Most services can log to files out of the box. Thus, we adopt a hybrid approach where we use log files to record object accesses but post-process the logs to store required permissions, R, to a database so as to permit a general-purpose query engine for analyzing permission gaps.

The Config. Parser is a service-specific component that generates the set of granted permissions G. If configuration files are used to define granted permissions (e.g., SSHD), it reads in configuration files and generates G. For others, like Unix file permissions, it queries the system for the information. Config. Parser also extracts a sequence of configuration settings, C, that are used by Config. Generator for discovering settings towards reducing permission gaps.

The DB Schema/Query Mapper is similar in spirit to tools like Django [20] in that it uses an input schema to generate initial tables for the database. We also use it to generate SQL queries from *query templates*, which provide simple ways of querying the database using highly expressive select-project-join (SPJ) queries [21] on entities and attributes in the configuration schema. Full SQL is also available. Users who wish to extend DeGap or make custom queries can either use templates or full SQL. The Config. Generator and Config. Evaluator internally make use of templates as well for direct queries on the database.

Config. Evaluator takes as input candidate configuration file (or settings) that a user would like to evaluate against R, the requests in the log files. It reports back whether the candidate configuration leads to a system that has a narrower gap than G without over-tightening.

Config. Generator uses specifications for configuration parameters (described in Section 5.1 and in Figure 2) as input and generates tighter alternatives for configuration settings. It then evaluates those modified settings using the Config. Evaluator to determine whether they tighten the permissions without over-tightening them. The subset of alternatives that are acceptable are presented to the user. Config. Generator can also apply a greedy algorithm (presented in

Section 5.1) to generate a sequence of configuration setting changes that is *maximal*; tightening any remaining setting further leads to an over-tightened system.

5.1 Permission Gap Analyzer

For DeGap to be useful, users should be able to evaluate the effect on permissions when a configuration setting is changed. Towards this end, the Permission Gap Analyzer (PGA) provides the following capabilities:

- *Evaluate a proposed configuration setting change:* PGA uses Over-Tightening Rule and Under-Tightening Rule (see Section 4) to help evaluate a proposed configuration setting with respect to R.
- *Generate a list of candidate configuration changes:* PGA uses the specifications for configuration generation to automatically iterate through possible one-step changes to configuration settings and identify the settings that can be tightened to reduce the gap.
- *Generate a sequence of configuration changes:* PGA can identify a full *sequence* of changes to a configuration file that provides a maximal solution to gap reduction. The solution is maximal and not necessarily optimal in that any further tightening will lead to over-tightening. But, there could be other sequence of changes that are longer in length or result in lower gap with respect to some objects. In general, finding an optimal sequence is likely to require exponential time as given n possible individual tightening steps, there can be 2^n combinations of tightening steps. We therefore focus on finding a maximal sequence rather than an optimal solution. Given that we are working with estimates of permission gaps, we believe this is a reasonable and practical strategy.

Now, we elaborate the features of PGA. PGA also permits direct queries on the database via query templates, as discussed in Section 5.2. They allow specific queries on the permissions database and support extensibility. In the following discussions, G refers to granted permissions, R refers to required permissions (derived from logs), and G' refers to a candidate for granted permissions. C and C' refer to the combinations of configuration settings that result in G and G' respectively.

```
field = {type = <type>, values = <value 1> | <value 2> | ... | <value n>,
         default = <default>}

PermitRootLogin = {type = oneof,
             values = yes | without-password | forced-commands-only | no,
             default = yes}
AllowUsers = {type = setof(subject), default = *}
```

Fig. 2. Configuration specification format and examples for `PermitRootLogin` and `AllowUsers`

5.1.1   Config. Evaluator

The Config. Evaluator E takes in C', G, and R, then computes the permissions G' that would be granted by configuration C'. It compares G' with G and R, and returns three possible results: tighter, tightest, and bad. C' is bad if G' is not a subset of G, or at least one permission in R is denied by G'. Otherwise, G' is tighter than G. To check if G' is the tightest possible set of permissions, in addition to the two conditions, we check that G' is not being over-tightened/under-tightened, i.e., $G' \setminus R \equiv \emptyset$ and $R \setminus G' \equiv \emptyset$.

5.1.2   Automatically Generating Alternative Configurations·

To assist PGA in generating alternative configurations, a user specifies the format of a configuration file, along with choices for each field, as shown in Figure 2. The current version of the system views configuration files as a sequence of fields, where each field can either have (i) a single value from a domain or a set of values, or (ii) a sequence of values from a domain. This can obviously be generalized to allow nested fields, but is adequate as a proof-of-concept.

Each specification has three parts: type, values, and default. Type is specified as either oneof or setof. We found these two types sufficient for analyzing permissions for SSHD and auditd, but more types can be easily added. If type is oneof, the values part is mandatory. It specifies the possible values for the configuration in increasing order of tightness and is delimited by '—'. In Figure 2, PermitRootLogin is specified as having type oneof and can take four values, yes, without-password, forced-commands-only, and no in order of increasing strictness. It is specified to have a default value of yes, thus, if PermitRootLogin is not present in the SSHD configuration file, the value yes will be used.

If the type is setof, the configuration takes a set of values, such as AllowUsers for SSHD. These configurations typically specify a range of values for two categories, subjects, or objects. Specifying a range of values for access rights is rare but possible. If a configuration affects only a subset of a certain category, computing permission gaps for permissions excluding those affected by the category is redundant. Towards optimization, we allow the user to augment the type with either subject, object, or right. Using this annotation, PGA pre-filters the permissions for the specified category for computing operations such as $G \setminus G'$. We will elaborate on type setof shortly.

The Config. Generator is used for tightening a single configuration setting from a given state. It provides a Python method *restrict_setting(c)* that generates a more restricted value for a field c. Repeated calls to the function return subsequent choices for that field (when choices are exhausted, the function returns None, which is equivalent to False in conditionals in Python). This function is used to automatically find the list of all possible configurations that only tighten a setting as well as a maximal solution of a sequence of configuration tightening steps using a greedy algorithm. The function *restrict_setting(c)* works as follows for the two types of fields that are currently supported:

Type `oneof` fields: Using the Config. Generator Specification, the function *restrict_setting(c)* returns the next (tighter) value for a field c in a configuration. If a configuration `type` is `oneof`, the generator returns the value that follows the current one. For example, if the current value for `PermitRootLogin` is `without-password`, then the function returns `forced-commands-only` on the first call, `no` on the second call, and finally Python's `None`.

Type `setof` fields: If the configuration `type` is `setof`, every time the function *restrict_setting(c)* is called to restrict a set, it removes one element in the set that has not been previously removed. For example, if `AllowUsers` were "user1, user2, user3", it would generate the following sequences: "user2, user3", "user1, user3", "user1, user2" and Python's None. Note that it only removes one value from the current list and does not generate all subsets. So, the procedure is linear in the size of the set.

In practice, sets can have special values such as `*`, which denote all possible values from a domain that are difficult to enumerate and apply the above strategy. For example, in `sshd_config`, if `AllowUsers` is missing, the default value for that can be considered to be `*`. The question then is how we represent G and generate alternatives for tighter configurations when the values of an attribute cannot be feasibly enumerated? To address the problem, we use a projection on R on the appropriate domain as the initial recommendation for the set of all granted permissions. There is no loss of generality since DeGap is concerned with reducing G towards R. For example, if `AllowUsers` is missing (equivalent to `*`) and two subjects `user1` and `user2` are the only ones who successfully logged in, the tool will recommend narrowing down `*` to the set $\{user1, user2\}$.

5.1.3   Greedy Algorithm for Discovering a Maximal Patch
The Config. Generator includes a greedy algorithm to compute a maximal patch to a configuration automatically. This is achieved by iteratively restricting each configuration and testing if the new set of granted permissions is a subset of the original one without rejecting any required permission.

5.2   DB Schema and Query Mapper

The DB Schema and Query Mapper loads a user query, then extracts tables and their attributes from the database, and dynamically generates an SQL query before submitting it to the database. A significant advantage of the Query Mapper is that the user does not have to manually craft SQL queries for basic uses. For our experiments, we found that the Query Mapper suffices for investigating permission gaps; however an advanced user may choose to query the database directly if it is required.

A user can make three kinds of queries. The first kind of queries are SPJ queries and are made by the Query Mapper on the database directly. The second and third kinds of queries are gap analysis and configuration change queries respectively.

```
Object.path = ?
Object.type = (LIKE,"%private key%")
ReqPerm = ?
Right.label = (=,"other-read")
```

Fig. 3. Query for files with types matching SQL pattern "%private key%" and read by others

SPJ queries allow users to leverage their domain knowledge and formulate their own queries. The user simply specifies constraints using pairs having the format (<operator>, <constraint value>), where <operator> is one of SQL's comparison operators. For example, if a user knows that files having types containing keywords "private key" may be possible attack targets, she may use the query template shown in Figure 3 to query for all other-read accesses on types matching "%private key%" for further analysis.

Gap analysis queries pertain to asking questions regarding permission gaps and how they may be reduced. There are two kinds of gap analysis queries that we have found useful. Firstly, given a specific change to a configuration setting, a user can ask what are the permission gap changes with respect to R. This is helpful for a user who is deciding if a change should be made. The Query Mapper may inform the user that the permission gap is (i) *under-tightened*, i.e., there are subjects who are granted permissions and did not previously access the object, (ii) *over-tightened*, i.e., there are subjects who were previously granted access but were denied given the change, or (iii) *no permission gap*, i.e., all subjects who were previously granted permissions and accessed the object still have the permissions, and all subjects who did not access the object are now denied.

The second gap analysis query we found useful is that the user can request for a list of possible one-step changes to the configuration settings that lead to reduction in the permission gap without over-tightening. There may be different ways to reduce permission gaps. For example, for SSHD, to disallow root login, the user can either set PermitRootLogin to "no", exclude root from AllowUsers, or both. The user may use the result to selectively modify the configuration file. One can think of this type of one-step analysis to have the same semantics as a breadth-first-search for a set of tightened configurations.

The last kind of queries, the configuration change queries, return a set of configuration settings that can reduce the permission gaps without over-tightening. This kind of queries provide a list of sequence of changes to the configuration settings that help reduce permission gaps without over-tightening. This uses results from the Greedy Algorithm discussed in Section 5.1.

6   Evaluation

We implemented DeGap in Python and used SQLite for the database for detecting permission gaps in SSHD, auditd, and user groups. The three scenarios have vastly different ways for specifying permissions. File permissions are specified in the file system's inode structure and retrieved using system calls. On the other hand, SSHD configurations and user groups are stored in configuration files. Also, the types of configuration values differ, i.e., binary versus ranges.

Additionally, for SSHD, certain configuration settings, such as PermitRootLogin and AllowUsers, interact to determine if a certain permission should be granted.

6.1   Case Study: Tightening SSHD Configurations

We considered SSHD as a single object and subjects to be users attempting to connect with the service. An access right could be either password or public-key authentication. The permissions were set in /etc/ssh/sshd_config. For simplicity, we only discuss AllowUsers, PermitRootLogin, PubkeyAuthentication, and PasswordAuthentication, whose uses were inferable from SSHD logs. We evaluated the SSHD logs from two servers, a source code repository and a web-server hosting class projects, in our department. Since accesses to SSHD are logged by default, we did not have to make any changes to the system.

```
PermitRootLogin = {type = oneof,
              values = yes | without-password | forced-commands-only | no,
              default = yes}
PubkeyAuthentication = {type = oneof, values = yes | no, default = yes}
PasswordAuthentication = {type = oneof, values = yes | no, default = yes}
AllowUsers = {type = setof(subject), default = *}
```

Fig. 4. Configuration generation rules used as input to DeGap

For both servers, we used the configuration generation rules in Figure 4 for hinting to the Config. Generator how the values for each field should be tightened. PubkeyAuthentication and PasswordAuthentication could be either yes or no. For PermitRootLogin, if without-password was used, root would not be able to login using a password. If forced-commands-only was used, only public-key authentication would be allowed for root. If AllowUsers was specified, only specified users would be granted access; otherwise, all users had access.

The second column of Table 1 shows part of the original configurations used by SSHD on the first server. Both publickey and password authentication methods were allowed. As specified by AllowUsers, four (anonymized) users, user1, user2, user3, and root were allowed SSHD access. DeGap computed the possible tightest configurations as shown in the third column of Table 1. We manually verified the results using traditional tools such as grep to search for keywords such as "Accepted" in the logs. Only user1 and root did access the server, suggesting that permission creep had occurred for two users. The server owner confirmed that the three suggested configuration changes should have been applied.

The fourth column of Table 1 shows part of the SSHD configurations used by Server 2. Except for AllowUsers, all configurations had a value of yes. The AllowUsers field was unspecified, implying that anyone could connect to Server 2 using either password or public-key authentication over SSH. DeGap suggested new configurations as shown in the last column of Table 1. DeGap recommended the AllowUsers field to be specified with user1 and user2, and the PasswordAuthentication and PubkeyAuthentication fields to retain their

Table 1. Partial SSHD configurations for Server 1 and 2, with their original and tightened values as suggested by DeGap

Configuration	Server 1		Server 2	
	Original	Suggestion	Original	Suggestion
PermitRootLogin	yes	without-password	yes	no
AllowUsers	user1 user2 root user3	user1 root	<unspecified>	user1 user2
PubkeyAuthentication	yes	yes	yes	yes
PasswordAuthentication	yes	no	yes	yes

original values of "yes". Again, we manually verified that user1 and user2 did access Server 2 using the public-key and password authentication methods respectively. The owner concurred with the suggestions.

6.2 Case Study: Tightening File Permissions Using auditd

In this section, we describe using DeGap for finding file permission gaps with auditd logs collected over seven days on 17 departmental servers that were installed with Fedora 15 and were patched regularly. We added a rule for recording execve and open syscalls on files, "-a exit,always -F arch=b64 -S execve -S open", to auditd's rule file. A successful call to open indicates that the calling process has acquired the read and write access rights specified by the open flags (O_RDONLY, O_WRONLY, O_RDWR). While one could log other syscalls such as read and write to ascertain the actual rights needed to access an object, the open flags already circumscribe these rights. Moreover, logging these syscalls leads to expensive disk operations. On average, we collected over 12 million file open and execute events for over 345,000 files by over 200 users for each server. The analysis was performed on two identical machines, both having two Dual-Core AMD Opteron 2218 Processors and 16GB RAM.

```
distinct = yes
count = ?
Right.label = "other-write"
GrPerm.has_gap = yes
```

Fig. 5. Query for finding number of files with other-write permission gaps

Leveraging Query Language Regex. We performed a query that leverages the query language's regular expression matching capabilities. We searched for files with types matching the SQL pattern "%private key%" using the query shown in Figure 3. On all the machines, we found that the RSA private keys for Dovecot, a popular IMAP and POP3 server, on all analyzed servers were world-readable. We verified this by checking Dovecot's SSL configuration file, which is also world-readable. If an attacker obtains the key, she can generate a fake certificate and launch a man-in-the-middle attack. In fact, it is highlighted on Dovecot's SSL configuration page that no users, except root, require access to the key file [22]. The administrator agreed that the other read permission should be removed.

File Permission Gaps. In this part of the analysis, we take a macro view on the permission gaps. Using the query shown in Figure 5, DeGap identified a large number of files with permission gaps. Figure 6 shows the number of files and directories that have the original read, write, or execute permission set with the number of files whose corresponding permissions were used. For files, respectively, only 0.592%, 0.00432%, and 2.59% of the group read, write, and execute permissions were used. More importantly, only 0.0592% and 0.181% of the other read and execute permissions were used. There were no writes by others. For directories, the percentages for group read (list), group write (modify), other read, and other write were 0.0128%, 0.0429%, 0.0354%, and 0.341% respectively.

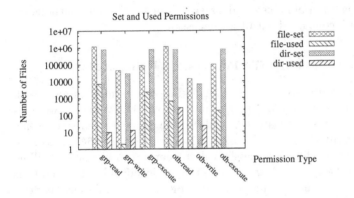

Fig. 6. Number of files and directories with permissions set and actually used

World-writable files presented a huge security risk since an adversary could easily modify the files while violating the non-repudiation principle. While there were 14,348 world-writable files, fortunately they belonged to only 17 users. These files include research data, exams, reports, etc.

The risks of world-readable files are not necessarily lesser than those of world-writable files. In total, we observed 1,133,894 world-readable files. Based on filenames in the `auditd` logs, some of the user files potentially contained sensitive information such as visa applications, (hashed and plain-text) passwords, and emails. For one user, while the inbox was not world-readable, the outbox was.

We applied DeGap towards generating configuration settings for reducing the permission gaps for files. DeGap was able to propose the correct suggestions for reducing the permission gaps. While it may be overly idealistic to remove every unused permission, the huge discrepancies in the number of files whose permissions were set and actually used illustrate the enormous potential for some of these redundant permissions to be removed. The large number of files may lead to manageability issues. The list can be fed into another system capable of extracting semantic information about the files to rank files according to potential criticality from access control perspective.

6.3 Case Study: Tightening /etc/group

The passwd and group files in the /etc directory are used to manage users on Unix-based OSes. We now discuss how DeGap can be used to identify dormant groups, which can possibly be removed from group, during the monitoring period. DeGap can also be used to tighten passwd. However, this is less interesting and can be achieved easily using other means. Thus, we will not discuss DeGap's usage for the purpose of tightening passwd in the interest of space.

We considered a group to be dormant if it was not used to access files. We used the same logs in Section 6.2 as inputs . However, we re-defined the object to be a collection of all the files (instead of each file being a single object). Also, there is only a single access (instead of read, write, and execute accesses).

The group files for all 17 servers were the same. This implied that a truly dormant group must be dormant across all servers. Thus, after finding the dormant groups for each server, we computed the intersection of these groups to determine a set of dormant groups for all servers. From this set, we removed groups having system users as members, since such groups are less likely to be susceptible to permission creeps. We identified system users as those whose home directories are not /, etc, bin, sbin, or var. 526 out of 565 groups were found to be dormant during monitoring. While it may be possible that there are false positives, as we acknowledged earlier to be a limitation of log-based approaches, it provides a starting point for administrators to tighten the group file.

7 Conclusion and Future Work

Permission gaps expose a system to unnecessary risks. This can lead to permission creep that is hard to eliminate in practice [23]. Without a second reference point, i.e., permissions that are actually needed, identifying and removing permission gaps is a challenge. Towards a framework using a common logic for extracting this information, we propose DeGap that estimates needed permissions from logs. We describe DeGap, and demonstrate its capabilities in real-life analysis of SSHD permissions, file permissions and user groups from logs.

From SSHD logs, DeGap found two users erroneously having access to a server, suggesting permission creep. Additionally, legitimate users only accessed a server using public key authentication. However, the server had allowed password authentication and was under password brute-force attacks. On another server, root was allowed access when it did not need it. DeGap proposed changes needed for the configuration settings to eliminate these gaps without over-tightening the permissions. The server owner concurred with the proposals.

From auditd logs, DeGap found that Dovecot's private key was world-readable on all servers, contradicting the recommendation on Dovecot's site [22]. DeGap also found a large number of user files with permission gaps for world-read or world-write, some of which contain sensitive information including passwords, suggesting that DeGap could be useful to both administrators and typical users for detecting permission gaps. DeGap also uncovered dormant user groups as candidates for removal from /etc/group.

Looking forward, DeGap currently automatically proposes the set of permissions that excludes operations not found in the logs. However, users may want more flexibility by specifying specific operations to exclude. Additional research is needed to achieve this flexibility.

Acknowledgements. This material is based upon work supported by the National Science Foundation under Grant numbers 0916126 and CNS-1318722.

References

1. Beckmann, A.: Debian 'openvswitch-pki' Package Multiple Insecure File Permissions Vulnerabilities (August 2012), http://www.securityfocus.com/bid/54789
2. Beckmann, A.: Debian 'logol' Package Insecure File Permissions Vulnerability (August 2012), http://www.securityfocus.com/bid/54802
3. Beckmann, A.: Debian 'extplorer' Package Insecure File Permissions Vulnerability (August 2012), http://www.securityfocus.com/bid/54801/info
4. Felt, A.P., Chin, E., Hanna, S., Song, D., Wagner, D.: Android permissions demystified. In: Proceedings of the 18th ACM Conference on Computer and Communications Security, CCS 2011, pp. 627–638. ACM, New York (2011)
5. Au, K.W.Y., Zhou, Y.F., Huang, Z., Lie, D.: Pscout: analyzing the android permission specification. In: Proceedings of the 2012 ACM Conference on Computer and Communications Security, CCS 2012, pp. 217–228. ACM, New York (2012)
6. Bartel, A., Klein, J., Monperrus, M., Traon, Y.L.: Automatically securing permission-based software by reducing the attack surface: An application to android. CoRR, abs/1206.5829 (2012)
7. Johnson, R., Wang, Z., Gagnon, C., Stavrou, A.: Analysis of android applications' permissions. In: SERE (Companion), pp. 45–46. IEEE (2012)
8. Molloy, I., Park, Y., Chari, S.: Generative models for access control policies: applications to role mining over logs with attribution. In: Proceedings of the 17th ACM Symposium on Access Control Models and Technologies, SACMAT 2012, pp. 45–56. ACM, New York (2012)
9. Bay31. Role designer (2013), http://www.bay31.com/role_designer
10. Smalley, S., Vance, C., Salamon, W.: Implementing SELinux as a Linux security module. NAI Labs Report #01-043, NAI Labs (December 2001) (revised May 2002)
11. Bauer, M.: Paranoid penguin: an introduction to novell apparmor. Linux J. 2006(148), 13 (2006)
12. Farmer, E.H.S.D.: The cops security checker system. In: USENIX Summer Conference, pp. 165–170 (June 1990)
13. Tiger analytical research assistant (2002), http://www-arc.com/tara/
14. The Bastille Hardening program: increase security for your OS, http://bastille-linux.sourceforge.net/
15. Files and file system security (June 2012), http://tldp.org/HOWTO/Security-HOWTO/file-security.html
16. Cannady, J.H.J.: A comparative analysis of current intrusion detection technologies. Technical report, Georgia Tech Research Institute, Atlanta, GA 30332-0800
17. Open Source Tripwire (2012), http://sourceforge.net/projects/tripwire/
18. Lampson, B.W.: Protection. In: Princeton University, pp. 437–443 (1971)

19. Gerhards, R.: Performance Optimizing Syslog Server (January 2004),
    http://www.monitorware.com/common/en/
    articles/performance-optimizing-syslog-server.php
20. Django: The Web framework for perfectioniss with deadlines (2012),
    http://www.djangoproject.com
21. Deshpande, A., Ives, Z., Raman, V.: Adaptive Query Processing 1 (2007)
22. Sirainen, T.: Dovecot SSL configuration (April 2012),
    http://wiki2.dovecot.org/SSL/DovecotConfiguration
23. Olzak, T.: Permissions Creep: The Bane of Tight Access Management (October
    2009), http://olzak.wordpress.com/2009/10/01/permissions-creep/

A Novel RSU-Aided Hybrid Architecture for Anonymous Authentication (RAHAA) in VANET

R.V. Pradweap and R.C. Hansdah

Department of Computer Science and Automation,
Indian Institute of Science, Bangalore, India
{pradweap,hansdah}@csa.iisc.ernet.in

Abstract. With the Intelligent Transportation System(ITS) projects gaining momentum all over the world, its backbone network VANET (Vehicular Adhoc Network) and its security architecture has become a prime research area in the recent past. With the VANET intending to improve the traffic efficiency and ensure comfort, safety and privacy of the users, meeting the complex security requirement of VANET has become an unenviable task. In this paper, we have proposed a novel Road Side Unit (RSU)-aided design which uses oneword CertificateLess SignCryption (CLSC), without pairing, to provide anonymous authentication. The hybrid approach ensures that the proposed scheme works efficiently even in the absence of RSU. Simulation study and security analysis of the protocol clearly demonstrate the efficiency and effectiveness of the protocol.

Keywords: RSU-aided, CLSC, Anonymous Authentication.

1 Introduction

The burgeoning economy and the rapid strides made in the fields of communication and information technology coupled with increased spending power among urban population has resulted in manifold increase in the number of vehicles plying on the road in every country. The resultant increase in traffic congestion and the fatalities on the road are a cause of major concern. This has forced countries to invest lot of time and effort for developing Intelligent Transport System(ITS), which is an integrated system of people, vehicle and infrastructure. It aims to provide safety, comfort and VAS (Value Added Services) to the users, improve traffic efficiency of transportation system and reduce carbon foot-prints. VANET is the backbone of an ITS and the unique security requirements of Vehicular Communication(VC) makes it a double-edged sword. It offers enormous opportunities to the designers and also presents scope for a variety of security attacks, which may defeat the very purpose of VANET. It is due to these unique security requirements, the possibility of self-navigating automobiles often seen in sci-fi movies are yet to become a reality. A handful of ITS has been tested so far including *PATH* of USA, *FLEETNET* of Germany and *AMTICS* of

A. Bagchi and I. Ray (Eds.): ICISS 2013, LNCS 8303, pp. 314–328, 2013.

Japan, but none of these initial projects catered for security. Recently, the European Union(EU)'s project like SeVeCom (Secure Vehicular Communication) [2] and PRESERVE (PREparing SEcuRe VEhicle to X communication System), and Smartway of Japan have focussed on implementing security architecture for VANET. A technical demonstration of PRESERVE, which is based on SeVe-Com, was given in Nov 2012[1].

1.1 Related Works

The usefulness of the VANET depends heavily upon its ability to provide security while safeguarding user privacy. A broader description of perceived security threats and security requirements in VANET is given in [1,3]. For anonymous authentication, Papdimitratos et al. [2], Raya [3] et al. have proposed a PKI based scheme where each OBU (On Board Unit) stores a set of public keys called pseudonyms and their certificates. This approach requires preloading a large number of pseudonyms and corresponding certificates for each vehicle. Interval for changing pseudonyms is a contentious issue, as short one results in frequent updating of pseudonym sets while longer interval may result in repeated use of the same pseudonym. Certificate management is also cumbersome. Zeng et al. have [5] proposed PKI+, which allows users to generate pseudonyms autonomously. However, user revocation requires the entire network of non-revoked users to be reconfigured after each such event. The bilinear pairing operation is computationally expensive. Perrig et al. have [6] proposed a TESLA based scheme with low computational and communication overhead, based on one-way hash chain. But hash-chain authentication, even though light weight, requires high-precision clock synchronisation. It also results in huge storage overhead as the messages had to be buffered till the time their key is revealed, which increases linearly with the number of vehicles.

To provide anonymity, Frediguer et al. [7] have proposed Mixed Zone approach, which uses designated points, where the pseudonyms of the vehicle will be changed. This method again fails to address the certificate revocation and pseudonym distribution issues. A major drawback is the symmetric key update, which occurs only when the zone has no vehicles. The issue of optimal placement of this mix-zone is also a design issue. Moreover most of the pseudonym-based schemes are vulnerable to sybil attack. SeVeCom has a hardware security module which limits the use of pseudonyms. Another issue with the pseudonym-based schemes, where a central authority issues pseudonyms to all the participating vehicles, is the time required to search the pseudonym database for assigning an unique pseudonym. Ateniese et al. [8] and Libert et al. [9] have proposed proxy-resignature based scheme which uses RSU as a proxy thereby optimising the certificate management. But it requires RSU to be present all along the network. Zhang et al. in [10] and later Lu et al. in [11] have designed the RSU-based scheme in such a way that it reduces the computational load on the vehicles. The scheme again depends solely on the RSUs for broadcasts. In [10], aggregated HASH is used to verify messages from multiple vehicles but it works only in the presence of RSU and any compromise of RSU will compromise the network as all the vehicles share their symmetric key with the RSU. Sun's [12] ID-based scheme reduces certificate overhead but pseudonym management remains an issue. ID-based schemes further suffer from key-escrow problem. In GSIS, which is a hybrid scheme, Lin et al. [13] have combined both Group and ID-based approaches. The schemes in [12,13] guarantee anonymous authentication and liability, but have shown linear increase in the verification time with the increased number of revoked vehicles in the network.

Chaurasia et al. [14] have proposed an RSU-based authentication method, but it incurs high computational delay due to multiple encryption/decryption during authentication and also requires the CA (Certification Authority) to be online continuously. It does not discuss the details of vehicular communication and certificate revocation. Hu et al. [15] have proposed an efficient HMAC based scheme which replaces signature with HMAC verification, and it is much faster than signature verification. But the scheme is not completely independent of bilinear pairing. The signature size is also quite high (more than 200 bytes). Since HMAC requires symmetric key establishment, the scheme does not guarantee non-repudiation and it also requires the Trusted Authority (TA) to be online. Bhavesh et al. [18] have proposed a novel scheme AMLA, which classified the users according to their privacy requirement and uses ID-based scheme based on bilinear pairing to reduce the communication overhead, but it again suffers from the computational overhead of pairing operation and is prone to sybil attack as vehicle can assume multiple identities and also suffers from key-escrow problem. In a broadcast environment like VANET, where messages are emitted every 100 to 300 ms, the communication overhead increases with the increasing number of vehicles. This would require a very small verification time, to reduce computational delay and a smaller signature size to reduce communication overhead. To provide liability, the vehicles/RSU would need to store the messages, the corresponding public key and the certificate it receives for a certain period of time. Qin et al. in [16] have estimated that this would amount to storing 8.4×10^8 signatures, keys and certificates, in PKI and 7.4×10^{10} under ECC, for one year, which is a huge overhead. This would be a herculean task in Indian scenario, if we have a single, centralized TA which would maintain the entire vehicle database or issue credentials to all the vehicles.

1.2 Our Contribution

In this paper, we propose an RSU-based hybrid design , which works even in the absence of RSU. The scheme is based on CertificateLess SignCryption (CLSC) scheme without pairing, proposed by Jing in [17], which reduces the communication overhead considerably, while providing the same level of security as PKI. Our design ensures inherent robustness of the system even in the face of compromise of Trusted Authorities(TA), by reducing the reliance on TAs as well as segregating their roles. It also solves the key-escrow problem, associated with

ID-based systems, as in our scheme, the TA is unaware of the final private key of the user. Signcryption provides authentication and confidentiality, simultaneously. The use of asymmetric keys provides non-repudiation which is a sore point in most of the efficient symmetric key authentication schemes. Our design also ensures that a vehicle can use at most one pseudonym at a time, which while providing anonymity also prevents the sybil attack. By adopting the method of classifying the users as per their privacy requirement [18] and off-loading most of the computation to RSU, we reduce the processing load at each vehicle. This feature combined with low computation cost for verification makes our system more efficient and practical than most of the earlier schemes, more so in the Indian scenario, with vast land mass to cover. Decentralised approach to anonymity also reduces the overhead in selection, storage and update of pseudonyms. The design ensures that the effect of compromise of a major entity like RSU is localized, in the worst case. We have also introduced the concept of Home and Foreign RSU, which greatly reduces the amount of data being maintained at each RSU and provides a more efficient way to trace a misbehaving vehicle.

2   System Architecture

In this section, we will discuss the system components that comprise the VANET, their communication model, CLSC scheme on which the protocol is based and the system design.

2.1   System Component

The system would comprise of the following entities :

(a) **Certificate Authority(CA):** It is the central authority who issues the initial credentials to the vehicles, during the registration of the vehicle. It loads the Real Identity(RID), Password(PWD) and the public parameters into the OBU of the vehicle, over secure channel, once. It need not be online always, unlike most existing designs. It also maintains a database, for liability purpose, to link the credentials to an unique user.

(b) **Road Side Unit (RSU):** It is the communication backbone of the network. Each RSU also plays the role of Regional Trusted Authority(RTA), by issuing temporary credentials to the vehicles within its communication range. It has much higher computation power and storage capacity than the vehicles. It processes all the related event notification messages received from the vehicles and broadcast them as a single event. We classify the RSUs into two types as follows:

– **Home RSU(HRSU):** Every vehicle will be registered with a HRSU, which would ideally be the one close to its place of residence or could be one of its choice, if privacy is of utmost importance to the user. HRSU will not be aware of the RID of the vehicle which is registered under it. It also maintains a database of all the vehicles registered with it.

- **Foreign RSU (FRSU)**: All RSUs other than the HRSU will be Foreign RSUs to a vehicle.

(c) **Vehicles(V)**: They are the users of the system and vehicle has an OBU, where it stores the credentials issued by RTA and CA.

2.2 Communication Model

The communication range of vehicle is around 300m and that of RSU is around 1000m. Other than the event notification messages and RSUs beacon messages, which are multi-hop, all the other messages are single hop broadcasts. The communication can be classified into the following two types:

1. **Vehicle-Vehicle (VV)**: It includes *beacon messages*(information on speed, location, direction, acceleration etc), which helps in neighbour discovery, *emergency messages*(information like applying sudden brakes, blind turn etc) and in the absence of RSU,*event notification*(occurrence of accident, traffic congestion etc). The vehicles process only the messages transmitted by their immediate neighbours.

2. **Vehicle-RSU (VR)**: All vehicles forward the *event notifications* messages to RSU, which processes them in batch and broadcasts consolidated event notification to all the vehicles in its zone. Each vehicle also sends out periodic *beacon messages*, which gives out its ID, public key etc. The RSUs get their credentials from the CA periodically over a secure channel.

2.3 CLSC without Pairing

The scheme in [17] involves three parties: a key generation centre (KGC), a sender and a receiver with identities ID_A and ID_B respectively. The scheme has the following phases:

1. *Setup:* Using a security parameter k, public parameters (p,q,n,g,P0,H1,H2,H3), where p and q are two primes such that $q > 2k$ and $q|(p-1)$, g is a generator of Zq^*, the KGC selects $s \epsilon Zq^*$, as the master key and compute its public key $P0=g^s$. H1,H2,H3 are secure one-way hash functions. n is the length of the message to be signcrypted.

2. *Partial Key Generation by KGC* : The KGC randomly selects $x_i \epsilon Zq^*$ and computes partial public key $X_i=g^{x_i}$. It takes as input(parameters,s,ID_i) and outputs partial private key $d_i = x_i+sQ_i$, where $Q_i = H1(ID_i, X_i)$.

3. KGC forwards the partial public and private key pair (X_i, d_i) to the user i.

4. *Final Key Generation by User* : The user takes as input (parameters,ID_i) and randomly outputs $y_i \epsilon Zq^*$, as the partial private key. It then calculates partial public key as $Y_i=g^{y_i}$. The final public key is (X_i, Y_i) and the final private key is (d_i, y_i)

5. *Signcrypt* : If A wants to send a message m to B, then it randomly selects $r \epsilon Zq^*$ and computes $R = g^r$. It then computes $k_A =(X_BY_BP0^{Q_B})^{d_A+y_A+r}$, $h_A = H3(R,k_A)$, $I = H2(ID_A,ID_B,R,k_A, m, h_A)$ and $c = h_A \oplus m$. The signcrypted message $\sigma =(R,I,c)$ is sent to B.

6. *Unsigncrypt* : To unsigncrypt σ, B computes $k_B = (RX_AY_AP0^{Q_A})^{d_B+y_B}$, h_B = H3(R,k_B),m =$h_B \oplus$ c and accepts m only if I = H2(ID_A,ID_B,R,k_B,m, h_B).

The correctness of the scheme is proved in [17] by showing $k_A = k_B$, and hence, $h_A = h_B$. As we can see from the above, the KGC is unaware of the partial private key generated by the user.

2.4 System Design

1. **User Privacy:** Even though VANETs security requirement demands user anonymity to preserve their privacy, in reality not all users would require the same level of privacy. The level of privacy for a public transport is far less than a VIP user. The pseudonym is changed on expiry of validity time or when the vehicle moves into a new RSU. Based on privacy requirement,we classify the users into three levels as follows:
   (a) *Level 0:* Lowest level of Privacy. It is provided free of cost. The pseudonyms have validity for 6 hours
   (b) *Level 1:* Mid level Privacy. A nominal fee is charged. The pseudonyms have validity for 2 hours
   (c) *Level 2:* Highest Level of Privacy. Premium service. The pseudonyms have validity for 20 mins
   The above classification of user privacy ensures that the privacy requirements of each user is met at the optimal possible way. This also ensures that an RSU will have adequate number of pseudonyms in its pool all the time, as level 2 users will be far less than other two categories of users.
2. **Access Control:** To avoid a user claiming to be away while his vehicle actively participated in a malicious attack or being misused by an adversary when the user is unaware, we need a strict access control to OBU. This could either be a biometric (retina or thumb scan) or a password protected USB-dongle, which needs to be plugged into the OBU for activation.
3. **Pseudonym Management:** Each RSU will play the role of pseudonym provider. It will maintain two sets of pseudonym pools, "Used" and "Free". Initially, when the system starts up, all the available pseudonyms will be in the free pool. As the vehicles enter the RSU zone, RSU starts assigning pseudonyms from the free pool and the corresponding pseudonyms are moved into used pool. A pseudonym is returned to free pool, on the expiry of its validity period or when the vehicle receives new pseudonym from the next RSU, whichever is earlier.
4. **Cross Authentication:** RSUs cross authenticate one another periodically, to detect any malicious/rogue entity among them. This ensures that a RSU cannot be compromised for more than a certain period of time "p".

2.5 Assumptions

1. Each vehicle has a tamper proof OBU and physical extraction of info from it is not feasible.

2. The RSUs cover all the zones in a congested area and are less frequently placed on highways and sparsely populated areas.
3. CA being centralized, is highly secure.
4. There exists a high speed secure communication among RSUs and between RSU and CA. Both RSUs and CA are honest and hard to compromise.

3   Proposed Authentication Protocol (RAHAA)

The proposed scheme has three phases : *Initial Setup, Registration at HRSU* and *Handover*. In the following paragraphs, we will discuss them in detail

1. **Initial Setup:** Before a vehicle V_i enters into the system for the first time, say, after it has been purchased by the user, CA would assign RID_i to V_i, accept a password(PWD) chosen by V_i and would load them along with public parameters(params) on to the OBU. It will also choose a One-Time ID-Key set, $(PID, d, X)_{OTP}$, to be used by the vehicles in case of emergency (like when it is unable to communicate using its present key set issued by the RSU) or when there is no RSU available. Simultaneously, the CA forwards the hash digest of (RID, PWD) and also the One-Time ID-Key set to HRSU, by encrypting it with the public key of the HRSU, to enable the registration of the vehicle.

   $CA \rightarrow V_i$: params,H(RID,PWD),$(PID, d, X)_{OTP}$
   $CA \rightarrow HRSU$: $Enc_{HRSU}(H(RID, PWD), (PID, d, X)_{OTP})$

   Once the OTP is used, a fresh set is issued by CA through HRSU, upon request. To prevent any misuse, an upper limit is fixed on the maximum number of such requests for a given duration. CA also maintains an RID database, as shown in Table 1, which associates H(RID,PWD) to a unique attribute of the vehicle like Engine Number. The database would contain an entry for each vehicle in the system. Even though CA's database would be large, query processing would be manageable, as it would be searched only in the event when arbitration is required. These entries are encrypted with CA's administration key.

Table 1. CA's RID Database

H(RID,PWD)	ENGINE NO
32 Bytes	2 Bytes

Table 2. Pseudonym Format

RSU ID	Random ID	TTL
2 Bytes	3 Bytes	1 Byte

2. **Registration at HRSU:** This phase occurs when a vehicle enters the VANET system for the first time. Since a vehicle usually starts from its home, the nearest RSU is normally the HRSU. The vehicle would send the hash digest of RID and PWD, along with a One-Time-Secret key, $s_k \in Zq^*$

and encrypt them with the public key of HRSU (also denoted as HRSU). A timestamp TS_i is sent along with the request to prevent replay attack. HRSU decrypts the incoming request and verifies the hash with the data in its database. If it finds a match, then the vehicle is a valid user and HRSU assigns it temporary credentials, which include a pseudonym PID_i and a partial public-private key pair (X_i, d_i), generated using the CLSC scheme. These are encrypted using s_k and sent to V_i. The format of PID is as given in Table 2.

$$V_i \rightarrow \text{HRSU} : Enc_{HRSU}(H(RID, PWD), s_k, TS_i)$$

If H(RID,PWD) is invalid, then return "Invalid Credentials", else generate (X_i, d_i)

$$\text{HRSU} \rightarrow V_i : Enc_{s_k}(PID_i, X_i, d_i)$$

Each PID_i is assigned a TTL (Time To Live), as in SeVeCom, based on the privacy level of the user. Before the expiry of TTL, the vehicle sends a "Refresh Credential" request to the RSU, using its existing credentials. HRSU maintains a pseudonym database, as given in Table 3. If the RSU does not receive the refresh credential request, it will maintain the current data till it receives the authentication request from the neighbouring RSU, to which the vehicle might have moved, or upto some threshold time "t1", whichever is larger. The PID column stores all the PID's the vehicle has assumed, across

Table 3. Pseudonym Database

H(RID,PWD)	$(PID, d, X)_{OTP}$	PID_i	(X_i, Y_i)
32 Bytes	262 Bytes	6 Bytes	256 Bytes

Table 4. Visitor Database

PID_j	(X_j, Y_j)	$HRSU_j$
6 Bytes	256 Bytes	2 Bytes

various RSUs, over a period "p", which will be used by the legal authorities in conjunction with CA to identify a mischievous node. The (X,Y) column would contain the corresponding public key pair. Like the CA, the RSU also encrypts its database.

3. **Handover:** When the vehicle moves from one RSU to another, it would send a message, which is signcrypted using the credentials provided by the PRSU and time stamp TS_i. The signcrypted message will be encrypted with public key of PRSU. The entire request is then encrypted with the public key of the New RSU(NRSU). NRSU would identify the PRSU from the vehicle's PID. After verifying the timestamp, NRSU decrypts the request and forwards the encrypted signcrypt to the PRSU, which verifies the signcrypt and if valid, it will return a "Valid" message as authentication. Once the NRSU obtains the authentication, it issues fresh credentials to V_i.

$$V_i \rightarrow \text{NRSU} : Enc_{NRSU}(Enc_{PRSU}(\sigma), TS_i, PID_i)$$
$$\text{NRSU} \rightarrow \text{PRSU} : (PID_i, Enc_{PRSU}(\sigma))$$

PRSU verifies the validity of σ and, on correct verification, sends the vehicles last known public key pair, which is stored in its pseudonym database and also sends the vehicles HRSU id. PRSU deletes the data corresponding to V_i from its database. It returns an error message on failure of verification.

$$\text{PRSU} \rightarrow \text{NRSU} : Enc_{NRSU}(X_i, Y_i, HRSU_i)$$

If the authentication is successful, New RSU will issue fresh Temporary Credentials to V_i, by encrypting it with (X_i, Y_i). NRSU intimates the HRSU about V_i's current credentials.

$$\text{NRSU} \rightarrow V_i : Enc_{(X_i, Y_i)}(PID_j, X_j, d_j)$$
$$\text{NRSU} \rightarrow \text{HRSU} : Enc_{HRSU_i}(PID_j, X_j, Y_j)$$

If a vehicle re-enters the system after the time "t1", i.e., after the last RSU has deleted the record of stored
credentials corresponding to the vehicle, then the vehicle can use its hash digest of (RID,PWD) to request for fresh credentials. The NRSU would send it to the HRSU of the vehicle for verification, before issuing temporary credentials to it. Each RSU maintains a secure Visitors database, as shown in Table 4, for the visiting vehicles for liability requirement. The details will be maintained for a duration "d".

4. **VV Communication in the Absence of RSU:** When the RSU is unavailable, either due to the sparse spacing or the RSU is down , vehicles communicate with each other using the One-Time ID-Key set, issued by the CA. A vehicle will start emitting its One-Time ID-Key, instead of its last assigned temporary credentials, when it no longer detects the presence of RSU. So all vehicles in the non-RSU area would be emitting their One-Time ID-Key set. This is easily recognisable as each such PID is prefixed with CAs ID. Once the Vehicle enters a RSU zone, it authenticates itself using the method described in "Handover" phase and then request for fresh One-Time ID-Key set through their HRSU. The CA changes its master key "s" periodically for better security and would update the One-Time ID-Key set of all vehicles through their HRSU.

5. **Renewal of Credentials:** As mentioned before, RSU will renew the credentials (PID,X,Y) of a vehicle before the expiry of the current credentials, upon receipt of request from the vehicle. This request is sent automatically from the vehicle. In a scenario when the number of Level-2 privacy users is less than an approved threshold r, and if n is the total number of vehicles in the region, then RSU, in order to ensure privacy, will renew the credentials of n-r lower level vehicles also.

4   Analysis of RAHAA

Security Requirements: RAHAA achieves authentication, confidentiality, integrity, non-repudiation and non-frameability, in one stroke, by employing the

CLSC scheme. It provides anonymity using pseudonyms. The key feature of our scheme is that the RTA is unaware of the private key of the users and hence, it need not be fully trusted.The scheme uses asymmetric key setup, and hence, provides non-repudiation among users. Unlike the previous schemes, KGC (in our case RTA) is unaware of the private key of the users. In addition, since the RTA cannot sign on behalf of the users, it also guarantees non-frameability. Liability is provided by the CA which maintains one half of the information (Unique Engine number)and HRSU which holds the other half(PID). These are discussed in detail in succeeding paragraphs. A comparison of security services provided by various schemes are given in Table 5. We present a comparison of a few RSU aided schemes in Table 6 and it can be clearly seen that our scheme is much more robust than others as it does not require round-the-clock presence of RSU, RTA, and CA.

Table 5. Comparison of Security Services

Services	RAISE	GSIS	HMAC	RAHAA
Authentication	Yes	Yes	Yes	Yes
Anonymity	Yes	Yes	Yes	Yes
Confidentiality	No	No	No	Yes
Integrity	Yes	Yes	Yes	Yes
Non-Repudiation	No	No	No	Yes
Non-Frameability	No	No	No	Yes
Liability	Yes	Yes	Yes	Yes

Table 6. Comparison of RSU aided schemes

Scheme	RSU	CA	TA Trust
RAISE [21]	Needed	Online	Fully
SMSS [19]	Needed	Online	Fully
HMAC[15]	Needed	Online	Fully
RAHAA	Not Always	Offline	Semi

Uniqueness of Pseudonyms: In our scheme, as the pseudonyms are assigned centrally by the RSU, from "Free Pool", with an unique RSUID prefixed to them, each vehicles PID would therefore be unique. The PIDs that expire can be reused optimally. The prefixing of RSUID ensures that the probability of two neighboring RSUs assigning same PID to two different vehicles is zero. The random assignment of pseudonyms from the free pool also provides better user privacy due to its uniform distribution.

Sybil Attack: In this scheme, each vehicle is assigned a pseudonym of certain lifetime and the associated credentials when it enters a RSU zone. At any point of time, the user will have only one set of credentials. The tamper proof OBU ensures that the user cannot retain or copy old credentials. The newly issued credentials overwrite the existing ones. This guarantees that the user will have only one valid pseudonym at any point of time. Another possibility is a that user trying to create his own public private key pair for the assigned PID. This is not feasible as each PID is bound to its private and public key pair and RTA's master secret key 's', as described in the section 3.3. So unless the user knows 's', finding of which is not computationally feasible, he would not be able to create a valid alternate public-private key pair for a PID issued by the RSU. Hence, a user can have only one valid credential associated with each PID, unlike schemes like PKI+, SeVeCom where each vehicle store multiple valid PIDs in its database. This effectively rules out sybil attack. The timestamping of messages also prevent replay attack.

Storage Requirement

Vehicles: Since each vehicle will have only one PID at any time, the storage requirement for pseudonyms and its credentials is much lower as compared to that in [18,5,2,4], which manage multiple pseudonym sets. In our scheme, a vehicle would require 820 bytes, including 8 bytes of RID, 518 bytes for the storage of temporary credentials (PID,X,Y), 32 bytes for hash digest of (RID,PWD) and 262 bytes for One-Time ID-Key set. Unlike the previous schemes, the vehicle would require to store only the emergency and beacon messages it receives from other vehicles for liability purpose. As all immediate neighbours of a vehicle do not change frequently, we need to store beacon messages from the same neighbors once in every few seconds. This considerably reduces the storage requirement.

RSU: Unlike in [18], in our scheme, each RTA maintains two databases, one for its home registered vehicles (pseudonym database) and another for the visiting vehicles (visitor database). In pseudonym database, each entry would be of length 556 bytes, and in the visitor database, it would be of length 264 bytes.

CA: Each entry in CA's database, as given in Table 1, would have a length of 34 bytes. This table will have a single entry for each vehicle on the system, indexed and sorted by the hash digest, making the query operations on a database of this size efficient and fast. Unlike previous schemes, as the pseudonyms are issued by RSU, CA would not have to maintain a central database of all pseudonyms, which takes enormous time to search while assigning a unique set of pseudonyms to a vehicle.

Anonymous Authentication: The design provides anonymous authentication(AA) inherently. We provide the following argument to substantiate it. AA will fail if either the anonymity or the authentication fails. The authentication is based on [17], which is proved to be secure under the CDH assumption. So if there exists an Adversary(A) who can break the authentication of our scheme in polynomial time, then there exists an algorithm (B), which can solve the CDH problem, which is not possible. Therefore, the authentication is provably secure [17]. Anonymity will fails under two cases:

1. *The adversary(A) is able to link PID to Engine No* : Consider a scenario when the vehicle V_i is in FRSU. The adversary can easily find out PID and FRSU. To find out the HRSU of V_i, A has to compromise FRSU and its visitor database, both of which are not trivial. Let the probability of compromising an RSU be ε_1. Adversary needs to compromise HRSU and pseudonym database to find H(RID,PWD) of V_i, which again has a probability of ε_1. The only place where a user can be uniquely identified is at CA, which links H(RID,PWD) to V_i's unique engine number. As CA is more secure than RSU, let the probability of compromising a CA be ε_2. Hence, the probability of A linking a PID to its engine number by compromising CA and RSUs is $\varepsilon_1 \times \varepsilon_1 \times \varepsilon_2$, which would be relatively small.

2. *The adversary is able to track change of PID continuously* : A PID is changed upon its expiry or when V_i enters a new RSU. In the first case, adversary(A) can easily find the PID and its expiry time. If PID_i is the only PID expiring at time t_i, then A can track it trivially, if there are k such PID's expiring simultaneously, then the probability of PID_j being assigned to V_i is $\frac{1}{k}$. As far as high privacy users are concerned, it is ensured that a threshold "t" users are always updated along with the high privacy user. Moreover, if V_i is the only vehicle entering the RSU zone, then A can track it trivially. But in a dynamic environment such as VANET, there will always be vehicles moving in and out of a RSU zone. So if there are "n" vehicles entering into an RSU, then the probability of PID_j being assigned to V_i is $\frac{1}{n}$. Hence, if both the events occur in a RSU, PID_j being assigned to V_i is $\frac{1}{k} \times \frac{1}{n}$, which would be small, if n and k are sufficiently large.

Hence, the scheme provides anonymous authentication and even the compromise of individual system components would not reveal any useful information to the adversary.

Liability: When a vehicle V_i is reported for misbehaviour, its signcrypted message σ is submitted along with its PID to the RSU, by the competent legal authority. The RSU will lookup its visitor database and finds $HRSU_i$ and sends "reveal identity" query to HRSU. HRSU will search its pseudonym database and forward H(RID,PWD) to the CA and requests "reveal identity". The CA would query its RID Database and would reveal the engine number to the legal authority.

Signature Size: Using a 1024 bit security, when a vehicle sends a signcrypted message σ =(R,I,c), where R is 128 bytes, I is 32 bytes and c is 32 bytes, the total size of σ is 192 bytes. If we remove the message part, i.e, 'c', the signature overhead is 192-32 = 160 bytes. If we add to this, a PID of 6 bytes and a timestamp of 1 byte we get a total overhead of 167 bytes. This is a huge reduction as compared to Public Key Cryptography Signature(PKCS) scheme like RSA which uses 1152 bytes. The GSIS protocol uses a group ID of 2 bytes,message ID of 2 bytes, timestamp of 4 bytes, TTL of 1 byte and signature of 192 bytes resulting in a message overhead of 201 bytes. We have given comparison of our protocol against some standard protocols in vogue in table 7.

Table 7. Signature Size Comparison

Scheme	Size
PKCS with RSA	1152 bytes
GSIS	201 bytes
HMAC [15]	200 bytes
Threshold	200 bytes
RAHAA	167 bytes

Table 8. Timing Comparison

Scheme	Signing Time	Verification Time
Kamat's IDB	117 ms	124 ms
GSIS	54 ms	52 ms
SeVeCom	0.6 ms	2.4 ms + c.N*
Threshold	10 ms	27 ms
RAHAA	10 ms	10 ms
AMLA	10 ms	10 ms

Time Analysis: The CLSC scheme used in our protocol involves three exponential operations for signing and two exponential operations for verification and no pairing operations, which reduces the time delay to a large extent. In a broadcast environment, a vehicle would verify much more messages than signing, and therefore, a smaller verification delay is a major requirement. Our scheme was implemented in Java SDK 1.7 on Intel core processor with 2.26 Ghz processor and it was observed that, on the average, the signing took 16 ms and verification took 10 ms for a 1024 bit prime number. The signing time can be reduced to 10 ms if we can pre-calculate and store a set of R (a 1024-bit number) in the vehicle. This reduced verification time combined with the RSU-based approach implies that each vehicle will be verifying relatively smaller number of messages in a lesser time frame. A comparison of signing and verification times of various standard schemes, as calculated in the original papers and in [20], are shown in Table 8, where N = number of entries in CRL, c = time to check one entry.

5   Simulation and Results

We used Qualnet and java code on JDK 1.7 to simulate the VANET traffic and calculate the traffic flow. We assumed a simulation area of 1000*1000 m which is large enough to cover 100 to 1000 vehicles. The simulation period was also varied from 5 to 60 seconds at a fixed datarate of 6 MBps. The vehicles are assumed to move at a speed from 10 to 80 Kmph and random way point mobility model is considered.

Message Overhead Analysis: In a broadcast environment like VANET, it is desired that the message overhead is as small as possible, to free up sufficient bandwidth for useful communication. In this section, we compare our protocol with Non-RSU aided protocol like SeVeCom, where messages do not rely on RSU for verification of event notification messages. As we can see in Figure 1, the system performance degrades linearly with increase in number of vehicles (100 to 1000). But our protocol is 48% better than SeVeCom at every stage of comparison and it in fact performs much better at maximum load (1000 vehicles). As we can see the curve for RAHAA has much lower gradient as compared to that for SeVeCom. Our system is efficient even in the absence of RSU, as RSU will not be present only at places with very low vehicle density, where the number of event notification messages would also be far less, keeping the verification delay within the acceptable limits.

Verification Delay Analysis: We compare RAHAA with schemes like Kamat's IDB and hybrid schemes like GSIS, based on the verification time given in Table 8 and the resultant graph is given in Figure 2. On the average, the verification delay of our scheme is 12 times better than that for GSIS and 29 times better than that for Kamat's IDB. Even in the absence of RSU, our scheme outperforms Kamat's IDB and Hybrid Schemes. This not only shows that our scheme has lesser verification delay, when all other parameters remain the same, but it also

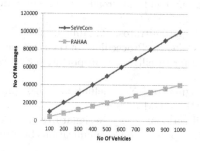

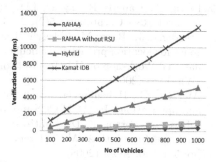

Fig. 1. Message Overhead Analysis   **Fig. 2.** Verification Delay Analysis

shows that RAHAA can efficiently handle more vehicles at any given time as compared to the other two schemes. This indicates that our scheme is robust and scalable.

6   Conclusion

In this paper, we have designed a noverl RSU-aided system for the VANET and proposed an efficient protocol for anonymous authentication based on CLSC, without pairing. The system possesses salient features like semi-trusted RTA, CA being offline, segregation of trust among trusted authorities, efficient pseudonym management and fast verification. It also reduces the database load at trusted authorities. The use of CLSC also improves the bandwidth utilization by doing away with the certificates, thereby freeing up bandwidth for useful communication. The signature size can be further reduced if we choose p using Elliptic Curve rather than Zp^*.

References

1. Lagana, M., Feiri, M., Sall, M., Lange, M., Tomatis, A., Papadimitratos, P.: Secure communication in vehicular networks - PRESERVE DEMO. In: Proceedings of the 5th IEEE International Symposium on Wireless Vehicular Communications (2013)
2. Papadimitratos, P., Buttyan, L., Holczer, T., Schoch, E., Ger, J.F., Raya, M., Ma, Z., Kargl, F., Kung, A., Hubaux, J.-P.: Secure vehicular communication systems: Design and architecture. IEEE Communications 46(11), 100–109 (2008)
3. Raya, M., Hubaux, J.-P.: The security of vehicular ad hoc networks. In: Proceedings of the 3rd ACM Workshop on Security of ad hoc and Sensor Networks, pp. 11–21. ACM (2005)
4. Alexiou, N., Lagana, M., Gisdakis, S., Khodaei, M., Papadimitratos, P.: Vespa: Vehicular security and privacy-preserving architecture. In: Proceedings of the 2nd ACM Workshop on Hot Topics on Wire less Network Security and Privacy (2013)
5. Zeng, K.: Pseudonymous PKI for ubiquitous computing. In: Atzeni, A.S., Lioy, A. (eds.) EuroPKI 2006. LNCS, vol. 4043, pp. 207–222. Springer, Heidelberg (2006)

6. Perrig, A., Canetti, R., Tygar, J.D., Song, D.: The tesla broadcast authentication protocol. RSA Cryptobytes 5(2), 2–13 (2002)
7. Freudiger, J., Raya, M., Felegyhazi, M., Papadimitratos, P., Hubaux, J.P.: Mix-zones for location privacy in vehicular networks. In: Proceedings of the First International Workshop on Wireless Networking for Intelligent Transportation Systems (Win-ITS) (2007)
8. Ateniese, G., Hohenberger, S.: Proxy re-signatures: New definitions, algorithms, and applications. In: ACM CCS, pp. 310–319. ACM (2005)
9. Libert, B., Vergnaud, D.: Multi-use unidirectional proxy re-signatures. In: Proceedings of the 15th ACM Conference on Computer and Communications Security, pp. 511–520. ACM (2008)
10. Zhang, C., Lin, X., Lu, R., Ho, P.H., Shen, X.: An efficient message authentication scheme for vehicular communications. IEEE Transactions on Vehicular Technology 57(6), 3357–3368 (2008)
11. Lu, R., Lin, X., Zhu, H., Ho, P.H., Shen, X.: ECPP: Efficient con- ditional privacy preservation protocol for secure vehicular communications. In: INFOCOM, pp. 1229–1237 (2008)
12. Sun, J., Zhang, C., Fang, Y.: An ID-based framework achieving privacy and non-repudiation in vehicular ad hoc networks. In: IEEE Military Communications Conference, MILCOM 2007, pp. 1–7. IEEE (2007)
13. Lin, X., Sun, X., Ho, P.-H., Shen, X.: Gsis: a secure and privacy preserving protocol for vehicular communications. IEEE Transactions on Vehicular Technology 56(6), 3442–3456 (2007)
14. Chaurasia, B.K., Verma, S.: Infrastructure based authentication in vanets. International Journal of Multimedia and Ubiquitous Engineering 6(2), 41–54 (2011)
15. Hu, C., Chim, T.W., Yiu, S.M., Hui, L.C.K., Li, V.O.K.: Efficient HMAC based secure communication for vanets. Computer Networks (2012)
16. Qin, B., Wu, Q., Domingo-Ferrer, J., Susilo, W.: Distributed privacy-preserving secure aggregation in vehicular communication. In: Intelligent Networking and Collaborative Systems (INCoS), pp. 100–107. IEEE (2011)
17. Jing, X.: Provably secure certificateless signcryption scheme without pairing. In: Electronic and Mechanical Engineering and Information Technology (EMEIT), vol. 9, pp. 4753–4756. IEEE (2011)
18. Bharadiya Bhavesh, N., Maity, S., Hansdah, R.C.: Authentication with Multiple Levels of anonymity (AMLA) in vanets. In: 2012 International Conference on Advanced Information Networking and Applications(AINA). IEEE (2013)
19. Zhu, L., Chen, C., Wang, X., Lim, A.O.: SMSS: Symmetric Masquerade Security Scheme for vanets. In: ISADS, pp. 617–622. IEEE (2011)
20. Liting Huang. Secure and privacy-preserving broadcast authentication for IVC. Master's thesis, Universiteit Twente (2012)
21. Zhang, C., Lin, X., Lu, R., Ho, P.-H.: RAISE: an efficient RSU-aided message authentication scheme in vehicular communication networks. In: IEEE International Conference on Communications, ICC 2008, pp. 1451–1457 (2008)

Recipient Anonymous Ciphertext-Policy Attribute Based Encryption

Y. Sreenivasa Rao and Ratna Dutta

Indian Institute of Technology Kharagpur
Kharagpur-721302, India
{ysrao,ratna}@maths.iitkgp.ernet.in

Abstract. Attribute Based Encryption (ABE) is a promising and increasingly versatile paradigm. Given the many potential uses of ABE schemes, constructing efficient schemes that provide recipient anonymity via policy hiding while ensuring constant-size secret key and ciphertext with strong security notion is a challenging task. In this paper, we propose a fully secure recipient anonymous Ciphertext-Policy ABE (CP-ABE) scheme using an AND-gate access policy. The secret key size, ciphertext size and computation costs are all *constant* in our scheme. To the best of our knowledge, this is the first fully secure CP-ABE scheme with hidden access policy as well as constant ciphertext length which preserves recipient anonymity. The security analysis is in non-selective model under four static assumptions over composite order bilinear groups.

Keywords: recipient anonymity, attribute based encryption, ciphertext-policy, composite order bilinear group.

1   Introduction

The practical deployment of public key encryption is to ensure that only the intended recipients can decrypt the data. Identity-Based Encryption (IBE) [2] is a major breakthrough in public key encryption that enables one-to-one communication, where encrypted data is intended for a specific recipient who is known to the sender in advance. However, several applications have demanded encryption of data according to some policy based on recipients' credentials, without prior knowledge of actual recipients, in such a way that only legitimate recipients are allowed to view the encrypted data. Attribute-Based Encryption (ABE), proposed by Sahai and Waters [3], is witnessed an increasing interest towards such goal. In ABE, each user is ascribed a set of descriptive attributes (or credentials), and secret key and ciphertext are associated with an access policy or a set of attributes. Decryption is then successful only when the attributes of ciphertext or secret key satisfy the access policy. ABE is classified as Key-Policy ABE (KP-ABE) [4] or Ciphertext-Policy ABE (CP-ABE) [5] according to whether the secret key or ciphertext is associated with an access policy, respectively. While the first ABE system [3] is considered as a KP-ABE with threshold access policy, the first CP-ABE system is devised by Bethencourt et al. [5] for monotone access

A. Bagchi and I. Ray (Eds.): ICISS 2013, LNCS 8303, pp. 329–344, 2013.

structures (MAS) which are more expressive access policies in nature. The proof of security is only analyzed in the generic bilinear group model. Consequently, several improved CP-ABE schemes [6–13, 17–24, 27] are suggested.

Goyal et al. [4] presented the first KP-ABE system that allows any monotone access structure, while Ostrovsky et al. [1] proposed the first KP-ABE scheme which allows any non-monotone access structure (nonMAS). Lewko et al. [14] further came up with efficient non-monotone KP-ABE construction which is an improvement of the work of [1] by employing the techniques from revocation systems. All the foregoing KP/CP-ABE constructions except [8] are proven to be *selectively* secure—the simulation starts with the announcement of the adversary's target that he intends to attack. Lewko et al. [8] presented the first *fully* (non-selective) secure KP-ABE (and CP-ABE) schemes using Linear Secret-Sharing Scheme (LSSS)-realizable MAS in the standard model over composite order bilinear groups. To achieve full security, they adapt the dual system encryption technique of Waters [16]. Regarding nonMAS, Okamoto and Takashima [15] proposed a KP-ABE (and a CP-ABE) scheme which is fully secure under the Decisional Linear (DLIN) assumption in the standard model over prime order groups. Attrapadung et al. [26] proposed the first constant-size ciphertext selectively-secure KP-ABE for MAS as well as nonMAS over prime order groups with constant number of pairings, further improved by Rao and Dutta [25].

Every ABE construction suffers from at least one of the following facts: (i) the number of secret key components *grows* linearly with the number of user attributes, (ii) the ciphertext size is *linear* in the number of ciphertext attributes, (iii) the number of exponentiations and pairing computations during encryption and decryption are *linear* in the number of required attributes and (iv) the access policy is sent along with the ciphertext (in CP-ABE), i.e., the scheme does not provide *recipient anonymity*. Moreover, most of the schemes are proven to be selectively secure. A comparison in properties and security levels of current ABE schemes are given in Table 1, 2.

The schemes which feature constant communication and computation cost are becoming ideal primitives where the resources have limited computing power and bandwidth is the primary concern (e.g., wireless sensor networks). In policy revealing CP-ABE schemes, an unauthorized user can learn the access policy ascribed to the ciphertext. The policy hiding schemes are useful in some applications such as military operations wherein the access policy must also be kept secret. Given the potential uses of ABE schemes, constructing an efficient ABE scheme that provides recipient anonymity via policy hiding while ensuring constant-size secret key, constant ciphertext length and constant computation cost with strong security level is a crucial problem. To the best of our knowledge, there is no such existing contstruction in the literature. We address these concerns in a ciphertext-policy setting.

Our Contribution. In this paper, we present the *first* fully secure recipient anonymous CP-ABE scheme whose secret key size, ciphertext size and computation costs are all constant regardless of the number of underlying attributes using an AND-gate access policy. To this end, we adopt the technique of [10].

Table 1. Comparison between previous work and our (here "$\sqrt{}$" and "×" denote the scheme possesses and the scheme does not possess the corresponding property, resp.)

Scheme	KP-ABE/ CP-ABE	Constant-Size Secret Key	Constant-Size Ciphertext	Recipient Anonymity	Security Model
[1, 3, 4]	KP-ABE	×	×	×	Selective
[25, 26]	KP-ABE	×	$\sqrt{}$	×	Selective
[8, 15]	KP-ABE	×	×	×	Full security
[6, 7, 24]	CP-ABE	×	×	×	Selective
[5, 8, 15]	CP-ABE	×	×	×	Full security
[11–13, 18, 20]	CP-ABE	×	$\sqrt{}$	×	Selective
[21–23]	CP-ABE	×	×	$\sqrt{}$	Selective
[19, 27]	CP-ABE	×	×	$\sqrt{}$	Full Security
[10, 17]	CP-ABE	$\sqrt{}$	$\sqrt{}$	×	Selective
Our	CP-ABE	$\sqrt{}$	$\sqrt{}$	$\sqrt{}$	Full Security

Table 2. Comparison of expressiveness of an access policy

Scheme	Access Policy
[3, 11, 13]	t-out-of-n threshold policy
[4, 5, 7, 27]	Tree-based policy
[1, 15]	Non-monotone policy
[6, 8, 25, 26]	Linear Secret-Sharing Scheme realizable policy
[17, 20, 24]	AND-gate on positive and negative attributes with wildcards
[19, 23]	AND-gate on multi-valued attributes with wildcards
[12, 22]	AND-gate on positive and negative attributes
[18]	AND-gate on positive attributes
[10, 21], Our	AND-gate on multi-valued attributes

In proposed scheme, the ciphertext consists of 3 group elements and the secret key consists of 2 group elements. Therefore, the size of ciphertext and secret key are independent of the number of attributes associated with it. No pairing computation is needed in encryption and only two pairing computations are required to decrypt a message. The number of exponentiations during secret key generation, encryption and decryption is independent of the number of underlying attributes. Hence, our construction achieves constant computation cost.

In policy hiding CP-ABE schemes, the encryptor conceals access policy and hence the decryption will be carried out without knowledge of ciphertext policy. In turn, an intermediate adversary cannot obtain any information about the ciphertext policy. However, the concealment of an access policy cannot simply provide recipient anonymity. Given an access policy W and a ciphertext, if an adversary is able to determine whether the ciphertext is encrypted under the given access policy W or not, then the scheme is said to provide *no* recipient anonymity. As noted by Emura et al. in [10], the CP-ABE scheme described in [10] is not recipient anonymous (for details see Section 2.4). By adopting the

Table 3. Comparative summary of constant-size ciphertext CP-ABE schemes

Scheme	KeyGen E_G	Encrypt E_G	E_{G_T}	Decrypt E_G	P_e	Secret Key Size	Ciphertext Size	EAP	RA
[11]	$O(|U|)$	$O(|U|)$	1	$O(\phi^2)$	3	$O(|U|)B_G$	$2B_G + B_{G_T} + \tau$	Threshold	No
[20]	$O(|U|)$	2	1	-	3	$O(|U|)B_G$	$2B_G + B_{G_T} + \tau$	AND	No
[12]	$O(|U|)$	2	1	-	2	$O(|U|)B_G$	$2B_G + B_{G_T} + \tau$	AND	No
[18]	$O(|L|)$	2	1	-	2	$O(|L|)B_G$	$2B_G + B_{G_T} + \tau$	AND	No
[13]	$O(|U|^2)$	2	1	$O(\phi)$	2	$O(|U|^2)B_G$	$2B_G + B_{G_T} + \tau$	Threshold	No
[10]	4	2	1	-	2	$2B_G$	$2B_G + B_{G_T} + \tau$	AND	No
[17]	$O(|U|)$	3	1	-	2	$2B_G$	$2B_G + B_{G_T} + \tau$	AND	No
Our	2	2	1	-	2	$2B_G$	$2B_G + B_{G_T}$	AND	Yes

E_G (or E_{G_T}) = number of exponentiations in a group G (or G_T, resp.), P_e = number of pairing computations, B_G (or B_{G_T}) = bit size of an element in G (or G_T, resp.), $|U|$ = number of attributes in the attribute universe U, ϕ = number of required attributes in decryption, $|L|$ = number of attributes which the user holds, τ = size of ciphertext policy, EAP = expressiveness of access policy and RA = recipient anonymity.

concept of dual system encryption introduced in [16], we accomplish recipient anonymous fully secure CP-ABE primitive in the standard model over composite order bilinear groups.

For our construction, the access policy is formulated by an AND-gate on multi-valued attributes, which is similar to the access policies used in [10, 21] and is a subset of the access policies used in [19, 23]. A crucial property of ABE systems is collusion-resistant, i.e., no two or more receivers can combine their secret keys to decrypt the encrypted data that they are not entitled to decrypt alone. The proposed scheme is collusion-resistant since in the key generation phase each user is given one group element as a secret key component corresponding to the set of all attributes which the user holds, no matter how many attributes the user attribute set is associated with. The user cannot extract the individual secret attribute keys from this single secret key component. Hence, different users cannot pool their secret keys in order to decrypt a ciphertext. In Table 3, we give a comparison of the size of secret key, ciphertext size and computation costs of our scheme with the previous CP-ABE schemes whose secret key size or ciphertext size or both are constant.

2   Preliminaries

2.1   Composite Order Bilinear Groups

Our construction depends on composite order bilinear groups first introduced in [28]. Let $\mathcal{G}(\cdot)$ be a group generator algorithm which takes as input the implicit security parameter κ and outputs a tuple $(N = p_1 p_2 p_3, G, G_T, e)$, where p_1, p_2, p_3 are distinct primes, G and G_T are cyclic groups of composite order $N = p_1 p_2 p_3$ and $e : G \times G \to G_T$ is a map satisfying the following properties: (Bilinearity) for all $u, v \in \mathbb{G}$ and $a, b \in \mathbb{Z}_N$, we have $e(u^a, v^b) = e(u, v)^{ab}$, and (Non-degeneracy) there exists $g \in \mathbb{G}$ such that $e(g, g)$ has order N in $\mathbb{G}_T$. Assume that the group operations in $\mathbb{G}$ and $\mathbb{G}_T$, and the bilinear map e are computable in time polynomial in κ. Let $\mathbb{G}_{p_1}, \mathbb{G}_{p_2}$ and $\mathbb{G}_{p_3}$ be subgroups of order p_1, p_2 and p_3 in $\mathbb{G}$, respectively. For any $u_i \in \mathbb{G}_{p_i}, u_j \in \mathbb{G}_{p_j}$, for $i \neq j$, we have $e(u_i, u_j) = 1_T$, where 1_T is the identity element in $\mathbb{G}_T$. This property is called *orthogonal property* of the subgroups $\mathbb{G}_{p_1}, \mathbb{G}_{p_2}$ and $\mathbb{G}_{p_3}$ (for details see [8]). It is used to implement semi-functionality in our security proof.

Each element $T \in \mathbb{G}$ can uniquely be written as $X_1 X_2 X_3$ (product of three elements), where $X_i \in \mathbb{G}_{p_i}$ and is referred to as the "$\mathbb{G}_{p_i}$ part of T", for $i \in \{1, 2, 3\}$. For $x, y, z \in \{1, p_1, p_2, p_3\}$, let $\mathbb{G}_{xyz}$ be the subgroup of order xyz in $\mathbb{G}$. A random element $u \in \mathbb{G}_{p_i}$ can be selected by choosing a random $\alpha \in \mathbb{Z}_N$ and setting $u = g_i^\alpha$, if g_i is a generator of $\mathbb{G}_{p_i}$, for $i \in \{1, 2, 3\}$.

We now state the complexity assumptions that we use to prove security of our scheme and these assumptions hold in the generic group model under the assumption that finding a non-trivial factor of N is hard. (Proof will be given in full version of this paper.)

Assumption 1. Given a group generator $\mathcal{G}(\cdot)$, we define the following distribution: $\Sigma = (N = p_1 p_2 p_3, \mathbb{G}, \mathbb{G}_T, e) \leftarrow \mathcal{G}(\kappa)$ and then choose random elements $g_1 \in \mathbb{G}_{p_1}, g_3 \in \mathbb{G}_{p_3}$ and set $D = (\Sigma, g_1, g_3)$. Choose random $T_0 \in \mathbb{G}, T_1 \in \mathbb{G}_{p_1 p_3}$. Now, the advantage of an algorithm $\mathcal{A}$ in breaking Assumption 1 is defined as

$$\mathsf{Adv}_\mathcal{A}^1 = |\Pr[\mathcal{A}(D, T_0) = 1] - \Pr[\mathcal{A}(D, T_1) = 1]|.$$

Assumption 2. Given a group generator algorithm $\mathcal{G}(\cdot)$, we define the following distribution: $\Sigma = (N = p_1 p_2 p_3, \mathbb{G}, \mathbb{G}_T, e) \leftarrow \mathcal{G}(\kappa)$ and then choose random $g_1 \in \mathbb{G}_{p_1}, X_1 X_2 X_3 \in \mathbb{G}, Y_1 Y_2 \in \mathbb{G}_{p_1 p_2}, g_3 \in \mathbb{G}_{p_3}$. Set $D = (\Sigma, g_1, X_1 X_2 X_3, Y_1 Y_2, g_3)$. Choose random $T_0 \in \mathbb{G}_{p_1 p_2}, T_1 \in \mathbb{G}_{p_1}$. Now, the advantage of an algorithm $\mathcal{A}$ in breaking Assumption 2 is defined to be

$$\mathsf{Adv}_\mathcal{A}^2 = |\Pr[\mathcal{A}(D, T_0) = 1] - \Pr[\mathcal{A}(D, T_1) = 1]|.$$

Assumption 3. Given a group generator algorithm $\mathcal{G}(\cdot)$, we define the following distribution: $\Sigma = (N = p_1 p_2 p_3, \mathbb{G}, \mathbb{G}_T, e) \leftarrow \mathcal{G}(\kappa)$ and then choose random $\alpha, s \in \mathbb{Z}_N, g_1 \in \mathbb{G}_{p_1}, X_2, Y_2, Z_2 \in \mathbb{G}_{p_2}, X_3, Y_3 \in \mathbb{G}_{p_3}$ and set $D = (\Sigma, g_1, g_1^\alpha X_2, X_3, g_1^s Y_2 Y_3, Z_2)$. Let $T_0 = e(g_1, g_1)^{\alpha s}$. Choose a random element $T_1 \in_\mathcal{R} \mathbb{G}_T$. Now, the advantage of an algorithm $\mathcal{A}$ in breaking Assumption 3 is defined to be

$$\mathsf{Adv}_\mathcal{A}^3 = |\Pr[\mathcal{A}(D, T_0) = 1] - \Pr[\mathcal{A}(D, T_1) = 1]|.$$

Assumption 4. Given a group generator algorithm $\mathcal{G}(\cdot)$, we define the following distribution: $\Sigma = (N = p_1 p_2 p_3, \mathbb{G}, \mathbb{G}_T, e) \leftarrow \mathcal{G}(\kappa)$ and then choose random $s \in \mathbb{Z}_N, g_1 \in \mathbb{G}_{p_1}, X_2, Y_2, Z_2 \in \mathbb{G}_{p_2}, g_3, X_3, Y_3, Z_3 \in \mathbb{G}_{p_3}$ and set $D = (\Sigma, g_1 X_3, g_1^s Z_3, g_1 X_2, Z_2, g_3)$. Let $T_0 = g_1^s Y_2 Y_3$. Choose a random element $T_1 \in_\mathcal{R} \mathbb{G}$. Now, the advantage of an algorithm $\mathcal{A}$ in breaking Assumption 4 is defined to be

$$\mathsf{Adv}_\mathcal{A}^4 = |\Pr[\mathcal{A}(D, T_0) = 1] - \Pr[\mathcal{A}(D, T_1) = 1]|.$$

Definition 1. *We say that $\mathcal{G}$ satisfies Assumption ℓ if for any polynomial time algorithm $\mathcal{A}$, $\mathrm{Adv}_{\mathcal{A}}^{\ell}$ is a negligible function of κ, for all $\ell \in \{1, 2, 3, 4\}$.*

Definition 2. *A function $f : \mathbb{N} \to \mathbb{R}$ is said to be a negligible function of κ if for each constant $\lambda > 0$, we have $f(\kappa) < \kappa^{-\lambda}$, for all sufficiently large κ.*

2.2   Access Policy

Our access policy is similar to AND-gate on multi-valued attributes access policy used in [10, 21]. We assume that there are n categories $\mathsf{Att}_1, \mathsf{Att}_2, \ldots, \mathsf{Att}_n$ of attributes and for each $i, 1 \leq i \leq n$, let $\mathsf{Att}_i = \{v_{i,1}, v_{i,2}, \ldots, v_{i,k_i}\}$ be the set of possible attributes in the i-th category. Note that $|\mathsf{Att}_i| = k_i$. Then the universe of attributes is $U = \bigcup_{i=1}^{n} \mathsf{Att}_i$. We also assume here that every user has n attributes with each attribute belonging to a different category. For our construction, we use an access policy W, denoted as $W = \bigwedge_{i=1}^{n} w_{i,j_i}$, where $w_{i,j_i} \in \mathsf{Att}_i$. Which is an **AND**-gate on n attributes subject to the condition that each attribute belong to a different category.

Given a set of attributes $L = [v_{1,j_1}, v_{2,j_2}, \ldots, v_{i,j_i}, \ldots, v_{n,j_n}]$, where $v_{i,j_i} \in \mathsf{Att}_i$, of a user and an access policy W, we say that L *satisfies* W, denoted as $L \models W$ if and only if $v_{i,j_i} = w_{i,j_i}$, for all $i, 1 \leq i \leq n$, and otherwise L does not satisfy W, denoted as $L \not\models W$. Note that the number of possible access policies is $\sigma = \prod_{i=1}^{n} k_i$.

2.3   Security Model

A CP-ABE scheme consists of four algorithms:

   1. **Setup**$(\kappa, U) \to (\mathsf{PK}, \mathsf{MK})$,   2. **KeyGen**$(\mathsf{PK}, \mathsf{MK}, L) \to \mathsf{SK}_L$,
   3. **Encrypt**$(\mathsf{PK}, M, W) \to \mathsf{CT}$,   4. **Decrypt**$(\mathsf{CT}, \mathsf{SK}_L) \to M$.

Following [19], we describe a full chosen plaintext security (CPA) model for ciphertext-policy hiding CP-ABE in terms of a game Game which is carried out between a challenger and an adversary $\mathcal{A}$.

Setup. The challenger runs the **Setup** algorithm and gives public key PK to $\mathcal{A}$.

Key Query Phase 1. The adversary is allowed to make queries for secret keys corresponding to sets of attributes $L_1, L_2, \ldots, L_{q_1}$. The challenger runs **KeyGen** algorithm and gives the corresponding secret keys $\mathsf{SK}_{L_1}, \mathsf{SK}_{L_2}, \ldots, \mathsf{SK}_{L_{q_1}}$ to $\mathcal{A}$.

Challenge. The adversary submits two equal length messages M_0, M_1 and two access policies W_0^*, W_1^*. These access policies cannot be satisfied by any of the queried attribute sets $L_1, L_2, \ldots, L_{q_1}$. The challenger flips a random coin $\mu \in \{0, 1\}$ and runs **Encrypt** algorithm in order to encrypt M_μ under W_μ^*. The resulting challenge ciphertext CT^* is given to the adversary $\mathcal{A}$.

Key Query Phase 2. The adversary queries the challenger for secret keys corresponding to sets of attributes $L_{q_1+1}, L_{q_1+2}, \ldots, L_q$ with the restriction that none of these satisfies W_0^* and W_1^*. The challenger now runs **KeyGen** algorithm and returns the corresponding secret keys $\mathsf{SK}_{L_{q_1+1}}, \mathsf{SK}_{L_{q_1+2}}, \ldots, \mathsf{SK}_{L_q}$ to $\mathcal{A}$.

Guess. The adversary outputs a guess bit $\mu' \in \{0, 1\}$ for the challenger's secret coin μ and wins if $\mu' = \mu$.

The advantage of $\mathcal{A}$ in this game is defined as $\mathsf{GameAdv}_{\mathcal{A}} = \Pr[\mu' = \mu] - \frac{1}{2}$, where the probability is taken over all random coin tosses during the game.

Definition 3. *A CP-ABE scheme is said to be fully CPA secure ciphertext-policy hiding (or recipient anonymous) if all polynomial time adversaries have at most a negligible advantage in the above security game.*

2.4   Emura et al. [10] CP-ABE Construction

Setup$(\kappa, U) \to (\mathsf{PK}, \mathsf{MK})$. On receiving the implicit security parameter κ, this algorithm generates a prime number p, a bilinear group $\mathbb{G}$, a random generator $g \in \mathbb{G}$ and a bilinear map $e : \mathbb{G} \times \mathbb{G} \to \mathbb{G}_T$, where $\mathbb{G}$ and $\mathbb{G}_T$ are multiplicative groups of order p. It then chooses randomly $h \in \mathbb{G}, \alpha \in \mathbb{Z}_p, t_{i,j} \in \mathbb{Z}_p$, for each attribute $v_{i,j} \in U, 1 \le i \le n, 1 \le j \le n_i$ and sets $Y = e(g,h)^{\alpha}, T_{i,j} = g^{t_{i,j}}, 1 \le i \le n, 1 \le j \le n_i$. Now, the public key and master secret key are $\mathsf{PK} = \langle p, g, h, Y, \{T_{i,j} | 1 \le i \le n, 1 \le j \le n_i\}\rangle$ and $\mathsf{MK} = \alpha$, respectively. Note that $\forall L_1, L_2$ with $L_1 \ne L_2$, $\sum_{v_{i,j} \in L_1} t_{i,j} \ne \sum_{v_{i,j} \in L_2} t_{i,j}$ is assumed (this assumption is natural, for details see *Remark 1*).

KeyGen$(\mathsf{PK}, \mathsf{MK}, L) \to \mathsf{SK}_L$. Let $L = [v_{1,j_1}, v_{2,j_2}, \ldots, v_{i,j_i}, \ldots, v_{n,j_n}]$, where $1 \le j_i \le k_i$, be the set of attributes of a user. This algorithm randomly chooses $r \in \mathbb{Z}_p$ and sets $D_1 = h^{\alpha} \cdot (g^{\sum_{v_{i,j_i} \in L} t_{i,j_i}})^r$ and $D_2 = g^r$. It outputs the secret key $\mathsf{SK}_L = \langle D_1, D_2\rangle$ associated with L.

Encrypt$(\mathsf{PK}, M, W) \to \mathsf{CT}$. Let $W = \bigwedge_{i=1}^{n} w_{i,j_i}$, where $w_{i,j_i} \in \mathsf{Att}_i$, be an access policy. Chooses a random $s \in \mathbb{Z}_p$ and sets $C = MY^s, C_1 = g^s, C_2 = (\prod_{w_{i,j_i} \in W} T_{i,j_i})^s$. The ciphertext $\mathsf{CT} = \langle C, C_1, C_2\rangle$.

Decrypt$(\mathsf{CT}, \mathsf{SK}_L) \to M$. This algorithm recovers the message M by computing $C \cdot e(D_2, C_2)/e(D_1, C_1)$, if $L \models W$.

Remark 1. (Secret Keys, $t_{i,j}$, Construction) *In construction of [10],* $\sum_{v_{i,j} \in L_1} t_{i,j} \ne \sum_{v_{i,j} \in L_2} t_{i,j}$, *for all L_1, L_2 with $L_1 \ne L_2$, is assumed. If there exists L_1 and L_2 such that $L_1 \ne L_2$ and $\sum_{v_{i,j} \in L_1} t_{i,j} = \sum_{v_{i,j} \in L_2} t_{i,j}$, then any user having the attribute set L_1 can decrypt a ciphertext encrypted under an access policy W, where $L_1 \not\models W$ and $L_2 \models W$. Note that the number of access policies is $\sigma = \prod_{i=1}^{n} k_i$. Following [10], the assumption holds with probability $\frac{p(p-1)\cdots(p-(\sigma-1))}{p^{\sigma}} > \frac{(p-(\sigma-1))^{\sigma}}{p^{\sigma}} > \left(1 - \frac{\sigma-1}{p}\right)^{\sigma} > 1 - \frac{\sigma(\sigma-1)}{p} > 1 - \frac{\sigma^2}{p}$. Therefore, if each secret key $t_{i,j}$ is chosen at random from $\mathbb{Z}_p$, the assumption is natural.*

We now argue why the foregoing CP-ABE scheme is not recipient anonymous. Some components C_1, C_2 of a ciphertext CT for attributes form a Decision Diffie-Hellman (DDH)-tuple $(C_1, C_2) = (g^s, g^{s \sum_{w_{i,j_i} \in W} t_{i,j_i}})$. Hence, it exposes some information about attributes. Precisely, given an access policy $W' = \bigwedge_{i=1}^{n} w_{i,j_i'}$, the adversary can run the DDH-test $e(C_1, \prod_{w_{i,j_i'} \in W'} T_{i,j_i'}) \overset{?}{=} e(C_2, g)$, which is same as $e(C_1, \prod_{w_{i,j_i'} \in W'} T_{i,j_i'})/e(C_2, g) \overset{?}{=} 1_T$, where 1_T is the identity element in $\mathbb{G}_T$, on the public keys of attributes occur in W' and the ciphertext components.

This in turn allows the adversary to determine whether the ciphertext CT is encrypted under the access policy W' or not. The scheme is then said to provide *no* recipient anonymity.

3   Our Construction

Our CP-ABE consists of the following four algorithms.

Setup$(\kappa, U) \to$ (PK, MK). This algorithm obtains a tuple $(p_1, p_2, p_3, \mathbb{G}, \mathbb{G}_T, e)$ by running the group generator algorithm $\mathcal{G}(\kappa)$, where p_1, p_2, p_3 are distinct primes, $\mathbb{G}$ and $\mathbb{G}_T$ are two cyclic groups of same composite order $N = p_1 p_2 p_3$ and $e : \mathbb{G} \times \mathbb{G} \to \mathbb{G}_T$ is a bilinear map. Note that $\mathbb{G}_{p_1}$ and $\mathbb{G}_{p_3}$ are subgroups of $\mathbb{G}$ of order p_1 and p_3, respectively. It randomly picks generators g_1, g_3 of $\mathbb{G}_{p_1}, \mathbb{G}_{p_3}$, respectively and selects random elements $P \in \mathbb{G}_{p_1}, R_0 \in \mathbb{G}_{p_3}$.

For each attribute $v_{i,j} \in U$, $1 \le i \le n, 1 \le j \le k_i$, a random exponent $a_{i,j} \in \mathbb{Z}_N$ and a random element $R_{i,j} \in \mathbb{G}_{p_3}$ are chosen. We assume that $\sum_{v_{i,j} \in L_1} a_{i,j} \ne \sum_{v_{i,j} \in L_2} a_{i,j}$, where L_1 and L_2 are two sets of attributes such that $L_1 \ne L_2$ (this assumption is similar to *Remark 1* with $t_{i,j} = a_{i,j}$ and $p = N$).

Now, it sets $Y = e(P, g_1)$, $A_0 = g_1 \cdot R_0$, $A_{i,j} = g_1^{a_{i,j}} \cdot R_{i,j}$, for all $1 \le i \le n$ and $1 \le j \le k_i$. The public key is PK $= \langle N, A_0, g_3, Y, \{A_{i,j} | 1 \le i \le n, 1 \le j \le k_i\}\rangle$ and the master secret key is MK $= \langle g_1, P \rangle$.

KeyGen(PK, MK, L) $\to$ SK$_L$. Let $L = [v_{1,j_1}, v_{2,j_2}, \ldots, v_{i,j_i}, \ldots, v_{n,j_n}]$, where $1 \le j_i \le k_i$, be the set of attributes of a user. This algorithm randomly chooses $r \in \mathbb{Z}_N$ and computes $D_1 = P \cdot \left(g_1^{\sum_{v_{i,j_i} \in L} a_{i,j_i}} \right)^r$ and $D_2 = g_1^r$.

Finally, it outputs the secret key associated with L is SK$_L = \langle D_1, D_2 \rangle$.

Encrypt(PK, M, W) $\to$ CT. Let $M \in \mathbb{G}_T$ be the message to be encrypted and let $W = \bigwedge_{i=1}^{n} w_{i,j_i}$, where $w_{i,j_i} \in$ Att$_i$, be an access policy. This algorithm chooses at random $s \in \mathbb{Z}_N$ and $R_0', R' \in \mathbb{G}_{p_3}$. It then computes

$$C = M \cdot Y^s, C_1 = A_0^s \cdot R_0' \text{ and } C_2 = \left(\prod_{i=1}^{n} A_{i,j_i} \right)^s \cdot R'. \text{ The ciphertext is}$$

CT $= \langle C, C_1, C_2 \rangle$. Where the access policy W is not embedded in CT.

Note that a random element $R \in \mathbb{G}_{p_3}$ can be selected by choosing a random $\alpha \in \mathbb{Z}_N$ and setting $R = g_3^\alpha$ (observe g_3 is publicly given).

Decrypt(CT, SK$_L$) $\to M$. The recipient decrypts the ciphertext CT using his own secret key SK$_L = \langle D_1, D_2 \rangle$ without knowing the access policy W by computing $C \cdot \frac{e(D_2, C_2)}{e(D_1, C_1)}$, which returns the correct message M, if $L \models W$.

If the user attribute set L satisfies the hidden access policy W of the ciphertext, the user can recover the message M correctly. In order to know whether the decryption was successful without knowing W, the user can use the technique outlined in [23]. The technique is that the encryptor selects at random key $\in \mathbb{G}_T$ and generates two uniform and independent ℓ-bit symmetric keys (key$_1$, key$_2$) from key. Then, it encrypts key under the public key PK and access policy W by running **Encrypt**(PK, key, W) = CT. On the other hand, the message M is encrypted under key_1 using a symmetric encryption scheme $\mathcal{E}_{\mathsf{key}_1}(M)$. The final ciphertext is of the form $\mathsf{CT}' = \langle \mathsf{key}_2, \mathsf{CT}, \mathcal{E}_{\mathsf{key}_1}(M) \rangle$. The user (or recipient) can use key_2 to check whether the decryption was successful after decrypting key from CT where the false positive probability is approximately $1/2^\ell$. If successful, the user decrypts M by using key_1 derived from key.

Recipient Anonymity. We now show how the proposed scheme provides recipient anonymity by employing composite order bilinear groups. Suppose the adversary is given an arbitrary access policy $W' = \bigwedge_{i=1}^n w_{i,j_i'}$, where $w_{i,j_i'} \in \mathsf{Att}_i$, and a ciphertext $\mathsf{CT} = \langle C, C_1, C_2 \rangle$ which is an output of the encryption algorithm Encrypt. Let CT is encrypted under an access policy $W = \bigwedge_{i=1}^n w_{i,j_i}$. The adversary then performs the DDH-test as follows.

$$
\frac{e\left(C_1, \prod_{i=1}^n A_{i,j_i'}\right)}{e(C_2, A_0)} = \frac{e\left(g_1^s R_0^s R_0', g_1^{\sum_{i=1}^n a_{i,j_i'}} \prod_{i=1}^n R_{i,j_i'}\right)}{e\left(g_1^{\sum_{i=1}^n s a_{i,j_i}} (\prod_{i=1}^n R_{i,j_i}^s) R', g_1 R_0\right)}
$$

$$
= \frac{e(g_1^s, g_1^{\sum_{i=1}^n a_{i,j_i'}}) \cdot e(R_0^s, R_{W'}) \cdot e(R_0', R_{W'})}{e(g_1^{s \sum_{i=1}^n a_{i,j_i}}, g_1) \cdot e(R_W^s, R_0) \cdot e(R', R_0)},
$$

where $R_{W'} = \prod_{i=1}^n R_{i,j_i'}$ and $R_W = \prod_{i=1}^n R_{i,j_i}$. Note that due to orthogonal property (see Section 2.1), some pairings in both numerator and denominator become identity in $\mathbb{G}_T$.

There are two possible cases.

- If $W' = W$, then $j_i' = j_i$ for all $i, 1 \le i \le n$, and hence $\sum_{i=1}^n a_{i,j_i'} = \sum_{i=1}^n a_{i,j_i}$ and $R_{W'} = R_W$. Therefore,

$$
\frac{e\left(C_1, \prod_{i=1}^n A_{i,j_i'}\right)}{e(C_2, A_0)} = \frac{e(R_0', R_{W'})}{e(R', R_0)}.
$$

- Suppose $W' \ne W$. Then, there exists at least one $k, 1 \le k \le n$ such that $j_k' \ne j_k$. Without loss of generality, we can assume that $j_i' = j_i$, for all $i, 1 \le i \le n$ except $i = k$. Then $a_{i,j_i'} = a_{i,j_i}, R_{i,j_i'} = R_{i,j_i}$, for all $i, 1 \le i \le n$, except $i = k$. Therefore,

$$
\frac{e\left(C_1, \prod_{i=1}^n A_{i,j_i'}\right)}{e(C_2, A_0)} = \frac{e(g_1^s, g_1^{a_{k,j_k'}}) \cdot e(R_0^s, R_{k,j_k'}) \cdot e(R_0', R_{W'})}{e(g_1^{s a_{k,j_k}}, g_1) \cdot e(R_{k,j_k}^s, R_0) \cdot e(R', R_0)}.
$$

In both the cases the DDH-test gives a random element of $\mathbb{G}_T$ so that the adversary cannot determine whether the ciphertext CT is encrypted under the access policy W' or not. Thus, our scheme *preserves* recipient anonymity.

4   Security Analysis

We use the dual system encryption technique introduced in [16] to prove full security of our scheme. In a dual system technique, secret keys and ciphertexts can either be normal or semi-functional. The semi-functional secret keys and ciphertexts are not used in a real scheme. Instead, they are used in a security proof. The normal secret keys can decrypt normal as well as semi-functional ciphertexts. The semi-functional secret keys can decrypt normal ciphertexts, but cannot decrypt a semi-functional ciphertext. Let us define formally semi-functional secret keys and ciphertexts as follows. We first choose random values $z_{i,j} \in \mathbb{Z}_N$, for each attribute $v_{i,j} \in U, 1 \leq i \leq n, 1 \leq j \leq k_i$. These values are common to both semi-functional ciphertexts and secret keys.

Semi-functional Ciphertext. Let g_2 be a generator of the subgroup $\mathbb{G}_{p_2}$ and let $W = \bigwedge_{i=1}^n w_{i,j_i}$, where $w_{i,j_i} \in \mathsf{Att}_i$, be an access policy. First run encryption algorithm **Encrypt** to obtain a normal ciphertext $\mathsf{CT} = \langle C, C_1, C_2 \rangle$. Then choose a random exponent $\delta \in \mathbb{Z}_N$, and compute the semi-functional ciphertext $\mathsf{CT}' = \langle C', C_1', C_2' \rangle$, where

$$C' = C, C_1' = C_1 \cdot g_2^\delta, C_2' = C_2 \cdot g_2^{\delta \sum_{i=1}^n z_{i,j_i}}.$$

Semi-functional Secret Key. Let $L = [v_{1,j_1}, v_{2,j_2}, \ldots, v_{i,j_i}, \ldots, v_{n,j_n}]$ be the set of attributes of a user for which a semi-functional secret key is computed. Firstly, run key generation algorithm **KeyGen** to obtain a normal secret key $\mathsf{SK}_L = \langle D_1, D_2 \rangle$ associated with the user attribute set L. Then choose two random exponents $\gamma_1, \gamma_2 \in \mathbb{Z}_N$ and compute the semi-functional secret key components as

$$D_1' = D_1 \cdot g_2^{\gamma_1 + \gamma_2 \sum_{v_{i,j_i} \in L} z_{i,j_i}}, \quad D_2' = D_2 \cdot g_2^{\gamma_2}.$$

The semi-functional secret key associated with L is $\mathsf{SK}_L' = \langle D_1', D_2' \rangle$.

It can be shown that if we use a legitimate semi-functional secret key to decrypt a semi-functional ciphertext, the $z_{i,j}$ terms will always be canceled but we are left with an extra term $e(g_2, g_2)^{\delta \gamma_1}$.

In order to prove full security of our scheme, we use a hybrid argument over a sequence of games under Assumptions 1, 2, 3, 4 given in Section 2.1. The sequence of games is as follows. Let q be the number of secret key queries made by the adversary.

$\mathsf{Game}_{\mathsf{Real}}$: This is the real security game (described in Section 2.3) in which the challenge ciphertext and all secret keys are normal.

Game_0 : In this game, the challenge ciphertext is semi-functional, but all secret keys are normal.

$\mathsf{Game}_k (1 \leq k \leq q-1)$: In this game, the challenge ciphertext is semi-functional; the first k secret keys will be semi-functional and the rest of the secret keys are normal.

Game_q : In this game, the challenge ciphertext and all secret keys are semi-functional.

$\mathsf{Game}_{\mathsf{Final}'}$: In this penultimate game, all secret keys are semi-functional and the challenge ciphertext is a semi-functional encryption of a random element in $\mathbb{G}_T$ which is independent of the two messages given by the adversary.

$\mathsf{Game}_{\mathsf{Final}}$: This final game $\mathsf{Game}_{\mathsf{Final}}$ is same as $\mathsf{Game}_{\mathsf{Final}'}$ except that in the challenge ciphertext, C_2' is chosen at random from $\mathbb{G}$. Hence, the ciphertext is independent of the ciphertext-policies provided by the adversary and adversary's advantage in this game is 0.

We will now prove in the following lemmas the indistinguishability of the above games.

Lemma 1. *Suppose that there exists a polynomial time algorithm $\mathcal{A}$ such that* $\mathsf{Game_{Real}Adv}_\mathcal{A} - \mathsf{Game_0Adv}_\mathcal{A} = \epsilon$. *Then we can build a polynomial time algorithm* $\mathcal{B}$ *with advantage* $\epsilon(1 - \frac{\sigma^2}{N})$ *in breaking Assumption 1, i.e.,* $\mathsf{Adv}^1_\mathcal{B} = \epsilon(1 - \frac{\sigma^2}{N})$.

Proof. We construct an algorithm $\mathcal{B}$ which has received $\langle \Sigma, g_1, g_3, T \rangle$, where T is either an element of $\mathbb{G}$ or an element of $\mathbb{G}_{p_1 p_3}$, from the challenger. It simulates either $\mathsf{Game_{Real}}$ or $\mathsf{Game_0}$ depending on the value of T and interacts with $\mathcal{A}$ to break Assumption 1 as described below. Note that a random element $u \in \mathbb{G}_{p_i}$ can be selected by choosing a random $\alpha \in \mathbb{Z}_N$ and setting $u = g_i^\alpha$, if g_i is a random generator of $\mathbb{G}_{p_i}$, for $i \in \{1, 2, 3\}$.

Setup. The algorithm $\mathcal{B}$ randomly selects $P \in \mathbb{G}_{p_1}, R_0, R_{i,j} \in \mathbb{G}_{p_3}, a_{i,j} \in \mathbb{Z}_N$, and sets $Y = e(P, g_1), A_0 = g_1 \cdot R_0, A_{i,j} = g_1^{a_{i,j}} \cdot R_{i,j}$, for all $1 \leq i \leq n$ and $1 \leq j \leq k_i$. It then sends $\mathcal{A}$ the public key $\mathsf{PK} = \langle A_0, g_3, Y, \{A_{i,j} | 1 \leq i \leq n, 1 \leq j \leq k_i\} \rangle$ and keeps the master key $\mathsf{MK} = \langle g_1, P \rangle$ secret to itself.

Key Query Phase 1 and Phase 2. The algorithm $\mathcal{B}$ can generate normal secret keys $\mathsf{SK}_L = \langle D_1, D_2 \rangle$ in response to $\mathcal{A}$'s secret key requests on sets of attributes L by using the **KeyGen** algorithm because it knows the master secret key $\mathsf{MK} = \langle g_1, P \rangle$.

Challenge. The algorithm $\mathcal{A}$ submits two equal length messages M_0, M_1 and two access policies W_0^*, W_1^* to $\mathcal{B}$. In order to compute the challenge ciphertext CT^*, $\mathcal{B}$ implicitly sets g_1^s to be the $\mathbb{G}_{p_1}$ part of T and randomly chooses $t_0, t \in \mathbb{Z}_N$. It then chooses a random $\mu \in \{0, 1\}$. Let $W_\mu^* = \bigwedge_{i=1}^n w_{i,j_i}$. Now, compute the challenge ciphertext as

$$\mathsf{CT}^* = \langle C', C'_1, C'_2 \rangle = \langle M_\mu \cdot e(P, T), T \cdot g_3^{t_0}, T^{\sum_{i=1}^n a_{i,j_i}} \cdot g_3^t \rangle.$$

We note that if there exists an L such that $(L \not\models W_0^*$ and $\sum_{v_{i,j_i} \in L} a_{i,j_i} = \sum_{w_{i,j_i} \in W_0^*} a_{i,j_i})$ or $(L \not\models W_1^*$ and $\sum_{v_{i,j_i} \in L} a_{i,j_i} = \sum_{w_{i,j_i} \in W_1^*} a_{i,j_i})$ holds, then $\mathcal{B}$ aborts. This probability is at most $\frac{\sigma^2}{N}$ as shown in *Remark 1*.

Guess. Finally, $\mathcal{A}$ outputs a guess $\mu' \in \{0, 1\}$ and wins the game if $\mu' = \mu$.

We note that for $i \neq j$, the values ρ modulo p_i are uncorrelated from the values ρ modulo p_j by the Chinese Remainder Theorem. So if $T \in \mathbb{G}_{p_1 p_3}$, CT^* is a properly distributed normal ciphertext and hence $\mathcal{B}$ will simulate the game $\mathsf{Game_{Real}}$. If $T \in \mathbb{G}$, let g_2^δ be the $\mathbb{G}_{p_2}$ part of T, i.e., $T = g_1^s g_2^\delta X_3$, where X_3 is a random element in $\mathbb{G}_{p_3}$. This implicitly sets $z_{i,j_i} = a_{i,j_i}$, and hence CT^* is a properly distributed semi-functional ciphertext and in this case $\mathcal{B}$ simulates the game $\mathsf{Game_0}$. Thus, $\mathcal{B}$ can use the output of $\mathcal{A}$ to break Assumption 1 with advantage $\epsilon(1 - \frac{\sigma^2}{N})$. $\square$

Lemma 2. *Let $1 \leq k \leq q$. Suppose that there exists a polynomial time algorithm $\mathcal{A}$ that makes at most q secret key requests such that* $\mathsf{Game_{k-1}Adv}_\mathcal{A} - \mathsf{Game_kAdv}_\mathcal{A} = \epsilon$. *Then we can build a polynomial time algorithm $\mathcal{B}$ with advantage $\epsilon(1 - \frac{\sigma^2}{N})$ in breaking Assumption 2, i.e., $\mathsf{Adv}^2_\mathcal{B} = \epsilon(1 - \frac{\sigma^2}{N})$.*

Proof. We build an algorithm $\mathcal{B}$ which has received $\langle \Sigma, g_1, X_1X_2X_3, Y_1Y_2, g_3, T \rangle$, where T is either an element of $\mathbb{G}_{p_1p_2}$ or an element of $\mathbb{G}_{p_1}$, from the challenger. It will simulate either Game_{k-1} or Game_k depending on the value of T and interacts with $\mathcal{A}$ to break Assumption 2 as described below.

Setup. The algorithm $\mathcal{B}$ selects randomly $R_0, R_{i,j} \in \mathbb{G}_{p_3}, \alpha, a_{i,j} \in \mathbb{Z}_N$, and sets $Y = e(g_1^\alpha, g_1), A_0 = g_1 \cdot R_0, A_{i,j} = g_1^{a_{i,j}} \cdot R_{i,j}$, for all $1 \leq i \leq n$ and $1 \leq j \leq k_i$. It then sends $\mathcal{A}$ the public key $\mathsf{PK} = \langle A_0, g_3, Y, \{A_{i,j} | 1 \leq i \leq n, 1 \leq j \leq k_i\} \rangle$ and keeps the master key $\mathsf{MK} = \langle g_1, \alpha \rangle$ secret to itself.

Key Query Phase 1 and Phase 2. In order to make first $k-1$ secret keys semi-functional, $\mathcal{B}$ chooses a random $\beta \in \mathbb{Z}_N$, and implicitly sets the $\mathbb{G}_{p_1}$ part of Y_1Y_2 as g_1^a and the $\mathbb{G}_{p_2}$ part of Y_1Y_2 as g_2^b, i.e., $Y_1Y_2 = g_1^a g_2^b$, and responds to each secret key request on a set of attributes L from $\mathcal{A}$ by setting

$$D_1' = g_1^\alpha \cdot (Y_1Y_2)^{\beta \sum_{v_{i,j_i} \in L} a_{i,j_i}}, \quad D_2' = (Y_1Y_2)^\beta.$$

This implicitly sets $z_{i,j_i} = a_{i,j_i}, r = a\beta, \gamma_2 = b\beta$ and $\gamma_1 = 0$, so D_1' and D_2' are properly distributed semi-functional secret key components. Note that the values z_{i,j_i} modulo p_2 are uncorrelated from the values of a_{i,j_i} modulo p_1 by the Chinese Remainder Theorem.

Since $\mathcal{B}$ knows the master secret key $\mathsf{MK} = \langle g_1, \alpha \rangle$, it can simply run the key generation algorithm **KeyGen** to make normal secret keys for the last $q-k$ secret key queries made by the adversary $\mathcal{A}$.

To make k^{th} secret key, $\mathcal{B}$ will implicitly set g_1^r as the $\mathbb{G}_{p_1}$ part of T and sets

$$D_1' = g_1^\alpha \cdot T^{\sum_{v_{i,j_i} \in L} a_{i,j_i}}, \quad D_2' = T.$$

If $T \in \mathbb{G}_{p_1}$, then this is a properly distributed normal secret key. If $T \in \mathbb{G}_{p_1p_2}$, let $T = g_1^r g_2^{\gamma_2}$ then this is a properly distributed semi-functional secret key. In this case, we implicitly set $\gamma_1 = 0$ and $z_{i,j_i} = a_{i,j_i}$.

Challenge. The algorithm $\mathcal{B}$ receives two equal length messages M_0, M_1 and two access policies W_0^*, W_1^* from the adversary $\mathcal{A}$. In order to compute the semi-functional challenge ciphertext CT^*, $\mathcal{B}$ implicitly sets g_1^s to be the $\mathbb{G}_{p_1}$ part and g_2^δ to be the $\mathbb{G}_{p_2}$ part of $X_1X_2X_3$, and randomly chooses $t_0, t \in \mathbb{Z}_N$. It then chooses a random $\mu \in \{0,1\}$. Let $W_\mu^* = \bigwedge_{i=1}^n w_{i,j_i}$. Compute the semi-functional challenge ciphertext $\mathsf{CT}^* = \langle C', C_1', C_2' \rangle$, where $C' = M_\mu \cdot e(g_1^\alpha, X_1X_2X_3), C_1' = (X_1X_2X_3) \cdot g_3^{t_0}, C_2' = (X_1X_2X_3)^{\sum_{i=1}^n a_{i,j_i}} \cdot g_3^t$. The first k semi-functional secret keys and the semi-functional ciphertext are properly distributed except that $\delta\gamma_1 = 0$ modulo p_2. So if a legitimate semi-functional secret key attempts to decrypt the semi-functional ciphertext, the correct message M will be recovered. But the adversary is not provided any secret keys whose sets of attributes satisfy either W_0^* or W_1^*. As in Lemma 1, if there exists an L such that $(L \not\models W_0^*$ and $\sum_{v_{i,j_i} \in L} a_{i,j_i} = \sum_{w_{i,j_i} \in W_0^*} a_{i,j_i})$ or $(L \not\models W_1^*$ and $\sum_{v_{i,j_i} \in L} a_{i,j_i} = \sum_{w_{i,j_i} \in W_1^*} a_{i,j_i})$ holds, then $\mathcal{B}$ aborts. This probability is at most $\frac{\sigma^2}{N}$.

Guess. Finally, $\mathcal{A}$ outputs a guess $\mu' \in \{0,1\}$ and wins the game if $\mu' = \mu$.

If $T \in \mathbb{G}_{p_1}$, then $\mathcal{B}$ has properly simulated the game Game_{k-1} and if $T \in \mathbb{G}_{p_1 p_2}$, then $\mathcal{B}$ has properly simulated the game Game_k. Thus, $\mathcal{B}$ can use the output of $\mathcal{A}$ to break Assumption 2 with advantage $\epsilon(1 - \frac{\sigma^2}{N})$. $\qquad \square$

Lemma 3. *Suppose that there exists a polynomial time algorithm $\mathcal{A}$ that makes at most q secret key requests such that $\mathsf{Game}_q \mathsf{Adv}_{\mathcal{A}} - \mathsf{Game}_{\mathsf{Final'}} \mathsf{Adv}_{\mathcal{A}} = \epsilon$. Then we can build a polynomial time algorithm $\mathcal{B}$ with advantage ϵ in breaking Assumption 3, i.e., $\mathsf{Adv}_{\mathcal{B}}^3 = \epsilon$.*

Proof. We build an algorithm $\mathcal{B}$ that is received $\langle \Sigma, g_1, g_1^{\alpha} X_2, X_3, g_1^s Y_2 Y_3, Z_2, T \rangle$, where $T = e(g_1, g_1)^{\alpha s}$ or a random element of $\mathbb{G}_T$, from the challenger. It will simulate either Game_q or $\mathsf{Game}_{\mathsf{Final'}}$ depending on the value of T and interacts with $\mathcal{A}$ to break Assumption 3 as described below.

Setup. The algorithm $\mathcal{B}$ randomly selects $R_0, R_{i,j} \in \mathbb{G}_{p_3}, a_{i,j} \in \mathbb{Z}_N$, and sets
$Y = e(g_1^{\alpha} X_2, g_1)$,
$A_0 = g_1 \cdot R_0, A_{i,j} = g_1^{a_{i,j}} \cdot R_{i,j}$, for all $1 \leq i \leq n$ and $1 \leq j \leq k_i$. It then sends $\mathcal{A}$ the public key $\mathsf{PK} = \langle A_0, g_3, Y, \{A_{i,j} | 1 \leq i \leq n, 1 \leq j \leq k_i\} \rangle$.

Key Query Phase 1 and Phase 2. In order to make the semi-functional secret keys on sets of attributes, $\mathcal{B}$ randomly chooses $r \in \mathbb{Z}_N$ and sets
$$D_1' = g_1^{\alpha} X_2 (g_1^r)^{\sum_{v_{i,j_i} \in L} a_{i,j_i}} Z_2^{\sum_{v_{i,j_i} \in L} a_{i,j_i}}, D_2' = g_1^r Z_2.$$
This implicitly sets $g_1^{\alpha} = P, g_2^{\gamma_1} = X_2, g_2^{\gamma_2} = Z_2$ and $z_{i,j_i} = a_{i,j_i}$. We note here that the values z_{i,j_i} modulo p_2 are uncorrelated from the values of a_{i,j_i} modulo p_1. So D_1' and D_2' are properly distributed semi-functional secret keys. Now, $\mathcal{B}$ sends $\mathsf{SK}_L' = \langle D_1', D_2' \rangle$ to $\mathcal{A}$.

Challenge. The algorithm $\mathcal{A}$ submits two equal length messages M_0, M_1 and two access policies W_0^*, W_1^* to $\mathcal{B}$. To compute the semi-functional challenge ciphertext CT^*, $\mathcal{B}$ will take s from the assumption term $g_1^s Y_2 Y_3$ and implicitly sets g_2^{δ} to be the $\mathbb{G}_{p_2}$ part of $g_1^s Y_2 Y_3$, and randomly chooses $t_0, t \in \mathbb{Z}_N$. It then chooses a random $\mu \in \{0, 1\}$. Let $W_{\mu}^* = \bigwedge_{i=1}^n w_{i,j_i}$. Compute the semi-functional challenge ciphertext components as
$$C' = M_{\mu} \cdot T, C_1' = (g_1^s Y_2 Y_3) \cdot g_3^{t_0}, C_2' = (g_1^s Y_2 Y_3)^{\sum_{i=1}^n a_{i,j_i}} \cdot g_3^t.$$
This implicitly sets $z_{i,j_i} = a_{i,j_i}$. Then the semi-functional challenge ciphertext $\mathsf{CT}^* = \langle C', C_1', C_2' \rangle$ is sent to $\mathcal{A}$. Note that since all the secret keys and the ciphertext are properly distributed semi-functional, no legitimate semi-functional secret key decrypts the semi-functional ciphertext, so the condition namely that there exists an L such that $(L \not\models W_0^*$ and $\sum_{v_{i,j_i} \in L} a_{i,j_i} = \sum_{w_{i,j_i} \in W_0^*} a_{i,j_i})$ or $(L \not\models W_1^*$ and $\sum_{v_{i,j_i} \in L} a_{i,j_i} = \sum_{w_{i,j_i} \in W_1^*} a_{i,j_i})$ is immaterial.

Guess. Finally, $\mathcal{A}$ outputs a guess $\mu' \in \{0, 1\}$ and wins the game if $\mu' = \mu$.

If $T = e(g_1, g_1)^{\alpha s}$, CT^* is a properly distributed semi-functional encryption of M_{μ} and hence $\mathcal{B}$ will simulate the game Game_q. Similarly, if T is a random element of $\mathbb{G}_T$, then CT^* is a properly distributed semi-functional encryption of a random element of $\mathbb{G}_T$ and therefore $\mathcal{B}$ simulates the game $\mathsf{Game}_{\mathsf{Final'}}$. Thus, $\mathcal{B}$ can use the output of $\mathcal{A}$ to break Assumption 3 with advantage ϵ. $\qquad \square$

Lemma 4. *Suppose that there exists a polynomial time algorithm $\mathcal{A}$ that makes at most q secret key requests such that $\mathsf{Game_{Final'}Adv_{\mathcal{A}}} - \mathsf{Game_{Final}Adv_{\mathcal{A}}} = \epsilon$. Then we can build a polynomial time algorithm $\mathcal{B}$ with advantage ϵ in breaking Assumption 4, i.e., $\mathsf{Adv}_{\mathcal{B}}^{4} = \epsilon$.*

Proof. We build an algorithm $\mathcal{B}$ that is received $\langle \Sigma, g_1 X_3, g_1^s Z_3, g_1 X_2, Z_2, g_3, T \rangle$, where $T = g_1^s Y_2 Y_3$ or a random element of $\mathbb{G}$, from the challenger. It will simulate either $\mathsf{Game_{Final'}}$ or $\mathsf{Game_{Final}}$ depending on the value of T and interacts with $\mathcal{A}$ to break Assumption 4 as follows.

Setup. $\mathcal{B}$ randomly selects $\alpha, a_{i,j} \in \mathbb{Z}_N$, and sets $Y = e((g_1 X_2)^{\alpha}, g_1 X_3)$, $A_0 = g_1 X_3$, $A_{i,j} = (g_1 X_3)^{a_{i,j}}$, for all $1 \leq i \leq n$ and $1 \leq j \leq k_i$. It then sends $\mathcal{A}$ the public key $\mathsf{PK} = \langle A_0, g_3, Y, \{A_{i,j} | 1 \leq i \leq n, 1 \leq j \leq k_i\} \rangle$.

Key Query Phase 1 and Phase 2. In order to make the semi-functional secret keys on sets of attributes, $\mathcal{B}$ randomly chooses $r \in \mathbb{Z}_N$ and sets

$$D_1' = (g_1 X_2)^{\alpha}(g_1 X_2)^{r \sum_{v_{i,j_i} \in L} a_{i,j_i}}, D_2' = (g_1 X_2)^r.$$

If $X_2 = g_2^{\ell}$, then this implicitly sets $g_1^{\alpha} = P, \gamma_1 = \alpha \ell, \gamma_2 = \ell r$ and $z_{i,j_i} = a_{i,j_i}$. We note here that the values z_{i,j_i} modulo p_2 are uncorrelated from the values of a_{i,j_i} modulo p_1. So D_1' and D_2' are properly distributed semi-functional secret keys. Now, $\mathcal{B}$ sends $\mathsf{SK}_L' = \langle D_1', D_2' \rangle$ to $\mathcal{A}$.

Challenge. The algorithm $\mathcal{A}$ submits two equal length messages M_0, M_1 and two access policies W_0^*, W_1^* to $\mathcal{B}$. To compute the semi-functional challenge ciphertext CT^*, $\mathcal{B}$ will take s from the assumption term $g_1^s Z_3$ and randomly chooses $t_0, t \in \mathbb{Z}_N$, a random element $\Lambda \in \mathbb{G}_T$. It then chooses a random $\mu \in \{0,1\}$. Let $W_{\mu}^* = \bigwedge_{i=1}^{n} w_{i,j_i}$. Compute the semi-functional challenge ciphertext components

$$C' = \Lambda, C_1' = (g_1^s Z_3) Z_2 g_3^{t_0}, C_2' = T^{\sum_{i=1}^{n} a_{i,j_i}} \cdot g_3^t.$$

This implicitly sets $Z_2 = g_2^{\delta}$ and $z_{i,j_i} = a_{i,j_i}$. Then the semi-functional challenge ciphertext $\mathsf{CT}^* = \langle C', C_1', C_2' \rangle$ is sent to $\mathcal{A}$.

Guess. Finally, $\mathcal{A}$ outputs a guess $\mu' \in \{0,1\}$ and wins the game if $\mu' = \mu$.

If $T = g_1^s Y_2 Y_3$, CT^* is a properly distributed semi-functional encryption of a random message in $\mathbb{G}_T$ and hence $\mathcal{B}$ will simulate the game $\mathsf{Game_{Final'}}$. Similarly, if T is a random element of $\mathbb{G}$, then CT^* is a properly distributed semi-functional encryption of a random element of $\mathbb{G}_T$ with C_2' is random in $\mathbb{G}$ and therefore $\mathcal{B}$ simulates the game $\mathsf{Game_{Final}}$. Thus, $\mathcal{B}$ can use the output of $\mathcal{A}$ to break Assumption 4 with advantage ϵ. $\qquad\square$

Theorem 1. *If Assumptions 1, 2, 3 and 4 hold, then our CP-ABE scheme is fully CPA secure ciphertext-policy hiding (or recipient anonymous).*

Proof. If Assumptions 1, 2, 3 and 4 hold, then we have shown by the previous lemmas that the real security game $\mathsf{Game_{Real}}$ is indistinguishable from $\mathsf{Game_{Final}}$, in which the advantage of adversary is negligible and hence the adversary cannot attain a non-negligible advantage in breaking our CP-ABE scheme. $\qquad\square$

Acknowledgement. The authors would like to thank the anonymous reviewers of this paper for their valuable comments and suggestions.

References

1. Ostrovksy, R., Sahai, A., Waters, B.: Attribute Based Encryption with Non-Monotonic Access Structures. In: ACM Conference on Computer and Communications Security, pp. 195–203 (2007)
2. Shamir, A.: Identity-Based Cryptosystems and Signature Schemes. In: Blakely, G.R., Chaum, D. (eds.) CRYPTO 1984. LNCS, vol. 196, pp. 47–53. Springer, Heidelberg (1985)
3. Sahai, A., Waters, B.: Fuzzy Identity-Based Encryption. In: Cramer, R. (ed.) EUROCRYPT 2005. LNCS, vol. 3494, pp. 457–473. Springer, Heidelberg (2005)
4. Goyal, V., Pandey, O., Sahai, A., Waters, B.: Attribute Based Encryption for Fine-Grained Access Control of Encrypted Data. In: ACM Conference on Computer and Communications Security, pp. 89–98 (2006)
5. Bethencourt, J., Sahai, A., Waters, B.: Ciphertext-Policy Attribute-Based Encryption. In: IEEE Symposium on Security and Privacy, pp. 321–334 (2007)
6. Waters, B.: Ciphertext-Policy Attribute-Based Encryption: An Expressive, Efficient, and Provably Secure Realization. Cryptology ePrint report 2008/290 (2008)
7. Ibraimi, L., Tang, Q., Hartel, P., Jonker, W.: Efficient and Provable Secure Ciphertext-Policy Attribute-Based Encryption Schemes. In: Bao, F., Li, H., Wang, G. (eds.) ISPEC 2009. LNCS, vol. 5451, pp. 1–12. Springer, Heidelberg (2009)
8. Lewko, A., Okamoto, T., Sahai, A., Takashima, K., Waters, B.: Fully Secure Functional Encryption: Attribute-Based Encryption and (Hierarchical) Inner Product Encryption. Cryptology ePrint report 2010/110 (2010)
9. Rouselakis, Y., Waters, B.: New Constructions and Proof Methods for Large Universe Attribute-Based Encryption. Cryptology ePrint report 2012/583 (2012)
10. Emura, K., Miyaji, A., Nomura, A., Omote, K., Soshi, M.: A Ciphertext-Policy Attribute-Based Encryption Scheme with Constant Ciphertext Length. IJACT 2(1), 46–59 (2010)
11. Herranz, J., Laguillaumie, F., Ràfols, C.: Constant Size Ciphertexts in Threshold Attribute-Based Encryption. In: Nguyen, P.Q., Pointcheval, D. (eds.) PKC 2010. LNCS, vol. 6056, pp. 19–34. Springer, Heidelberg (2010)
12. Chen, C., Zhang, Z., Feng, D.: Efficient Ciphertext Policy Attribute-Based Encryption with Constant-Size Ciphertext and Constant Computation-Cost. In: Boyen, X., Chen, X. (eds.) ProvSec 2011. LNCS, vol. 6980, pp. 84–101. Springer, Heidelberg (2011)
13. Ge, A., Zhang, R., Chen, C., Ma, C., Zhang, Z.: Threshold Ciphertext Policy Attribute-Based Encryption with Constant Size Ciphertexts. In: Susilo, W., Mu, Y., Seberry, J. (eds.) ACISP 2012. LNCS, vol. 7372, pp. 336–349. Springer, Heidelberg (2012)
14. Lewko, A., Sahai, A., Waters, B.: Revocation Systems with Very Small Private Keys. In: IEEE Symposium on Security and Privacy, pp. 273–285 (2010)
15. Okamoto, T., Takashima, K.: Fully Secure Functional Encryption with General Relations from the Decisional Linear Assumption. In: Rabin, T. (ed.) CRYPTO 2010. LNCS, vol. 6223, pp. 191–208. Springer, Heidelberg (2010)
16. Waters, B.: Dual System Encryption: Realizing Fully Secure IBE and HIBE under Simple Assumptions. In: Halevi, S. (ed.) CRYPTO 2009. LNCS, vol. 5677, pp. 619–636. Springer, Heidelberg (2009)

17. Doshi, N., Jinwala, D.: Hidden Access Structure Ciphertext Policy Attribute Based Encryption with Constant Length Ciphertext. In: Thilagam, P.S., Pais, A.R., Chandrasekaran, K., Balakrishnan, N. (eds.) ADCONS 2011. LNCS, vol. 7135, pp. 515–523. Springer, Heidelberg (2012)

18. Jinguang, H., Willy, S., Yi, M., Jun, Y.: Attribute-Based Oblivious Access Control. The Computer Journal, 1–14 (2012)

19. Lai, J., Deng, R.H., Li, Y.: Fully Secure Cipertext-Policy Hiding CP-ABE. In: Bao, F., Weng, J. (eds.) ISPEC 2011. LNCS, vol. 6672, pp. 24–39. Springer, Heidelberg (2011)

20. Zhou, Z., Huang, D.: On Efficient Ciphertext-Policy Attribute Based Encryption and Broadcast Encryption. Cryptology ePrint report 2010/395 (2010)

21. Balu, A., Kuppusamy, K.: Privacy Preserving Ciphertext Policy Attribute Based Encryption. In: Meghanathan, N., Boumerdassi, S., Chaki, N., Nagamalai, D. (eds.) CNSA 2010. CCIS, vol. 89, pp. 402–409. Springer, Heidelberg (2010)

22. Yu, S., Ren, R., Lou, W.: Attribute-Based Content Distribution with Hidden Policy. In: NPSec 2008, pp. 39–44 (2008)

23. Nishide, T., Yoneyama, K., Ohta, K.: Attribute-Based Encryption with Partially Hidden Encryptor-Specified Access Structures. In: Bellovin, S.M., Gennaro, R., Keromytis, A.D., Yung, M. (eds.) ACNS 2008. LNCS, vol. 5037, pp. 111–129. Springer, Heidelberg (2008)

24. Cheung, L., Newport, C.: Provably Secure Ciphertext Policy ABE. In: ACM Conference on Computer and Communications Security, pp. 456–465 (2007)

25. Rao, Y.S., Dutta, R.: Computationally Efficient Dual-Policy Attribute Based Encryption with Short Ciphertext. In: Reyhanitabar, R. (ed.) ProvSec 2013. LNCS, vol. 8209, pp. 288–308. Springer, Heidelberg (to appear, 2013)

26. Attrapadung, N., Libert, B., de Panafieu, E.: Expressive Key-Policy Attribute-Based Encryption with Constant-Size Ciphertexts. In: Catalano, D., Fazio, N., Gennaro, R., Nicolosi, A. (eds.) PKC 2011. LNCS, vol. 6571, pp. 90–108. Springer, Heidelberg (2011)

27. Müller, S., Katzenbeisser, S.: Hiding the Policy in Cryptographic Access Control. In: Meadows, C., Fernandez-Gago, C. (eds.) STM 2011. LNCS, vol. 7170, pp. 90–105. Springer, Heidelberg (2012)

28. Boneh, D., Goh, E.-J., Nissim, K.: Evaluating 2-DNF Formulas on Ciphertexts. In: Kilian, J. (ed.) TCC 2005. LNCS, vol. 3378, pp. 325–341. Springer, Heidelberg (2005)

Error Correction of Partially Exposed RSA Private Keys from MSB Side

Santanu Sarkar[1], Sourav Sen Gupta[2,*], and Subhamoy Maitra[2]

[1] Chennai Mathematical Institute, Chennai, India
sarkar.santanu.bir@gmail.com
[2] Indian Statistical Institute, Kolkata, India
sg.sourav@gmail.com, subho@isical.ac.in

Abstract. The most popular public key cryptosystem to date has been RSA, whose security primarily relies on the unfeasibility of factoring the modulus, which is a product of two large primes, and on the secrecy of certain RSA parameters. In 2009, the cold-boot attack by Halderman et al presented an important cryptanalytic model where a portion of the secret parameters may be exposed. In this direction, Heninger and Shacham (Crypto 2009) introduced the problem of reconstructing RSA private keys when few random bits from each are known. Later, Henecka, May and Meurer (Crypto 2010) introduced the problem of error-correction in the RSA private keys when all the bits are known with some probability of error. Their approach attempted error-correction from the least significant side of the parameters. In this paper we provide a novel technique for error-correction that works from the most significant side of the parameters. Representative experimental results are provided to substantiate our claim.

Keywords: cryptanalysis, RSA, cold-boot attack, partial key exposure, private keys, error-correction.

1 Introduction

RSA has been the most well known and commercially used public key cryptosystem since its inception in 1978 by Rivest, Shamir and Adleman. One can find a complete description of the RSA scheme in [17]. Let us briefly state the algorithm, as follows.

Let $N = pq$ where p and q are primes. By definition of the Euler totient function, $\phi(N) = (p-1)(q-1)$.

- KeyGen: Choose e co-prime to $\phi(N)$. Find d such that $ed \equiv 1 \bmod \phi(N)$.
- KeyDist: Publish public key $\langle N, e \rangle$ and keep private key $\langle N, d \rangle$ secret.
- Encrypt: For plaintext $M \in \mathbb{Z}_N$, ciphertext $C = M^e \bmod N$.
- Decrypt: For ciphertext C, plaintext $M = C^d \bmod N$.

* Supported by DRDO sponsored project Centre of Excellence in Cryptology (CoEC), under MOC ERIP/ER/1009002/M/01/1319/788/D(R&D) of ER&IPR, DRDO.

A. Bagchi and I. Ray (Eds.): ICISS 2013, LNCS 8303, pp. 345–359, 2013.
© Springer-Verlag Berlin Heidelberg 2013

To accelerate the decryption process of RSA, one can use CRT-RSA [15], a variant of the original scheme that uses Chinese Remainder Theorem (CRT). In CRT-RSA, one uses $d_p = d \bmod (p-1)$ and $d_q = d \bmod (q-1)$, instead of d, for the decryption process. Decryption becomes more efficient if one pre-calculates the value of $q^{-1} \bmod p$. Thus, in PKCS [14] standard for the RSA cryptosystem, it is recommended to store the RSA private keys as a tuple

$$PK = (p, q, d, d_p, d_q, q^{-1} \bmod p),$$

which we shall henceforth refer to as the *private key* of RSA. Note that there are other ways of speeding up RSA by choosing bit patterns in the primes (as a non-exhaustive list, one may refer to [3,10,19] and the references therein), but CRT-RSA is the most convenient and widely popular variant in practice.

RSA and CRT-RSA have been put through extensive cryptanalysis over the last three decades. An important model of cryptanalysis is the side channel attack, such as fault attacks, timing attacks, power analysis etc., by which an adversary may obtain some information about the private key PK. In this paper, we concentrate on the partial information about the private key PK retrieved using side channel attacks, and how this information may be exploited to mount an attack on RSA. This type of attacks on RSA or CRT-RSA, based on certain 'partial information' about the private keys, is popularly known as 'partial key exposure' attacks.

1.1   Cold-Boot Attack on RSA

The cold-boot attack, a new paradigm of partial key exposure side-channel attacks on cryptographic primitives, was introduced by Halderman et al [4] in 2009. It is assumed that the attacker has physical access to the system, and he/she can run a 'cold reboot' to restart the machine without destroying its memory contents. The main idea of the attack thereafter is to exploit the data remanence property of the memory, usually based on DRAM or SRAM technologies, to extract relevant information about the cryptosystem functioning on the machine. In [4], it was experimentally verified that a generic computer memory retains a considerable portion of its data even minutes after the cold-boot; thus allowing the attacked to successfully recover sensitive information.

This technique was exploited in [4] to identify and extract fully-retained AES and RSA keys from the memory, even after a few minutes of the cold-boot. The method was further extended to attack practical disk encryption systems like BitLocker, FileVault, TrueCrypt, dm-crypt and Loop-AES [4]. Detailed information about the motivation and consequences of cold-boot attack is presented by the authors of [4] at `https://citp.princeton.edu/research/memory/`.

Partial Key Exposure from Cold-Boot Attack: Note that all the attacks in [4] exploit the fact that identification and extraction of fully-retained keys are possible from the computer memory. However, the attacker may not be as lucky; he/she may only get a partial information about the secret keys from the memory.

In fact, this is the most practical case to assume, considering that the attacker may retrieve the remanent information from the memory after a certain amount of time, and some parts of the memory may have already decayed. In such a scenario, the cold-boot attack motivates a side channel cryptanalysis on RSA where some bits of PK are revealed but not the entire private key. This provides a natural motivation for partial key exposure attack on RSA.

Previous Partial Key Exposure Attacks on RSA: Rivest and Shamir [16] pioneered partial key exposure attacks by factoring the RSA modulus $N = pq$ given a contiguous two-third fraction of the bits from the least significant side of one of the primes p or q. Later, a seminal paper [2] by Coppersmith proved that factorization of the RSA modulus can be achieved given half of the MSBs of a factor. His method used LLL [11] lattice reduction technique to solve for small solutions to modular equations. This method triggered a host of research in the field of lattice based factorization, e.g., the works by Howgrave-Graham [8], Jochemsz and May [9].

Note that these results require knowledge of contiguous blocks of bits of the RSA private keys. However, in an actual practical scenario of cold-boot attacks, it is more likely that an adversary will gain the knowledge of random bits of the RSA parameters instead of contiguous blocks. In this model, the application of the earlier factorization methods prove insufficient, and one requires a way to extract more information out of the random bits obtained via the side channel attacks. In [7], it has been shown how N can be factored with the knowledge of a random subset of the bits (distributed over small contiguous blocks) in one of the primes. But still, that did not address the case of partial random-bit key exposure in case of cold-boot attacks; the following did.

Reconstruction of RSA Private Key from Random Bits.

In Crypto 2009, the cold-boot partial key exposure attack [4] was exploited for the first time against RSA by Heninger and Shacham [6]. In this work, the random bits of both the primes are considered unlike the earlier works (e.g., [2,1,7]) where knowledge of the bits of a single prime have been exploited. The authors proved that the attacker can factor N in time $\text{poly}(e, \log_2 N)$ if he/she has

$\delta \geq 0.27$ fraction of random bits of p, q, d, d_p, d_q, or
$\delta \geq 0.42$ fraction of random bits of p, q, d, or
$\delta \geq 0.59$ fraction of random bits of p, q.

The algorithm proposed in [6] exploits a modified brute force search of the unknown bits in the RSA private keys with the help of smart pruning of wrong solution paths in the search tree. This pruning is done using the partial knowledge of the random bits in PK; hence the fraction of required known bits decreases as we increase the number of parameters involved in the pruning process.

Error-Correction of RSA Private Key.

In Crypto 2010, Henecka et al [5] studied the case when all the bits of PK were known, but with some probability of error in each bit. One may consider that each bit of the parameters in PK is flipped with some probability $\gamma \in [0, \frac{1}{2})$. In [5], the authors proved that one can correct the errors in key PK in time $\text{poly}(e, \log_2 N)$ when the error rate is

$\gamma < 0.237$ when p, q, d, d_p, d_q are known with error, or
$\gamma < 0.160$ when p, q, d are known with error, or
$\gamma < 0.084$ when p, q are known with error.

The algorithm proposed in [5] guesses the bits of one of the primes and uses the reconstruction approach of [6] as a subroutine to get approximations of the other parameters in PK. The verification of each guess is done by comparing the Hamming distance of the guess with the erroneous version of PK obtained through side-channel attacks. This is equivalent to pruning the search space towards the correct solution, and hence more bit-error can be corrected if one uses more parameters from PK during the pruning phase. A similar avenue was followed in [13] to recover noisy RSA keys using coding-theoretic techniques.

Reconstruction versus Error-Correction of RSA Secret Keys: Note that the cold-boot attack generally allows the attacker to extract remanent data from the memory, but the attacker may never be sure of the authenticity of this data. As the pattern of decay is quite unpredictable across the different parts of the memory, it is more likely for the attacker to obtain a 'noisy' information about the secret key, rather than a fragmented information without any noise. From this practical consideration, one should focus more on error-correction of 'noisy' secret keys of RSA, compared to reconstruction from partially recovered random bits. This issue has been highlighted earlier in [5,13], and we follow the same principle by paying more attention to error-correction of RSA secret keys, rather than reconstruction of the same.

1.2   Motivation of This Paper

Both reconstruction [6] and the error-correction [5] routines start from the least significant side of the PK parameters and moves through the complete length towards the most significant side. This is implicitly based on the assumption that the density of the random bits available for reconstruction is the same throughout the parameters and the error-rate for the bits are uniform over the length of each PK entity.

We already have existing algorithms for factorization having either the least significant half [1] or the most significant half of bits [2]. The existing works [6,5] consider certain information about the bits through the complete length of the secret parameters. For example, in [6], one requires the knowledge of certain proportion of bits over the complete bit representation of the primes and the target is to recover all the bits. The algorithm of [6] proceeds from the least significant bits of the private keys and build them moving towards the most significant side. In [12], we noted that the process can be terminated just after recovering the least significant half of the primes, as after that we can indeed use the existing strategy [1] to recover the remaining bits. That is the reason we revisit the existing strategy [6] with the motivation of recovering only the least significant half of the primes and in such a case, no information is required from the most significant side of the private keys. Following the work of [6], we revisited this idea in [12].

Given this, a natural question is how the respective algorithms perform when we move from the most significant side and have some information from that portion. In [18], we considered the idea for implementing brute-force reconstruction and error-correction on the keys starting from the most significant side. This, in general, seems to be difficult, as the "carries" from multiplication would seem to interfere. Our strategy of [18] overcomes this difficulty by (i) bounding the length of a carry chain and (ii) adopting an iterative approach where a fraction of bits of the private key are guessed. Once the most significant half of a prime is known, the factorization is immediate following the idea of [2].

1.3   Contribution of This Paper

This is a follow-up work of [18], where we present further results towards error-correction of RSA private key PK. While in [18], the reconstruction idea has been studied in algorithmic form and detailed experimental results have been presented, the idea of error-correction from MSB side was introduced only. Detailed algorithmic or experimental results had not been presented in [18].

In this paper, we present the complete algorithm for correcting the bit-errors in RSA private key, starting from the MSB side of the parameters. Suppose that all the bits of the private key PK are known, but with some probability of error γ for each bit. Then using our technique, one can correct the errors in the private key PK efficiently when the error rate is of the order of [5] where the problem has been tackled for LSB side.

2   Background: Reconstruction from MSB Side [12,18]

In this section, we explain the existing ideas of reconstructing partially correct RSA secret keys that are required for understanding our strategy.

2.1   Brief Description of [12]

We first refer to [12, Section 4] that explains reconstructing the most significant half of the primes p, q given the knowledge of some blocks of bits. Let us recall at this point that, $N = pq$, and the primes p, q are of the same bitsize. We start with the following.

Definition 1. *Define $X[i]$ to be the i-th most significant bit of X with $X[0]$ being the MSB. Also define X_i to be the partial approximation of X where X_i shares the most significant bits 0 through i with X.*

The Idea for Reconstruction. If one of the primes, p say, is completely available, one can easily obtain $q = N/p$. Now, if a few MSBs of p are known, then one can get an approximation p' of p. This allows us to construct an approximation $q' = \lceil N/p' \rceil$ of the other prime q as well. The idea is to use the known blocks of bits of the primes in a systematic order to repeat this approximation process until we recover half of one of the primes.

Outline of the Idea. Suppose that the MSBs $\{0, \ldots, a\}$ of the prime p are known. This gives an approximation p_a of p, and hence an approximation $q' = \lceil N/p_a \rceil$ of q. Let us consider that q' matches q through MSBs $\{0, \ldots, a-t-1\}$, i.e., $q' = q_{a-t-1}$, with some probability depending on t.

Further, given the MSBs $\{a-t, \ldots, 2a\}$ of q, an improved approximation q_{2a} may be constructed using q_{a-t-1} and these known bits. Again, q_{2a} facilitates the construction of a updated approximation $p' = \lceil N/q_{2a} \rceil$, which may be expected to satisfy $p' = p_{2a-t-1}$ with some probability depending on t.

With the knowledge of MSBs $\{2a-t, \ldots, 3a\}$ of p, it is once again possible to obtain an improved approximation p_{3a} of p. This process of constructing approximations is recursed until one can recover the most significant half of one of the primes. The reconstruction idea is illustrated in Fig. 1.

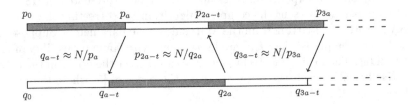

Fig. 1. The feedback mechanism in MSB reconstruction

The Reconstruction Algorithm. Let $S = \{0, \ldots, T\}$ denote the set of bit indices from the most significant halves of the primes. Assume that $k = \lfloor T/a \rfloor$ is odd in this case. Consider $U, V \subseteq S$ such that

$$U = \{0, \ldots, a\} \cup \{2a-t, \ldots, 3a\} \cup \cdots \cup \{(k-1)a-t, \ldots, ka\},$$
$$V = \{a-t, \ldots, 2a\} \cup \{3a-t, \ldots, 4a\} \cup \cdots \cup \{ka-t, \ldots, T\}.$$

Further, consider that $p[i]$'s are available for $i \in U$ and $q[j]$'s are also known for $j \in V$. Then, Algorithm 1 can reconstruct T many contiguous most significant bits of the prime q.

The subroutine Correct presented in Algorithm 1 takes as input a partial approximation Y of X and a set of contiguous known bits, $X[i]$ for $i \in \Sigma$, say. It outputs an improved approximation Z of X by correcting the bits of the partial approximation Y using the knowledge of the known bits. This subroutine works as described is Algorithm 2.

Input: N, T and $p[i], q[j]$ for all $i \in U$ and $j \in V$
Output: Contiguous T many MSBs of q

1 Initialize: $p_0 := 2^{l_p-1}$, $q_0 := 2^{l_q-1}$;
2 $p_a := \mathsf{Correct}(p_0, p[j]$ for $j \in \{1, \ldots, a\} \subset U)$;
3 $q_{a-t} := \lceil \frac{N}{p_a} \rceil$;
4 **for** i *from* 2 *to* $k-1$ *in steps of* 2 **do**
5      $q_{ia} := \mathsf{Correct}(q_{(i-1)a-t}, q[j]$ for $j \in \{(i-1)a - t, \ldots, ia\} \subset V)$;
6      $p_{ia-t-1} := \lceil \frac{N}{q_{ia}} \rceil$;
7      $p_{(i+1)a} := \mathsf{Correct}(p_{ia-t-1}, p[j]$ for $j \in \{ia - t, \ldots, (i+1)a\} \subset U)$;
8      $q_{(i+1)a-t-1} := \lceil \frac{N}{p_{(i+1)a}} \rceil$;
end
9 $q_T := \mathsf{Correct}(q_{ka-t-1}, q[j]$ for $j \in \{ka - t, \ldots, T\} \subset V)$;
10 Return q_T;

Algorithm 1. MSB reconstruction algorithm using random blocks of bits from p, q when k is odd [12]

Input: Y and $X[i]$ for $i \in \Sigma$
Output: Z, the correction of Y

1 **for** j *from* 0 *to* l_X **do**
2   **if** $j \in \Sigma$ **then** $Z[j] = X[j]$;   // Correct j-th MSB if $X[j]$ is known
     else $Z[j] = Y[j]$;   // Keep j-th MSB as $X[j]$ is not known
end
3 Return Z;

Algorithm 2. Subroutine Correct used in Algorithm 1 [12]

In the case where $k = \lfloor T/a \rfloor$ is even, Algorithm 1 needs to be tweaked a little to work properly. One may use a slightly changed version of $U, V \subseteq S$ such that $U = \{0, \ldots, a\} \cup \{2a - t, \ldots, 3a\} \cup \cdots \cup \{ka - t, \ldots, T\}$ and $V = \{a - t, \ldots, 2a\} \cup \{3a - t, \ldots, 4a\} \cup \cdots \cup \{(k-1)a - t, \ldots, ka\}$. As discussed earlier, $p[i]$'s are known for $i \in U$ and $q[j]$'s are known for $j \in V$.

The work in this section explains in detail the work of [12, Section 4]. The idea is to reconstruct the primes from the MSB side where blocks of bits had to be known. The question remains open whether one can reconstruct the private keys from the MSB side if the random bits are known, but they are not available as contiguous blocks. This problem has been tackled in [18] as we describe below.

2.2 Brief Description of [18]

In this section we explain the algorithm RecPK from [18] that recovers the RSA private key PK from its partial knowledge. It is assumed that some random bits of PK are known through some side channel attack on the system. The goal is to recover the top $\frac{1}{2}\log_2 p$ many MSBs of prime p and then use the lattice based approach of Coppersmith [2] to factor N.

It is clear if the attacker knows any one of $\{p, q, d, d_p, d_q\}$, he/she can easily factor N. There are four RSA equations connecting these five variables:

$$N = pq, \quad ed = 1 + k\phi(N), \quad ed_p = 1 + k_p(p-1), \quad ed_q = 1 + k_q(q-1) \quad (1)$$

Now when e is small (within the range of a brute force search), one can capture k, k_p, k_q easily as each of these is smaller than e. One can write $d = d_1 + d_2$, where $d_2 = d \bmod 2^{(\log_2 N)/2}$ and $d_1 = d - d_2$. It is also well known that when e is small, one can find around half of the MSBs of d, that is the portion d_1 (see [1] for details). Hence in Equation (1), there are five unknowns p, q, d_p, d_q and d_2.

The Idea for Reconstruction. Consider the case when few random bits are known from the upper halves of p, q, d_2, d_p, d_q, and assume that we know the first a many contiguous MSBs of p. According to the algorithm proposed in [12], one can recover the first $(a - t)$ many contiguous MSBs of q with probability greater than $1 - \frac{1}{2^t}$.

The situation is, however, different than the one considered in [12]. Here, we only know a few random bits of the RSA parameters from the MSB side, not contiguous blocks. That is, in the parameters p, q, d, d_p, d_q, we know about δ fraction of the bits at random (where $0 \le \delta \le 1$). One can further assume that the known bits of the private keys are distributed uniformly at random, i.e., we know δa many bits in each block of size a, and $a(1 - \delta)$ bits are unknown.

The idea for reconstruction provides a two-part solution to this problem. One can perform two steps iteratively over the bits of prime p, starting at the MSB:

- Guess the missing bits in a block (of size a, say) to obtain all possibilities.
- Filter using the known bits of q, d_2, d_p, d_q to recover the correct option.

In the Guess routine, one considers all options for the unknown $a(1-\delta)$ many bits in a specific block of p, and construct $2^{a(1-\delta)}$ possibilities for the block. Using each of these options, one can mimic the reconstruction idea of [12] to find the first $(a - t)$ many MSBs of q, d_p, d_q, d_2. In the Filter stage, one can utilize the bits known from q, d_p, d_q, d_2 to discard obvious wrong options.

Reconstruction Illustrated Using p and q. Suppose that we know δ fraction of the bits of p and q each, distributed uniformly at random, as discussed. Now, the reconstruction algorithm is as follows.

Step 0: In the Guess routine, one generates $2^{a(1-\delta)}$ options for the first a MSBs of p, pads the remaining by 0's, and stores in an array A, say. The Filter algorithm is performed on $A = \{\tilde{p}_1, \tilde{p}_2, \ldots, \tilde{p}_k\}$ where $k = |A| = 2^{a(1-\delta)}$.

Step 1: For each option $\tilde{p}_i \in A$, one reconstructs the first $(a-t)$ MSBs of q using the idea of [12], i.e., $\tilde{q}_i = \lfloor \frac{N}{\tilde{p}_i} \rfloor$. Store these options in an array B. It is expected that the first block of $(a - t)$ MSBs of $\tilde{q}_i$ will correctly correspond to $\tilde{p}_i$ with probability $1 - \frac{1}{2^t}$ in each of these cases (t is the offset).

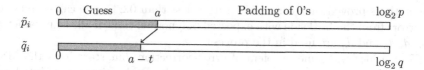

Step 2: Match the known bits of q from this block (first $(a-t)$ MSBs of q) with the corresponding ones in each of these reconstructions $\tilde{q}_i$. If for some $1 \leq l \leq a - t$, the bit $q[l]$ is known but $q[l] \neq \tilde{q}_i[l]$, then there is a mismatch, and one can discard $\tilde{q}_i$ from B, and hence $\tilde{p}_i$ from A. If all the known bits of q match with those of $\tilde{q}_i$, then only one retains $\tilde{p}_i$ in A. After this match-and-discard stage, the number of remaining options in $A = \{\tilde{p}_1, \tilde{p}_2, \ldots, \tilde{p}_x\}$ is x, which is considerably lower than the initial number of options $k = 2^{a(1-\delta)}$.

Step 3: Each remaining option has some correctly recovered block of MSBs. One attempts to find the initial contiguous *common portion* out of the x options, i.e., to find the maximum value of c such that c many initial MSBs of all the options are same. If there is only a single option left in A (i.e., $x = 1$), we evidently get $c = a$.

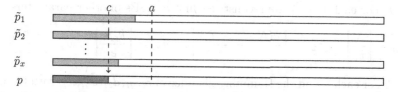

Iterate: Now, one can take the next block of a bits of p starting at the $(c+1)$-th MSB, and repeat the Guess and Filter routines using the first $(c+a)$ MSBs of p.

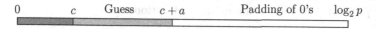

The last two steps above (Step 3 and Iterate) constitute the 'sliding window' technique that filters adaptively over the length of p. This process is continued until half of p is recovered from the MSB side.

One may refer to [18] for detailed idea in this regard. We now present how one can modify and refine these ideas for handling the case when each bit may be erroneous with some probability.

3   Error-Correction from MSB Side

In case of our second problem, instead of knowing a few bits, we consider the situation where all the bits of the private key PK are known, but there is a probability of error associated with each bit. This scenario was introduced in [5].

The authors proved that when error rate is less than 0.237, one can correct the bit errors from the LSB side with expected polynomial time, if all the parameters p, q, d, d_p and d_q are used in the process.

We consider the same problem of error-correction, but start from the MSB side and correct the error in the top half of the RSA primes as pointed out in [18]. Suppose that the upper halves of all RSA private keys p, q, d_2, d_p, d_q are given, but with some error probability γ associated with each bit. We call the available values of the parameters p', q', d_2', d_p', d_q', each of which is erroneous to some extent. We correct the errors from the MSB side using the following idea.

3.1   Idea for Error-Correction

Choose the parameters a (blocksize) and t (offset) for reconstruction, and further choose a threshold $T_{a,t,\gamma}$ (depending on the chosen parameters a, t and the error rate γ) for error to be used in this approach.

Step 0: In the **Guess** routine, we generate 2^a (all possible) options for the first a MSBs of p, pad the remaining portion by 0's, and store in an array A, say.

Step 1: For each $\tilde{p}_i \in A$, we reconstruct first a MSBs of other parameters:

$$\tilde{q}_i = \left\lfloor \frac{N}{\tilde{p}_i} \right\rfloor, \quad \tilde{d}_{2i} = \left\lfloor \frac{k(N - \tilde{p}_i - \tilde{q}_i)}{e} \right\rfloor, \quad \tilde{d}_{p_i} = \left\lfloor \frac{k_p \tilde{p}_i}{e} \right\rfloor, \quad \tilde{d}_{q_i} = \left\lfloor \frac{k_q \tilde{q}_i}{e} \right\rfloor$$

Step 2: For each i, find the Hamming distance of $\tilde{p}_i, \tilde{q}_i, \tilde{d}_{2i}, \tilde{d}_{p_i}, \tilde{d}_{q_i}$ with the available values p', q', d_2', d_p', d_q' and calculate the sum of all these Hamming distances. The Hamming distance is calculated only for the concerned block of size a in all the parameters, and the sum is considered to be a measure for error. If this sum is less than the predefined threshold $T_{a,t,\gamma}$ we retain $\tilde{p}_i$ in A, and otherwise we discard $\tilde{p}_i$ from A to reduce the number of options.

Step 3: Suppose that there are x options remaining in array A after the threshold based filtering has been performed. Find the maximum value of c such that c many initial MSBs of all the options are same. As we have chosen the common bits of all possibilities, these c bits of p are correctly recovered.

Iterate: We take the next block of a bits of p starting at the $(c+1-t)$-th MSB, and repeat the **Guess** and **Filter** routines using the first $(c+a-t)$ MSBs of p.

The Guess and Filter processes are continued until half of p is error-free from the MSB side. After this, one can factorize N using the lattice based idea of Coppersmith [2], as it is done in case of reconstruction as well. The next section presents the formal algorithm for error-correction using all parameters of PK.

3.2   The General Error-Correction Algorithm

In this section, we present the complete algorithm for error-correction of RSA private keys p, q, d, d_p, d_q. Suppose that all bits of PK are known, but each one has a probability γ of being correct. In other words, there is an error probability γ associated with each bit in PK. In such a scenario, Algorithm 3 recovers the top half of the RSA prime p using the idea described above.

Input: N, e, k, k_p, k_q, the erroneous approximations p', q', d_2', d_p', d_q', , and the percentage of error γ.
Output: Top half of the MSBs of p, corrected.

1   Choose parameters $a, t, b = 0, c_{old} = 1$;
2   Choose threshold $T_{a,t,\gamma}$ depending on a, t, γ;
3   **while** $b < \frac{l_N}{2}$ **do**
4 | For first $(a + b)$ MSBs of p, choose all possible options $\tilde{p}$ and store in an array A;
5 | $A = \text{Filter}(N, p', q', d_2', d_p', d_q', A, a, t, b, \gamma, T_{a,t,\gamma})$;
6 | If the array A remains unaltered, increase a and go to Step 4;
7 | **if** $|A| = 1$ **then**
8 | | Set first $(a + b - t)$ MSBs of $\tilde{p} = A[1]$ as those of prime p;
9 | | Set $b = a + b - t$ and $c_{old} = a + b - t$;
    | **end**
10 | **else**
11 | | Find $c \leq a + b$ such that the first c MSBs of all members of A are same;
12 | | If c remains unaltered $(c = c_{old})$, decrease $T_{a,t,\gamma}$ and go to Step 4;
13 | | Set $b = c - t$ and $c_{old} = c - t$;
    | **end**
    end

Algorithm 3. CorPK: MSB error-correction algorithm using p, q, d_2, d_p, d_q

---

Choice of Threshold: One may note that in Step 2 of Algorithm 3, we need to choose a threshold $T_{a,t,\gamma}$ based on a, t and γ. Theoretically, in case with all five RSA parameters p, q, d, d_p, d_q, one should have a threshold $T_{a,t,\gamma} \geq 5(a - t)\gamma$ to accommodate for the correct values to be within the search range. However, as we use the Hamming distance for $5a$ bits for filtering, the threshold should be increased to $T_{a,t,\gamma} \geq 5a\gamma$.

Input: N, the erroneous approximations p', q', d_2', d_p', d_q', array A, parameters
   a, t, b, and the percentage of error γ.
Output: Modified array A of bit strings.

1 **for** $i = 1$ *to* $|A|$ **do**
2 | $\tilde{p} = A[i]$;
3 | Calculate $\tilde{q} = \lfloor \frac{N}{\tilde{p}} \rfloor$, $\tilde{d}_2 = \lfloor \frac{k(N - \tilde{p} - \tilde{q})}{e} \rfloor$, $\tilde{d}_p = \lfloor \frac{k_p \tilde{p}}{e} \rfloor$, $\tilde{d}_q = \lfloor \frac{k_q \tilde{q}}{e} \rfloor$;
4 | Calculate the Hamming distance of block of MSBs $[b, (a + b)]$ of p' with $\tilde{p}$,
   | q' with $\tilde{q}$, d_2' with $\tilde{d}_2$, d_p' with $\tilde{d}_p$, and d_q' with $\tilde{d}_q$ respectively;
5 | If the sum of all Hamming distances is more than threshold $T_{a,t,\gamma}$, discard
   | corresponding $\tilde{p}$ from A;
   end
6 Return A;

Algorithm 4. Subroutine Filter used in CorPK algorithm

In practice, we start with a very high value of the threshold $T_{a,t,\gamma} \approx 5a(0.5+\gamma)$, and gradually decrease it during runtime in each step where the sliding-window approach does not provide a new pivot point c (as in Step 12 of Algorithm 3). Similarly, we choose $T_{a,t,\gamma} \approx 2a(0.5+\gamma)$ in the p, q case, and $T_{a,t,\gamma} \approx 3a(0.5+\gamma)$ in the p, q, d case. The initial choices of $T_{a,t,\gamma}$ are verified and finalized through extensive experimentation.

3.3   Experimental Results for Error-Correction

We support our claim with the help of some representative cases of practical reconstructions. The average performance of the algorithm over 100 runs in each of the representative cases is presented in Table 1.

We have implemented using C programming language (with GMP library for processing large integers) on Linux Ubuntu 11.04. The hardware platform is an HP Z800 workstation with 3GHz Intel(R) Xeon(R) CPU. In these experiments, we have taken 1024 bit N, and $e = 2^{16} + 1$ in all cases. The average performance of the algorithm over 100 runs in each case is presented in Table 1.

In case of practical experiments with our idea for error-correction, we have successfully corrected approximately 6% bit error in the p, q case, 11% bit error in the p, q, d case, and 18% bit error in the case with all the PK parameters p, q, d, d_p, d_q. In the last case, 18% error could be corrected using $a = 16$, offset $t = 3$ and an initial threshold $T_{a,t,\gamma} = 54$.

Comparison with Previous Works: Note that our result is competitive with the results published in [5] where the experimental values were 8%, 14% and 20% in the three respective cases where the algorithms proceeded from the least significant side of the secret parameters. Further, our work is the first in studying the scenario from the most significant side and the algorithms are completely different from that of [5].

Table 1. Experimental data for error-correction algorithm CorPK

		Erroneous approximations of p and q known			
a	t	Threshold $T_{a,t,\gamma}$	Error γ (%)	Success probability	Time T (sec)
12	3	12	3	0.34	4.0
		12	4	0.15	4.2
14	3	14	3	0.39	12.2
		15	4	0.22	12.4
		16	3	0.59	38.5
16	3	17	4	0.41	42.8
		17	5	0.11	43.2
		19	3	0.74	216.3
18	3	19	4	0.42	224.8
		19	5	0.24	231.2
		19	6	0.10	235.6

		Erroneous approximations of p, q and d known			
a	t	Threshold $T_{a,t,\gamma}$	Error γ (%)	Success probability	Time T (sec)
12	3	20	7	0.23	7.9
		20	8	0.10	8.4
		23	7	0.48	20.1
14	3	24	8	0.26	21.1
		24	9	0.20	21.9
		25	10	0.10	22.4
		27	7	0.66	62.2
		27	8	0.58	62.6
16	3	28	9	0.31	62.8
		28	10	0.17	59.0
		29	11	0.10	59.9

		Erroneous approximations of p, q, d, d_p and d_q known			
a	t	Threshold $T_{a,t,\gamma}$	Error γ (%)	Success probability	Time T (sec)
12	3	38	14	0.28	21.8
		39	15	0.13	21.8
		44	14	0.44	60.7
14	3	45	15	0.32	57.1
		46	16	0.15	58.3
		46	17	0.10	53.5
		51	14	0.69	167.0
		52	15	0.46	165.5
16	3	52	16	0.29	168.1
		53	17	0.19	162.6
		54	18	0.12	163.1

4   Conclusion

In this paper, we study error-correction in RSA private key PK when all the bits are known with some probability of error. We propose a new strategy for correcting the bit-errors in RSA private key, starting from the MSB side of the parameters. Suppose that all the bits of the private key PK are known, but with some probability of error γ for each bit. Our experimental results show that one can correct the errors in the private key PK efficiently when the error rate is

- $\gamma \leq 0.18$ when p, q, d, d_p, d_q are known with error, or
- $\gamma \leq 0.11$ when p, q, d are known with error, or
- $\gamma \leq 0.06$ when p, q are known with error.

Future Scope: As a future direction of research, it will be nice to look into the theory behind reconstruction and error-correction. Improved algorithms, both from least and most significant side of the secret parameters, will be of interest to the community.

Acknowledgments. The authors would like to thank the anonymous reviewers for their valuable comments that helped improve the quality of the paper.

References

1. Boneh, D., Durfee, G., Frankel, Y.: An attack on RSA given a small fraction of the private key bits. In: Ohta, K., Pei, D. (eds.) ASIACRYPT 1998. LNCS, vol. 1514, pp. 25–34. Springer, Heidelberg (1998)
2. Coppersmith, D.: Small solutions to polynomial equations, and low exponent RSA vulnerabilities. Journal of Cryptology 10(4), 233–260 (1997)
3. Graham, S.W., Shparlinski, I.E.: On RSA moduli with almost half of the bits prescribed. Discrete Applied Mathematics 156(16), 3150–3154 (2008)
4. Halderman, J.A., Schoen, S.D., Heninger, N., Clarkson, W., Paul, W., Calandrino, J.A., Feldman, A.J., Appelbaum, J., Felten, E.W.: Lest we remember: cold-boot attacks on encryption keys. Commun. ACM 52(5), 91–98 (2009)
5. Henecka, W., May, A., Meurer, A.: Correcting errors in RSA private keys. In: Rabin, T. (ed.) CRYPTO 2010. LNCS, vol. 6223, pp. 351–369. Springer, Heidelberg (2010)
6. Heninger, N., Shacham, H.: Reconstructing RSA private keys from random key bits. In: Halevi, S. (ed.) CRYPTO 2009. LNCS, vol. 5677, pp. 1–17. Springer, Heidelberg (2009)
7. Herrmann, M., May, A.: Solving linear equations modulo divisors: On factoring given any bits. In: Pieprzyk, J. (ed.) ASIACRYPT 2008. LNCS, vol. 5350, pp. 406–424. Springer, Heidelberg (2008)
8. Howgrave-Graham, N.: Finding small roots of univariate modular equations revisited. In: Darnell, M.J. (ed.) Cryptography and Coding 1997. LNCS, vol. 1355, pp. 131–142. Springer, Heidelberg (1997)
9. Jochemsz, E., May, A.: A strategy for finding roots of multivariate polynomials with new applications in attacking RSA variants. In: Lai, X., Chen, K. (eds.) ASIACRYPT 2006. LNCS, vol. 4284, pp. 267–282. Springer, Heidelberg (2006)

10. Lenstra, A.K.: Generating RSA moduli with a predetermined portion. In: Ohta, K., Pei, D. (eds.) ASIACRYPT 1998. LNCS, vol. 1514, pp. 1–10. Springer, Heidelberg (1998)
11. Lenstra, A.K., Lenstra Jr., H.W., Lovász, L.: Factoring polynomials with rational coefficients. Mathematische Annalen 261, 515–534 (1982)
12. Maitra, S., Sarkar, S., Sen Gupta, S.: Factoring RSA modulus using prime reconstruction from random known bits. In: Bernstein, D.J., Lange, T. (eds.) AFRICACRYPT 2010. LNCS, vol. 6055, pp. 82–99. Springer, Heidelberg (2010)
13. Paterson, K.G., Polychroniadou, A., Sibborn, D.L.: A Coding-Theoretic Approach to Recovering Noisy RSA Keys. In: Wang, X., Sako, K. (eds.) ASIACRYPT 2012. LNCS, vol. 7658, pp. 386–403. Springer, Heidelberg (2012)
14. Public-Key Cryptography Standards (PKCS) #1 v2.1: RSA Cryptography Standard. RSA Security Inc. (2002), http://www.rsa.com/rsalabs/node.asp?id=2125
15. Quisquater, J.J., Couvreur, C.: Fast decipherment algorithm for RSA public-key cryptosystem. Electronic Letters 18(21), 905–907 (1982)
16. Rivest, R.L., Shamir, A.: Efficient factoring based on partial information. In: Pichler, F. (ed.) EUROCRYPT 1985. LNCS, vol. 219, pp. 31–34. Springer, Heidelberg (1986)
17. Rivest, R.L., Shamir, A., Adleman, L.M.: A method for obtaining digital signatures and public-key cryptosystems. Communications of the Association for Computing Machinery 21(2), 120–126 (1978)
18. Sarkar, S., Sen Gupta, S., Maitra, S.: Reconstruction and error correction of RSA secret parameters from the MSB side. In: Workshop on Coding and Cryptography (2011)
19. Shparlinski, I.E.: On RSA moduli with prescribed bit patterns. Designs, Codes and Cryptography 39, 113–122 (2006)

Efficient Enforcement of Privacy
for Moving Object Trajectories

Anuj Shanker Saxena[1], Vikram Goyal[2,*], and Debajyoti Bera[2]

[1] National Defence Academy, Khadakwasla, India
[2] Indraprastha Institute of Information Technology Delhi, New Delhi, India
{anujs,vikram,dbera}@iiitd.ac.in

Abstract. Information services based on identity and current location is already very popular among Internet and Mobile users, and a recent trend that is gaining acceptance is those based on annotated routes of travel, which we call as trajectories. We are motivated by the need of some users to reveal neither their identity nor location. This is not impossible since exact location can be substituted by an enclosing region, and the identity can be anonymised by relaying all queries through a proxy. However, when users are continuously making queries throughout a session, their queries can contain sufficient correlation which can identify them and/or their queries. Furthermore, a large region will fetch unnecessary search results degrading search quality. This problem of guaranteeing privacy, using smallest possible enclosing regions is NP-hard in general. We propose an efficient greedy algorithm which guarantees a user specified level of location and query privacy, namely k-anonymity and l-diversity, throughout a session and all the while trying to not significantly compromise service quality. Our algorithm, running on the proxy, makes use of trajectories to find similar users whose trajectories are also close by (using appropriate notions of similarity and closeness) for privacy enforcement. We give an indexing structure for efficiently storing and retrieving past trajectories, and present extensive experimental results comparing our approach with other similar approaches.

1 Introduction

We call as trajectory the sequence of locations visited by a continuously moving user, with additional annotations (like, time at a location, nearby shops, photos taken, activities done, etc.) possibly present for each location. Trajectory data of users are finding a lot of use in today's service oriented economy. From a consumer point of view, they find most usage in trip recommendation systems, viz., obtaining suggestion of a suitable trajectory based on user preference. For example, a user can request suggestion for a trip which visits a preferred set of places, and/or allows some preferred activities.

There are several online services which use customer trajectory data, either directly or subvertly. These services are becoming easier to deploy thanks to the proliferation of the Internet, and easy availability of affordable mobile devices. They are also very popular among users due to the immense value they add; essentially, all one needs is

---

* The author acknowledges the support from Fast Track Scheme for Young Scientist, Department of Science and Technology, India for this work.

A. Bagchi and I. Ray (Eds.): ICISS 2013, LNCS 8303, pp. 360–374, 2013.

a mobile phone with a proper data plan. Simultaneously however, users are becoming concerned with privacy of their personal information and behaviour. Sophisticated data mining algorithms running on powerful computing machinery has brought to the limelight the issue of privacy in online services.

It is now the need of the hour to have proper privacy protection mechanism for all such services (commonly known as *location-based services (LBS)*. The usual protocol of LBS is that a user submits to a service provider her current location and relevant query parameters ("nearest cafe", "closeby people who like to hike", "neighborhood shopping malls selling tuxedos") and the latter replies her with matching service availability). For example, a broker could be offering a ride-share service, allowing users who have a car to advertise route information and request names of interested passengers. Lacking a better word, we will use adversary to refer to a nosy individual with access to the user requests (the service provider can very well play this role) who may try to extract sensitive information about users. It is clear that privacy violations can occur from two basic information, "where she is (at what time)" and "what query did she make", and the research community studies them separately as *location privacy* and *query privacy*. In the above example, a paranoid user may not want to disclose to the broker that he wants to offer a ride, nor her exact location.

One simple approach for location privacy is to report a larger region (called as *cloaked region*) as location instead of the exact location. There are a few issue however; first, the user may end up with a query result bloated with services in the nearby locations as well, and secondly, this may not suffice if the adversary knows that no other user is present in the larger region, and lastly, if a user is continuously taking service (such as in our case of trajectories), then by correlating successive regions one can get a better estimate of the actual location. Similarly, a user can make queries under a different name or add redundant random keywords to ensure query privacy. This also has similar problems in continuous query scenarios. The work on location and query privacy mostly rely on the notions of k-anonymity, l-diversity and m-invariance. k-anonymity hides a user among $k - 1$ other users so that adversary can not isolate an individual user out of the group of k users. However, k-anonymity alone does not suffice for query privacy, e.g., if all the users in that group make the same query. This can be prevented by ensuring l-diversity which requires that set of queries are diverse enough (at least l). Again both of these fall short during continuous queries, thereby necessitating m-invariance. In m-invariance it is necessary that a set of m different queries remain unchanged at every instant for the complete session (in addition to l-diversity).

The techniques above are applicable for different scenarios. Specifically, there can be two kinds of adversaries: *location-unaware* (the default) and *location-aware*. A location-aware adversary has additional knowledge about the exact position of every user; m-invariance suffices for query privacy for such adversaries [1]. However, location unaware adversaries may also try to infer exact locations, and our main contribution is a strategy to ensure both location and query privacy by enforcing k-anonymity (using an invariant set of users throughout a session) and m-invariance (using an invariant set of activities throughtout a session).

A previous work [2] used historical trajectory data but for only applying k-anonymity. Another relevant work [1] showed how to efficiently implement m-invariance, however their algorithm does not use trajectories of users. It uses only current locations of users, which, as we show later, is prone to larger cloaked regions (when user does not move along the guessed trajectory) compared to our solution.

In this paper, we design an algorithm to find an anonymised activity-trajectory for given user's activity-trajectory which 1) satisfy user specified privacy constraints i.e. k-anonymity, l-diversity and m-invariance; and 2) try not to compromise service quality. To meet these objectives, information from past trajectories is used (via a suitable inference system[3], which we use as an external module) to select users (a) whose predicted trajectories will be close to the trajectory of the user, and (b) whose trajectories will most likely have enough diverse activities. There are several difficulties in designing the inference system and so the algorithm-First, trajectories (in trajectory database) have different length, and secondly, it is not clear how to define the notion of closeness among annotated trajectories. Finally, it is computationally expensive to search for a group of users (k or more), with enough (l or more) diversity in their activities, who can be grouped together in a small region in a consecutive manner. Thus, for solving this problem, we propose an index for trajectory data and define the distance function to measure the closeness. Our extensive experimental study shows that our proposed indexing method and our algorithm gives better results than before.

1.1 Related Work

Gruteser and Grunwald [4] considered the problem of privacy breaches for location-based services nearly a decade ago and proposed a solution by modifying the spatial and temporal information. Since then, this area has seen intense research effort producing a large gamut of solutions. Most strategies try to either mask the exact spatial location (obfuscation, aka. cloaking) or the identity in a way so that it is difficult for someone to correlate a user with a query or a user with his location (or both).

Most of the solutions which target user anonymity, do so based on the central idea of k-anonymity: the region reported by the user query should contain at-least k users so that the requesting user is indistinguishable from the other $k - 1$ users [5]. One of the earlier notable works were by Gedik and Liu [6] who proposed an algorithm Clique-Cloak to find the smallest obfuscated area called Clique-Cloak based on a personalized k-anonymity model. Mokbel proposed a grid-based algorithm to determine the optimal obfuscated area based on his Casper framework [7]. Bamba et al. [8] proposed PrivacyGrid which tries to preserve both k-anonymity and l-diversity (extension of k-anonymity to avoid query privacy attack when each user in the k-anonymous group have same query). All these solutions were primarily proposed for ensuring privacy of user identity [9,10] and even though they work well with respect to location privacy for snapshot queries, they fail in the case of continuous queries [11,1].

Another method to introduce confusion in a user's path is based on an identity anonymisation concept called *mixzone* proposed by Beresford and Stajano [12]. Users in a mixzone are assigned identities in such a way that it is not possible to relate entering individuals with exiting individuals. This idea has even been extended to urban road networks by [13]. The objective of the mixzone-based approach is to prevent the adversary from figuring out the complete path of any user. Similar to mixzones, where users do not avail service to ensure location privacy, Saxena et al. [11] considered skipping service once in a while. Their Rule-based approach gave a heuristic which determined, at a particular location along the known complete user path, whether it is safe to take service or not. They do suggest limited modifications in the path during the middle of the journey.

As extensions of the notions of k-anonymity and l-diversity, other notions like historical k-anonymity and m-invariance impose other constraints of invariancy of users and queries throughout the session, respectively. Dewri et. al in their paper [1] show that for preserving query privacy in continuous query scenario only enforcing m-invariance is sufficient in the case of location-aware adversary. However, for the case of location-unaware adversary where location privacy is equally important, there is a need to enforce historical k-anonymity. In [2], the authors consider past visited locations (footprints) of the user as well as trajectories of other users to anonymise the trajectory of the current user and enforce historical k-anonymity. In this paper, for location-unaware adversary, we implement historical k-anonymity and m-invariance over users trajectories using proposed hierarchical inverted trajectory index.

2   Preliminaries

In this section we review necessary concepts and definitions related to (activity) trajectories that are required in the rest of the paper.

2.1   Trajectories

We denote the location of a user by (x, y, t), where x and y are the latitude and longitude, respectively, and t is the timestamp when the user was at this coordinate. $p.x$, $p.y$ and $p.t$ will denote the respective coordinates. A trajectory of a moving user can be defined as a finite sequence of locations visited by him. We denote a trajectory by $T = < p_1, p_2, \ldots, p_n >$, where p_i is the user's i^{th} location on his route.

Activity trajectories are an extension of trajectories where each location on a trajectory is annotated with textual attributes; for us, these attributes represent the activities performed (or, can be performed) by the user at that location. In this paper we restrict ourself to the LBS scenario where every user is performing a single activity during a session. For example a user may be looking for a movie show of his interest somewhere on his route; thus he sends a request for movie shows which are within a kilometer of places he is passing through during his journey.

Definition 1 (Session based Activity Trajectory). *A session based activity trajectory, denoted by $AT = < T, A >$, comprises of a user's trajectory (T) and a single activity of interest (A) for the entire session along T.*

2.2   User Privacy

The objective in the paper is to protect both *location and query privacy* of users by modifying the the users' service requests (specifically, using techniques of anonymization and location blurring) efficiently with the help of historical data.

Goal: For a user's known AT and using historical session based activity- trajectory data set $\mathcal{D}$, the goal is to hide the location and activity information in AT from an adversary by mixing AT with past activities trajectories from $\mathcal{D}$.

It is important at this point to observe that the protection of sensitive information depends upon adversary's knowledge and effectiveness of using $\mathcal{D}$. Our technique requires an inferencing engine, which can reliably predict from $\mathcal{D}$ accurate activity trajectories of a set of users at any point of time in the future. Our algorithm shares the same failure rate of this inferring engine. Exact knowledge of an adversary may be hard to estimate, but typically, adversaries can make strong inferences about exact locations and preferred activities by correlating different queries in a single session. If an adversary does not have any information about users' movement pattern, mixing an activity trajectory with $k-1$ other "close by" activity trajectories makes it hard to infer the activity. On the other hand, if an adversary knows even some locations on a user's path, he can identify the user's trajectory among a group of k trajectories. We can also consider that situation when the adversary has prior knowledge about users' likes and dislikes towards various activities – is the user still protected?

To solve these privacy disclosures, we need to first understand an adversary's knowledge. We assume that adversaries are *location-unaware*, i.e., they don't have exact location information of any user at any time. However, the adversary may have background knowledge which he can used to make inferences; for example, an adversary may know a user's house and office, and he may also know at what time user leaves the house and at what time he reaches the office. Thus for a query with a location close enough to user's house or office at proper times can be used by adversary to infer user identity and thereby, help him to know about user's other locations and queries.

We protect privacy of the user against adversaries like above by generating a k-anonymous trajectory having l-diverse activities, where k and l are user supplied parameters representing *levels of privacy*. From a given user's activity trajectory $AT =< T, A >$, an anonymous activity trajectory, denoted by $AT^* =< T^*, A^* >$, is the grouping of T with at least $k-1$ other trajectories such that neither can an adversary relate the user to his trajectory with significant confidence (with probability more than $\frac{1}{k}$) nor can he relate the user to activities in his query (with probability more than $\frac{1}{l}$).

Definition 2 (Anonymization of trajectory). *For a trajectory $T =< p_1, p_2, \ldots, p_n >$, its anonymization $T^* =< \langle \mathcal{R}_1, p_1.t \rangle, \langle \mathcal{R}_2, p_2.t \rangle, \ldots, \langle \mathcal{R}_n, p_n.t \rangle >$ consists of a sequence of regions such that for all $p_i.t$, the corresponding spatial location $(p_i.x, p_i.y)$ is contained in the region $\mathcal{R}_i$. If T^* is an anonymization of T we denote it by $T \subset T^*$.*

For any i, $\mathcal{R}_i$s as in the definition above are called the minimum bounding regions (MBR) corresponding to the ith location $p_i.(x, y)$. To ensure privacy, T^* needs to satisfy the k-anonymity and/or l-diversity conditions.

Definition 3 (k-anonymous trajectory). *An anonymization T^* of T is a k-anonymization of T if the cardinality of the set $\{tr | tr \subset T^*\}$, denoted by $|T^*|$, is greater or equal to k.*

In case of a AT, say $AT =< T, A >$, we say $AT^* =< T^*, A^* >$ is k-anonymous if $|T^*| \geq k$ i.e. the cardinality of the set $\{< tr, A >\in \mathcal{D} | tr \subset T^*\}$ is greater or equal to k. Here $A^* = \{A | < tr, A >\in \mathcal{D} \text{ and } tr \subset T^*\}$.

Definition 4 (*k*-**anonymous** *l*-**diverse Activity Trajectory (kl-AT)**). *An activity trajectory* $AT^* =< T^*, A^* >$ *is said to be a kl-AT of an activity trajectory* $AT =< T, A >$ *if*

1. $T \subset T^*$ *and* $A \in A^*$
2. $|T^*| \geq k$ *and* $|A^*| \geq l$

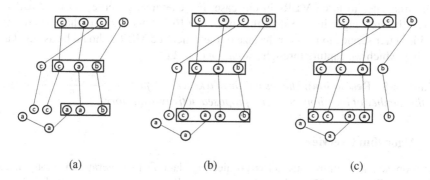

(a)   (b)   (c)

Fig. 1. Illustration of 3-anonymity and 2-diversity on trajectories (a) 3-anonymity and 2-diversity not satisfied; (b) and (c) 3-anonymity and 2-diversity satisfied; (c) has low resolution as compare to (b)

It can be observed easily that any arbitrary grouping of activity trajectory from $\mathcal{D}$ to get a kl-AT of user's trajectory may violate the k-anonymity or/and l-diversity requirement. For example, as in figure 1(a), the grouping of the trajectory is 3-anonymous 2-diverse corresponding to each of the user's movement, but an adversary having knowledge of the trajectory can identify that the set of trajectories at time $t = 1$ is different from the set of trajectories at time $t = 2$ and that of at time $t = 3$. This correlation discloses the user's trajectory. Also the set of activities at time $t = 1, 2, 3$ are respectively $A_1^* = \{a, a, b\}$, $A_2^* = \{c, a, b\}$ and $A_3^* = \{c, a, c\}$ which are 2-diverse at respective times. Knowing the fact that the user is present in each of the MBR, and $\cap_i A_i^* = \{a\}$ discloses the user's activity. It is therefore suggested to generate AT^* for a given AT by selecting a set of activity trajectory such that each trajectory has at least one location in each MBR $\mathcal{R}_i$ of T^*. The AT^* so generated will satisfy the k and l requirement, and thus a $kl - AT$. For example ,as in figure 1(b) and 1(c), the reported AT^* are both 3-anonymous and 2-diverse.

2.3 Service Model

The service model to ensure both location and query privacy is a standard modification of the usual user—proxy—provider model. Users send their queries to the proxy. The proxy waits until it has collected enough queries to ensure privacy, and then, it sends a consolidated query, to the service provider. The latter sends the query results to the proxy, who filters the results for each user and sends them filtered result relevant to their query. The consolidated query is what we refer to here as kl-AT, and this consolidation is our main focus in this paper.

2.4 Quality of Anonymization

We had hinted earlier that privacy does not come for free; it may degrade service quality, which translates to large MBRs in our case. For example, observe that the MBR in figure 1(b) are bigger in size than that of figure 1(c). This suggests that in order to provide better service to the user the size of the generated MBR's should be as small as possible, which we capture through *resolution* of a AT^*.

Definition 5 (Resolution). *The resolution of a kl-AT is defined as* $\frac{\sum_{i=1}^{n} area(\mathcal{R}_i)}{n}$*, where n is the number of locations on user's proposed activity-trajectory.*

2.5 Algorithm Overview

Our proposed algorithm uses activity-trajectory data $\mathcal{D}$ to generate an anonymised $AT^* =< \langle \mathcal{R}_1, \mathcal{R}_2, \dots \mathcal{R}_n \rangle, A^* >$ from a given $AT =< \langle p_1, p_2, \dots p_n \rangle, A >$, such that the following holds. Here, k and l are privacy parameters representing k-anonymity and l-diversity respectively.

1. $\mathcal{R}_i$ is an MBR corresponding to each location p_i of the user.
2. There are at least $k-1$ other activity trajectories, called candidate trajectories, such that each candidate trajectory has at least one location in $\mathcal{R}_i$ for all i.
3. The activity set of the candidate trajectories, denoted by A^*, is l-divergent. i.e there are at least l different activities which are performed over those $k - 1$ additional trajectories.
4. In session based activity trajectory, as same activity is performed at all the locations of the trajectory, the l-diverse activity sets at anonymised locations of the trajectory (i.e. A_i^* for each $\mathcal{R}_i$) are all same, and therefore l-diversity directly imply l-invariance.
5. The resolution of the MBR's thus generated is kept low.

AT^* is essentially an efficient (last property) kl-AT (first three properties). The efficiency of the algorithm to find it depends upon efficient retrieval of candidate trajectories and choosing the best possible out of them. In section 3, we define a grid index on activity trajectories for this purpose. We also define a distance function to measure distance between any two activity trajectory. It is obvious that the spatially closer trajectories will give low resolution. We also develop a tighter lower bound distance over all partially seen (unseen) trajectory in the database for early termination with best k-trajectories satisfying kl-AT. In section 4, we discuss the proposed algorithm to find kl-AT for given user's activity trajectory. Section 5 reports the experimental observations and section 6 concludes the paper.

3   Indexing Structure

In this section we discuss our proposed grid index for activity trajectories. We divide the entire spatial region into $2^n \times 2^n$ cells , called a n-Grid. Each cell of this n-Grid, called *leaf-cell*, contains a list of elements of the form $(tr.id, tr.A, tr.p)$ corresponding to trajectories which pass through that leaf-cell; here $tr.id$ is the trajectory id, $tr.A$ is the activity performed on the trajectory and $tr.p$ is the location on the trajectory which lie in the leaf-cell. On top of the n-Grid, we build $(n-1)$-Grid, $(n-2)$-Grid,..., 1-Grid,0-Grid (see figure-2) as a hierarchy of cells – called intermediate cells. The 0-Grid consists of the entire region (also called the root-cell). Apart from the address of the child cells, each intermediate cell contains a bitmap of size equal to the total number of activities in $\mathcal{D}$. Activity of all the activity trajectories which has a location in the current intermediate cell is reflected in this bitmap. These bitmaps help us in verifying whether further probing of children cells is required. If the cell under consideration does not have any trajectory having different activities than that of those already grouped, then we need not to further investigate this cell. Each cell starting from n-Grid to 0-Grid is assigned a unique cell-id using an appropriate space filling curve. For example in figure 2, 2-Grid cells are numbered from 1 to 16, 1-Grid cells are numbered from 17-20, and 0-Grid denoting the entire region is numbered as 21.

The candidate selection algorithm works similar to the R-tree based method, i.e., finding the spatially closest trajectories to the query trajectory. There are, however, two important modifications, towards efficiency and low resolution. We will denote a query by $Q =< P, A >$, where P is the sequence of locations and A is the requested activity.

1. Before probing the children cells of a cell, the algorithm checks the bitmap of the cell to decide if further probing will lead to trajectories that improve the diversity of the set of activities. If not, then the cell under consideration and its children are

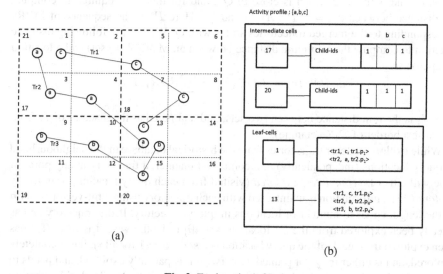

(a)

(b)

Fig. 2. Explanation of Index

immediately pruned. This increases the efficiency of the algorithm as fewer cells are examined as compare to an R-tree based technique in which no decision at intermediate level is taken to prune the cells.

2. A global heap is maintained to ensure that the browsing speed to search the candidate trajectories with respect to the query locations are almost same. This is implemented by storing in a global min-heap one tuples of the form $< \langle d, cell - id \rangle, i >$ corresponding to each query location $Q.P_i$. The distance d, of $Q.P_i$ from the cell $cell - id$, is minimum for the ith location over all unexplored cells implies $cell - id$ is the closest cell to be explored next from location i. The min-heap over d ensures that the next cell picked corresponding to the query location from where the exploration is least (in term of d) as compare to all query locations.

Before we discuss our algorithm to find a group of trajectories satisfying kl-privacy corresponding to given user query, we first discuss the notion of distance of an activity trajectory from the query activity trajectory. It is obvious that by choosing activity trajectories that are spatially closer to the user's query, we generate MBRs having low resolution. The distance of Q from $tr =< T, A >$ is defined as the sum of the pointwise spatial distance between $Q.P$ and $tr.T$, i.e.,

$$d_{tr}(Q, tr) = d_p(P, T) = \sum_i d(P_i, T_i)$$

where, P_i is the ith location on the trajectory $Q.P$, T_i is the ith location on the trajectory T, d_p is the distance between two sequence of locations and d represents the Euclidean distance between two locations.

Our algorithm generates a $kl - AT$ by successively merging other AT from $\mathcal{D}$ to Q. At any intermediate stage, it would have had merged a few ATs with Q (call the merged anonymous trajectory Q^*, which may not yet satisfy $kl - AT$). At this stage, it has to find a $tr \in D$ which is close to Q^*, and for this it is required to compute the distance between $Q^* =< P^*, A^* >$ and tr . Here P^* is the sequence of MBRs corresponding to the merged trajectories so far with Q. We use the following distance function to compute the minimum distance between an MBR $\mathcal{R}_i$ (a set) and a location (singleton set).

$$d_{tr}(Q^*, tr) = d_p(P^*, T) = \sum_i d_s(\mathcal{R}_i, T_i)$$

Here d_s is the min distance between two sets, and computed as the distance of T_i from the closest border of $\mathcal{R}_i$ (rectangle).

While exploring closer trajectories from the historical database in the neighbourhood of query locations (independently) in a controlled manner, a trajectory at any point of time will either be *completely explored* (visited from each query location) or *partially explored*. This information is maintained with each trajectory using a bit-vector $tr.seen$ of the length equal to number of locations in query trajectory. If the trajectory tr has already been explored from the ith location, $seen[i]$ is 1 otherwise it is zero. If it has been explored from each of the query location (i.e $seen[i] = 1$ for all i), it is completely explored, and is either in Q^* or pruned. Otherwise it is partially explored, and needs to be stored only if it is a probable *candidates* to be in Q^* in future. To decide whether a partially explored trajectory is a candidate, we need to define, compute and store the partial-distance of partially explored trajectories.

We maintain the set of partially seen trajectory in the priority queue PS, using partial distances as key, and storing triples $< d, tr, seen >$ corresponding to each partially explored trajectory tr. The partial distances of $tr \in PS$ from Q and Q^* are:

$$d_{tr}(Q, tr) = d_p(P, T) = \sum_{seen[i]=1} d(P_i, T_i) + \sum_{seen[i] \neq 1} r(P_i)$$

$$d_{tr}(Q^*, tr) = d_p(P^*, T) = \sum_{seen[i]=1} d_s(R_i, T_i) + \sum_{seen[i] \neq 1} r(P_i)$$

for query locations from where the trajectory tr is unseen, the distance is approximated by $r(P_i)$ which is the distance of the closest unexplored cell from the ith location (radius of browsing wave front). Clearly, this is a lower bound of the distance as the trajectory unseen from the ith location (i.e. P_i) cannot have better distance than the current *radius of the wave front ([14])* from P_i.

We want to avoid complete exploration of all active trajectories in $\mathcal{D}$ if possible. For early termination to find best k activity trajectories, we maintain and update the lower bound distance LB over the partially explored trajectories in PS and the upper bound distance UB over completely explored trajectories stored in a priority queue CS(completely seen). The lower bound distance LB is the distance of the first element in PS; formally, $LB = min\{d_{tr}(Q, tr)|tr \in PS\}$.

CS is a max-priority queue of completely explored trajectories, having entries as $< d, tr >$, where, the complete distance of tr from Q is denoted by d, and keys as d. Therefore, the first element in CS is the farthest trajectory completely seen so far from the user query Q, and the corresponding distance is represented by UB. The values LB and UB are updated with every insert or delete in PS or CS. Also $LB > UB$ implies that no partially seen trajectory can be as close as the farthest completely seen trajectory. As we are exploring trajectories by increasing the wave front from all the query locations in a controlled manner, all the unseen trajectories will be even farther than the partially seen trajectories and therefore cannot have lesser distance than that of the lowest distant partially seen trajectory in PS. Therefore, when $LB > UB$, we can terminate successfully without exploring the remaining trajectories in $\mathcal{D}$.

In the next section we discuss our proposed algorithm for finding the best grouping of trajectories which satisfy the kl-AT requirement also ensuring a small resolution.

4   Algorithm

The proposed greedy algorithm to find a group of activity trajectories from the historical activity trajectory data for a given user query is given in Algorithm 1; it satisfies kl-AT and ensure a small resolution of the obfuscated MBR.

To find a satisfying group of trajectories, the quad tree of cells over the space(as discussed in Section 3) is scanned from each of the query location $Q.P_i$. This is done by maintaining a min heap H_i for each query location i using distance d of the query

---

Algorithm 1. Algorithm to generate kl-AT for given user Query Q

Input: Historical AT Data $\mathcal{D}$ and the user request $Q =< P, A >$
Output: Anonymous Activity Trajectory $AT^* =< P^*, A^* >$
State: H_i : Min-Heap of cells for i^{th} query location; key as $d(Q.P_i, cell - id)$
              H^G : Min-Heap to maintain controlled unraveling of cells from query location
              PS : List of partially seen trajectories
              CS : Set of completely seen AT so far which satisfy kl-AT
              P^*: Sequence of MBRs as per current best k AT in CS
              A^*: Set of Activities corresponding to current best k AT
              LB : Lower bound distance for all partially explored trajectories
              UB : Upper bound distance for all completely explored trajectories

Method:

1: Initialize $PS \leftarrow \phi; CS \leftarrow Q.P; LB \leftarrow 0; UB \leftarrow 0; A^* \leftarrow Q.A; P^* \leftarrow MBR(CS);$ ⎫ Initia-
2: **for** each query location i in Q.P **do**   ⎬ lisation
3:     $H_i \leftarrow$ insert $< 0,$ root-cell$>$ ⎭
4:     $H^G \leftarrow$ insert $<< 0,$ root-cell$>, i >$

5: **while** true **do**
6:     $node \leftarrow H^G.pop()$
7:     **if** $node$ is corresponding to i^{th} query location **then**
8:         delete root of H_i
9:     **if** $node$ is an intermediate-cell **then**
10:         **for** each child-cell of $node$ **do**
11:             **if** diverse(child-cell.bitmap, A^*) **or** $(|A^*| \geq l)$ **then**
12:                 $H_i \leftarrow$ insert $< d(Q.P_i,$child-cell), child-cell$>$
13:     **else**
14:         **for** each tr in $node$ **do**
15:             **if** $tr.id$ is seen first time from i^{th} location **then**
16:                 update $tr.id.seen[i], d_{tr}(P^*, tr.id)$
17:             **if** tr.id is seen completely **then**
18:                 remove $tr.id$ from PS ⎫
19:                 **if** $|CS| == k$ **and** $d_{tr}(P^*, tr.id) < CS.top().d$ **then**   ⎪
20:                     replace top of CS by $tr.id$, its activity by $tr.A$ in A^* ⎬ Validating tr
21:                     update P^*, UB ⎪ to be a candidate
22:                 **else if** $|CS| < k$ **then**   ⎪
23:                     insert $tr.id$ into CS, update A^*, P^*, UB ⎭
24:             **else**
25:                 insert $tr.id$ in PS, update LB
26:     $H^G \leftarrow$ insert $< H_i.top(), i >$
27:     **if** $LB > UB$ **then**
28:         return $< P^*, A^* >$

---

location from the unexplored cells as key. Each H_i contains the information of the unexplored cells as a tuple $< d, cell - id >$. We initialize H_i (line 3) corresponding to each query location $Q.P_i$ as $< 0, 0 - cell >$, where $0 - cell$ is the root cell (root cell represents the entire space and hence contains every location). When we explore any intermediate cell corresponding to H_i (as in line 9-10), we insert its children cells into heap H_i for further exploration at a later stage. These child cells are inserted into H_i only if its bitmap (storing the information of the activities performed over trajectories having locations in $cell - id$) meet the l-diversity requirement taken in conjunction with the activities (A^*) of the current grouped trajectories. This is done using a helper function $diverse$ (line 11) which checks if two bit-vectors of the size equal to number activities (namely, bitmap and A^*) for having one at different positions.

To control the exploration from each query location, we maintain a heap H^G containing information of the nearest unexplored-cell corresponding to each query location (initialized in line 4). In H^G, we store for each query location i, the top of H_i associated with the index of the query location. H^G is a min heap where distance d of the nearest unexplored cell from the query location is used as the key. By choosing the minimum of those nearest unexplored cells (from query locations) in H^G to be explored next (as in line 6), we maintain the balanced exploration from query locations.

When we get a leaf-cell as the next cell to be explored (line 13), we process its included trajectories, some of which may be partially seen and others will be completely seen (with respect to all the query locations). To maintain this record, we have two priority queues PS and CS for partially seen and completely seen trajectories, respectively. We initialize PS as empty and CS as $Q.P$ (line 1), and update them corresponding to each trajectory when we explore a leaf cell. In PS corresponding to each partially seen trajectory tr, we add the information $< d, tr, seen >$ keeping the record of its partial distance, trajectory id and the record of its $seen$ status from query locations. Its counterpart CS, at any stage, contains the trajectories which are considered to be part of the anonymized group of trajectories, and stores $< d, tr >$, where d is the distance of all completely seen trajectories tr.

For every trajectory in a leaf-cell (line 15), we update its $seen$ and compute its distance from the sequence of MBR (as in P^*) corresponding to current CS (if it is seen first time from the query location). The function MBR returns a sequence of MBRs for given set of points (used for each query location corresponding to CS). If tr is partially seen, the distance in line 16 is partial distance, otherwise complete distance.

We validate the seen status of tr in line 17 to decide whether we need to insert it in CS or in PS. If it is completely seen and is a *valid candidate* we insert it in CS and remove its entry from PS (line $17 - 23$). tr is a valid candidate if either k trajectories are not selected in CS or if k trajectories are already selected then the current trajectory is closer (as compare to the farthest trajectory in CS). If tr is not completely seen its entry is updated in PS (as the distance d_{tr} might have changed) as in line 25.

As an when a trajectory is inserted in PS or CS we also update LB and UB. LB is the lower bound distance of all partially seen trajectory in PS and UB is the upper bound of all completely seen trajectory in CS. Since PS is maintained as a priority queue in increasing d and CS is maintained as a priority queue in decreasing d, LB and UB are the distance of the first element in PS and CS respectively.

A set of activities corresponding to all completely seen trajectory in CS is maintained in A^*. It is initialize with the user's requested activity and updated every time a completely seen trajectory is added or deleted from CS (line 20, 23).

The initialization of the variables has been done in the lines from 1 . The helper functions $MBR()$ and $diverse()$ are omitted due to their simple nature. Loop from line 5 to 29 runs until we find required group of trajectories and therefore $\langle P^*, A^* \rangle$, which is decided by verifying the condition in line 27. If LB of the partially seen trajectory is greater than the UB of the completely seen trajectories then no trajectory from PS can be as close as the farthest trajectory in CS, and therefore we can terminate successfully.

5   Experimental Evaluation

We conducted extensive experiments to evaluate the performance of proposed index and algorithm. We used one real dataset from Foursquare®for the experiments. The dataset contains actual activity trajectories representing users' check-in records on Foursquare®. Each check-in record has a user's ID, her geo-location, time of check-in, and the tips. We randomly picked a word from tips to mark it as an activity for the entire trajectory; the latter was obtained by putting together the records belonging to the user in a chronological order. The dataset consists of 31557 trajectories and 215614 locations.

Experimental Setup: We compare our method with m-invariance method adapted to enforce historical k-anonymity on the basis of query overhead (resolution) and absolute computation time. Our hierarchical index is created by partitioned the space into $2^6 \times 2^6$ cells. Values for other parameters are 5 for trajectory size, 4 for diversity, and 7 for K. A query trajectory for the experiment is generated by randomly choosing a trajectory from the database and then selecting the desired number of locations. We generate 50 different queries for each experiment and report the average of the performance time and resolution. The experiments were conducted on a laptop with Intel Duo core 3GHz CPU and 8GB memory.

Effect of Trajectory Size: Figure 3 shows the effect of trajectory size on resolution and evaluation time, respectively. It can be seen that our approach performs consistenly better than the adaptive m-invariance approach with respect to resolution; this is due to our use of extra information of complete trajectories for deciding the member of the group. For computation time, the adaptive m-invaiance approach takes constant time whereas our algorithm time increases as the query trajectory size increase. The constant time for m-invariant approach is due to the reason of using only first location of the trajectory for its decision making; however, we use all locations for better quality.

Effect of K: As like trajectory size parameter, we can see in figure 4 that the performace of our algorithm is better in terms of resolution time. The time for m-invaiance is almost constant due to doing simple partition of already given sorted sequence of trajectories on the basis of their hilbert index. We, however, spend more time to choose best group and indeed performs better consistently for all value of K.

Effect of Diversity: We see that our algorithm again performs better than m-invariance for resolution and efficiency with respect to diversity (see figure 5).

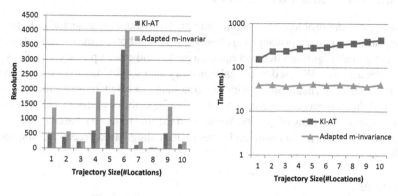

Fig. 3. Effect of Trajectory Size on Performance

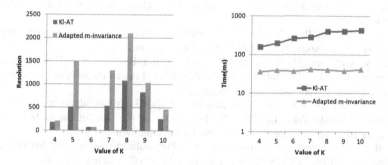

Fig. 4. Effect of K on Performance

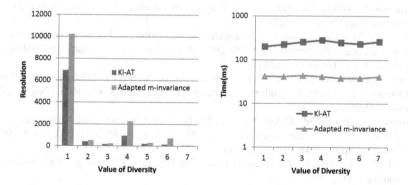

Fig. 5. Effect of Diversity on Performance

6   Conclusions and Future Work

We investigated the problem of grouping and anonymising user trajectories to protect users' location and query privacy. This being an NP hard problem, we have designed an *efficient greedy algorithm* that can run on a proxy, and ensure privacy as well as low loss of service quality. We used historical trajectory data sent to the proxy to find similar nearby trajectories to ensure anonymity. We conducted an extensive experimental study and showed that our greedy approach due to using trajectories performs better than the baseline approach in terms of quality. We wish to explore trajectory based optimization in other similar scenarios in future and investigate scaling based greedy techniques for large datasets.

References

1. Dewri, R., Ray, I., Ray, I., Whitley, D.: Query m-invariance: Preventing query disclosures in continuous location-based services. In: IEEE MDM (2010)
2. Xu, T., Cai, Y.: Exploring historical location data for anonymity preservation in location-based services. In: INFOCOM 2008: Proceeding of 27th Conference on Computer Communications (2008)
3. Jeung, H., Yiu, M.L., Zhou, X., Jensen, C.S.: Path prediction and predictive range querying in road network databases. The VLDB Journal 19(4), 585–602 (2010)
4. Gruteser, M., Grunwald, D.: Anonymous Usage of Location-Based Services Through Spatial and Temporal Cloaking. In: MobiSys 2003: Proceedings of the 1st International Conference on Mobile Systems, Applications and Services (2003)
5. Chow, C.-Y., Mokbel, M.F., Liu, X.: A peer-to-peer spatial cloaking algorithm for anonymous location-based service. In: GIS 2006: Proceedings of the 14th Annual ACM International Symposium on Advances in Geographic Information Systems (2006)
6. Gedik, B., Liu, L.: Protecting Location Privacy with Personalized k-Anonymity: Architecture and Algorithms. IEEE TMC: IEEE Transactions on Mobile Computing 7 (2008)
7. Mokbel, M.F., Chow, C.-Y., Aref, W.G.: The new Casper: query processing for location services without compromising privacy. In: VLDB 2006: Proceedings of the 32nd International Conference on Very Large Data Bases (2006)
8. Bamba, B., Liu, L., Pesti, P., Wang, T.: Supporting anonymous location queries in mobile environments with privacygrid. In: WWW 2008: Proceeding of the 17th International Conference on World Wide Web (2008)
9. Bettini, C., Mascetti, S., Wang, X.S., Jajodia, S.: Anonymity in Location-Based Services: Towards a General Framework. In: MDM 2007: Proceedings of the International Conference on Mobile Data Management (2007)
10. Chow, C.-Y., Mokbel, M.F.: Enabling private continuous queries for revealed user locations. In: Papadias, D., Zhang, D., Kollios, G. (eds.) SSTD 2007. LNCS, vol. 4605, pp. 258–275. Springer, Heidelberg (2007)
11. Saxena, A.S., Pundir, M., Goyal, V., Bera, D.: Preserving location privacy for continuous queries on known route. In: Jajodia, S., Mazumdar, C. (eds.) ICISS 2011. LNCS, vol. 7093, pp. 265–279. Springer, Heidelberg (2011)
12. Beresford, A.R., Stajano, F.: Location Privacy in Pervasive Computing. IEEE Pervasive Computing 2(1) (2003)
13. Palanisamy, B., Liu, L.: Mobimix: Protecting location privacy with mix-zones over road networks. In: 27th ICDE 2011 (2011)
14. Shang, S., Ding, R., Yuan, B., Xie, K., Zheng, K., Kalnis, P.: User oriented trajectory search for trip recommendation. In: EDBT (2012)

An Administrative Model for Spatio-Temporal Role Based Access Control

Manisha Sharma[1], Shamik Sural[1], Vijayalakshmi Atluri[2],
and Jaideep Vaidya[3]

[1] School of Information Technology, IIT Kharagpur, India
[2] National Science Foundation and MSIS Department, Rutgers University, USA
[3] MSIS Department, Rutgers University, USA
{manishas,shamik}@sit.iitkgp.ernet.in,
atluri@rutgers.edu, jsvaidya@business.rutgers.edu

Abstract. In the present computing environment, access control decisions are often based on contextual information like the location of users and objects as well as the time of making an access request. Several variants of Role based Access Control (RBAC) have recently been proposed that support spatio-temporal policy specifications. However, unlike the administrative models available for RBAC, there is no reported literature on complete administrative models for spatio-temporal role based access control. In this paper, we introduce an administrative model for the recently proposed ESTARBAC (Enhanced Spatio-temporal Role based Access Control) model and name it as ADMINESTAR (Administrative model for Enhanced Spatio-Temporal Role based Access Control). ADMINESTAR defines a broad range of administrative rules and administrative operations. An instance of the set of administrative rules frames the currently effective administrative policy for the system. Administrative rules specify which administrative role can change which ESTARBAC entity. These ESTARBAC entities together define the system state which can be changed by administrative operations upon their successful execution under the control of defined administrative policies. ADMINESTAR would help in practical deployment of spatio-temporal role based access control systems and also provide a means for their formal security analysis.

Keywords: Administrative Model, Spatio-Temporal Access Control, Administrative Rules, Administrative Operations, Role Hierarchy.

1 Introduction

The Role based Access Control (RBAC) [1] model is capable of capturing many access control policies like Mandatory Access Control (MAC) [2] policies and Discretionary Access Control (DAC) [3] policies as well as the Principle of Least Privilege and the well-known Separation of Duty (SOD) based policies. In many protected systems, however, access control decisions cannot be made only on the basis of the role an individual possesses in the organization. They require

A. Bagchi and I. Ray (Eds.): ICISS 2013, LNCS 8303, pp. 375–389, 2013.

access permissions be given based on the access request time, user location and object location as well. The classical RBAC needs spatio-temporal extensions to express such requirements. Over the last few years, several access control models have been developed that impose temporal [9][16], spatial [12][13] and spatio-temporal constraints [4][5][6] over RBAC.

Of the above-mentioned spatio-temporal extensions, STRBAC [4] (Spatio-temporal Role based Access Control) defines two separate functions *RoleEnable Loc(r)* and *RoleEnableDur(r)*, which specify the sets of locations and the sets of durations for enabling a role r. It also makes use of *Role Allocation* and *Role Enabling* operations. A role is said to be allocated when it satisfies the temporal and spatial constraints needed for role assignment. A role can be assigned once it has been allocated. A role is said to be enabled if it satisfies the temporal and location constraints needed to activate it. A role can be activated only if it has been enabled. In ESTARBAC (Enhanced Spatio-temporal Role Based Access Control) [6], which is an extension of the STARBAC model [5], the concept of *RoleExtents* associates a role with a (*location, interval*) pair. It defines spatio-temporal domains for permissions as well. This enables ESTARBAC to specify granular spatio-temporal access control policies. Concrete access control evaluation algorithms are included in ESTARBAC for determining whether a particular access can actually be granted on a resource at a given spatio-temporal point.

Along with the development of various extensions of RBAC, administrative models were proposed that can be used for administering deployed RBAC systems and also enable formal security analysis [7], [8]. The URA97 (User-role assignment) component of the ARBAC97 (Administrative RBAC) model [7] was used to carry out RBAC security analysis in [14] and [15]. So far, limited work has been done towards security analysis of spatio-temporal role based access control systems. Toahchoodee and Ray [10][11] specify and analyze various properties of the STRBAC model. They use Alloy, a formal language based on first-order logic, for the purpose of security analysis. The analysis, however, is not based on a formal administrative model.

It is thus observed from the literature that no complete administrative model is currently available that can suitably be used for carrying out formal security analysis of spatio-temporal RBAC similar to what has been done for classical RBAC [14] [15] and also for managing a spatio-temporal role based access control deployment. In order to overcome these shortcomings, in this paper, we propose an administrative model for ESTARBAC, which is named as AD-MINESTAR (Administrative model for Enhanced Spatio-Temporal Role based access control). It may be noted that, while ADMINESTAR is meant specifically to administer ESTARBAC systems, similar models can be developed for other spatio-temporal access control models like STRBAC [4].

ADMINESTAR is used to manage all ESTARBAC entities, namely, role extents, permission extents, set of logical locations, set of intervals, role to role extent mapping and permission to permission extent mapping. In addition, we also introduce two types of role hierarchies: *Role Activation Hierarchy* and *Permission Invocation Hierarchy*, which are not present in ESTARBAC.

ADMINESTAR has two main components: *Administrative policy*, which is a set of administrative rules ($Rule_1$ to $Rule_{15}$), and A*dministrative operations* (Op_1 to Op_{15}). For each administrative operation Op_{id}, there exists a corresponding administrative rule $Rule_{id}$ in the system. We also specify an algorithm for authorization check which is called prior to the execution of any operation. This algorithm verifies whether the user (assigned to an administrative role) who invoked the operation Op_{id} is authorized to perform it. If this algorithm returns *true*, then only the operation can be performed, otherwise the operation fails. It may be noted that we consider the set of roles assigned to ordinary users to be distinct from the set of roles that can be assigned to administrative users. The latter is denoted as the set of administrative roles.

The rest of the paper is organized as follows. In Section 2, Preliminaries on ARBAC97 as well as various components of ESTARBAC are briefly described. We introduce the proposed administrative model for ESTARBAC in Section 3 and its administrative operations in Section 4. Finally, Section 5 concludes the paper providing directions for future research.

2 Preliminaries

This section introduces some of the basic concepts required for understanding the proposed ADMINESTAR model. The first sub-section gives an overview of ARBAC97 - an administrative model for RBAC [7] and the second sub-section introduces the basic components of ESTARBAC [6].

2.1 ARBAC

ARBAC97 [7], an administrative model for RBAC [1], has three main components, namely, URA97-user to role assignment, PRA97-role to permission assignment and RRA97-role to role assignment. URA97 controls modifications made to the UA (user-role assignment) relation by using assignment and revocation rules defined by Can_{assign} and Can_{revoke}, respectively. PRA97 controls modifications made to the PA (role-permission assignment) relation by using assignment and revocation rules defined by $Can_{assignp}$ and $Can_{revokep}$, respectively. RRA97 defines a relation Can_{modify} for changing the role hierarchy.

Other administrative models for RBAC include ARBAC99 [17] and ARBAC02 [18] of which ARBAC99 incorporates the notion of mobile and immobile users and permissions. ARBAC02 defines user and permission pools based on organizational structure which are independent of roles and role hierarchies. A bottom-up approach is introduced for permission to role assignment. Instead of prerequisite roles, user organization structure and permission organization structure are used to specify which roles a user must have before being assigned another role and similarly for permissions.

2.2 ESTARBAC

ESTARBAC [6] is a spatio-temporal extension of the role based access control model in which access control decisions are based on contextual information such as user location, access time and object location. Roles and permissions are associated with spatio-temporal extents. The spatio-temporal access control policies are defined using the notion of spatio-temporal role extent and spatio-temporal permission extent. In general, a user gets a required access to a requested object only when the appropriate role is spatio-temporally available to him and the requisite permission is spatio-temporally available to that role. These spatio-temporal extents require some mechanism to represent space and time as discussed next.

In ESTARBAC, the physical points p_i represent granular points in space. The set of all physical points is represented by E where $E = \{p_1, p_2, p_3,....,p_m\}$. A *logical location* L_j is defined as a collection of physical points in the system, i.e., $L_j = \{p_{j1}, p_{j2}, p_{j3},....,p_{jn}\}$, where each $p_{jk} \in E$. An interval element is represented by a set of periodic time instants which are expressed using periodic expressions P [9]. A periodic expression represents an infinite set of periodic time instants and an interval $[begin, end]$ imposes upper and lower bounds on instants in P. *Intervals* is a set of all time intervals that participate in at least one spatio-temporal access control policy specification.

ESTARBAC consists of the basic components of RBAC, namely, users, roles and permissions (permissions are represented as operations on objects), but they are associated with either spatial extents or spatio-temporal extents. Users and objects are associated with spatial extents since their location may vary with time. Roles and permissions can be available only at specific locations and during specific time intervals. Hence, roles and permissions are also associated with spatio-temporal extents, namely, role extents denoted by *RoleExtents* and permission extents denoted by *PermExtents*. These components are discussed in detail below.

i. *Users* and *Objects*

The set of all users, who could be mobile, is denoted as *Users*. The current association of *Users* with *Locations* is expressed as:

$$UserLocations \subseteq Users \times Locations$$

Objects are also associated with locations expressed as:

$$ObjLocations \subseteq Objects \times Locations$$

ii. *RoleExtents*

In ESTARBAC, a role is available to a user only at its spatio-temporal extents called role extents. The set *RoleExtents* is derived from the sets *Roles*, *Locations* and *Intervals*. The following functions return the different components of a role extent *re*.

$$re \in RoleExtents$$

$$RERole : RoleExtents \longrightarrow Roles$$

$$RELoc : RoleExtents \longrightarrow Locations$$

$$RETime : RoleExtents \longrightarrow Intervals$$

$$Extent(re) =< RELoc(re), REtime(re) >$$

iii. *PermissionExtents*

Permissions are available to a role only at specific locations and during specific intervals. The set *PermExtents* is derived from the sets *Permissions*, *Locations* and *Intervals*. The following functions return the different components of a permission extent *pe*.

$$pe \in PermExtents$$

$$PEPerm : PermExtents \longrightarrow Permissions$$

$$PELoc : PermExtents \longrightarrow Locations$$

$$PETime : PermExtents \longrightarrow Intervals$$

$$Extent(pe) =< PELoc(pe), PETime(pe) >$$

iv. *PermLocs*

In ESTARBAC, it is considered that the objects can be also be mobile in nature. In order to spatially constrain the mobile objects accessed through permissions, each permission specifies the allowable locations for objects represented by the following relation:

$$PermLocs \subseteq Permissions \times Locations$$

The set of users, roles and permissions in ESTARBAC are administered using the relations specified in the ARBAC97 [7] model described in Sub-section 2.1. The other components of ESTARBAC described in Sub-section 2.2 that are spatio-temporal in nature are administered using the relations presented in the next section.

3   ADMINESTAR

In this section, we present details of the proposed administrative model for ESTARBAC named as ADMINESTAR. It can be used to administer role extents, permission extents, set of logical locations, set of intervals, role to role extent mapping and permission to permission extent mapping. It may be noted that, ADMINESTAR in itself uses an ESTARBAC model to manage ESTARBAC. We also introduce two types of role hierarchies not present in ESTARBAC, namely, *Role Activation Hierarchy* and *Permission Invocation Hierarchy*, which are described first.

3.1 Role Activation Hierarchy and Permission Invocation Hierarchy

In ESTARBAC [6], each user has his own context. A user context has the following components:

– *coordinate*: the current location value of the user collected when the user makes an access request
– *refresh Time*: the last time when the user coordinate value was refreshed in the system

Role Activation Hierarchy: A user assigned to a role can activate its junior role if and only if the user's context satisfies the junior role's spatio-temporal extent. A user's context is updated if a sufficiently long time has passed since the last refresh time.

Permission Invocation Hierarchy: A senior role can invoke the permissions of its junior role if and only if the following conditions hold:

– User assigned to a senior role can activate the junior role and
– User assigned to a senior role satisfies the spatio-temporal extent of the permissions associated with the junior role.

The administrative components of ADMINESTAR are discussed next.

3.2 ADMINESTAR Components

ADMINESTAR consists of the following components:

– *Administrative Policies*: They specify which administrative role is authorized to modify ESTARBAC entities of which regular role range. ESTARBAC entities include role extents, permission extents, set of logical locations, set of intervals, role to role extent mapping and permission to permission extent mapping. All ESTARBAC entities together define the system state, which changes when one or more of the entities change.
– *Administrative Operations*: The administrative operations change the system state upon their completion only if the administrative policies allow.

An administrative policy governs a set of administrative rules which control the modifications that can be made to the entities of an ESTARBAC system. In other words, these types of rules determine the administrative roles that are authorized to change the spatio-temporal extents associated with regular roles and permissions. Overall, the set of identified administrative rules and administrative operations provides a comprehensive coverage for all the management tasks required to administer an ESTARBAC system. Table 1 lists the data structures used in the ADMINESTAR Model. The administrative policies are described in detail below.

A broad range of administrative rules (denoted by $Rule_{id}s$) are included in ADMINESTAR which define the administrative policy of a spatio-temporal RBAC system. An administrative rule defines which administrative role is authorized to modify which ESTARBAC entity. The exhaustive set of administrative

Table 1. Data structures used in administrative policy and administrative operations

Data Structure	Description
Roles	Set of regular roles
AdminRoles	Set of administrative roles
Permissions	Set of permissions
Objects	Set of Objects
Users	Set of users
Locations	Set of logical locations
Intervals	Set of predefined intervals
RE	Set of role extents
RoleExtent [r]	Set of role extents associated with role r
PE	Set of permission extents
PermExtent [p]	Set of permission extents associated with permission p
PermLocs	2D matrix whose rows are permissions and columns are locations, where each permission specifies the allowable location for the objects

rules is listed in Table 2. The administrative rules are classified into the following categories:

1. *Admin Role Extents*: It includes those types of rules which control the modifications that can be made to the set of role extents RE. It comprises of the following:

- *CanUpdate_RoleExtent_Loc* (a, re_set): The user assigned to an administrative role a can update the location of any role extent which belongs to the set re_set, where $re\_set \subseteq RE$.
- *CanUpdate_RoleExtent_Interval* (a, re_set): The user assigned to an administrative role a can update the time interval of any role extent which belongs to the set re_set, where $re\_set \subseteq RE$.
- *CanAdd_RoleExtent* (a): The user assigned to an administrative role a can add a new role extent to the set RE.

2. *Admin Permission Extents*: It includes those types of rules which control the modifications that can be made to the set of permission extents, PE. It comprises of the following:

- *CanUpdate_PermExtent_Loc* (a, pe_set): The user assigned to an administrative role a can update the location of any permission extent which belongs to the set pe_set, where $pe\_set \subseteq PE$.
- *CanUpdate_PermExtent_Interval* (a, pe_set): The user assigned to an administrative role a can update the time interval of any permission extent which belongs to the set pe_set, where $pe\_set \subseteq PE$.
- *CanAdd_PermExtent* (a): The user assigned to an administrative role a can add a new permission extent to the set PE.

Table 2. Administrative rules of ADMINESTAR

$Rule_{id}$	Description
$Rule_1$	CanUpdate_RoleExtent_Loc (a, re_set)
$Rule_2$	CanUpdate_RoleExtent_Interval (a, re_set)
$Rule_3$	CanAdd_RoleExtent(a)
$Rule_4$	CanUpdate_PermExtent_Loc (a, pe_set)
$Rule_5$	CanUpdate_PermExtent_Interval (a, pe_set)
$Rule_6$	CanAdd_PermExtent(a)
$Rule_7$	CanUpdate_Locations $(a, locs)$
$Rule_8$	CanAdd_Location(a)
$Rule_9$	CanUpdate_Intervals (a, I)
$Rule_{10}$	CanAdd_Interval(a)
$Rule_{11}$	CanAssign_RoleExtent (a, r)
$Rule_{12}$	CanRevoke_RoleExtent (a, r)
$Rule_{13}$	CanAssign_PermExtent (a, p_set)
$Rule_{14}$	CanRevoke_PermExtent (a, p_set)
$Rule_{15}$	CanUpdate_PermLocs (a)

3. *Admin Space*: It includes those types of rules which control the modifications that can be made to the set of logical locations, *Locations*. It comprises of the following:

- *CanUpdate_Locations* $(a, locs)$: The user assigned to an administrative role a can update the mapping of logical location l to physical points, where $l \in locs$ and $locs \subseteq Locations$.
- *CanAdd_Location* (a): The user assigned to an administrative role a can add a new logical location to the set *Locations*.

4. *Admin Time*: It includes those types of rules which control the modifications that can be made to the set of time intervals, *Intervals*. It comprises of the following:

- *CanUpdate_Intervals* (a, I): The user assigned to an administrative role a can update any interval which belongs to the set I, where $I \subseteq Intervals$.
- *CanAdd_Interval* (a): The user assigned to an administrative role a can add a new interval to the set *Intervals*.

5. *Admin Role to RoleExtent Mapping*: It includes those types of rules which control the modifications that can be made to role to role extent mapping. It comprises of the following:

- *CanAssign_RoleExtent* (a, r): The user assigned to an administrative role a can assign a role extent from the set RE to any regular role which belongs to the role range r.
- *CanRevoke_RoleExtent* (a, r): The user assigned to an administrative role a can revoke a role extent from any regular role which belongs to the role range r.

6. *Admin Permission to PermExtent Mapping*: It includes those types of rules which control the modifications that can be made to permission to permission extent mapping. It comprises of the following:

- *CanAssign_PermExtent* (*a*, *p_set*): The user assigned to an administrative role *a* can assign a permission extent from the set *PE* to any permission which belongs to the set *p_set*, where $p\_set \subseteq Permissions$.
- *CanRevoke_PermExtent* (*a*, *p_set*): The user assigned to an administrative role *a* can revoke a permission extent from any permission which belongs to the set *p_set*, where $p\_set \subseteq Permissions$.

7. *Admin Permission to Location Mapping*: It includes a rule which controls the modifications that can be made to the values in *PermLocs*.

- *CanUpdate_PermLocs* (*a*): The user assigned to an administrative role *a* can update the matrix *PermLocs*.

In the next section, the administrative operations are discussed in detail.

4   Operations in ADMINESTAR

Like regular roles, the administrative roles are also associated with spatio-temporal extents. Thus, administrative roles have role extents and administrative rules represent their permissions to modify the spatio-temporal extents associated with regular roles and permissions. We assume that these administrative permissions have $< ANYWHERE, ANYTIME >$ permission extent, where *ANYWHERE* includes all logical locations and *ANYTIME* includes all time intervals. The role extents of administrative roles are administered by a single security officer who is senior to all administrative roles. For each administrative rule, there exists an administrative operation (denoted by Op_{id}) which changes one of the data structures given in Table 1 under the control of its corresponding administrative rule, $Rule_{id}$. Table 3 lists all the administrative operations.

When a user requests the system to perform an operation, an authorization check is first done to determine whether the user is authorized to use the same. If the authorization check succeeds, then only the operation can be performed. The algorithm for authorization check is given as Algorithm 1 whose parameters are operation Op_{id} and rule $Rule_{id}$. In this algorithm, $UserLoc$ is the current location of the user u who wants to perform the operation Op_{id} and a' is the administrative role assigned to u. For the execution of operation Op_{id}, the corresponding administrative rule $Rule_{id}$ is considered. If the role a' is senior to role a and user's spatio-temporal context meets spatio-temporal extent of role a then the further conditions for authorization check are evaluated in a separate boolean function named $check(Op_{id}, Rule_{id})$, where a' and a are the parameters of Op_{id} and $Rule_{id}$ respectively. The algorithm for *check* is given in Algorithm 2. In the function *check*, there exists a condition block for each administrative

---

Algorithm 1. authorization_check $(Op_{id}, Rule_{id})$

INPUT: $Op_{id}, Rule_{id}$
OUTPUT: True OR False
if $(a' \geq a)$ then
    for all $(re \in RoleExtent[a])$ do
        if $((userLoc \subseteq reLoc)$ && $(accessTime \subseteq reTime))$ then
            if $(check(Op_{id}, Rule_{id})$ ==True) then return True
            end if
        end if
    end for
end if
"User is not authorized to perform the requested operation."
return False

Algorithm 2. check $(Op_{id}, Rule_{id})$

INPUT: $Op_{id}, Rule_{id}$
OUTPUT: True OR False
if $(Op_{id}==Op_1 \parallel Op_{id}==Op_2)$ then
    if $(re' \in re\_set)$ then return True
                      $\triangleright$ re' and re_set are parameters of Op_{id} and $Rule_{id}$ respectively
    else return False
    end if
else if $(Op_{id}==Op_3 \parallel Op_{id}==Op_6 \parallel Op_{id}==Op_8 \parallel Op_{id}==Op_{10} \parallel Op_{id}==Op_{15})$ then
return True
else if $(Op_{id}==Op_4 \parallel Op_{id}==Op_5)$ then
    if $(pe' \in pe\_set)$ then return True
                      $\triangleright$ pe' and pe_set are parameters of Op_{id} and $Rule_{id}$ respectively
    else return False
    end if
else if $(Op_{id}==Op_7)$ then
    if $(loc_i \in locs)$ then return True
                      $\triangleright$ loc_i and $locs$ are parameters of Op_{id} and $Rule_{id}$ respectively
    else return False
    end if
else if $(Op_{id}==Op_9)$ then
    if $(i_i \in i)$ then return True
                      $\triangleright$ i_i and i are parameters of Op_{id} and $Rule_{id}$ respectively
    else return False
    end if
else if $(Op_{id}==Op_{11} \parallel Op_{id}==Op_{12})$ then
    if $(b \in r)$ then return True
                      $\triangleright$ b and r are parameters of Op_{id} and $Rule_{id}$ respectively
    else return False
    end if
else if $(Op_{id}==Op_{13} \parallel Op_{id}==Op_{14})$ then
    if $(p \in p\_set)$ then return True $\triangleright$ p and p_set are parameters of Op_{id} and $Rule_{id}$
respectively
    else return False
    end if
end if

Table 3. Administrative operations of ADMINESTAR

Op_{id}	Description
Op_1	Update_RoleExtent_Loc (a', re', loc_{new})
Op_2	Update_RoleExtent_Interval (a', re', I_{new})
Op_3	Add_RoleExtent (a', re')
Op_4	Update_PermExtent_Loc (a', pe', loc_{new})
Op_5	Update_PermExtent_Interval (a', pe', I_{new})
Op_6	Add_PermExtent (a', pe')
Op_7	Update_Locations (a', loc_i, phy)
Op_8	Add_Location (a', loc_{new})
Op_9	Update_Interval (a', I_i, I_{new})
Op_{10}	Add_Interval (a', I_{new})
Op_{11}	Assign_RoleExtent (a', b, loc, I)
Op_{12}	Revoke_RoleExtent (a', b, loc, I)
Op_{13}	Assign_PermExtent (a', p, loc, I)
Op_{14}	Revoke_PermExtent (a', p, loc, I)
Op_{15}	Update_PermLocs (a', p_i, loc_i)

operation and it returns *True* if those conditions are met. If the authorization succeeds, then Algorithm 1 returns true, otherwise it returns false.

The administrative operations are explained in detail below:

1. Op_1: Update_RoleExtent_Loc (a', re', loc_{new}): The user u assigned to the administrative role a' wants to update the location of role extent re' to a new location loc_{new}. Before this operation proceeds, the function *authorization_check* with parameters Op_1 and $Rule_1$ is called to verify whether the user u is authorized to perform this operation. If u is authorized (*authorization_check()* returns *true*), then only the location of role extent re' is changed to loc_{new} provided loc_{new} belongs to the set *Locations*, otherwise the operation fails.

2. Op_2: Update_RoleExtent_Interval (a', re', I_{new}): The user u assigned to the administrative role a' wants to update the interval of role extent re' to a new interval I_{new}. Before this operation proceeds, the function *authorization_check* with parameters Op_2 and $Rule_2$ is called to verify whether the user u is authorized to perform this operation. If u is authorized, then the interval of role extent re' is changed to I_{new} if and only if I_{new} belongs to the set *Intervals*, otherwise the operation fails.

3. Op_3: Add_RoleExtent (a', re'): The user u assigned to the administrative role a' wants to add a new role extent re' to the set *RE*. Before this operation proceeds, the function *authorization_check* with parameters Op_3 and $Rule_3$ is called to verify whether the user u is authorized to perform this operation. If u is authorized, then only the new role extent re' is added to the set *RE*.

4. Op_4: Update_PermExtent_Loc (a', pe', loc_{new}): The user u assigned to the administrative role a' wants to update the location of permission extent pe' to

a new location loc_{new}. Before this operation proceeds, the function *authorization_check* with parameters Op_4 and $Rule_4$ is called to verify whether the user u is authorized to perform this operation. If u is authorized, then only the location of permission extent pe' is changed to loc_{new} provided loc_{new} belongs to the set *Locations*, otherwise the operation fails.

5. Op_5: Update_PermExtent_Interval (a', pe', I_{new}): The user u assigned to the administrative role a' wants to update the interval of permission extent pe' to a new interval I_{new}. Before this operation proceeds, the function *authorization_check* with parameters Op_5 and $Rule_5$ is called to verify whether the user u is authorized to perform this operation. If u is authorized, then only the interval of permission extent pe' is changed to I_{new} provided I_{new} belongs to the set *Intervals*, otherwise the operation fails.

6. Op_6: Add_PermExtent (a', pe'): The user u assigned to the administrative role a' wants to add a new permission extent pe' to the set *PE*. Before this operation proceeds, the function *authorization_check* with parameters Op_6 and $Rule_6$ is called to verify whether the user u is authorized to perform this operation. If u is authorized, then only the new permission extent pe' is added to the set *PE*, otherwise the operation fails.

7. Op_7: Update_Locations (a', loc_i, phy): The user u assigned to the administrative role a' wants to update the mapping of logical location loc_i to a set of physical points represented by phy. Before this operation proceeds, the function *authorization_check* with parameters Op_7 and $Rule_7$ is called to verify whether the user u is authorized to perform this operation. If u is authorized, then only the logical location loc_i is mapped to phy, otherwise the operation fails.

8. Op_8: Add_Location (a', loc_{new}): The user u assigned to the administrative role a' wants to add a new logical location loc_{new} to the set *Locations*. Before this operation proceeds, the function *authorization_check* with parameters Op_8 and $Rule_8$ is called to verify whether the user u is authorized to perform this operation. If u is authorized, then only the new logical location loc_{new} is added to the set *Locations*, otherwise the operation fails.

9. Op_9: Update_Intervals (a', I_i, I_{new}): The user u assigned to the administrative role a' wants to update the interval I_i to a new interval I_{new}. Before this operation proceeds, the function *authorization_check* with parameters Op_9 and $Rule_9$ is called to verify whether the user u is authorized to perform this operation. If u is authorized, then only the interval I_i is changed to I_{new}, otherwise the operation fails.

10. Op_{10}: Add_Interval (a', I_{new}): The user u assigned to the administrative role a' wants to add a new interval I_{new} to the set *Intervals*. Before this operation proceeds, the function *authorization_check* with parameters Op_{10} and $Rule_{10}$ is called to verify whether the user u is authorized to perform this operation. If u is authorized, then only the new interval I_{new} is added to the set *Intervals*, otherwise the operation fails.

11. Op_{11}: Assign_RoleExtent (a', b, loc, I): The user u assigned to the administrative role a' wants to assign a role extent, whose set of locations is the set *locs* and set of intervals is the set I, to the regular role b. Before this operation

proceeds, the function *authorization_check* with parameters Op_{11} and $Rule_{11}$ is called to verify whether the user u is authorized to perform this operation. If u is authorized, then only the operation proceeds, otherwise it terminates. If there exists a role extent in RE whose set of locations is the set *locs* and set of intervals is the set I, then that role extent is added to the set RoleExtent[b], otherwise the operation fails.

12. Op_{12}: Revoke_RoleExtent (a', b, *loc*, I): The user u assigned to the administrative role a' wants to revoke the role extent, whose set of locations is the set *locs* and set of intervals is the set I, from the set RoleExtent[b]. Before this operation proceeds, the function *authorization_check* with parameters Op_{12} and $Rule_{12}$ is called to verify whether the user u is authorized to perform this operation. If u is authorized, then only the operation proceeds, otherwise it terminates. If there exists a role extent in RoleExtent[b] whose set of locations is equal to the set *locs* and set of intervals is equal to the set I, then that role extent is deleted from the set RoleExtent[b], otherwise the operation fails.

13. Op_{13}: Assign_PermExtent (a', p, *loc*, I): The user u assigned to the administrative role a' wants to assign a permission extent, whose set of locations is the set *locs* and set of intervals is the set I, to the permission p. Before this operation proceeds, the function *authorization_check* with parameters Op_{13} and $Rule_{13}$ is called to verify whether the user u is authorized to perform this operation. If u is authorized, then only the operation proceeds, otherwise it terminates. If there exists a permission extent in PE whose set of locations is equal to the set *locs* and set of intervals is equal to the set I, then that permission extent is added to the set PermExtent[p], otherwise the operation fails.

14. Op_{14}: Revoke_PermExtent (a', p, *loc*, I): The user u assigned to the administrative role a' wants to revoke the permission extent, whose set of locations is the set *locs* and set of intervals is the set I, from PermExtent[p]. Before this operation proceeds, the function *authorization_check* with parameters Op_{14} and $Rule_{14}$ is called to verify whether the user u is authorized to perform this operation. If u is authorized, then only the operation proceeds, otherwise it terminates. If there exists a permission extent in permExtent[p] whose set of locations is equal to the set *locs* and set of intervals is equal to the set I, then that permission extent is deleted from the set PermExtent[p], otherwise the operation fails.

15. Op_{15}: Update_PermLocs (a', p_i, loc_i): The user u assigned to the administrative role a' wants to update the value at PermLocs[p_i][loc_i]. Before this operation proceeds, the function *authorization_check* with parameters Op_{15} and $Rule_{15}$ is called to verify whether the user u is authorized to perform this operation. If u is authorized, then only the value at PermLocs[p_i][loc_i] is updated provided $p_i \in Permissions$ and $loc_i \in Locations$, otherwise the operation fails.

5   Conclusion and Future Direction

Although several administrative models for RBAC exist, no work has yet been done on the development of administrative models for its spatio-temporal extensions. ADMINESTAR, as proposed in this paper, is the first such administrative model. It employs ESTARBAC itself to manage ESTARBAC systems. ADMINESTAR includes *Administrative Policies* - a set of administrative rules used to specify the administrative roles that can modify the spatio-temporal extents of different regular roles and permissions along with *Administrative Operations*. The various ESTARBAC entities define the system state and the administrative operations cause a state transition upon their successful execution under the control of corresponding administrative rule. We also define two types of role hierarchies, namely, Role Activation Hierarchy and Permission Invocation Hierarchy which play an important role in specifying administrative policies. ADMINESTAR can be used for two major purposes, namely, managing real-life deployment of ESTARBAC systems and security analysis of ESTARBAC.

Similar to ADMINESTAR, administrative models can be built for other extensions of RBAC like GEO-RBAC [12], LRBAC [13], STRBAC, etc. In future, we plan to carry out formal analysis of security properties of ESTARBAC using the relations defined in the administrative model proposed in this paper. In addition, we will analyze the proposed set of administrative operations of ADMINESTAR to show that this set is minimal and complete.

Acknowledgement. This work is partially supported by the National Science Foundation under grant numbers CNS-0746943 and 1018414.

References

1. Sandhu, R., Coyne, E., Feinstein, H., Youman, C.: Role-based access control models. IEEE Computer, 38–47 (1996)
2. Osborn, S.: Mandatory access control and role-based access control revisited. In: Proc. of the 2nd ACM Workshop on Role-Based Access Control, RBAC 1997, pp. 31–40 (1997)
3. Osborn, S., Sandhu, R., Munawer, Q.: Configuring role-based access control to enforce mandatory and discretionary access control policies. ACM Transactions on Information and System Security (TISSEC), 85–106 (2000)
4. Ray, I., Toahchoodee, M.: A spatio-temporal role-based access control model. In: Proc. of the IFIP WG11.3 Conference on Data and Applications Security and Privacy (DBSec), pp. 211–226 (2007)
5. Aich, S., Sural, S., Majumdar, A.: STARBAC: spatio temporal role based access control. In: Meersman, R. (ed.) OTM 2007, Part II. LNCS, vol. 4804, pp. 1567–1582. Springer, Heidelberg (2007)
6. Aich, S., Mondal, S., Sural, S., Majumdar, A.K.: Role based access control with spatio-temporal context for mobile applications. Transactions on Computational Science IV, 177–199 (2009)
7. Sandhu, R., Bhamidipati, V., Munawer, Q.: The ARBAC97 model for role-based administration of roles. ACM Transactions on Information and System Security (TISSEC), 105–135 (1999)
8. Li, N., Mao, Z.: Administration in Role-Based Access Control. In: Proc. of the 2nd ACM Symposium on Information, Computer and Communications Security (ASIACCS), pp. 127–138 (2007)
9. Bertino, E., Bonatti, P., Ferrari, E.: TRBAC: A temporal role based access control model. ACM Transactions on Information and System Security, 191–233 (2001)

10. Toahchoodee, M., Ray, I.: On the formalization and analysis of a spatio-temporal role-based access control model. Journal of Computer Security, 399–452 (2011)
11. Toahchoodee, M., Ray, I.: Using alloy to analyse a spatio-temporal access control model supporting delegation. IET Information Security, 75–113 (2009)
12. Bertino, E., Catania, B., Damiani, M.L., Perlasca, P.: GEO-RBAC: A spatially aware RBAC. ACM Transactions on Information and System Security, 29–37 (2007)
13. Ray, I., Kumar, M., Yu, L.: LRBAC: A Location-Aware Role-Based Access Control Model. In: Bagchi, A., Atluri, V. (eds.) ICISS 2006. LNCS, vol. 4332, pp. 147–161. Springer, Heidelberg (2006)
14. Li, N., Tripunitara, M.: Security analysis in role-based access control. ACM Transactions on Information and System Security, 391–420 (2006)
15. Jha, S., Li, N., Tripunitara, M., Wang, Q., Winsborough, W.: Towards formal verification of role-based access control policies. IEEE Transactions on Dependable and Secure Computing, 242–255 (2008)
16. Joshi, J.B.D., Bertino, E., Latif, U., Ghafoor, A.: A generalized temporal role-based access control model. IEEE Transactions on Knowledge and Data Engineering, 4–23 (2005)
17. Sandhu, R., Munawer, Q.: The ARBAC99 model for administration of roles. In: Proc. of the 15th Annual Computer Security Applications Conference, ACSAC 1999, pp. 229–238 (1999)
18. Sandhu, R., Oh, S.: A model for role administration using organization structure. SACMAT 2002. In: Proc. of the 7th ACM Symposium on Access Control Models and Technologies, pp. 155–162 (2002)

A UC-Secure Authenticated Contributory Group Key Exchange Protocol Based on Discrete Logarithm

Yasser Sobhdel and Rasool Jalili

Data and Network Security Laboratory,
Department of Computer Engineering,
Sharif University of Technology, Tehran, Iran
{Sobhdel@alum.,Jalili@}sharif.ir

Abstract. Authenticated key exchange protocols allow parties to establish a common session key which in turn is fundamental to building secure channels. Authenticated group key exchange protocols allow parties to interact with each other and establish a common group session key and avoid peer to peer key exchange; in other words they pave the way to build a broadcast channel.

We construct an authenticated group key exchange protocol over UC framework which has the contributiveness property; i.e., the output is not biased by inputs of any party. Our protocol uses CRS model and discrete logarithm. Other protocols over UC framework either are defined over RO model [19] or benefit from a non-standard hardness assumption [16].

Keywords: Authenticated Group Key Exchange, Universal Composability Framework, Contributiveness.

1 Introduction

Parties in an insecure network can generate a common shared key through authenticated group key exchange (AGKE) protocols. This key which is also called the session key, enables those participating parties to securely communicate with each other and transmit information while they are assured that the recipients of the key is the ones which they assume, hence these protocols are called authenticated GKE protocols. Importance of these protocols are evident to us, since daily growth of communication and specially the need for secure interaction of users make authenticated key exchange protocols one of the key elements of building secure communications.

The two-party case of AKE protocols are extensively analyzed [4,3,5,11,12,15], but since seminal work of Katz and Shin [20] more effort has been made on GKE protocols [2,16,19,20], though there had been various articles on the subject in the past specially by Bresson et al. [8,7]. Katz and Shin in [20] modeled insider attacks on GKEs and proposed a protocol over universal composability framework [10]. Their protocol benefitted from "Ack" property which stems from

A. Bagchi and I. Ray (Eds.): ICISS 2013, LNCS 8303, pp. 390–401, 2013.

seminal work of Canneti and Krawcyzk [11]. Informally speaking, the "Ack" property states that given only the session key and public information of the protocol, internal session of all parties must be "simulatable" by the time the first party outputs the session key [11]. It is good to mention that the protocol of Katz and Shin required at least 3 rounds of interactions. Another feature which was introduced by Bohli et al.[6] and Bresson et al.[9] is "contributiveness" property; a GKE protocol which has the contributiveness property lets every party interact equally in process of generating session key, therefore predetermining the session key is far out of consideration.

Bohli et al. [6] proposed a two-round AKE protocol which has the contributiveness property. Furukawa et al. [16] proposed a protocol based on bilinear pairing which does not satisfy the contributiveness property, meanwhile they introduced a new hardness assumption which they call it "Linear Oracle Bilinear Diffie-Hellman" or LOBDH in short which is not a standard hardness assumption. In 2009 Choundary Gorantla et al. [19] proposed a two-round protocol which satisfied the contributiveness property. They defined a new functionality which had the mentioned properties and their approach to benefit from the functionality was to use the concept of "non-information oracles" which was introduced in the work of Cannet et al. [10]. Informally speaking, a non-information oracle is a turing machine with the property that for every PPT adversary with which interacts, its local output remains indistinguishable from random [11]. They call a non-information oracle for each party and this oracle computes output of every party in the same manner. Finally they use a game-based approach for proof of security. Armknecht et al. [2] introduced a lower bound on the communication effort of secure GKE protocols and proposed a two-round protocol which lacks contributiveness. Abdalla et al. [1] proposed a generic construction of password-authenticated GKE protocol from any two-party password-authenticated key exchange protocol.

ORGANIZATION. In section 2 we give an overview of universal composability framework. In Section 3 we first define an ideal functionality and then propose our protocol and prove its security under regulations of UC framework. Comparison of our work with other proposed protocols is stated in section 4. Future works are suggested in section 5.

2 Universal Composability Framework

Universal composability framework or in short UC was formulated by Canetti [13,10] and benefits from ideal/real paradigm, in which security of protocol is defined by comparing the protocol run in real world to an ideal process and stems from "trusted party paradigm" [18]. An algorithm is defined for trusted party which is called "functionality" and to prove a protocol is secure with respect to a given task, it must be proved that running the protocol with a real adversary "emulates" the trusted party.

In this framework, real world includes parties running the protocol and an adversary $\mathcal{A}$ who has ability of controlling the link (and ability to block some messages) and corrupting the parties. In the ideal world, a trusted party and set of dummy parties exist where every party hands its input to the trusted party (who runs an ideal functionality called $\mathcal{F}$) and receives its output. An interactive distinguisher called environment $\mathcal{Z}$ is introduced and a protocol is called secure if no environment $\mathcal{Z}$ can distinguish between a real execution with real adversary $\mathcal{A}$ and ideal execution with ideal adversary (simulator) $\mathcal{S}$ with probability better than negligible[1]. So, a protocol π is said to securely realize an ideal functionality $\mathcal{F}$ if for any real world adversary interacting with $\mathcal{Z}$ and participating parties, there exist an ideal world simulator $\mathcal{S}$ interacting with the environment $\mathcal{Z}$, the ideal functionality $\mathcal{F}$ and dummy parties such that no poly-time environment $\mathcal{Z}$ can distinguish whether it is interacting with real world adversary $\mathcal{A}$ or ideal world adversary $\mathcal{S}$ [13,10,20].

If a protocol, say π, can invoke any number of copies of an ideal functionality, say $\mathcal{F}$, this protocol is called "$\mathcal{F}$-hybrid". Suppose that a hybrid protocol π^ρ is result of initiating a protocol π and replacing every call to functionality $\mathcal{F}$ with a new instance of protocol ρ. A theorem is proved in [10] stating that running protocol π^ρ without accessing the functionality $\mathcal{F}$, has the same effect of $\mathcal{F}$-hybrid protocol π. This theorem is called **universal composition theorem**. In a special case, it means that if π securely realizes a $\mathcal{G}$ functionality, then $\pi^\mathcal{G}$ securely realizes $\mathcal{G}$ functionality. At last, it is good to mention that security of given protocol in UC framework requires straight line simulatability, which means the simulator cannot be rewound.

3   Proposed Protocol

The proposed protocol is based on common reference string model and existence of a public key infrastructure and a trapdoor bit commitment is assumed which nobody is aware of the trapdoor (except for the simulator). It should be mentioned that these requirements are in conformance with extended universal composability framework which is introduced to cover weakness of traditional UC framework in providing adaptive soundness and deniability features when parameters are public. It is customary to assume a higher level protocol provides some level of information to the called sub-protocol such as session identifier or knowledge of other parties public keys.

3.1   Prerequisites

We show every party by ϕ_i in which $i \in \{1, 2, \ldots, n\}$ and n is number of protocol participants. We assume that every party has an index i and these indexes form a group. Said otherwise, by ϕ_i we mean $\phi_{(i \bmod n)}$, by this approach every party

---

[1] A function is negligible in a (security) parameter k if for any $c \in \mathbb{N}$ there exists $k_0 \in \mathbb{N}$ such that for all $k > k_0$ we have $|f(k)| < K^{-c}$ [10].

has left and right neighbors; that means the left neighbor of ϕ_1 is ϕ_n and the right neighbor will be ϕ_2.

Through out our protocol, p is a prime number and $\mathbb{Z}_p^*$ is a group with g as its generator. Both p and g are public parameters and can be provided by higher level protocols and are assumed part of common reference string. Broadcasts are handled using peer to peer connection between nodes, as assumed in the universal composability framework. Each party has it own public and private keys (PK_i, SK_i) which are his long-term keys; Therefore it can be used to sign messages. It is good to know that in many similar protocols two key pairs are used, one long-term key pair for signing messages and an ephemeral key pairs (short-term) which is used for verification of messages.

The $\in_R$ symbol is used for random (uniform) selection of a member of a set or a group; when no special set or group is not explicitly stated, the natural numbers are assumed. Meanwhile $\xleftarrow{\text{BCast}}$ is used for broadcasting messages.

Trapdoor Bit Commitment. A commitment scheme is used for a single bit which benefits from a trapdoor. The algorithms used for this scheme are key generation algorithm "Gen", commitment "Com", verification "Ver" and opening of a commitment "$Open$". The "Gen" algorithm outputs a public parameter "$Param$" and its (private) trapdoor "tdr" on input 1^k in which k is the security parameter $((1^k, tdr) \leftarrow Gen(1^k))$. The "$Com$" algorithm on input $Param$, a binary value $b \in \{0,1\}$ and accessing a random tape, outputs the values of "com" and "decom". The "Ver" algorithm on input "$Param$", "com", and "decom" outputs either values of $b \in \{0,1\}$ or $\perp$ which indicates an error has occurred. Accepting "$Param$", $b' \in \{0,1\}$ "com", and "decom", the "$Open$" algorithm (with access to "tdr") outputs "decom'" which fits in the $b' = Ver(Param, \text{com}, \text{decom}')$. The trapdoor bit commitment used in the protocol has completely hiding, binding, and equivocation properties [17] .

3.2 Group Key Exchange Functionality

The universal composability framework follows the ideal/real paradigm, hence stating a functionality of ideal group key exchange is required. The following functionality is improved functionality of [20] which benefits from contribution of parties in generating the key as well. Since definition of the functionality is adequate in [16], we will restate it here without major modifications.

$\mathcal{F}_{\mathcal{GKE}}$ Ideal Functionality

$\mathcal{F}_{\mathcal{GKE}}$ interacts with instances of parties $\phi_1, \phi_2, \ldots, \phi_n$ and ideal adversary $\mathcal{S}$ with security parameter κ. This ideal functionality records set of ready-to-participate-in-the-protocol messages "$Ready(Pid)$", corruption messages "$Corr$" and generated keys "$Keys$" as its internal state.

Request to participate in the protocol: After receiving a request to participate in the protocol "$(Pid, (\phi, piid), NewSession)$" from party ϕ_i, the $\mathcal{F}_{\mathcal{GKE}}$ first checks whether $\phi \in Pid$. if (and only if) this holds, it adds the party identity "$(\phi, piid)$" to the "$Ready(Pid)$" set, then $\mathcal{F}_{\mathcal{GKE}}$ sends the "$(Pid, (\phi, piid))$" to $\mathcal{S}$.

Key generation: when $\mathcal{F}_{\mathcal{GKE}}$ receives a (Pid, sid, OK) from $\mathcal{S}$, it first checks that session identifier contains identities of the parties "$sid = \{(\phi_i, piid_i)\}_{i=1,2,...,n}$" and all parties have sent the corresponding message-to-participate-in-the-protocol "$sid \subseteq Ready(Pid)$". In case of error, the functionality aborts.

If all instances of parties "$(\phi_i, piid_i) \in sid$" are uncorrupted, $\mathcal{F}_{\mathcal{GKE}}$ randomly chooses the key "κ" and adds the "(Pid, sid, OK)" to "$Keys$" set. If any of the party instances "$(\phi_i, piid_i) \in sid$" are corrupted, the functionality $\mathcal{F}_{\mathcal{GKE}}$ adds "(Pid, sid)" to "$Corr$" set, but saves nothing in the "$Keys$".

Generating corrupted keys: After receiving the "(Pid, sid, key, κ)" from $\mathcal{S}$, the $\mathcal{F}_{\mathcal{GKE}}$ first checks whether "$(Pid, sid) \in Corr$" or not. If so, the functionality clears this entry from the "Corr" set and adds "(Pid, sid, κ)" to "Keys" set.

Key delivery: if $\mathcal{S}$ has sent "$(Pid, sid, deliver, (\phi, piid))$", and "$(Pid, sid, \kappa)$" exists, and also information of party instance is present in the session identifier "$(\phi, piid) \in sid$", then sends the "$((\phi, piid), Pid, sid, \kappa)$" to party ϕ.

Corrupting party instance: $\mathcal{S}$ can request to corrupt any party "$(\phi_i, piid_i) \in sid$", and when corruption takes place that party will remain corrupted to the end of the protocol run. Furthermore, if there exist a tuple "$(Pid, sid, \kappa) \in Keys$" but the message "$((\phi_i, piid_i), Pid, sid, \kappa)$" has not sent to party ϕ_i yet, while party ϕ_i is being corrupted, the key "κ" is sent to $\mathcal{S}$, in any other case no information is sent to $\mathcal{S}$ during corruption.

What distinguishes this functionality from previous functionalities is the ability to freely choose participating parties by the functionality. Furthermore, unlike the functionality presented in [16], the security parameter is chosen from $\{0,1\}^k$ because the proposed protocol benefits from standard discrete logarithm assumption. This functionality is secure with respect to EUC model and consequently is secure in universal composability framework with joint states.

3.3   Proposed Protocol

In this section we explain each round of protocol. Transferred messages in each round are shown between two lines and extra comments are provided afterward.

First round

---

for each ϕ_i
$$b_i \in_R \{0,1\}, \ x_{i_0} \in_R \mathbb{Z}_p^*, \ x_{i_1} \in_R \mathbb{Z}_p^*$$
$$\text{Set } y_{i_0} := g^{x_{i_0}}(mod \ p), \ y_{i_1} := g^{x_{i_1}}(mod \ p)$$
$$(\text{com}_i, \text{decom}_i) := Com(Param, b_i)$$

$$\text{Set } \mathcal{M}_i^1 := \{\phi_i; \ PID, \ (\phi_i, piid), \ y_{i_0}, \ y_{i_1}, \ C_i = \mathsf{com}_i\}$$
$$\text{Set } \sigma_i^1 := E_{SK_i}(\mathcal{M}_i^1 \parallel PID)$$
$$\phi_i \xrightarrow{\text{BCast}} (\mathcal{M}_i^1 \parallel \sigma_i^1)$$
$$\text{Set } st_i^1 := (PID, \ (\phi_i, \ piid_i), \ y_{i_0}, \ y_{i_1}, \mathsf{com}_i, \ \mathsf{decom}_i, \ b_i, \ x_{i_0}, \ x_{i_1})$$

We restate that in this protocol "$piid$" is the Party Instance Identifier. In concurrent execution of protocols, each party assumes an identifier for every protocol run which must not be confused with session identifier (sid) or Partner identifier (PID). In this protocol, each party and instance of protocol run are assumed as a symbol of a participating party and are shown as $(\phi_i, piid_i)$.

In this round every party chooses two exponents, one real exponent shown as "x_{b_i}" and a fake exponent, commits to the real exponent and sends the generator "g" to the power of these exponents along with commitment to the index of its real exponent to others.

In the end of first round, each party verifies the integrity of received message in the form of $\mathcal{M}_i^1 \parallel \sigma_i^1$. Furthermore, before broadcasting the $\mathcal{M}_i^1 \parallel \sigma_i^1$, each party updates its internal state with $st_i^1 := (PID, \ (\phi_i, \ piid_i), \ y_{i_0}, \ y_{i_1}, \mathsf{com}_i, \mathsf{decom}_i, \ b_i, \ x_{i_0}, \ x_{i_1})$.

Second round

each party calculates the following variables:
$$sid := \{(\phi_i, \ piid_i)\}_{i=1,2,\ldots,n}$$
$$\text{Msgs} := (PID, sid, \{y_{i_0}, \ y_{i_1}, \mathsf{com}_i\}_{i=1,2,\ldots,n})$$

for each ϕ_i
$$\text{Set } Y_{Left} := < y_{(i-1)_0}^{x_{b_i}}(\mathrm{mod} \ p), \ y_{(i-1)_1}^{x_{b_i}}(\mathrm{mod} \ p) >$$
$$\text{Set } Y_{Right} := < y_{(i+1)_0}^{x_{b_i}}(\mathrm{mod} \ p), \ y_{(i+1)_1}^{x_{b_i}}(\mathrm{mod} \ p) >$$
$$\text{Set } \mathcal{M}_i^2 := (Y_{Left_i}, Y_{Right_i}, b_i, decom_i, x_{1-b_i})$$
$$\text{Set } \sigma_i^2 := E_{SK_i}(\mathcal{M}_i^2)$$
$$\phi_i \xrightarrow{\text{BCast}} (\mathcal{M}_i^2 \parallel \sigma_i^2)$$
$$\text{Set } st_i^2 := ((\phi_i, \ piid_i), \ \text{Msgs}, \ b_i, \ Y_{Left}, \ Y_{Right})$$

In this round every party raises the received messages from its left and right neighbor to the power of his real "x" shown as "x_{b_i}". It must be mentioned that every party before setting its internal state st_i^2, erases his real exponent x_{b_i}".

Key generation

1. Each party ϕ_i verifies the signature σ_j^2 of the message $\mathcal{M}_j^2$ which is received from every party ϕ_j where $i \neq j$. If this verification fail, the signature is invalid and ϕ_i aborts.

2. ϕ_i verifies that the commitment sent in the first round decommits to b_i received from the same party:

$$\forall j \in PID \setminus \{i\}, b_j = Ver(com_j, decom_j)$$

3. While received the x_{1-b} of both his left and right neighbor, ϕ_i first makes sure that received exponent and index are correct in the following way:

ϕ_i raises $g^{x_{b_i}}$ (his real exponent) to the power of $x_{1-b_{i+1}}$ (fake exponent of his right neighbor) and $x_{1-b_{i-1}}$ (fake exponent of his left neighbor) separately and compares the results to the values in the previous round. Said otherwise, he compares $(g^{x_{b_i}^{x_{1-b_{i+1}}}}, g^{x_{b_i}^{x_{1-b_{i-1}}}})$ with Y_{Left_b} and Y_{Right_b}. in case of inequality, ϕ_i aborts.

4. In this stage, for each party, ϕ_i raises the received g^{x_b} of the party to the power of x_{1-b} (fake exponent) of his neighbors and XOR them with the received message and sent messages in the second round:

$$\text{Set } Y_{Left \oplus Right} := \bigoplus\nolimits_{i \in PID}(Y_{Left_i} \oplus Y_{Right_i})$$

$$\text{Set } Y_{Real}^{Fake} := \bigoplus\nolimits_{i \in PID}(g^{x_{b_{i-1}}^{x_{1-b_i}}}, g^{x_{b_{i+1}}^{x_{1-b_i}}})$$

if $Y_{Left \oplus Right} \oplus Y_{Real}^{Fake} = 0$ is not satisfied, ϕ_i aborts.

5. Calculates the key from the following formula:

$$\kappa := \bigoplus_{i \in PID} g^{x_{b_i}}$$

Then outputs the following and erases his internal state st_i^2:

$$output := (\phi_i, piid_i, PID, sid, \kappa)$$

3.4   Proof of Security

We suppose existence of public key infrastructure and bit commitment scheme which nobody knows its trapdoor. These are the general settings which EUC requires. However, as mentioned in [16], this kind of protocol does not deal with deniability and adaptive soundness of EUC model. Even if a participant can prove to some one else that he has exchanged a key, this protocol is still secure. Meanwhile adaptive soundness is not a problem because in the proof of security of the protocol, we don't use any parameter from the default settings of the protocol. Therefore, we prove the protocol is secure in the standard universal composability framework and we do not consider the settings of the EUC.

To prove the protocol is secure, we must prove that for every environment $\mathcal{Z}$, real adversary $\mathcal{A}$, and ideal adversary $\mathcal{S}$, distinguishing between real and ideal run is possible only with negligible probability. So, we will describe $\mathcal{S}$ and concentrate on the abort conditions of it; these aborts take place when the received messages are not in order and simulator lacks enough information to proceed[2].

---

[2] The proof of security here is much like the proof of security in [16].

Description of Simulator. Ideal adversary has black box access to real adversary $\mathcal{A}$. Messages of $\mathcal{Z}$ to $\mathcal{S}$ ($\mathcal{Z}$ supposes it is sending to $\mathcal{A}$) are sent for $\mathcal{A}$ and messages sent from $\mathcal{A}$ to $\mathcal{S}$ ($\mathcal{A}$ believes it is sending to $\mathcal{Z}$) are sent to $\mathcal{Z}$. Moreover, $\mathcal{S}$ simulates all (dummy) parties as well. In the beginning of simulation, $\mathcal{S}$ generates public and private key pairs (PK_ϕ, SK_ϕ) for each party and hands over the public keys to $\mathcal{A}$. Then it runs the "Gen" algorithm to generate the public parameter and its trapdoor "$(Param, tdr)$", and sends the "$Param$" to $\mathcal{A}$. When $\mathcal{S}$ received the "$(Pid, (\phi, piid), NewSession)$" from $\mathcal{A}$ and ϕ is not corrupted, it simulates a party ϕ with $piid$ instance for $\mathcal{A}$; which means it does the computation of the first round for $(\phi, piid)$. From now on, what ever message is received from $\mathcal{S}$ for $(\phi, piid)$ is processed by $\mathcal{S}$ and the output is sent to $\mathcal{A}$ in a way that mimics a real $(\phi, piid)$ exists. Furthermore, the ideal adversary $\mathcal{S}$ (simulator) proceeds the simulation as follows:

1. **Generating session keys**
   Suppose that a simulated party $(\phi, piid)$ has output a session key $((\phi, piid), Pid, sid, \kappa)$. If a party wants to take part in two sessions with a common Pid (that means all parties are the same in both sessions), $\mathcal{S}$ aborts. In formal statement, if $\mathcal{S}$ has previously sent (Pid, sid', ok) to $\mathcal{F}_{\mathcal{GKE}}$ in which $sid \neq sid'$ and if there is no corrupted party $(\phi', piid') \in sid \cap sid'$, then $\mathcal{S}$ aborts. If this is not the situation, $\mathcal{S}$ verifies whether any of the party instances $(\phi', piid') \in sid$ is corrupted:
   (a) **without corruption**
       If none of the party instances $(\phi', piid') \in sid$ are corrupted, then:
       i. **without "OK" message**
          If $\mathcal{S}$ has not sent (Pid, sid, ok) message to $\mathcal{F}_{\mathcal{GKE}}$, then $\mathcal{S}$ verifies that it has received the whole $(\phi, piid) \in sid$ messages from $\mathcal{F}_{\mathcal{GKE}}$. If it is not so, $\mathcal{S}$ aborts, else sends (Pid, sid, ok) to the $\mathcal{F}_{\mathcal{GKE}}$ and after that sends $(Pid, sid, deliver, (\phi, piid))$ to the functionality.
       ii. **with "OK" message**
          If $\mathcal{S}$ has already sent (Pid, sid, ok) to $\mathcal{F}_{\mathcal{GKE}}$, this means that a party instance $(\phi', piid') \in sid$ has already generated a session key κ'. If $\kappa \neq \kappa'$ then $\mathcal{S}$ aborts, else $\mathcal{S}$ sends $(Pid, sid, deliver, (\phi, piid))$ message to $\mathcal{F}_{\mathcal{GKE}}$.
   (b) **with corruption**
       If some of party instances $C \subseteq sid \setminus \{(\phi, piid)\}$ are corrupt then:
       i. **without "OK" message**
          If $\mathcal{S}$ has not sent (Pid, sid, ok) message to $\mathcal{F}_{\mathcal{GKE}}$, it sends $(Pid, (\phi', piid'), NewSession)$ message to the functionality on behalf of all corrupted parties $(\phi', piid') \in C$ which has not yet sent this message to the $\mathcal{F}_{\mathcal{GKE}}$. If after sending the previously stated messages, $\mathcal{S}$ didn't receive $(Pid, (\phi', piid'))$ for each instances $(\phi', piid') \in sid$, it aborts. If abort condition is not met, $\mathcal{S}$ sends (Pid, sid, ok), (Pid, sid, key, κ) and $(Pid, sid, deliver, (\phi, piid))$ messages to $\mathcal{F}_{\mathcal{GKE}}$.

     ii. **with "OK" message**

If S has already sent (pid, sid, ok) message to $\mathcal{F}_{\mathcal{GKE}}$, according to description of functionality, it has sent (Pid, sid, key, κ') to $\mathcal{F}_{\mathcal{GKE}}$. If $\kappa \neq \kappa'$ then S aborts, else S sends $(Pid, sid, deliver, (\phi, piid))$ message to $\mathcal{F}_{\mathcal{GKE}}$.

2. **corruption**

When $\mathcal{A}$ corrupts a party instance $(\phi, piid)$, S sends internal state of the party to $\mathcal{A}$ according to the following:

(a) **without "OK" message**

If S has not sent (Pid, sid, ok) message to $\mathcal{F}_{\mathcal{GKE}}$ for a (Pid, sid) which $(\phi, piid) \in sid$, then S sends to $\mathcal{A}$ current internal state of $\mathcal{A}$.

(b) **with "OK" message**

Now we consider a situation in which S has already sent (Pid, sid, ok) to $\mathcal{F}_{\mathcal{GKE}}$.

     i. **without erasing internal state**

If S has not sent $(Pid, sid, deliver, (\phi, piid))$ message (in which $(\phi, piid) \in sid$) to $\mathcal{F}_{\mathcal{GKE}}$, it verifies that $(\phi, piid)$ has $st^2_{(\phi, piid)}$ internal state, that means the second round is complete. If this not so, S aborts, else it uses the trapdoor tdr and calculates internal state of the corrupted party and hands it over to $\mathcal{A}$.

     ii. **with erasing internal state**

If S has already sent $(Pid, sid, deliver, (\phi, piid))$ message to $\mathcal{F}_{\mathcal{GKE}}$, due to forward secrecy of the protocol, S sends nothing to $\mathcal{A}$ (i.e., it returns empty internal state to $\mathcal{A}$).

$\square$

4   Comparison with Previous Works

Authenticated contributory group key exchange protocols which are proposed over UC framework are so limited that only two works can be compared with the proposed protocol. We review cons and pros of each one of them and compare them with the proposed protocol. Furukawa et al. [16] proposed a two-round group key exchange protocol based on bilinear pairing over elliptic curves and used non-interactive proof for ACK property. Furthermore their protocol benefits from common reference string model and to distribute a session key among n parties, $2n + 1$ pairing operation is needed per party; Therefore (at least) $2n^2 + 2$ pairings are needed for a complete operation of their protocol. As we know pairing is a costly operation (comparing with exponentiation) and this amount of pairing operation leads to an inefficient protocol. Furthermore their protocol makes use of LO-BDH (Linear Oracle - Bilinear Diffie-Hellman) hardness assumption which is not a standard assumption and we are unaware of its cons and pros.

Gorantla et al. [19] proposed a protocol based on discrete logarithm hardness assumption; their proof of security uses a relaxed form of security called non-information oracle and it is a gamed-based proof. Their protocol is proposed over random oracle model which is a very powerful model but finding a hash function which can completely replace the oracle in real world is trouble-some. Furthermore the simulator which is used to prove security of the protocol, invokes a non-information oracle per party. Every oracle performs every calcu-lation of that party like hashing and XOR etc. except for signing messages with parties' private keys. Said otherwise, the oracle defined is the same as the main protocol except for signing the messages, because there is no need to do so in the simulator. So for polynomially many parties, their protocol is not the most efficient because every operation (except for signing) is done twice.

The proposed protocol makes use of common reference string model, as Fu-rukawa's protocol, and benefits from discrete logarithm hardness assumption. Furthermore, its proof of security uses non-interactive proof to prove ACK prop-erty. Due to using trapdoor commitment mechanism and exponentiation of a fake value along with committed value, the proposed protocol has twice modular ex-ponentiation as Gorantla's protocol (of course till key generation stage); but except for the XOR operation which is common in both, the proposed protocol does not require any hashing. Meanwhile, due to benefiting from common refer-ence string model, it can be implemented more easily and may not have trouble finding a fitting hash function at all. Overall comparison of these protocols is shown in table 1.

Table 1. Comparison of proposed protocol with works of others

Protocol	Hardness assumption	Security model	Operations per party
Gorantla et. al. [19]	Discrete Logarithm	Random Oracle	$3E+(n+4)H$
Furukawa et. al. [16]	LO-BDH	Common Reference String	$(2n+1)BP + 2E$
Proposed scheme	Discrete Logarithm	Common Reference String	$(2n+6)E$

It is good to mention that in table 1 "LO-BDH" stands for Linear Oracle - Bilinear Diffie-Hellman and "E" represents modular exponentiation, "H" means hashing and "BP" is short form of bilinear pairing. According to table 1, pro-posed protocol has a major improvement over its counterpart in CRS model and regarding the fact that the prerequisites of CRS is less than random oracle, the imposed overhead is natural. Our protocol does not support joining single party or a group of parties as supported in [1] and every thing must be started from scratch.

5   Future Works

Secure key exchange protocols are still a challenging topic and the way of using these protocols to reach an efficient secure public broadcast channel has remained a challenge. In general, one of the goals of authentication protocols is to provide a secure channel between two parties. With growth of number of participants , this concept is extended and becomes a type of broadcast channel.

With a group key exchange in place, it is so important to let other parties join the group or even leave it with logical cost. Enhancing the protocol to enable joining and leaving a single member or even a group of parties can be quite challenging. A good example of join capability is shown in [1]. Also memory tokens can be put to use of GAKE to further simplify such operation, [14] is a very efficient example of such protocol for two parties.

References

1. Abdalla, M., Chevalier, C., Granboulan, L., Pointcheval, D.: Contributory password-authenticated group key exchange with join capability. In: Kiayias, A. (ed.) CT-RSA 2011. LNCS, vol. 6558, pp. 142–160. Springer, Heidelberg (2011)
2. Armknecht, F., Furukawa, J.: On the minimum communication effort for secure group key exchange. Journal of the ACM (JACM) 38(1), 108–115 (2009)
3. Bellare, M., Canetti, R., Krawczyk, H.: A modular approach to the design and analysis of authentication and key exchange protocols (extended abstract). In: Proceedings of the Thirtieth Annual ACM Symposium on Theory of Computing, pp. 419–428. ACM (1998)
4. Bellare, M., Rogaway, P.: Entity authentication and key distribution. In: Stinson, D.R. (ed.) CRYPTO 1993. LNCS, vol. 773, pp. 232–249. Springer, Heidelberg (1994)
5. Bird, R., Gopal, I., Herzberg, A., Janson, P., Kutten, S., Molva, R., Yung, M.: Systematic design of two-party authentication protocols. In: Feigenbaum, J. (ed.) CRYPTO 1991. LNCS, vol. 576, pp. 44–61. Springer, Heidelberg (1992)
6. Bohli, J., González Vasco, M., Steinwandt, R.: Secure group key establishment revisited. International Journal of Information Security 6(4), 243–254 (2007)
7. Bresson, E., Chevassut, O., Pointcheval, D.: Dynamic group diffie-hellman key exchange under standard assumptions. In: Knudsen, L.R. (ed.) EUROCRYPT 2002. LNCS, vol. 2332, pp. 321–336. Springer, Heidelberg (2002)
8. Bresson, E., Chevassut, O., Pointcheval, D., Quisquater, J.: Provably authenticated group diffie-hellman key exchange. In: Proceedings of the 8th ACM Conference on Computer and Communications Security, pp. 255–264. ACM (2001)
9. Bresson, E., Manulis, M.: Securing group key exchange against strong corruptions. In: Proceedings of the 2008 ACM Symposium on Information, Computer and Communications Security, pp. 249–260. ACM (2008)

10. Canetti, R.: Universally composable security: A new paradigm for crypto-graphic protocols. In: Proceedings of Foundations of Computer Science (FOCS), pp. 136–145. IEEE (2002)
11. Canetti, R., Krawczyk, H.: Analysis of key-exchange protocols and their use for building secure channels. In: Pfitzmann, B. (ed.) EUROCRYPT 2001. LNCS, vol. 2045, pp. 453–474. Springer, Heidelberg (2001)
12. Canetti, R., Krawczyk, H.: Universally composable notions of key exchange and secure channels. In: Knudsen, L.R. (ed.) EUROCRYPT 2002. LNCS, vol. 2332, pp. 337–351. Springer, Heidelberg (2002)
13. Canetti, R.: Universally composable security: A new paradigm for cryptographic protocols. Cryptology ePrint Archive, Report 2000/067 (2000), http://eprint.iacr.org/
14. Dagdelen, Ö., Fischlin, M.: Unconditionally-secure universally composable password-based key-exchange based on one-time memory tokens. IACR Cryptology ePrint Archive 2012 (2012)
15. Diffie, W., Oorschot, P., Wiener, M.: Authentication and authenticated key ex-changes. Designs, Codes and Cryptography 2(2), 107–125 (1992)
16. Furukawa, J., Armknecht, F., Kurosawa, K.: A Universally Composable Group Key Exchange Protocol with Minimum Communication Effort. Security and Cryptog-raphy for Networks 36(2), 392–408 (2008)
17. Goldreich, O.: Foundation of Cryptography: Basic Tools. Cambridge University Press (2001)
18. Goldreich, O., Micali, S., Wigderson, A.: How to play any mental game. In: Pro-ceedings of the nineteenth Annual ACM Symposium on Theory of Computing, pp. 218–229. ACM (1987)
19. Gorantla, M., Boyd, C., Nieto, J.: Universally composable contributory group key exchange. In: Proceedings of the 4th International Symposium on Information, Computer, and Communications Security, pp. 146–156. ACM (2009)
20. Katz, J., Shin, J.: Modeling insider attacks on group key-exchange protocols. In: Proceedings of the 12th ACM Conference on Computer and Communications Se-curity, pp. 180–189. ACM (2005)

Author Index